Otto Dix and the First World War

GERMAN VISUAL CULTURE

VOLUME SIX

SERIES EDITOR

Dr Christian Weikop
Senior Lecturer
Edinburgh College of Art
University of Edinburgh

PETER LANG
Oxford • Bern • Berlin • Bruxelles • New York • Wien

OTTO DIX AND THE FIRST WORLD WAR

Grotesque Humor, Camaraderie and Remembrance

MICHAEL MACKENZIE

PETER LANG
Oxford • Bern • Berlin • Bruxelles • New York • Wien

Bibliographic information published by Die Deutsche Nationalbibliothek.
Die Deutsche Nationalbibliothek lists this publication in the Deutsche Nationalbibliografie; detailed bibliographic data is available on the Internet at http://dnb.d-nb.de.

A catalogue record for this book is available from the British Library.

Library of Congress Cataloging-in-Publication Data:

Names: Mackenzie, Michael, 1965- author.
Title: Otto Dix and the First World War : grotesque humor, camaraderie and remembrance / Michael Mackenzie.
Description: Oxford ; New York : Peter Lang, 2019. | Includes bibliographical references and index.
Identifiers: LCCN 2018018396 | ISBN 9783034317238 (alk. paper)
Subjects: LCSH: Dix, Otto, 1891-1969--Criticism and interpretation. | World War, 1914-1918--Art and the war. | World War, 1914-1918--Germany. | Art and society--Germany--History--20th century.
Classification: LCC N6888.D5 M24 2018 | DDC 701/.03--dc23 LC record available at https://lccn.loc.gov/2018018396

Cover image: Otto Dix, *The War* [Der Krieg], oil and tempera on wood panel, 1928–1932, Staatliche Kunstsammlungen, Dresden, Galerie Neue Meister. © Otto Dix / Artists Rights Society (ARS), New York / VG Bild-Kunst, Bonn. Photo Art Resource, NY / Erich Lessing, used with permission.

Series cover design by Brent Meyers. Cover design by Peter Lang Ltd.

ISSN 2296-0805
ISBN 978-3-0343-1723-8 • ISBN 978-1-78874-334-1 (ePDF)
ISBN 978-1-78874-335-8 (ePub) • ISBN 978-1-78874-336-5 (mobi)

Published by Peter Lang Ltd, International Academic Publishers,
52 St Giles, Oxford, OX1 3LU, United Kingdom
oxford@peterlang.com, www.peterlang.com

This publication has been peer reviewed.

Contents

Figures

Acknowledgments

This project began unexpectedly several years ago, when my wife, Anne Harris, a medievalist, suggested that we read Bakhtin together. Our children were no longer quite so small, and we had a little time every evening after they went to bed. As we read, it occurred to me that Bakhtin's story about the humor of grotesque realism and the fascination with the "lower bodily stratum" as strategies for warding off the fear of death, and also for undermining the cultural authority of official representation, might explain some things that had long puzzled me about Otto Dix's depictions of the First World War and its veterans. Specifically, a similar strategy on Dix's part might explain how and why those images were at one and the same time so horrendously grotesque and so irreverently humorous. I reasoned that the communities of soldiers on both sides must have filled their own speech with the humorous grotesque and the lower bodily stratum, and when it turned out that their soldier's slang was well documented, I knew that I could support my thesis. And so the person I need to thank the most at the outset is Anne, for suggesting Bakhtin, and then for encouraging this nascent project, and for countless other forms of support.

As I began writing, several people read early versions of what became second and third chapters, especially Riccardo Marchi, and also several of my colleagues at DePauw: Julia Bruggemann; David Alvarez; Christopher Wells; Peter Graham; Hillary Kelleher; and Meryl Altman. I thank them for all of their close reading and generous, detailed feedback. As I began to present material at conferences, especially the early work on the grotesque in Dix's imagery, Jim van Dyke, Dennis Crockett, and Elizabeth Otto all took the time to offer very useful responses.

DePauw University supported me generously as I undertook research to develop the idea into a book on all of Dix's images of the war, with time to research and write, space to work, and financial support for research. Some of this support came in the form of the Rieth Faculty Fellowship, and I am grateful to Mr. Blair Anderson "Andy" Rieth Jr. and his family for this support. My colleagues Carrie Klaus and Tamara Beauboeuf, who each took a turn as dean of faculty during the long gestation of this book, were unflagging and creative in finding ways to support the work, and I am very grateful to them. Likewise Brooke Cox, librarian, and Misti Scott, administrative assistant, are owed my gratitude for their help with images, especially. Andy Cullison and the staff of the Prindle Institute for Ethics at DePauw provided space to work and support during a leave. The students in my seminar on the art and literature of the First World War thought with me about some of the ideas presented here, and I am grateful to them, also. I am fortunate indeed to have the support of the staff, administration, my fellow faculty, and the students at DePauw.

As I set out to do further research on Dix and his work representing the war, I was warmly welcomed and encouraged above all by the generous and knowledgeable director of the Kunstmuseum Albstadt, Veronika Mertens, her staff, and her family. I have much to thank Doctor Mertens for, including access to the extensive collection of Dix's work in Albstadt, especially works on paper, for permission to reproduce works from their collection, and also the opportunity to go through Dix's field notebook from the war. The chance to hold that notebook, which had been with Dix in the trenches, was a highpoint of my research for its sheer auratic and material presence. I am also grateful to Doctor Mertens for the opportunity to present some of my findings at the colloquium on images of the First World War which she organized in 2015. At that colloquium, I benefitted from the insights of Simone Fleischer and Ulrike Lorenz. I am indebted to the staff of the Deutsches Kunstarchiv at the Germanisches Nationalmuseum in Nuremberg for the access they gave me to Dix's papers and correspondence. I was able to peruse the other side of the correspondence between Dix and his gallery dealer Karl Nierendorf in the archives of the Galerie Nierendorf in Berlin, thanks to the generosity of its director Florian Karsch. Alas, I am too late to thank Dr. Karsch here for his help and guidance.

I also owe a debt of gratitude to the staffs of the Kupferstich-Kabinett in Dresden, the Kupferstichkabinett in Berlin, the Kunstmuseum Stuttgart, the Hamburg Kunsthalle, Doctor Birgit Dalbajewa of the Staatliche Kunstsammlungen Dresden, the Kunstsammlung Chemnitz, and the staff of the David and Alfred Smart Museum in Chicago, all of which gave me access to the works, and especially the graphic works, of Otto Dix and others in their collections. Most especially I'd like to thank Bettina Dix and Rainer Pfefferkorn, who welcomed me into their home and gave me access to the works in the Otto Dix estate.

For his encouragement and good example in all things, and for listening to my ideas about this topic, I would like to thank my brother-in-law, the cultural historian of the Khrushchev-era Soviet Union, Steven Harris, his wife Gina, and Henry and Emmett. And for always having room and time for me, I thank Michael and Claudia Wiese.

Finally, I am indebted to Laurel Plapp and the editorial team at Peter Lang, who have been helpful, encouraging, and endlessly patient as I worked to bring this project to completion. Without all of these people and their generosity, this project would never have been realized.

To return to where the project began, I would like to dedicate this book to my wife, Anne, and our children, Oliver, Iris, and Eleanor, who cannot remember a time when I was not writing it.

Greencastle, September 2018

Introduction

"War is really something brutal. Hunger, lice, mud, these insane noises. It's really something else."[1] This is how Otto Dix described the First World War, nearly half a century after he lived through it as a young soldier. Even towards the end of his life, after the Weimar Republic, Nazism and the division of Germany into East and West, this experience continued to preoccupy him, to haunt him, and one might even suspect to define him, as a man, as a German, as an artist. It's a telling list of plagues: parasites; intolerable physical conditions; extreme emotional states. Perhaps surprisingly, it doesn't mention the violence: being shot at; gassed and bombarded; stormed by the enemy. It doesn't acknowledge that the soldier's job was to kill – and as a machine gunner, Dix must have slaughtered countless oncoming enemy soldiers, mostly at close range. No, the list only indicates physical and psychological suffering. It presents the soldier as a victim, but specifically the victim of natural elements, not of enemy soldiers, sadistic officers, or mendacious politicians. It is a list of things to do with unpleasantly earthy, undignified, degrading physical states – the very opposite of the classical beauty that had once been considered the proper subject of artists. It points instead to the kinds of bodily conditions that folk cultures – including that of soldiers – have always mined for grotesque humor (the kind of ironic humor that the good Sergeant Dix himself displayed in a letter from the front when he referred to his stretch of the front as "the lovely lousy-slimepagne," combining into one grotesque, disparaging term lice and the slimy mud of Champagne).[2] Interestingly, it is a list of things

1 "Der Krieg ist eben etwas Viehmäßiges: Hunger, Läuse, Schlamm, diese wahnsinnigen Geräusche. Ist eben alles anders." Recorded in 1963, cited in Diether Schmidt, *Otto Dix im Selbstbildnis* (Berlin: Henschelverlag, 1981), 252. All translations are my own, unless otherwise noted.

2 The portmanteau combining "slime" and "Champagne" works better in German: "die schöne, Läuse-Schlampagne." Postcard from the field to Helene Jakob (4 June 1916),

that can't be easily seen or represented. After a long career as a visual artist, a career partially spent depicting the war, Otto Dix still wrestled with the difficulty of *visually* representing a front experience that resisted depiction. These are the things he still hasn't managed to show us! During the war and for two decades after, that struggle had forced him to push figurative art past the limits of social acceptability, in an effort to tell what he and many of his fellow veterans saw as the truth about the war, in a way that he hoped would finally hammer it home for those who hadn't been there.

Otto Dix is one of the best-known German artists of the 1920s, both for German and for English-speaking audiences, and his work has enjoyed a rapidly increasing exposure and familiarity, both in and outside of Germany, during the past 20 years – and in the past ten years especially.[3] During the 1920s and early 1930s he returned again and again to the subject of the war. A phenomenally gifted but also a difficult artist, he transgressed a wide array of cultural limits and taboos, representing sexuality, especially prostitution, violence (not least against women and combined with sex), and marginal existence and figures of all kinds, from sailors to circus performers to proletariat slum dwellers. Prostitutes whose physical decline showed through their makeup were a favorite theme, as were former soldiers permanently disabled or disfigured in the war. He depicted with uncompromising frankness and vibrant immediacy scenes that the educated bourgeoisie didn't discuss or acknowledge in polite

---

reproduced in Ulrike Rüdiger, *Grüsse aus dem Krieg. Die Feldpostkarten der Otto-Dix-Sammlung in der Kunstgalerie Gera* (Gera: Kunstgalerie Gera, 1991), 31–32. Rüdiger transcribes the phrase as "*blöde* Läuse-Schlampagne": "stupid" rather than "lovely"; Bernd Ulrich among others reads it as "schöne" [lovely], Bernd Ulrich, "'Dann gehts wieder in die schöne Läuse-Schlampagne.' Otto Dix im ersten Weltkrieg," in Dalbajewa, Birgit, Simone Fleischer, and Olaf Peters, *Otto Dix. Der Krieg – Das Dresdner Triptychon* (Dresden: Sandstein Verlag, 2014), 35–45. Dix included in this postcard a drawing of his machinegun inside a concrete pillbox.

3 His most recent major exposure has been, in Germany, the exhibition *Das Auge der Welt. Otto Dix und die Neue Sachlichkeit*, at the Kunstmuseum Stuttgart in 2012, and in the U. S. the exhibition *Otto Dix* at the Neue Galerie in New York City, 2010. See the exhibition catalogs, Kunstmuseum Stuttgart, *Otto Dix and the New Objectivity* (Stuttgart: Hatje Cantz, 2012), and Olaf Peters, ed., *Otto Dix* (Munich: Prestel, 2010).

company: portside brothel scenes; sadomasochistic rituals; sex murders; street battles. But this book is not about the entirety of Otto Dix's life and career. It is tightly focused on his prolonged and productive engagement with the theme of his experiences in the First World War, and the central place that the production of a public memory of the war had throughout the 1920s and into the 1930s – both in Dix's work and in the society of which he was an active and highly visible member.

The war was a defining experience for Dix, as it was for many of his generation, and I will not argue here, as many have done, that he made art about the war in order to condemn it and all war and militarism. Instead, I will argue that he made artworks that were very public statements about the war because he wanted this experience to be recognized *as* defining, defining for him, and because he felt uniquely qualified to show the public the truth about the war – *his* truth, and the truth of his generation. It is what I will refer to, somewhat awkwardly, as the Social Democratic truth of the war, because it hewed closely (though not absolutely) to the "truth" of the war espoused after 1924 by the *Reichsbanner*, an organization of Social Democrat veterans. I say "awkwardly" because Dix was not a member of the Social Democratic – or any other – party. But he did come from a family and a neighborhood with a strong Social Democrat tradition and culture. And as I argue through close readings of his works and comparisons with other representations of the war, Dix's own "truth" of the war, which he still espoused at the end of his life, was closest to, if not identical with, that of the organization of Social Democratic veterans. There were also tens of thousands of other German veterans for whom the truth of the war was not victimization, but heroism, or the forging in combat of an ethnic nation led by a new elite of veterans of the front. This was the conservative nationalist view espoused by such veterans groups as the *Stahlhelm*. The Social Democrats said that the "truth" of the war was indeed the German soldier's victimization, at the hands of a vicious officer class and political elite. The extreme right also said that the "truth" of the war was the German soldier's victimization, but at the hands of the Jews, while the communists said that it was at the hands of industrialists and war profiteers. The "truth" of the war, of the meaning of its intense experiences, its sacrifices, and its loss, was the elusive object of bitter contention throughout the interwar period. A major claim of the present book is that Otto Dix was not above or apart from this fray, but that he lived in it, with an ever-evolving idea about what the war had meant. It has become a truism in the literature on Dix that he compulsively returned again and again to the theme of the war out of his own private, individual trauma. But I argue here instead that he was doing what many other veterans did – both nationalists and center-leftists – and intentionally encouraged each other to do: repeatedly telling the story of the war in public, conveying to the public what it had "really" been like at the front, lest the enormity of the experience be forgotten.

Otto Dix entered the German army in 1914 at the age of 23, and spent nearly four years as a machine gunner fighting in the trenches.[4] He saw and experienced combat much more than any of the other well-known war artists of the period, whether German, French, or British, more even than the great novelists of the war, Erich Maria Remarque or Henri Barbusse.[5] When he returned to civilian life he completed his education as a painter and became one of the foremost artists of the Weimar Republic. Although he was renowned as a chronicler of the modernity and the contradictions of the world around him between the wars, he remained deeply marked by the war, and returned to it often in his art. Coming from a proletariat background and with, at first, only an education in applied arts, Dix was fairly bursting with an ambition that far outstripped his humble origins, and after the war he attended the prestigious Dresden Art Academy, where he acquired a proper education in figure drawing and history painting. He set about realizing his stated ambition to become "either a famous or an infamous" artist at a moment when the exalted, Cubism-inflected pathos of second-generation Expressionism was ubiquitous in Germany.[6] He set aside his classical skills

4 Otto Dix military pass, Deutsches Kunstarchiv, Germanisches Nationalmuseum, Nuremberg (hereafter DKA), I, A, 2. Dix was registered 22 August 1914.

5 Linda F. McGreevy, *Bitter Witness: Otto Dix and the Great War* (Peter Lang, 2003), and Simone Fleisher, "Der Künstler und der Krieg," in Dalbajewa, Fleischer, and Peters, eds. *Der Krieg*, 14–33.

6 For recent biographies of Dix see Olaf Peters, *Otto Dix. Der unerschrockene Blick* (Stuttgart: Reclam, 2013) and Philipp Gutbrod, *Otto Dix, The Art of Life* (Stuttgart: Hatje Cantz, 2010).

for the formal vocabulary of Expressionism and the typical cosmic themes featured in the pictures by the artists he considered his peers, reproduced in the art journals of that year, themes which he represented more often than not with semi-abstracted self-portraits and female nudes. This was followed by a brief Dadaist phase, which saw Dix exhibiting a large scale collage-and-paint caricature of war cripples in the streets of post-war Germany at the First International Dada Fair, a Berlin exhibition of politically charged and generally provocative paintings, objects, slogans, and photo-collages. As Germans tried to make sense of the war, tried to frame the memory of it, the massive loss of life it caused, the loss of the war and the resulting transformations of their society, they shaped competing narratives and constructed competing images. Otto Dix contributed periodically to this public work of remembrance in artworks that were shocking, brutal, and that insisted on their eyewitness status and hence their claims to truth.[7] But soon enough artists who, like Dix, rejected non-objective, or abstract, painting, returned to traditional forms of art, to the depiction of solid sculptural volumes and bodies in a precise (often overly precise or exaggerated, airless) pictorial space, with a strong emphasis on surface information and details. Where Expressionism was characterized by high-keyed and hot color contrasts and expressive brushwork, the return to objectivity (dubbed *Neue Sachlichkeit* in Germany, although the sudden reversion was international), was characterized by balanced color harmonies and smooth, unemotive surfaces. This rejection of emotive distortion and reversion to the art historical models of Nicolas Poussin and J. A. D. Ingres was led by Pablo Picasso himself already during the war. Otto Dix was well equipped for this return to objective, observational painting, and was soon acknowledged as one of the foremost exponents of *Neue Sachlichkeit*.[8]

He steadily increased his mastery of traditional materials and painting techniques, learning to paint with a combination of oil and tempera on panel, and even working from cartoons, full-scale drawings transferred

7 Jay Winter, "War Memorials. A Social Agency Interpretation," in Jay Winter, *Remembering War. The Great War Between Memory and History in the Twentieth Century* (New Haven, CT and London: Yale University Press, 2006), 135–153.

8 Dennis Crockett, *German Post-Expressionism. The Art of the Great Disorder 1918–1924* (University Park: Penn State University Press, 1999).

directly to the canvas or wood panel support. But if Dix seemed to embrace traditional values and skills in his technique, his subject matter in the first half of the 1920s was all the more shocking and even offensive to bourgeois propriety. In the mid-1920s, at a time when many painters had returned to traditional painting materials and methods, Dix was acknowledged as a master, being called back to teach large-scale painting at the very Dresden Art Academy from which he had so recently graduated. His imagery, too, was steeped in tradition, combining depictions of prostitutes with baroque allegories of *vanitas*, for example, and German Renaissance representations of Venus, or "Death and the Maiden." Every self-portrait had its reference to Albrecht Dürer, every painting of a child had its reference to Phillip Otto Runge or Hans Baldung Grien. Even a painting of his young family – artist, wife, and eldest child gathered around their newborn – was both shocking in its frankness, and sly in its reference to the Flemish master Petrus Christus (*The Artist's Family*, 1927, Städel Museum). Otto Dix was seen as a force to be reckoned with, the most prestigious German painter of the 1920s and early 1930s except perhaps Max Beckmann – a position the two artists continue to occupy relative to each other to this day.[9] His large-scale paintings, such as the triptych *Metropolis* [Großstadt] (1927–1928) (see Figure 1), but also his portraits of such quintessential figures of German modern urban culture as *The Dancer Anita Berber* (1925, Kunstmuseum Stuttgart) and *The Journalist Sylvia von Harden* (1925, Centre Pompidou, Paris), became emblematic of certain aspects of the transformations of modern life taking place in Weimar Germany.[10] Meanwhile, Dix became a highly sought-after society portraitist, despite the fact that his depictions of his sitters were often quite unflattering.

9 Compare the exhibition *Die Neue Sachlichkeit*, at the Kunsthalle Mannheim in 1925, and the more recent exhibition, *Dix/Beckmann. Mythos der Welt*, 2014. Buderer, Hans-Jurgen, "Die Geschichte einer Ausstellung, 1923, 1925, 1933" in Manfred Fath, ed., *Neue Sachlichkeit: Bilder auf der Suche nach der Wirklichkeit: Figurative Malerei der zwanziger Jahre* (Munich: Prestel, 1994), 15–37, and Ulrike Lorenz, Beatrice von Bormann, and Roger Dierden, eds., *Dix/Beckmann. Mythos der Welt* (Munich: Hirmer, 2014).

10 Birgit Schwarz, *Otto Dix. Großstadt* (Frankfurt: Insel, 1993); James van Dyke, "Otto Dix's philosophical metropolis," in Olaf Peters, ed., *Otto Dix* (Munich: Prestel, 2010), 178–197; Susan Laikin Funkenstein, "Anita Berber: Imaging a Weimar Performance Artist," *Woman's Art Journal*, 26/1 (2005), 26–31.

The son of the German working class, expressing his class resentment through provocative subject matter, unflattering portraits of his patrons, and coarse manners, but also gaining commissions and a high-profile teaching post, dressing like a dandy, competing in dance competitions with the good bourgeois wife he stole away from one of his patrons; Otto Dix was the consummate Weimar "outsider as insider."[11]

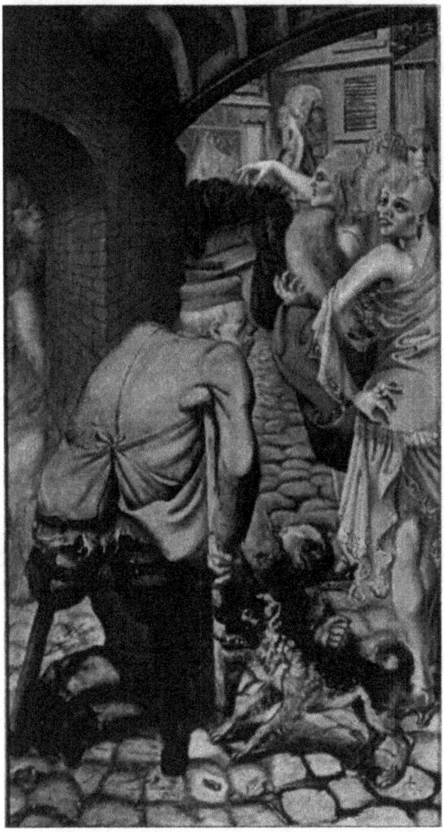

Figure 1. Otto Dix, *Metropolis* [die Großstadt], left panel, 1928, mixed oil and tempera on wood, 540 × 300 cm, Kunstmuseum Stuttgart. © Otto Dix / Artists Rights Society (ARS), New York / VG Bild-Kunst, Bonn. Digital file: author's own scan.

11 Peter Gay, *Weimar Culture. The Outsider as Insider* (New York: Harper and Row, 1968).

He courted scandal in the early 1920s. Some gallerists refused to exhibit his work due to its often salacious nature. The gallerist Hans Goltz, a well-known supporter of modern art, rejected most of Dix's work, declining to exhibit his "bordellos, whores, gunned-down communists, street filth."[12] A painting of prostitutes parading before a client in a brothel (*Salon II*, 1921, lost) was confiscated on charges of immorality, and another, a painting of a young woman – certainly another prostitute – seen from behind admiring herself in front of a mirror (*Girl at the Mirror*, 1921, destroyed), and which allegorizes the *vanitas* theme by showing in the mirror her reflection as an old crone, landed the artist in serious legal jeopardy.[13] But the biggest, most public, and stubbornly lingering scandal of all was over a painting that depicted, not a brothel scene or prostitutes, but a trench in the First World War, filled with mangled and mutilated dead bodies. It was the lurid, graphic nature of the representation – and its complete lack of any gesture of heroism or even of the supposed nobility of self-sacrifice – which offended many critics. This painting was *The Trench* [Schützengraben] (1920–1923) (see Figure 2), finished in 1923 and purchased by the prestigious Wallraf-Richartz Museum in Cologne, which was eventually forced to return it to the artist.[14]

12 Letter from Hans Goltz to Dix, dated 2 February 1922, DKA, I, C 268.

13 Dix was tried for the "distribution of obscene images," of which charge he was acquitted. Dietrich Schubert, *Otto Dix* (Reinbek: Rowohlt, 1980, revised edition, 2001), 52 f., and Gutbrod, *Otto Dix*, 54.

14 Dennis Crockett, "The Most Famous Painting of the 'Golden Twenties'?," *Art Journal* 51/1 (Spring 1992), 72–80.

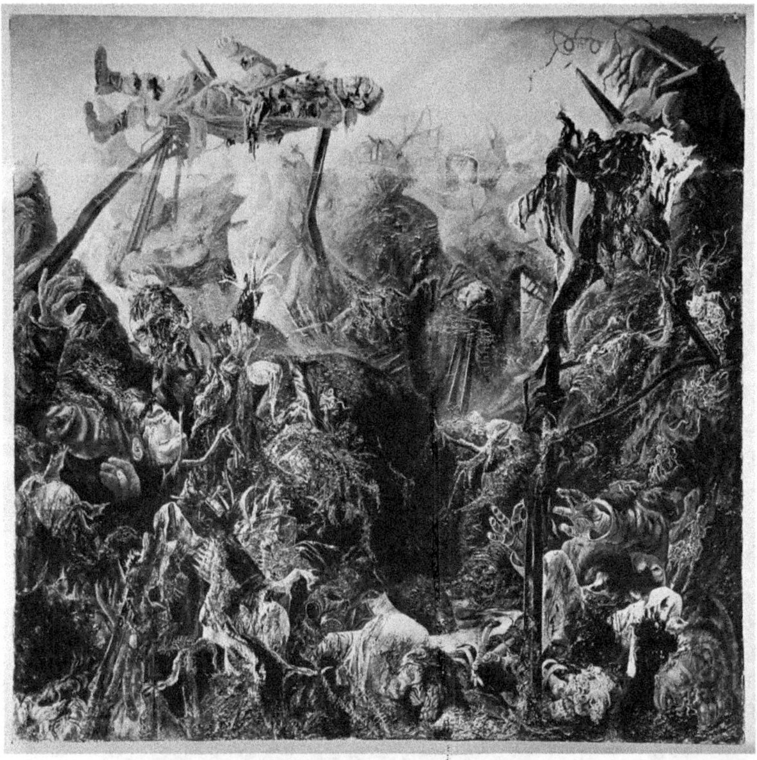

Figure 2. Otto Dix, *The Trench* [Schützengraben], oil on hessian, 1920–1923, lost, presumed destroyed. © Otto Dix / Artists Rights Society (ARS), New York / VG Bild-Kunst, Bonn. Photo © Rheinisches Bildarchiv Cologne, rba_64673, used with permission.

Otto Dix would return to this subject repeatedly throughout the 1920s and 1930s, each time aiming to make a high-profile contribution to the ongoing, and ever-evolving, public debate about the meaning of the war, and about who could claim to tell the truth of the war experience.[15] In 1932 Dix completed another such work, this one a massive and complex multi-panel composition, *The War* [Der Krieg] (1928–1932) (see Figure 3), which ranks with *Metropolis* as one of the central monuments of German painting from between the wars.

15 Paul Fox, "Confronting Postwar Shame in Weimar Germany: Trauma, Heroism, and the War Art of Otto Dix," *Oxford Art Journal*, 29/2 (2006), 247–267.

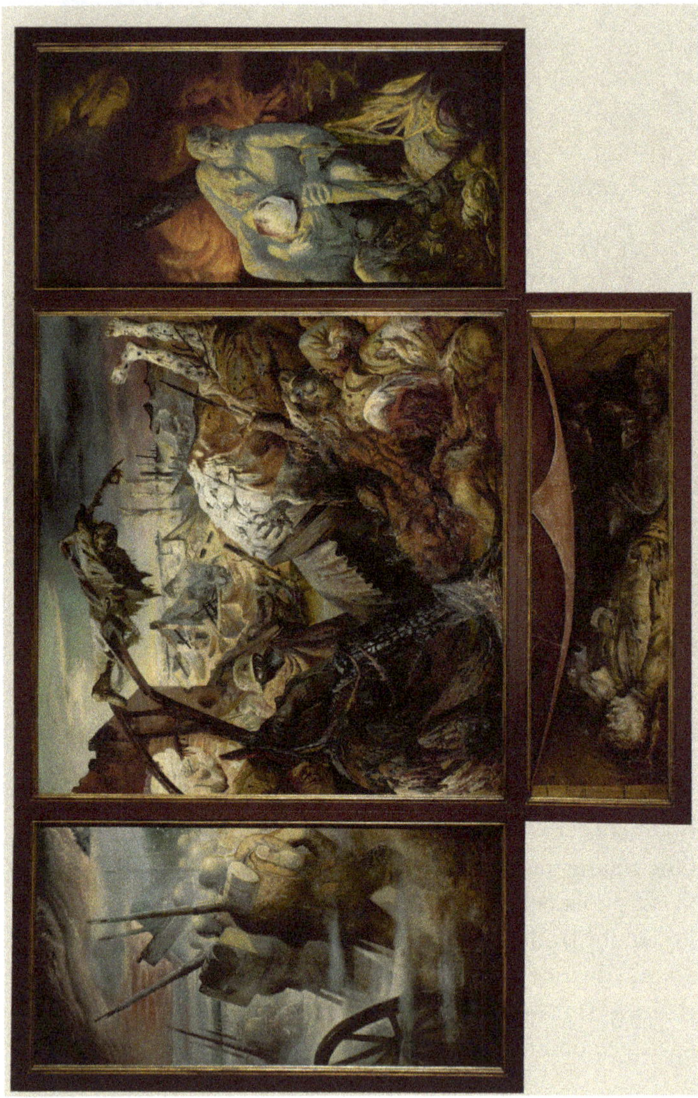

Figure 3. Otto Dix, *The War* [Der Krieg], oil and tempera on wood panel, 1928–1932, Staatliche Kunstsammlungen, Dresden, Galerie Neue Meister. © Otto Dix / Artists Rights Society (ARS), New York / VG Bild-Kunst, Bonn. Photo Art Resource, NY / Erich Lessing, used with permission.

It clearly broadcasts its intended status as an important public statement, but it came almost too late. In 1933, after the National Socialist seizure of power, the Nazis claimed a monopoly on the public work of remembrance. Otto Dix, whose competing interpretation of the war they had long resented, would not be allowed to participate in this conversation any longer. The Nazis had neither forgiven nor forgotten the affront to their own remembrance of the war which he presented with *The Trench* in 1923. That early painting had come to be associated, rightly or wrongly, with the political pacifism movement, and the Nazis accused him of practicing painting as an act of sabotage. They made *The Trench* a centerpiece of the notorious Degenerate Art exhibition in 1937, under the headline "*gemalte Wehrsabotage*," or "a painted act of military sabotage," before dispensing with it for good.[16] The public defamation of this particular painting could be said to be the first example of the right-wing practice of decrying modernist art and artists as an affront to healthy, normal, popular values and ethno-nationalist sentiment, cultural resentment as a form of the populist politics of outrage, a practice which has continued periodically to this day. The genealogy of twenty-first-century umbrage about "artists today" undermining the virtues and standards of Western European culture with their infamous disdain for skill and beauty, and their supposedly puerile desire to shock and scandalize, can be traced more or less directly back to the public media controversy over *The Trench*, and its rumination on the nature and meaning of the First World War.

Dix's representations of the war are, like all of his work of the 1920s, characterized by their unstinting realism. At times they border on caricature, and at others they are aggressive in their pitiless depictions of the grizzly realities of the first modern, mechanized war. They are always provocative in their refusal to glamorize warfare. In German art history,

16 It was exhibited in the "Degenerate Art" exhibition in Munich in 1937, and published in the exhibition guide under this slogan. The page from the exhibition guide is reproduced in Stephanie Barron, ed., *Degenerate Art. The Fate of the Avant-Garde in Nazi Germany* (Los Angeles, CA: Los Angeles County Museum of Art, 1991), 373.

Otto Dix has been understood as a protestor of war and militarism, either as an uncompromising individualist or as a committed antifascist, depending on whether his history was written in West Germany or in East Germany (or by West German art historians sympathetic to socialism), respectively. His combination of provocation and grotesque realism was routinely taken, even in his own day, as an unambiguous rejection of war and militarism and of the political culture that produces war and militarism, at first that of Kaiser Wilhelm and his caste, and then later the militarism of the Nazis. This understanding of Dix's provocative realism fit a certain conservative cultural narrative that was influential in the Weimar era, a narrative which diagnosed modern art, leftism, and pacifism as related symptoms of cultural decay. The Nazis reiterated the conservative interpretation of Dix as a provocative antiwar artist, and used it with insidious efficiency to defame modern art and pacifism simultaneously. After the Second World War, during the Cold War, the combination of those qualities of provocation and antimilitarism which had been ascribed to Dix comfortably fit a liberal ideology of the artist as sovereign and incorruptible. Otto Dix occupied a useful place in West German art history, as an artist who had made his art in determined and highly individual opposition to illiberalism and militarism. Because he was featured prominently by the Nazis in their "Degenerate Art" exhibition of 1937, the successor states, both East and West Germany, embraced him as a protestor, an antifascist, and an antiwar artist. In West Germany his individualism and seeming commitment to individual resistance or protest was celebrated, although his insistence on figurative art even late in life made it a challenge to assimilate him into the narrative of modern art.[17] In East Germany, where opposition to war was equated with antifascism, his depictions of the First World War were praised as antiwar propaganda: "It is the most tendentious painting that any German artist has created in a long time, because there is an open declaration behind

17 See the thorough overview of Dix reception through the 1980s in Ursula Zeller, "The Reception of Dix's Work," in Keith Hartley and Sarah O'Brien Twohig, eds., *Otto Dix, 1891–1969* (London: Tate Gallery, 1992), 49–60.

it. 'Make war on war,' that's the motto of this picture."[18] But these are all oversimplifications of his depictions of the front experience, tendentious interpretations which suited the political and ideological needs of the critic's or the art historian's own historical moment. And they all have in common a modernist image of the artist as highly individual, isolated from and mostly in opposition to public discourse and public opinion.

Otto Dix is a widely written-about artist, although primarily in German. I have endeavored as much as possible to make this narrative accessible to readers who are not steeped in the history of Weimar Germany, or in the career of Otto Dix. I must of course engage with the extensive existing literature, which has its own history, shaped by the needs of authors on either side of the Cold War divide and the consensus of the post-Cold War political order. But I have tried to avoid an obsessive preoccupation with the historiography of Dix studies, which is sizable in English and enormous in German. Most books take into account the entirety of his career, concentrating especially on the decade of the 1920s, the decade of his greatest prominence and most historically significant work. Monographs and exhibitions foreground his depictions of Weimar urban society; the war as a theme is considered primarily because of his representation of "war cripples" in the streets of postwar cities, or as a symptom of the era's fatal social contradictions. To date, his depictions of the war have been the subject of fewer studies. Most of those were written during the Cold War, when Otto Dix was claimed by both Germanies as a part of their two distinct "usable pasts." Fritz Löffler, a prominent East German art historian who had known Dix during the 1920s, placed his images of the war in the tradition of antifascism and political pacifism reaching back to the 1920s.[19] Otto Conzelmann, a West German art historian who was the first to write a monograph on Dix after the Second

18 "Es ist die tendenziöseste Darstellung, die seit langem ein deutscher Künstler geschaffen hat, weil hinter ihr das offene Bekenntnis steht. Krieg dem Kriege, das ist die Devise des Bildes." Horst Jähner, "Vor dem wie steht das was: Zu den Bildern über den Krieg von Otto Dix," *Bildende Kunst*, 6 (1957), 370–375, here p. 372.

19 Fritz Löffler, *Otto Dix. Life and Work* (R. J. Hollingdale, trans., New York and London: Holmes and Meier, 1982).

World War, separated Dix from any political intention whatsoever, and most especially any leftist politics, and emphasized instead the artist's individuality and existentialist emphasis on experience and a Nietzschean ideal of the artist as *übermensch*.[20] For Conzelmann (who, like Löffler, knew Dix personally), the depictions of the war experience were simply powerfully personal depictions of extremes of the human experience, and of the human spirit under great duress.[21] There have also been art historians in the west, sympathetic to Marxism even during the Cold War, who celebrated Dix as a political artist committed to socialism. Dietrich Schubert in particular has written tirelessly (and with great scholarly rigor) for decades in support of this vision of Dix's career and interpretation of his depictions of the war.[22] More recently, there have been a small number of monographs in German on individual works representing the war, especially the etching portfolio of 1924 and the triptych *The War* in Dresden.[23] The 1980s in particular saw an increasingly politicized dispute over whether Dix had been a committed Leftist or an apolitical artist (and therefore available to conservative writers and custodians of German culture).[24]

In English, the most sustained and important study of the war pictures is Linda McGreevy's monograph, *Bitter Witness*, from 2001.[25] As the title suggests, the artist's presumed embitterment about the war is a central theme. But it may be an unwarranted assumption, unduly influenced by Paul Fussell's reading of the British war poets, to think that this is the message of Dix's war pictures. McGreevy also emphasized the

20 Otto Conzelmann, *Otto Dix* (Hannover: Fackelträger, 1959).

21 Otto Conzelmann, *Der andere Dix – Sein Bild vom Menschen und vom Kriege* (Stuttgart: Hatje-Cantz, 1983).

22 See especially Schubert, *Otto Dix*.

23 Verein August Macke Haus, *Otto Dix. "Der Krieg" Radierwerk, 1924* (Bonn: August Macke Haus, 1999), and Dalbajewa, Fleischer, and Peters, eds., *Der Krieg*.

24 See Otto Karl Werckmeister, "Radical Art History," in: *Art Journal*, Vol. 42, No. 4 (Winter 1982), pp. 284–291, and, for an overview, Brigid S. Barton, "Die Entstehung eines Künstlerrufs: Otto Dix und Der Schützengaben," in: *Dix zum 100. Geburtstag: Symposium*, Albstadt: Galerie Albstadt, 1991, pp. 47–60.

25 McGreevy, *Bitter Witness*.

theme of trauma, a popular one in English-language scholarship in recent decades, and one taken up soon after by Paul Fox.[26] For McGreevy, the most important question seems to have been, "How true and accurate were Dix's depictions of the war?" The answer, according to her, was that they were very true, and she verifies his depictions with reference to histories of the war and written accounts of the conditions of the fighting, with an emphasis on the misery of the soldiers and the high casualty rates. This is a useful and excellent monograph, but accepts uncritically Dix's own rhetorical claims to the truthfulness and accuracy of his work, which he often claimed was guaranteed by his status as an eye-witness and a participant. Her study begs the question, what was the political, social, and ideological content of claiming to speak the truth about the war in the years after? I will follow Jay Winter in the present book, and view the very claims of truth-telling by individual eye-witnesses as part of the structure of public memory – not so much a guarantee of singular objective veracity, but rather part of a collective, discursive process.[27] In this way, where McGreevy located the meaning of the artworks in the period 1914–1918 and the events depicted in work, I will locate their meaning in the period 1919–1937, the years when the works were made and exhibited publicly. She wrote about what the works represent, with an emphasis on the artist's inner life and trauma, in his isolation, whereas I write here about the social context in which the works were meaningful, and about the larger social trends in which the artist participated. The present book treats the corpus of Dix's war images as an evolving process, rather than as a unified and monolithic statement of a single, consistent, and unambiguous message (of anti-war resentment and bitterness). I try to understand that process as part of the wider, social production of memory and meaning, and the search for a value in its sacrifices, rather than as exclusively the product of an individual artist's own inner psychological trauma, political clarity, or unchanging, unbending artistic and moral integrity in the face of a conflicted and flawed society.

26 Fox, "Confronting Postwar Shame."

27 See especially Winter, *Remembering War.*

Another characteristic of scholarship on Dix, especially since the 1980s, is a strong emphasis on the importance of the writer Friedrich Nietzsche for Dix and his work. The attention to the influence of Nietzsche and ecstatic vitalism on Dix has led to an overemphasis on the individuality of the person of the artist, suggesting a man in isolated, heroic struggle against the titanic forces of war and society. This image was first and forcefully set out by Otto Conzelmann, who used Nietzsche explicitly to depoliticize Dix's work.[28] For Conzelmann, Dix embraced his experiences of war and combat as an opportunity to observe man under extreme circumstances. The theme of Nietzsche's influence was also taken up by Dietrich Schubert, a West German art historian who is in every other way opposed to Conzelmann's presentation of Dix as apolitical.[29] For Schubert, Dix was obviously a committed communist, even if he never joined the party.[30] Art historian and curator Olaf Peters, who on the whole has a more balanced view of Dix's political outlook, has also strongly emphasized the importance of Nietzsche for the interpretation of his art.[31] Most recently, the theme of Nietzsche's importance for Dix's self-image is explored by Änne Söll, although more as an influence on his habitus as an avant-garde artist and a warrior than as a source for his iconography, which had previously been the focus of art historians preoccupied with Nietzsche.[32]

28 Conzelmann, *Der andere Dix*, and, following Conzelmann's emphasis on Nietzsche, Mathias Eberle, *World War I and the Weimar Artists. Dix, Grosz, Beckmann, Schlemmer* (New Haven, CT: Yale University Press, 1985).

29 See especially Schubert, *Otto Dix*; "Nietzsche-Konkretionsformen in der bildenden Kunst," Müller-Lauter and Volker Gerhardt, eds., *Nietzsche-Studien*, 10/11 (1981/82), 278–327; and "Die Verfolgung des Gemäldes *Schützengraben* (1923) von Otto Dix," Rolf Kloepfer and Burckhard Dücker, eds., *Kritik und Geschichte der Intoleranz* (Heidelberg: Syncron, 2000), 351–370.

30 See especially Schubert, *Otto Dix*, and also Schubert's open letter to Klett-Cotta, the publisher of Conzelmann's book, published in *Kritische Berichte*, as "Betrifft: O. Conzelmann, Der 'Andere' Dix," *Kritische Berichte* 12/1 (1984), 84–94.

31 See especially Olaf Peters, *Neue Sachlichkeit und Nationalsozialismus. Affirmation und Kritik 1931–1947* (Berlin: Reimer, 1998).

32 Änne Söll, *Der Neue Mann? Männerporträts von Otto Dix, Christian Schad und Anton Räderscheidt, 1914–1930* (Paderborn: Wilhelm Fink, 2016).

I want to present here an understanding of Dix's war pictures that is less focused on the artist's individualism. Far from personifying a singular and isolated moral rectitude, Dix actually expressed sentiments that were in line with the those of a majority of his fellow veterans, in particular those who shared his working-class, socialist background. Rather than simple pacifism, his pictures of the war experience expressed a much more complex mix of responses and sentiments, a mix which valued solidarity and sought meaning in his generation's collective experience. We need to be skeptical of the idealizing notion that Dix was somehow possessed of an exceptional moral clarity about the war, its causes and results, even clairvoyant about the coming catastrophe that would be brought on in part by nostalgia and revanchism.[33] We should resist the tendency to ascribe to Dix our own feelings about German militarism and our perspective on the First World War, informed as it is in hindsight by the rise of fascism, the Second World War, and the long ensuing history of modern military conflict. I also want to resist here the notion that the works representing the war were transcriptions of Dix's private experiences of 1915–1918. I am not concerned with measuring the accuracy of his representations against other accounts of those battles. Instead, I am concerned with the context in which these artworks were made – Germany society in the 1920s and into the 1930s, as it struggled to come to terms with all that had transpired. The artworks were his contributions to the public construction of a collective memory, and a public discourse about the meaning of the war, two related processes that unfolded in the period 1919–1937. The artworks may have represented events in the past, but they were very much about their own present.

For the next generation of art historians, who were trained towards the end of the Cold War or after, including Olaf Peters, Ulrike Lorenz,

33 Art historians continue to be wedded to the belief that Dix was clairvoyant about politics. See most recently Olaf Peter's otherwise quite balanced biography of the artist, *Otto Dix. Der unerschrockene Blick* (Stuttgart: Reclam, 2013), where he refers to him as a, "hellsichtiger politischer Beobachter," p. 169. Peters explores the theme of the artist as seer at length in *Neue Sachlichkeit und Nationalsozialismus*, 82 ff.

James van Dyke, Birgit Dalbajewa, and Kira van Lil, among others, the urgent ideological needs thrown up by the conflicts of the Cold War era are historical artefacts. Released from the need to find an ideological ally in this artist, and to claim him for "our" side, they are instead inclined to see a more balanced, nuanced picture of what the man was doing with his art, and to reconstruct the historical, cultural context in which his art originally made sense. The present study owes more to the growing literature on memory and the social construction of the memory of the Great War, and in particular the work of Jay Winter, and behind it Maurice Halbwachs, than to the ideological contests of the Cold War.[34]

In the English-speaking world a vivid and brutal depiction of the horrors of the war was primarily seen in the context of the English war poets, whose own vivid depictions of those horrors was so clearly meant as an indictment, not only of the generation which had sent their own sons off like lambs to the slaughter, but also of those who refused still to see the war for what it was. The British war poets – Siegfried Sassoon, Edmund Blunden, Robert Graves, Wilfred Owen, and others, had been steeped as schoolboys in the glories of the heroic Greeks before the walls of Troy, and were shocked by the reality of what had been so mystified for them by their Classics professors. They felt they had been lied to, and they were embittered about it. The combination of irony and bitter anger was identified by Paul Fussell as the root stock not only of modernist poetry but of the modern outlook on life itself.[35] Haunted by the sight of a gas victim, Wilfred Owen wrote, explicitly as an indictment (of Jessie Pope, author of widely published, pro-war poems, as it turns out), the lines,

> If in some smothering dreams, you too could pace
> Behind the wagon that we flung him in,

34 Jay Winter, *Sites of Memory, Sites of Mourning: The Great War in European Cultural History* (Cambridge: Cambridge University Press, 1995); Maurice Halbwachs, *On Collective Memory* (Chicago: University of Chicago Press, 1992, Lewis A. Coser, ed. and translator).

35 Paul Fussell, *The Great War and Modern Memory* (New York: Oxford University Press, 1975).

> And watch the white eyes writhing in his face,
> His hanging face, like a devil's sick of sin;
> If you could hear, at every jolt, the blood
> Come gargling from the froth-corrupted lungs,
> Obscene as cancer, bitter as the cud
> Of vile, incurable sores on innocent tongues,—
> My friend, you would not tell with such high zest
> To children ardent for some desperate glory,
> The old Lie: *Dulce et decorum est*
> *Pro patria mori.*

Verse such as this, scathing, condemnatory, and lurid, established for English-speaking audiences an indissoluble link between the unstinting depiction of the true human cost of the war, seen up-close and reported in the first-person, and of the hypocrisy that refused to see war for what it was. The British war poets taught us the lesson that any harrowingly realistic depiction of the war and its effects must of necessity also be a full-throated condemnation of it. But this is not necessarily the lesson of Otto Dix. The tendency to confuse Dix's response to the First World War with our own persists because it makes Dix politically and morally unambiguous, and possessed of an admirable clarity of foresight as well.[36] But our own unambiguous ideas about the First World War – that it was a horrible, senseless, and pointless mass slaughter – overlooks what was almost certainly the most common response of veterans to their memories of the war. The widespread sentiment among the veterans of the war was that, while it was a horrible experience that one would never wish to repeat, it was nonetheless meaningful, even a defining moment in one's biography, and an event that should above all be *actively remembered*. I will take as my starting point here the assumption that Otto Dix most likely shared the attitudes of his contemporaries, at least those from his own milieu

36 See, for example, Philippe Dagen, "The Morality of Horror," in Annette Becker, ed., *Der Krieg / The War* (Peronne: Historial de la Grande Guerre, 2003), 9–23. For Dagen, Dix was not only a pacifist and a war protestor, he was also a communist in all but official membership. This is a misrepresentation.

and background. Assuming, or better, *wishing* that he had anticipated our own judgments has colored our reading of his works.

Alerted by Mikhail Bakhtin to the importance of carnivalesque humor and grotesque realism in folk culture, a humor which aimed to keep the fear of death at bay, as well as at undermining the cultural authority of classicism, I will read Dix's provocative, humorously grotesque images of the war as expressions of a working-class culture among enlisted men, a language of the trenches which sustained the soldiers in their daily struggle against death, the working conditions at the front, and the officer class.[37] Bakhtin, a Russian literary theorist, was a contemporary of Dix, and wrote an exuberantly celebratory study of the continued vitality in Renaissance literary language of medieval folk culture, with its wit, earthiness, and degradation of elevated culture and social hierarchy.[38] The importance of the cultural elements he identified, in particular grotesque humor and earthy realism, for the countercultural and even revolutionary activity of the Berlin Dadaists after the war (a group which briefly included Dix), has been identified by the work of Christian Weikop.[39] But the sardonic wit and grotesque humor of Dada already characterized the verbal culture of the soldiers in the trenches on all sides during the war, as was widely remarked-upon already at the time. The chaotic, carnivalesque speech that Bakhtin would identify as the continuity of subversive medieval popular culture into the Renaissance and beyond had bloomed again in the glossaries of soldiers' slang and the humorous newspapers published by the soldiers themselves at the front. It served the soldiers in the trenches, expressing in ribald, excessive and often vulgar language the truth about the

37 Mikhail Bakhtin, *Rabelais and His World* (Bloomington: Indiana University Press, reprint edition 1984, Hélène Iswolsky, translator). Originally written in 1940 as a dissertation.

38 Bakhtin, *Rabelais and His World*.

39 Christian Weikop, "Berlin Dada and the Carnivalesque. *Jedermann sein eigner Fussball* (1919) and *Der Dada* (1919–1920)," in Peter Brooker and Andrew Thacker, eds., *The Oxford Critical and Cultural History of Modernist Magazines: Europe 1880–1940* (Oxford: Oxford University Press, 2014), 816–854.

war experience that official newspapers and other accounts, written in approved, elevated verbal and visual languages, could not or would not express. Following Bakhtin, it is possible to identify his category of the "lower bodily stratum" as the source of most of the soldier's slang, and to identify as one of the main functions of that slang the establishment of a society apart. Erich Maria Remarque confirms both of these theses in *All Quiet on the Western Front*, when he writes that three-quarters of the soldier's slang

> is derived from ... his stomach and intestines. ... they give an intimate flavor to expressions of his greatest joy as well as of his deepest indignations. It is impossible to express oneself in any other way so clearly and pithily. Our families and our teachers will be shocked when we go home, but here it is the universal language. (p. 8)

Remarque wrote this in 1927, but already during the war linguists had begun to collect and publish soldiers' humorous slang terms in German, French, and English. Dix himself collected several specimens in his field notebook. Although Remarque, writing in 1928, claimed that the earthy humor was increasingly tinged with bitterness as the war went on, earlier in the 1920s Dix was using it to craft a nuanced and complicated message addressed specifically to his fellow veterans, as I will argue, and one that was much more than simply a shared bitterness about the war. After the war, Dix sought to fashion a visual equivalent to this verbal language, one that, far from isolating him as a voice in moral opposition to society, actually established a connection between Dix and his fellow veterans, a community apart from the older generation and from civilians.

As the 1920s progressed, the provocation and the grotesque humor fell away in Dix's work, to be displaced by a greater level of artistic craft and mastery as well as complexity of meaning and art historical associations. There was also an increasing concern with the central virtues that had by that time emerged as the collective meaning of the war for many veterans: comradeship and solidarity between enlisted men; faithfulness to duty; and a normative masculinity. Following Jay Winter, I emphasize here the collective work of remembrance, rather than the isolated individuality of trauma. Otto Dix did not work in intellectual, cultural, or moral isolation. He participated in and responded to the public discourse about the meaning and the legacy of the war in Germany, especially in the socialist, center left milieu into which he had been born. As that discourse and work of remembrance evolved over the course of the 1920s and early 1930s, Dix's monumental works of art evolved with them. At the same time, all of his work, including his depictions of contemporary life in Germany, increasingly emphasized craft and art historical references, while growing less and less provocative. His art continued to emphasize monumentality, as if to present itself as a modernist alternative to the traditional language of war memorials, and it continued to emphasize a combination of craft, art history (especially German Renaissance art historical precedents), the virtue of solidarity, and an increasingly complex tension between normative masculinity and tenderness and (non-genital) physical intimacy between men under fire.[40] The message and procedures of Dix's work was not static; it did not remain unchanged throughout the interwar period. Indeed, it changed significantly over the years, and in ways that can to a great extent be mapped onto the changes in the larger public discourse. How could works of great craftsmanship and art historical ambition, such as *The War*, or *Flanders* (1934–1936) (see Figure 4), be seen as the continuation of the earlier satirical, Dadaistic works, which had been so hostile to the material conventions of high art? In the past, the answer given to this question has always been the supposed unity of their clear, unambiguous, and unchanging message of anti-militarism and bitterness about the war.[41] Yet this is too simple – and too static. Here I construct instead a narrative of the artist's own evolving attitudes, which were in dialog with rapidly changing social attitudes in German society about the war, and in which the meaning is shifting, never quite as unambiguous as art historians have made it out to be.

40 Santanu Das, "Wilfred Owen and the sense of touch," in Das, *Touch and Intimacy in First World War Literature* (Cambridge: Cambridge University Press, 2005), 137–174.

41 See for example McGreevy, *Bitter Witness*.

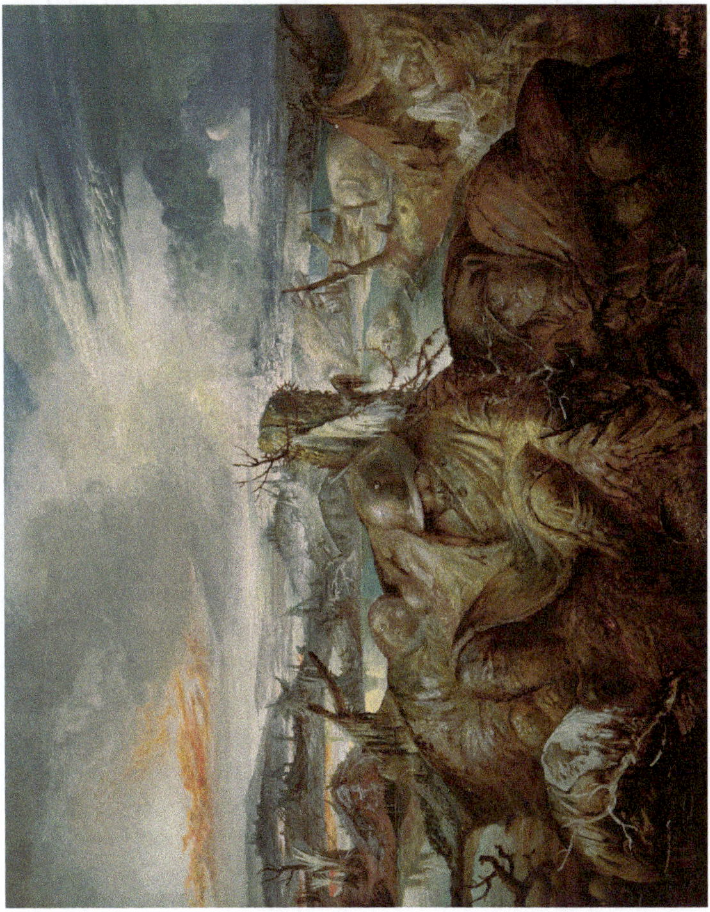

Figure 4. Otto Dix, *Flanders* [Flandern], oil and tempera on canvas, 1934–1936, Natonalgalerie, Staatliche Museen zu Berlin: B 658. © Otto Dix / Artists Rights Society (ARS), New York / VG Bild-Kunst, Bonn. Photo © akg-images / Jörg P. Anders, used with permission.

Otto Dix partook in a discourse of memory creation that had clear ground rules and standards. In written texts, such as Remarque's *All Quiet on the Western Front*, those rules and standards demanded, in the analysis of Thomas F. Schneider,

> that the author should be a veteran; that the events described in the text should have been experienced by the author; and that the events should be verifiable (and, therefore, exact dates and locations had to be given). Further, these standards prevented fiction about the war from formulating interpretations of the war. ... valid texts about the war should show no obvious tendency or political meaning.[42]

If we allow "valid texts" to include visual images, then it is possible to say that Dix followed these rules scrupulously. Except that there was a political tendency – but it was in a way so mainstream as to be overlooked. My reading of the war pictures, especially after 1923, finds evidence that Dix shared the attitudes of the largest organized group of veterans, which was affiliated with the left-liberal Social Democrats, the cultural identity that Dix brought from his working-class background. I draw here on the work of Benjamin Ziemann, who has reconstructed the attitudes about the war expressed by Social Democrat veterans' organizations.[43] Dix shared many of the concerns and attitudes of this group, although he could also differ from them in significant ways.

None of this is to say that his pictures were pro-war pictures. They certainly were not. But what that meant for Dix and his audience in the period between the wars might not be what we think it meant. The "meaning of the war" in Germany was a rhizomic discourse, sometimes disappearing from view for a time, but always continuing to grow and change underground, as it were, and make new, unexpected connections, popping up again when it was supposed to have been buried and forgotten. The

42 Thomas F. Schneider, "The Weimar Republic and the Literature of the Great War," in Brian Murdoch, ed., *Critical Insights.* All Quiet on the Western Front *by Erich Maria Remarque* (Pasadena, CA: Salem Press, 2011), 23–37, here p. 28.

43 See especially Benjamin Ziemann, *Contested Commemorations, Republican War Veterans and Weimar Political Culture* (Cambridge: Cambridge University Press, 2012).

discourse of the left and the discourse of the right were at times quite distinct, and at times similar, and the artworks of Otto Dix were part of this discourse, connected to it at several points, in places branching off from it, but never wholly outside of, or in total opposition to that discourse.

But did Otto Dix express in his art a condemnation of war in general, or even of the First World War in particular? This is an important question to answer, but a surprisingly difficult one.[44] Dix was not a wordy artist, and did not write personal statements about his work or his social or political positions. His reflective statements made in interviews after the Second World War are unreliable guides to his work from the 1920s, made as they were in a very different (and complicated) political situation, at a very different time in his life, and in a very different mood. Yet his statement to friends in the 1960s that he "was not really a pacifist" seems straightforward enough.[45] Part of the difficulty in interpreting what appears at first to be the central problem of the work stems from the fact that "pacifism" in the postwar, nuclear age has for a long time now meant something different than it did in the period between the world wars. The fascist war of aggression and total destruction and of genocide gave to the question of pacifism a more universally recognized and urgent moral cast beginning in the 1950s. Add to this the broad popularity of the antiwar movement in the era of the Vietnam War, and the moral complexity of the question in the post-Cold-War era of UN interventions (or non-interventions), neo-Imperialism, and ISIS, and the meaning of the term "pacifism" is very different, in its moral resonance, than it was a century ago. Pacifism meant something narrower, and much more problematic, in Germany in the 1920s and early 1930s than it does to us. To gain a definite sense of what Dix's

44 A good overview – though now out of date – of the literature on this specific question is given in Jorg Martin Merz, "Otto Dix' Kriegsbilder. Motivationen – Intentionen – Rezeptionen," *Marburger Jahrbuch für Kunstwissenschaft* 26 (1999), 189–226. More recent is Kira van Lil, "Ein perfekter Skandal. Der 'Schützengraben' von Otto Dix zwischen Kritik und Verfemung," in Uwe Fleckner, ed., *Das verfemte Meisterwerk. Schicksalswege moderner Kunst im "Dritten Reich"* (Berlin: Akademie Verlag, 2009), 49–74.

45 Maria Wetzel, "Professor Otto Dix – Ein harter Mann, dieser Maler," *Diplotamischer Kurier* 14 (1965), 731–745. Reprinted in Schmidt, *Otto Dix im Selbstbildnis*, 269–270.

representations of the war meant to a German audience in his own day, specifically with regard to the question "pacifism" or "anti-militarism," we will need to be specific about what those positions were at that time. And so in this book I define pacifism in a strict way, as the radical rejection of some commonly held beliefs: that a nation-state or a people should defend itself, sometimes militarily; and that it was morally right for soldiers in uniform to abide by their duty to hold their line, remain under arms, and defend themselves, their nation, and each other. These ideas were not widely questioned in the 1920s. But the true, radical pacifist viewed all armed conflict as immoral and criminal, and rejected categorically such ideas as duty, honor, and even national defense as part of the web of lies spun by the ruling class, officer caste, and war profiteers, or as an expression of man's worst and most primitive impulses. The true pacifist dreams of a utopic world without armies or armed conflict, in which the spirit of the universal brotherhood of man triumphs over all struggle between states. But the radical pacifist is also the one who takes concrete steps to end or even prevent armed conflict, by striking in the munitions factory, dodging the draft, and, in Weimar Germany, exposing the illegal buildup of the German army beyond the sharp limits set by the Versailles Treaty. When the Nazis exhibited two of Dix's paintings about the war under the rubric "painted military sabotage" they were accusing him of being just this sort of radical, activist – and treasonous – pacifist. Such radical pacifists were in the minority, and because they advocated breaking the law in the service of pacifism, they were often arrested and prosecuted for treason. There were public figures during and after the First World War who answered to this description, such as Bertrand Russell in Britain, Émile Arnaud (who coined the term "pacifism") in France, and Kurt Tucholsky in Germany. But they held a fringe position.

The pacifist movement, with its slogan "Nie Wieder Krieg" [Never Again War] was strongest and most popular in Germany in the months immediately following the end of the war, but continued in the margins of German political life until the National Socialists came to power in 1933 and brutally suppressed it. A more common sentiment – distinct from political "pacifism," was the opposition to a vaguer phenomenon called "Prussian militarism," meaning the glorification of military display and an exaggerated reverence for hierarchy and obedience, as well as a belief in the natural order of aristocratic privilege and the officer caste. The rejection of "Prussian militarism" was widely viewed as sort of normal, healthy skepticism, akin to resenting aristocrats or the rich, and was not only confined to Germany. One could reject Prussian militarism and still believe in the need for a standing army to defend the nation, even an army larger than the one allowed under the terms of the Versailles Treaty. The rejection of the spirit of Prussian militarism, combined with an emphasis on the suffering of the front soldier during the war, or on the grief of those whose sons, brothers, and husbands had been killed, wasn't so much pacifism as a resentment of the conditions of the world war specifically. Radical pacifism on the other hand was a much more extreme position and was widely viewed with suspicion. Tucholsky wrote in 1928, in "Healthy Pacifism," an essay that appeared under one of his many pseudonyms, that the only true pacifist was an individual who, like himself, "struggled against war by *every* means," including illegal means such as dodging the draft or striking in the munitions factory.[46] Tucholsky was joined in his extremism by the radical pacifist Kurt Hiller, who founded in 1926 the *Gruppe Revolutionärer Pazifisten* [Group of Revolutionary Pacifists], which aimed at ending war and rearmament through both political and direct action.

The political pacifist movement in Germany sought to enlist Dix to their cause, but he kept them at arm's length. Kurt Hiller wrote enthusiastically to Dix, hoping for the artist's support (it was not forthcoming).[47] Dix's gallery dealer Karl Nierendorf, who handled the promotion of *The Trench* and, after it, the portfolio of 50 etchings titled *The War*, was more receptive, allowing a pacifist organization to reproduce *The Trench* on the cover of a brochure titled "*Nie wieder Krieg*." Dix had grown up in a time when pacifism even in the weak sense, as a desire to avoid armed conflict and find less violent means of settling disputes between nation states, was viewed with deeply felt disapproval, even moral revulsion. A desire to avoid

46 Ignaz Wrobel (pseud. of Kurt Tucholsky), "Gesunder Pazifismus," *Das Andere Deutschland* (31 March 1928), 4.

47 Letter from Kurt Hiller, written on the stationery of the Gruppe Revolutionärer Pazifisten, dated 17 October 1926, DAK, I, C, 343.

war was seen by a generation that had never known a European land war as a form of cowardice; it did not conform to normative conceptions of masculinity. During the Eulenburg Affair that embroiled the monarchy of Kaiser Wilhelm II and the German nation in the first decade of the twentieth century (when Otto Dix was an adolescent), a strong and lasting negative link was forged in the German public imagination between pacifism and negatively viewed homosexuality.[48] Note that Tucholsky, in his writings promoting pacifism, characterizes his brand of pacifism as "healthy," to distinguish it from the "unnatural" pacifism still associated with Prince Eulenburg and the "camarilla" around Kaiser Wilhelm. But Tucholsky's efforts to cleanse pacifism of its disrepute were in vain. In the German public imagination, even after the war, radical pacifism was viewed in the 1920s as politically extreme, criminal, and tainted by associations with homosexuality. There is no reason to suppose that Otto Dix did not share the broader public sentiment of homophobic and political revulsion, other than an ahistorical projection of our own progressive values onto the protagonists of our narratives.

Dix expressed in his artworks what might be called a "weak" form of pacifism: the subjective, individual sentiment that war is a calamity, and that its primary qualities are unnecessary suffering, destruction and death, rather than gallantry, glory and political advantage. Dix created realistic representations of war, as the painful mangling and violation of bodies, rather than a romanticizing emphasis on glamorous uniforms, gallant gestures, and men on horseback. His were the most extreme version of this artistic position that anyone had ever seen, which is why his artwork about the war remains relevant and powerfully affecting to this day. But there is little evidence that Dix was a pacifist in the strong sense of the term, in the sense of pacifism as a political program and plan of action, of action that included refusing to serve, hindering the production of munitions – or making public statements that encouraged others to do these things. His artwork did not aim to motivate people to embrace the radical politics of pacifism. This is what the critic Alfred Solmony meant when he wrote that

48 Norman Domeier, *The Eulenburg Affair. A Cultural History of Politics in the German Empire* (Rochester, NY: Camden House, 2015), 206 f.

Dix's most notorious painting of the war, *The Trench* (1920–1923) was *not* pacifist propaganda, "The picture is not tendentious, but only a pedantically precise, objective depiction."[49] But the National Socialists would in fact accuse Dix of the crime of sabotage for painting it.

Organization of the book

This book proceeds chronologically, beginning with the paintings Dix made of himself as a soldier in training, when he was still only anticipating what the front might be like, proceeding through the work he made while actually at the front, and on to the work he made about the war experience after the war was over. He made art during the four years of the war, and then went on, after the war ended, to return to the themes and images of combat over the next 17 years. Only a second world war, another period in uniform, and almost a year spent as a prisoner of war among the French, finally ended the work of remembrance of the First World War. Hence the bulk of this book will actually be about the period between 1919 and 1936, and only the first chapter will be about the period of the war itself.

In the first chapter I cover the artwork done during the years of the war, both before Dix arrived at the front and then while he was there. Even within this era we can see a dramatic and rapid evolution of the art, from Expressionist pathos and crudity to sober observational drawing, to mythic distillations of war itself, rendered again in an Expressionistic vocabulary. I emphasize the disunity in Dix's work, as he went from one idea to another about what it even meant to represent the war. As his ideas about this changed, his means of representation changed, too, from naturalistic drawings done strictly from life to imaginative, expressive, even symbolic

49 "Das Bild kennt keine Tendenz, nur peinlich genaue sachliche Schilderung: so ist Krieg." Alfred Salmony, "Die neue Galerie des 17. Bis 20. Jahrhunderts im Museum Wallraf-Richartz in Köln," *Der Cicerone* 16/1, 6–11.

distillations of the very essence of combat violence. I also emphasize the degree to which Dix had the ambition to exhibit his work and was responsive to his audience, even this early in his career, as well as his relationship to, and differences from, his artistic peers. The art Dix made during the war changed and evolved to follow three primary issues: the changing and evolving national conversation about what the war was really like; what it meant; and who had the right to talk about it. The first shift was from the depiction of the war while it was happening, the life of the soldier and the world of barracks, trenches, landscapes, shelling, and bodies, to an exploration of the essence of armed combat. At first, Dix recorded, surprisingly, anything *but* the scenes of actual violence and drama, fear and carnage. The horrors of war became, however, the overwhelming focus of the later work of remembrance.

After the war, Dix turned to the depiction of those unfortunate men who returned from the war having lost limbs, having suffered disfiguration of their faces, blindness, or shell shock. This is the subject of the second chapter. In 1920 Dix evolved again, rapidly, from a "second-generation German Expressionist" interested in ecstatic states and cosmic themes, to a Dadaist, toying with collage and social critique. During this time, between 1919 and 1921, he seemed preoccupied, obsessed even, with the question of nerves, the loss of nerve (and why he himself had kept his nerve when others had not), and sexual potency. But I will show that he was also preoccupied with the language and attitude of the front soldier, the grunt or *Frontschwein*, and that he sought in Dadaist collage and humor an opportunity for a visual equivalent to the earthy, vulgar, humorous slang of the trenches.

In the third chapter I discuss *The Trench*, the central painting of the entire complex and a key painting in the political contest over "shocking" modernist art. It's shadow would stretch over the rest of Dix's public career until the Second World War. It, too, partakes of the language of the comic grotesque. The public debate over this painting will be an important factor in my discussion, enabling us to consider it as part of the public, collective work of remembrance. At the same time, the partnership between the artist and his gallery dealer, Karl Nierendorf, a partnership with a mix of cooperation and conflict, will be an important part of the story – all against the backdrop of the Allied occupation of the Rhineland, undertaken to secure the payment of the onerous reparations schedule set down in the Versailles Treaty.

In the fourth chapter I discuss the portfolio of 50 etchings on the subject of the war which Dix made in 1924. With this massive project, Dix moved away from the provocative, transgressive form of grotesque humor, to a more somber tone. At the same time, he began to emphasize in his work what had come to be identified as the primary virtue of the war, the thing that gave it meaning: *Kameradschaft* or camaraderie. Dix produced the 50 images for this portfolio at a significant moment in the ongoing work of public memory about the war. The publication of *All Quiet on the Western Front* by Erich Maria Remarque in 1928 is often mentioned as a turning point in the public discussion in Germany of the war and its legacy. I will look instead to the founding of the center-left *Reichsbanner* in 1924, which would be the largest veterans' group in Germany. It publicly presented an understanding of the war quite distinct from that of the nationalist counter-revolutionaries like the *Stahlhelm*. The different veterans' groups made *Kameradschaft* into the central virtue of the war (it was well established by the time Remarque cited it in the opening pages of his novel in 1928), although they argued over who was included in its embrace; was it German officers and enlisted men both, or was it just enlisted men – possibly from both sides of no-man's-land? The emphasis on camaraderie, however, excluded many who had suffered through the war: women in particular, and non-combatants of all kinds.

Dix continued to work through these questions and conflicts in the largest of his artworks, a kind of public monument, the multi-panel altarpiece *The War*. This work is the subject of Chapter 5. In this complicated painting, which went through an equally complicated process of becoming, Dix again claimed his right, as an eye-witness, to make public statements about the truth and the meaning of the war experience. By now a professor of, essentially, history painting, he created a modern-day public salon-piece with layered symbolic references and art-historical associations. It is little wonder that this painting in particular has generated so many interpretations which make of it a complex allegory. My own effort to interpret it eschews the Nietzschean and philosophical readings in favor of a comparison with actual public monuments.[50] Following Jay Winter again, I compare the triptych to war memorials which were themselves created to express social agency.[51] It was a somewhat paradoxical attempt by an individual artist, working without a public commission, to create a moment of social agency. But Dix was also working in a social environment which included popular books and films about the war, of which he was certainly aware. In his long process of working on this triptych, begun as early as 1927 and exhibited in Berlin in 1932, at the Autumn Salon of the Prussian Academy (of which he was by then a member), he sometimes included, and then sometimes again painted out, references to films and other popular narratives alongside art historical precedents redolent of specifically German associations.

In the sixth and final chapter, I consider the last painting Dix made about the experience of the First World War, another monumental painting, *Flanders*. This painting continues to emphasize the virtue of camaraderie, in dialog with other kinds of monuments. But this painting in particular emphasizes a physical tenderness between two soldiers. At the same time, Dix continues to emphasize heteronormativity in his construction of the memory of the front, and of camaraderie. This chapter also discusses the seizure of power by the National Socialist party, a turn of events that was calamitous for Otto Dix. The artist's very public remembrance of the war experience was very much at odds with that espoused by nationalist conservatives like the Nazis. They fully intended to enforce their cultural monopoly on the public process of remembrance, and one way in which they accomplished this was by marginalizing Otto Dix. The artist's efforts to maintain a professional career as a public artist – and the Nazis' determination to prevent him from doing so – is a narrative which is entwined

50 For a specifically Nietzschean interpretation of this painting and its iconography, see Olaf Peters, "Die ewige Wiederkehr des Gleichen. Zur Geschichtsauffasung des Gemäldes 'Der Krieg' von Otto Dix," in Uwe Fleckner, ed., *Bilder machen Geschichte: Historische Erignisse im Gedächtnis der Kunst* (Berlin: DeGruyter, 2014), 305–318.

51 Jay Winter, "War Memorials. A Social Agency Approach," in Jay Winter, ed., *Remembering War. The Great War Between Memory and History in the Twentieth Century* (New Haven, CT: Yale University Press, 2006), 135–153.

with his efforts to articulate a specific memory in *Flanders*, and also with his turn to landscape painting. It was not by chance that the landscape came to dominate the composition of *Flanders*. Dix was not able to exhibit the painting in Germany during the Third Reich, and spent his time in a kind of exile in rural southern Germany, finally deprived of his public audience. Yet war was not done with him. He ended the Second World War in uniform, in a French POW camp, painting altarpieces for his fellow prisoners as a last, concrete gesture of camaraderie. That is where the book ends. Dix lived out his final years, from 1946 to 1969, in his bourgeois villa on the southernmost shore of Germany, painting and making prints, moving between East and West Germany, neither of which had much use for his late artwork. The First World War no longer concerned him, and thus the last 24 years of his life do not concern this book.

CHAPTER 1

Dix in Uniform: The First World War and the Front Experience

When the First World War began, Otto Dix was 22 years old and had just completed four years of study at the *Kunstgewerbeschule* [School of Arts and Crafts] in Dresden. He was almost completely unknown. Unlike many German artists whose works can be found in museums today, such as Max Beckmann, Ernst Ludwig Kirchner, or Hermann Max Pechstein, Dix had no connections and no way to avoid fighting at the front as an enlisted man; he was in uniform, training and in and out of combat on both the Eastern and Western fronts for four years.[52] During the course of the war, he made more than 600 drawings on paper, as well as 72 gouaches, a remarkable achievement. Dix was already conversant with the formal languages of modernist experimentation and over the course of the war he tried a wide variety of stylistic directions.[53] Too little has been made of these different techniques and formal diversity, and in particular it has been little remarked that the works fall into clearly distinguishable periods. Dix did not simply try one

52 Or perhaps he did. After he was inducted it would be 13 months before he was shipped to the front, as he underwent first one sort of training and then another, a very curious circumstance. Bernd Ulrich has suggested that it might have been Bruno Alexander Roscher, who sat for a portrait by Dix in 1915 (and whom Ulrich identifies as an NCO in the artillery), who protected the young and obviously talented artist during that first year. Bernd Ulrich, "'Dann gehts wieder in die schöne Läuse-Schlampagne'. Otto Dix im Ersten Weltkrieg," in Birgit Dalbajewa, Simone Fleischer, and Olaf Peters, *Otto Dix. Der Krieg – Das Dresdner Triptychon* (Dresden: Sandstein, 2014), 35–43.

53 Fritz Löffler, *Otto Dix und der Krieg* (Leipzig: Reclam, 1986); Otto Conzelmann, *Der andere Dix – Sein Bild vom Menschen und vom Kriege* (Stuttgart: Hatje-Cantz, 1983); Dietrich Schubert, *Künstler im Trommelfeuer des Krieges* (Heidelberg: Wunderhorn, 2013).

thing alongside another in aimless eclecticism. Rather, to judge by the work, he went through different phases of thinking about what it meant to represent war. These different phases were separated by interruptions to his time at the front, pauses that must have afforded him moments of self-reflection. Yet in the literature on Otto Dix, his work tends to be characterized as a coherent body of work, unified by a single underlying meaning, whether that meaning comes from his Nietzschean embrace of unbridled human impulses or his fascination with or abhorrence of the destructive energy of the war machine.[54] What has mattered most, it often seems, is to present Dix as an artist of integrity and authenticity, a paragon of the modernist ideology of the individualistic creator, a figure of single-minded opposition to what we now see as the absolute pointlessness of the First World War. I will instead emphasize the ways in which Dix was attuned to his audience and responded positively to his situation and even to the experience of the war itself – but avoiding what has become an overemphasis on an individualistic, Nietzschean celebration of the primal human condition. In what follows I emphasize instead the different phases of his production, and what I see as the underlying differences in meaning as the young artist moved from one idea about the representation of war to another. Significantly, comparisons with the work of other artist-soldiers reveal some surprising and significant differences between Dix's representations of his wartime experiences and theirs.[55] Dix is often treated in splendid isolation from his contemporaries, but it will be instructive to return him to the fold of his peers.

The pictures Dix made in 1914–1918 are often treated as precursors to his later, most historically significant representations of the war, again emphasizing the unity of his work and of its meaning.[56] But there are some

54 Brigid S. Barton, "Die Entstehung eines Künstlerrufs: Otto Dix und *Der Schützengraben*," in Rainer Beck, *Otto Dix, 1891–1969: Zeit, Leben, Werk* (Konstanz: Stadler, 1993); Mathias Eberle, *World War I and the Weimar Artists. Dix, Grosz, Beckmann, Schlemmer* (New Haven, CT: Yale University Press, 1985).

55 Other scholars who have made such comparisons include Linda McGreevy, *Bitter Witness: Otto Dix and the Great War* (Bern: Peter Lang, 2003), esp. 144–171, and Schubert, *Künstler im Trommelfeuer*, but they draw different conclusions.

56 Kira van Lil, "Ein perfekter Skandal. Der 'Schützengraben' von Otto Dix zwischen Kritik und Verfemung," in Uwe Fleckner, ed., *Das verfemte Meisterwerk. Schicksalswege*

profound differences between the drawings done at the front during the war and his most famous monumental depictions of it done from memory during the 1920s. The most significant difference turns out to be, on closer inspection, the near total absence of the violence of the war from his drawings, especially the most naturalistic drawings done in 1915–1916, whereas the works done in the 1920s emphasize to an extraordinary degree the violence done to the human body. Other artists who also fought in the trenches, by comparison, often emphasized the violence of the war in their drawings done at or near the front. But like other artists who saw and represented the war, Dix was crafting his depiction of it with an eye to his audience, and with his evolving style and emerging career always in mind.

From art student to soldier

Wilhelm Heinrich Otto Dix was born in 1891, in the small industrial city of Gera in what is today the state of Thuringia in southeastern Germany, although at the time it was the primary town of a tiny, sovereign principality within the German Empire, Reuss-Gera. His father, Ernst Franz Dix, born in Untermhaus (which was later incorporated into Gera) in 1862, was a skilled iron worker, a die-caster in a foundry; he had bought a small parcel of land abutting the St. Marien Church in Untermhaus and had built the house in which Otto Dix and his brother and sister would grow up. Their mother, Louise Pauline, née Amann, was a seamstress. The family did not belong to the working poor of industrial Europe, but to a better-off segment of the working class. After completing his primary school education, Dix spent three years, from 1907 to 1910, as an apprentice decorative painter in the provincial city of Gera. His apprenticeship had been a traditional one, and included such duties as grinding pigments and cleaning the hen house

---

moderner Kunst im "Dritten Reich" (Berlin: Akademie, 2009), 49–74; Olaf Peters, "Die Erfahrung des Krieges, 1914–1918," in Dalbajewa, Fleischer, and Peters, eds., *Der Krieg*, 47–53.

(which produced the eggs needed for tempera painting, as well as food). After this traditional education in the trade of decorative art, Dix received a stipend from the Prince of Reuss-Gera to study at the *Kunstgewerbeschule* [School of Arts and Crafts] in nearby Dresden, in the much larger neighboring state of Saxony. Despite coming from somewhat better circumstances than the families of most industrial workers, Dix could hardly have expected to finance his continuing education himself. The stipend from the Prince of Reuss-Gera (who counted the Dix family among his 150,000 or so subjects) enabled this young man of obvious talent to pursue what was supposed to be a practical career in applied art. At the Dresden School of Arts and Crafts he studied figure drawing as well as ornament, and continued his practice of observational drawing from nature, a habit begun in grade school. Although he was a student of the School of Arts and Crafts, rather than the more prestigious Dresden Academy of Art (where he would in fact study after the war), he was nonetheless an ambitious young artist, and frequently visited both the old master collections of Dresden's famous Gemäldegalerie Alte Meister, and the exhibitions of avant-garde art that were taking place with increasing frequency in the city. Dix already had an ambition to be an avant-garde artist. And he would achieve his goal; in the late 1920s he would be named a professor of painting at the Dresden Art Academy, and two of the monumental paintings of the war for which he became famous, *The Trench* and triptych *The War*, would enter the Dresden art museum's collections. It would be a remarkable career.

Dix's father was politically active, a lifelong member of the German Socialist Party in an area where the production of machinery was an important part of the economy, and the workers' movement an important part of the culture. Presumably, Otto Dix's world view was indelibly stamped by this formative political orientation, and although he later achieved considerable financial as well as social success as an artist, and enjoyed the private circumstances of a well-to-do bourgeois, he would throughout his life refer to his working-class background and the values he had received growing up in the industrial proletariat. Dix was unusual among artists in this regard; most artists in the late nineteenth or early twentieth centuries, especially those who felt they could afford to court the notoriety of being avant-garde, came from more privileged backgrounds. It is certainly a sign of Dix's talent and ability, as well as the strength of his will, that he successfully followed this career path and climbed up the social hierarchy of what was a highly stratified society. In the army, too, he would rise, but only as far as *Vizefeldwebel* [sergeant] – the highest rank obtainable by somebody without a formal secondary education (art school didn't count). Dix was often aggressive in his anti-bourgeois stance, and often displayed a preoccupation with his own social status, and with the income from his art, especially in his dealings with his gallery representatives; Olaf Peters has plausibly suggested that this demeanor was the result of his origins.[57]

Dresden at that time was a regional, rather provincial metropolis of the German Empire, the capital of the state of Saxony, which was a nominally independent kingdom in Imperial Germany. In the late seventeenth and early eighteenth centuries Dresden had been the residence of the Electors of Saxony (including Augustus the Strong, 1694–1733, who was also King of Poland), and that had been the period of its greatest cultural florescence; its glittering Baroque architecture remained its greatest treasure. By the early twentieth century its finest days were behind it. Yet it was the birthplace of the Expressionist group *Brücke* (which included the painters Ernst Ludwig Kirchner, Erich Heckel, and Karl Schmidt-Rottluff) in 1905. Otto Dix was able to see the work of these and other modern artists in Dresden; in 1912 there was an exhibition of the work of Vincent van Gogh at the Galerie Arnold, as well as the Cubists (also at the Galerie Arnold in 1912), and the Italian Futurists (at the Kunstsalon Emil Richter, in 1913). These exhibitions were extremely important for Dix, who in his ambition to join the avant-garde emulated their effects in his own painting.[58] In 1914 Ludwig Meidner, an Expressionist artist from Berlin, moved to Dresden, and Dix came to know him personally. Meidner combined the visual drama and aggressive, energetic, slashing brushwork of German Expressionism with the strong compositional diagonals and rhythmically repeating lines and shapes of Futurism. Each of these artists or groups of artists provided the young Dix with exciting new formal possibilities which he would explore, especially in the drawings and paintings he made during his time in uniform.

57 Peters, *Otto Dix. Der unerschrockene Blick* (Stuttgart: Reclam, 2013), 14.
58 Löffler, *Otto Dix und der Krieg*, 6.

Dresden was also one of the centers of the various reform movements that swept the German Empire in the early twentieth century, including the clothing reform and nudist movements that had been so important to the early development and self-identity of the *Brücke* artists. Dix for a time followed the teachings of the American Otto Hanisch, called "Mazdaznan," an eclectic mixture of yoga breath control, dietary reform, utopianism, and racial fantasies of an original "Aryan" people. With his good friends and fellow artists Otto Baumgärtel and Kurt Lohse, Dix practiced for a while vegetarianism and the avoidance of alcohol in keeping with Mazdaznan.[59] Hanisch, who was doubtless influenced by the popularity of Nietzsche's works, claimed to have founded his lifestyle teachings partly on the ancient Persian religion of Zoroastrianism and its prophet Zarathustra. Famously, Dix also read the works of Nietzsche – indeed, he made a plaster bust of him in a manner reminiscent of Rodin's portraits of great writers – and this has encouraged art historians to see Nietzsche's philosophy as a kind of key to Dix's own understanding of the First World War, and to his representations of the war.[60] But his reading of Nietzsche should probably be seen in the context of his other reform-movement enthusiasms: as part of the wide spectrum of counter-cultural lifestyle commitments available in the early twentieth century, appealing above all to young Germans seeking to distance themselves from the staid and confining customs, politics, and religion of Wilhelmine society. Dix was equally enthusiastic about Esperanto, the invented language which was intended to foster universal understanding and therefore peace among nations. He shared this enthusiasm, too, with a friend, Helene Jakob, the daughter of the building manager of the Arts and

59 Olaf Peters, *Der unnerschrockene Blick*, 33, and Peters, "Otto Dix – Otto Baumgärtel – Marga Kummer. Biographische Bemerkungen zum Frühwerk, zu Nietzsche, Mazdaznan und Ernst Haeckel," in Ulrike Lorenz, ed., *Dix avant Dix. Das Jugend- und Frühwerk 1903–1914* (Jena: Glaux, 2000), 280–292.

60 Most recently Olaf Peters, "Die Erfahrung des Krieges 1914–1918," in Dalbajewa, Fleischer, and Peters, eds. *Der Krieg*, 47–53, Dietrich Schubert, "Death in the Trench: The Death of the Portrait? Otto Dix's Wartime Self-Portraits, 1915–1918," in Peters, ed., *Otto Dix* (Munich: Prestel, 2010), 33–55, and Änne Söll, *Der Neue Mann? Männerporträts von Otto Dix, Christian Schad und Anton Räderscheidt, 1914–1930* (Paderborn: Wilhelm Fink, 2016), 26–31.

Crafts College (Dix also was a border in their home). The two kept up a correspondence throughout the war, much of it in Esperanto.

Otto Dix also eagerly explored the various stylistic options and painting techniques available for him to study, both in the Galerie Alte Meister and in the exhibitions of avant-garde art in the Galerie Arnold and the Kunstsalon Richter, trying his hand at all of them. He had a prodigious talent and was able to express something compelling in each mode he tried. He also enjoyed a robust self-confidence. In 1912 he painted a self-portrait (*Self-Portrait with Carnation*, Detroit Institute of Arts) in which he holds a small, deceptively simple flower, in imitation of Albrecht Dürer's famous *Self-Portrait Holding a Thistle* from 1493, in the Louvre. Like his hero Dürer, Dix advertises the precision of his observational drawing in a plant specimen presented like a botanical illustration, the complexity of its tiny foliage recorded with scientific care. The figure is precisely outlined against a featureless, bluish-green background, a device borrowed from the portraiture of Holbein and Cranach, of which many examples hung in the Dresden Galerie Alte Meister. In 1913 he tried out the effects of Ludwig Meidner and Vincent van Gogh, painting nocturnal Expressionist cityscapes with starbursts around the streetlights (*Street With Gas Lanterns*, 1913, Kunstsammlung Chemnitz, Museum Gunzenhauser), done alla prima, in complete contrast to his painstaking handling of materials the previous year.[61] Dix rendered homage to van Gogh with a painting of ravens alighting on a field, seen against the bursting rays of the setting sun (*Sun Setting over a Winter Landscape with Ravens*, 1913, Städtische Galerie Dresden). He was exploring more direct, expressive ways of handling his paint, energetically pushing it around with the charged brush.

And then, the following year, on 31 July 1914, Kaiser Wilhelm stepped out onto the balcony of his palace in Berlin and declared to the gathered crowd, "A momentous hour has struck Germany. Jealous rivals everywhere force us to legitimate defense. The sword has been forced into our hand." On 1 August, Germany declared war on Russia. The next day, 2 August, the Kaiser again appeared on his balcony, proclaiming his hope that "the good

61 Conzelmann notes that Dix borrowed the device of halos around gas lanterns from van Gogh, but doesn't mention Meidner. Otto Conzelmann, *Otto Dix* (Hannover: Fackelträger, 1959), p. 12.

German sword will emerge victorious" and that party politics had ceased, and that henceforth he only recognized German brothers, not political opponents. On 3 August, Germany declared war on France, and on 4 August, Great Britain declared war on Germany. The Great War had begun. One of the persistent myths of the war is that young men across Europe rushed to volunteer in a wave of war euphoria that swept the continent, and there is a parallel myth that the young Otto Dix volunteered as part of this wave. More recent social historians have established that volunteering for the army in August 1914 was not actually quite so popular, and a closer reading of Dix's military record suggests that he may not have actually volunteered, either.[62] Dix had already been mustered into the reserves of the Royal Saxon Army in 1911–1912, at the age of 20, while still a student at the Arts and Crafts College; when war was declared in 1914, there would have been no need to volunteer.[63] On 5 September 1914, Otto Dix was sworn in.

Dix had been mustered into the reserve regiment of an entity called the "Royal Saxon Army" because, just as Saxony was its own kingdom within the German Empire, so too was the Royal Saxon Army its own army. It had existed since the late seventeenth century, and retained some limited autonomy within the greater German Imperial Army, of which it nonetheless formed a part (besides the Iron Cross second class, Dix would be awarded the Friedrich-August Medal in silver, a decoration specific to the Saxon Army, by the King

62 Simone Fleischer, "Der Künstler und der Krieg," in Dalbajewa, Fleischer, and Peters, eds. *Der Krieg*, 14–33. For an explosion of the myth of universal war euphoria and mass volunteering, see Jeffrey Verhey, *The Spirit of 1914. Militarism, Myth and Mobilization in Germany* (Cambridge: Cambridge University Press, 2000). The quotation is from a speech delivered by Kaiser Wilhelm on 31 July 1914.

63 Otto Dix archive, "Personalien," DKA, I, A, 2, and cited in Fleischer, "Der Künstler und der Krieg." The details of Dix's military career that follow are taken from Fleischer's careful reconstruction, which is based on the remaining archival records for the XII. Reservekorps of the Saxon Army, held in the Central State Archives of Saxony (Sächsischen Hauptstaatsarchiv) in Dresden, and on the published history of the Royal Saxon Army in the First World War, as well as on Dix's own military papers and his wartime notebook, discussed in further detail below. See also his Curriculum Vitae, handwritten MS., private collection, cited in Fleischer, Schubert, and elsewhere.

of Saxony on 24 June 1917).[64] Dix was first sent to be trained for the field artillery (48th Field-Artillery Regiment, Dresden), at their recruit depot in Dresden. By mid-October, he was transferred to another field artillery regiment (12th), still in Dresden, where he was trained on the heavy field howitzer; he remained there for nearly four months (20 October to 12 February).

While in the reserves in Dresden, Dix continued to paint. Evidently fascinated by his own appearance in uniform, but also continuing his formal experimentation with the visual languages of Expressionist painting, he painted what may well have been another homage to van Gogh, *Self-Portrait as Soldier* [Selbstbildnis als Soldat] (1914) (see Figure 5).

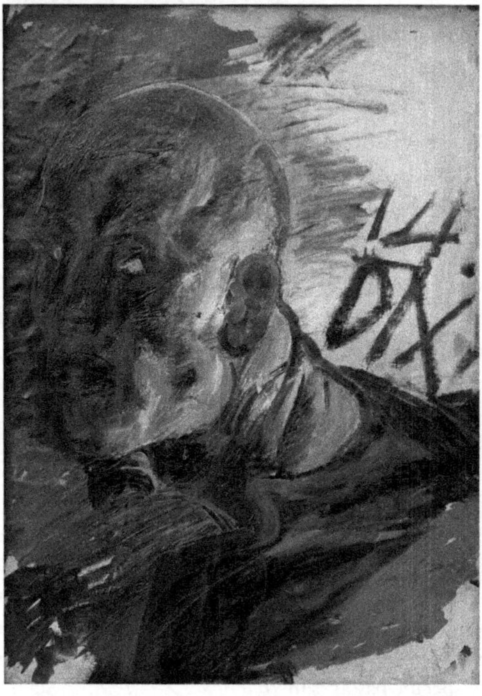

Figure 5. Otto Dix, *Self-Portrait as Soldier* [Selbstbildnis als Soldat], oil on paper, 1914, Kunstmuseum Stuttgart. © Otto Dix / Artists Rights Society (ARS), New York / VG Bild-Kunst, Bonn. Photo © akg-images, used with permission.

64 Dix archive, "Personalien," DKA.

The recruit's shaved head juts into the picture much like van Gogh's *Self-Portrait as Bonze* (1888), which Hugo von Tschudi had bought for the Nationalgalerie in Berlin in 1906, and which had been the object of some debate in Germany between conservative and progressive arbiters of taste; Dix had clearly chosen sides in this debate. The self-portrait as soldier also shows the artist's efforts at understanding the work of Emil Nolde, with his wild, even violent clashes of color and aggressively crude application of paint.[65] The same is true of the self-portrait Dix painted on the reverse side, the *Self-Portrait Wearing an Artillery Helmet* [Selbstbildnis mit Artillerie-Helm]. Dix's admiration for the work of Ludwig Meidner is evident here as well; in both self-portraits the bravura brushwork seems to conjure the artist's own visage out of the pictorial field. This doubled self-portrait of the artist with and without his helmet has been extensively mined for clues to the young artist's feelings about militarism and the war.[66] Looking at these paintings now, it is hard not to read them in the light of what followed: the enormity of the war experience and Dix's ongoing preoccupation with that experience in the years after the war. Yet they may have more to do with the young artist's attempts to master the expressive techniques of Nolde and Meidner than with the fact that the artist found himself – for a brief time, he would have supposed – in uniform. After all, the war was not expected to last past Christmas.

65 Schubert has suggested a strong link between this self-portrait as a soldier and Dix's plaster bust of Nietzsche, emphasizing the importance of that writer's work for understanding Dix's art; Schubert, "Death in the Trench," 35. But there is very little stylistic or formal similarity. Olaf Peters elaborated on this idea, in Peters, "Die Erfahrung des Krieges," 48. In particular, the iconography of the artillery helmet has been related to specific passages in *Thus Spake Zarathustra*; Schubert, *Otto Dix*, 27, and Söll, *Der neue Mann?*, 44. I think a more immediate connection is with other self-portraits by painters that Dix admired just as much as he did Nietzsche: van Gogh and Meidner, and Emil Nolde.

66 Eberle, *World War I and the Weimar Artists*, 22, Richard Cork, *A Bitter Truth. Avant-garde and the Great War* (New Haven, CT: Yale University Press, 1994), 93–94, and Änne Söll, *Der Neue Mann?*, 41–44.

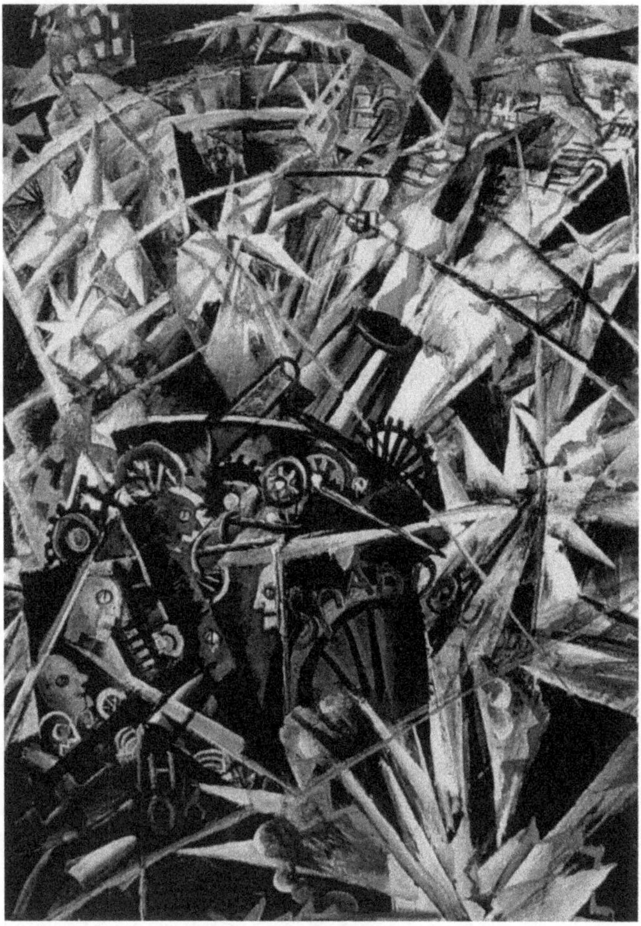

Figure 6. Otto Dix, *The War (The Artillery Piece)* [Der Krieg (Das Geschütz)], oil on cardboard, 1914, Städtische Sammlung Düsseldorf. © Otto Dix / Artists Rights Society (ARS), New York / VG Bild-Kunst, Bonn. Photo: author's own scan.

It was undoubtedly during this period that he painted the picture *The War (The Artillery Piece)* [Der Krieg (Das Geschütz)] (1914) (see Figure 6), which depicts just the kind of field howitzer that he was training on at the time, set at the center of another Cubo-Futurist composition. Around the stubby barrel of the howitzer a chaotic composition rotates, with starburst explosions, burning buildings, and billowing smoke. The rectangular field is crisscrossed by Futurist "lines of force," which in turn subdivide the howitzer itself, breaking it up into overlapping elements; the wheel of the gun, along with the various traversing and elevation wheels and toothed gears, create a strong circular motif which underscores the round muzzle at the center of the composition. The wheel, which gave the field howitzer its mobility, is emphasized by the name "Spandau" written around its perimeter in a manner that anticipates Gino Severini's more exuberant *Gun in Action* (painted in Paris in 1915, now in the Museum Ludwig, Cologne). Spandau was where Krupp manufactured these guns, and the name would have been inscribed on each one. Five small faces – the crew – are drawn with cartoonish crudeness around the breech, in the lower left quadrant. A zigzag tongue of red flame emerges from the muzzle, and a shell follows its trajectory towards the upper right; it is somewhat lost against the chaos of the bombarded town in the background. In its Cubo-Futuristic conceptualization of the picture plane as well as in its dark palette heightened by carmine reds, cadmium yellows, and green-gray tinted whites, this picture is closely related to another self-portrait, the *Self-Portrait as Mars* [Selbstbildnis als Mars] (1915) (see Figure 7), painted the following year.

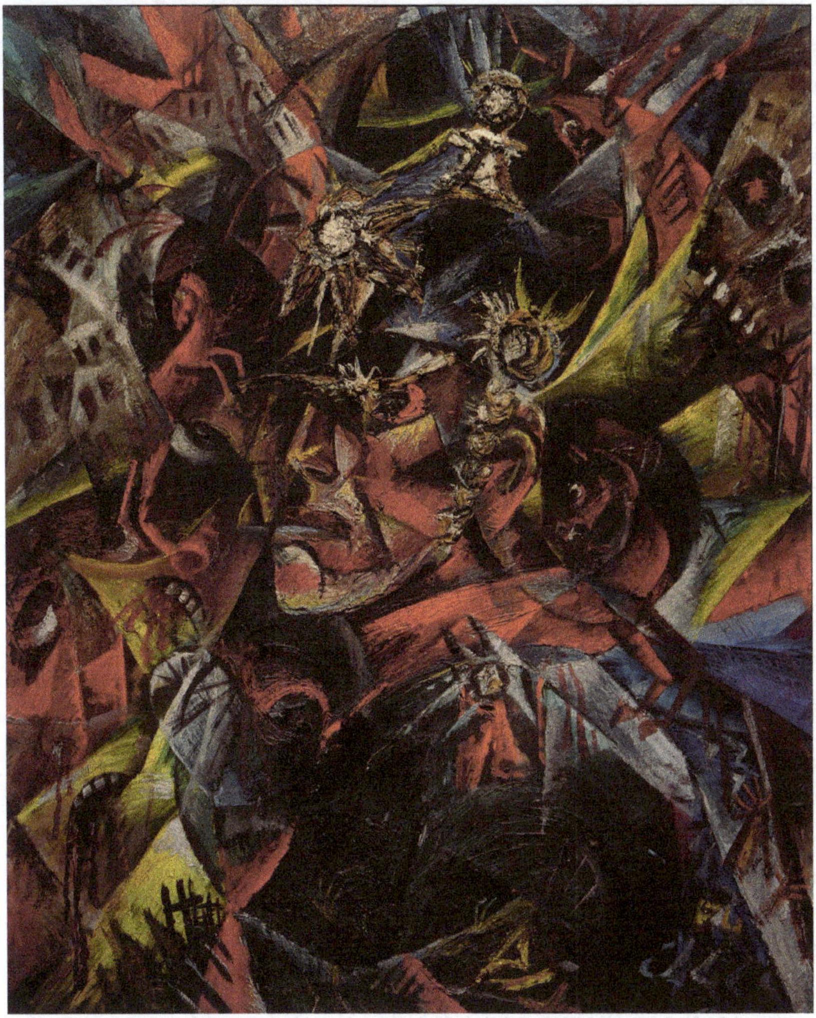

Figure 7. Otto Dix, *Self-Portrait as Mars* [Selbstbildnis als Mars], oil on paper, 1915, Städtische Sammlungen Freital, Schloss Burgk. © Otto Dix / Artists Rights Society (ARS), New York / VG Bild-Kunst, Bonn. Photo © akg-images, used with permission.

This self-portrait was also painted in oil, and so must have been painted soon after *The Artillery Piece*, early in 1915, while Dix still had space and materials to complete such a work, and because the two are so similar stylistically. *Self-Portrait as Mars* is filled with the imagined glory and horror of the war: the same destroyed rows of houses; blood pouring from disembodied mouths; horses rearing up in fright (a soldier in the field artillery would have been well acquainted with the sight of horses doing the work of war, as they were employed to pull the guns). In the self-portrait, Dix's strong jaw is the exact counterpart to the muzzle of *The Artillery Piece*: it is the anchor of the composition around which all of the other chaos and starbursts spin, along with the somewhat undigested references to Ludwig Meidner and Franz Marc. The contrast between the face in the foreground and the catastrophic city in the background recalls especially Meidner's own self-portrait, *Ich und die Stadt* [I and the City], of 1913, a painting which Meidner very likely brought with him when he moved to Dresden in April 1914. Meidner also provided further examples of a Cubo-Futurist depiction of urban destruction in his portfolio *Krieg*, produced in Dresden in 1914. Dix seems to have learned a lot from Meidner about how to create a chaotic city scene of tumbling, shattered houses piled on top of each other in a dynamic, rotational composition. Also in 1915, Dix painted yet another portrait of himself in uniform, in which he tried out the deliberate naiveté of Henri Rousseau, a popular affectation among the avant-garde, *Self-Portrait as Shooting Target* [Selbstporträt als Schießscheibe] (1915) (see Figure 8).

This particular self-portrait seems to express a personal disposition towards the war very different from the spirit of *Self-Portrait as Mars*, while also experimenting with a very different visual form. If the self-portrait as the god of war expresses blood-thirstiness and determination, conveyed by the trademark lantern jaw at the center of the composition, and the explosive gleam of the brass fittings on his artillery uniform, then the self-portrait as shooting target displays a good deal of self-irony, and a black humor that is in dramatic tension with the fear of death, or rather seems to disarm that fear even while acknowledging it.

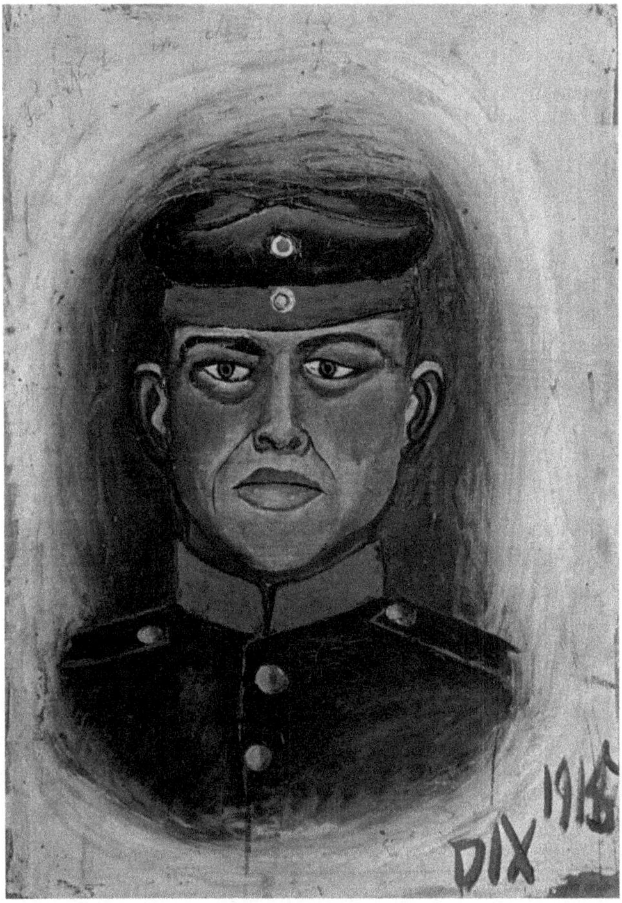

Figure 8. Otto Dix, *Self-Portrait as Shooting Target* [Selbstbildnis als Schießscheibe], oil on paper mounted on plywood, 1915, Otto Dix Stiftung, Vaduz. © Otto Dix / Artists Rights Society (ARS), New York / VG Bild-Kunst, Bonn. Digital file: author's own scan.

Portraits of officers, even the Kaiser himself – and self-portraits – were popular motifs for shooting targets, and this may be an early example of Dix quoting a form of barracks humor specific to his fellow soldiers, a topic to which I will return in the following chapter.[67]

67 Änne Söll, *Der neue Mann?*, 38–46.

During this period of artillery training in Dresden Dix was obviously searching for the form that would not only allow him to express his self-identity as a soldier and his embrace of the excitement of the war (seen from a safe distance in Dresden) and the glamour of his uniform (much as Ernst Ludwig Kirchner, mobilized as a reserve artillery officer, did in Berlin at the same time, in photographs he staged in his studio). Dix was also searching for the formal painting vocabulary that would best suit his ambition of becoming an avant-garde artist, of the sort he had seen exhibited in Dresden over the previous three years.[68] As Dix himself wrote back home to his girlfriend Marga Kummer, "Despite being a soldier I still have high-flown artistic plans."[69] Above all, Dix seems to be having fun in these pictures, pleased by the figure he cuts in his artillery uniform, using the mirror to explore his artistic persona and his stylistic experiments, much as van Gogh had done a quarter century before him. Dix had not yet experienced the reality of war at the front when he made these works. All he had seen of war so far was life in camp.

68 On Dix's self-portraits in uniform: Peters, "Die Erfahrung des Krieges"; Schubert, "Death in the Trench"; Schubert, "Rezeptions- und Stilpluralismus in die frühen Selbstbildnissen des Otto Dix", in Werner Hager and Norbert Knopp, eds., *Beiträge zum Problem des Stilpluralismus* (Munich: Prestel, 1977), 203–224; Diether Schmidt, *Otto Dix im Selbstbildnis* (East Berlin: Henschel, 1981).

69 "Ich habe trotz ich Soldat bin, immer noch hochfliegende Kunstpläne." Letter to Marga Kummer (January 1915) in Ulrike Lorenz, ed., *Otto Dix. Briefe* (Cologne: Wienand, 2013), 438.

Masculinity and the erotics of the uniform

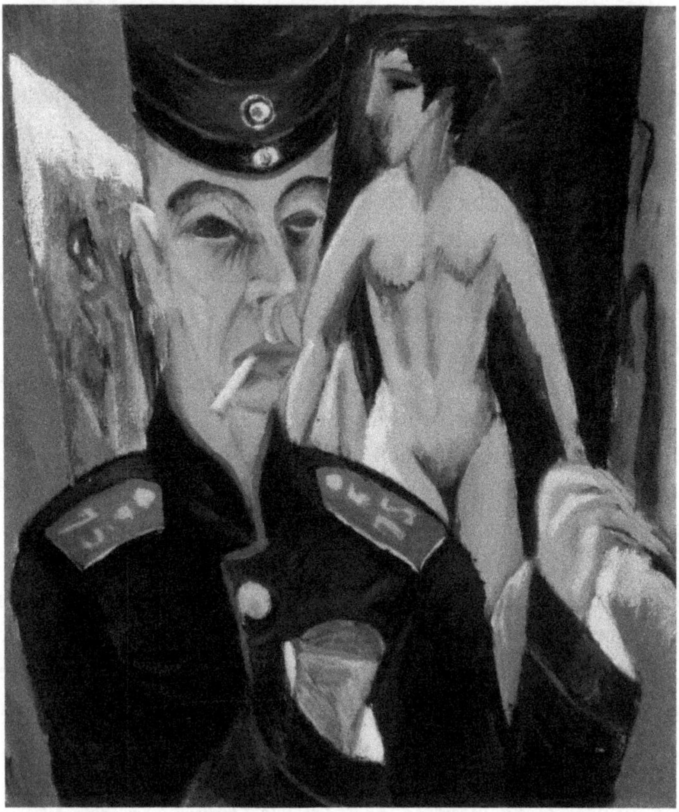

Figure 9. Ernst Ludwig Kirchner, *Self-Portrait as Soldier* [Selbstbildnis als Soldat], oil on canvas, 1915 Allen Memorial Art Museum, Oberlin College. Digital file: author's own scan.

But then, barracks life had been more than enough for some better-connected artists. Kirchner was so put off by the realities of barracks life that after just few months he had wrangled a temporary medical discharge. It was at this moment that Kirchner painted his well-known *Self-Portrait as Soldier* [Selbstbildnis als Soldat] (1915; the painting was on view in Dresden at the Städtische Galerie as of 1916, and is now at the Allen Memorial Art Museum, Oberlin College) (see Figure 9), in which a sallow and melancholy artist sits in his studio, wearing his artillery reservist's uniform, brandishing the hideous stump of his (purely imaginary) amputation. The standard interpretation of this painting has read it as an expression of traumatic anxiety and fear of artistic and sexual impotence brought on by the war, an interpretation that Peter Springer has recently and convincingly demonstrated is untenable.[70] In fact, Kirchner dreaded being yanked from his studio and returned to active duty: "who knows if they will put me back in, in which case I won't be able to work anymore – I'm worse off than any prostitute."[71] He apparently meant the comparison seriously, because he made it again a year later, as his anxiety about being called up and perhaps killed at the front persisted, "Right now I'm like the prostitutes I painted. Whisked away, gone the next time."[72]

The Kaiser's brandished sword and his boasts and Kirchner's brandished stump and his prostitutes; these are the markers staking out a field of the cultural imaginary in which Dix would bring forth the representations of his own experience of the war. The Kaiser as crusading medieval warrior and the Brücke artist as sickly modern neurasthenic were seemingly at opposite ends of the range of available forms of masculinity which a soldier and/or artist might perform. Allen Frantzen has shown that the image of the chivalrous Christian knight, far from withering away in the reality of mechanized warfare, lived on in popular imagery during and after the war, and continued to inform soldiers' image of themselves.[73] As we will

70 Peter Springer, *Hand and Head. Ernst Ludwig Kirchner's Self-Portrait as Soldier* (Berkeley: University of California Press, 2002, Susan Ray, translator). For the older interpretation, Donald Gordon, *Ernst Ludwig Kirchner* (Cambridge: Cambridge University Press, 1968), 20 ff.

71 Kirchner to Carl Hagemann (3 December 1915), quoted in Gordon, *Ernst Ludwig Kirchner*, 25.

72 Kirchner to Gustav Schiefler (12 November 1916), quoted in Wolfgang Henze, ed., *Ernst Ludwig Kirchner – Gustav Schiefler, Briefwechsel 1910–1935/38* (Stuttgart: Belser, 1990), 83.

73 Allen Frantzen, *Bloody Good. Chivalry, Sacrifice, and the Great War* (Chicago: University of Chicago Press, 2004).

see in the next chapter, Dix would use his art to mock, without any apparent mercy or empathy, German veterans crippled by the loss of limbs or the shattering of nerves – in sharp contrast to Kirchner's use of the image to express his own self-pity. What did this suggest about Dix's own self-image? Perhaps that in his self-perception his masculinity had remained intact, although chivalry was notably absent from his portraits of himself and other soldiers, and that firm soldierly masculinity was proven on the bodies of prostitutes and other women reduced exclusively to erotic objects.

Susan Grayzel has recently reiterated the degree to which the coming of war in 1914 provided men of all class backgrounds with an unprecedented opportunity to perform an idealized image of masculinity, and the torment of those who feared that they might not live up to that image.[74] This particular masculinity turned especially on the link between the supposed sexual desirability of the appearance of a uniform, and the presumed need to defend women against the sexual rapaciousness of the enemy. Even the socialist press in Germany proclaimed its support for the war with phrases about preventing the wives and children of the working class from being, "sacrificed to the bestialities of the Cossacks."[75] In posters, postcards, and popular songs, it was not only the virginally pure wives and daughters whose sexuality circulated in the economy of national and gender identity, but also the slattern, who invited men to complete the equation of manly virility and soldierly virtue on their willing bodies.[76] In reality women were not simply passive victims or prizes for the men of opposed armies – indeed, their potential role as desiring subjects, and specifically their sexual desire for men in uniform, was played on by propagandists hoping to motivate men to volunteer. And women in countries on both sides of the war were mobilized into industry, especially the armaments industry, into the organization and logistics of the war, as nurses in the field, and as ambulance drivers – and

74 Susan R. Grayzel, "Women and Men," in John Horne, ed., *A Companion to World War I* (Oxford: Wiley & Blackwell, 2010), 263–278.

75 Friedrich Stampfer, quoted in Hew Strachan, *First World War*, Vol. 1, *To Arms* (New York: Oxford, 2001), 121–122.

76 Grayzel, "Women and Men," 263–278.

also as prostitutes, professionally or informally, on the home front or nearer the lines. Women organized, publicly expressed their support for or opposition to the war, and published their own memoirs, poetry, and novels about their experiences. If the wartime mobilization of women was experienced as destabilizing to the kind of gender ideology exploited at the outset of the war to justify and further it, then all the more reason for an artist like Dix to reiterate and exaggerate gender identities in his art.

Yet even the Kaiser's own projection of an ideal of German manliness was a symptom of his denial of his own neurasthenia. He was suspected of being nervous to the point of physical and mental collapse, and his capacity to command the ship of state in the era of gunboat diplomacy had always been doubted by those around him.[77] On the world stage he might draw attention away from his shame about his withered arm by rattling his saber with the other hand, but it was said in stage whispers behind his back that he lacked the courage and decisiveness to lead the German Empire into war, or the bluff needed to achieve a colonial empire. Thus, only when he finally made war would he succeed in demonstrating his mettle and his manliness.[78] The pressure exerted on the Kaiser by this fatal logic only increased with the discovery that his inner circle of friends and advisors were nearly all homosexuals, a discovery which was turned into a political scandal.[79] Prince Philip Eulenburg, General Kuno von Moltke, and the circle around them were viewed as soft on France and not enthusiastic enough about Germany's naval buildup. Theirs were supposedly voices of moderation which had already held the Kaiser back from the brink of European war in the Morocco Crises of 1906 and 1911. The revelation of the secret erotic life of this inner circle of aristocrats, peers of the realm, and high military commanders of noble birth gave a hawkish (and homophobic)

77 Joachim Radkau, *Das Zeitalter der Nervosität. Deutschland zwischen Bismarck und Hitler* (Munich: Propyläen Taschenbuch, 2000), 296 ff.

78 Radkau, *Zeitalter der Nervosität*, 299.

79 Norman Domeier, *The Eulenburg Affair. A Cultural History of Politics in the German Empire* (Rochester, NY: Camden House, 2015), and Martin Kohlrausch, *Der Monarch im Skandal: Die Logik der Massenmedien und die Transformation der wilhelminischen Monarchie* (Berlin: DeGruyter, 2005), 176–186.

press the leverage they needed to push for military action in Germany's foreign policy. Thus the popular press strengthened the equation between a normative heterosexual masculinity and an aggressively forward military posture in Germany's relations with the other European powers. In this rhetorical context in the first months of the war, it is significant that Dix's *Self Portrait as Mars* emphasizes an aggressive and even sexualized masculinity, enhanced by the celebrated sexual appeal of a uniform.

Military training and the machine gun

In February of 1915, nearly six months after being called up, Dix was transferred to the 102nd Reserve Infantry Regiment of the Saxon Army, and to the garrison in Bautzen, not far from Dresden, where he would remain for the next six months. Instead of the field howitzer, Dix was now training to fire a heavy Maxim machinegun, model 1908. The importance that the machine gun would have in the stalemate war of attrition had become increasingly clear to the generals over the course of the first months of the war, while Dix had still been in Dresden, and the number of machine gun companies was being increased on all sides, not least the German.[80] The Royal Saxon Army was stationed on the Western Front, in Champagne, where the stalemate of trench warfare had established itself into a pattern of attack and counter-attack with high casualty rates and little or no ground gained. It was a form of warfare in which defensive tactics dominated, including the use of trench systems in depth, barbed wire, and reinforced machinegun nests. Defensive positions were everything, and the heavy machinegun, which sat immobile on a tripod, was a defensive weapon. Even artillery bombardments using shrapnel shells, later high-explosive shells, that lasted for days on end and had a horrendous effect on fragile

80 Fleischer, "Der Künstler und der Krieg," 15, and John Ellis, *The Social History of the Machine Gun* (Manchester, NH: Ayer, 1975).

human bodies and minds, were primarily intended to destroy the defensive arrangements of barbed wire and trench systems.

But as yet, Dix had not experienced any of this first hand. While he was garrisoned in Bautzen, he continued to draw, primarily landscapes but also portraits of his fellow recruits, working on small, square-format paper. Other avant-garde artists strove to convey something of the strangeness and even brutality of garrison life, as Kirchner did in a painting of his fellow artillerymen naked and vulnerable in the shower, under the strict discipline of a uniformed officer, in *Artillerymen* [Soldatenbad], (1915, oil on canvas, Guggenheim), which in turn recalls Eugène Chaperone's *Soldier's Bath, Regimental Barracks* [La Douche au régiment] (1887), with similar themes.[81] But Dix focused instead on mastering the principles of Cubo-Futurist composition, using the hilly landscape around Bautzen. These drawings were strongly reminiscent of the early Cubist landscapes of Pablo Picasso and Georges Braque, and also of Jean Metzinger, all of which had been shown in Dresden, in an exhibition of Cubism at the Galerie Arnold in 1912 and in a Picasso exhibition at the Kunstsalon Emil Richter in January of 1914.

Promoted to *etatmässige Gefreiter* (equivalent to private first class or corporal) on 17 September 1915, Dix became the leader of a heavy machinegun crew. A heavy machinegun needed a crew of five soldiers: a commander (this was Dix); one to carry it (the gun weighed 23 kilos) and to fire it; one to help load it and to carry the sledge that it was mounted on (37 kilos); two to carry the ammunition and to spot targets, and to serve as backup (in case the operator was wounded or killed); and one to remain with the platoon commander, who in turn maintained command and control over the other machinegun crews in the platoon (between two and six).[82] A Maxim gun could fire continuously as long as the operator held the trigger, up to 500 rounds per minute, at a distance of up to 2,000 meters. With continuous fire the barrel would get hot; the gun was water cooled,

81 Reproduced in Richard Thomson, *The Troubled Republic* (New Haven, CT: Yale University Press, 2004), 30.

82 Friedrich von Merkatz, ed., *Unterrichtsbuch für die Maschinengewehr-Kompagnien. Gerät 08*. (Berlin: Eisenschmidt, 1917), 204.

and four liters of water were carried along with the ammunition. It was the job of one of the crew to make sure the hose for the cooling water was connected to the jacket that encased the barrel, and even to change out the barrel when it overheated. In general, each infantry regiment contained one machinegun company, although Dix was part of a reserve division (the 23rd Reserve Division, part of the XII Royal Saxon Reserve Corps, which in turn made up the Third Army – the Royal Saxon Army, stationed in Champagne), and reserve divisions tended to be weaker, with fewer regiments and fewer machinegun companies than was standard for regular divisions. At the outset of the war, the 102nd Reserve Infantry Regiment, to which Dix was attached since being moved to Bautzen, did not have a machinegun company of its own.[83] In Champagne, where the 23rd Reserve Division and the rest of the Third Army was stationed, the French were preparing for a major offensive in the autumn, designed to break through the heavily entrenched German positions. The 23rd Division would need more machine guns, and in September new platoons were formed up. One of these was the Field Machinegun Platoon 390 [*Feld- M. G. Zug* 390], which included Dix. It was formed on 21 September 1915, and sent directly to Champagne, west of Reims, to fight in what would be called the Second Battle of Champagne.[84] And so, in the early autumn of 1915, Dix entered the fighting of the Western Front.

The French attack was prepared with an artillery barrage that began on 22 September. Thousands of guns fired their shells in rapid succession day and night in what the Germans called "*Trommelfeur*," a deafening drumroll barrage. Up to 200,000 high-explosive shells fell on the section of the front covered by Dix's division in a single day, each capable of blasting a crater 5 to 6 meters deep and wide. Soon all that was left of the surrounding woods was a stubble of shattered tree stumps, and the ground was reduced to a moonscape. The complicated system of trenches with their forward listening posts, dugouts, shallow communication trenches, and subterranean

83 Hermann Cron, *Imperial German Army 1914–1918: Organisation, Structure, Orders-of-Battle* (Gliwice: Helion & Co., 2002, reprint of 1937 edn.), 308.

84 Fleischer, "Der Künstler und der Krieg," 16; Dix archive, "Personalien," DKA.

shelters was annihilated.[85] It was into this inferno that Otto Dix and his machinegun crew entered. On the morning of 25 September the artillery barrage lifted and the French attacked the German defensive line with 20 divisions, 400,000 men attacking ten men to a meter. The German Third Army had only six divisions, but with well-prepared defenses and a reserve position further back. The French broke through in several places, and the Germans fell back to their reserve line, which was undamaged by the artillery barrage. The exhausted and thinned French divisions could not take this second line, and in most places were quickly beaten back by a counter-attack that came four days later. The French Commander-in-Chief, Marshall Joffre, called off the offensive on 3 October. Dix had just survived a major battle that had cost 50,000 German lives and 25,000 soldiers taken prisoner, and 145,000 French casualties. It was almost a year to the day since the painter August Macke, who had exhibited with Kandinsky and Marc in the *Blaue Reiter*, had been killed in an assault on the French positions in the very same sector.[86]

As a machine gunner, Dix enjoyed a certain advantage; he didn't have to attack across no-man's-land, but could instead wait for the enemy to come, whereupon he would open fire. But his job was nonetheless deadly dangerous. The heavy machinegun had to be brought into position despite sometimes thick artillery fire, and manned continuously despite being a target for the enemy. The Second Battle of Champagne also saw the use of poison gas by the French (the Germans had first used it in April and May of that year in Flanders), which threatened everybody on the line. From 12 to 18 October Dix and two others participated in an attack on a "nest" of French troops who had captured a stretch of German trench in a commanding position and were stubbornly holding it. The "French Nest" was

85 Artur Baumgarten-Crusius, *Sachsen in großer Zeit. Geschichte der Sachsen im Weltkrieg*, Vol. II (Leipzig: Minerva, 1920), 246, cited in Fleischer, "Der Künster und der Krieg," 16. See also McGreevy, for an impressionistic description of the battlefields of Champagne and Dix's first day at the front, *Bitter Witness*, 35–39.

86 Macke was killed on 26 September 1914, in an assault on the French position near Perthes-les-Hurlus, south of Somme-Py. Macke had been drafted into his old unit, Infantry Regiment 160 (9th Rhineland Regiment), Fourth Army, VIII. Army Corps.

recaptured on 15 October, and in the midst of battle, Dix and his team brought their machinegun into position to hold off a counterattack during a further three days of fighting. For this and for their courage in the fighting of 30 September to 4 October, Dix and the other two members of his team were recommended for the Iron Cross, second class.[87] The medal was officially bestowed upon him on 12 November; he jotted down in his field notebook, without elaboration, that he received the actual medal on 17 November. He did not record who gave it to him; it may well have been the King of Saxony himself, who personally appeared before troops from the 23rd Reserve Division, including some from the 102nd Reserve Infantry Regiment whom he singled out for their part in recapturing the "French Nest."[88] In all likelihood, Dix was among them. On 24 November, Dix was taken ill, and remained in the field hospital until 7 December.

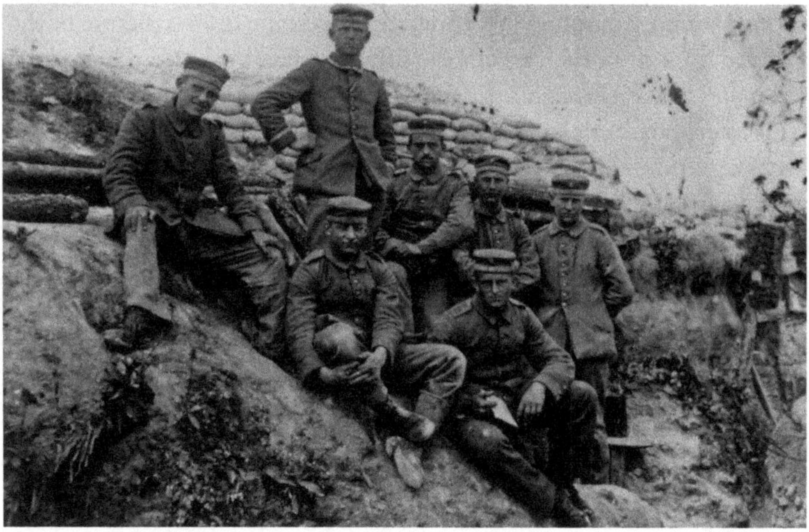

Figure 10. Otto Dix with Comrades, field postcard to his brother Fritz, 1916, Kunstsammlung Gera. © Otto Dix / Artists Rights Society (ARS), New York / VG Bild-Kunst, Bonn. Digital file: author's own scan.

87 Fleischer, "Der Künstler und der Krieg," 16–17.
88 Fleischer, "Der Künstler und der Krieg," 17–18.

In the early months of 1916, Dix's division remained stationed in Champagne, in the area around St. Souplet and St. Martin in Champagne, east of Reims. A postcard sent by Dix to his brother Fritz in 1916 shows Dix with his platoon on the Western Front, the ribbon of his Iron Cross visible (see Figure 10). Place names from this area, Tahure and St. Marie sur Py, would show up in his portfolio of etchings done almost a decade later. After the failed attempt at a breakthrough by the French, this became a relatively "quiet" sector, meaning that there were no large-scale attacks or heavy fighting. But the artillery never entirely fell silent, and the enemy would have kept up a constant harassing fire of small arms and even trench mortars. Much later, in an etching of 1924, Dix would represent soldiers standing on the firing parapet of their trench, with a title that sounded like a field-manual directive: "At night the watch shall keep up a continuous fire." Dix's job would have also included keeping his machinegun in working order, sometimes in a concrete pillbox; he drew a picture of the cramped interior of such a pillbox, with the machinegun standing at the center and a view through a slit across no-man's-land, on the back of one of his many postcards to Helene Jakob. The routines and daily life of the machinegun crew is recorded in Dix's field notebook: making coffee; firing practice; keeping watch; making coffee again.[89] The routines of work were described by Otto Lais (1897–1988), another artist who was also a machine gunner, in a Bavarian infantry regiment:

> "Ora et labora" – pray and work. "Curse and work" was our trench saying in the position near Bapaume in Artois! This saying referred to the "eternal" digging, to the laying of barbed wire, to the never ending construction of belowground dugouts. We cussed, cursed, and groaned as we hauled coils of wire by night, and the iron posts and wooden frames for the wire, and all the other "treasured" things in an infantry soldier's life.[90]

89 Otto Dix Field Notebook, held in the Kunstmuseum Albstadt, 44–45.

90 Otto Lais' narrative of first day of the Battle of the Somme, translated and edited by Jack Sheldon, *The German Army on the Somme 1914–1916* (Barnsley, England: Pen & Sword Military, 2005), 142–143. The original runs as follows: "'Ora et labora' – Bete und arbeite. 'Schimpfe und arbeite' war unsere Grabenlosung in den Stellung vor Bapaume in Artois! Diese Losung bezog sich auf das 'ewige' Schanzen, auf das

The German troops constantly expanded their network of trenches – the strength of the fallback trench, which had kept the French from breaking through in September, had proven the wisdom of this practice – and they dug their dugouts deeper and deeper below ground, reinforcing them with corrugated iron sheeting and steel rails. They kept the trenches in good condition. Dix noted in a postcard to Helene Jakob that his unit's trench "is neatly reinforced with concrete and is swept out twice a day. Very German, isn't it?"[91] But Lais in his memoir goes on to note that the machine gunner was exempt from some of the more physically exhausting jobs like carrying heavy mortar rounds up into position. Troops would stay in position in the forward trench for several days, and then would be sent back to the rear, often an occupied town, to rest. Dix's regiment would be stationed in Pont Faverger or Auberive; the field hospital was in Béthenville – place names written on several of the drawings he did while in the rear. Regiments would periodically be moved to a different section of the trench, in order to keep troops alert – and to break up the informal truces that would get established between a unit and their enemy counterparts in the opposite trench. In a letter home to Helene Jakob, Dix offered a vivid description of life in such a "quiet" sector.

> Yesterday afternoon the enemy artillery entertained us with a three-hour long barrage. At times the fire increased to drumroll-fire. We huddled in our underground bunkers. "Highest Alert," an attack was expected. In one section the front was a dangerous corner, at night there are six machineguns in place here. But the Frenchies never attacked. The result was some wounded, buried and shot-up trenches.
> Right next to our bunker is a fortified artillery observation post, reinforced with 30 cm thick, iron-reinforced concrete plate, supported by railway rails. A direct hit busted through the rails and the concrete slab.

Drahtverhauziehen, auf den nicht endenwollenden Unterstandsbau. Geflucht, geschimpft, gestöhnt wurde beim nächtlichen Schleppen der Drahtrollen, der spanischen Reiter, der Rahmenhölzer und all der anderen 'geschätzten' Dinge im Leben eines Infanteristen." Otto Lais, *Maschinengewehr im Eisernen Regiment, 8. Badisches Infanterie-Regiment Nr. 169* (Karlsruhe: G. Braun, 1935), 1.

91 Field postcard to Helene Jakob, 4 June 1916, Ulrike Rüdiger, *Grüsse aus dem Krieg. Die Feldpostkarten der Otto-Dix-Sammlung in der Kunstgalerie Gera* (Gera: Kunstgalerie Gera, 1991), 84.

> The air pressure knocked us back, and the trench was left literally strewn with iron shrapnel. Tonight it's pitch black and I have patrol duty until midnight. Somebody is constantly attacking and it's a mercy when the flares go up. The infantry is firing as always. The French bullets fly whistling over our trenches, otherwise everything is quiet. The boredom, the lice and the fleas, eat you up in secret [*heimlich*] when you're not watching. Other than that, there is absolutely nothing, except the drum-roll fire, that's strange [*un*heimlich] to a soldier.[92]

Dix thanked Jakob for sending him pencils and an eraser, but complained that he found it difficult to do any drawing while in the front lines, "It's sad, it annoys me, that I draw relatively little when I'm in position, by contrast, in reserve, I do more."[93] Yet Dix did find time to draw and even to paint some small gouaches on paper. He illustrated his postcards to Helene Jakob (which were still partly written in Esperanto) with sketches, some of which correspond closely to the larger, more finished drawings. And he wrote of exhibiting the artworks publicly. When he met up with another artist and old friend from Dresden, Otto Griebel, near the Loretto Heights, Dix hauled out his drawings and showed

92 "Gestern nachmittag hat uns die feindliche Artillerie mit einem drei volle Stunden dauernden Feuerüberfall unterhalten. Das Feuer war stellenweise bis zum Trommelfeuer gesteigert. Wir hockten in unseren Unterständen drin. 'Höchste Bereitschaft,' es wird ein Angriff erwartet. Auf einen kurzen Abschnitt war die Front eine gefährliche Kurve, nachts stehen hier 6 Maschinengewehre. Die Franzmänner griffen aber nicht an. Der Erfolg war einige Verwundete, Verschüttete und zerschossenen Gräben. Direkt neben unserem Unterstand liegt ein überbauter Artilleriebeobachtungsstand, der durch eine 30 cm starke Eisenbetonplatte und durch Eisenbahnschiene gestützt ist. Durch Volltreffer wurde die Eisenbahnschiene durchgehauen und die Betonplatte … durchschlagen. Der Luftdruck setzte uns natürlich bald hin, der Graben war nachher von Eisensplittern buchstäblich besät. Heute ist die Nacht stockdunkel und ich habe bis 12 Uhr Patrouilledienst, man rennt fortwährend an und es ist eine Wohltat, wenn Leuchtkugeln aufsteigen. Die Infanterie schießt wie immer. Pfeifend schwirren die französischen Kugeln über unsere Gräben, sonst ist alles ruhig. Die Langeweile, die Läuse und die Flöhe, das frißt einen alles *heimlich* auf. Sonst ist außer der Trommelfeuer überhaupt nichts *un*heimlich für einen Soldaten." Emphasis in the original.
Letter to Helene Jakob, dated 7 January 1916, Lorenz, *Otto Dix. Briefe*, 440.

93 "Es ist traurig, es ärgert mich, daß ich verhältnismäßig wenig zeichne, wenn ich in der Stellung bin, dagegen in Reserve mache ich mehr." Letter to Helene Jakob, dated 7 January 1916, Lorenz, ed., *Otto Dix. Briefe*, 440.

them to Griebel, joking about what his comrades in the trenches made of it all. Decades later, Griebel recalled, "I could hardly comprehend that somebody could finish so much work in the trenches; I myself found little opportunity to do so."[94] No doubt the relief from some duties afforded to machine gunners helped. An example of a drawing done in the reserve towns shows two soldiers sleeping, exhausted, in a drawing labeled "Pont Faverger, Nov 2 15."[95] Later Dix wrote again to Jakob, "Right now I haven't managed to draw in days, the weather was heavy snow and wind. Besides that, I had a stomach-lining infection and had to lay in the underground bunker for two days and sustain myself with "Großer Form," *Feld zwieback* and coffee. Besides, Frenchy's been flashing the little town something awful, until art just leaves you. You see such horrible things!"[96] In the same letter, he worried that he might not be able to exhibit his work during the war, "I don't think I'll be able to exhibit anything before the end of the war, because it's so difficult when you can't take care of it yourself."[97] But in fact he would find opportunities to do so.

By now Dix had started to pepper his letters to Helene Jakob with some trench slang, like "funken" to fire an artillery barrage, and "Großer Form." He did not shy away from describing the ever-present mortal danger. Nonetheless, a circumspect phrase like "You see such horrible things" hid some of the truly devastating violations of the human body, the kinds of things that the English poet and junior officer Siegfried Sassoon detailed in his poem "Counter-Attack," in which he describes a captured German trench,

94 "Mir erschien es kaum begreiflich, dass man so vieles im Graben fertigbringen konnte, den ich selbst fand nur wenig Möglichkeit dazu." Otto Griebel, "Erlebnis und Vorbild – Otto Dix," *Bildende Kunst* 11 (1966), 581–586, here 582, cited in Annegret Jürgens-Kirchhoff, *Schreckensbilder. Krieg und Kunst im 20. Jahrhundert* (Berlin: Reimer, 1993), 68. See also Otto Griebel, *Ich war ein Mann der Straße. Lebenserinnerungen eines Dresdner Malers* (Altenburg: DZA, 1995, 2nd edn.), 33.

95 Dresden, Kupferstichkabinett, C 1989–152.

96 "Ich bin jetzt tagelang nicht zum Zeichnen gekommen, das Wetter war garstig, Schnee und Wind. Außerdem mußte ich wegen Magen-Darm-Katarrh 2 Tage im Unterstand liegen und mich von 'Großer Form' u. Feldzwieback und Kaffee ernähren." Letter to Helene Jakob, 13 February 1916, Lorenz, *Otto Dix, Briefe*, 444.

97 "Ich denke, dass ich vor ende des Krieges nichts ausstellen kann, es ist so schwierig, wenn man die Sachen nicht selbst besorgen kann." Lorenz, *Otto Dix. Briefe*, 444.

> The place was rotten with dead; green clumsy legs
> High-booted, sprawled and groveled along the saps
> And trunks, face downward, in the sucking mud,
> Wallowed like trodden sand-bags loosely filled;
> and naked sodden buttocks, mats of hair,
> Bulged, clotted heads slept in the plastering slime.
> And then the rain began, – the jolly old rain![98]

Dix, too, complained about the rain (like all soldiers), in his letters home, "It rains and rains all the time here. The artillery fire is sometimes very heavy. We are installed to the right of the village of Aubérive."[99] But in his field notebook he recorded more horrible things, like the pile of dead French soldiers that served as a kind of makeshift bulwark in a captured trench, a grisly image that would reappear in his work in the 1920s.[100] Sassoon's equation of dead bodies with sandbags suggests that the English officer and poet had seen similar things.

The aesthetic challenge of representing the war pictorially

In his letter to Helene Jakob of 18 February 1916, Dix also described the view of no-man's-land from his position, and the French lines beyond it: "The French position lies before us like an enormous map. Deathly still, emptiness, nothing but the labyrinthine trenches and corridors, which are a contrasting white against the gray-green field."[101] He painted two landscapes that resembled

98 "Counter-Attack," Siegfried Sassoon, 1918

99 "Bei uns regnet und regnet es immerzu. Das Feuer der Artillerie ist von Zeit zu Zeit sehr stark. Unsere Unterkünfte sind rechts des Dorfes Aubérive." Letter to Helene Jakob, 18 February 1916, Lorenz, *Otto Dix. Briefe*, 444.

100 Entry for 7 November 1915. The image of the fighter who uses dead bodies as a makeshift barricade reappears in the portfolio *Death and Resurrection* [Tod und Auferstehung], 1922, number IV, *The Barricade* [Die Barrikade].

101 "Die Französ. Stellung liegt hier vor uns wie eine Mächtige Landkarte. Totenstille, Leere, nur die labyrinthischen Gräben und Gänge, die sich weiß aus dem graugrün des Bodens abheben."

this verbal description, in gouache on the same sketch paper that he used for his drawings, , *Trenches in Front of Reims I* [Gelände vor Reims I] (1915) (see Figure 11) and *Trenches in Front of Reims II* [Gräben vor Reims II] (1915).[102]

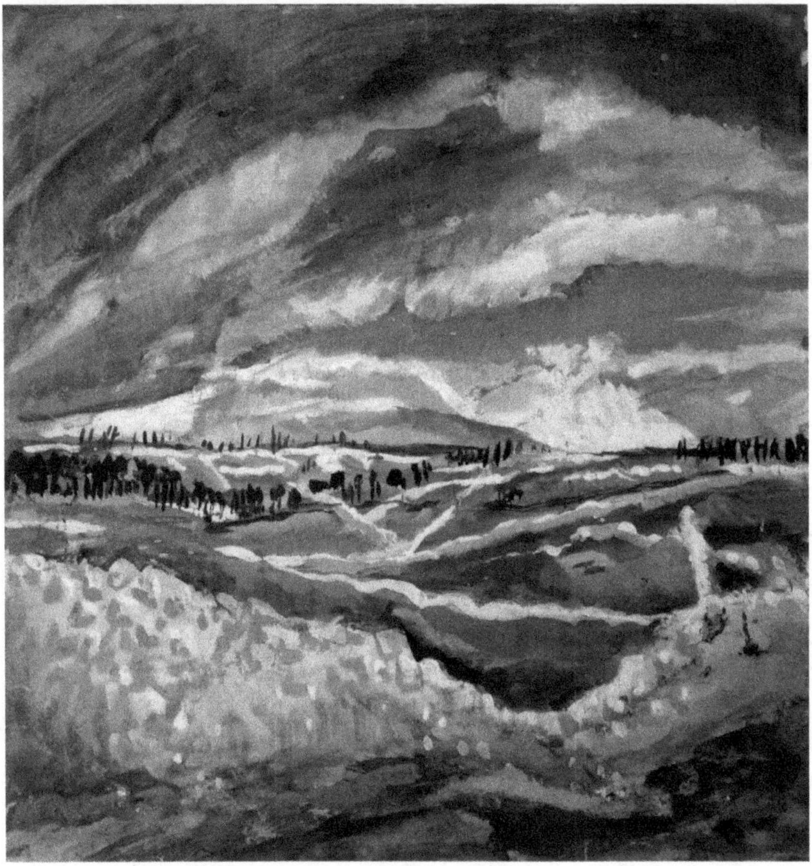

Figure 11. Otto Dix, *Trenches in Front of Reims I* [Gelände vor Reims I], gouache on paper, 1915 or 1916, private collection. © Otto Dix / Artists Rights Society (ARS), New York / VG Bild-Kunst, Bonn. Digital file: author's own scan.

102 Both reproduced in Suse Pfäffle, *Otto Dix. Werkverzeichnis der Aquarelle und Gouachen* (Stuttgart: Hatje, 1991), 262.

Both are pictures of an empty landscape with a low horizon and gently rolling hills under heavy skies, loosely indicated in expressionistic color juxtapositions of red, blue, green and ochre. The landscape is empty; nothing moves in it; it does indeed look dead. But it is crisscrossed by a network of white lines indicating the forward and connecting trenches, or more specifically, the white soil thrown up along the lip of the trenches as they were dug out of the white chalky ground of Champagne. Dix is here grappling in word and image with one of the fundamental challenges to every artist who attempted to depict the Great War through observational and representational art, whether through naturalistic, or modernist, post-Impressionist means. The challenge was that there was very little to see, outside of the big battles; there was only empty landscape, the stumps of trees and the posts of barbed wire entanglements (either or both might be indicated in this gouache by the rows of stubby black lines along the horizon), and sky.[103] Invisible to the eye – whether the eye of the artist or the observing sentries who constantly scrutinized this landscape through periscopes peeking up over the edge of the trench – were the thousands of enemy soldiers who constantly moved, unseen, through the trenches on the other side of no-man's-land. The landscape of Champagne was in fact full of activity: on both sides there was a constant business of digging, improving trenches and positions, making connecting tunnels to the rear and saps or listening posts pushed out into no-man's-land. Equipment, ammunition, and food was being brought up, guns were being sited, and of course there was a steady firing of artillery and small arms. But nothing was visible to the observer's eye. By war's end art critics would already be theorizing about the need to reconceptualize the depiction of war in art; modern warfare might have its characteristic motifs, but there was no longer any "battlefield" with its traditional action to depict.[104] Warfare had once taken the form of

103 Philippe Dagen, *Le Silence des Peintres* (Paris: Fayard, 1996, reprint Paris: Éditions Hazan, 2012), 81–104.

104 Robert de La Sizeranne, *L'Art pendant la guerre 1914–1918* (Paris: Hachette, 1919), 222–240, cited in Dagen, *Le Silence des peintres*, 100 ff.

a highly visual arrangement of ordered columns and rows of soldiers in distinctive dress, seen from a commanding height by the general and his staff. But modern warfare had replaced all that with desolate, cratered moonscapes, villages reduced to dust, burnt up forests, and muddy fields. The visual excitement of cavalry charges seen from close quarters had given way to an invisible war of tunneling, camouflage, machineguns fired from half-hidden nests, and high velocity shells fired from long-range guns secreted away in positions in the rear. In the nineteenth century, tourists could turn out to watch the spectacle of great battles, as at the First Battle of Bull Run in the American Civil War in 1861, and the battles of the Franco-Prussian War. As recently as the Boer War (1899–1902) so many tourists came to watch the fighting that they interfered with the conduct of the battle.[105] Despite the use of firing trenches, those battles had retained a visual spectacle allied with the traditions of battle painting, and had unfolded dramatically in a single day, or at most a few days. But by the First World War, the quantity of firepower and high-explosive artillery and the sheer scope of the battlefield – which in Champagne stretched nearly 80 kilometers from Reims to the Aisne river – and the long duration of battles of attrition, made both tourism, and the spectacle it presupposed, a thing of the past.

The First World War began as a war of rapid movement and cavalry or infantry charges, led by young officers out in front, but the machinegun and the German decision to dig in and keep the territory they had gained, rather than to retreat, soon changed all that. Yet even in 1915, a professional battle painter like Eugène Chaperone (1857–1938) could produce shamelessly propagandistic images of an engagement such as the Battle of Morhange (near Nancy, 20 August 1914), which depicts enthusiastic French troops charging with bayonets, sweeping bewildered and discouraged German troops before them; an officer astride a rearing horse, saber drawn, links the composition firmly to the

105 David Lloyd, *Battlefield Tourism: Pilgrimage and the Commemoration of the Great War in Britain, Australia, and Canada, 1919–1939* (London: Bloomsbury Academic, 1998), 21.

most traditional battle scenes, and shrapnel shells bursting overhead add a bit of color.[106] In Chaperone's war, only German soldiers seem to die.[107] Chaperone's painting was published in the illustrated weekly *Le Panorama de la Guerre*; there appeared in the same issue a photograph of an armored train, mounted with an artillery piece. Chaperone never painted such a modern, unpicturesque thing, but Gino Severini did, in the same year, in his famous Futurist painting now at MoMA (*Armored Train in Action*, 1915). A greater contrast is hardly imaginable than that between the traditional cavalry charge and an armored train speeding across the entire theater of the war, and the gulf between Chaperone's and Severini's paintings is just as wide. German artists, too, painted old-fashioned, heroic images, which were circulated as postcards for use by soldiers to send home. One represented a machinegun platoon decimating an attack by French Zouaves in an action that took place near Soissons on 17 September 1914. The postcard reproduces an illustration by another professional battle painter, Rudolf Trache (1866–1948, studied at the Dresden Art Academy), *Attack of the Zouaves on a German Machinegun Unit Near Soissons, 17 September* [Sturmangriff der Zuaven auf eine deutsche Maschinengewehrabteilung bei Soissons, 17. September], 1914. At least this image represents a machinegun and its effects on a traditional infantry charge, in this case of mixed European and colonial troops. The British artist Richard Caton Woodville (1856–1927, studied at the Düsseldorf Painting Academy and in Paris under Gérôme) painted Bengal cavalry lancers, albeit dismounted, but charging with their lances, their distinctive Bengali headdresses adding an orientalist panache to the romance of a lance charge (*Bengal Lancers Attack German Trenches, Ramscapelle, Belgium, near the Yser River, October 24, 1914*, reproduced in *The Illustrated War News*, 18 November 1914). Chaperone, Trache, and Woodville were already in their fifties and sixties when they painted their pictures, intended for reproduction and mass circulation in the press. In most

106 Eugène Chaperone, *A Morhange, près Nancy*, *Le Panorama de la Guerre* 33 (13 May 1915, Supplément 12).

107 *Le Panorama de la Guerre* 33 (13 May 1915), 281.

cases they hadn't seen the actual fighting or gotten within earshot of the front, relying instead on written dispatches and the visual rhetoric of battle painting they had learned in the nineteenth century.

As the conflict petrified into a defensive war of stalemate and attrition, the local actions these older artists depicted became increasingly irrelevant, and with them the visual codes of nineteenth-century battle painting. The terrible artillery duels between hidden, long-range gun batteries (in attempts to preemptively knock out the enemy's artillery) and week-long barrages intended to cut barbed-wire entanglements and cave in trench systems did not lend themselves to the kinds of compositions taught by professors of battle painting in the old academies of Germany and France. Those old-fashioned compositions centered around small groups of impetuously charging men, tautly posed between the inevitable wounded comrade and the undaunted officer pointing the way forward from atop his rearing steed. Philippe Dagen has demonstrated that such paintings were reviled by the men at the front especially, and were in any case superseded by the advent of amateur photography practiced by those soldiers. Their photographs of the real conditions of the front and of the mangled, unburied dead were reproduced in the same weekly news magazines, where they gave the lie to the fatuous battle paintings of the arrière-garde.[108]

So for example, while the French and British press reported in early October 1914, that at Soissons their troops had captured the German position "in one of the fiercest trench – encounters in the whole history of war," just as important at Soissons was "a long-range artillery duel between our guns and those of the French on our left and the enemy's artillery on the hills [which] continued during the greater part of the day (the 12th), and did not cease until nearly midnight. The enemy had a very large number of heavy howitzers in well-concealed positions."[109] Yet such an action, while it may have been just as newsworthy as the troops

108 Dagen, *Silence des peintres*, 72 ff.

109 "Great Siege-Battle of the Aisne: Panoramas of the British, French, and German Positions" *The Illustrated London News* (16 October 1914), 22.

capturing an enemy trench, simply did not avail itself to traditional depiction. How should such actions be represented to the public? The illustrated news magazines solved this problem by publishing panoramic photographs and even topographical drawings of the front lines observed from a distance, with labels written onto the pictures indicating the locations of invisible enemy batteries and trenches.[110] These images had originated as reconnaissance information for use by artillery gunners, done by officers, probably in the artillery companies, who scrutinized the battlefield from this distant perspective (later in the war the production of observational photographs for use in such counter-battery artillery barrages was the key function of aerial reconnaissance, and in turn the primary cause of aerial combat). The panoramic images were more akin to maps of the terrain – which were published in the illustrated weeklies alongside them – than to battle paintings. To the untrained eye such panoramic drawings simply look like sketches of not particularly interesting landscapes, much like Dix's gouaches titled *Trenches in Front of Reims*. The problem Dix faced as an artist wishing to depict the battlefield was not so different from the problems faced by artillery spotters.

Official war artists

The military leadership of the belligerent countries continued to see value in representing the war in the language of history painting, and they began to send artists to the actual front as official war artists, now nominally part of the armed forces and often theoretically in uniform, in order to create more meaningful and convincing history paintings of the war, often but not always done from life rather than from written

110 Paul Gough, "'Calculating the Future'. Panoramic sketching, reconnaissance drawing and the material trace of war," in Nicholas J. Saunders and Paul Cornish, eds., *Contested Objects. Material Memories of the Great War* (Abingdon: Routledge, 2009), 237–250.

reports. But the days of battlefield tourism were over, and the real action mostly did not lend itself to figurative representation. The front was also indiscriminately dangerous. And so artists went to those places that were relatively safe and accessible to them, looking for moments which presented the courage, dignity, and suffering of the individual soldier, and which could be translated into figurative compositions that told narratives of courage and sacrifice. The artillery battery and the gun crew at work loading the heavy shells into the breech became a common motif. The most notable – and biggest at 364 x 591 cm – work on this theme was probably *The Battle of Vimy Ridge*, by Richard Jack (the first official Canadian war artist), painted in his London studio in 1918–1919 for the Canadian War Records Office (1919, now in the Canadian War Museum) (see Figure 12).

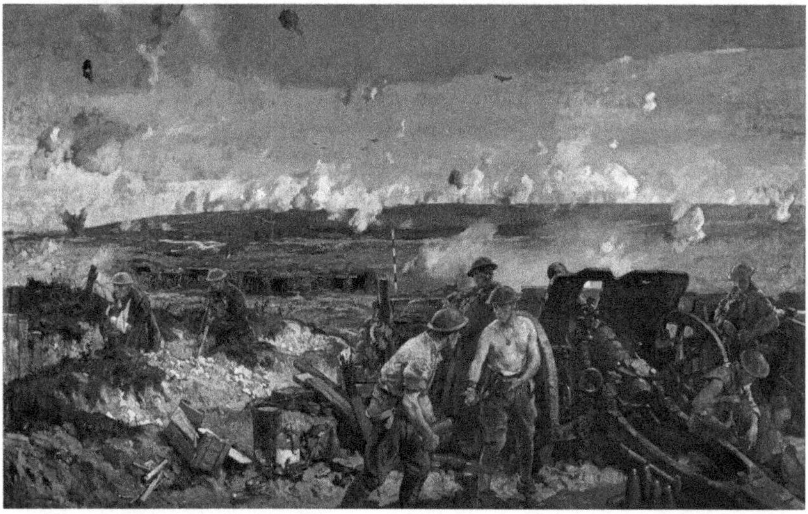

Figure 12. Richard Jack, *The Taking of Vimy Ridge, Easter Monday 1917*, oil on canvas, 1919. CWM 19710261–0160, Beaverbrook Collection of War Art, Canadian War Museum. Photo: Canadian War Museum, used with permission.

The monumental figures of the gunners dominate the foreground; the rest of the painting consists of nothing but a featureless plain and the crest of Vimy ridge on the horizon, wreathed in cordite smoke. But the motif had already become prevalent in 1914, as can be seen in the example of a painting reproduced in *Le Panorama de la guerre de 1914*, which featured the dead bodies of several gunners killed at their posts, and included a narrative text describing the heroism of the sole surviving gunner who continued to load and fire even when he was the last man standing.[111] Other subjects favored by official war artists were: care for the wounded (the most famous is undoubtedly John Singer Sargent's *Gassed*, painted in 1919 for the British, although C. R. W. Nevinson's *The Doctor* of 1916 is equally affecting; both are now at the Imperial War Museum; neither reproduces the hackneyed compositions of the more conventional battle painters); the ruined buildings and churches of French and Belgian towns destroyed by shelling; soldiers marching or at rest. After 1916 the bizarre lunar landscape of no-man's-land was represented in official war art more and more often, as its appearance became increasingly familiar through photographs, and as the scope and scale of the artillery barrages preceding the offensives increased exponentially, especially at the battles of the Somme and Verdun. The rain-filled craters and flooded landscapes that characterized Flanders came to function as an image of the seeming endlessness and inhuman vastness of the war (Nevinson's *After a Push* of 1917 and Paul Nash's *The Menin Road*, 1919, are important examples). In France the former avant-gardists associated with the Nabis, Felix Vallotton and Maurice Denis, now established names, were also commissioned to make paintings of the war. Denis also depicted soldiers at work behind the lines and in reserve towns, but Vallotton produced one of the most remarkable paintings of the war, a dramatic scene of an artillery barrage at Verdun with a beautiful, Symbolist-inflected surface as decorative as any Byzantine icon, as well as an affecting set of wood engravings entitled "*C'est la Guerre!*" (1915–1916) with inventive, appealing compositions that on closer inspection reveal horrible scenes of violence, debauchery, and decaying corpses. The print portfolio may well have served as a model for Dix when he set about achieving a similar effect, seven years later, although in the 1920s,

111 "Jusq'au but!" *Le Panorama de la guerre de 1914* 6, 136.

in peacetime, Dix did not vilify the enemy, as Vallotton so emphatically did in his portfolio produced in the midst of the war.

In Champagne and Arras: Eye-witness accounts vs. "genre scenes"

Unlike the official war artists, Otto Dix was not limited to motifs seen at the rear, but was familiar with the whole range of the war's experiences. Freed of the constraints placed on official war artists by the dangers of the front (or rather, unable to avoid those dangers), what did he choose to make pictures of? While stationed in Champagne in late 1915 and the first half of 1916, and then in the area of the Somme in the second half of 1916, he took the landscape and the life of the soldier at the front as his subject, recording the scenes he had before him during the quieter hours when he had time to draw, and practicing a naturalistic, observational drawing style. Most of the drawings were obviously very concerned with issues of line weight and compositional problems to do with the square format of the paper. The trenches themselves were one of his favorite subjects, depicted from the perspective of somebody standing just above and looking down into them, or else standing in them and looking down their length. Trenches were routinely built with angles and zigzags to avoid enfilading fire should the enemy break into them, and these zigzags become an important compositional device and the primary picturesque interest of Dix's drawings. Although these drawings are considerably more conventional than his earlier experiments in Cubist landscape done while in the barracks at Bautzen, Dix is nonetheless still engaged in creating compacted, condensed spatial effects. In the drawing *Soldier in a Trench* [Soldat im Schützengraben] of 1916 (see Figure 13), Dix depicts a sentry at the end of a trench, spying through a peephole in the sandbag defenses, keeping a lookout against enemy troops attacking across no-man's-land.

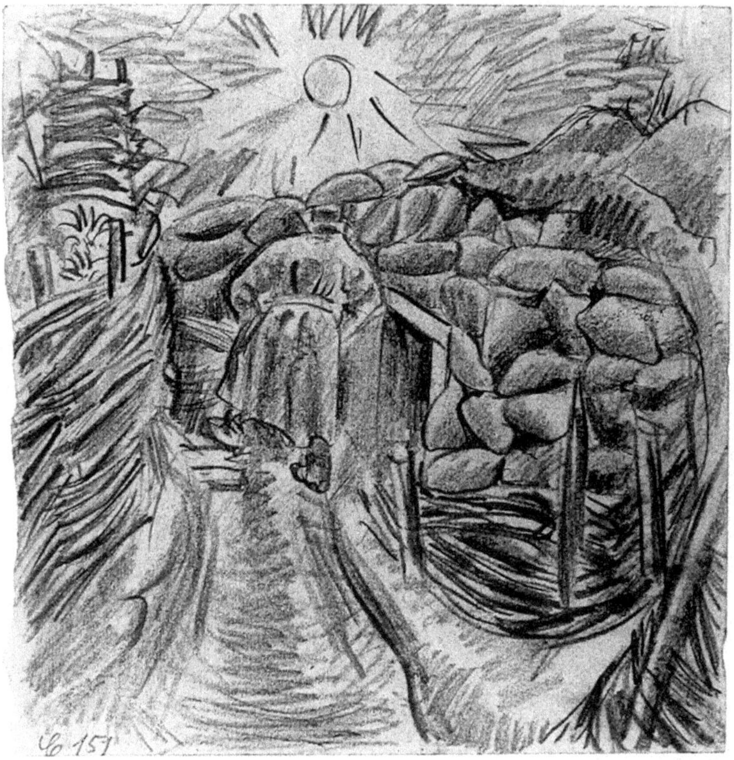

Figure 13. Otto Dix, *Soldier in a Trench* [Soldat im Schützengraben], graphite and charcoal, 1916, Kunstmuseum Albstadt, Stiftung Sammlung Walter Groz, SWG 1976–554. © Otto Dix / Artists Rights Society (ARS), New York / VG Bild-Kunst, Bonn. Photo © Kunstmuseum Albstadt, used with permission.

Many details of trench construction are observed and recorded: sandbags; revetments fashioned out of branches woven together; the higher parados on the left – opposite the enemy side; and the reinforced entrance to the dugout on the right, on the side facing no-man's-land (so that attacking troops can't fire directly into it). The sun is setting, the hour of stand-to, and this soldier has just emerged from the dugout to keep watch until dark; it is cold in the trench, colder than in the dugout, and he shoves his hands into the pockets of his great coat. Nothing much is happening, and the sentry must stand there until night falls; Dix takes advantage of the situation to draw a model from life. The point of view is emphatically from within the trench itself; beyond the lip of the trench only the sky is visible; we do not see what the sentry sees, but only what Dix, the observant artist, sees.

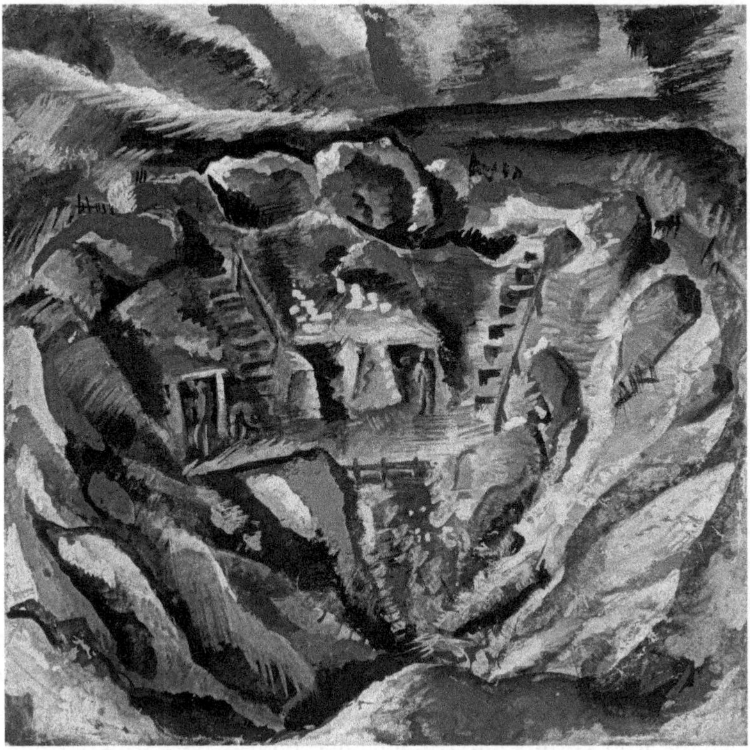

Figure 14. Otto Dix, *Jägertrichter near Vimy ridge* [Jägertrichter in Vimy], gouache, 1917, Kupferstich-Kabinett, Dresden, C1946-62. © Otto Dix / Artists Rights Society (ARS), New York / VG Bild-Kunst, Bonn. Photograph © Kupferstich-Kabinett, Staatliche Kunstsammlungen, Dresden / Herbert Boswank, used with permission.

In both his drawings and his gouaches, Dix also depicted the ruined towns destroyed by shelling and the cratered landscape, including some truly spectacular craters like the so-called *Jägertrichter* (named "Central Crater" by the British), a hole 52 meters in diameter and 11 meters deep. Dix depicted this enormous crater in the gouache *Jägertrichter near Vimy ridge* [Jägertrichter in

Vimy] (1916 or 1917) (see Figure 14).[112] This wonder had been made by a mine blown by German engineers beneath the British lines on 28 April 1916, as part of the tunneling and mining war between the Germans and British, who were vying with each other for the strategically important Vimy Ridge. Once they had blown this and other mines, the Germans had seized the ridge and used the resulting craters along the crest as strongpoints, connecting them with communication trenches.[113] In the gouache Dix has indicated these improvements being made to the position. But a year later, in the terrible Battle of Vimy Ridge of April 1917, the Canadians finally ejected the German army from this strategic point. It was this battle, so important in Canadian national consciousness, that the official Canadian war artist Richard Jack would depict in 1918 (see Figure 12). The contrast between Jack's gargantuan battle panorama and Dix's tiny gouache is instructive. Jack's is a Realist painting in the mode of Courbet, foregrounding war's labor and the soldier's laboring body. It emphasizes the heroic figures, muscled male bodies stripped to the waist, straining at their work, their poses obviously staged in the artist's London studio. The landscape is blank but its scale is clearly indicated by the black and white striped rods placed at regular intervals by the gun crews for use in registering their targets. In contrast to Jack's studio-based practice, Dix painted his little picture on the spot, a motif in which the cyclopean alteration to the landscape is the object of interest, not the laboring bodies of the gunners. The view is from the lip of a crater sublime in scale, but rendered on a sheet of paper small enough to fit into the artist-soldier's haversack. Dix reduces the soldiers in his picture to tiny, almost comically antic specks in a landscape transformed a second time, through the artist's brush, into Cézannesque, proto-Cubist slabs of paint. It is the artist's labor, not the gunners', which is made heroic here.

112 Dix noted in his field notebook that he saw the "Jägertrichter" while in the Artois region in late August 1916 (entry of 29 August 1916). The gouache is likely to date to this occasion, and not 1917, as stated in the inventory of the Dresden Küpferstich-Kabinett. Dix was in the Artois again between 2 March and 15 March 1917, but no mention is made in the record of Vimy Ridge specifically; see Fleischer, "Der Künstler und der Krieg," 24–26.

113 Philip Robinson and Nigel Cave, *The Underground War: Vimy Ridge to Arras*, Vol. 1 (South Yorkshire: Pen and Sword Military Press, 2011), 72 ff.

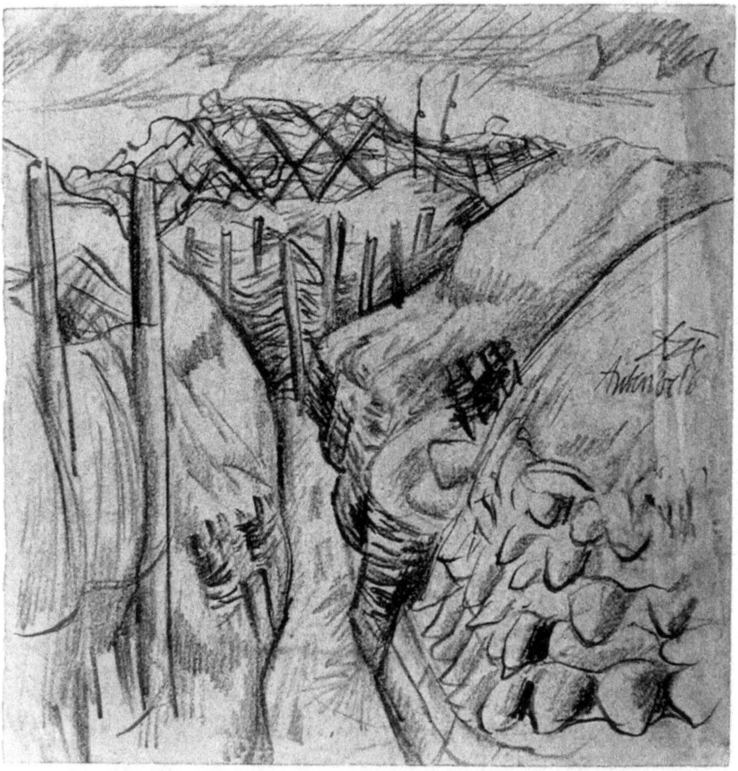

Figure 15. Otto Dix, *Aubérive*, graphite and charcoal, 1916, Kunstmuseum Albstadt, Stiftung Sammlung Walter Groz, SWG 1976–559. © Otto Dix / Artists Rights Society (ARS), New York / VG Bild-Kunst, Bonn. Photo © Kunstmuseum Albstadt, used with permission.

Back in the trenches, Dix continued to draw what I will call the "genre scenes" of the foot soldier's life, such as *Aubérive* (1916) (see Figure 15), with its observed details of sandbags, barbed wire entanglements, and revetment walls of woven branches. Portraits of his fellow soldiers, the work they had to do, the trenches they lived in, and the picturesque views offered by ruined villages and farming hamlets; the subject matter could have been borrowed from seventeenth-century Dutch painting. In numerous drawings of ruined villages and farmhouses the compositions are unified by the heavy outline of the jagged silhouettes of buildings ruined by artillery fire, and careful consideration is given to line weight and distinct differences in the tonality given by shading. In some of these scenes, Dix begins to reintroduce some of the lessons learned from his experiments in Cubist landscape done at Bautzen.

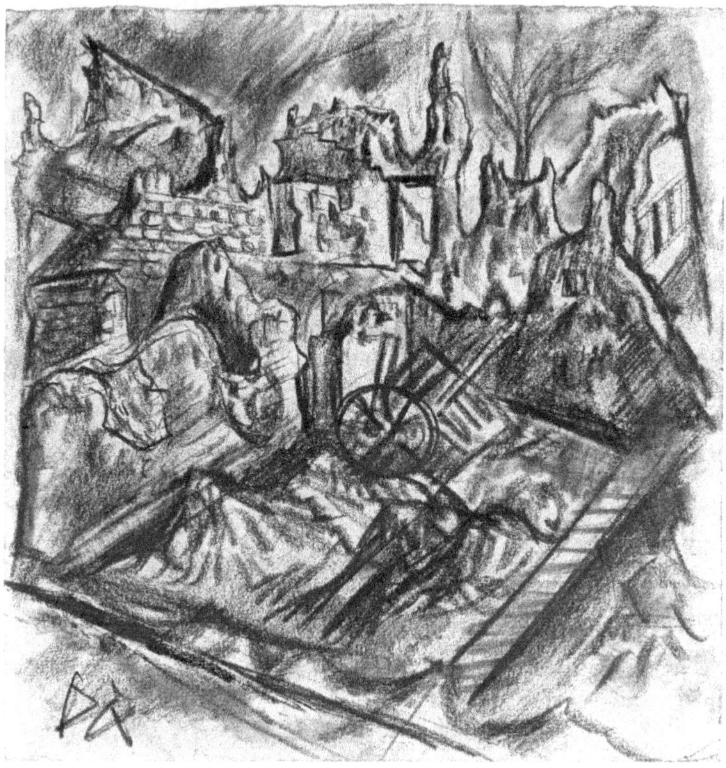

Figure 16. Otto Dix, *Ruins* [Trümmer], red chalk on paper, 1915, Kupferstich-Kabinett, Dresden, C 1968–382. © Otto Dix / Artists Rights Society (ARS), New York / VG Bild-Kunst, Bonn. Photo © Kupferstich-Kabinett, Staatliche Kunstsammlungen, Dresden / Estel/Klut, used with permission.

In *Ruins* [Trümmer] (1915) (see Figure 16), an extraordinarily rich and complex composition done in red chalk, Dix combines two different perspective systems, two-point perspective for the square courtyard of the farmstead in the foreground and single-point for the ruins in the background, into a complexly layered composition. The foreground frames a striking circle-and-square motif, the hand-cart with its wheel sitting at the center of the courtyard. The walls that would have enclosed the courtyard (and depicted in a related drawing of the same motif) have been omitted, leaving an inverted triangle reaching down to the bottom edge of the page. The lower corners of the page are left essentially blank. The upper corners, by contrast, are filled in with the shapes of buildings that don't correspond to the perspective systems of the rest of the drawing, but do suggest that the ruins of the town stretch on indefinitely. The artist's interest is clearly held primarily by the compositional challenges presented by such motifs.

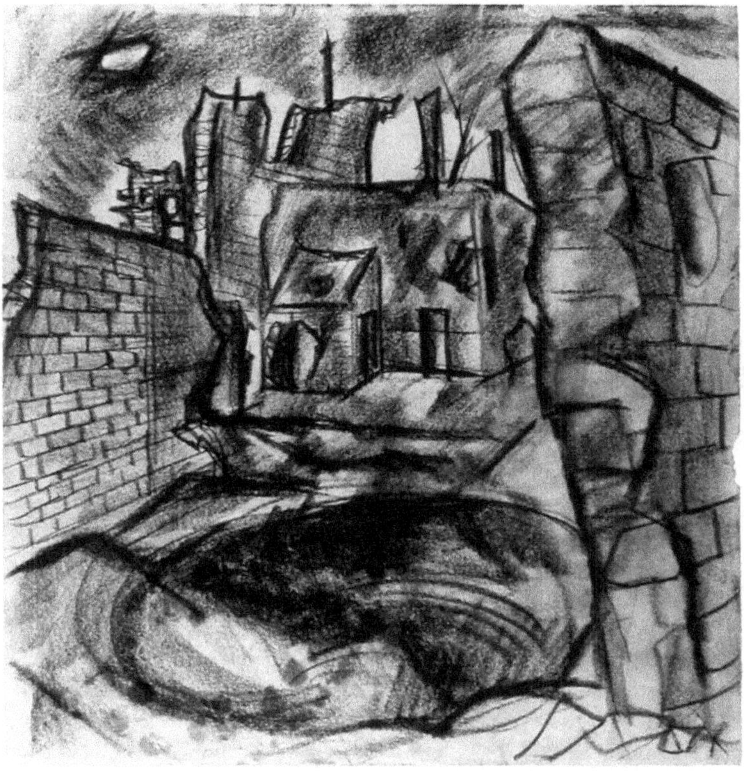

Figure 17. Otto Dix, *Shell Hole in a House* [Granattrichter im Haus], graphite and charcoal, 1916, Kunstmuseum Albstadt, Stiftung Sammlung Walter Groz, SWG 1976–557. © Otto Dix / Artists Rights Society (ARS), New York / VG Bild-Kunst, Bonn. Photo © Kunstmuseum Albstadt, used with permission.

One motif which seemed to fascinate Dix in its bizarreness, and which seems to have suggested a kind of emotional content to him, was the crater in the middle of a building, *Shell Hole in a House* [Granattrichter im Haus] (1916) (see Figure 17), and the related motif of trenches zigzagging through the middle of a town in *Communication Trench in the Village Street of Aubérive* [Laufgraben in der Dorfstrasse von Aubérive]. Dix sketched similar motifs in several of his postcards to Helene Jakob from Aubérive, and on the backs of two of them he wrote a lengthy and somewhat poetic description:

> Shell holes in villages are full of elemental fury. Everything roundabout is subordinate to these powerful, symmetrical craters. They are the eye sockets of the earth, and what circles around them are strange, painful, fantastic [continued on the next postcard] lines. They aren't houses anymore, nobody honestly thinks so. They are living beings of a peculiar sort, with their own natural laws and conditions of life. There are only holes with stones around, or only skeletons. It's a special kind of beauty that is expressed here. I salute you *samideane*. Dix.[114]

There is one more category of image which Dix sought to represent in both his drawings and his postcards during the months he was stationed in Champagne: the activities and spaces hidden beneath the earth in the deep dugouts. In some drawings, the entirety of the underground room, including its structural elements such as posts and interior walls, is seen as if from an impossible vantage point outside of the room but beneath

114 "Voll elementarer Wucht sind Granattrichter innerhalb Dörfern. Alles in der Umgebung scheint der Dynamik dieser gewaltigen symmetrischen Trichter zu unterliegen. Es sind die Augenhöhlen der Erde, was darum herum kreiselt sind irre schmerzlich phantastische / Linien. Häuser sind das nicht mehr, niemand glaubt das im Ernst. Es sind Lebewesen von besonderer Art mit eigenen Gesetzen und Lebensbedingungen. Es sind lauter Löcher mit Steinen herum, oder lauter Skelette. Es ist eine eigenartige seltene Schönheit, die hier redet. – Ich grüße Sie samideane. Dix." "Samideane" is the Esperanto greeting that Dix often used in his postcards to Jakob, and means "likeminded." Postcards nos. 13 and 14, (1916). Rüdiger, *Grüsse aus dem Krieg*, 50–52.

the earth, as if by a mole with x-ray vision.[115] In *Stairway to a Dugout*, the stairway is seen in a similar fashion, with several soldiers sitting on the stairs, either waiting out an artillery barrage or simply taking shelter from the incessant rain.

Amateur soldier-artists

Otto Dix was far from the only artist in uniform to make pictures during his moments of free time between battles and the endless work of war. By "artist in uniform" I mean specifically those artists who were *not* commissioned as official war artists. But besides young soldiers who were already well-known and successful artists, such as Franz Marc and August Macke, Ernst Ludwig Kirchner, Max Beckmann, Hermann Max Pechstein, Umberto Boccioni, Fernand Léger, and others, there were young, unknown artists, some trained and some amateurs, who not only produced art during the war, but who managed to get it exhibited. There were exhibitions in both Germany and France, such as the "Salon des Armées," December 1916 to February 1917, at the Jeu de Paume in the Tuilleries, organized by the *Bulletin des armées de la République*, which according to a publicity poster was "reserved for artists of the front." The "Salon des Armées" combined works by various artist soldiers with objects from the front: canons and artillery shells, but also the small objects of handicrafts that soldiers made from recovered materials, shell casings and the like, in order to pass the tedious hours between actions. And not all of the artworks on display were made by trained artists. Thus the

115 See for example, *Unterstand*, Dresden Küpferstich-Kabinett, C 1968–379, Lehmann, Hans-Ulrich, *Otto Dix: Die Zeichnungen im Dresdner Kupferstich-Kabinett: Katalog des Bestandes* (Dresden: Kupferstich-Kabinett, 1991), 61, and *Sieben Meter unter der Erde*, Dresden Küpferstich-Kabinett, C 1968–381.

exhibition was a curious but undoubtedly effective amalgam of reportage and relics, conveying a sense of immediate, physical connection with the men at the front. In this context, the sketches sent from the front combined the facticity of eye-witness account with the materiality of the relic, fashioned by the very hand of the soldier at the front. In Dresden, the exhibition "Dresden Artists Who are In the Army" [Ausstellung Dresdener Künstler, die im Heeresdienste stehen], where Dix exhibited his drawings from the field, was one of the most important venues in Germany. Dix showed several drawings from his time in Champagne at this exhibition, including *Communication Trench in the Village Street of Aubérive*, *In the Trench Near Aubérive*, and *Stairway to a Dugout*. This last was reproduced in the catalog.[116]

Young artists in uniform often developed visual strategies to emphasize the immediacy of their sketches done at the front, the fact that they had "seen it with their own eyes," in the tradition of Francisco Goya's "Yo lo vi," or "I saw it."[117] These signs of immediacy often make the rhetorical claim that the works were done on the spot, at the very moment when the depicted motif was viewed, a claim that is self-contradictory, as an artist could not both make a drawing and be on the move, attacking or retreating or even defending a position. These visual signs include marks of haste in execution, where the rapidity of the marks underwrites the truthfulness of observed details, and claims them as the artist-soldier's own lived experience. One such young artist in uniform was Otto Schubert, who during the war published a portfolio of 24 lithographs based on drawings made at the front, *24 Lithos from the Western Front*, including *Defense* [Abwehr] (1917) (see Figure 18).[118]

116 *Zweite Ausstellung Dresdener Künstler, die im Heeresdienste Stehen. Galerie Arnold, Sept. 27 – Oct. 29, 1916* (Dresden: Galerie Arnold, 1916).

117 From the *Disasters of War* series, 1810–1820. Dix would later make a specific reference to this image, in his own print series from 1923; this phrase is often cited in conjunction with Dix's drawings of the war.

118 *24 Lithos vom Krieg im Westen*, 1917, Robert Gore Rifkind collection.

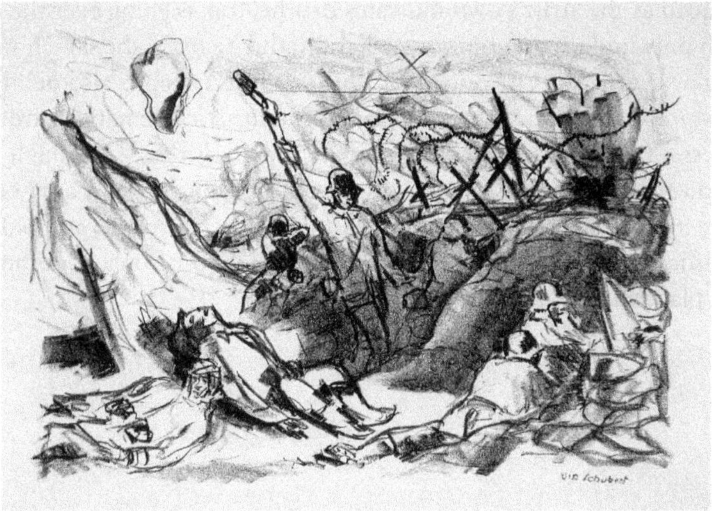

Figure 18. Otto Schubert, *Defense* [Abwehr], lithograph on laid paper, 1917, Los Angeles County Museum of Art, The Robert Gore Rifkind Center for German Expressionist Studies. Photo © 2018 Museum Associates/ LACMA. Licensed by Art Resource, NY, used with permission.

Another was Henri Camus, whose *Charging for a hand-to-hand attack. Grenadiers of my squad (scared shitless)* [Départ d'un coup de main. Grenadiers de mon escouade (la trouille aux fesses)] (1916–1917) (see Figure 19) depicts not only great immediacy, but also closely observed detail – such as how a soldier holds himself, extending an arm to keep his balance as he clambers over the side of a low trench, encumbered by his heavy coat, helmet, and the haversack slung over his shoulder. This particular drawing also includes another sign of its supposed immediacy and status as an eye-witness document, namely the inscription that Camus, like other artists, wrote directly on the page. Such inscriptions heighten the directness of the expression, and also of the artist's connection to the image and the events depicted.[119] In this instance, the identification of

119 Henri Camus (1893–1989) was a young medical student. He drew more than 500 sketches in his sketchbooks, and although he was not a professional artist, he did exhibit these drawings in the "Salon des Armées" in the Tuileries.

the squad as the artist's own indicates that he, too, is going over the top, which only underscores the contradiction; did he make the sketch while going over the top? Of course not. But this inscription is also painfully honest – the idiomatic expression in the parenthetical remark "la trouille aux fesses" could be loosely translated as "scared shitless." Although Dix would very often use his signature as a compositional device, only rarely did he include any such inscription within the picture plane, and only in the earliest stages of his project of drawing while at the front; one example is the place name Aubérive.

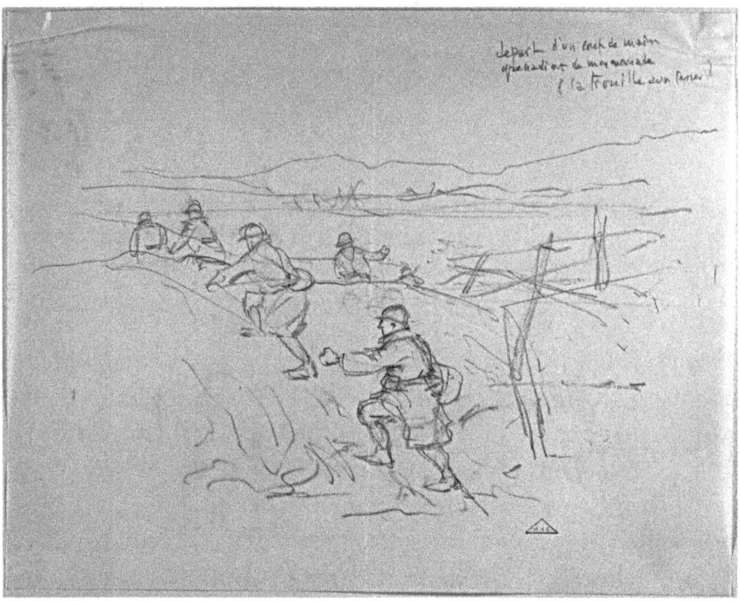

Figure 19. Henri Camus, *Charging for a hand-to-hand attack. Grenadiers of my squad (scared shitless)* [Départ d'un coup de main. Grenadiers de mon escouade (la trouille aux fesses)] watercolor and pencil on paper, 1916–1917, La Contemporaine, Nanterre. Photo © La Contemporaine, Nanterre, used with permission.

Camus provides another example, in *Seen at the bottom of the communication trench Desaix, without being able to stop and help* [Vu au fond du boyau Desaix sans pouvoir s'arrêter pour l'aider] (1917) (see Figure 20).

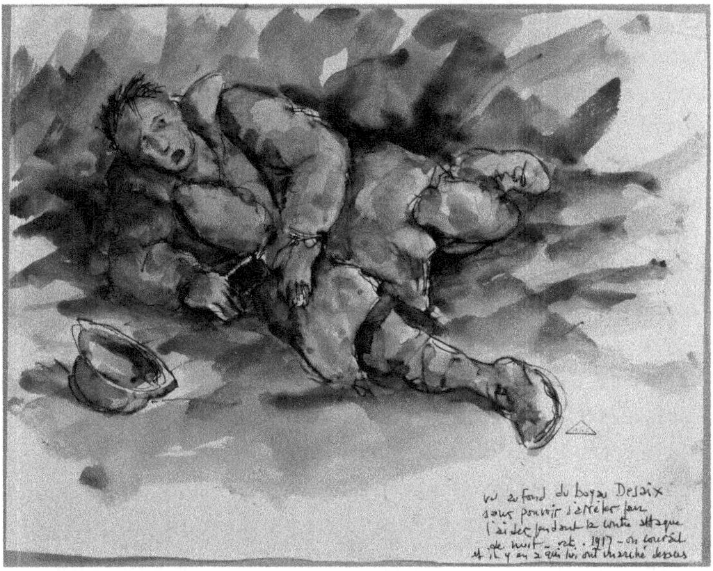

Figure 20. Henri Camus, *Seen at the bottom of the communication trench Desaix, without being able to stop and help* [Vu au fond du boyau Desaix sans pouvoir s'arrêter pour l'aider], watercolor and pencil on paper, 1917, La Contemporaine, Nanterre. Photo © La Contemporaine, Nanterre, used with permission.

The image is so immediate that it is easy to forget that it is a fiction, but if the artist didn't have time to stop and offer aid, he didn't have time to make this little watercolor sketch, either. He made it later, from what must have been a very vivid memory. Even during the war, the powerful emotional bonds between soldiers who had suffered and fought and feared together were presented, in the drawings of Camus and any number of other soldier-artists, as something at least as powerfully important as his own fear of dying. Whether this was true or not, it was part of the story of physical and emotional experience which soldier artists and writers on all sides sought to put across to their audience, not least their civilian audience back home. The French critic Le Rousseur, writing in *Le Crapouillot* during the war stated categorically that only the artist who was also a soldier, and had lived through the experience of a bombardment or who had himself gone over the top, could give an honest visual representation of such an experience, and then only in sketches done immediately afterward, not in a large-scale battle paintings done later in the studio. In other words, only pictures which deliberately created the false impression of having been done on the spot could hope to attain the status of truthful documents – truthful in the way that mattered most, which was as a genuine document of combat and death made by somebody who had experienced the front in all its intensity.[120] The artist-soldier had to try to, "translate the sensations, the emotions of these guys – and make them comprehensible to the philistines," by which he meant of course civilians and others not at the front.[121] And the most dramatic sign of immediacy and witness was also the most contradictory kind of sign: the claim, written right onto the picture, that the artist had not had time to respond to the suffering of his comrades in a normal, human fashion. This was presented as its own kind of agony, the agony of the soldier who could not save or even comfort his comrade in arms, or give his corpse the dignity it deserved.

By contrast with other artist-soldiers like Camus, Otto Dix did not seem especially interested in conveying such emotional authenticity or the suffering of the frontline soldier – a claim that will surprise anyone familiar with the his representations of the war experience done later, after the war. Let me try to back this claim up by triangulating his work with that of two German artists, Otto Schubert and Adolf Erbslöh, whose works are dissimilar to each other in a significant way. Like Camus, Otto Schubert (another soldier-artist whose work would be exhibited alongside Dix's in Dresden in 1916), included detailed information in his small watercolors such as *Battle Near Béthincourt, Dead Man's Hill, Hill 304* [Schlacht bei Béthincourt, Höhe Toter Mann, Höhe 304] (1916) (see Figure 21), a picture of part of the Battle of Verdun.[122]

120 Audoin-Rouzeau has noted that the "eye wash" which characterized official reporting of the war was the source of much resentment and despair of soldiers at the front. Stéphane Audoin-Rouzeau, *Men at War 1914–1918: National Sentiment and Trench Journalism in France During the First World War* (Oxford: Berg, 1992), 92 f.

121 "[T]raduire les sensations, les Émotions des bonshommes – à les faire comprendre aux philistines." Le Rousseur, *Le Crapouillot*, cited in Dagen, *Le Silence des peintres*, 114, without further information.

122 The inscriptions says, "Die Schlacht bei Béthincourt. Links der tote Mann. In der Mitte das Dorf Béthincourt unter dem deutschen Trommelfeuer. Im Hintergrund

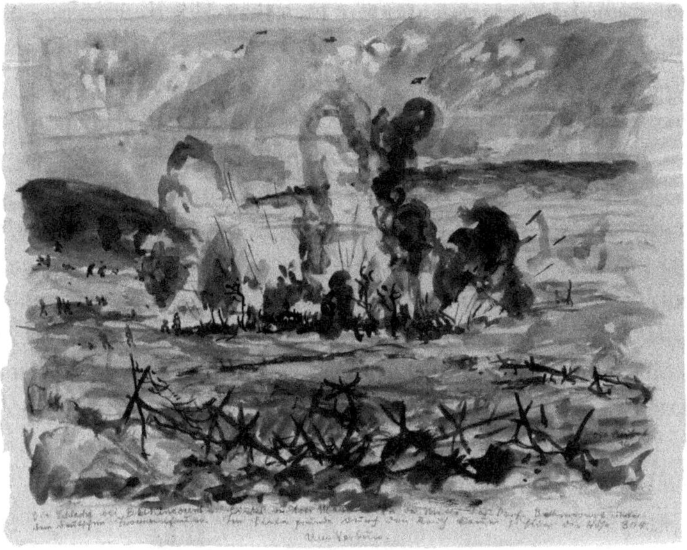

Figure 21. Otto Schubert, *Battle Near Béthincourt, Dead Man's Hill, Hill 304* [Schlacht bei Béthincourt, Höhe Toter Mann, Höhe 304], watercolor and pencil on paper, 1916, Kupferstich-Kabinett, Dresden, C 1973–17. © Kupferstich-Kabinett, Staatliche Kunstsammlungen, Dresden / Herbert Boswank, used with permission.

In one of the largest and most horrible battles of the war, under some of the heaviest artillery barrages ever seen (during which the village of Béthincourt was completely wiped from the map), we see the difficulty faced by an artist like Schubert who wanted to convey such an experience with immediacy and eye-witness authenticity. The watercolor depicts a barbed wire entanglement in the foreground and an empty middle ground; in the distance are the two visually unremarkable but strategically vital heights, the "Dead Man" hill and "Hill 304." Between them is a vague knot of fire and smoke: the village of Béthincourt being annihilated. The figures are mere flecks, too small to make out; they appear to be French, judging by the color of their uniforms. By contrast, in late 1916 or early 1917 Adolf Erbslöh, a semi-official German

durch den Rauch kaum sichtbar die Höhe 304. Um Verdun." Schubert, *Künstler im Trommelfeuer*, 373.

war painter who had been an important member of the Munich avant-garde alongside Franz Marc and August Macke (both killed in combat by then) and who was 10 years older than Dix, painted a small oil, *Ruins near Béthincourt* [Ruinen bei Béthincourt] (1916–1917) (see Figure 22); it could be any early Expressionist landscape. This is a good example of the contrast between artist soldiers like Schubert, who made small drawings and watercolors of actual combat, however short they may have fallen of conveying the overwhelming enormity of the combat and artillery barrages, and the official war painters who didn't get near the front, but concentrated instead on quiet and even somewhat conventionally picturesque images such as ruins. But what I want to draw attention to here especially is the surprising fact that Dix's pictures of the war, at least in the period while he was fighting in Champagne in 1916, had more in common with the genre scenes of Erbslöh, including the picturesque motifs of ruined houses and other results of the war, than with the attempts by his fellow soldier-artists to convey the immediate violence of combat.

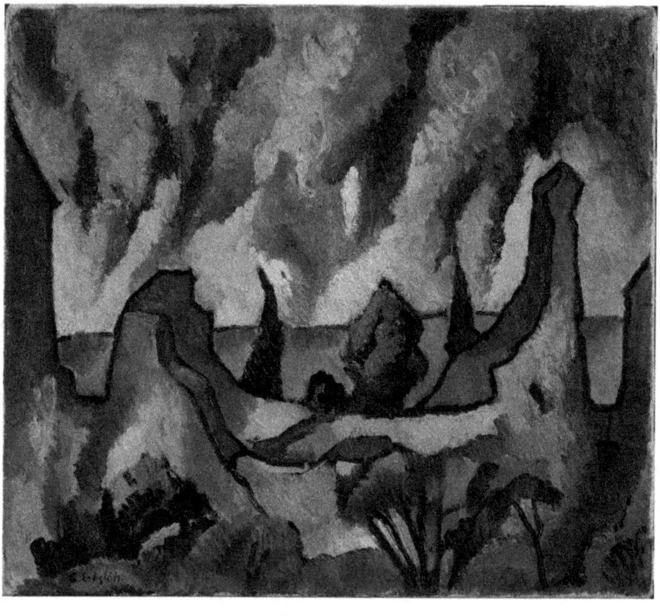

Figure 22. Adolf Erbslöh, *Ruins near Béthincourt* [Ruinen von Béthincourt], oil on canvas, 1916–1917, Museum Kunstpalast, Düsseldorf, 0.1968.5586. Photo: © Museum Kunstpalast / Horst Kolberg / ARTOTHEK, used with permission.

The point here is that although Otto Dix was a soldier in the fighting, like Camus and Schubert, unlike them he did not make pictures meant to convey the experience of modern combat, unimaginable to the "philistines" back home. Instead, he concentrated on the kinds of motifs, such as ruined houses and villages, which could really and truly be drawn from life, on the spot, in a manner similar to the official war artists like Erbslöh or Denis. There is evidence that he was concerned to get his genre drawings "right," with an eye towards showing them to a (civilian) public. In the dozen or so miniature landscape sketches Dix drew in his field notebook, he corrected some, using the same violet pencil he used to correct his written statement about artistic creation.[123] Even in his postcards home to his fiancé, Otto Schubert often tried to capture scenes of combat (unlike Dix), although he also depicted the French countryside, the waiting in dugouts, and the work of war.[124] In one of his postcards, Schubert conveys the image of German soldiers defending their trench with grenades, while in the distance artillery explosions send flames, smoke, and clods of earth into the sky, "spouting dark earth and wire with gusts from hell."[125] In contrast, Dix focused on the still landscapes and inert objects around him in his postcards to Helene Jakob, just as in his drawings.[126] In the drawings that Schubert exhibited in the 1916 Galerie Arnold exhibition, alongside Dix, he represented both scenes of combat, such as *First Assault Wave* [Erste Sturmwelle] as well as genre scenes of the war. The same is true of Schubert's lithographs, published in the portfolio *24 Lithos from the War*, which included scenes of direct combat, such as *Defense* [Abwehr] (see

123 He changed the heading of a draft for an artistic statement from "Entstehung eines Kunstwerks", to "Entstehung eines Erlebnises." This may have been written around the time of the first exhibition of his drawings, in the Galerie Arnold exhibition in October 1916. Dix, Field Notebook, Albstadt, 40.

124 A recent exhibition (2014–2015) displayed a cache of nearly 50 of these postcards, which are in a private collection in the US, "Postcards from the Trenches. Germans and Americans Visualize the Great War." <http://postcardsfromthetrenches.com/postcards> Accessed 19 May 2015.

125 See Otto Schubert, postcard in the Kupferstich-Kabinett, Dresden, C.1973–9. The line is from Sassoon's poem *Counter-Attack* again.

126 Rüdiger, *Grüsse aus dem Krieg*.

Figure 18) and *Hand-to-Hand Fighting* [Nahkampf].[127] In 1916 Schubert produced an entire portfolio of images of horses suffering in the war (see Figure 23) (also a subject he represented in at least one postcard, *Horses under Shrapnel Fire* dated 11 March 1916), a very effective way to convey the animal-like fear and pain experienced in combat, as explored even recently in the play and movie *War Horse*.[128]

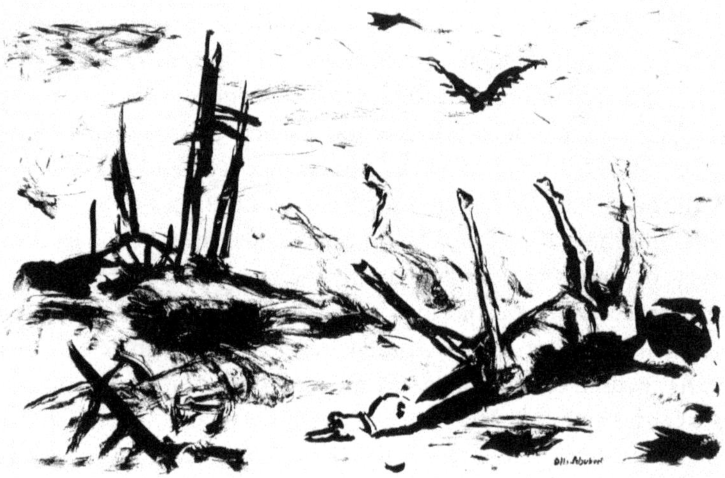

Figure 23. Otto Schubert, *Death* [Tod], lithograph on laid paper, 1917, Los Angeles County Museum of Art, The Robert Gore Rifkind Center for German Expressionist Studies. © Otto Dix / Artists Rights Society (ARS), New York / VG Bild-Kunst, Bonn. Photo © 2018 Museum Associates/ LACMA. Licensed by Art Resource, NY.

After the war, and after Schubert and Dix had worked side by side for a time in the Dresden avant-garde group *Sezession Gruppe 1919*, Dix would make etchings based on similar themes and with similar objectives. But during his first year at the front, throughout 1916, Dix stuck to motifs that he could draw or paint from life, concentrating on stylistic and formal issues rather

127 Schubert, *24 Lithos vom Krieg im Westen*, 1917.

128 Schubert, *Die Leiden der Pferde im Krieg*, Dresden, 1917. *War Horse*, novel by Michael Morpurgo (1982); play by Nick Stafford (premier 2007); film by Steven Spielberg (2011).

than emotional ones.[129] This is perhaps surprising in light of the enormous importance that Dix would put on conveying "what it was really like" at the front during battle and the most affective, horrible sensations. Only in the 1920s would Dix begin to deploy the strategies used by artists like Camus: the very specific place names, the claims to have "seen it myself," as well as the overwhelming images of human suffering. Dix would use these techniques to great effect, especially in his series of etchings in the portfolio, *The War*. But for him these preoccupations arose only after the war.

Battle of the Somme

On 24 July 1916, the 23rd Reserve Division, including Dix's machinegun platoon, was transferred to the Battle of the Somme, which had begun on 1 July. Here the British and the French armies together tried to do what they had not been able to do in Champagne in September of the year before: to mass their troops and overwhelm the German defenses. The attack was preceded by an eight-day-long artillery barrage of a magnitude never seen before, which the planning staff hoped would not only destroy the German trenches and barbed wire emplacements, but also kill most of the defenders. But the German army had dug their bunkers deep enough and reinforced them strongly enough that they were able to survive the barrage in enough numbers to defend their positions, especially in the stretch opposite the British army (the French artillery fire had been more effective). When the British soldiers advanced across no-man's-land on 1 July, instead of finding the German line essentially undefended, as had been expected, they were met with devastating machinegun fire. The

129 One other artist in uniform who similarly stuck to genre scenes done from life was the Frenchman Mathurin Méthuet, whose hundreds of drawings done at the front can be seen in the Musée Méthuet in Lamballe, France. His drawings were published in *L'Illustration* (26 August 1916). Interestingly, Méthuet was, like Dix, trained as a decorative artist, a career he continued after the war (unlike Dix).

machineguns had been carefully positioned so that their lines of fire crisscrossed, creating a deadly effect. As each wave of British soldiers fell, the next was sent out according to the pre-determined timetable; the officers in the rear, confident that the Germans had been decimated, were unaware of the disaster unfolding in front of the German trenches. The result was the bloodiest day in British military history: 57,470 casualties, of whom 19,240 were killed.[130] It was the Maxim machinegun which did the bulk of this industrialized killing. The idea that all 80 divisions of British infantry casually walked across no-man's-land in loose formation, like lambs to the slaughter, is firmly embedded in the British national consciousness and has most recently been represented in Joe Sacco's remarkable panoramic drawing of that day, *The Great War: July 1, 1916, The First Day of the Battle of the Somme* (2013).[131] While it may not have actually happened like this – most of the divisions did not simply stroll into the hail of bullets – it has been pointed out that, in the face of the enfiladed fire of the German machineguns, it mattered very little how the British soldiers approached the German lines; as long as they were out of their trenches, they didn't stand a chance. In fact, the effective range of the machinegun of the sort that Dix operated was so great that a significant number of British soldiers on that first day were killed while still in the rear, before they could even reach their *own* trenches to form up.[132] This is not to say that a German machine-gunner wasn't also in great danger on that day and in the subsequent weeks of July. The British and French did gain ground, and in the French sector of the battle, to the south of the bend in the Somme River, where Dix would eventually be stationed, the Germans were driven back a couple of kilometers. On the first day of the battle, another soldier-artist, Otto Lais (8th Baden Infantry Regiment), who, just like Dix, was a machine-gunner and *Unteroffizier* [sergeant] of a machinegun platoon, was defending a trench opposite the British

130 Robin Prior and Trevor Wilson, *The Somme* (New Haven, CT: Yale University Press, 2005), 112.

131 Sacco, Joe, *The Great War: July 1, 1916, The First Day of the Battle of the Somme. An Illustrated Panorama* (New York: W. W. Norton, 2013).

132 Prior and Wilson, *The Somme*, 114 ff.

army near Serre, where the British were dealt their heaviest losses. After the war Lais published a vivid description of his experience on that day. It is worth quoting at length, because it gives a sense of the extreme peril faced even by a machine-gunner in his defensive position, as well as how a gunner went about his work. It also has some of the earthy humor that characterize such combat narratives, and that I will emphasize in Dix's own postwar imagery.

> The machine gunners, who lived a privileged life at quiet times and were envied for being able to avoid jobs such as carrying heavy mortar rounds forward, were earning their pay today. Belt after belt was fired. 250 rounds – 1,000–3,000. 'Pass up the spare barrels!' shouts the gun commander. Barrels are changed – fire on! 5,000 rounds. The barrel must be changed again. It's red hot and the cooling water is boiling – the hands working the weapon are scorched and burned […] The cooling water turns to seething steam with the continuous firing. In the heat of battle, the steam overflow hose slips out of its fixing on the water jacket. With a great hiss, a jet of steam goes up, providing a superb target for the enemy. […] We fire on endlessly […] The cooling water has almost steamed away. 'Where's the water?' bawls the gunner. 'Get the mineral water out of the dugout!' 'There's none left Unteroffizier!' It all went during the eight day bombardment.
>
> The British keep charging forward. Despite the fact that hundreds are already lying dead in the shell holes to our front, fresh waves keep emerging from the assault trenches over there. We have got to fire! A gunner rushes into the crater with the water container and urinates into it. A second pisses into it too – quick, refill! The British have closed to grenade throwing range and hand grenades fly to and fro. The barrel change is complete, the water jacket refilled. Load! Hand and rifle grenades burst close to the weapon. Just keep calm, get the tangle sorted out and load! Speak loudly, slowly and clearly to yourself. 'Forward! – Down! – Back! (Working parts forward – Belt on – Working parts back). The same again! – Safety catch to the right! – Fire!' … Tack! – Tack! – Tack! – Tack! … […][133]

Lais ends his highly narrativized reminiscence with a consideration of the British dead, ruing his own handiwork. Dix happened to have missed

133 Otto Lais, *Maschinengewehr im Eisernen Regiment (8. Badisches Infanterie-Regiment No. 169)* (Karlsruhe: G. Braun, 1935). 3, translation, Jack Sheldon, *The German Army on the Somme, 1914–1916* (South Yorkshire: Pen & Sword Military, 2005), 142–143.

that first day and the first, bloody weeks of the battle, but on his first day in position, 24 July, his regiment, the 102nd, came under heavy fire, and then had to fend off an enemy attack. The trenches and dugouts were nearly destroyed, and the regiment had to take shelter mostly in shell holes and a few remaining dugouts, while they came under a heavy French drumroll barrage.[134] He spent the rest of July and the first part of August 1916 in the Battle of the Somme, partly in a position in the notorious Monacu Farm, directly overlooking the Somme river – a place name that would appear in his etchings in 1923. It was a hellish business. A machine gunner might survive the devastating artillery barrages and the defense of a position against waves of troops. But then falling back when the enemy broke through, and moving forward again in the wake of a successful counter-attack or to provide reinforcement to units under attack, often over open ground or scurrying from one shell hole to the next, put him in mortal peril. On 12 August Dix's division, the 23rd Reserve Division, was relieved and sent to the village of Maurois, 50 km to the rear, for rest, before being sent to the Artois region from 23 August to 23 October. In a letter to Helene Jakob dated 15 August, Dix described the fighting.

> Thank God the horrible days on the Somme are over. We were relieved there by the Bavarians on the 12th. Our position was to the right of the notorious Monacu Farm. Our company was deployed there for three weeks, relieving each other every two days. The first two days that the 102nd Reg. was there ran their course relatively quietly. We still had two trenches there, one behind the other. Of course there were no communication trenches. I lay there with five other machineguns in the position "Brown Earth" … [In] the second position, where the 102nd Reg. had deepened the trenches by night according to old custom. Frenchy was on the commanding height and could observe everything just fine, and began on the third day to lay down a drumroll barrage with his twenty-eights, and sometimes his fifteens and smaller calibers. It was horrible! The b. position was so plowed up, you couldn't make out the trenches anymore. I sat with my gun and my men in a reinforced pillbox. Our little den threatened to collapse with every shell. As it got worse, my three men pulled out. And I was left sitting there with just one. I was determined to stay. Suddenly, a twenty-eight shell threw so much dirt into our hole that we were stuck up to our

134 Fleischer, "Der Künstler und der Krieg," 21.

chests. The gun was buried, impossible to dig it out fast enough. So I pulled out, into the next pillbox to the left (the firing had started on the right). Now it started from the left, too. Soon the gun in the second pillbox was hit by a shell and the machine gunner, who was standing in the entrance, had both eardrums burst by it. Fall back! I moved farther to the left – the others ran like crazy to the rear. I lay for hours in the barrage in a foxhole one meter deep and two meters long with another soldier. In the evening it got quieter and I went to the rear. In total we lost 12 machineguns; the Frenchies got two of them. On the 10th I lay with a gun (we had to leave the Brown position and had dug ourselves in under an overhang 30 mtr farther back). There, among the Grenadier Reg. 100, a drumroll barrage of twenty-eights from 10:30 in the morning until nine in the evening. This time at the overhang – the losses of this reg. are terrible. In the evening the enemy attacked. Because of the fog, a gun battery fired too short, and fired into our overhang. Horrible dismay terrible losses. The bodies lay all around, arms and legs were flying. From the 6. Comp. of this Reg. just 9 men were left. Every time it was a feeling of relief, when the red flares went up (meaning, "enemy attack") and we could move up with our gun and fire. But what use are all of these details to you? You certainly can't imagine such a thing. Now we're far to the rear of that Hell, in a place called Maurois. Maybe I'll get a leave soon. So many good comrades were left out there, it's a shame about those boys. Hearty greetings, *Via samideano*.[135]

135 Transcribed in Fritz Löffler, *Otto Dix und der Krieg*, 10–11, reprinted in *Otto Dix. Briefe*, 448–449, with the place name "Maurois" corrected. "Gott sei Dank sind die furchtbaren Tage an der Somme vorüber. Wir sind am 12. Durch Bayern dort abgelöst worden. Unsere Stellung war rechts des viel genannten Gehöftes Monacu. Unsere Kompagnie war drei Wochen dort eingesetzt und wir lösten unter uns alle 2 Tage ab. Die ersten beiden Tage an welchem Reg. 102 dort lag verliefen verhältnismäßig ruhig. Wir hatten dort noch 2 Gräben hintereinander. Verbindungen durch Laufgräben gibt es natürlich nicht. Ich lag mit noch 5 anderen M. G. in der Stellung 'Braune Erde' [Auf] die zweite Stellung wo das Reg. 102 nach altem Brauch nachts die Gräben vertieft hatte, fing der Franzmann, der auf der Höhe liegt und alles herrlich beobachten kann, am 3ten Tage an mit 28igern zu trommeln, dazwischen 15er und kleiner Kaliber. Es war furchtbar! Die b. Stellung wurde so umgeackert, daß man keinen Graben mehr sah. Ich saß mit meinem Gewehr und meinen Leuten in einem minierten Stollen. Bei jedem Schuß drohte unsere Bude zusammen zu fallen. Als es immer schlimmer wurde, rückten 3 meiner Leute ab. Da saß ich nun noch mit einem. Ich war entschlossen zu bleiben. Plötzlich haut uns eine 28er so viel Dreck ins Loch, daß wir bis an die Brust drinsteckten. Das Gewehr war verschüttet, ausgraben in der Eile unmöglich. Ich rückte also und zwar in den nächsten Stollen von weiter links (von rechts fing die Schießerei an). Jetzt

Dix was again rotated out of the ongoing Somme battle during the month of September, a bloody month when casualties on all sides combined surpassed 100,000.[136] In the end the battle, which was originally conceived as a mere diversionary tactic to draw German troops away from Verdun, lasted a full six months, and one accounting puts the number of German soldiers killed at 164,055, with the number of combined French and British killed at 146,431.[137]

Between 24 October and 4 December Dix's 102nd Regiment was back on the Somme front (by then the battle was finally over), near Bapaume, to help defend the line against continued Allied assaults; Dix had been promoted to platoon leader of the 390th Machinegun Platoon. On 4 December Dix's 23rd Reserve Division was sent to winter quarters in the rear, near Arras. On 17 December Dix fell ill, and was sent to a military hospital in Hénin, near Lens, in an area occupied by the German

---

ging's auch von links los. Bald war das Gewehr des zweiten Stollen zerschossen und dem Gewehrführer, der am Eingang stand, schlug es beide Trommelfelle durch. Ausreißen! Ich rücke etwas weiter links – die anderen rennen in wilder Flucht nach hinten. In einem kleinen Erdloch 1 mtr. hoch 2 mtr lang lag ich noch alleine mit einem Infanteristen stundenlang im Trommelfeuer. Am Abend wurde es ruhiger und ich ging zurück. Die folgenden Tage waren fast noch furchtbarer. Im ganzen sind uns 12 Maschinengewehre verlorengegangen, 2 davon haben die Franzer. Am 10. Lag ich mit einem Gewehr (wir hatten die braune Stellung verlassen müssen und uns 30 mtr weiter hinten an einem Steilhang eingegraben). Dort zwischen Gren. Reg. 100 Trommelfeuer von früh ½ 11 bis abends neuen mit 28ern. Diesmal nach dem Steilhang – die Verluste dieses Rgts. sind furchtbar. Am Abend griff der Feind an. Wegen des Nebels schoß eine Batterie zu kurz und schoß in unseren Steilhang. Furchtbare Bestürzung schreckliche Verluste. Die Leichen lagen herum, Arme und Beine flogen. Von der 6. Komp. dieses Reg blieben 9 Mann übrig. Es war jedes mal ein befreiendes Gefühl, wenn die roten Leuchtkugeln aufstiegen (heißt 'Feind greift an') und wir konnten mit unserem Gewehr vorrücken und feuern. Was aber nützen Ihnen all diese Einzelheiten? Vorstellen wie so was ist können Sie sicher nicht. Jetzt sind wir weit hinter dieser Hölle im Ort Maurois. Vielleicht erhalte ich nun bald mal Urlaub. Es sind viele gute Kameraden draußen geblieben, Schade um die Kerle. Recht viele Grüße Via samideano."

136 Military pass, DKA, Nuremberg. See also Fleischer, "Der Künstler und der Krieg," 22–24.

137 J. H Boraston, *Sir Douglas Haig's Despatches* (London: Dent, 1920 edn.), 53.

army since the start of the war. During his recovery he must have been in Méricourt, near Lens, because he painted a gouache of a quiet street in this town, seen from an upper-story window, quite likely the window of a room in which he was billeted.[138]

1917 and a new conception of art in the trenches

During all this time, Dix continued to draw and paint when he could, probably in those moments when his unit was out of the trenches, in the reserve line, or in the reserve towns. From the military hospital in Hénin he wrote to his friend and colleague in Dresden, Otto Baumgärtel, with whom he had once practiced the Mazdaznan diet and breathing exercises, asking him to go see about exhibiting Dix's work at Gerstenberger's in Chemnitz, a prosperous industrial town near Dresden, and mentioning the positive reception of his work in the exhibition at the Galerie Arnold.[139] In August of 1917 he had drawings in an exhibition in the Lennéstrasse in Dresden, and in September he again had work in a group show at the Galerie Arnold.[140] Once Dix was well enough to return to the front in early 1917, he returned to drawing and painting again as well, but with a difference. Gone were the drawings and gouaches of his surroundings, the trenches, and ruins, done from life in a manner that was essentially naturalistic, even if it utilized to some degree the

138 *Mericourt*, 1916 or 1917, Museum Gunzenhauser, Chemnitz, GUN-Z-0156, reproduced in Pfäffle, *Werkverzeichnis der Aquarelle und Gouachen*, 70.

139 Letter to Otto Baumgärtel, 1917. "Würdest Du die Gütte haben und Dich mal (möglichts Bald) bei Gerstenberger – Chemnitz erfragen ob ich in nächster Zeit eine Anzahl Zeichnungen und Stücke aus dem Felde dort ausstellen Kann?" *Otto Dix. Briefe*, 449.

140 Herbst Ausstellung Gemälde – Aquarelle – Graphik, opened 2 September 1917. See Negendanck, *Die Galerie Ernst Arnold*, p. 470. The Lennéstrasse exhibition is mentioned in a letter to Helene Jakob of 14 August 1917, in *Otto Dix. Briefe*, 450.

vocabularies of Cubism or Expressionism. Dix now began to represent something more abstract, the very concept of the violence of the war, in the form of a typology of combat moments: hand to hand fighting; exploding artillery shells; drumroll bombardments; the machinegun. The style has become much more strongly Cubo-Futurist, similar to the contemporaneous work of Wyndham Lewis, Christopher Nevinson, and Henri Gaudier-Brzeska.[141] He could hardly have known the work of these artists; rather, they had all been independently developing the formal possibilities opened up by the pre-war work of the Cubists and the Futurists. There are still portraits of fellow soldiers, but just as often we see a caricature of the type of the dehumanized, animalistic warrior, represented without any obvious pathos or criticism. Dix is not representing the dehumanized soldier ruefully observed as it were by the last man to have retained his humanity. On the contrary – he seems to have relished, even identified with the dehumanization. If Dix drew his own self portrait in 1915 as the melancholy artist, aping Dürer's pose with his head resting on his hand and his elbow propped on a table, then in 1917 he depicted himself as a grinning animal of prey, his smile revealing sharp canine fangs.

This abrupt break in his style and his whole approach to the project of representing the war came after several months of very hard fighting, and then an illness and rather lengthy recovery. Clearly, the lengthy pause afforded Dix an opportunity to reflect on his experiences of the previous 15 months. Surprisingly, the distinct change in his art, and its connection to his three months away from the front, has gone unremarked in the literature on Dix.[142] Whereas before his drawings

141 Conzelmann, "Mißverständnis und Wahrheit um Otto Dix," in Galerie der Stadt Stuttgart, Katalog zum 80. Geburtstag von Otto Dix, Stuttgart: Galerie der Stadt Stuttgart, 1971), 13–18.

142 It has been associated instead, by Ulrike Lorenz (née Rüdiger), with Dix's time on the Russian front, and with the landscape there, at least as far as his drawings on postcards sent to Helene Jakob are concerned. Rüdiger, *Grüsse aus dem Krieg*, 17. Linda McGreevy follows Lorenz here, *Bitter Witness*, 177 ff. See also Löffler, *Otto Dix und der Krieg*, 13.

and paintings had been single-minded in their focus on formal questions and their concentration on working from life, and whereas Dix had only selected motifs that he could paint from life, the genre scenes of the war, now he sought to convey the very essence of modern warfare in heightened, almost allegorical form. These scenes of modern warfare still did not make any claim to represent specific combat actions; they are still quite different in this regard from the work of Camus or Otto Schubert. Rather, they depict the artillery barrage *as such*; the attack as the *pure idea* of the attack.

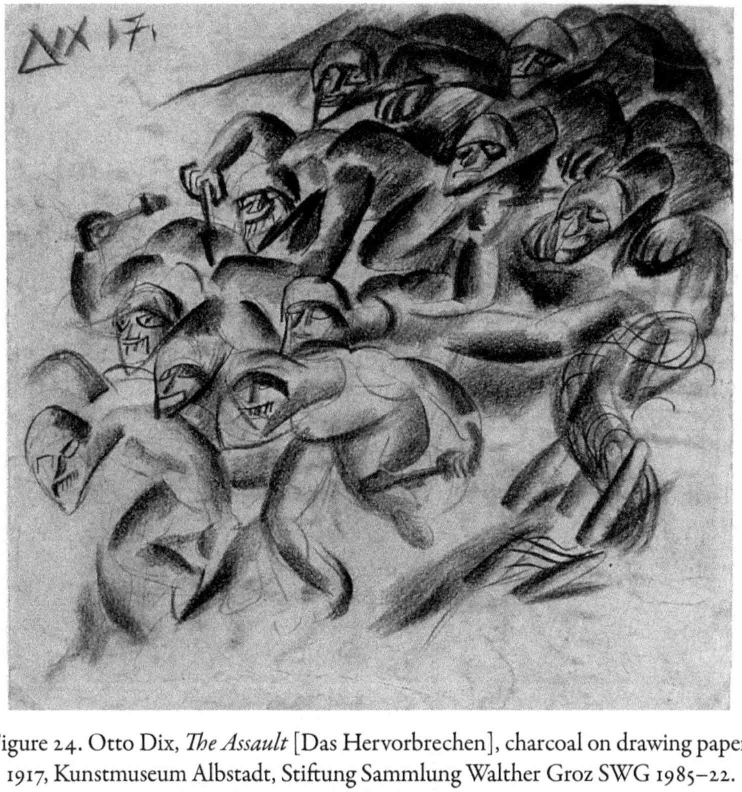

Figure 24. Otto Dix, *The Assault* [Das Hervorbrechen], charcoal on drawing paper, 1917, Kunstmuseum Albstadt, Stiftung Sammlung Walther Groz SWG 1985–22. © Otto Dix / Artists Rights Society (ARS), New York / VG Bild-Kunst, Bonn. Photo © Kunstmuseum Albstadt, used with permission.

The Assault [Das Hervorbrechen] (1917) (see Figure 24) depicts a wedge of advancing troops (the helmets and the shape of the hand grenades indicate that they are German, but this fact is downplayed), with unnaturally leering eyes and hungry, toothy mouths. A stylized barbed wire emplacement outlines the silhouette of their unified mass; otherwise, no particulars are given. It is an image of abject dehumanization and bloodlust; it conveys however no sense at all of dismay or disgust, and suggests neither empathy for the victims nor distance from the killers. It is war reduced to its most elemental instinct. The act of machinegunning the enemy is generalized and abstracted in *Rows Falling in Machinegun Fire* [Fallende Reihe im MG-Feuer] (1916 or, more likely, 1917) (see Figure 25). In this remarkable image, the bullets issue from Dix's signature in the lower right hand corner; the machinegun itself and its operator are not pictured. One motif in particular seems to have been especially important to Dix, because he made several closely related versions of it: the shell hole wreathed by mangled corpses and dismembered arms and legs. Then there was the quintessential motif of this war, the exploding shell with its attendant cone-shaped fountain of earth, smoke, and flying body parts, and every artist tried to capture it, from avant-gardists like Max Pechstein and Felix Vallotton to more conventional battle painters. But any visual representation, including photographs, only caught the visual aspect of such a detonation, the flash and the earth and materiel which it sent up into the air. It could not however capture the concussion or the terrible sound of the explosion. In his own versions, Dix captured something of the chaos by depicting the explosion not as the conventional inverted cone, but as spiraling, expanding energy.[143]

143 See for example *Schwerer Granateinschlag*, in two versions: Kunstmuseum Stuttgart and the Zeppelinmuseum Friedrichshafen, reproduced in Schubert, *Künstler im Trommelfeuer*, 364, 399, and *Volltreffer*, Kunstmuseum Stuttgart, Inv. Nr Z-1150, reproduced often, most recently in Dalbajewa, Fleischer, and Peters, ed. *Der Krieg*, 58.

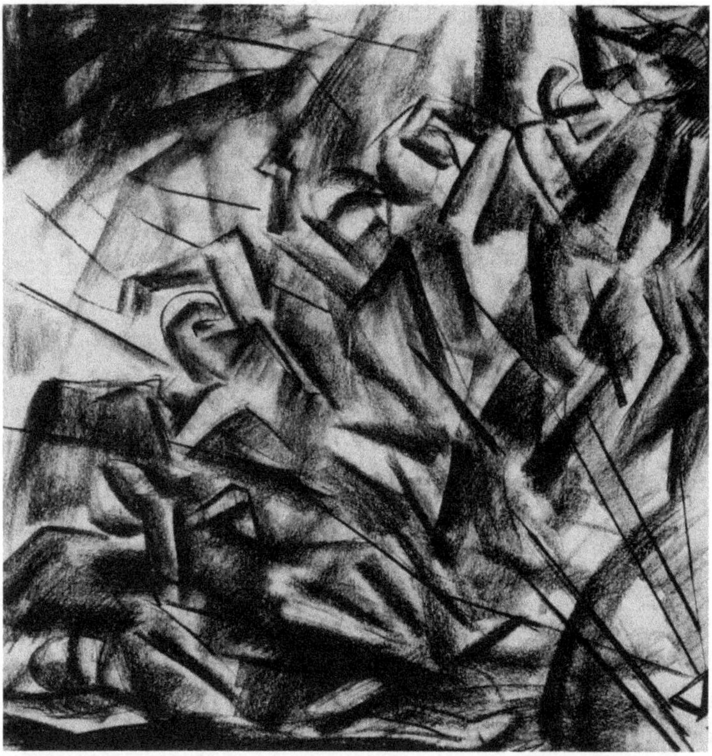

Figure 25. Otto Dix, *Rows Falling in Machinegun Fire* [Fallende Reihe im MG-Feuer], charcoal on drawing paper, 1916–1917, Otto Dix Stiftung, Vaduz. © Otto Dix / Artists Rights Society (ARS), New York / VG Bild-Kunst, Bonn. Digital file: author's own scan.

Another theme emerged in the expressionistic and Cubo-Futurist drawings of 1917, one that was also raised to the level of allegory: the female nude and sexuality, depicted in works such as *Fruit Dish* [Fruchtschale] (ink, 1917) and *Spring Day* [Frühlingstag] (1917 or 1918).[144] Voluptuous female nudes and embracing nude couples are depicted in these ink drawings in

144 *Fruchtschale* (Salzburg Museum Rupertinum), reproduced in Schubert, *Künstler in Trommelfeuer*, 261; *Frühlingstag* reproduced in Conzelmann, *Handzeichnung* (Hannover: Fackelträger, 1968), no. 15. Dietrich Schubert, "Otto Dix Zeichnet im Ersten Weltkrieg," in Wolfgang Mommsen, ed., *Kultur und Krieg, Die Rolle der*

a manner that recalls the early Cubism of Braque and Picasso or the salon Cubism of Henri Le Fauconnier. These were certainly not depictions of the observed reality at the front, but rather an elevation of the imagery of the war to the mythic. Here, too, Dix was trying to convey what he considered to be a fundamental truth about the war; as he had already written in his journal, he imagined that "All war is centered on the vulva."[145] Dix had not forgotten the sexualized imagery with which the men been encouraged to enlist at the outset of the war, or the related fantasies of sexual potency conferred on the warrior by his uniform. The juxtaposition of war and sexuality, and of male and female sexuality, would only intensify in Dix's work after the war, as we will see in the next chapter.

The gouaches underwent a similar transformation, although the jarring, somewhat crude color contrasts and brushwork had always made these more expressionistic, less controlled than the drawings. Now they became even bolder and more energetic in their handling of paint and color, and often more mythic or allegorical in their subject matter as of late 1916 and early 1917, just as with the drawings. The gouache *Flare* [Leuchtkugel], perhaps the most often reproduced of the wartime gouaches, depicts a group of dead soldiers caught in a barbed wire entanglement at night, surrounded by an eerie green glow and spectrally lit by the red and white signal flares over the battlefield.[146] The figure of the dead soldier caught in the barbed wire and left to die, belonged to the standard motifs of the war's imagery. But Dix raised what had already become a convention to the level of the mythic or the allegorical. That he himself saw the allegorical quality of this gouache is confirmed by the print he made for the *War* portfolio in 1923, that more or less directly reworks this image, and to which he gave a title reminiscent of baroque allegory: *Dance of Death Anno 1917* [Totentanz Anno 1917].

Intellektuellen, Künstler und Schriftsteller im Ersten Weltkrieg (Berlin: de Gruyter, 2015), 179–194.

145 Entry for 30 May 1916. This particular page is reproduced in Fleischer, "Der Künstler und der Krieg," 20.

146 1917, Kunstmuseum Albstadt, reproduced in Pfäffle, *Werkverzeichnis der Aquarelle und Gouachen*, 95, and Fritz Löffler, *Otto Dix, Life and Work*, plate 14.

Deployment in Flanders and the Eastern Front

When he returned to the fighting in mid-March 1917, Dix was deployed to the Siegfried Line, a well-prepared defensive line along the Western Front. Dix's regiment was engaged in fighting south of Arras where they had to help hold off a major British attack, and then after ten days of fighting his division was moved by train to Bruges, in German-occupied Belgium. For most of 1917 Dix's regiment alternated between guard-duty on the border between Belgium and Holland, and fighting in the trenches in Flanders, on the Yser River and Wijtschaete, and near Pilkem, not far from the devastated city of Ypres, with occasional periods of more significant rest in Bruges.[147] The region was notoriously wet, and the trenches were often flooded, which figures in a gouache painted by Dix probably in 1917.

In *Flooded Barbed Wire* [Überflutetes Drahtverhau] (given the date 1916 in Pfäffle, more likely 1917) (see Figure 26) the composition is structured and unified by bands of whitish green – viridian and white painted over a red ground – representing banks of poisonous gas clouds as anonymous figures advance on the viewer through the pickets of barbed wire. The landscape is a murky field without horizon line or recession, making it, like so many of the gouaches, a flat, solid composition. As with the *Dance of Death* image, this one would be reworked in the *War* portfolio in 1923, as *Storm Troops Advancing Under Cover of Gas* [Sturmtruppe geht unter Gas vor] (see Figure 27), where the figures would be closer, and clearly identifiable as German soldiers. In the original gouache they remain anonymous – their nationality is indeterminate, the identifying details of their uniforms deliberately suppressed. Presumably they are wearing gasmasks, but no indication is given. The most shocking detail in this image is the soldiers drowning in the flooded trenches or shell hole of the foreground. At around the same time, Dix was decorated with the Friedrich August Medal (silver; 23 May) and the Silver Service Medal of the House of Reuss, Gera (30 July).[148]

147 Fleischer, "Der Künstler und der Krieg," 26–29.
148 Fleischer, "Der Künstler und der Krieg," 27 f.

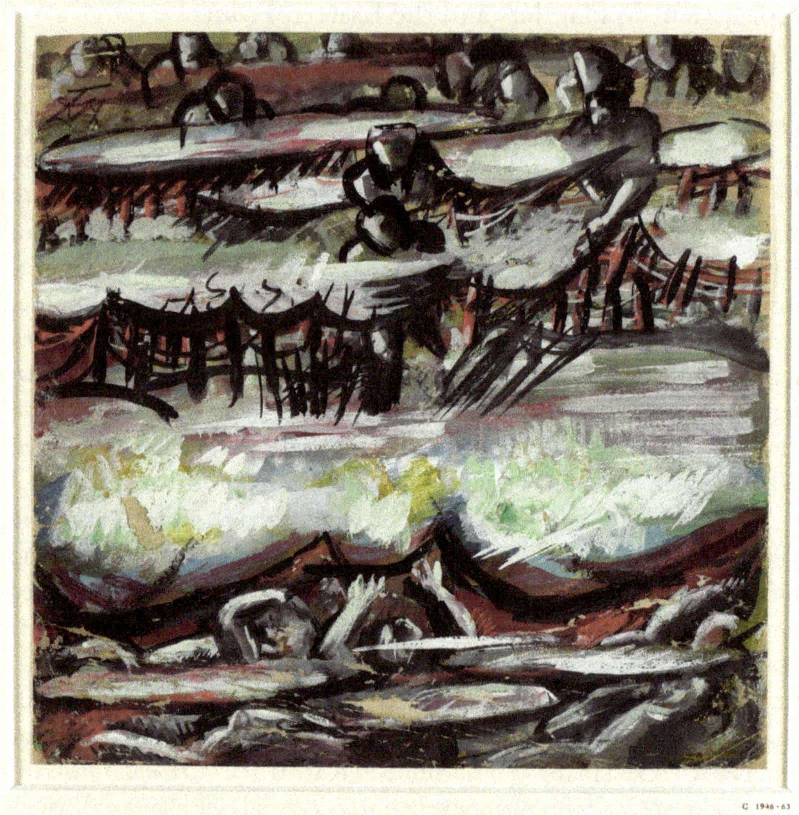

Figure 26. Otto Dix, *Flooded Barbed Wire* [Überflutetes Drahtverhau], gouache, 1916, Kupferstich-Kabinett, Dresden, C 1946–63. © Otto Dix / Artists Rights Society (ARS), New York / VG Bild-Kunst, Bonn. Photo © Kupferstich-Kabinett, Staatliche Kunstsammlungen, Dresden / Estel/Klut, used with permission.

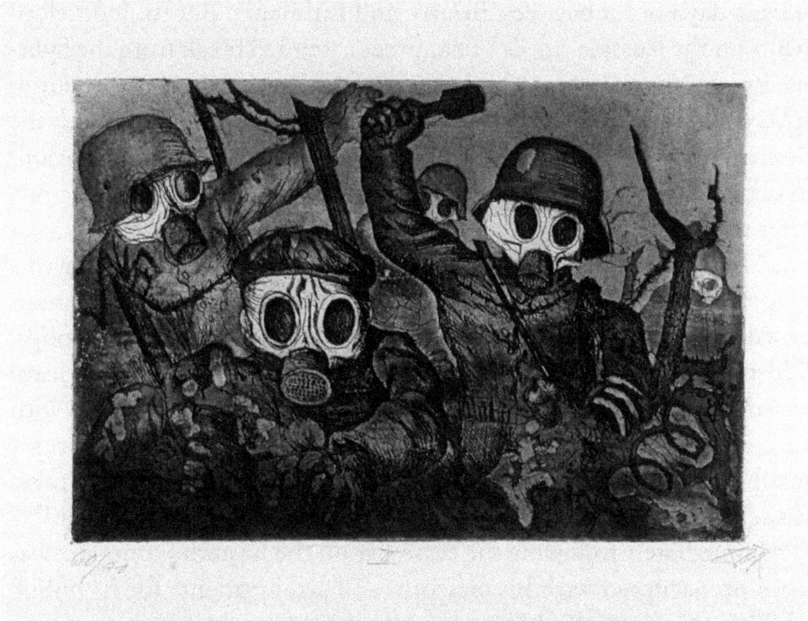

Figure 27. Otto Dix, *Storm Troopers Advancing Under Gas* [Sturmtruppe geht unter Gas vor] from *The War* [Der Krieg] (folio II, no. 12), etching, aquatint, and drypoint, 1924, Kunstmuseum Albstadt, Stiftung Sammlung Walther Groz SWG 1976–653. © Otto Dix / ARTISTS RIGHTS SOCIETY (ARS), Artists Rights Society (ARS), New York / VG Bild-Kunst, Bonn. Photo © Kunstmuseum Albstadt, used with permission.

As the war dragged on, Dix was drawn into other areas of it. In August of 1917 he took part in a week-long training course on using the heavy machinegun to shoot down airplanes – something he and his men had tried in a less systematic way to do since at least 1916.[149] On 1 October 1917, the 23rd Reserve Division, and with it Dix's regiment, was transported to the Russian front, where they were involved in fighting close to the

149 Dix mentions their practice of firing at aircraft with their machineguns in a postcard (written in Esperanto) to Helene Jakob, 22 June 1916. *Otto Dix, Briefe*, 448. He also admits that they had not yet brought down any aircraft in this way.

present-day border between Belarus and Lithuania. But soon developments on the Russian side led to another extended break from the fighting. By late November 1917, in the wake of the Bolshevik seizure of power in St. Petersburg, the Russian troops had begun to make peace with the German troops in the trenches opposite them, including Dix's division; an official cease-fire came into effect on 29 November. Dix wrote in a letter to Helene Jakob,

"There is finally a cease-fire! Yesterday our regimental band played a concert standing on the edge of the trench, facing the line. The Russians crowded through our barbed wire and shook hands with our troops. A historic moment, tailor-made for the newsreels. I'm going on leave beginning of February at the latest."[150] He followed this description with the mention that he was being considered for transfer to the air corps – possibly as a machine gunner in a two-seater, although it's unclear. He was sent to German-occupied Vilnius for (physical?) examination.[151]

Immediately following the cease-fire on the Eastern Front, Dix was again preoccupied with his artwork, and arrangements for its public exhibition in Germany. He wrote in the same letter to Jakob,

> Please have the superintendent of the Arts and Crafts School make a simple portfolio for me, 75 cm x 75 cm, with bands to bind it. I'm up to my eyeballs in my work, and I don't know what to do with it. Yesterday I received a personal invitation to the Nassau Art Society in Wiesbaden, to exhibit five pictures there. I wrote to [the Gallery] Arnold right away, which has all of my work, and asked them to frame it and send it there. The exhibition begins early January, hopefully I'll manage it. My "fame" already extends beyond Dresden!?![152]

150 "Jetzt ist nun endlich Waffenstillstand! Gestern machte unsre Regimentskapelle auf dem Grabenrand stehend vor der Linie Konzert. Die Russen kam[en] in Scharen durch unser Drahtverhau und schüttelten sich mit unsren Landsern die Hände. Also ein historischer Moment reif fürs Kino. Anfang Februar spätestens fahre ich auf Urlaub." Letter of 12 December 1917, *Otto Dix, Briefe*, 450 f.

151 "Ich denke, daß ich bald zu den Fliegern versetzt werde, am 17. muß ich nach Wilna zur endgültigen Untersuchung." Letter of 12 December 1917, *Otto Dix, Briefe*, 450 f.

152 "– Ich habe heute eine Bitte und zugleich Bestellung an Sie. Lassen Sie doch bitte für mich beim Hausverwalter K. G. Sch. [Kunstgewerbeschule] zwei einfachen

He was indeed sent on leave to his hometown of Gera, as he had hoped, as early as Christmastime, but fell ill there, so that his leave was extended, possibly until mid-February.[153] Thus he was once again away from the war for two months, and once again, there followed a sharp change in his manner of painting and drawing, and even of medium. The new style which Dix developed after this break was very strongly expressionistic and abstracted. The ink drawings *The Clinging Mud* [Der zähe Schlamm] (1918) and *Great Black Birds* [Große schwarze Vögel] (1918) (see Figure 28) both feature simple, strongly graphic motifs, skulls in one instance and the spread of a carrion birds' wings in the other, repeated in a way that is additive rather than pictorial.[154] The motifs in these works of 1918 are imagistic, suggestive, drawn in an elliptical way, connoted more than described. Done with brush and ink wash, usually in three different tonalities ranging from the full black of undiluted ink to a light wash, with an intermediary tone, the compositions are densely built up out of strongly rhythmic, repeated shapes. The high contrast and chiaroscuro of Dix's ink wash technique underscores the menace of these motifs, which become memento mori as much as representations of some of the more unpleasant aspects of the landscape of the front: slimy mud and rotting corpses.

Mappen machen, Größe 75 cm x 75 cm, mit Bänden zum Zubinden. Meine Arbeiten wachsen mir fast über den Hals zusammen, ich weiß fast nicht mehr wohin damit. Gestern erhielt ich eine persönliche Einladung des Nassauischen Kunstvereins Wiesbaden mit der Bitte, 5 Bilder nach dorthin einzusenden. Ich habe sofort an Arnold geschrieben, der meine sämtliche Arbeiten hat, und bat ihn, diese einrahmen zu lassen und sie nach dort zu senden. Die Ausstellung beginnt schon Anfang Januar, hoffentlich komm ich noch zurecht. Mein ‚Ruhm' geht also schon über Dresden hinaus!?!" Letter of 12 December 1917, *Otto Dix, Briefe*, 450 f.

153 Fleischer, "Der Künstler und der Krieg," p. 31.

154 Both are in the Kunstmuseum Albstadt.

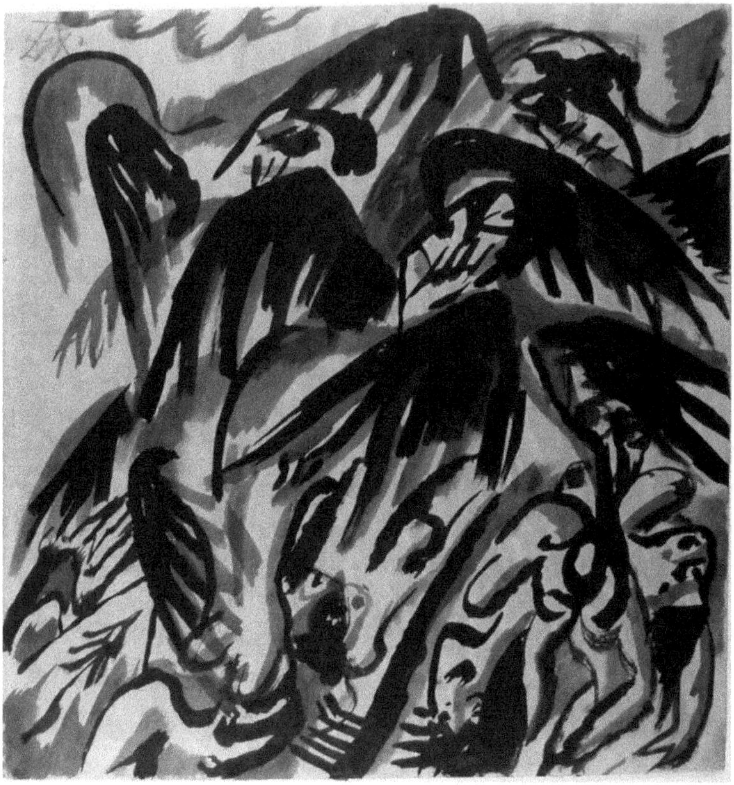

Figure 28. Otto Dix, *Great Black Birds* [Große schwarze Vögel], ink on paper, 1918, Kunstmuseum Albstadt, 1980–103. © Otto Dix / Artists Rights Society (ARS), New York / VG Bild-Kunst, Bonn. Photo © Kunstmuseum Albstadt, used with permission.

On 18 February 1918, fighting broke out again between the German and the Russian armies, as the German army scrambled to capture as much Russian territory as possible before the signing of the final peace treaty. Dix was involved in the capture of Dünaburg (today Daugavpils, a city in Latvia), followed by a push of 100 km up the Duna river deep into Belarus, from 19 February to 3 March, which devolved into un-co-ordinated fighting between isolated bands of Russian and German soldiers.[155] On 3 March,

155 Dix's military pass, DKM, Nuremberg.

the treaty of Brest-Litowsk was signed between Imperial Germany and Bolshevik Russia, ending the war in the East.[156] Dix's division was returned to the Western Front just in time for the Spring Offensive of 1918, the so-called "Kaiserschlacht." They fought in the "Michael Offensive" in Flanders, near Arras, and then north of Bapaume. The Kaiserschlacht led to some breakthroughs, but was not decisive, and the war continued to drag on, now with the Americans arriving and with few strategic options and little hope left for Germany. Dix was wounded on the neck by shrapnel on 8 August 1918, and took until 12 September to recover. He was then sent back yet again to his unit at the front in Flanders. On 8 October 1918, Dix was promoted to *Vizefeldwebel* [senior NCO]. By this time, the German army was steadily retreating. Dix's regiment continued to fight rearguard actions, most significantly near Oudenaarde, Belgian Flanders, on 31 October. But on 6 November, Dix was transferred from the 102nd Reserve Infantry Regiment to a reserve air division, and sent to the East.[157] Two days later came the cease-fire. The war was finally over. Dix was released from his new air unit and sent home to Gera on 22 December 1918.[158]

We have seen that pictures made by artists in uniform, soldiers who were soldiers first, and who made art in their spare moments, typically made their art in order to tell the truth of how it really was, to make it understandable to the public back home. This art was intended to contradict the official art made by official war artists (which continued to reach a mass audience through, for example, luxury volumes with full-color reproductions of the work of official war artists), and any representation which fell short of the truth of the artist's own experience.[159] It was made for "philistines" who, in Dix's words, "certainly can't imagine such a thing." Nonetheless, it was clearly important for soldiers to try to represent the experience, to try to communicate something of it, regardless of how futile the attempt may have seemed.

156 John Keegan, *The First World War* (New York: Vintage, 2000), 341 ff.

157 Fleischer, "Der Künstler und der Krieg," 32 f.

158 Dix's military pass, DKM, I, A 2.

159 For example, Baumgarten-Crusius, Artur, *Sachsen in großer Zeit. Geschichte der Sachsen im Weltkrieg*, Vol. II (Leipzig: Minerva, 1920), dedicated to the Royal Saxon Army, with double-page color spreads of paintings by war artists from Saxony.

Significantly, Otto Dix displayed a complete lack of interest in this function of pictures made at the front. His interest was much more in developing his skills of drawing, painting, and composition, and in developing and evolving a formal vocabulary. Dix produced four distinct and coherent bodies of work while fighting in the war: the early, essentially naturalistic and observational drawings of the trenches and ruins of the front, and soldiers on guard duty or resting; the more expressionistic and geometric drawings that applied the compositional lessons of Futurism to the themes of the war raised to abstract categories; the gouaches with their bold use of expressionistic color contrasts which follow the same thematic development as the drawings; and the late brush and ink images with their strongly rhythmic, abstracted meditations on almost allegorical themes related to the war, themes such as violence, mud, and carrion. Jean Cassou, the first art historian to have the opportunity to write about these drawings, characterized the entire corpus as "expressionistic" rather than "Cubist," by which he meant emotive rather than analytic, an immediate, visceral response to a "horrible reality."[160] He could hardly have mischaracterized them more drastically. At no time did Dix depict what were presented as first-hand accounts of specific combat actions, unlike most other artists who were serving as soldiers in the war. His interest was obviously in perfecting his craft and developing a specific formal vocabulary – often quite Cubist in structure – not in immediacy. What he presented to audiences back home – and he was constantly engaged in exhibiting his work back in Germany – was his mastery of traditional and avant-garde visual languages, not "what the war was really like." It was only after the war that he would discover a desire to give his testimony of the horrors and intensity of the war, and to proclaim his membership in the elect community of front soldiers. Cassou also wrote that, in the drawings, the spirit of the tragic was confounded with the spirit of the grotesque and caricature. Again, this does not describe the work Dix made during the war, but looks ahead to the work he did in 1920. It is to caricature and the grotesque which I will turn in the next chapter, where I will examine the work Dix made after he returned home from the war.

160 Jean Cassou, "Otto Dix," in Galerie "Im Erker," *Otto Dix: Der Krieg* (St. Gallen: Galerie "Im Erker," 1962), 12.

CHAPTER 2

Dix and Dada: War Cripples and Neurasthenics, Soldier's Slang, and the Humor of Grotesque Realism

After Otto Dix was demobilized, he returned to Dresden and once again took up his art education, but this time as a student at the Art Academy, a much more prestigious institution than the Arts and Crafts College. His ambition to become a serious artist, a painter, was now very clear. He joined one of the many avant-garde groups which proliferated throughout Germany in the wake of the Great War and Germany's defeat. For a brief time, nearly every German city with an art school or a community of artists had such a group, mostly oriented towards a Cubo-Futurist formal vocabulary and a subject matter that tended towards the ecstatic, the cosmic, and the millennial. Dresden was no exception, and Dix joined the group there, the *Gruppe 1919*. It included Conrad Felximüller and Lasar Segall, and held its first group exhibition in the Galerie Emil Richter in 1919. Like similar groups of Expressionists in other German cities, this one wrote the motto "Brotherhood" on its banner, but it was focused less on politics and more on securing exhibition venues. Felixmüller, the most politicized member of the group, soon left for this reason.

Neurasthenia and *Moon Woman*, 1919

Dawn, the birth of a new humanity, and a generalized, archetypal conception of gender and sexuality were common themes among all of the local German Expressionist groups in 1919, and Dix was able to fit his work seamlessly into this general direction. The theme of gender and sexuality had become inextricable in Dix's mind from the experience of being a soldier at the front, having written in his field notebook, "All war is centered on the vulva."[161] As we saw in the previous chapter, the soldier's masculinity, as constructed in relation to the sexuality of women (and other men), was widely invoked at the outset of the war. And as we shall recall in this chapter, mobilization and occupation during the war often provided the soldiers with opportunities for sex, typically in the form of prostitution in sanctioned brothels and in the reserve towns behind the lines. Sexuality, and the sexuality of the female body, had emerged as a central theme in Dix's allegorization of the war experience in his work in late 1918, and he seems to have been trying to elevate the twinned themes of sexuality and violence in these pictures to a cosmic, universalizing level. They continued to hold a central place in his work in his brief Expressionist phase in 1919. As we will see in this chapter, the damaged and neutered body of the returned veteran displaced the sexualized female body in his Dadaist work in 1920 and 1921. Patricia Anne Simpson has clearly articulated the connection between national and gender identity in war time. "The culture of war uses the rhetoric of national identity to mobilize sentiment in support of war. As a correlate, this discourse exerts regulatory influence over potentially threatening or unstable gender identities."[162] The First World War in particular was, among other things, the culmination of a gender ideology around soldiering that emerged, concomitant with national armies of citizen-soldiers, in the Napoleonic period. As we saw at the outset of the previous chapter, Dix painted a number of self-portraits in uniform early on in the war, images strongly coded with a heterosexual male gender ideology. If the First World War was a nineteenth-century war fought with twentieth-century weaponry, to catastrophic effect, then the gender ideology

161 Otto Dix Field Notebook, held in the Kunstmuseum Albstadt, entry for 30 May 1916. Reproduced in Fleischer, "Der Künstler und der Krieg," in Birgit Dalbajewa, Simone Fleischer, and Olaf Peters, *Otto Dix. Der Krieg – Das Dresdner Triptychon* (Dresden: Sandstein, 2014), 20. Olaf Peters relates this painting to Dix's reading of various vitalist writers and their world view, in particular Salomo Friedländer, Friedrich Albert Lange, and of course Friedrich Nietzsche. Peters, *Otto Dix* (Munich: Prestel, 2010), 58 f.

162 Patricia Anne Simpson, *The Erotics of War in German Romanticism* (Lewisburg, PA: Bucknell University Press, 2006), 24.

expressed in Dix's early work was originally a nineteenth-century ideal of militarized masculinity here expressed with a modernist formal aesthetic.

In 1919 Dix painted what could be seen as a companion to the self-portrait as Mars (see Figure 7), an oil painting of a female nude, *Moon Woman* [*Mondweib*] (1919) (see Figure 29).[163]

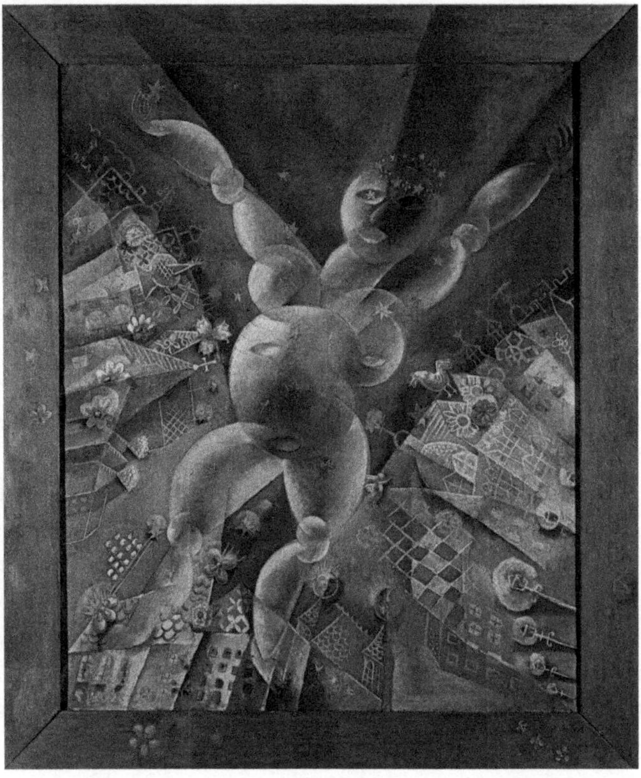

Figure 29. Otto Dix, *Moon Woman* [Mondweib], 1919, oil on canvas, frame painted by artist, 1919, National Gallery, Berlin. © Otto Dix / Artists Rights Society (ARS), New York / VG Bild-Kunst, Bonn. Author's own scan.

163 Strictly speaking, there is a self-portrait, done at the same time and in similar style to Moon Woman, that could be an actual pendant, titled *Sehnsucht* [Longing] (Galerie Neue Meister, Staatliche Kunstsammlungen Dresden). The painting features a (male) crescent moon and a (female) sun. At 53.5 x 52 cm, it is only half the size of *Moon Woman*.

The title already announces the elevation of the sexualized female body to a cosmic level (it should be noted that the moon, in German, is male, while the sun is its female counterpart). Depicting a figure swollen with fecundity and erotic promise, it was a large picture, 120 cm x 100.5 cm, and was clearly an ambitious statement.[164] The Moon Woman ascends into the heavens, her head crowned by a wreath of stars; her naval sits above her spherical belly, while below it her vulva is also emphasized, echoing the shape and color of her mouth. The world (a role played here by a provincial German city) bursts outwards in a dynamically radiating composition from her womb – the source of all human existence and experience. In order to fully understand the implications of this female nude for the returning soldier, we need to return briefly to the comparison made at the beginning of the previous chapter between Dix's self-portrait in uniform as the god of war (see Figure 7), and Ernst Ludwig Kirchner's self-portrait in uniform as an amputee (see Figure 9).

In the terms current in the discipline of psychiatry at the time, Kirchner depicted himself as a neurasthenic; in military psychiatry the neurasthenic soldier was labeled a "war-neurotic," unfit for duty and in need of rehabilitation and demobilization. In the late nineteenth century the condition of neurasthenia had enjoyed a certain respect as a sign that the (male) subject had been enduring the rigors of the forefront of modernity, a status that the avant-garde artist continued to claim into the early twentieth century.[165] By the time of the war, however, the neurasthenic had been demoted to the (male) hysteric, the malingerer, whose weak nerves threatened to undermine the war effort. Steadiness

164 The painting was exhibited in the second exhibition of the Dresdner Sezession Gruppe 1919, in the galleries of Emil Richter, the same venue as some of the first Brücke exhibitions. Roland März, "Das Gemälde 'Mondweib' von Otto Dix aus dem Jahr 1919. Eine Neuerwerbung der Nationalgalerie" *Forschungen und Berichte* 25 (1985), 71–81.

165 See for example Patricia Berman, "Edvard Munch's Self-Portrait with Cigarette: Smoking and the Bohemian Persona," *The Art Bulletin* 75/4 (December 1993), 627–646. Munch served in turn as an important model for Kirchner.

of nerves was the new manly virtue. The war, it was claimed repeatedly in public and medical discourse, was a war of nerves, and would be won by the side with the steadiest nerves.[166] Kirchner was diagnosed with war neurosis; at the beginning of the war, the usual treatment involved a rest period in a sanatorium far from the front, and Kirchner spent his in a clinic in Königstein in the Taunus Mountains, which had been expanded to include a ward for war neuroses and war hysteria under the care of a neurologist and a psychologist. In these early months it was not unusual for men who, like Kirchner, had not actually seen any fighting or been near the front to nonetheless suffer and be treated for symptoms of war neurosis.[167] As the number of cases of war neuroses, or shell shock as the British called it, rose sharply during the war, medical professionals switched to treatments that were intentionally punitive, such as painful electroshock therapy.[168] While neurasthenia indicated a certain importance in the cultural vanguard for intellectuals of Kirchner's generation, Dix was clearly on the other side of a generational divide on this issue, although he was only 11 years younger than Kirchner. The divide was also one of class, and carried markers of gender as well. For Dix and his generation, war neurosis or hysteria was a weakness which a former proletariat making a public reputation for himself could ill afford. Rather, it was steadiness of nerves which was called for. And it was this steadiness of nerves that Dix had performed in his self-portraits in uniform. Even

166 Hans Georg Hofer, *Nervenschwäche und Krieg. Modernitätskritik und Krisenbewältigung in der österreichischen Psychiatrie (1880–1920)* (Vienna: Böhlau, 2004), 32–35.

167 For a thorough recounting of Kirchner's brief military career and his illness, see Peter Springer, *Hand and Head. Ernst Ludwig Kirchner's Self-Portrait as Soldier* (Berkeley: University of California Press, 2002, Susan Ray, translator), 22–42.

168 Paul Lerner, *Hysterical Men. War, Psychiatry, and the Politics of Trauma in Germany, 1890–1930* (Ithaca, NY: Cornell University Press, 2003); Linda F. McGreevy also discusses the cruel approach to shell shock, although not specifically in relation to Dix's art during or after the war, Linda McGreevy, *Bitter Witness* (Bern: Peter Lang, 2003), 124–126.

in the recent literature this performance of steady nerves continues to be viewed uncritically and found convincing.[169]

In 1919, after he finished *Moon Woman*, Dix wrote to a fellow artist, "In the meantime I have once again made new things which for weak nerves will be the cause of a shock to the nerves [*Nervenschocken*]," repeating the term "nerves" twice.[170] The implication is clear: Dix himself was made of stronger stuff, not given to shell shock, and his ability to paint the over-ripe, hyper-sexualized *Moon Woman* proved it.[171] For those with weaker nerves, it would only be another damaging assault on the psyche. The standard interpretation of *Moon Woman* is that it mocks bourgeois pedants steeped in the nineteenth-century lunar imagery of Romantic longing – people like Fritz Glaser, Doctor of Law, who nonetheless purchased the painting when it was exhibited in 1919, and who then went on to commission Dix to paint a portrait of himself and his impeccably bourgeois family. But in the context of public debates about weak and hypersensitive nerves, debates which only intensified during and even after the war, these references to weak and broken nerves can only be meant to indicate those among Dix's fellow veterans whose malady had, by some estimations, cost Germany the war. Dix is playing the role of military psychiatrist, delivering his own version of electroshock therapy to weak-nerved malingerers. At precisely the same moment, in Berlin, Raoul Hausmann and George Grosz were doing similar things in their

169 "His painter colleagues Max Beckmann and George Grosz suffered nervous breakdowns after serving; Dix's mental and physical toughness, however, allowed him to survive the inferno to which he felt impelled to bear witness," writes Sabine Rewald, Ian Baruma, and Matthias Eberle, *Glitter and Doom: German Portraits From the 1920s* (New Haven, CT: Yale University Press, 2006), 56.

170 "Ich habe einstweilen wieder neue Sachen gemacht, die für schwache Nerven Gelegenheit zum Nervenschocken sind ..." Dix, letter to the painter Kurt Günther, c. 1919, cited in März, "Mondweib," 73, and Schmidt, *Otto Dix im Selbstbildnis*, 201. The other paintings he is referring to are probably *Leda and the Swan*, *Resurrection of the Flesh*, and *Pregnant Woman*. See Fritz Löffler, Emilio Bertonati, and Johann Heuzinger von Waldegg, *Dresdner Sezession 1919–1923* (Munich: Galleria del Levante, 1977), 74.

171 März, "Mondweib," 74.

Dadaist collages.[172] During and after the war, to speak of weak nerves was to speak of soldiers and veterans, and it is just such veterans whom Dix was addressing – targeting – with his painting *Moon Woman*. Like many, Dix seems to have been strikingly unsympathetic to those suffering war neurosis. Indeed, his stated intention here was to inflict more of the same!

The formal devices and spiritual themes of Expressionism dominated modern art in Germany in the months after the war and the revolution, and in the visual culture generally. But this bubble soon burst, and their stock fell as sharply as it had risen. Dix quickly abandoned this vocabulary, too, and joined the newer, more radical direction of the avant-garde, Dadaism. In the summer of 1920 he participated in an exhibition of German Dada in Berlin, the so-called *Erste Internationale Dadamesse* [First International Dada Fair] (20 June – 25 August). He began experimenting with one of Dadaism's most innovative and productive formal strategies: collage. Although he continued to paint in oil on canvas, collage elements became an important component of his picture-making, always deployed with wit and contributing to the meaning of the work. He also adopted Dadaism's fundamental mode of address: effrontery, with the dignity of the urban bourgeoisie as the prime target. Finally, he adopted one of Dadaism's main thematic concerns, namely, the chaos and dislocation caused by the lost war, by the end of monarchy and empire, and by catastrophic inflation. Specifically, Dix made a series of works depicting the ubiquitous presence in Germany's streets of veterans, disfigured, often multiple amputees who were either reduced to begging for change or marching in protest of their shabby treatment by the state.[173] These were often large-scale paintings, obviously intended for public exhibition

172 Brigid Doherty, "'See, We Are All Neurasthenics!' or, the Trauma of Dada Montage," *Critical Inquiry* 24/1 (Autumn 1997), 82–132.

173 On the politically disruptive presence of thousands of returned invalided soldiers, see Sabine Kienitz, "Beschädigte Helden. Zur Politisierung des kriegsinvaliden Soldatenkörpers in der Weimarer Republik," in Jost Dülffer and Gerd Krumeich, eds., *Der verlorene Frieden. Politik und Kriegskultur nach 1918* (Essen: Klartext, 2002), 199–214.

and even the walls of museums, in contrast to the small watercolors, priced within reach of private collectors, with which Dix was primarily earning his meager living as an artist at the outset of his career (Dix may not have expected to sell these large paintings yet, and produced much more affordable etchings of all four compositions, each included in a portfolio of five other plates, in editions of 20). The watercolors were mostly images of sexuality: prostitutes and circus performers, or hyper-masculine and hyper-sexualized sailors visiting whores in port-side brothels.[174] There is a relationship between these two themes that needs to be uncovered.

The cycle of "War Cripples" pictures

In 1920 Dix painted four large-format, grotesque pictures of "*Kriegskrüppel*" [war cripples] (or, more respectfully, "*Kriegsinvaliden*," [war invalids]), some still wearing their uniforms, others wearing their Iron Crosses and other military decorations, engaged in typical activities of such unfortunates after the war: playing the popular card game *skat* at their *Stammtisch* (*Skat Players*); selling matches on the street corner (*Match Seller*); begging (*Prague Street*); or marching in the street (*War Cripples, 45% Employable*). In the cycle, markers of class difference and former rank are clearly legible, for example in a meeting between two legless veterans, one a former enlisted man, now reduced to begging, and the other a former officer, who wears a suit and enjoys the relative advantage of a wheeled platform, providing him some mobility.

174 Änne Söll, "Neue Männlichkeit. Die Matrosenbilder von Otto Dix," in Nils Büttner and Daniel Spanke, eds., *Das Auge der Welt. Otto Dix und die Neue Sachlichkeit* (Stuttgart: Hatje Cantz, 2012), 48–61.

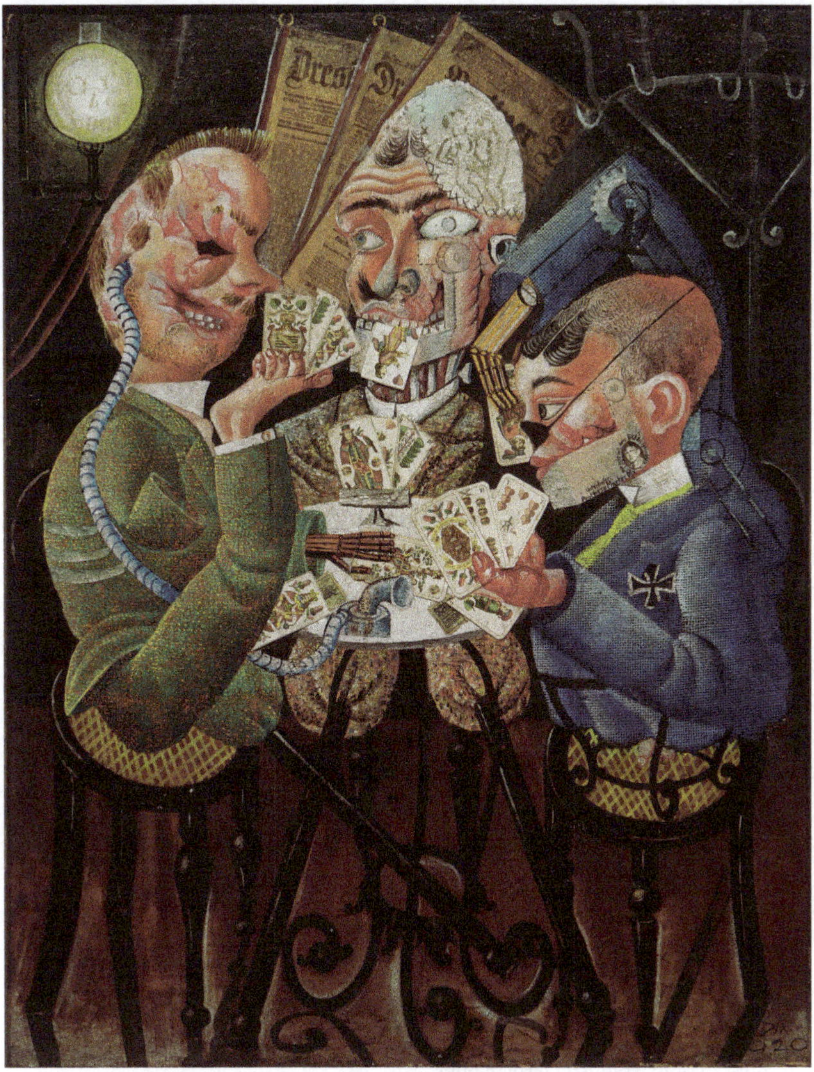

Figure 30. Otto Dix, *Skat Players* [Die Skatspieler], oil and collage on canvas, 1920, National Gallery, Berlin, FNG 74/95, property of the Association of Friends of the Nationalgalerie. © Otto Dix / Artists Rights Society (ARS), New York / VG Bild-Kunst, Bonn. Photo © Joerg P. Anders / akg-images, used with permission.

Skat Players [Die Skatspieler] (1920) (see Figure 30) depicts three veterans, probably officers, gathered at their weekly table to play cards. They are not destitute on the street, but are comparatively comfortable in their café; a preparatory drawing includes a sign on the table indicating that it was their regular table, or *Stammtisch*.[175] Skat is a card game for specifically three players, popular in Germany, and was an important pastime among soldiers during tedious unoccupied hours.[176] The painting is marked on the back "Skatklub ehemaliger 342er," meaning that this is the Skat Club of former members of the 342nd Regiment; they are reliving their army days and maintaining their bonds. Nostalgia for the camaraderie of the war is built into the scenario. So are specific references to Dresden and southeastern Germany: the collaged Dresden newspapers and the particular version of the skat deck – with suits of bells, leaves, acorns and hearts – in use in Saxony.[177] All three figures have been catastrophically mutilated, and then cobbled back together from a junk drawer's worth of odds and ends. Their wounds are horrific: not only missing arms and legs, but gaping facial wounds, missing eyes, ears, noses, and jaws. Such wounds were real, and veterans bearing them were a common sight after the war. Few essays on these collages neglect to reproduce contemporary photographs of horrible, nauseating facial and head wounds so bad that it is a wonder their victims still lived. But Dix has transformed these horrors into absurd caricature. The figure on the left uses his foot in place of a hand and holds his cards between his toes. His face is badly mangled; his eye is an empty socket – more of a gash, and his teeth are permanently exposed, giving him an aggressive-looking sneer. His left hand – a prosthetic contraption made of jointed wooden dowels, is placed palm down on the table, right

175 Private collection, reproduced in Rewald and Buruma, *Glitter and Doom*, 54. The sign that reads "*Stammtisch*," hanging above the three men, is of the sort that one finds in old-fashioned German pubs.

176 The novel *All Quiet on the Western Front* provides an indication of how much time soldiers at the front spent in their dugouts playing Skat.

177 Roland März, "Ja, das ist doch auch eine Lust am Grotesken," *Museumsjournal: Berichte aus Museen, Schlossern und Sammlungen in Berlin und Potsdam* 9/4 (October 1995) 52–55. März identified the various newspapers as the *Dresdner Anzeiger*, the *Dresdner Neueste Nachrichten*, and the *Berliner Tageblatt*, from 3 May 1920.

next to his elaborate hearing aid, which is a funnel connected by a metal tube to the scarred spot where his ear should be. The middle figure has a mechanical jaw and a false eye, and holds his cards in his teeth; we guess that he, too, lacks both arms. And the man to the right is somehow even worse off than the other two; his body below the waist is gone entirely, and not only his jaw is missing but his nose as well. As with the first figure, his right hand –with which he is about to play his trump card – is a flimsy mechanical affair. Dix reveals the clockwork arm and spine beneath his coat.

This picture has become the most well-known and often reproduced from this group of four collages, decorating, most recently, the cover of a book on disabled German veterans, and a French high school textbook on German history, to name just two examples. It has become representative not only of Dix's work, but of what are taken to be the general attitudes in Weimar Germany about the war and its consequences. But I suspect that this is an oversimplification, reducing a complicated statement to straightforward irony, as if it expressed an unmitigated bitterness about the war. This is a misrepresentation, and misses the most significant and troubling element of the picture: its humor. Dix has invented a situation of grotesque, absurdist humor, and the closer one looks, the more details one notices, both witty and vulgar, so that the overall effect grows both more shocking and also funnier. The foot that holds the cards like a hand extends from a pant leg that is finished like a sleeve, complete with a shirt cuff; the card hidden up this "sleeve" reveals that the player is cheating. The central figure has a prosthetic neck, as though his head itself has perforce been reattached, which is absurd. The mechanical jaw of the figure on the right contains a little collaged oval portrait photo of Dix himself, as the trademark on the device, wittily conflating collage-making and prosthetics construction. And there is the deliberate confusion of the wooden legs of the invalids with the table and chair legs; comparison with the preparatory drawing shows that Dix intentionally heightened this visual confusion. Then there are the dirty jokes. The central figure has had, as the result of a bad head wound, part of his skull replaced by a plate, represented here by some silver foil pasted down onto the surface of the canvas. Look closely and you can see that it is also painted over with images of naked ladies – which is evidently what the card player is thinking about. The figure on the right, though missing both legs, has a tiny pink penis and testicles, which are exposed here for no good reason (this was not the case in the preparatory drawing, where at least he still had the stumps of both his legs). Once again the picture is animated by Dix's preoccupation with sexual potency, or lack of it, among war invalids, and their evident inability to balance the sexual equation of the war that linked women's desire and the sexual appeal of the soldier in uniform, or the soldier's sexual appetites with the brothels of occupied cities.[178]

The use of collage and the theme of prosthetics are related. As has often been noted, the one functions as an ironic metaphor for the other. But the collage elements themselves are significant, and bear closer inspection. As with his other collages, Dix does not use newsprint and printed papers merely as random textures or pictorial elements, as in the collages of Pablo Picasso and Georges Braque – works which he had opportunity to see in Dresden. The picture makes fun of Parisian Cubism, which it directly quotes in several ways, beginning with the playing cards and newspapers and the café setting, as well as the circular table at the center of the composition. The chair caning is an unmistakable reference to Picasso's *Still Life with Chair Canning* (1912). But in contrast to the Cubists, Dix uses collaged elements either to represent themselves, or as some kind of witty, humorous, and often disparaging commentary on the scene. So, for example, while the real newspapers and cards "stand in for" the newspapers and playing cards within the depicted scene, and emphasize the milieu of café and pub, the pasted-in portrait of Dix himself draws attention to the persiflage of the whole affair. The blue suit of the man on the right has been identified as ersatz cloth made from paper pulp fiber, which was actually used in the postwar period to make cheap suits.[179] It recalls in

178 Brigid Doherty considers at length the Berlin Dadaists' concern with the theme of disruption of sexual function and potency through the traumas of the war, in particular shell shock. In her reading of several of the pictures made by Grosz and Heartfield, there is a fixation on and confusion of the genitals of male figures, whether by conscious intention or unconscious anxiety and hesitation. Doherty, "'See, We Are All Neurasthenics!' or, the Trauma of Dada Montage," *Critical Inquiry* 24/1 (Autumn 1997), 82–132.

179 März, "Lust am Grotesken," 54.

turn the impoverishment and debasement of the German diet as a result of the Allied blockade and postwar economic sanctions. A heavy reliance on ersatz foodstuffs reduced the German diet to a third of the required daily calories, a situation which itself suggested to many a debasement of the entire culture. Some Germans bemoaned, "We have become an *Ersatz* nation, and have lost in consequence many of our good qualities. *Ersatz* butter, *Ersatz* bread, *Ersatz* jam, *Ersatz* clothing – everything is becoming *Ersatz*."[180] As we will see, ersatz bread, butter, and jam was something with which Dix would have been familiar as a soldier.

This scurrilous picture, with its mordent wit, was shown at the exhibition of the Dresden Secession in the Galerie Arnold in October and November of 1920. The bitter irony, here turned into a brutal joke for the viewing public, is that the disfigurement and disability of these veterans will forever prevent their full and seamless reentry into peacetime society, and obviously belies their idyllic memories of their time in the military. The time of comradeship in the war, as the object of nostalgia, was widely referred to with the phrase "der grosse Zeit" – something like "glory days," which could be pronounced either straight or inflected with irony, depending on the speaker's attitude. The standard interpretation of this work is that it uses the means of Cubism to make a socially critical statement about the pointless destruction of men's bodies in a pointless war.[181] I am offering a different interpretation: that it combines a parody of Cubism and a grotesque, vulgar humor with a startling contempt for men who came back from the war with their bodies – and their masculinity – shattered. The main effect which the picture aims at is not indignation, but laughter.

180 Harry A. Franck, *Vagabonding Through Changing Germany* (New York: Harper and Brothers, 1920), 64. Franck was an American traveling in Germany after the war; the quotation is unattributed and may well be apocryphal, but it undoubtedly captured a mood.

181 See, as only two examples, Roland März, who even interprets the progress of the card game as an allegorical indictment of the exploitation of these men by the war and its generals, März, "Lust am Grotesken," and Sabine Rewald, catalog entry, *Glitter and Doom*, 56 f., where one can read that this is a "ferocious … antiwar image." The image is frequently reproduced with minimal commentary to illustrate what is taken to be the self-evident point: that the German public was embittered by the war and its results.

Of course the reality which these four paintings refers to was tragic and horrible. Tens of thousands of men returned to Germany maimed and disabled by the war, as was the case in Britain, France, and all of the other combatant nations. In Germany the soldiers suffered the added indignity of having fought on the losing side, and then saw their already paltry pensions further diminished by the runaway inflation of the postwar period. Enormous efforts by the medical professions of all nations resulted in a wide range of ameliorative measures: developments in prosthetic limbs designed to enable men to return to productive work; physical therapy designed to help them do the same; and even prosthetic masks, nosepieces, eyeglasses, and imitation hands, all designed to hide the horror of their disfigured faces and allow them to go out in public. But the world to which they returned was not particularly sympathetic to them, and for many their presence on the street, especially if they were protesting or begging, was seen as an affront to public decency. Deborah Cohen's comparative history of disabled veterans in Britain and Germany tells the story of German soldiers and their families embittered not only by what they saw as the government's insufficient financial support, but even more so by the general public's lack of gratitude or care. This enmity, which quickly became mutual, may well have been the result, in Cohen's telling, of Weimar government policies severely restricting the sort of private philanthropic work that had provided relief to disabled soldiers and their families in previous wars, and that continued to provide the bulk of relief in Britain. The new German government wanted to establish a state monopoly on charity work and so burnish its image as a welfare state.[182] Many historians have blamed the excessive bureaucratization of the pension system in the Weimar state for the bitterness of German veterans in general and disabled veterans in particular.[183] Cohen suggests that it was

182 Deborah Cohen, *The War Come Home. Disabled Veterans in Britain and Germany, 1914–1939* (Berkeley: University of California Press, 2001), esp. Chapter 2, "The Nation Accused. German Veterans and the State Regulation of Charity," 61–97.

183 Robert Weldon Whalen, *Bitter Wounds. German Victims of the Great War, 1914–1939* (Ithaca, NY: Cornell University Press, 1984), 164–165, and Michael Geyer, "Ein Vorbote des Wohlfahrtsstaates," *Geschichte und Gesellschaft*, 9/2, Vol. 9 (1983), 230–277, esp. 257–258.

the lack of charity from the public that embittered Germans more than the veterans of other nations.[184] But it took until the second half of the 1920s for this resentment to become so marked. In 1920, the veteran's organizations still felt that the public was with them in their struggle to secure sufficient support and recognition from the state bureaucracy.[185] And here the question must simply be asked: Did Otto Dix represent such veterans in his Dadaist pictures because he was sympathetic to them, as a fellow veteran, or because he held them in contempt, as so many others did? Their presence in artworks and on the walls of the Dada-Fair are on one, almost technical level a gesture of Dadaist spleen, besmirching the sacred precincts of the art world with the reviled, the unwanted, the detritus of the city street. But beyond this, is it meant to express the artist's bitterness over the war and its consequences, as visited on the bodies of the proletariat, or is it an uncharitable expression of relief at having been himself spared such pain and humiliation? Are we being invited to feel rage at an unjust war and an unfair social order, or to laugh at the grotesque sight of these bodies and their shattered masculinity? The widely accepted and reassuring interpretation of these works is that they express the artist's anger and empathy.[186] This question was debated already by art critics in the early 1920s. Gustav Hartlaub, who coined the term "Neue Sachlichkeit," suggested that Dix and George Grosz were motivated by cynicism, and were obsessed with the grotesque, the deviant, and the criminal. He had in mind not only the Dadaist "war cripple" pictures, but also the later, "verist" paintings with their "*Polizeispitzelblick*" – meaning, roughly, the

184 Cohen, *War Come Home*, 90 ff.

185 Cohen, *War Come Home*, 91.

186 See for example Matthias Eberle, *World War I and the Weimar Artists. Dix, Grosz, Beckmann, Schlemmer* (New Haven, CT: Yale University Press, 1985), "In his pictures of cripples and invalids, Dix attacked with a bitter anger only a veteran could feel, the indifference of civilians to the suffering of the war-victims," 38. And more recently, Frances S. Connelly, in her excellent study on the grotesque, *The Grotesque in Western Art and Culture. The Image at Play* (Cambridge: Cambridge University Press, 2012), calls these pictures a, "truly outraged and outrageous indictment of the social values, public leadership, and private interests that produced this tableau," 113. This interpretation of the pictures as statements of "bitter anger" and "indictment" is also the entire thrust of Linda McGreevy's thorough study, *Bitter Witness*.

gaze of the police snitch.[187] The art critic Paul Ferdinand Schmidt defended Dix against this criticism with an ad hominem attack on Hartlaub, whom he essentially dismissed as having bourgeois taste.[188] If critics who knew Dix personally, as Schmidt did, couldn't quite bring themselves to claim that his work was anti-militarist, they would at least imply that there was something high-minded, or at least principled in their "objective" depiction of contemporary reality ("he [Dix] has a clear vision of life in its contemporaneity").[189] This positive view of Dix as a principled, progressive critic of German militarism was only strengthened through the decades of postwar German division and the Cold War competition over Dix's legacy.[190] I am convinced, however, that the obvious if grotesque humor of the Dadaist "war cripple" pictures is not the laughter of bitter irony, but of coldhearted mockery. These wounded soldiers are simply the butt of a joke, a joke about their nullified masculinity. It is a joke, however, which Dix meant to share with other veterans. And it is a joke that draws its humor from the realm of the grotesque body, with its wounds, scars, deformities, and purulations, and from mocking references to its mangled masculinity and sexuality.

187 Gustav Hartlaub, "Der Zynismus als Kunstrichtung?," *Frankfurter Zeitung* (13 September 1924), cited in Dietrich Schubert, "Krüppeldarstellungen im Werk von Otto Dix nach 1920: Zynismus oder Sarkasmus?," in Gertrude Cepl-Kaufmann and Gerd Krumeich, eds., *Krieg und Utopie* (Düsseldorf: Klartext, 2006), 293–308. I thank Professor Schubert for bringing his essay to my attention.

188 Paul Ferdinand Schmidt, "Die deutschen Veristen," *Das Kunstblatt* 8 (1924), 373. Schubert brings this debate up again to frame the interpretation of the war- cripple pictures as a choice between cynicism – Hartlaub's term – and sarcasm, where "sarcasm" indicates an attack on the social forces of militarism which caused the mutilation of these veterans in the first place.

189 "[M]an hat den Blick für das Leben und seine Gegenwärtigkeit ..." Schmidt, "Die deutschen Veristen," p. 373.

190 The relentless criticism of Dix's war and "war cripple" pictures by the Nazis only made this postwar interpretation more plausible and morally compelling, and is repeatedly brought up by Schubert in particular as evidence of the progressive, socially critical content of the artworks. But of course the Nazi's demonization of his art as anti-militarist (which in their world view was an alien and subversive position) always served their own political agenda.

In the summer of 1920, the Berlin Dadaist artists and agitators George Grosz, John Heartfield, and Raoul Hausmann organized an exhibition that was at the same time a countercultural action, the First International Dada Fair, in the rooms of the gallerist Otto Burchard in Berlin. They invited 25 other artists, including Otto Dix, to show work in the exhibition. Dix sent a large painting, *War Invalids, 45% Employable!* [Kriegskrüppel, 45% Erwerbsfähig!] (1920) (see Figure 31), one of the largest works in the show.[191]

It had several important elements in common with several other objects on display: collage or assemblage, humor, and mockery of the military.[192] The painting, which was apparently destroyed by the Nazis after they came to power, depicts a row of men in uniform, each afflicted with grievous bodily harm sustained in the war. Their sad parade is like a carnival scene from a Bosch painting, and it mocks – there is no other word for it – the war invalids who marched in Berlin and Dresden, among other cities, as early as December of 1918, protesting the inadequacy of their support by the state.[193] One figure seems to have lost both arms and both legs; he is being pushed in a wheel chair by another man with a prosthetic jaw and who – we see with the aid of a kind of x-ray vision through his clothing – has a mechanical arm and a mechanical leg. The group is being led by an officer, who is decorated with an Iron Cross medal. He, too, is horribly disfigured, most of his nose is missing and his face is badly scarred; he is left with the use of only one good hand, his other hand and both legs being replaced by the crudest of prosthetics. The second figure in the row is missing a leg and walks with the aid of a crutch; his peg leg is far too short, forcing him to walk along as though on his knees. The jittery lines of his arm and head make him seem to shiver and shake uncontrollably. He represents a continuation with Dix's earlier concern with the figure of the neurasthenic, and with weak nerves and shocks to the nerves.

191 According to Conrad Felixmüller, Dix subtitled this painting "Four of These Don't Add Up To a Whole Man." Quoted by Eberle, *World War I and the Weimar Artists*, 44.

192 Helen Adkins, "Erste Internationale Dada-Messe," in *Stationen der Moderne: Die bedeutenden Kunstausstellungen des 20. Jahrhunderts in Deutschland* (Berlin: Berlinische Galerie, 1988), 157–183.

193 Whalen, *Bitter Wounds*, 117–129.

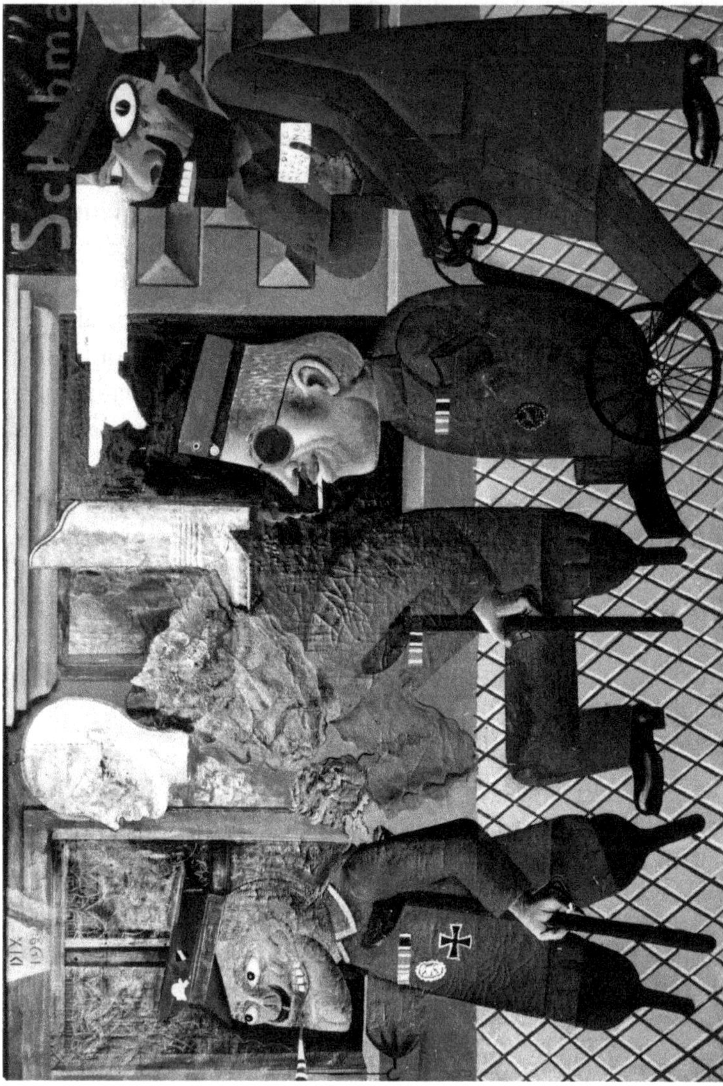

Figure 31. Otto Dix, *War Invalids, 45% Employable* [Kriegskrüppel, 45% Erwerbsfähig!], oil and collage on canvas, 1920, lost. © Otto Dix / Artists Rights Society (ARS), New York / VG Bild-Kunst, Bonn. Photo, akg-images, used with permission.

The traumatic neurosis which Ernst Ludwig Kirchner and thousands of others suffered from had a notoriously shifting symptomology, but the most recognizable symptom was a dramatic, debilitating trembling or shaking, with various kinds of involuntary contortions, contractions, and other muscle movements, and even stuttering. In German, the lay term used by public and doctors alike for this violent and uncontrollable shivering (already before the war) was *zittern*, and the men who suffered, claimed to suffer, or believed themselves to be suffering from this affliction (depending on the varying opinions of psychiatrists, neurologists, generals, and politicians), were called *Zitterer*, a term more dismissive than empathetic.[194] The *Zitterer* became a recognizable type within a few months of the start of the war, and by the end of the war he was as iconic as the amputee.[195] Debate about the *Zitterer*, about the authenticity of their malady, continued into the 1920s.[196] The debate centered around a single vexing question, and one that proved difficult to decide medically: to what extent was the victim of traumatic neurosis suffering from a genuine malady, and to what extent was he simply malingering? Was he really disabled by an external shock or trauma, or was he simply unwilling, consciously or not, to carry out his duty and return to the front? In fact, in the early years of the war, the central question for the doctors was whether or not traumatic neurosis was caused by injury to the physical tissue of the nervous system, or if it even had any organic basis at all. By 1916, the official position of the medical professionals was that it did not.[197] The goal of the German doctors became convincing the enlisted men that their symptoms were all in their heads, "curing" them of their

194 Josef Pelnár, *Das Zittern. Seine Erscheinungsformen, seine Pathogenese und klinische Bedeutung* (Berlin: Springer, 1913).

195 Films of these men, made by military psychiatrists to document their remarkable symptoms, can be readily found on the internet.

196 See especially Lerner, *Hysterical Men*, and, on the similar situation and attendant public debates in Austria, Hans Georg Hofer, *Nervenschwäche und Krieg*.

197 Lerner, *Hysterical Men*, 62–79.

delusions by making them admit this either to themselves or to the doctors, and then shipping them back to the front.[198]

It seems incomprehensible now that physicians during and after the war were unwilling to credit the awesome destructive power of industrialized warfare with the potential to cause real trauma in men serving at the front. But this reluctance was rooted in the nineteenth-century discourse of nerves and nervous trauma in Germany. Medical discourse in Germany in the nineteenth century had originally labeled nervous trauma as *neurasthenia*, a concept and a term taken from the American physician Beard, who popularized it in the early 1880s, which was essentially viewed as a symptom of an unfinished process of modernity, and so suffered by the bourgeois men charged with transforming Germany into a modern, industrial and bureaucratic nation state. On the one hand, it gave expression, in medical terms of "nerves" and "nervousness," to the sense that the individual was increasingly subjected to an onslaught of overstimulation and physical danger in the modern, urban world.[199] At the same time it gave German bourgeois men especially a culturally and morally sanctioned means of temporarily laying down the heavy burden of their responsibilities for guiding the modern German economy, as they began the ritual of taking time away to restore their "nerves." "Neurasthenia" was a condition with positive associations; it was also very gendered. While its symptomology looked nearly indistinguishable from "hysteria," a diagnosis traditionally reserved for women and cited as evidence of women's constitutional incapacity for public life, "neurasthenia" was pointed to as evidence that bourgeois men were at the forefront of modern life and were exposed, as a result of their important positions of responsibility, to its taxing effects.[200] But when Chancellor Bismarck introduced the world's first accident insurance scheme to offset the losses incurred by, in particular, railway

198 Lerner, *Hysterical Men*, and also Andreas Killen, *Berlin Electropolis: Shock, Nerves, and German Modernity* (Berkeley: University of California Press, 2006).

199 Joachim Radkau, *Das Zeitalter der Nervosität. Deutschland zwischen Bismarck und Hitler* (Munich: Propyläen Taschenbuch, 2000).

200 Hofer, *Nervenschwäche und Krieg*, 32 ff., and Lerner, *Hysterical Men*.

accidents, the disabilities covered included neurasthenia and nervous trauma. As a result, the prevalence of "nervousness" spread downward in the class hierarchy of Wilhelmine society, at great monetary cost to the Wilhelmine state. The discourse of nervous trauma grew explosively, matching the industrial and economic growth of Germany, and as a consequence the symptomology lost greatly in prestige. Faced with an enormous payout, politicians and physicians found it convenient to believe that the epidemic of nervous trauma in Germany in the late nineteenth century was due to a (possibly unconscious) desire to benefit from the system, and by the end of the nineteenth century, the German medical profession was all but unanimous in its contention that the symptoms of nervousness in general were "functional" in nature –that is, it was nothing more than the effect of a desire, conscious or unconscious, to collect a pension and avoid work. The goal of doctors became returning men to productive work; in the war it would be returning them to the work of fighting at the front. Once the war was over, the goal became, once again, employment – a fact evoked directly by the title, *45% Employable*.[201] Even before the war, *hysteria* – with its associations with the female body – became the preferred diagnosis for the symptoms of nervous trauma when they appeared in working-class men, as opposed to *neurasthenia*, with its positive dimension, which was diagnosed in bourgeois men. For the industrial proletariat in the Germany of Dix's childhood, nervous trauma and weak nerves were an affliction associated with the lower stratum of the female body, a failing of masculinity, a failure of the will in the face of the demands of modern industrial work, and a form of unmanly malingering, whereas for bourgeois men traumatic neurosis was an intellectual matter, a privilege

201 The psychiatrist Robert Sommer, for one, converted his prewar practice of identifying and "curing" the psychosomatic symptomology of neuroses caused by traumatic accidents to the treatment of shell shock. Sommer, "Beseitigung funktioneller Taubheit besonders bei Soldaten durch eine experimental-psychologische Methode," *Schmidts Jarhbücher der in- und ausländischen gesamten Medizin* 84 (February 1917) 65–75, cited in Doherty, "See, We Are All Neurasthenics!," 122 f.

reserved for men who needed a pause from running the affairs of the state and the economy.[202] These associations of class and gender were carried into the public discussion of traumatic neurosis during the war. By then, the habit of calling a soldier, a man from the working class, who revealed himself to be unfit for the work of industrial warfare, a hysteric, womanly, grotesque, was well established among the public as well as the medical profession.[203]

In two more works from this group of oil paintings with collage, Dix focused on the figure of the disabled veteran reduced to begging in the streets of Dresden. In the first, *The Matchbook Seller* [Der Streichholzhändler] (1920) (see Figure 32), a rump of a man is selling matches. He is armless and legless, with dark glasses over his blinded eyes, and calls out to passers-by on the street. The words coming out of his mouth, scrawled like graffiti across the surface of the canvas, reads, "Streichhölzer! Echte Schwedenhölzer! ("Matches! Genuine Swedish Matches"; Swedish matches were considered the best sort). Actually, what is written is, "*Sch*treichhölzer!" in imitation of the soft, slurred pronunciation of the Saxon dialect. Dix's signature and the year 1920 are also written in chalk on the curbstone – by the gutter. Elegantly dressed passers-by pay the invalid no heed; a little dachshund offers the final indignity of lifting its leg to piss on him; Dix has carefully painted an exuberant yellow stream of urine arcing from the dog's little red-tipped penis. The second painting, *Prague Street* [Prager Strasse] (1920) (see Figure 33) has a much denser composition and set of references.

202 Lerner, *Hysterical Men*, 64.

203 Dora Apel, "'Heroes' and 'Whores': The Politics of Gender in Weimar Antiwar Imagery," *The Art Bulletin* 79/3 (Sep. 1997), 366–384.

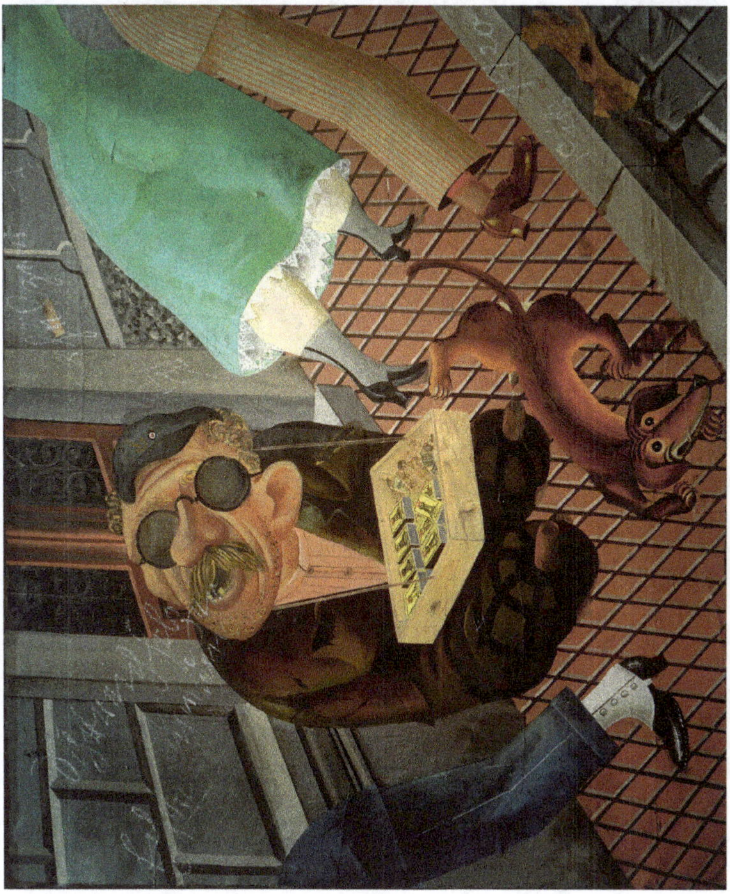

Figure 32. Otto Dix, *Matchbook Seller* [Streichholzhändler], oil and collage on canvas, 1920, Staatsgalerie, Stuttgart. © Otto Dix / Artists Rights Society (ARS), New York / VG Bild-Kunst, Bonn. Photo akg-images, used with permission.

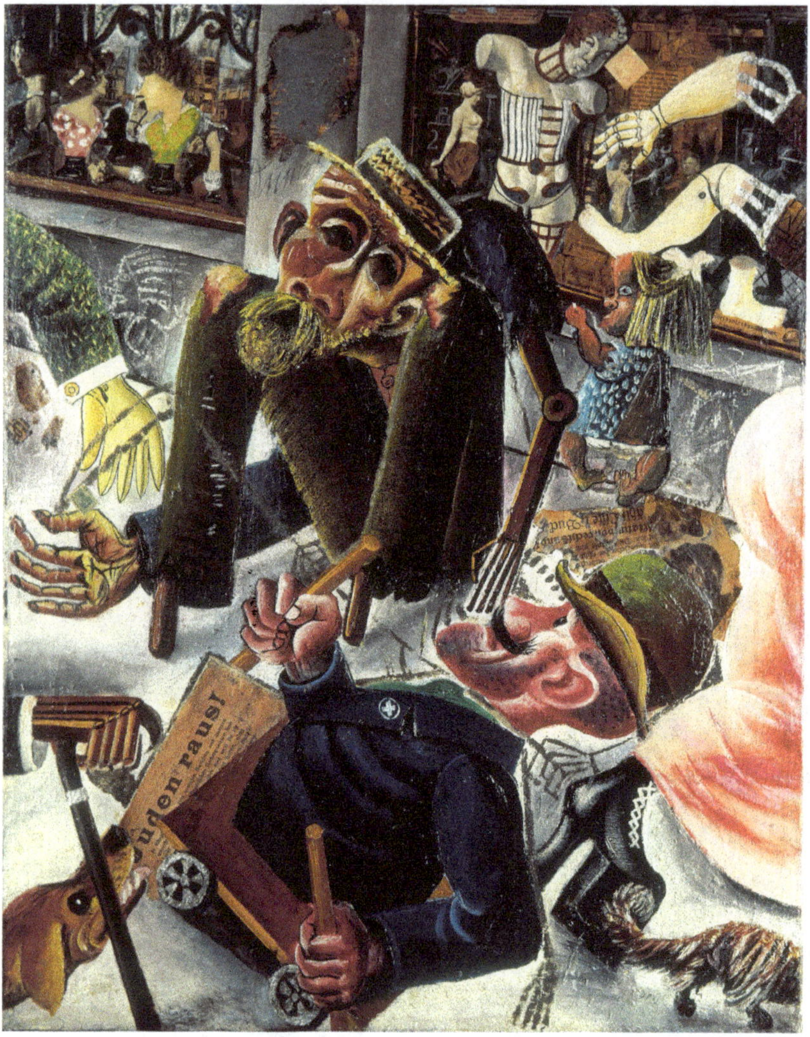

Figure 33. Otto Dix, *Prager Strasse*, oil and collage on canvas, 1920, Kunstmuseum Stuttgart. © Otto Dix / Artists Rights Society (ARS), New York / VG Bild-Kunst, Bonn. Photo © Alinari / akg-images, used with permission.

This painting was exhibited together with *Skat Players* in the Dresden Secession exhibition in the Galerie Arnold in 1920. A beggar with a wooden, prosthetic arm and two peg legs accepts a coin (actually, a real postage stamp, pasted directly onto the canvas) dropped into his outstretched palm by a hand clad in a yellow deerskin glove – all the passers-by in both paintings are dressed with conspicuous elegance, though only their legs or hands are shown as they hurry down the main boulevards of Dresden. In this painting a second crippled veteran also passes the beggar by, but this second fellow is well-dressed and wears an officer's mustache; he is clearly better-off than the beggar whom he disdainfully ignores, even though his own legs and lower torso are missing. He rolls along on a little wheeled platform, propelling himself with two sticks which he uses like ski poles. The shop windows of Dresden's elegant Prager Strasse are filled with mannequins displaying what looks like a mix of prosthetics and medical devices and beauty aids; the hairdresser's next door displays heads sporting wigs in the latest styles, represented by real hair used as a collage element. The general effect is a blackly funny counterpoint to the pitiable condition of the beggar. Like the dog pissing on the matchbook seller, it is a vulgar joke told at the expense of the veteran's dignity, and to the degree that the humor works, it is hard to reconcile with the notion that Dix might be here expressing his empathy with these men. Both pictures contain small collaged elements, unobtrusive at first, but significant, for they are part of a deliberate strategy to undermine the cultural authority and dignity of oil painting on canvas. The collage elements in *Prague Street* include, besides the hair on the mannequin's head, the money in the matchbook tray, and that quintessential collage material of synthetic Cubism, the printed page.

Whereas Picasso and Braque cut out and often inverted their bits of newspapers, interrupting their editorial coherence and fragmenting the words of their headlines (it remains an open question whether or not we are meant to read them), Dix has pasted an entire page of print onto the canvas of *Prague Street* (although partially painted over), right side up, so that its offensive and hateful headline, "Juden Raus!" [Jews Out!] is clearly legible. Rather than being converted to mere texture and tonality, as it would have been in Parisian Cubism, here the text is allowed to convey its strident verbal message clearly, collapsing the fictive pictorial space into the picture plane, and disrupting the reading of the image itself. I am unconvinced by the frequent argument that Dix is exposing, with a clear-sighted political acumen, the hypocrisy of a bourgeois society that is already scapegoating Jews, and that he was already alive to the worst implications of fascism; that seems like wishful thinking.[204] Rather, the shrill ugliness of the flyer's headline, like the graffiti/dialect of the matchbook seller, an affront to civil discourse, is here utilized directly for its shock value, to function as an affront to the dignity and integrity of oil painting, of high art. The function of the racist headline, like the graffiti scrawls and the match seller's cry, was to incorporate low, vulgar speech acts into the precinct of high culture, speech acts that belong in the street – in the gutter, to be precise. Here they disrupt the elevated cultural tone of salons and museums.[205] The picture is full of collaged elements referring to the lower bodily stratum, to newspaper advertisements for condoms and gynecological medical equipment – juxtaposed with both prosthetic limbs and limbless mannequins modeling beauty aids (such as bust enlargers and corsets). These are, in turn, juxtaposed with the limbless veterans. The effect is one of low comedy.[206] An outraged

204 See as just one example the catalog of the Tate Gallery survey exhibition of Otto Dix, in 1991, in which the authors write about this flyer that Dix "adroitly locates the beginnings of Fascism in the politico-economic turmoil of 1920." Keith Hartley and Sarah O'Brien Twohig, *Otto Dix: 1891–1969* (London: Tate Gallery, 1992), 98.

205 The poster which Dix has pasted directly onto the canvas was actually a campaign poster for the Social Democrat list in Dresden, for the Reichstag elections in 1920; the headline, obviously meant to grab attention, was actually the Social Democrat's *parody* of the racist politics of the nationalists. The poster is reproduced and discussed in detail in Ulrich Weitz, "Kriegskrüppel, Kapp-Putsch und Kunstlump-Debatte," in Galerie der Stadt Stuttgart, *Dix* (Stuttgart: Hatje, 1991), 95–100.

206 Hartley and Twohig, in their text for an exhibition catalog of 1991, read these various scraps and their placement in the picture plane as direct references to the political debates of 1920 over whether or not to legalize abortion and contraception. Undoubtedly influenced by Patricia Leighten's novel interpretive move of reading the actual newspaper texts in Picasso's collages for their first-order political content,

sense of social justice, and empathy for the former soldiers mutilated by the war and then thrown away by the country they fought for, are not what's on offer in these pictures. Rather, what is on offer are humorous speech acts, vulgar jokes, burlesque humor shared with a knowing audience. This is an important point, and I will return to it presently.

There is another form of vulgar humor being retailed here, and it turns on the contrast between the damaged bodies of the men, both of whom are cut off at the waist, and the prominent backsides of the women walking down the street. As with *Moon Woman*, we have here again to do with Dix's evident preoccupation with the sexuality of the soldier in uniform, and its relationship to the sexualized female body. The women's buttocks and thighs are clearly visible beneath their clothes, roundly modeled and emphasized. Their sex is on offer; the war has been fought, in Dix's words, "for the vulva"; and yet these soldiers are in no position to make good on their claim; like the character of Jake Barnes in Ernest Hemingway's novel *The Sun Also Rises*, their own sexuality has been nullified by the injuries they sustained in the war. In reality, impotence was a common complaint among the sufferers of war neurosis.[207] But there is another figure here who, in contrast to these disabled veterans, *can* make good on his claim, and that is Dix himself – who pasted a photograph of himself in the shop window. In other paintings, too, Dix celebrated his own aggressive sexual appetite with a maximum of vulgarity. He painted the same sorts of female figures, naked in brothels or naked in his studio, while he himself is dressed like one of the dandies walking past his crippled fellow veterans on Prague Street.

in a book published just three years prior, Hartley and Twohig add together these references to taboo sexual subjects and the blaring anti-Semitic political slogan to get a registration of Dix's "anger," an anger which, in their reading, has expanded beyond the poor treatment of Germany's war invalids to now include the conservative political positions with regard to women's reproductive rights. This despite the fact that there is absolutely no evidence that Dix had progressive – or really, any – political views on these subjects. Keith Hartley and Sarah O'Brien Twohig, eds., *Otto Dix, 1891–1969* (London: Tate Gallery, 1992); Patricia Leighten, *Re-Ordering the Universe: Picasso and Anarchism, 1897–1914* (Princeton, NJ: Princeton University Press, 1989).

207 Eric J. Leed *No Man's Land. Combat and Identity in World War I* (Cambridge: Cambridge University Press, 1979), 183–186.

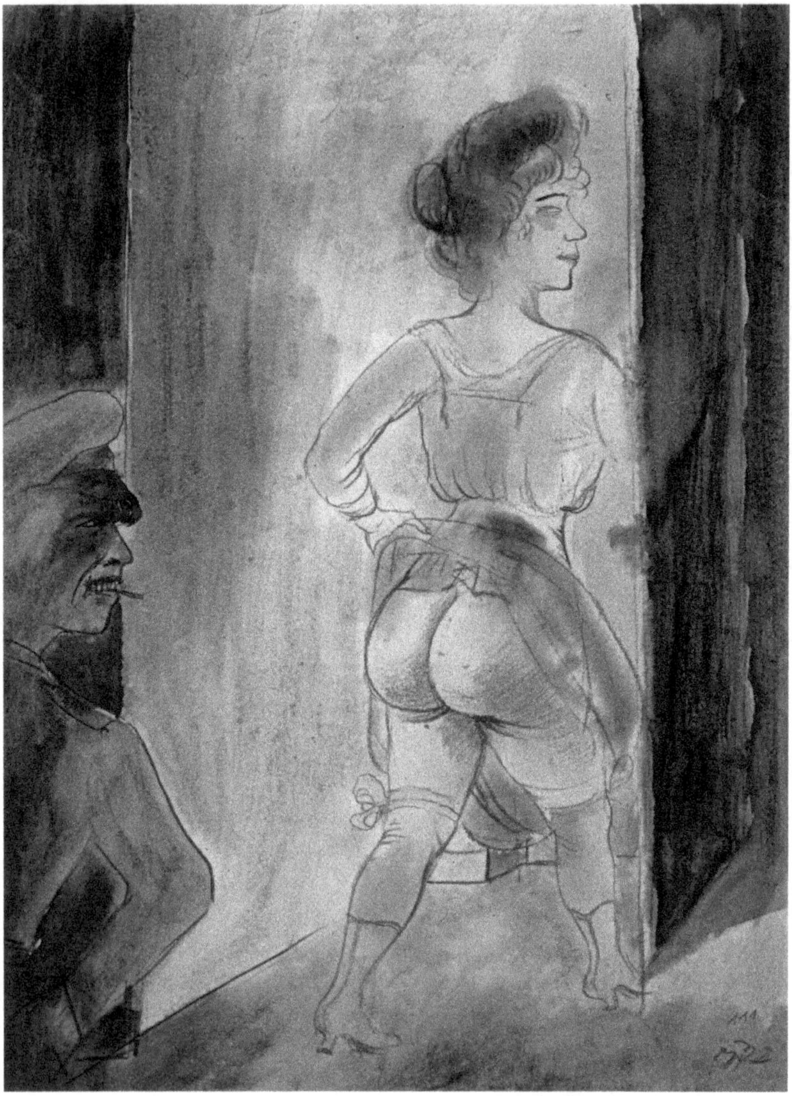

Figure 34. Otto Dix, *Me in Brussels* [Ich in Brüssel], watercolor, 1922, Otto Dix Stiftung, Vaduz. © Otto Dix / Artists Rights Society (ARS), New York / VG Bild-Kunst, Bonn. Digital file: author's own scan.

In a key watercolor, *Me in Brussels* [Ich in Brüssel] (1922) (see Figure 34), he also depicted himself in uniform, on leave in Brussels, leering at the whores of the occupied city who expose their large rear ends to him, proffering their wares; in this self-portrait, Dix, the conquering soldier, leers at his spoils. A much more empathetic view of prostitution in occupied Belgium can be found in Heinrich Wandt's book, *Etappe Gent*, of 1926, a frank indictment of the brutality of the German occupying army's sexual exploitation of Belgium. The mass incarceration and deportation of the male Belgian population led the women and children, in Wandt's account, directly to the brink of starvation. Women – mostly factory workers and seamstresses and the servant class in the cities of Ghent and Brussels – saw themselves left with no alternative but to prostitute themselves, whether in brothels or on the streets, for prices ranging between 20 Marks and 3 Marks, or for a loaf of army-issue bread. "The soldiers were amazed by the wholesale supply of prostituted women and girls," Wandt states. "They gave no thought to the systematic way in which militarism had delivered them to this shame."[208] The relish with which Dix depicts himself as triumphant in the moment of exploitation clearly indicates that he belonged to the amazed and delighted soldiery, not to the progressive and enlightened social critics such as Wandt. The scenario depicted in *Prague Street* and *The Match Seller* is simply the continuation of this same war economy in which women's bodies are available for a price, and soldiers or veterans are either fit to exploit the situation or not. The two paintings are at the same time continuations of the vulgar, grotesque humor, centered on the lower bodily stratum, in which the soldiers would have framed their narratives of their sexual exploits in Brussels and other occupied towns.

208 Heinrich Wandt, *Etappe Gent* (Vienna and Berlin: Agis, 1926), 151. "Die deutschen Soldaten wunderten sich über dieses Massenangebot prostituierter Frauen und Mädchen. Sie bedachten nicht, mit welcher systematischen Grausamkeit diese Unglücklichen vom Militarismus der Schande überliefert worden waren, und dass diese Bedauernswerten, denen der lange Krieg jede andere Verdienstmöglichkeit raubte, eben einfach keine andere Wahl hatten, wenn sie nicht Hungers sterben wollten," 156.

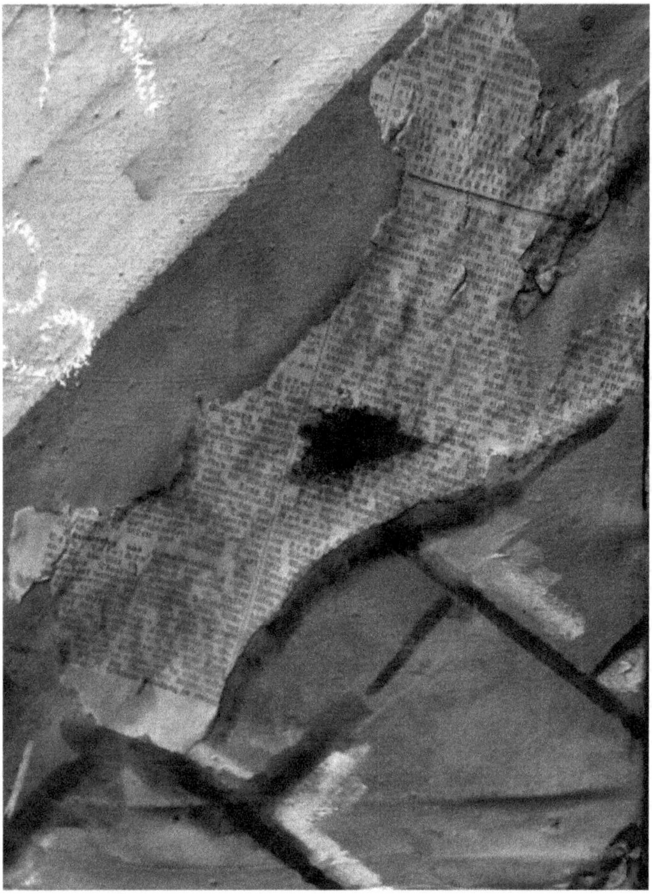

Figure 35. Otto Dix, *Matchbook Seller* (detail of newspaper scrap), oil and collage on canvas, 1920, Staatsgalerie, Stuttgart. © Otto Dix / Artists Rights Society (ARS), New York / VG Bild-Kunst, Bonn. Photo: the author.

The Matchbook Seller harbors one more joke here which needs to be pointed out, related to a public scandal often referred to as the "*Kunstlumpdebatte*," which involved the street fighting of 1920 and the Dadaists' professed disdain for high art. The reference would have been obvious to the art-viewing public in 1920. A scrap of newspaper lies in the gutter, already soiled and soon to be further sullied by the stream of urine from the dachshund (see Figure 35). Here there can be no question but that we are meant to read, or at least recognize, the newsprint of this bit of paper. It is the printed text of Oskar Kokoschka's open letter to the two armed groups who had engaged each other in the streets of Dresden in March of 1920 – the striking workers who opposed the Kapp Putsch and the local militia who supported it. The brief battle had unfolded within gunshot range of the Zwinger Palace and its art treasures. In the course of the battle a stray bullet had gone through one of the windows of the galleries and put a hole in a painting by Pieter Paul Rubens, *Bathsheba at the Fountain*. In response, Kokoschka, now a painting professor at the Dresden Art Academy, had written this letter asking the two sides to take any further armed conflict elsewhere, in order to keep Dresden's cultural heritage safe. Kokoschka had the letter printed as a flier and pasted around town; it was also reprinted in several Dresden newspapers.[209] Kokoschka and his plea were met with loud derision, not least from the Dadaists, who saw here the perfect opportunity to marry their (vague) revolutionary sympathies with their hostility towards traditional high art, and their contempt for their Expressionist predecessors like Kokoschka. John Heartfield and George Grosz published a response to Kokoschka, filled with humor, sarcasm, and derision.[210] Putting Kokoschka's own letter in the gutter was perhaps an even more direct statement of Dix's feelings on the matter. But it is only half of his statement. If one looks closely at the canvas, which is of poor quality and stitched together out of scraps at the edges, there is a small, square, heavily patched spot in the center of the match seller's chest (see Figure 36).

209 Ulrich Weitz, "Kriegskrüppel," 95 ff.

210 George Grosz and John Heartfield, "Der Kunstlump," *Der Gegner* 1/10–12 (Berlin: Malik, 1920), 48–56. Translated as "The Art Scab," in Anton Kaes, Martin Jay, Edward Dimendberg, eds., *The Weimar Republic Sourcebook* (Berkely: University of California Press, 1994), 483–486. The essay in *Der Gegner* includes the entirety of Kokoschka's letter. See also Beth Irwin Lewis, *George Grosz. Art and Politics in the Weimar Republic* (Princeton, NJ: Princeton University Press, 1991), 96, and Brigid Doherty, "The Work of Art and the Problem of Politics in Berlin Dada," *October* 105 (Summer 2003), 73–92.

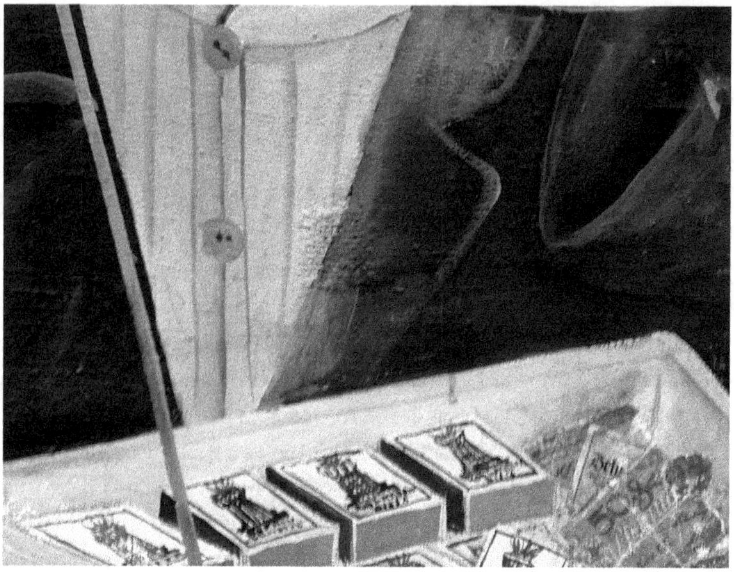

Figure 36. Otto Dix, *Matchbook Seller* (detail of patch), oil and collage on canvas, 1920, Staatsgalerie, Stuttgart. © Otto Dix / Artists Rights Society (ARS), New York / VG Bild-Kunst, Bonn. Photo: the author.

The patch is clearly visible beneath the paint indicating shirt and jacket lapel, just where the man's heart would be, as though a hole had been made there and then somewhat clumsily patched up and painted over. It is immediately adjacent other collaged elements, specifically the currency pasted into his box of matchbooks. Has the downtrodden soldier-turned-beggar caught a bullet? Has the painting? Is this Dix's response to the question, Who is more deserving of our concern and solidarity, the downtrodden working class and disaffected veterans, or Rubens' voluptuous nudes? Certainly this complicates my account, which has so far argued that Dix displayed little empathy for his wounded compatriots (the painting carries an inscription on the back, "Dedicated to my contemporaries" [*meinen Zeitgenossen gewidmet*], an ambiguous dedication that avoids words like "veteran," "victim," "comrades," or "capitalism").[211] A hole deliberately made in the canvas

211 Noted by Fritz Löffler, *Otto Dix und der Krieg* (Leipzig: Reclam, 1986), 17.

and then patched – or even just a false patch suggesting a bullet hole that isn't there, would be very much in keeping with his practice at the time of making holes and tears in his pictorial supports, marks and punctures which conveyed private or public meanings with wit and what was often vulgar humor, a practice which James van Dyke has analyzed in detail in multiple examples.[212] Van Dyke has identified another instance of Dix implying a puncture in a canvas, where there is no actual hole: the faux nail head in the portrait of Conrad Felixmüller and his wife and child (*The Felixmüller Family*, 1919) in the St. Louis Art Museum, which indicates a nail that isn't really there – with possible implied meanings based on puns and vulgar witticisms.[213] And Dietrich Schubert states that in the related work *Barricade* [Barrikade, 1920, destroyed] one of the corpses lying on a barricade made up from the detritus of European culture, both high and low, has an actual hole bored by Dix right through the canvas to indicate the bullet wound.[214] Nails, patches, holes real and false, belonged to his repertoire of collage elements. *The Matchbook Seller* and *Prague Street* intermingle in complicated and, perhaps, inconsistent and contradictory ways, Dix's response to the sight of his former comrades disabled and reduced to begging on Dresden's streets, his sexualized mythology of the war and his own masculinity, both in uniform and dressed as a dandy, his solidarity with the Dadaists and their hostility to established art and cultural authority, and his own desire for recognition as an artist – a desire which would, in a few short years, be gratified when he was appointed to the very academy where Kokoschka had lately taught. It was the response of an outsider who both resented, and desired entry into, the confines of high art and high society, and of the veteran who had seen his comrades maimed and killed in endless numbers, and who was elated to have survived the violence intact.

212 James van Dyke "Erasure and Jewishness in Otto Dix's *Portrait of the Lawyer Hugo Simons*," in Warren Carter, Haran Barnaby, Frederic J. Schwartz, *et al.*, eds., *Renew Marxist Art History* (London: University College, 2013), 362–381.

213 James van Dyke, "The Vulgarity of Otto Dix's Facture," presented at the 106th Annual College Art Association conference in Los Angeles, 24 February 2018.

214 Dietrich Schubert, *Otto Dix*, 43.

Grotesque humor

Graffiti, dirty pictures and dirty jokes, pasted paper and matchbooks, racist slogans, street cries and cat calls; Dix was scoffing at high art and the polite society which it was supposed to flatter and adorn. But the humor all comes at the expense of the disabled veterans. The dirty jokes and sexual innuendo serve to remind the viewer that Dix himself, who came away from the war intact, is free to satisfy his sexual appetites. As with his comments about *Moon Woman*, the point is rather a contempt for the physical infirmity of others, a contempt which is intimately mixed up with his preoccupation with his own sexuality, and with sexual conquest and competition. The laughter which this picture elicits is of a very particular sort. It is what Mikhail Bakhtin termed "carnival laughter," the laughter at the world turned upside down, at the mockery of cultural and social authority, at grotesque bodies displayed for the degradation of cultural ideals.[215] It is the laughter of grotesque realism.

I want to be clear here about what I mean by "grotesque" and grotesque humor. Although the term "grotesque" was coined in late fifteenth-century Italy and has meant a wide variety of things in modern European aesthetic discourse, in a variety of languages, including exaggerated mannerism, and the combination of disparate elements to create decorative motifs, as well as the misshapen and the ugly, it is the last quality which has come to be firmly associated with the term since the late nineteenth century.[216] The ugly and misshapen grotesque, especially when it appears in caricature and other forms of "low" culture, can often elicit laughter, and it is this humorous, caricatural form of the grotesque which Dix employs in his pictures of "war cripples."[217] Bakhtin's analysis of François Rabelais (originally written

215 Mikhail Bakhtin, *Rabelais and His World* (Bloomington: Indiana University Press, reprint edition 1984, Hélène Iswolsky, translator).

216 Frances S. Connelly, "Introduction," in Frances S. Connelly, ed., *Modern Art and the Grotesque* (Cambridge University Press, 2009), 1–19. Connelly in fact uses Dix's *Skat Players* to illustrate her discussion of the carnivalesque.

217 A version of this thesis was presented by the author at the German Studies Association conference, Minneapolis, 2008, "'Wie ein Frontschwein malt': Otto Dix, Grotesque Realism, and the Language of the Trenches."

in the 1930s) is still the dominant account of grotesque humor and the carnivalesque. Originating in medieval popular culture, the humorous grotesque is full of references to the base and the bodily, including wounds and hybrids, as well as excrement, sex, eating, expelling – taking in and spewing out. Bakhtin said that it draws heavily on what he termed the "lower bodily stratum," and rejoices in everything to do with the belly and eating, digesting, defecation and urination, as well as sexual intercourse and birth. The carnivalesque is also excessive, reveling in exaggeration, including long lists of objects, and substitutions for limbs and facial features. Its typical language was not the elevated diction of official culture, but the low speech of the marketplace, fairs, and festivities, social forms outside of official culture, where the popular imagery of folk culture lived on, in Bakhtin's analysis, well into the early modern era. Marketplace speech included forms of abuse and ribald insults that often used expressions of wounding or dismembering the body, with great verbal attention lavished on the specificity of the body parts to be broken or dismembered (think of the Ballad of John Barleycorn, contemporaneous with Rabelais but which may have originally functioned as a kind of advertisement for beer, sung in the marketplace). Bakhtin points to passages in Rabelais that contain "long and detailed anatomic list[s] of wounded members and organs, broken bones, and joints … based on the grotesque image of the dissected body."[218] The substitutions which Dix practiced in his collaged images of prosthetic body parts recall Rabelais' lengthy, grotesque descriptions of bodies assembled out of long lists of substitutions of inanimate objects for body parts.[219] Frances S. Connelly, who has closely traced the divergent histories of various strains of the grotesque in European art from the Renaissance on, asserts that both the carnivalesque and the "diablerie" – the "fascination with the demonic and the endless ways to depict the monstrous" carry forward the popular culture of medieval peasants and merchants, but that neither "play a direct role in

218 Bakhtin, *Rabelais*, 194.

219 For example Rabelais' figure Quaresmeprenant. Like Dix's skat players, the lists of Quaresmeprenant's qualities is incoherent and disintegrated; his chains of associations are base and vulgar, they give rise to ribald laughter; the comparisons dwell on putrefaction and repugnant formlessness.

the grotesque-comic of twentieth-century German art."[220] I would assert that, in the case of Dix's cycle of "war cripple" pictures, they do indeed play a direct role. Dix was deeply familiar with and admired the work of Matthias Grünewald, Hieronymus Bosch, and Hans Holbein the Younger, whom Connelly cites as examples of diablerie, and with their reinterpretations of "traditional medieval subjects of temptation, dances of death, and other diabolical incursions into the world."[221] Heinrich Schneegans, who in the late nineteenth century wrote a history of the humorous grotesque in Germany, included this visual tradition and suggested that it drew its power from its opposition to Catholicism – a circumstance that would have fit with Dix's Protestant background.[222]

The grotesque, in its various forms, was a lively tradition within German popular culture by the beginning of the twentieth century, and certainly enriched the semantic play and anti-classical, countercultural attitudes of the Berlin Dadaists.[223] Christian Weikop has demonstrated the importance of the Bakhtinian carnivalesque specifically for Berlin Dada.[224] And Thomas O. Haakenson has argued that Salomo Friedländer (who wrote under the name "Mynona"), and who was close to the Berlin Dadaists, deployed the grotesque as a weapon against conventional, unreflective modes of viewing and observing, and to unsettle the unquestioning acceptance of the rational, categorizing knowledges produced by science, especially in the

220 Frances S. Connelly, "Profound Play: The Image Tradition of the Comic Grotesque," in Kort, ed., *Comic Grotesque*, 195–209, here p. 197.

221 Connelly, "Profound Play," 198.

222 Heinrich Schneegans, *Geschichte der Grotesken Satire* (Strasbourg: Karl Trübner, 1894), 366 ff. On anti-Catholicism among German soldiers, Apel, "Heroes" and "Whores."

223 See Pamela Kort's exhibition catalog for the exhibition *Comic Grotesque. Wit and Mockery in German Art, 1870–1940* (Munich: Prestel, 2004), especially the essays by Peter Jelavich, "Grotesque and Carnivalesque: Negation and Renewal around 1900," 89–129, and Hanne Bergius, "Dada Grotesque," 155–170.

224 Christian Weikop, "Berlin Dada and the Carnivalesque. *Jedermann sein eigner Fussball* (1919) and *Der Dada* (1919–1920)," in Brooker, Peter, and Andrew Thacker, eds., *The Oxford Critical and Cultural History of Modernist Magazines: Europe 1880–1940* (Oxford: Oxford University Press, 2014), 816–854.

fields of anatomical pathology. In other words, the humorous grotesque was intended by Friedländer to open up a philosophical position for the acceptance of physical difference.[225] But this is quite different from what Dix was trying to do in response to the war invalids' own anatomical pathologies. Contrary to Friedländer/Mynona (whose essay, "Grotesk," he could have seen in the journal *Der Einzige* in 1919), Dix did not use grotesque humor to encourage the viewer's empathy with the war invalid, but to elicit laughter, and so to render harmless the memory of the physical threats of the war – of which the invalid on the street was a constant reminder.[226] Dix's use of grotesque humor is more in line with the function that Walter Benjamin ascribed to slapstick in Charlie Chaplin's films, which were popular in Germany later in the same decade: as a collective form of repression of or redemption from "the chaos of modernity." Thomas Haakenson reminds us that Benjamin saw a connection between Dada and Surrealism and what Germans called the *Groteskfilme* of Charlie Chaplin.[227] Benjamin undoubtedly had his beloved Baudelaire in mind here, who had written that caricature elicits laughter by representing the physical misfortunes of others. Baudelaire explained that, when a fellow human being falls on the ice or stumbles on the sidewalk, it makes us laugh involuntarily, despite our better judgment. "Nevertheless the laugh has gone forth, sudden and irrepressible." He pinpointed the cause of such laughter as

> a certain unconscious pride at the core of the laugher's thought. That is the point of departure. "Look at me! *I* am not falling," he seems to say. "Look at me! *I* am walking upright. *I* would never be so silly as to fail to see a gap in the pavement or a cobblestone blocking the way."[228]

225 Thomas O. Haakenson, "'The Merely Illusory Paradise of Habits': Salomo Friedländer, Walter Benjamin, and the Grotesque," *New German Critique*, 36/1 (106) (Winter 2009), 119–147.

226 Salomo Friedländer, "Grotesk" (signed "Mynona"), *Der Einzige* (1919), and *Der Querschnitt* (1921), cited in Haakenson, "The Merely Illusory Paradise of Habits," 144 f.

227 Haakenson, "The Merely Illusory Paradise of Habits," 140 f.

228 Michele Hannoosh, *Baudelaire and Caricature. From the Comic to an Art of Modernity* (University Park: Pennsylvania State University Press, 1992), 157.

The laughter elicited by Dix's "war cripples" is of just this Baudelairean sort. It is as though Dix were saying, "Look at me! I would never be so foolish as to be crippled or rendered impotent by the war!"

In Bakhtin's exuberant analysis of the use and representation of carnival humor and "marketplace speech" in the novels of Rabelais, laughter at the grotesque was intended both to resist cultural and social authority (a tension which is present on several levels in the "war cripples" collages) and to ward off the terror of death (which haunts the *Skat Players* in the form of a spectral death's head appearing in the gas lamp painted in the upper left-hand corner and, in a more general sense, in the figures of the disabled veterans themselves, and indeed the whole theme of the memory of the war).[229] For Bakhtin, these forms of humor are characterized by a forthright, even joyous embrace of the messy, undignified, and excessive condition of the real human body, and real bodily existence. Marketplace speech places a special emphasis on the body rent to pieces, which Bakhtin demonstrates "is the origin of all swearing," and long lists of wounds and physical abuses appear in folk tales, songs, and even barker's cries – as well as in Rabelais.[230] Curses, profanities, and oaths are part of the fund of marketplace speech, according to Bakhtin, as are the exaggerations of quacks and hawkers of medicines and the "*cris de Paris*" (the rhymed advertisements for wares sung out in the streets and marketplaces of Paris and other towns). All of these speech acts drew their grotesque imagery from the lower bodily stratum, the ironic exaggeration of the virtues of the wares, and the sarcastic exaggeration of the qualities of king and other exalted figures.[231] One thinks here of the cries of the *Match Seller*, rendered in dialect and equated with graffiti, scrawled in chalk on the surface of the canvas, a degradation of the cultural authority of oil painting

229 Bakhtin also ascribed a genuine revolutionary function to marketplace speech, but most later commentators agree that its function was more to maintain the status quo by offering a clearly delimited moment and space in which authority could be safely mocked without actually questioning its place in an unassailable natural order. Certainly in the military, the soldier's version of such mocking speech functions to help the soldier accommodate himself to the rigid hierarchy, and to clearly establish his own place near the bottom of it.

230 Bakhtin, *Rabelais*, 193 f.

231 Bakhtin, *Rabelais*, 151–153.

(as was collage). In marketplace speech, the imagery of food and excessive overeating is a frequent theme, also related to the lower bodily stratum. A drawing which Dix made late during his time in the army, and which seems out of keeping with the rest of his drawings from the period discussed in the previous chapter, takes on a central significance in this regard. It is a drawing of a fellow soldier, but quite different from the other, numerous portraits of comrades which Dix drew and painted during the war.

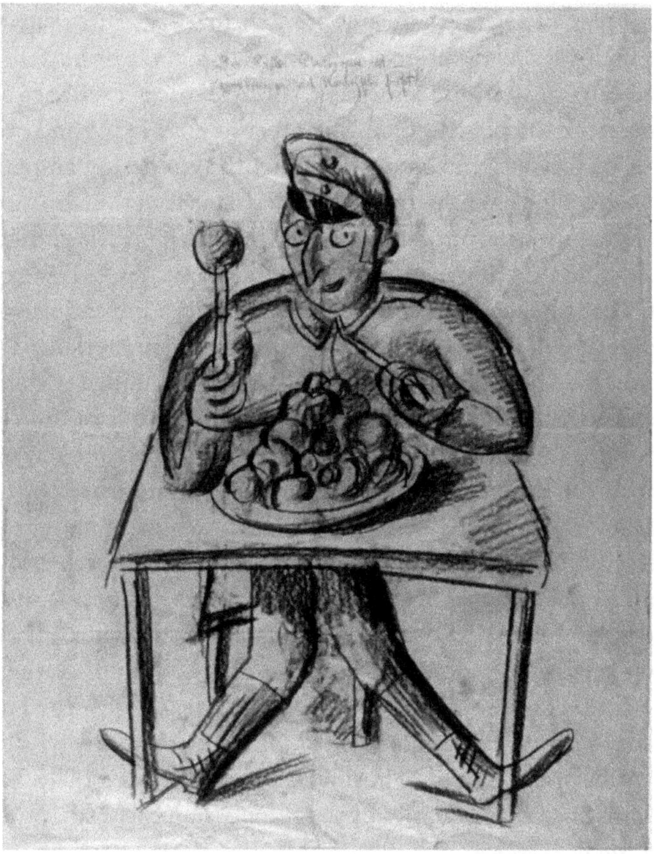

Figure 37. Otto Dix, *Portrait of Ludwig Preller*, charcoal on paper, 1918, Kunstmuseum Albstadt, Stiftung Sammlung Walther Groz SWG 1983–070. © Otto Dix / Artists Rights Society (ARS), New York / VG Bild-Kunst, Bonn. Photo © Kunstmuseum Albstadt, used with permission.

This particular drawing, of his friend Ludwig Preller (around 1918) (see Figure 37), has the humorous qualities of a caricature, and depicts this soldier seated, fork in hand, before an enormous pyramid of potatoes which he is about to consume with great relish. The humor of this carnivalesque excess is heightened by a rhymed couplet, written by somebody, not Dix, right on the picture, which reads, "Der Preller Philosophe ist / Trotzdem er viel Kartoffeln frist!" [Preller is a philosopher, despite guzzling lots of potatoes]. This seemingly minor work is in fact a key to the entire complex of Dadaist collages done in 1920, because it marks the first real use of Rabelaisian humor in Dix's depiction of his fellow soldiers, and obviously commemorates a barracks-room exchange of such humor between soldiers. As Bakhtin observed, overeating and excessive quantities of food are mixed up in turn with butchering animals, and intestines and tripe have a particularly central place in the carnivalesque, combining as they do butchering, sausage making, eating, digesting, excrement, and disemboweling, slaughter and murder.[232] Dix explored just such a concatenation of the themes of butchery and eating, soldiers, violence, and food in his painting *Butcher Shop* [Fleischerladen] (1920) (see Figure 38), where the butchers are visually confounded with the animals they slaughter, disembowel, and sell to people to feast on. That the butchers are former soldiers is announced by their regimental tattoos; the name of the Kaiser is introduced as well, in diminished form, as an inscription on the sailor's hat worn by the boy buying meat from the hairy-armed butcher's wife. Degradation, defecation, birth and death, are all ambivalent images that destroy and renew simultaneously, and that lead to a hearty, ribald laughter. In Bakhtin's account, all of these things are related to each other in the grotesque humor of the carnivalesque, and all aim at replacing the fear of death with the laughter at the body's lower stratum, and with giving birth to the world in an image that becomes a kind of cosmic, swollen, birthing belly. Dix was already engaging the thematics of the Rabelaisian carnivalesque in the painting *Moon Woman*.

232 Bakhtin, *Rabelais*, p. 162 f.

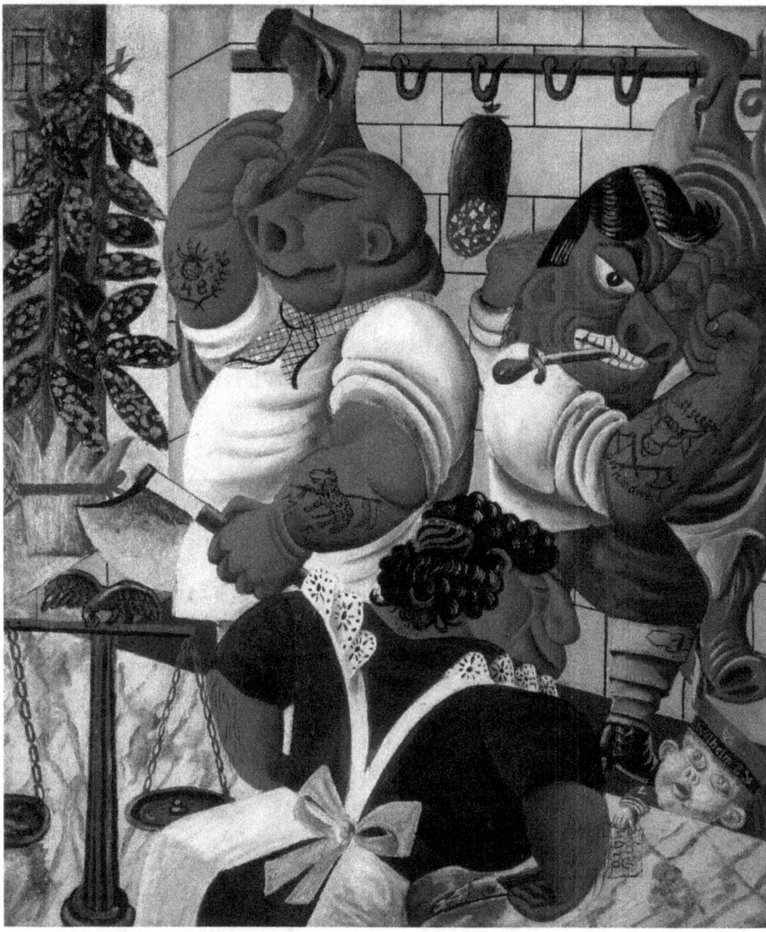

Figure 38. Otto Dix, *Butcher Shop* [Fleischerladen], oil on canvas, 1920, private collection. © Otto Dix / Artists Rights Society (ARS), New York / VG Bild-Kunst, Bonn. Digital file: author's own scan.

My argument is that Dix was fashioning in his Dadaist pictures, in the "war cripple" and related pictures, a visual equivalent to the speech of soldiers, which contemporary observers called "*Soldatensprache*" and "trench slang."[233] The carnivalesque, humorous and disparaging speech of soldiers is a well-known phenomenon, present in armies everywhere and probably in all epochs, but especially when men are conscripted and subjected to rigid, authoritarian, and often inefficient or even misguided discipline.[234] It was therefore an especially prevalent phenomenon in the mass mobilization of the Great War. This "trench slang" was a particular species of marketplace speech; part of a genuine folk culture, it drew heavily on the same funds of the humorous grotesque and the lower bodily stratum. "Wherever men laugh and curse, their speech is filled with bodily images," Bakhtin knew, especially when they must live intimately with each other. "The body copulates, defecates, overeats, and men's speech is flooded with genitals, bellies, defecations, urine, disease, noses, mouths, and dismembered parts."[235] The absurd displacements and replacements of body parts in Dix's "war cripple" pictures, the promiscuous substitutions of prosthetics and collage, the vulgarity of the sexual jokes and displays, all recall the carnivalesque humor of soldiers, as expressed in their own particular argot. That argot was characterized, like marketplace speech, by, "excessiveness, superabundance, tendency to transgress all limits, endless enumerations and accumulations of synonyms."[236] And surely the functions of such grotesque humor in the soldiers' slang were the same as Bakhtin's marketplace speech: to ward off the fear of death; to debase and bring low the hierarchies of military discipline, the officer class, and king and Kaiser.[237] It could also express the joy of still

233 Theodor Imme, *Die deutsche Soldatensprache der Gegenwart und ihr Humor* (Dortmund: Ruhfus, already in its second printing in 1918).

234 Two more recent examples are Tom Dalzell, *Vietnam War Slang. A Dictionary on Historical Principles* (London: Routledge, 2014), and Klaus-Peter Möller, *Der wahre E. Ein Wörterbuch der DDR-Soldatensprache* (Berlin: Lukas Verlag für Kunst- und Geistesgeschichte), 2000.

235 Bakhtin, *Rabelais*, 319.

236 Bakhtin, *Rabelais*, 306.

237 In Ulrich Böhme's analysis of the stylistic character of Ernst Jünger's *Stahlgewittern*, by contrast, especially the first version published in 1920 and again in 1922, the diction consistently echoes the Prussian military tone of absolute discipline and what Böhme terms the "jargon of the officer's club," a coldblooded and pretentious idiom characterized by foreign words and objective, statistical expressions – essentially the

being alive after the moment of danger has passed. Each of the significant elements in Dix's collage pictures had its counterpart in the carnivalesque humor of the soldiers' speech: the bricolage of the caricatured prosthetics; collaged replacements of body parts with mechanical parts and ersatz materials; the ribald humor of the vulgar jokes and sexual innuendos; the mockery of all kinds of cultural and military authority; the slapstick comedy of the disabled soldier. And most of all, his revelry in the grotesque body, with all of its wounds, orifices, exposed sexual organs, formless lesions, and misshapen, bulging stumps of amputations, recalls the carnivalesque humor and language of the marketplace and of diableries, the populist culture of medieval and early modern Europe, reborn in the language of the soldiers who had such need of it in the trenches.[238] All of Dix's grotesque bodies, vulgar jokes, affronts to authority, and Rabelaisian substitutions formed a kind of visual dialect, an equivalent of the soldier's slang.

In his Dadaist pictures of "war cripples," Dix was directly addressing his fellow veterans in a language that was familiar to them from the context of the war. That language and its humor marked out a community of fellow soldiers, distinct from the civilian world. It defined itself by the belief that civilian society could never understand the experiences which separated it from the social customs and moral codes of civilian life, a life to which the soldiers in many ways felt they could not fully return. And he was addressing his fellow veterans about a topic that mattered to them – the happy fact of their physical survival. The thrust of the "war cripple" pictures, and also of *Moon Woman* and *Butcher Shop*, is not moral condemnation; nothing could have been more out of character for Dix. It is the

---

opposite of "trench slang." Ulrich Böhme, *Fassungen bei Ernst Jünger* (Meisneheim am Glan: Hain, 1972), 13–17. This idiom was systematically eliminated in Jünger's later revisions of the text – although not to be replaced with carnivalesque humor. We now know that carnivalesque humor did appear in his actual journal written in the trenches, on which the memoir was based, and was expunged by Jünger early on. Ernst Jünger, *Kriegstagebuch 1914–1918* (Stuttgart: Klett-Cotta, 2014).

238 Bakhtin emphasizes "the boundary between the body and the world, and points of interchange: nose, mouth, anus, sexual organs, body parts that are enlarged, or that can even detach themselves from the body and lead a secondary life, for they hide the rest of the body, as something secondary." Bakhtin, *Rabelais*, 317.

joy of being alive, of having survived intact. In his novel of the war, *Under Fire*, Henri Barbusse relates the shocking laughter and joking of a column of men returning from a stint in the trenches – laughing for sheer joy at not having been killed this time, though so many of their comrades had been. Like soldiers everywhere, Dix has expressed this very particular joy in the popular folk language of revelry, in all that is low, bodily, generative, sexual, excessive, fluid, ambivalent, and above all humorous. "When death and birth are shown in their comic aspect, scatological images in various forms nearly always accompany the gay monsters created by laughter in order to replace the terror that has been defeated."[239] At the same time Dix was also speaking to his fellow art cognoscenti about concerns that he shared with them: the *Kunstlumpdebatte* and the emergence of collage as an avant-garde art practice, using imagery of degradation, defecation, urination, and the lower body to dethrone Parisian Cubism and German Expressionism. Dix was signaling his resentment of an art market which favored French over German art, and the art of older, established figures like Kokoschka over younger men such as himself.

The work of killing, and the destruction of the landscape, of bodies, of the entire known world, created a new, separate world apart, isolated from modern, ordered civil society. The special code of the soldiers' slang defined their community, based on shared experiences and new values which were radically alien to normative civilian society, and the soldiers themselves identified the exclusion of outsiders as an important function of their argot.[240] As one soldier in the world war said, "Just the fact that the uninitiated couldn't understand the words motivated the company to adopt them."[241] The special language and grotesque humor of the soldier would have functioned in Dix's pictures as a marker of inclusion or exclusion, signaling to fellow soldiers

239 Bakhtin, *Rabelais*, 151.

240 Bakhtin also identified the function of distinct subcultural dialects as defining and communicating a group's identity, values, and "sense of shared experiences." Caryl Emerson, "The Outer Word and Inner Speech: Bakhtin, Vygotsky, and the Internalization of Language" *Critical Inquiry* 10/2 (December 1983) 254–264.

241 "Gerade der Umstand, daß ein Uneingeweihter die Wörter nicht versteht, hat die Kompagnie bewogen, sie sich anzueignen." Quoted by Imme, *Soldatensprache*, 7.

(some of whom, it must be remembered, were also fellow artists or art critics) that they were supposed to be in on the joke.

Black humor and the mockery of death and danger were an important strategy for the psychological survival of the front, a phenomenon that was already being discussed by clinical psychologists in 1920.[242] And already during the war, linguists were fascinated by *Soldatensprache*, and began trying to document it, creating lexicons of various sorts. The Germans, French, and later the Americans all produced such lexicons.[243] As the lexicographers noted, the soldier's slang was rich in humor, satire, and self-irony, and performed a hygienic function for the nerves.[244] The German soldier's slang in the First World War is characterized by several elements familiar from Bakhtin's analysis of marketplace speech and carnivalesque humor. It substitutes inanimate objects for the body's internal and external parts, or for other familiar objects such as the soldier's weapon, so that, for example, a mouth becomes a "feeding machine," and a machinegun becomes a "coffee grinder." It is fixated on the lower bodily stratum, including food and defecation. The anus for example was a site of great linguistic productivity, enriching the German soldier's lexicon with many synonyms: *Mündung* (opening, derived from *Mund* – "mouth"); *Furzkasten* [fart box]; *Pfeffermühle* (peppermill, perhaps playing on the frequent use of "pepper" in expressions for artillery and machine gun fire); and *Auspuffrohr* [exhaust pipe].[245] A striking number of their terms for body parts were derived from the world of machines: *Propeller* [arms]; *Fressmaschine*, *Kommisbrotvertilgungsmaschine*

242 W. Ludwig, "Beiträge zur Psychologie der Furcht im Kriege" in W. Stern and O. Lipmann, eds., *Beihefte zur Zeitschrift für angewandte Psychologie* 21 (1920), 125–172, cited in Alexander Watson, *Enduring the Great War. Combat, Morale, and Collapse in the German and British Armies, 1914–1918* (Cambridge: Cambridge University Press, 2008), 92.

243 Besides Imme, *Soldatensprache*, see for example Otto Maußer, *Deutsche Soldatensprache. Ihr Aufbau und ihre Probleme* (Strasbourg: Trübner, 1917); François Déchelette, *L'Argot des Poilus. Dictionnaire humoristique et philologique* (Paris: Editions de Paris, 2004 reprint, originally 1918).

244 Maußer, *Deutsche Soldatensprache*, 6–8.

245 Imme, *Soldatensprache*, 104. *Auspuffrohr* is the only expression not already found in Horn, *Die deutsche Soldatensprache* (Giessen: Töpelmann, second edition, 1905).

("gobble machine"; "army-bread-consumption-machine," both meaning "mouth").[246] Food and eating were of course central. Bread, and the margarine and marmalade given to spread on it, produced what Bakhtin terms "endless enumerations and accumulations of synonyms."[247] "Marmalade" in turn was used to signify an expansive range of other things, such as particularly sticky mud, which soldiers had to move through, dig into, live in. Trench slang often ironized the imagery of heroism and the glorification of the monarchy, as in *Heldenfett* or *Heldenbutter* [Hero's Butter] for margarine – ersatz butter – and *Kaiserwilhelmgedächtnisbutter* – "Kaiser Wilhelm Memorial Butter" (mocking the Kaiser Wilhelm Memorial Church in Berlin specifically and the monarchy generally).[248] As Bakhtin observed, "'exalted' and 'sacred' things were combined with images of the lower bodily stratum."[249] Like the hawkers in the marketplace, soldiers described their daily foodstuffs with an exaggerated praise that mixed in sarcastic references to exalted figures.[250] *Heldenkeller* [Hero's Cellar] was an ironic term for a dugout, while the common term for mortar shells was "marmalade tins" [*Marmaladeneimer*]. Substitution, slippage, and confusion were the working operations of such linguistic wit, always combining high and low, the elevated and the vulgar – much as Dix would later do in his collages. In his field notebook Dix kept his own list of trench slang terms, including *Heldenfett*, under the heading "recently overheard in the brigade," begun while he was recuperating in the field hospital near Bethenville. The terms he jotted down had to do with the field hospital itself (*Karbolenbunker*, literally "carbolic bunker" makes reference to the use of carbolic acid as a disinfectant), and with artillery fire (*befunken* means to lay down a bombardment; a large caliber shell, which howled noisily as it crossed low over no-man's-land, is a "freight train" [*Güterzug*]).[251]

246 Imme, *Soldatensprache*, 102. The absurd length of some of these terms is itself reminiscent of marketplace speech, as Bakhtin describes it.

247 Bakhtin, *Rabelais*, 306.

248 Imme, *Soldatensprache*, 197.

249 Bakhtin, *Rabelais*, 192.

250 Bakhtin, *Rabelais*, 160 f.

251 Entry marked 25 October 1915, 14–15, 17, and again later on 54–55. Otto Dix Field Notebook, Kunstmuseum Albstadt.

Although the lexicons of *Soldatensprache* published during the war were cleaned up for the audience back home, leaving out nearly all references to sex and to defecation, we can safely assume that the Great War soldier's slang drew as liberally on these resources for humor as did the argot of every other soldiery.[252] Erich Maria Remarque writes, in *All Quiet on the Western Front*, "The terror of the front sinks deep down when we turn our back upon it; we make grim, coarse jests about it, when a man dies, then we say he has nipped off his turd [literally "pinched his ass together" MM], and so we speak of everything; that keeps us from going mad; as long as we take it that way we maintain our own resistance."[253] In Dix's own, private list of terms from the soldier's argot, scatological references are quite prominent: a hospital orderly is a "chamber-pot-slinger" [*Nachtschusselschwenker*], and a machinegun – the tool of Dix's own trade – is a "runny-shit-gun" [*Dünnschißkanone*], while weak coffee is "butt-cheek-brew" [*Arschbackenbrühe*]. The humor to be found in references to latrines and everything to do with them played an important role in the representation of the Great War in Germany in the 1920s (the word "latrine" itself appears in the term *Latrinenbefehle*, literally: "latrine orders"; translation: army rumors). The infamous "latrine" scene in Remarque's *All Quiet on the Western Front*, a scene in which three soldiers combine the pleasurable pastimes of sitting on the latrines and playing skat at the same time, caused much umbrage in 1928.[254] Another novelist of the war, Ludwig Renn, recounts in his own narrative the day when, having just received the Iron Cross, he was directed by his comrades to the latrine where they matter-of-factly told him to help in the group effort to "build a tower" of shit higher than a rival company's.[255] In his wartime journal, Ernst Jünger

252 Dalzell's and Möller's lexicons richly document this phenomenon for the American soldiers in Vietnam, and the East German *Volksarmee* in their barracks, respectively.

253 "Das Grauen der Front versinkt, wenn wir ihm den Rücken kehren, wir gehen ihm mit gemeinen und grimmigen Witzen zuliebe; wenn jemand stirbt, dann heißt es, daß er den Arsch zugekniffen hat, und so reden wir über alles, das rettet uns vor dem Verrücktwerden, solange wir es so nehmen, leisten wir Widerstand." Remarque, *Im Westen nichts neues*, 142, translation in Wheen, *All Quiet*, 105.

254 Remarque, *Im Westen*, 13–14; *All Quiet*, 8–9.

255 Ludwig Renn, *Krieg* (Berlin: Aufbau, 2014, originally 1928), 149.

recorded a humorous anecdote which combined sitting in the latrine with the lucky near-miss of an artillery shell (the latrine was destroyed by a shell just as he was walking away from it, having finished his business). It was the combination of defecating and the unpredictable, arbitrary chance of life and death which gave the anecdote its force and its humor, inducing Jünger to laugh for the sheer joy of still being alive.[256] Jünger left this anecdote out of his published memoir, *Storm of Steel* [In Stahlgewittern], which is markedly free of humor. It would be too easy, however, to draw from this contrast the conclusion that, because Jünger's mirthless book conveyed a politically reactionary mythologization of the war, that Remarque's and Dix's use of the humorous grotesque therefore necessarily conveyed an antiwar sentiment. Their joyous embrace of the lower bodily stratum was simply a utilization of what is, from a sociological standpoint, a very conventional but specific form of humor, even if it was conveyed with highly unconventional formal means, in the case of Dix, and was unusual in being presented to the broadest public, rather than simply uttered in private like most ribald war stories. It is true, however, that the political reactionaries who lauded Jünger's memoir hated the grotesque humor in Dix's paintings and Remarque's novel, a subject to which I shall return in later chapters.

In Bakhtin's analysis of carnivalesque humor, the grotesque body is explicitly contrasted with the idealized classical body, and all it represents: order; rationality; cultural authority; and social hierarchy.[257] Mynona (Salomo Friedländer) articulated very clearly for his audience, which included the Berlin Dadaists, the distinction between "the disfigured, contorted … abnormal, ugly" and the "beautiful, orderly, right, proportioned."[258] It is instructive in this regard to compare Dix's *Skat Players* with a painting by Jean Metzinger, *Soldier Playing Chess* [Soldat

256 Ernst Jünger, *Kriegstagebuch 1914–1918* (Stuttgart: Klett-Cotta, 2014), entry for 6 July 1916.

257 For Peter Fuß, too, the grotesque, real body and the classical ideal are opposed terms. Peter Fuß, *Das Groteske. Ein Medium des kulturellen Wandels* (Cologne: Böhlau, 2001), 61.

258 Friedländer, "Grotesk," cited in Haakenson, "The Merely Illusory Paradise of Habits," 144 f.

jouant aux échecs] (1916) (see Figure 39), which he painted probably while on leave from the front.

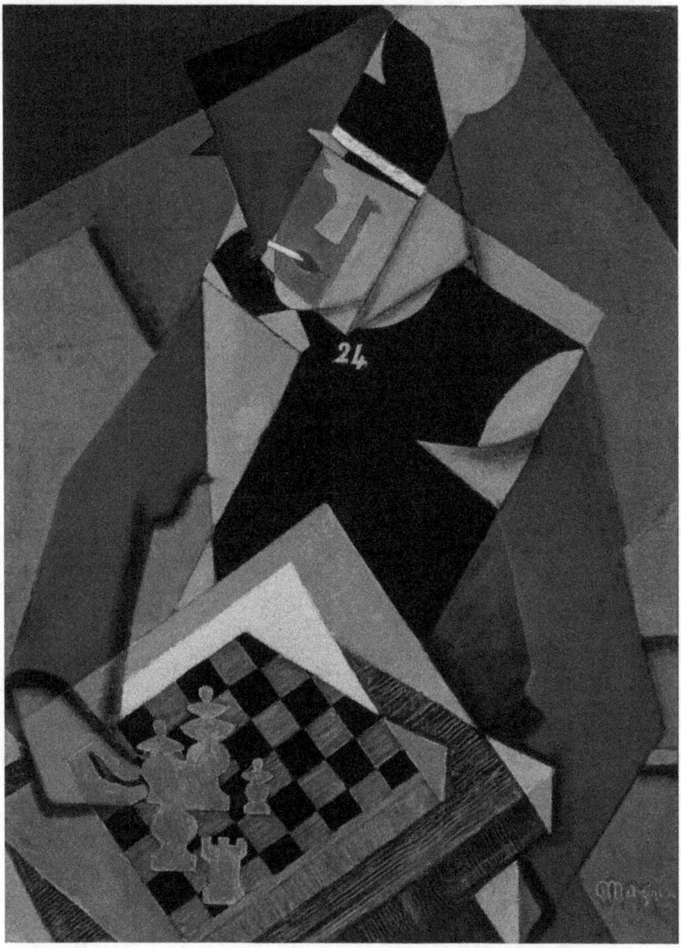

Figure 39. Jean Metzinger, *Soldier Playing Chess* [Soldat Jouant aux échecs], oil on canvas, 1915–1916, David and Alfred Smart Museum of Art, 1985.21. The David and Alfred Smart Museum of Art, The University of Chicago; Gift of John L. Strauss, Jr. in memory of his father, John L. Strauss. © Artists Rights Society (ARS), New York / ADAGP, Paris. Photo ©2018 courtesy of The David and Alfred Smart Museum of Art, The University of Chicago.

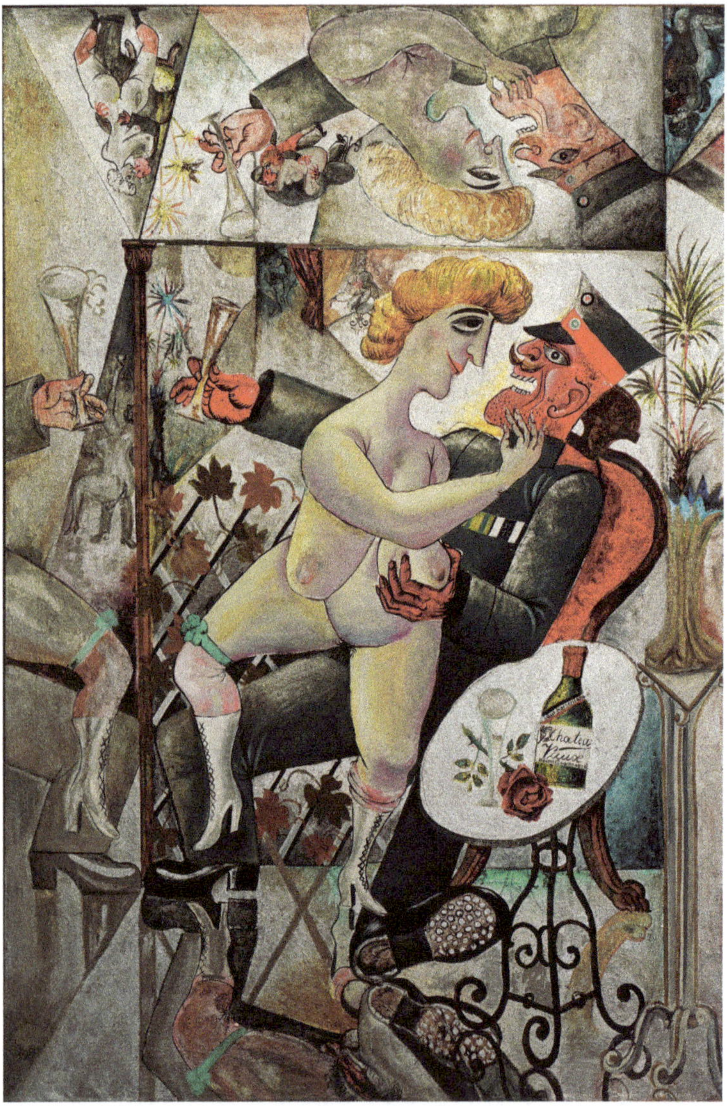

Figure 40. Otto Dix, *Memory of the Hall of Mirrors in Brussels* [Erinnerungen an die Spiegelsäle von Brüssel], oil on canvas with collage, 1920, Musee National d'Art Moderne, Centre Georges Pompidou, Paris, AM 1999–178. © Otto Dix / Artists Rights Society (ARS), New York / VG Bild-Kunst, Bonn. Photo © Georges Meguerditchian / CNAC/ MNAM / Dist. RMN-Grand Palais / Art Resource, NY, used with permission.

Soldier Playing Chess emphasizes the rationality which was so important to Metzinger's practice and that of the rest of the "Puteaux Group" of Cubists. In Metzinger's version of Cubism, the overlapping of the various planes constituting the pictorial structure suggests order (in contrast to the deliberate clutter of Dix's composition), with an underlying geometry, and a clear division of the composition according to the ratios of the Golden Mean, the very essence of classical order and beauty. At the intersection of the vertical axis of symmetry and the division between the upper third and the lower two thirds of the painting Metzinger has placed the golden number of the soldier's regiment. This cipher suggests both the rational order of mathematics and a well-ordered military organization and hierarchy. But the deepest difference is between chess and skat, between a game of intellect and rationality and a more populist game, one of chance and the subversive possibility of cheating fate and each other. As with the cartoon of Preller, who both philosophizes and eats comically excessive mounds of potatoes, the contrast between the use of the intellect and the business of the lower half of the body is meaningful.

Compare Metzinger's *Soldier Playing Chess* with another painting Dix made the same year, entitled *Memory of the Hall of Mirrors in Brussels* [Erinnerungen an die Spiegelsäle von Brüssel] (1920) (see Figure 40). This painting does not depict the contemporary postwar scene with disabled veterans marching or begging on the streets of Dresden. Rather, it is a scene from the war itself, one that is now, as per the title, being recalled to memory. In the center of the composition an officer in uniform is seated in a brothel with a prostitute on his knee. His cheeks are flushed with drink and he leers at her with an animalistic lust, grabbing her breast, while the fleshy overabundance of her body is emphasized. He is clearly enjoying himself, while she goes about her work of flattering him. The couple recalls Rembrandt's *Self-Portrait with Saskia* (1635). To return to Bakhtin once more, and to his analysis of Rabelaisian, carnivalesque humor: the woman's body, in both its fleshiness and its reproductive function, was understood as inherently more grotesque and more subversive than the male body, which by implication was taken to be closer to the rational, the ordered, and to polite culture. The heavy, hanging breasts; swollen belly; projecting hips and buttocks, are all excessive. Bakhtin speaks of "Woman" as an entity: "She is the inexhaustible vessel of conception, which dooms all that is old and terminated ... she lifts her skirts and shows the parts through which everything passes (the underworld, the grave) and from which everything issues forth."[259] Dix seems to have regarded the female body in similar ways.

But I want to emphasize here the special meaning that this painting would have had for Dix's fellow veterans, and the terms with which it would have elicited not only their memories, but also their sense of communal bonds, and the special role that a brothel scene would have played in the evocation of community and memory. Next to the couple is depicted a round table that once again recalls a Cubist still life with its champagne bottle (the label on the bottle, "Chateau Vause, Reims (Champagne)," is clearly legible, and makes unmistakable reference to a theater of the war). The rest of the painting also recalls – or better, satirizes – the compositional devices of Cubism, with its pattern of lozenges and its fracturing and fragmentation of the central motif, here accomplished through the mirrored surfaces of the walls, ceiling, and even floor of this brothel. Or rather, some of the repetitions of the central motif are reflections of the couple, while others turn out to be, upon closer inspection, other couples in various stages of their commercialized sexual transactions. Such "Mirrored Salons" were a popular feature of posh German officer's brothels throughout occupied Belgium, where the wine and liquor flowed freely; when the private bedrooms were all taken, the officers and the ladies carried out their business on the stairs and in the hallways. They were indeed the object of a vivid nostalgia among former officers for years after the war.[260] Such reminiscences – the ribald stories traded between veterans to reinforce the bonds of this special community, are in fact the subject and function of the painting, alongside the mockery of a specifically French modernism. War stories in general serve, among other functions, to assert a difference between those, including the teller of the

259 Bakhtin, *Rabelais*, 240 f.
260 Wandt, *Etappe Gent*, 162.

tale, who were there, who experienced it first-hand, and those who did not. The purpose of such stories is, as one veteran has remarked, "not to enlighten but to exclude; its message is not its content but putting the listener in his place. I suffered, I was there. You were not. Only those facts matter. Everything else is beyond words to tell."[261] And the kind of story represented here in particular is what the linguist and ethnologist Scott Kiesling has called the "fuck story," the kind of speech act designed to establish and perform male heterosexuality. Kiesling stresses the role such stories play in the formation and maintenance of group cohesion.[262] This is a story of the type recounted by soldiers to constitute and perform an identity of aggressive, heterosexual male subjugation of the vanquished population and of the years spent outside of the conventions of normative civil society.[263] The aggression implied by the scenario, the sexual exploitation of the female population as an integral part of military conquest and occupation, is not denied, but is simply made into a dirty joke, degrading not only the woman, but also Cubist painting and that other Hall of Mirrors, in Versailles, where momentous episodes of German history unfolded.

As with the *Skat Players*, the final emphasis on the lower bodily stratum, the genitalia, is only discovered after some close looking. This is part of the witty but dirty joke of both this painting and the *Skat Players*, which like any ribald joke elicits laughter through that special combination of expectation and surprise, the withholding and the revealing, the

261 Cited by Joanna Bourke, "Introduction 'Remembering' War," *Journal of Contemporary History* 39/4 (Oct. 2004), 473–485, here p. 477.

262 Scott F. Kiesling "Playing the Straight Man: Displaying and Maintaining Male Heterosexuality in Discourse," in Kathryn Campbell-Kibler, Robert J. Podesva, Sarah J. Roberts, *et al.*, eds., *Language and Sexuality. Contesting Meaning in Theory and Practice* (Stanford, CA: CSLI Publications, 2002), 249–267, here p. 256.

263 Joshua Goldstein summarizes arguments about the relationship between the social disruption of normal life and the suspension of conventional mores in the army during wartime, promiscuous sexuality, and aggression. Joshua Goldstein, *War and Gender: How Gender Shapes the War System and Vice Versa* (Cambridge: Cambridge University Press, 2001), 333–336.

elaborately formal device and the lower bodily stratum (think of dirty limericks). And what soldier's repertoire of carnivalesque humor would have lacked such dirty jokes? Here it is the mirrored floor which reveals quite graphically the woman's vagina, where the viewer discovers it at the very bottom edge of the canvas, only after having failed to find it where he expected to see it. Heightened with red, it is immediately juxtaposed with the hobnailed sole of the German's boot, the sign of his function as oppressor and military occupier. Dix has displaced the most telling details to the margin, as he very often did. The arrangement on the tabletop – champagne bottle, red rose, and champagne glass, feints with a more sentimental story in the conventional language of still life painting. But the joke at the heart of the painting – displaced to the lower edge of the picture – exposes the real relationship between the occupier and his conquest.[264]

The pornographic wound

And this brings us, through an unexpected association, to another motif in Dix's pictures of the war. To draw on Bakhtin once more, the classical ideal of the body is firmly outlined, uninterrupted, and hides away all orifices; the inside of the body is kept well out of sight, and its surface is smooth and without blemish. The humor of the grotesque body, by contrast, consists of exaggerated bulges and protrusions (including gargantuan breasts and buttocks of women), and the revelation of the inside of the body through orifices – and through wounds.[265] At the same time

264 Dora Apel addresses the relationship of these images to military occupation and aggression, and is one of the few art historians who discusses with specificity the politics of gendered representations of soldiers and prostitutes in Dix's works, but she overlooks the Rabelaisian humor at the heart of his Dadaist depictions of war invalids or prostitutes. Apel, "'Heroes' and 'Whores'.

265 Bakhtin, *Rabelais*, 318.

that Dix was making his large Dadaist collages for public exhibition, he was also painting watercolors for private collectors. These were mostly sexual in content: pictures of prostitutes, sailors with prostitutes, circus performers, and other disreputable types. These watercolors often crossed the line into pornography, as the *Memory of the Hall of Mirrors* finally reveals itself to do, as well. But occasionally Dix took another subject, the wounded veteran with a disfigured face. Whereas the facial wounds in the *Skat Players* are either covered, with patches for example, or with silver foil, or downplayed – at least in contrast to what we are about to see, in the more private watercolors they are fully exposed for the viewer to stare at. In the watercolor *War Wounded* [Kriegsverletzter] (1922) (see Figure 41), there is an invitation to look closely at the opening that must normally remain hidden, out of sight.[266] Whereas the rest of this painting is done in thin, transparent washes carefully contained by pen lines, the uneven, messy edges of the wound are lavishly built up with thick, impasto watercolor paint. In contrast to the rest of the picture, the richness of the color and texture, the formless, viscous fluidity of the thick pigment here insists on its own materiality to the point that it threatens to occlude its function as representation, just as the inchoate mass of the wounds, without clear outline or tonal modeling, defy the outlines of conventional figure representation.

266 Bernhard Maaz, "Otto Dix' 'Kriegsverletzter.' Zu einer Neuerwerbung des Dresdner Kupferstich-Kabinetts," in Dalbajewa, Fleischer, and Peters, eds., *Der Krieg*, 96.

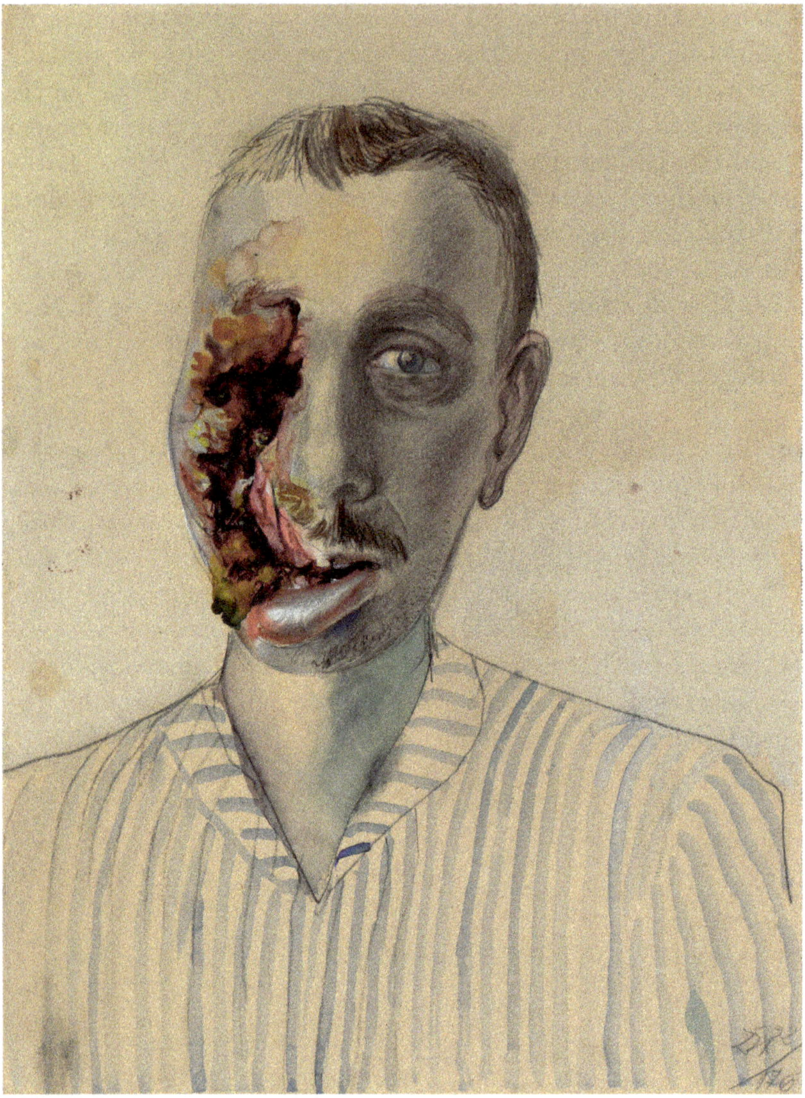

Figure 41. Otto Dix, *War Wounded* [Kriegsverletzter], watercolor and pencil, 1922, Kupferstich-Kabinett, Dresden, C 2014–64. © Otto Dix / Artists Rights Society (ARS), New York / VG Bild-Kunst, Bonn. Photo © Kupferstich-Kabinett, Staatliche Kunstsammlungen, Dresden / Herbert Boswank, used with permission.

In public, men would indeed wear patches or masks of various sorts to cover up these awful wounds, which were unsightly in the truest sense of the word – they could not be exposed to public sight. After the war, soldiers who had suffered such facial wounds were hidden away in hospitals and sanitaria, unable to confront a public that was unprepared to look at them. But there was also a strong but contradictory impulse to simultaneously looks closely and look away. On the one hand, a small industry sprang up for the production of masks to hide facial wounds certain to evoke revulsion in others. Most of these were clumsy and made of rubber, but some were made by professional sculptors of thin copper plate and painted to look as naturalistic as possible, an uncanny doubling of natural faces with their artificial simulacra.[267] These "portrait masks … worked to conceal the magnitude of horror," and were, "an appropriate metaphor for the unutterable," in the words of Claudine Mitchell.[268] At the same time, the most horrible facial wounds were represented in wax and plaster models, originally painted to be more life-like, and exhibited to the public in the Musée du Val-de-Grâce, Paris, which opened in 1917. However, these models were part of what Amy Lyford has identified as a larger "therapeutic narrative," displaying the medical profession's success at reconstructive surgery.[269] It was at this hospital that the future Surrealists André Breton and Louis

267 The producers of these metal masks, made as illusionistic as possible, were the British sculptor Francis Derwent Wood (who went on to produce the *Machine Gun Corps Memorial* in London and a representation of the legendary "Crucified Canadian") working in London, and the American sculptor Anna Coleman Ladd, working in Paris, with several assistants, mostly women. Caroline Alexander, "Faces of War," *Smithsonian Magazine* (February 2007). See also David M. Lubin, "Masks, Mutilation, and Modernity: Anna Coleman Ladd and the First World War," *Archives of American Art Journal* 47/3–4 (2008), 4–15.

268 Claudine Mitchell, "Facing horror: women's work, sculptural practice and the Great War," in Valerie Mainz and Griselda Pollack, eds., *Work and the Image, Volume II: Work in Modern Times: Visual Mediations and Social Processes* (Burlington: Ashgate, 2000), 33–55, here p. 45.

269 Amy Lyford, *Surrealist Masculinities. Gender Anxiety and the Aesthetics of Post-World War I Reconstruction in France* (Berkeley: University of California Press, 2007), 48–54. See also Sophie Delaporte, *Les Guelles Cassés. Les blesées de la face de la Grande Guerre* (Paris: Éditions Noêsis, 1996).

Aragon met, while they were both working as physicians in training, and Lyford speculates that it was here that they "started to see as surrealists."[270] But Otto Dix's drawings and watercolors of men's hideously disfigured faces do not engage in any such dialectic of looking and looking away, or even surrealist sublimation; he forthrightly invites the viewer to look and look closely. The sculptors who fabricated "portrait masks" for the victims of facial wounds intended to help them regain their identity, often figured as specifically masculine, as husbands and as successful reentrants into the workforce. The goal of the masks was to enable the wearer to escape notice, to walk the street without being seen or looked at.[271] But Dix invites us to stare directly, and to satiate if possible our horrified fascination.

The wounds in their richly painted detail threaten to occlude the men's identities, putting them in direct and dramatic tension with the specificity of what are at another level portraits, rendered by an artist who was a gifted and successful portraitist. The gaping wounds and irregular, lumpy flesh become the parallel of the vagina exposed in *Memory of the Hall of Mirrors*. They are grotesque – although now without much humor – because they violate the idealized, sculptural surface of the body, opening the interior of the body outward. Perhaps this is the reason why Dix once depicted a veteran with a mutilated face alongside a prostitute, *Prostitute and War Wounded* [Dirne und Kriegskrüppel] (1923).[272] This picture, which was commissioned by John Heartfield for publication in *Die Pleite*, is often interpreted as Dix's indictment of the parallel exploitation of men, as soldiers, and women, as prostitutes.[273] But I see little expression of solidarity in either Dix's representations of war invalids or of prostitutes (by contrast, what Heartfield had asked for was a picture of hungry, striking workers contrasted with fat bourgeoisie, or a strike broken up by the

270 Lyford, *Surrealist Masculinities*, 54.

271 Mitchell, "Facing horror," 44 f.

272 Published in *Die Pleite*, a Berlin Dada-aligned journal with a pronounced communist orientation, under the title *Two Victims of Capitalism* (which title it was given by the editors, George Grosz and John Heartfield), *Die Pleite* 2/7 (July 1923), 24.

273 See for example Maria Tatar, *Lustmord: Sexual Murder in Weimar Germany* (Princeton, NJ: Princeton University Press, 1993), 81.

army or fascists).[274] This double portrait points instead to one of the main complaints of those with facial wounds; that the sight of their hideously wounded faces provokes revulsion in women in particular, thus damaging still further their own masculinity.[275]

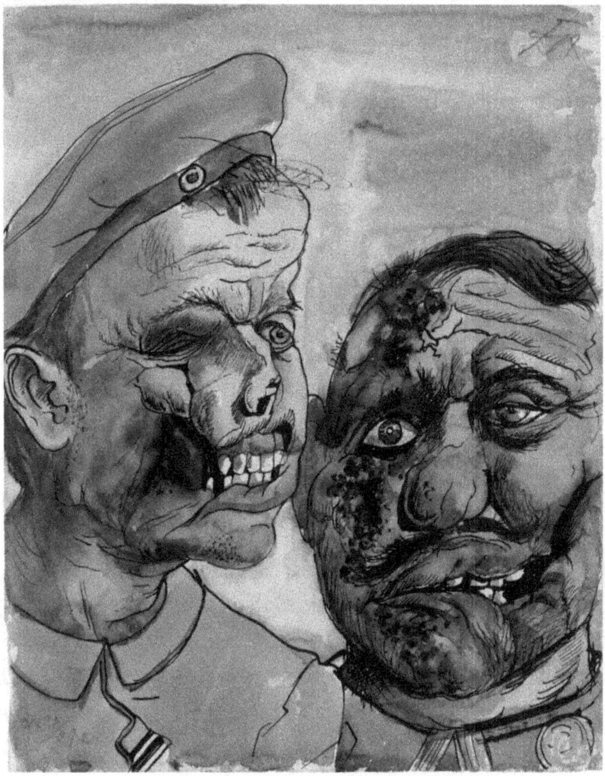

Figure 42. Otto Dix, *Memory of the Glory Days* [Erinnerung an die Grosse Zeit], pen, ink and watercolor, 1923, Kupferstich-Kabinett, Dresden C 1969–83. © Otto Dix / Artists Rights Society (ARS), New York / VG Bild-Kunst, Bonn. Digital file: author's own scan.

274 Letter from John Heartfield to Dix, on Malki Verlag letterhead (9 June 1923), Deutsches Kunstarchiv, Germanisches Nationalmuseum, Nuremberg, I, B 12 t.

275 One grateful recipient of Ladd's masks wrote a letter of thanks to her, in which he said, "The woman I love no longer finds me repulsive, as she has a right to do." Cited in Alexander, "Faces of War."

In a second double portrait, this time of two soldiers in uniform, the subjects display their wounds along with their medals; their wounds recall the carnivalesque fixation on openings and orifices, the exuberant violation of classicism's enclosed, smooth bodies and idealized features. Significantly, the watercolor is entitled *Memory of the Glory Days* [Erinnerung an die Grosse Zeit] (1923) (see Figure 42), suggesting not only the ironic mockery of nostalgia for the war, but also his ongoing preoccupation with remembrance and identity as a veteran within a community of veterans. As we have seen, memory is also bound to a preoccupation with the sexual adventures (read: exploitation of the female populations in occupied towns) of the war. Throughout the large body of watercolors Dix produced – and sold – in 1922 and into 1923, so many of which feature prostitutes, the bodies of women are exaggerated, their ample breasts and buttocks pushed to the point of caricature.[276] Their difference is emphasized and made comical – their difference from the bodies of men (often Dix's own, well-dressed and self-confident), their difference from the classical ideal, sometimes from the bodies of Europeans, as in *Dutch East India*, a picture of a white sailor and a dark-skinned prostitute.[277] There were watercolors of female sadists with their torture chambers where women's bodies were pulled at and inverted. Women's bodies are violated even more aggressively in the pictures of sex murders, or *Lustmord*, a topic which is too complex to discuss at length here, but which relies on a similar shocking, carnivalesque humor as the collages of war invalids.[278] There were also watercolors that mocked the naked bodies of men who were obviously homosexuals, as in *The God of Hair Dressers* [Der Gott der Friseure] (1922) (see Figure 43).[279]

276 James A. van Dyke, *On the Grotesque Body in a Double-Sided Drawing by Otto Dix*, in Bettina Mathias, Eliza Garrison, and James A. van Dyke, eds, *Approaches to the Body in Early Twentieth-Century German and Austrian Art* (Hanover: University Press of New England, 2015), pp. 61–77.

277 Reproduced in Suse Pfäffle, *Otto Dix. Werkverzeichnis der Aquarelle und Gouachen* (Stuttgart: Hatje, 1991), 166.

278 Eva Karcher, *Eros und Tod im Werk von Otto Dix* (Munster: Lit, 1984), 51–55.

279 Änne Söll, "'An die Schönheit' – Selbst, Männlichkeit und Moderne in Otto Dix Selbstbildnis von 1922" in Annette Geiger, ed., *Der Schöne Körper: Mode und Kosmetik in Kunst und Gesellschaft* (Cologne: Böhlau, 2008), 149–166.

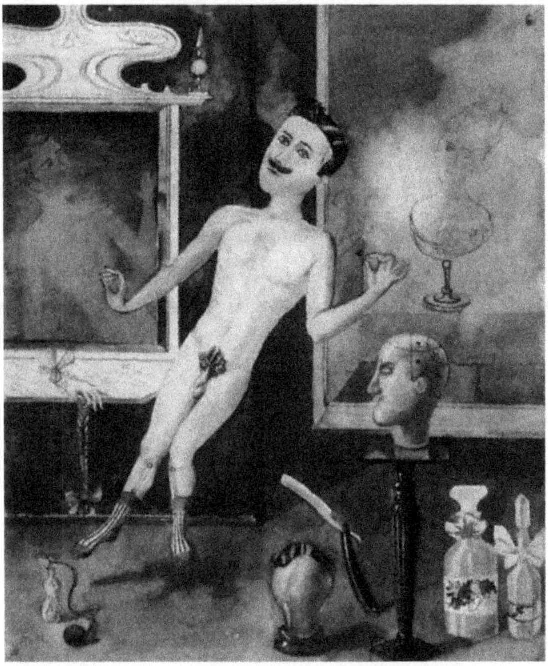

Figure 43. Otto Dix, *The God of the Hair Dressers* [Der Gott der Friseure], pencil and watercolor, 1922, Buchheim Museum der Phantasie, Bernried am Starnberger See. © Otto Dix / Artists Rights Society (ARS), New York / VG Bild-Kunst, Bonn. Digital file: author's own scan.

The misogyny and homophobia of these pictures fairly leaps off the page, and cannot be explained away as attempts empathize with the marginalized of German society, or as attempts to dismantle the integrity of the bourgeois art object.[280] Much more plausible is the possibility that they expressed what has been termed the "consensus of homophobia" that characterized German society, with continuity from the Wilhelmine era, through the Weimar Republic, and into the Third Reich.[281] At the center of the entire

280 Olaf Peters, *Otto Dix*. For a more critical view of the prevalence of the theme of sex murders in German art in the 1920s, see Tatar, *Lustmord*.

281 Susanne zur Nieden, "Homophobie und Staatsräson," in Susanne zur Nieden, ed., *Homosexualität und Staatsräson. Männlichkeit, Homophobie und Politik in*

complex of linked themes, worked over repeatedly in the watercolors and also in large paintings, is the image of Dix himself – as sex murderer, as impeccably dressed dandy, as artist with nude model and as rake with prostitutes. In *Me in Brussels*, he is the soldier, leering aggressively at the exaggerated behind of a prostitute on the street. In none of them is he himself the object of laughter. The object of laughter is either the woman, or men whose masculinity and sexual potency is either exaggerated to the point that it becomes carnivalesque (the sailors), or is made the direct object of derisive laughter, as drunken officers, homosexuals or as war invalids.

Deutschland 1900–1945 (Frankfurt: Campus, 2005), 17–51. See also Daniel Morat, "Kalte Männlichkeit? Weimarer Verhaltenslehren im Spannungsfeld von Emotionen- und Geschlechtergeschichte," in Manuel Borutta and Nina Verheyen, eds., *Die Präsenz der Gefühle. Männlichkeit und Emotion im 19. und 20. Jahrhundert* (Bielefeld: Transcript, 2010), 153–177.

CHAPTER 3

Dix in Düsseldorf: The Scandal of *The Trench* and Business with Karl Nierendorf During the Inflation Years

Beginning as early as 1920, while still in Dresden, Dix started working on a large-scale, ambitious picture of a grizzly scene of industrialized death in the trenches: *The Trench* [Schützengraben] (1920–1923, lost, presumed destroyed) (see Figure 2 and detail, Figure 44).

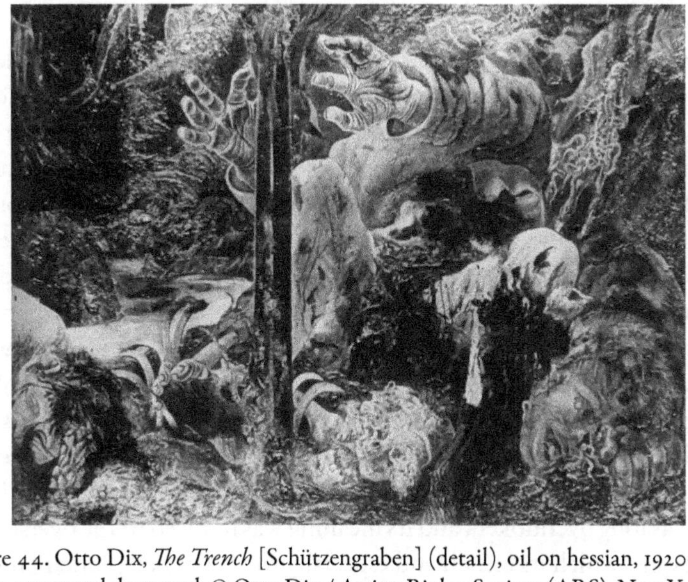

Figure 44. Otto Dix, *The Trench* [Schützengraben] (detail), oil on hessian, 1920–1923, lost, presumed destroyed. © Otto Dix / Artists Rights Society (ARS), New York / VG Bild-Kunst, Bonn. Digital file: author's own scan.

This painting would prove to be a turning point in Dix's career, and especially in his public reputation – and it was undoubtedly intended as such. The work depicted, in carefully painted and grisly detail, the shattered and confused remnants of a trench after an artillery barrage. At 2.27 x 2.50 meters, it was an ambitiously scaled work, comparable to the history paintings of an earlier century. However, rather than depict a heroic armed confrontation or even a heroic death, as was the norm for history painting since the eighteenth century, Dix depicted a grotesque carnage of bodies torn apart, brains and intestines spilling out into the muck and mud of the trench itself. It showed grotesque depictions of gaping wounds, bodies flung into undignified positions, and the merging of shapeless human viscera with formless mud and effluent. There are both fresh corpses and older ones, already in an advanced state of decay, indicating that the shelling of the trench has plowed up bodies which were already buried here after an earlier battle, months before. When the painting was finished, in 1923, it was positioned by the artist's new dealer and promoter, Karl Nierendorf, as a public statement worthy of prominent display in a public museum, and in fact he succeeded in the remarkable feat of convincing the director of the Wallraf-Richartz museum in Cologne, Hans-Friedrich Secker, to purchase and display it. Secker was just completing a reorganization of the museum, and he purchased the monumental picture by Dix to complete in dramatic fashion the installation of the contemporary art collection. The critics were sharply divided over its quality and by its deliberately provocative representation of the war, at a time when public opinion about the war itself was still in dynamic flux. In particular, people who were busily salvaging the culture of German militarism from the disrepute into which it had fallen, who were mythologizing the war experience and promoting the "stab-in-the-back legend," hated it. A decade later, when the Nazis came to power, they still resented the provocation of this painting, exhibiting it as "Degenerate Art" and accusing the painter of having "sabotaged the nation's fighting spirit." Then it disappeared, presumably destroyed, never to be seen again. As a direct result, the painting's importance for Dix's career was long overlooked, and its meaning was reduced to the oversimplified message which its critics, and especially the Nazis had pinned on it: as simple anti-war propaganda.

As the importance of Dix's work for the cultural history of the Weimar Republic continued to grow, on both sides of the Cold War divide, this lost painting was viewed – when remembered at all – as a transitional work, a precursor to the more famous triptych on the subject of the war, painted in 1928–1932 (which will be the subject of Chapter 5). To a great extent, the research done on this painting by Denis Crockett, especially on the critical debate that raged around it in 1923 and 1924, is responsible for our current understanding of its importance in Dix's career and in the public discourse of the Weimar Republic.[282] But the painting continues to be presented primarily as evidence of the consistency of Dix's attitudes about the war, which are usually understood to be wholly negative and critical. By contrast, in this chapter I will examine the painting (based on photographs and eyewitness accounts), the history of its making and, especially, its promotion and exhibition by Nierendorf, and the record of its stormy reception in the 1920s, as evidence of both the artist's evolving rather than static attitudes about the war experience and ideas about how to convey that experience, and of the complicated and fluid patterns of the wider public discussion about the war and its meaning. In both this and the next chapter I will also seek to reintegrate *The Trench* into the narrative of Dix's other artworks about the war, especially his well-known portfolio of etchings, simply titled *War*, which he started working on while the controversy around this painting was still playing out in public. I will also highlight the productive and largely successful – but often very contentious – relationship between Dix and Nierendorf, a relationship which both enabled Dix's work on the war and was often tested by it. I will highlight the collaboration between the artist and his dealer in part because it is central to the story I want to tell about the relationship between the artist's expressions about the war and the wider German public debate about that war, and not least of all because it was Nierendorf who actively positioned the painting as part of the anti-war movement, such as it was in the mid 1920s, and so contributed to its reception and durable reputation as an anti-war document. I will argue here that the actual message of *The*

282 Dennis Crockett, "The Most Famous Painting of the 'Golden Twenties'?," *Art Journal* 51/1 (Spring 1992), 72–80. See also Olaf Peters, *Neue Sachlichkeit und Nationalsozialismus. Afirmation und Kritik 1931–1947* (Berlin: Reimer, 1998), 194–205, and Dietrich Schubert, "Die Verfolgung des Gemäldes *Schützengraben* (1923) von Otto Dix," in Rolf Kloepfer and Burckhard Dücker, eds., *Kritik und Geschichte der Intoleranz* (Heidelberg: Syncron, 2000), 351–370.

Trench was not pacifism or condemnation, but the representation of the actual experience of the war, made visible to the entire public, but expressed in the particular idiom of soldier: grotesque realism, with its black, gallows humor. For the returned soldier in 1923, the solemnity and pathos of public memorial was just as false as the heroic battle paintings of the nineteenth century. But what *The Trench* accomplished by contrast was to represent the soldier's experience – which was horrible and grizzly – in the soldier's own idiom. That idiom used the humor of irony, exaggeration, and caricature, of the metamorphic and the lower bodily stratum, to acknowledge the painful realities of the suffering body while at the same time warding off the fear that the sight of such suffering would otherwise inspire.

Düsseldorf

Dix brought this unfinished painting with him when he moved to Düsseldorf in 1921, where he continued to work on it until 1923. Dix moved to Düsseldorf at the instigation of his friend the avant-gardist Conrad Felixmüller. The latter opened several possibilities to Dix, not all of which he seized. He introduced Dix to the art patron and gallerist Johanna Ey (affectionately called "Mutter Ey," because she looked after her young artists in a matronly way), who financed Dix's move to the Rhineland and financed his career there, introducing him in turn to a circle of collectors. Felixmüller also introduced Dix to a circle of avant-garde artists, who became Das Junge Rheinland. He became a master student at the Düsseldorf Art Academy [Kunstakademie Düsseldorf], and as such enjoyed the use of a studio in the academy. Finally, Felixmüller suggested to Dix that the latter join the Communist Party. Famously, the proletariat artist supposedly told Felixmüller that he'd rather spend the money on visits to the brothel than party dues. The story may be apocryphal, but it's not disputed that Dix visited brothels often, and that he never joined the party.

After moving to Düsseldorf, in 1921, Dix met the urologist Hans Koch, who became a patron, and who had Dix paint his portrait. Dix and Koch's wife Martha began an affair, while Koch himself was in turn having an affair with Martha's sister Maria. Maria was having another affair at the same time, with the art dealer Karl Nierendorf, and this is probably how Dix came to know Nierendorf. By 1922 this complicated set of relationships resolved itself: Martha divorced her husband and married Dix; the same year they moved to Düsseldorf together and had their first of three children; meanwhile, Martha's sister ended her relationship with Nierendorf and married Hans Koch. Relations between the newlywed Dixs and Koch and his new wife Maria seemingly remained warm. And finally, Nierendorf became Dix's exclusive dealer, while the artist ended his business relationship with Johanna Ey.[283]

Nierendorf was immediately taken by Dix's work, and suggested an exclusive contract; Dix hesitated at first, but eventually agreed to such an arrangement.[284] The contract stipulated that Nierendorf would have no say about the formal elements of the work – which did not stop him from pointing out that people did not want to buy works with a lot of negative space that seemed too, "unfinished, sketch-like."[285] Nierendorf was an enthusiastic supporter of Dix and his work, as one can see from his letters to the artist in 1922, as he was still negotiating an exclusive contract. The art dealer was traveling the length and breadth of Germany, visiting potential collectors in their homes and showing them Dix's works, finding some success in selling them, especially watercolors, to those collectors with whom he had some sway.[286] In October, the Galerie Nierendorf held its first exhibition of Dix's work, followed by another in January of the next year. Although he represented important contemporary artists

283 Anja Walter-Ris, *Die Geschichte der Galerie Nierendorf. Kunstleidenschaft im Dienst der Moderne. Berlin / New York 1920–1995* (Freie Universität Berlin, dissertation, 1999).

284 Letter from Nierendorf to Dix, 14 April 1922, and later, undated letters from the same year, Deutsches Kunstarchiv, Germanisches Nationalmuseum, Nuremberg, Otto Dix archive (hereafter DKA), I, C 524a.

285 Letter to Dix from Nierendorf, Frankfurt, undated but probably late June or early July 1922. Nierendorf was still traveling, showing Dix's work to potential collectors in their homes; he reported in the same letter that he had already sold the works *Alte Frauen, Matrose und Mädchen, Am Morgen*, and *Artistin*.

286 Letters from Nierendorf to Dix from 1922, DKA, I, C 524a.

working in Germany, including Vassily Kandinsky and George Grosz, Nierendorf's close working relationship with, even devotion to Dix was famous in these circles, earning him the sobriquet "Nierendix." His efforts to promote Dix's work met at first with resistance. Collectors told him frankly that they could never hang Dix's works in their living rooms. And yet Nierendorf quickly built a small but faithful circle of collectors, which soon included several museum directors.[287] Despite all of these efforts, it is clear from Nierendorf's letters to Dix that the art dealer had to constantly defend himself against his artist's complaints, suspicions, jealousies, and accusations that Nierendorf was not doing enough to further his career.

By late 1923, Nierendorf was able to negotiate the purchase of *The Trench* by the Wallraf-Richartz Museum in Cologne under the direction of Hans Secker, who wrote to Dix in late October of 1923 to congratulate not only the artist, but also himself, writing that, "It took fighting tooth and nail to incorporate your war picture into the Wallraf-Richartz museum"[288] It is difficult to know if the opposition Secker faced was directed more against the nature of the painting, or against the expense and the difficulty of paying for it – or the combination of the two. Dix wrote from Berlin to his wife Martha in Düsseldorf on 23 October to give her the news, and in the same breath to inform her that their trip to Sicily was now "assured."[289] The price agreed on between Nierendorf and Secker was 10,000 marks, at a time when paying for anything of significant value in Germany was extraordinarily difficult, and the financing of the purchase was a complex affair. Secker could only pay for the painting by selling works from the museums' collection to Nierendorf in exchange, for the value of 10,000 Goldmarks. Nierendorf did not receive any actual cash for the picture, and in order to pay Dix for it he had to ask a bank to extend a line of credit to the artist; here his training as a banker was useful.[290] When Secker was forced by the negative reaction to the painting's content and

287 Undated letter from Nierendorf to Dix, 1922, DKA, I, C 524a.

288 "Es ist nicht ohne Hängen und Würgen gelungen, Ihr Kriegsbild dem museum Wallraf-Richartz einzuverleiben." Letter from Hans Secker to Dix, 31 October 1923, DKA, I, B 12 r.

289 Letter from Dix to Martha, *Otto Dix, Briefe*, 76.

290 Letter from Nierendorf to Dix, 29 December 1923, DKA, I C 524 d.

style to return it to Nierendorf, the dealer had to reimburse various parties, including in some instances the artists of the other works for the value of their paintings, while continuing to pay interest on the credit extended to Dix by the bank. This complicated arrangement was necessitated by the ever-worsening inflation in Germany, and was itself to be the source of conflict between Dix and Nierendorf for years to come, even after the painting was returned.[291]

The Trench was in many ways a striking departure from the Dadaist collages of the period 1920–1921. It was large – of a size clearly intended for public display – and carried out in the traditional medium of oil on canvas, a painting ready for a museum's walls. It contained no collaged elements, no provocative challenge to the primacy of the medium of the Flemish and Dutch Masters and the German Renaissance. Nor did it utilize the self-consciously modernist visual vocabulary of Expressionism (as had *Moon Woman*, Figure 29, for example), which had since fallen out of fashion, but instead displayed the return to conventional, representational proportions, spatial relations, and local color that would soon enough be labeled "*Neue Sachlichkeit*" [New Objectivity]. And in contrast to the Dadaist pictures, which represented the present, the aftermath of the lost war with its social disruptions, its crippled beggars in uniform on the contemporary streets of Dresden and Berlin, *The Trench* returns to the war itself, which now existed only in memory. But soldiers' memories were increasingly the occasion of conflicts over the war's meaning.

Yet for all of these differences, there were some elements of *The Trench* which were carried over from the immediately preceding artworks. In many ways, Otto Dix continued in his efforts to identify and speak to his fellow former soldiers through the humorously grotesque, that is, through a visual equivalent of the soldier's earthy, vulgar, anti-hierarchical language which had functioned as an antidote to the rigid military discipline, phony heroism,

291 "Im Kriegsbild stecken für mich 4200.-M und die irrsinnigen Bankzinsen von einem Jahr. Dazu muss ich tausende aufbringen, um der Stadt Köln die ausgewählten Werke zu bezahlen, die ich als Gegenleistung für die Bankzahlung liefern muss. Otto Mueller verlangt z. B. 2000 –M für das Bild, das Secker gekauft hat und ich muss es beschaffen, während ich von dem Geld der Stadt keinen Pfennig in die Finger bekomme. Es wurde direkt an die Bank bezahlt und ich schulde aus der Affaire jetzt noch ausserdem 2500. – M dem Bankhaus Seligmann." Letter from Nierendorf to Dix, 1 April 1925, DKA I, C, 524 g.

and ever-present fear of death which was the soldier's lot. In painting, the anti-hierarchical is translated into an anti-classical aesthetic, while the earthy and the vulgar become the inclusion of the repulsive details of wounds and putrefaction pushed to the point of caricature and obscenity. As we shall see, the public conflict over the painting was polarized around just this visual vocabulary of the humorous grotesque.

To begin with, the color of *The Trench* was evidently lurid to the point of bad taste. Although we only have black and white photographs of it, critics found it necessary to comment on the lurid color often, and on the way it apparently highlighted to sickening effect the spilled brains and splayed bowels of dead soldiers. Wrote art critic Alfred Salmony, "The pool of phosphor forms the center of the color composition. Intestines, flesh and blood are hanging everywhere."[292] The longer one looked, the more details and fragments of heads, bodies, and organs emerged from the formless, glistening mud and ooze. Fritz Löffler wrote, "The painterly application of *The Trench* did not prevent Dix from losing himself in the most loving way in the details of the depicted horrors."[293] And whereas it had been an important part of the tradition of history painting that the lifeless body of the hero be presented in such a way as to resemble a Greek sculpture – lithe, perfectly proportioned, often marble-white (for example in Gavin Hamilton's *Achilles Mourning the Death of Petroclus*), as though transformed by death into the classical ideal, the bodies in *The Trench* are distorted and disfigured almost beyond recognition. The only corpse visible in its entirety, maintaining more or less the complete contour of a body, is the one skewered on the twisted and exposed iron beams, and this corpse in particular seems to mock the tradition of the hero's body in repose that is at the heart of the language of history painting.[294]

292 "Die Phosphorpfütze bildet den Farbmittelpunkt. Gedärm, Fleisch und Blut hängen umher." Alfred Salmony, "Die neue Galerie des 17. Bis 20. Jahrhunderts im Museum Wallraf-Richartz in Köln," *Der Cicerone*, 16/1, 6–11.

293 "Der malerische Vortrag im *Schützengraben* hat Dix aber nicht gehindert, sich in liebesvollster Weise in die Details der geschilderten Schrecklichkeiten zu versenken." Löffler, *Otto Dix und der Krieg*, 21.

294 The beams were repurposed railway rails used as supports for the concrete roofs of dugouts buried underground, as described in Ludwig Renn, *Krieg*, 152.

Death triumphs over all, in a theme that suggests the diablerie of early modern German carnivalesque imagery. Behind this skewered corpse held aloft above the lip of the trench is a suggestion of a landscape, with a distant and featureless no-man's-land rendered in lighter tonalities. Apparently a rainbow was visible in the sky, but its arc can be discerned only with difficulty in the black and white reproductions we have. Besides the obvious irony, it would have suggested an analogy between the "storm" of the bombardment and an actual thunderstorm, in keeping with Dix's feeling that the war was like a "natural phenomenon" [*Naturereignis*]. One reviewer described, "the play of colors, most clearly there where the sulfurous green and yellow in the puddles at the bottom of the trench are taken up again, transformed, in the rainbow above."[295] Another wrote, "Like a smile from Hell, a poisonous sulfur-yellow pool glints in the depths [and above,] a pale, ironic rainbow, the Biblical declaration of peace."[296]

The sides of the trenches have collapsed, stove in by the artillery barrage, and it appears almost as if a vitrine had been filled up with the dregs of the battlefield. Alfred Salmony emphasized the randomly piled details with a Rabelaisian list: "Shredded materiel is mixed up with shredded bodies, shivered wooden posts, bent iron beams, barbed wire. Gasmasks and wristwatches are left intact."[297] Closer examination reveals that we are ourselves situated within the trench, the bottom of which is indicated by a puddle that was, apparently, a sickly yellow, identified (by those critics, like Salmony, who shared Dix's battlefield experience) as the condensed residue of poison

295 "Nun ist in der Form zweifellos versucht, das Übergewicht der Stofflichkeiten durch Farbenspiel aufzugeben, am deutlichsten etwa dort, wo das schweflige Grün und Gelb in der Pfütze der Grabensohle in dem Regenbogen hochoben aufgenommen und verklärt wird." *Kölner Stadtanzeiger* (unsigned), "Zur Neuordnung des Wallraf-Richartz-Museums," *Unterhaltungsbeilage der Stadt-Anzeigers für Köln und Umgebung* (2 December 1923).

296 "Wie ein Lächeln der Hölle blinkt in der tiefe eine giftige schwefelgelbe Lache ... ein blasser, ironischer Regenbogen, die biblische Friedensurkunde." Dr. Walter Schmits, "Ein Bild des Krieges," *Kölnische Zeitung* (7 December 1923).

297 "Material mischt sich zerfetzt mit zerfetzen Leibern, Holzstützen zersplittert, Eisenstangen verbogen, Draht. Gasmaske und Armbanduhr blieben unversehrt." Salmony, "Die neue Galerie."

gas often seen covering the surface of standing water after a gas attack. The bulk of the pictorial field is filled up with a disordered heap of inchoate fragments, pushed right up to the picture plane, much darker in value than the sky with its rainbow, and apparently limned in the pale bluish-pink of dawn's light.[298] A dark void at the center of the composition can be read as the receding depths of the trench, or perhaps the entrance into a dugout; no living being emerges from it, and nothing seems to have survived the bombardment. There is not a sign of life anywhere – again in conscious defiance of the conventions of history painting, where there are always secondary actors to mourn the heroes, to contemplate the beauty, honor and dignity of their idealized corpses, and sometimes to swear their vengeance. Here the artillery shelling has indiscriminately mutilated the bodies of both the already dead and those who had, until recently, still been alive. "Some of the bodies are decomposed, white worms crawl from them; others seem fresh."[299] In some places, it is simply impossible to make out what is being depicted. Fritz Löffler, who had seen the painting in person, stated that the painting was done alla prima, and that the paint was in places a centimeter thick.[300]

It was, in short, a tour-de-force of what Mikhail Bakhtin called the lower bodily stratum: it is in places shapeless and undefined, without the proper contours – of bodies, of embankments, of passageways – that should have held the composition in place. It depicted internal organs, with emphasis on intestines and reproductive organs; it was set in the mud, below the surface of the earth, looking up at the sky from between the collapsed walls of a trench. It blurred and obliterated boundaries – the boundaries between bodies and between the organic and the inorganic, mud, metal and human tissue. Even the impasto of the paint exhibited an excess of fatty matter. And it blurred the boundaries between the lowest forms of bodily

298 Ernst Kállai described a "fahle[n] blaurosa Beleuchtungseffekt." Ernst Kállai, "Dämonie der Satire," *Das Kunstblatt* 11 (1927), 97–104.

299 "Ein Teil der Leichen verwest, weiße Würmer kriechen aus, einige scheinen Frisch." Salmony, "Die neue Galerie."

300 Löffler, *Otto Dix und der Krieg*, 21. He also stated that Dix had done numerous preparatory drawings, including anatomical studies done in the dissection rooms of the Friedrichstadt Hospital in Dresden.

existence and the high register of history painting, between the sacred, the elevated, the glorifying, the official state sanctioned forms of history painting and the disgusting, grotesque experiences of actual fighting and death in mechanized warfare. Hans Secker, the director of the Wallraf-Richartz, clearly realized that the painting would be controversial, and hung it behind a gray curtain so that visitors would not immediately be shocked by its graphic depiction of mutilated bodies.[301] Visitors who wished to see it could go behind the curtain. One assumes that this would have had the effect of heightening the sense of the picture's shocking nature.

The response to the painting centered to a great extent on its supposed realism, both in terms of its aesthetic, and what is depicted: the bloody, undignified and inglorious reality of modern warfare. This response must be seen in relation to the widespread discussion during the war itself about the phoniness of so many official and semi-official representations of the war. Also, there had been an imperative during the war for actual soldiers at the front to represent the war in their own manner, on their own terms. It will be recalled from Chapter 1 that Dix disregarded this imperative, creating art at the front that was primarily concerned with drawing and painting from life, and which therefore did not represent combat at all. Later in the war, Dix began making art that elevated violence and conflict to the level of myth, but still neglected to represent the reality of combat. It was only now, in 1923, that Dix was gripped by the imperative to represent "what it was really like." But he represented that reality in a version of the exaggerated, even caricatured idiom he had developed as a visual equivalent for the soldier's speech, and that he had used in his Dadaist collages of war cripples. The intersection of this manner of painting and the subject matter of the work made *The Trench* controversial; in fact, it became the most controversial and notorious painting in Germany in the 1920s.[302] After it was exhibited at the annual Academy exhibition in Berlin, the controversy became sharp and, as was only to be expected, took on a politicized tone.

301 Dennis Crockett, "The Most Famous Painting"; Heijo Klein, "Kállais Interpretation des 'Schützengrabenbildes" von Otto Dix im Vergleich mit zeitgenössischen und gegenwärtigen Deutungen," *Acta Historiae Artium* 36 (1993), 180–188.

302 Crockett, "The Most Famous Painting."

The inflationary period

The period during which *The Trench* was painted, sold, and exhibited, in late 1922 and 1923, was a time of widespread crisis in Germany generally, with a catastrophic devaluation of the Mark, Germany's default on its payments of war reparations to the Allies, and the ensuing occupation of the Rhineland by Allied troops and confiscation of coal shipments to France. Not surprisingly, these conditions made it increasingly difficult for Nierendorf to do business. In September of 1922 Nierendorf put pressure on Dix to produce more of his watercolors, which he was selling relatively quickly despite the general crisis of the art market.[303] He also pressured Dix to finish *Acrobats and Circus* [Artisten und Zirkus], his second major etching portfolio (after *Death and Resurrection* [Tod und Auferstehung]), and get it ready for printing, as each day increased the final cost of printing and paper.[304] By August of 1923, with inflation out of control, Dix couldn't get his checks from Nierendorf cashed at the bank, and Nierendorf had to resort to sending cash, in increasingly large sums – in the millions by August. Nierendorf in turn found it difficult to get paid for works he sold. He was forced to frequently raise the prices on Dix's works, from hundreds of marks to thousands; already by January of 1923 he was charging between 8,000 and 10,000 marks for a watercolor; in February he suggested to Dix raising his prices to 60,000 marks for the *Death and Resurrection* portfolio and 100,000 for the *Acrobats and Circus* portfolio.[305] Finally, he simply switched to dealing in American dollars when he could, both for selling works and for paying Dix, and the distortion of the Germany economy is shockingly evident in the contrast between prices he charged in dollars as against the prices in marks: 2 dollars for a watercolor; 100 for the oil painting of *Adalbert Trillhaas*.[306] It is impossible to translate the ever-changing prices of artworks in 1923 into anything meaningful, as

303 Evidenced by the balance sheet which Nierendorf drew up for Dix at the end of 1922, which included a long list of watercolors sold. DKA I, C, 524 b.

304 Letter from Nierendorf to Dix, 27 September 1922, DKA I, C, 524 b.

305 Letter from Nierendorf to Dix, 2 February 1923, DKA I, C, 524 c.

306 Letters of 16 January 1923 and 3 October 1923, respectively. DKA, I, C, 524 d.

the prices of more conventional commodities increased literally on a daily basis. But a picture of the daily experience of inflation can be gained from the postage on the postcards that Nierendorf often used to correspond with Dix: the postcard of 2 February 1923, in which Nierendorf suggested raising the prices of the print portfolios to 60,000 and 100,000 marks, already carried 80 marks worth of postage; one month later, on 3 March 1923, it cost 730 marks; by 1 October of that year, it cost 800,000 marks to mail a postcard; by the nineteenth of that month, the price had increased to 2 million marks. Finally, on 15 November 1923, Nierendorf spent 5 *billion* marks to send Dix a postcard.[307] In an effort to stabilize the economy, the currency of the Rentenmark was introduced (on 15 November 1923); it was in this currency that the price of 10,000 marks was settled upon for the monumental painting *The Trench*. Even as late as March of 1924, Nierendorf complained that, "One can only do business these days through personal arrangements. The Rentenmark may be stable, but nobody's got any."[308]

The inflation crisis wasn't the only thing that made it difficult for Nierendorf and Dix to conduct the business of bringing art to the market in 1923. The occupation of the Rhineland by allied troops also set up very real barriers. Nierendorf wasn't even able to travel from Cologne, where he had his gallery, to Düsseldorf (no more than 20 kilometers further down the Rhine), where Dix was living, without a pass issued by the British Army of the Rhine.[309] More importantly, shipping Dix's artwork to the Jury Free Exhibition in Berlin in late 1923 was a bureaucratic nightmare. Not only did Nierendorf need special permission from the French authorities to ship the work "across the border" between the occupied Rhineland and unoccupied Germany, there were restrictions as to how *The Trench* was to be transported.[310]

307 Postcard from Nierendorf to Dix, 15 November 1923, DKA I, C, 524 c.

308 "Man kann heute nur Geschäft durch persönliche Beziehungen machen. Die Rentenmark ist zwar stabil, aber niemand hat welche." Letter from Nierendorf to Dix, 19 March 1924, DKA I, C, 524 f.

309 Postcard of 11 August 1923 and pass issued to Nierendorf on 20 August, 1923, DKA I, C, 524 c.

310 Letter of 1 October 1923, DKA I, C, 524 c.

The stress of this situation took its toll on the relationship between artist and dealer, and Nierendorf complained about the vituperative tone that Dix was taking in their correspondence, calling him mistrustful and suspicious.[311] Dix's coarse idiom in general often became a theme in their correspondence, alongside regular disputes about expenses such as shipping and import/export fees and the lack of cash to pay them. By the end of 1923, the situation brought the two into open conflict, with Dix accusing Nierendorf of conspiring with Hans Secker, the director of the Wallraf-Richartz, to cheat him. Nierendorf again complained of the tone Dix used and asked, "Were you actually drunk when you wrote that ridiculous letter?"[312] The language in which Dix often harangued his dealer was not only colorful, but in Nierendorf's opinion at least it had too much of the soldier's diction. Already in the summer of 1922 Nierendorf complained of his "tone, which one would expect rather from a Prussian drill sergeant."[313] Later, in 1924, Nierendorf would be even sharper: "you unload your repressed subaltern-complex on me."[314] Dix was in fact quite conscious of the language that he used in his correspondence, and seems to have been pleased that it annoyed Nierendorf. He wrote, "You've got no damn reason to be irritated if I'm coarse sometimes. It seems like you're already so ruined by your business as an art peddler [literally, "so weit verkunsthändlert"] that you can't understand me anymore." The colorful, colloquial-sounding neologism "*verkunsthändlert*" is deployed by Dix as a marker of the discursive distance between himself and Nierendorf. It's precisely because Nierendorf is *verkunsthändlert* that he can no longer understand Dix's own barracks idiom. Clearly Dix made a connection

311 Nierendorf called him "misstrauisch" and "argwohnig." Undated letter, DKA I, C, 524 c.

312 "Warst Du eigentlich besoffen als Du mir den lächerlichen Brief schreibst?" Letter from Nierendorf to Dix, undated (right before Christmas, 1923); in his irritation Nierendorf returned the letter to Dix, who kept it with the rest of his correspondence, which is why it is in the Dix archive, DKA I, C, 524 e.

313 "Ton, dem man sonst nur von preuss. Unteroffizieren erwarte sollte." Undated letter from Nierendorf to Dix, late July 1922, DKA I, C, 524 a.

314 "Alle verdrängten Unteroffizier-Komplexe werden an mir ausgelöst." Undated letter from Nierendorf to Dix, December 1924, DKA I, C, 524 f.

in his own mind between the language of the front soldier and artistic authenticity. Refusing to accept these terms, Nierendorf responded by pointedly recommending to Dix a more literary model for his letters: "I warmly recommend that you read Zola's *Letters to My Friends*, because they prove that one can be a great and true artist, without adopting the manners of a prima donna or a film star."[315] If Dix points to his experience as a front soldier in the war as the source of both his idiom and his artistic authenticity, Nierendorf tries to shift the discussion to other models in his effort to delegitimize Dix's performance, comparing him to (female) opera stars and film stars, figures that, while more glamorous, were also likely to irritate Dix's class resentments and aggressively heterosexual identity, and in any case enjoyed less cultural influence in Weimar Germany.

Conventional and unconventional memorials

The Trench was, in many ways, a kind of public memorial, although it was an unconventional one and certainly created a counter-narrative, at odds with the typical narrative expressed by most war memorials. The installation of the painting behind a curtain (and what's more, in what had been a chapel), must have lent the work a sacral element, and underscored its memorial function. Considering that Dix's next monumental painting on the same subject – using some of the same motifs, took the form of a triptych with predella – a common format for late medieval altarpieces depicting the crucifixion – the notion of *The Trench* as a quasi-sacred work should not seem far-fetched. Like a triptych that remains closed except for

315 "Du hast verdammt keine Ursache geärgert zu sein wenn ich mal grob werde. Du scheinst aber schon so weit verkunsthändlert zu sein dass Du mir nicht mehr verstehst." This was in the letter Dix sent Nierendorf at Christmastime in 1923, which Nierendorf returned with the note, "Ich will Dir sehr empfehlen Zola, ‚Briefe an meine Freunde' zu lesen, die beweisen, dass man ein grosser, echter Künstler sein kann ohne die Manieren einer Primadonna oder eines Filmstars." Letter of 29 December 1923, DKA I, C, 524 d.

certain feast days, this depiction of mortal sacrifice was originally displayed hidden from view, at the end of its chapel.

While Dix was painting *The Trench*, monuments and memorials were being publicly dedicated and used all over Germany, including in Düsseldorf, and the appropriateness of their formal vocabularies, as well as of their supplementary texts, was being debated both in public and in the art press. It makes sense to consider these as the backdrop against which a young and ambitious painter with something to say about the war would consider his own formal choices. There were many more sculptural monuments to consider than large-scale history paintings of the war.[316] The conventional memorials I am contrasting this "unconventional memorial" with are the funerary sculptural monuments which dotted European public spaces, and which were being erected in large numbers after the Great War. They may or may not contain figurative elements, were done in noble materials such as stone or bronze, were almost universally classicizing, and were commissioned from a professional artist by a corporate body – possibly the local government, possibly a regiment, but somebody with a stake and a budget, or at least a fundraising campaign. It is often stated that the Weimar Republic was unable to create a national memorial for the Great War during the interwar period, in contrast to other nations. But local memorials – put up by towns, military units, or groups of private individuals – proliferated across Germany. Such monuments usually featured classicizing elements in both pedestals and architectural elements, and also in the representation of the human figure, dignifying and even glamorizing death. Figures were often generalized and idealized by their nudity; their death resembles sleep or repose.[317] An example might be Karl

316 The exception would be the large painting, *Der Verwundete* (1920) by Gert Wollheim, which could be seen in Dusseldorf in Johanna Ey's gallery; Wollheim and Dix were both members of the circle around Ey, were both veterans, and were both originally from the Dresden area.

317 Although the designs for many monuments were chosen by competition, to which individual artists or architects applied, others were chosen from set designs or the combination of set elements offered by companies that specialized in war monuments and memorials.

Hilger's *Warrior Memorial* [Kriegerdenkmal] (see Figure 45), dedicated in 1892 to commemorate fallen German soldiers of the Franco-Prussian War, and located in the Hofgarten in Düsseldorf, the same city where Dix was working between 1921 and 1925 while painting *The Trench.*

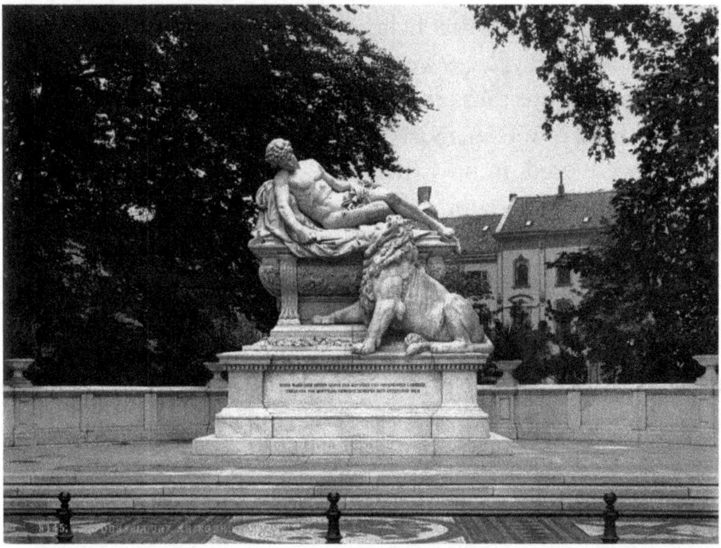

Figure 45. Karl Hilgers *Warrior Memorial* [Kriegerdenkmal], marble, 1892, Düsseldorf, Düsseldorf Hofgarten. Wikimedia commons.

Dix could hardly have been unfamiliar with it or the type and style it exemplified. Such monuments functioned by producing meanings within specific public discursive spaces, constituted not only by their physical surroundings (a public park in the case of Hilgers' monument, which is also typical), but also by public events such as their unveiling and other ceremonies. Timothy Ashplant has termed these discursive spaces "arenas of articulation," by which he means "those socio-political spaces within which social actors advance claims for the recognition of their specific war memories, and for whatever other benefits they seek to derive from such recognition."[318] Ashplant also uses

318 Timothy G. Ashplant, Graham Dawson, Michael Roper, *The Politics of War Memory and Commemoration* (Abingdon, UK: Routledge, 2000), 17. See also Jay Winter,

the term "agencies of articulation" for those who caused such monuments to be made. Agencies of articulation operated at any scale, from "the networks of families" to "the public sphere of nation-states." In Germany after the First World War, the agencies of articulation, the bodies which commissioned war memorials, tended to be veterans' organizations, which were often in turn organized by regiment or other fighting unit, whereas in France it was the citizenry of towns and villages who commissioned them, and the memory of dead combatants was thus centered in the town they had come from.[319]

The meaning of war memorials consisted as much in the manner in which they were used, in how their audience – the community which they initially addressed – approached them physically, and interacted with them – as in their actual form, whether figurative or non-figurative, and the iconography of the figures, and in their inscriptions. Some monuments were modest, located at the margins of cities or in smaller communities, and were intended to involve as many small donors as possible. Such small monuments invited an individual to contemplate a single dead loved one. Other monuments, such as those commissioned by the veterans' organizations of particular regiments, were often located in a larger town square, deliberately providing a place for larger crowds to assemble for memorial ceremonies, held annually or even more often.[320]

After the Great War, the range of ritual uses to which a community of memory – a community of mourning – could put a conventional monument sited in a public space, whether a figurative sculpture or a simple pylon with an inscription – could vary greatly. These different uses were often determined by the nature of the community that came together to

---

"War memorials and the mourning process," in Jay Winter, *Sites of Memory, Sites of Mourning: The Great War in European Cultural History* (Cambridge: Cambridge University Press, 1994), 78–116.

319 Michael Jeismann and Rolf Westheider, "Wofür stirbt der Bürger?," in Reinhart Koselleck, ed., *Der politische Totenkult. Kriegerdenkmäler der Moderne* (Munich: Fink, 1994), 23–49.

320 Susanne Brandt, "Trauer und fortgesetzter Krieg. Totengedanken zwischen Trauer und Kriegsverherrlichung in Düsseldorf nach dem Ersten Weltkrieg," in Jost Dülffer and Gerd Krumeich, eds., *Der verlorene Frieden. Politik und Kriegskultur nach 1918* (Essen: Klartext, 2002), 243–260.

commission the monument, and was often built into the design. Compare two contrasting examples, again from Düsseldorf. In 1921 a cenotaph was commissioned through a civilian citizens' initiative for the outlying neighborhood of Urdenbach, a community which had lost 102 men. Completed by the sculptor Siegfried Meinardus in 1931, the cenotaph took the form of a simple sarcophagus, topped by an Iron Cross but otherwise unornamented. The sober und dispassionate inscription reads "Unseren im Weltkrieg gefallenen Söhnen 1914–1918" [To our sons, fallen in the World War 1914–1918] (1931).[321] According to Susanne Brandt, the point of this sort of monument was not to celebrate martial virtues, but rather to form a community around mourning, and it was the explicit goal of the organizers to fund it through small donations, so that as many donors as possible had the chance to count themselves among that community.[322] By contrast, the local veteran's organization in Rath, another neighborhood of Düsseldorf, situated their own memorial – a spare, straight-sided modernist pylon in brick with the simple inscription "Unseren Gefallenen 1914–1918" [Our Fallen 1914–1918] in sans serif – in front of a large town square (now located at the sports stadium "Waldstadion"; the years 1939–1945 have been added to the original inscription). Its original location made it the focus of parades and war memorial ceremonies that functioned to create a sense of the meaning for the war, and to convey that meaning and its obligations to a younger generation in the 1930s.[323] The differences in the way these two memorials commemorated the war had more to do with how they were used than with their formal elements.

Likewise, a monument's meaning could be shifted, even dramatically altered, by the rituals through which its audience interacted with it, as well as by changing attitudes about the war. For example, Benno Elkan (1877–1960), a sculptor whose formal vocabulary (reminiscent of Aristide Maillol's) was praised in the conservative press as "Germanic," and whose preferred material, granite, was seen as "Nordic," (although Elkan himself was of Jewish descent), had one of his sculptures purchased by the city of

321 Brandt, "Trauer und fortgesetzter Krieg," 243–260.

322 Brandt, "Trauer und fortgesetzter Krieg," 250.

323 "Aufmarschplatz zu Kriegsgedächtnisfeiern," cited in Brandt, "Trauer und fortgesetzter Krieg," 252.

Frankfurt in 1920 and placed in a busy street near the city center to function as a war memorial.[324] The base was given the inscription "Den Opfern" [To the Victims] (1913–1914, dedicated 1920) (see Figure 46).

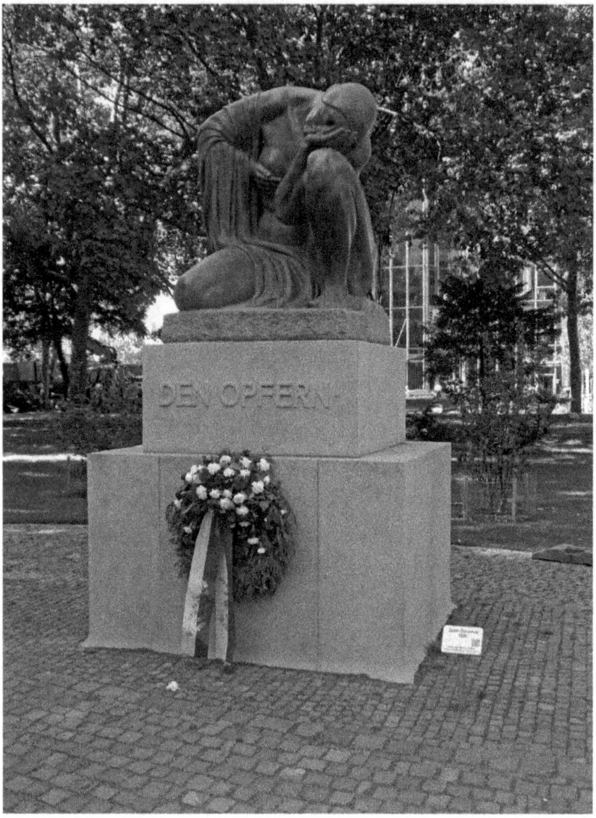

Figure 46. Benno Elkan, *Hero's Lament* [Heldenklage], bronze sculpture, 1913–1914, atop a pedestal of Swedish granite, dedicated 1920, Frankfurt. Wikimedia commons.

324 See Kathrin Hoffmann-Curtius, "Sieg ohne Trauer – Trauer ohne Sieg: Totenklage auf Kriegsdenkmälern des Ersten Weltkrieges," in Gisela Ecker and Maria Kublik-Kramer, *Trauer Tragen – Trauer Zeigen: Inszenierungen der Geschlechter* (Munich: Wilhelm Fink, 1999), 259–286, here 275 ff. According to Hoffmann-Curtius, the sculpture, minus the inscription, was originally exhibited in the Werkbund exhibition of 1914 in the "Friedhofabteilung," with the title *Heldenklage.*

It represented the figure of a mourning female figure down on one knee, holding her face in one hand and her nurturing breast in the other; this pose was typical for Elkan's funerary work.[325] In France, by way of comparison, women were often depicted in war memorials as the wives to whom the soldiers returned, sometimes together with their children; the sanctity of the family rather than maternal sorrow was the focus of France's own cult of the dead and the meaning of the war, at least in official discourse and cultural memory.[326] Dix by contrast used images of women as prostitutes and as the subjects of ribald stories and dirty jokes in order to address specifically male communities of memory, suggesting that, for him, the meaning of the war was the formation of social bonds between men, and an undiminished and unbridled sexual potency. The inscription "Den Opfern" was added to the Frankfurt monument when it was dedicated by the city of Frankfurt in 1920. Since the German word *Opfer* can mean both "victim" and "sacrifice," as in to sacrifice oneself willingly, the term binds together the losses of the war with a salvific notion that such losses had an inherent, even redemptive and sacred meaning. Although Elkan's work generally was at first identified with "Germanic" and "Nordic" qualities, this figure and its inscription now represented in 1920, at least to a writer for the *Frankfurter Zeitung*, "[a] rebuke and reminder. It is elegiac and pacifistic, a remembrance of the victims and a warning."[327] And according to *Der Cicerone*, "This monument is a memorial to the soldiers that successfully breaks with the old conception and understanding of the glorification of battle, heroism, glory, and honor. It is a lament for the dead, if you will, a lamentation

325 See also the Denkmal für die Stadt Völklingen, 1925, destroyed 1935, and the "Denkmal zur Befreiung der Rheinlande, Mainz, 1930, destroyed, both reproduced in Hoffmann-Curtius, "Sieg ohne Trauer," 279 and 281.

326 For a comparison between Germany and France, see, Reinhart Koselleck and Michael Jeismann, eds., *Der politische Totenkult: Kriegerdenmäler in der Moderne* (Munich: Fink, 1994).

327 "Klage und Mahnung. Es ist elegisch und pazifistisch, Opfergedächtnis und Warnung.," *Frankfurter Zeitung* (6 October 1920), cited in Hoffmann-Curtius, "Sieg ohne Trauer," 278, footnote 79.

of the horrible experience of the war."[328] If the work's meaning as a war memorial was shaped partly by its inscription, it was given even more specific anti-war associations through the way it was used, with several leftist and pacifist women's groups organizing a "Ceremony of grief for the victims of war" [Trauerfeier für die Kriegsopfer] – with a specifically pacifist message – in front of the monument on 1 November, All-Soul's-Day, 1920.[329] The rituals and inscription added to the work were supplementary texts which effectively altered the work's meaning in the public's mind.[330] But the mood in Germany with regard to mourning shifted over the next decade such that by 1930 Elkan's mourning figure was lambasted in Paul Westheim's journal of art criticism, *Das Kunstblatt*, for its *failure to glorify* the sacrifice to which it was dedicated. Just as significantly, the pose of the figure was now characterized as a "collapse" [*Zusammenbruch*], rather than as a gesture of maternal nourishing and mourning, more suited to a "private cemetery, where a widow can lament her own."[331] A memorial's meaning was not fixed, but determined partly at least by use and the changing public discourse.

The location of a memorial was also significant and could generate different meanings for different audiences in that space. Regimental monuments were often located in front of the regimental barracks, which

328 "Als Kriegerdenkmal bricht dieses Monument mit gutem Erfolg mit der alten Auffassung der Verherrlichung von Schlacht, Heldentum, Ruhm und Ehre. Es ist eine Klage um die Toten, wenn man will, eine Anklage gegen das furchtbare Erlebnis des Krieges." Sascha Schwabacher, "Frankfurter Kunstschau," *Cicerone*, 1920, p. 794, cited in Hoffmann-Curtius, p. 278.

329 Hoffmann-Curtius, "Sieg ohne Trauer," 280, and *Cicerone* (1920), 794, cited in Hoffmann-Curtius, "Sieg ohne Trauer," 278 ff..

330 Today, there is still a supplementary text guiding the viewer's understanding of this sculpture, which is located in the Gallusanlage, beneath the skyscrapers of Frankfurt's banking quarter: a QR code displayed alongside the sculpture links to a text which states that Elkan, "blieb ... seiner pazifistischen Linie treu und widersetzte sich auch während des Nationalsozialismus den propagierten Heldenkult in seinen Werken widerzugeben," Nicola Netzer, 2015.

331 "Privatfriedhof, auf dem eine Witwe ihren einzigen beklagen kann." Bruno Jaspert, "Benno Elkan: Den Opfern," in *Das Kunstblatt* 14 (1930), 178–180, cited in Hoffman-Curtius, "Sieg ohne Trauer," 282 f.

were often in working-class neighborhoods. A memorial to fallen comrades for the members of the regiment, they were often felt to be a provocation by the working-class residents.[332] In Düsseldorf in the 1920s however, the city council went out of its way to avoid monuments that could be seen as "polarizing," and fought more than once with veterans' organizations over designs and locations for monuments (a significant example is the equestrian monument commissioned by the Westphalian Ulan Regiment, created by Richard Langer – who taught sculpture at the Düsseldorf Art Academy while Dix was a student there; it is now located on the Joseph-Beuys-Ufer).[333] Many memorials, especially those commissioned by military units, expressed a conservative, nationalist and revanchist, even monarchist message. This could be effectively conveyed by their supplementary texts: ceremonies; speeches; and marches with the black, red, and white Imperial flag instead of the black, red, and gold Reich flag. This, too, was seen as a provocation in working-class neighborhoods dominated by Social Democrats, who by and large supported the Republic and its flag, as I will discuss at greater length in the next chapter. By contrast, few public monuments in Germany in the 1920s communicated an overtly anti-war or pacifist message. One exception was erected in 1922 in Annweiler in der Pfalz in 1922, at a time when the "Nie Wieder Krieg" [never again war] movement was still active, and in fact the inscription on that monument read "Nie Wieder Krieg." The monument was controversial, led to the notoriety of the city, and was finally torn down by local Nazi officials in April 1933.[334]

Although *The Trench* was a painting, it was also similar to sculptural monuments in that it was a large-scale work, clearly intended for a public space, and did the work of public remembrance. A decade later, in 1933, when the painting had been confiscated by the Nazis and was being exhibited in the first of the so-called "Degenerate Art" exhibitions, in Dresden, a painting professor at the Dresden Art Academy (and a former

332 Christian Saehrendt, *Der Stellungskrieg der Denkmäler im Berlin der Zwischenkriegszeit 1919–1939* (Bonn: Dietz, 2004), 37 ff.

333 Brandt, "Trauer und fortgesetzter Krieg," 252–253.

334 Jeismann and Westheider, "Wofür stirbt der Bürger," 29.

teacher and colleague of Dix's at that institution), Richard Müller, wrote about the painting as a "degradation of the German soldier who fell at the front," and explicitly identified it as an inversion of a proper memorial. "The German front soldier deserves to have a memorial raised to him that does him honor. Such a hymn to German heroism and heroic sacrifice can only by written by a person of inner maturity."[335] Müller compared Dix's painting – which he also faulted for what he saw as its technical shortcomings – to a low, sensationalistic commercial attraction in a wax-works display. Sensationalistic wax-works attractions were popular in Germany, and many included scenes of death and remembrance, such as Bismarck kneeling at the death-bed of Kaiser Wilhelm I.[336] Müller went on, complaining that it was a short step from *The Trench* to Dix's more pornographic representations of, "bordello scenes, pimps, and whores in the most outrageous positions."[337] Both of these comparisons, to wax-works and pornography, were already being made in criticism of *The Trench* 1923, as we shall see shortly.

The commissioning, ritual use, and written criticism of public memorial sculptures across Germany is the context in which statements made by the critics about *The Trench* were intelligible. If they found Dix's

335 "… eine Entwürdigung des gefallenen deutschen Frontsoldaten … der doch verdient, daß man ihm nach seinem Heldentode ein ihn ehrendes Denkmal setzt. Das hohe Lied des deutschen Heldenmutes und –todes können nur innerlich reife Menschen schreiben." Richard Müller, "Spiegelbilder des Verfalls in der Kunst," *Dresdner Anzeiger* (29 September 1933), cited in Kira van Lil, "Ein perfekter Skandal. Der 'Schützengraben' von Otto Dix zwischen Kritik und Verfemung," in Uwe Fleckner, ed., *Das verfemte Meisterwerk. Schicksalswege moderner Kunst im "Dritten Reich"* (Berlin: Akademie, 2009), 49–74, here 68.

336 Eva Giloi, *Monarchy, Myth, and Material Culture in Germany 1750–1950* (Cambridge: Cambridge University Press, 2011), 233 f.

337 "Eine Schilderung des Krieges, wie sie irgendein rühriger Panoptikumsbesitzer als Attraktion seiner 'Kriegsabteilung' einverleiben könnte in der Hoffnung, ein gutes Geschäft zu machen. […] Von diesen Motiven ist der Schritt nur klein zu denen, die für Dix charakteristisch sind und die er zahlreich abgewandelt hat – Bordellszenen, Zuhälter, Dirnen in gewagtesten Stellungen …" Richard Müller, "Spiegelbilder des Verfalls," in van Lil, "Ein perfekter Skandal," 69. Also cited in Schubert, "Verfolgung," 361.

representations of soldiers' bodies inappropriate, or his message offensive, antimilitarist, or exceptionally truthful, it is because of the difference between his figures and those of artists like Elkan, Langer, or even Hilger. Yet Dix was not directly given the charge of designing a war memorial by any particular community – he had given himself this brief, and the creation of his work was not itself a community effort involving fund-raising among stakeholders in the project of memorializing the dead. Furthermore, an oil painting, however large and public, was not predestined for an unveiling ceremony specifically directed at a preselected audience of veterans and surviving family. This gave him the advantage of independence – he did not need approval of his work ahead of time by a city council or other group. By contrast, in Düsseldorf where Dix worked, monument proposals were often rejected because of their polarizing political expressions. The discourse around his "monument" would not take the form of public speeches, which needed to be submitted to the censorship of allied military occupation authorities. And Dix was under no pressure to communicate a clear and unambiguous message to his audience, whether one of individual mourning, revanchism, pacifism, or any other sort.

Reception of *The Trench*

At first the public discussion of *The Trench* unfolded locally, in the Cologne daily papers, as part of the discussion of Walter Secker's rehanging of the Wallraf-Richartz-Museum collection.[338] Already the response to *The Trench* turned on the question of whether or not it was legitimate to incorporate such grotesque imagery into a painting, and one answer to this question was the legitimacy of such a mode of painting would

338 "Zur Neuordnung."

derive entirely from the fact that Dix himself had experienced such gruesome scenes first hand.

> Nobody can doubt that what is presented by the picture in material form, a heap of tattered bodies, shredded over and over again by shells, even after death, of impaled heads, of the stumps of limbs gnawed by rats, of contorted fingers, was really there, thousands of times over, and is therefore true. There is no affront to the idea of heroism here, because the only ones who can claim this idea are those who, actually confronted with such a scene, would leap into the inferno, time and again, and risk a grisly death and conquest by the unleashed, savage machines.[339]

According to this reviewer, the possible moral content of the painting, framed in terms of its truthfulness, is underwritten by the fact that Otto Dix himself not only experienced the things he has chosen to represent, but had presumably risked his own life in doing so. Dix is presented as a "truth-teller," in Jay Winter's sense.[340] But it also seems as though the author of the review cannot help trying to match the painting's emphasis on the grotesque with his own graphic language; he is challenged, seduced even, by the visceral horror of the painting into responding with his own grotesque turns of phrase. This would be a pattern in the response to *The Trench*. Another reviewer, Walter Schmits, wrote an even more exalted verbal description a few days later in the *Kölnische Zeitung*,

> The trench is completely filled with grizzly, dismembered corpses and bits of men. Brains spill from opened skulls like dark red grits; torn limbs, innards, shreds of uniforms, and spent shells are piled into a devastated mound, and if you were to cut a section of it out, with its puzzling forms and strong, slick and shiny colors, you

339 "Es kann keiner daran zweifeln, dass das, was das Bild stofflich gibt, in seiner Häufung zerfetzter, nach dem Tode abermals von Granaten zerfetzter Leiber, von aufgespießten Köpfen, von rattenbenagten Gliedstümpfen, von verkrampften Fingern in Wirklichkeit abertausende Male dagewesen und also wahr ist; es kann auch keine Verletzung heldischer Denkart darin liegen, denn nur die dürfen sich zu ihr bekennen, die, vor ein solches Bild gestellt, abermals den Sprung ins Inferno, grauenvollsten Tod und die Unterwerfung unter die wild und selbstherrlich gewordene Maschine wagen würden." "Zur Neuordnung."

340 Winter, *Sites of Memory*.

> would mistake it for a picture of a tropical aquarium full of startling creations, half animal, half plant.[341]

But the anonymous reviewer for the *Kölner Stadtanzeiger* turns against the painting, condemning it with comparisons to Matthias Grünewald and "the Brussels torture chamber" of Antoine Wiertz, which have little in common except for one thing: they are both examples of the grotesque. Grünewald, too, would become a common theme in the response to Dix's paintings of the war, both *The Trench* and the later triptych *War*. Grünewald would become a positive association, but this reviewer characterizes the similarity to this German exemplar of the early Renaissance grotesque as the "tragedy of German painting."[342] The reference to Wiertz's horrors is a little more surprising, and deserves some exploration. The Belgian Antoine Joseph Wiertz (1806–1865) was an academically trained painter specializing in nightmarish scenes focused on violent death and dismemberment, as well as madness, often spiced with women in peril.[343]

341 "... sonst ist der Graben ausgefüllt von gräßlich verstümmelten Leichen und Menschenfragmenten. Aus geöffneten Schädeln quillt das Gehirn gleich dicker roter Grütze; zerrissene Glieder, Eingeweide, Uniformfetzen, Patronenkapseln bilden einer wüsten Haufen, den man, wenn man ein Stück daraus herausschnitte, mit seinen rätselhaften Formen und starken, schleimig gleißenden Farben vielleicht für die Darstellung eines Salzwasseraquariums voll abenteuerliche Gebilde, halb Tieren, halb Pflanzen, halten würde." Dr. Walter Schmits, "Ein Bild des Krieges," *Kölnische Zeitung* (7 Dec., 1923, early morning edition).

342 "Zur Neuordnung."

343 G. Hermans, *Musée Wiertz, Album Illustré* (Antwerp: Hermans, c. 1900).

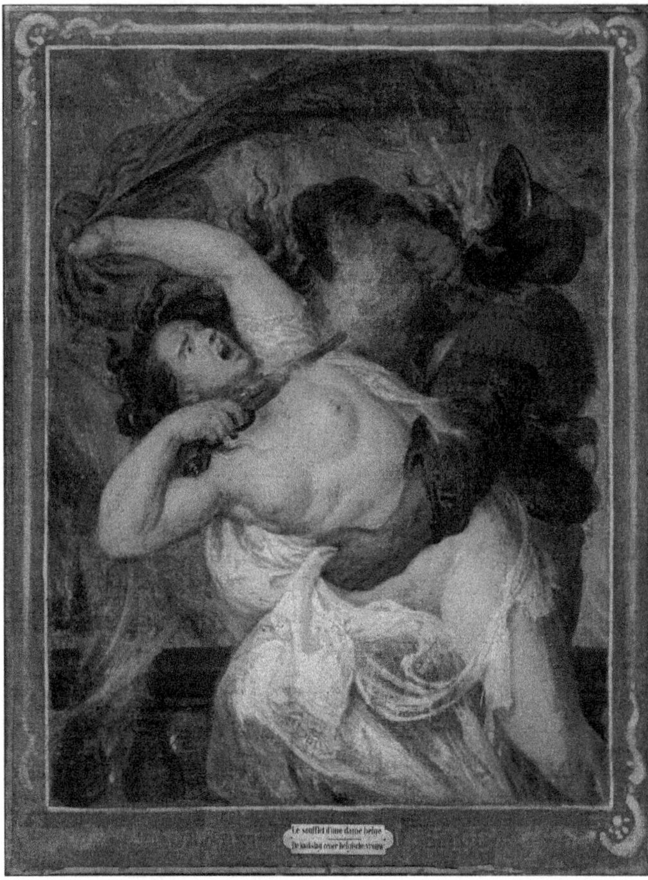

Figure 47. Antoine Wiertz, *A Belgian Lady Strikes a Blow* [Le Soufflet d'une dame belge], oil on canvas, 1861, Musée Wiertz, Brussels. © Royal Museums of Fine Arts of Belgium [RMFAB], Brussels / Photo: J. Geleyns Art Photography.

In one painting, *A Belgian Lady Strikes a Blow* [Le Soufflet d'une dame belge] (1861) (see Figure 47) a nude woman uses a pistol to shoot her would-be rapist, a soldier, in the head; his brains and blood are sprayed across the canvas. In another, *Hunger, Madness, Crime* [Faim, Folie, Crime] (1853), a poor mother, visibly maddened by starvation, is in the process of cutting up and cooking her infant; the fire is fueled by chair legs, indicating her destitution. The little corpse is mostly concealed, but a pudgy leg and foot hang out of the pot.[344] Wiertz may be largely forgotten today, but he had given his entire oeuvre to the Belgian state upon his death, with the stipulation that his vastly oversized works be displayed in perpetuity in his purpose-built shed, the "Musée Wiertz," where they can still be seen to this day, near the center of Brussels, not so far from Cologne. Indeed, Dix may have well seen them while he was stationed in Brussels, and the comparison is an apt one and not at all far-fetched. The reference did not in any case strike other reviewers in 1923 as too obscure, because later reviewers refer, knowingly, to the comparison, "Art historians say 'Grünewald' and appear contented; the outraged claim, 'Musée Wiertz,' and look away."[345]

The reference by Walter Schmits in the *Kölnische Zeitung* to a tropical aquarium, "full of startling creations, half animal, half plant," vividly suggests another aspect of the grotesque: the fantastic, metamorphic creatures of the French caricaturist J. J. Grandville (1803–1847), which combine the organic and inorganic into fantastic creatures inhabiting unsuspected worlds, thus constituting another form of grotesque humor. For Baudelaire, at least in Michele Hannoosh's reading of him, this sort of recombinatory grotesque, bringing together elements from seemingly opposed realms of nature, is more profound, more creative than the humor of mere slapstick.[346] Schmits clearly senses that *some* form of humor is intended by *The Trench*. "It would be instructive to discover," he writes, "how many vulgar jokes are made in front of Dix's picture, just to release the tension it creates, to find release in a word."[347] Just so! Schmits conjures up a scenario – perhaps unintentionally – of the grotesque humor embedded in the caricature calling out especially to initiated viewers (that

344 See Émile de La Veleye, *Catalogue du Musée Wiertz, précédé d'une Notice Biographique extraite de la 'Revue des Deux Mondes* (Bruxelles : Weissenbruch, 1875), cat. nos. 26 and 21, respectively.

345 "Kunsthistoriker sagen Grünewald und sehen dann sehr zufrieden aus, Entrüstete behaupten Musée Wiertz und blicken weg." Alfred Salmony, "Die neue Galerie," 8.

346 Michele Hannoosh, *Baudelaire and Caricature. From the Comic to an Art of Modernity* (University Park: Pennsylvania State University Press, 1992), 157.

347 "Es wäre lehrreich, festzustellen, wie viel rohe Witze vor dem Dixschen Bilde gerissen werden, einfach aus dem Drang heraus, den Alpdruck, den das Bild ausübt, zu verscheuchen, ein 'befreiendes Wort' zu finden." Schmits, "Ein Bild des Krieges."

is, other veterans) to respond with their own humorous vulgarities.[348] As Martina Kessel has recently shown, humor played a particular role in the political debate over what constituted a "correct" memorialization of the war in Germany in the Weimar Republic. Many authors used humor to recall the camaraderie of the trenches, and deployed it in the struggle over the memorialization of the war, in collections of soldiers' humor.[349] One author of such collections of humor from the "good old army days," "Krieger" Kröger claimed that the humor of the barracks had compensated for the horrors of the war.[350] And the satirical trench newspapers, of which the British paper *Wipers Times* is the most famous for English-speaking audiences, did not hesitate to include representations of the horrors of the war that soldiers were accustomed to seeing, such as "bursting skulls and intestines hanging on trees like ivy."[351]

For Schmits, the central, and linked, questions for an art critic to answer were: was the painting well-executed or not; and was the subject appropriate for painting. The first question he answered in the affirmative, declaring Dix among the best living German artists, as demonstrated by the drawing and the color composition of *The Trench*.

> Even the picture acquired by the museum [the Walraf-Richartz], whose terrible seriousness is not diminished by satirical distortions, proves the great ability of the painter, as does the design – one must assume that it was the explicit intention of

348 Jorg Merz has suggested that the painting contains a very specific vulgar joke, a phallic image. I am not suggesting anything so literal – in contrast to the earlier "war cripple" pictures. Jorg Merz, "Otto Dix' Kriegsbilder. Motivationen – Intentionen – Rezeptionen," *Marburger Jahrbuch für Kunstwissenschaft* 26 (1999), 189–226.

349 Martina Kessel, "Gewalt Schreiben. 'Deutscher Humor' in den Weltkriegen," in Wolfgang Hardtwig, ed., *Ordnungen in der Krise; Zur Politischen Kulturgeschichte Deutschlands 1900–1933* (Munich: Oldenbourg, 2007), 229–258.
Kessel cites Sigmund Graff, *Dicke Luft! Eine neue Ladung Frontwitze* (1926) and Carl-Albrecht Oertel, *Hurra bei Landsersch! Ernstes und Heiteres aus großer Zeit* (1932). Deutscher Humor, 236–239.

350 *Hanseaten im Westfronthumor. Lustige Episoden aus ernster Zeit*, cited in Kessel, "Deutscher Humor," 248 f.

351 Cited in Kessel, "Deutscher Humor," 245.

> the artist to render part of the composition a chaotic, formless mass – and also the color composition.[352]

But Schmits answered the second question with a clear "no." To begin with, he states, the viewer has no need to be reminded that war, and death in war, is nothing like its romanticized representation in traditional painting (for Schmits this was a good argument for continuing traditional forms of romanticized history painting). Furthermore, terror and disgust were not worthy emotions for painting to depict, and they rendered the "enjoyment of the artwork" impossible, recalling the well-known arguments of Gotthold Ephraim Lessing's essay of 1766, *Laocoön*. Lessing, it will be recalled, argued that figures in art should not be shown with their mouths open, no matter how terrible their pain might be. This is just the cultural principle – the classicism of smooth exterior surfaces and bodies without wounds or orifices – that Bakhtin said the comic grotesque rejected, the better to ward off fear of death with laughter at the degraded and undignified, opened-up body.[353] But Schmits was fully on the side of Lessing, complaining that the effect of terror and disgust was not one of art, but more like the artless "objectivity" [*Sachlichkeit*] of the scenes in a wax museum, in a "thoroughly unartistic wax-works diorama."[354] As we have already seen, the comparison with a wax-works would be made again, years later, when

352 Schmits, "... seine besten Bilder rücken ihn durch ihre schlagende Charakteristik und ihr von starken Eigenart zeugendes künstlerisches Können mit in die ersten Reihen der lebenden deutschen Künstler. Auch das vom Museum erworbene Bild, dessen grausamer Ernst nicht durch satirische Verzerrungen entstellt wird, beweist das große Können des Malers sowohl in dem zeichnerischen Entwurf – man muß wohl annehmen, daß der Künstler einen Teil des Gemäldes mit bestimmter Absicht als wirre Masse ohne klare Form gebildet hast – als auch namentlich in der farbigen Komposition." Schmits, "Ein Bild des Krieges."

353 Gotthold Ephraim Lessing, *Laocoön: An Essay on the Limits of Painting and Poetry* (Baltimore: Johns Hopkins University Press, 1984, Edward Allen McCormick, translator).

354 "Mit Recht darf man auch die Frage aufwerfen, ob sich der Gegenstand überhaupt für die bildende Kunst eignet. Wir möchten die Frage verneinen. Das Grausen und der Ekel – sittlich keineswegs wertvolle Empfindungen – sind so stark, dass sie bei den meisten Beschauern einen Kunstgenuss unmöglich machen und auf sie mit der

the painting was being publicly defamed by the Nazis. Ernst Kállai, writing in 1927, made a similar reference to wax-works chambers of horrors, in reference to Dix's work generally.[355] A wax-works was a decidedly low, popular form of entertainment and visual culture with which to associate *The Trench*, and was closely related to carnivals and side-shows in its unabashed gratification of the desire to gaze upon the body, whether famous, beautiful, alien and other, or monstrously grotesque. It was, one could argue, a "carnivalesque" form in Bakhtin's sense, a kind of modern-day folk culture, complete with its ambiguous celebrations of the high and mighty and its detailed depictions of bodily torments. The most famous wax museum in Germany was probably Castan's Panopticum, with its main gallery in the Pschorr-Haus in Berlin, on the Potsdammer Platz which had just closed after more than 50 years, and which had branches in Cologne and Dresden. Besides famous figures from history, Castan's displayed such horror scenes as torture chambers and monstrously grotesque, misshapen figures. The voyeuristic impulse built into this form of popular visual culture is close to that of pornography, as I suggested in the previous chapter's discussion of Dix's depictions of the facial wounds of some veterans. Schmits himself made the comparison between pornography and Dix's painting, emphasizing the contrast between art on one side, and on the other both pornography and *The Trench*.[356]

There are several preoccupations here, and not only in Schmits' essay. The difficult-to-pin down humor is one; the appropriateness of such a mode of painting for the subject – the commemoration of the war – is another; a third is the question of whether or not Dix was a skilled painter at all, and we will see that critics were strongly divided over this issue, too, presenting Dix as either one of the best or one of the worst painters of his generation. And behind these preoccupations was the issue of the formation of a kind

brutalen Sachlichkeit einer durchaus unkünstlerischen Panoptikumsgruppe wirken werden." Schmits, "Ein Bild des Krieges."

355 "Eine harmlose Atelierkammer etwa wird zur panoptikalen Schreckenskammer." Kállai, "Dämonie der Satire."

356 "… weil dann die lebhafte Vorstellung der Wirklichkeit die Dichtung überwiegen würde. Ähnlich steht es mit sexuellen Darstellungen." Schmits, "Ein Bild des Krieges."

of group identity around the painting, with some veterans identifying positively with the work, while critics like Schmits, self-appointed guardians of the traditional, romanticizing language of history painting, rejected it. This specific constellation of issues suggests that, in creating what amounted to a kind of counter-memorial, Dix had, deliberately or not, engaged in an essentially social and dialogical process of collective memory, in the sense outlined by Maurice Halbwachs. As Halbwachs explained, individual memories cannot exist isolated in the individual's consciousness, but only through communication within a particular social group. Even the most personal memories can only be thought about within a social framework, formed and informed by thoughts and ideas that are part of a social milieu, and their meaning is a social meaning.[357] Furthermore, language and linguistic conventions play an essential role in the formation of collective memory, both in communicating memories and in stabilizing their meanings.[358] As Jan Assmann has phrased it, "What is circulated here is cultural meaning that is coded and articulated through shared language, knowledge, and memory; it is a store of common values, experiences, expectations, and interpretation.[359] One could say therefore that communities of memory are also at the same time sociolinguistic groups, circumscribed by a sociolect which mediates, among other things, their memories, circulating them within the community and pressing them to conform to the groups' particular values and ideas. In the previous chapter I endeavored to relate the imagery of Dix's pictures of crippled soldiers to the argot of soldiers at the front, and suggested that both were recognizable and comprehensible to a community of memory made up of veterans in general in Germany. Likewise, the imagery of *The Trench* – like any proper argot – was incomprehensible to those who were not part of this community of memory, and so both shut outsiders out, and worked to define the community itself, even as it sought to reproduce certain ideological elements within the community. In the

357 Maurice Halbwachs, *On Collective Memory* (Chicago: University of Chicago Press, 1992, Lewis A. Coser, ed. and translator), 43–53.

358 Halbwachs, *On Collective Memory*, 45.

359 Jan Assmann, *Cultural Meaning and Early Civilization: Writing, Remembrance, and Political Imagination* (Cambridge: Cambridge University Press, 2011), 121.

"war cripple" pictures, those ideological elements had to do with gender and sexuality, class and place within the military hierarchy, and attitudes towards the fear of death and pain. In *The Trench*, the ideological elements had much more to do with telling "the truth" about what the soldier's experience at the front had been like. It was presented as a counter discourse to the emerging official memory of the war.

Jan and Aelita Assmann have developed Maurice Halbwachs' concept of collective memory, positing two distinctly different forms: *communicative* memory and *cultural* memory. Communicative memory is informal, primarily oral, and without fixed roles, but limited to the living participants in the events being actively remembered, whereas *cultural* memory – or history – is characterized by fixed rituals of commemoration that take place on fixed calendar dates, and above all by a fixed narrative.[360] Cultural memory represents "normative and formative versions of the past."[361] The narrative of communicative memory is by contrast fluid, constantly recreated and altered by dialog within the community of memory. It is actively produced to fulfill the needs of the community and its constituents, and is often contested. An important aspect of communicative memory is that roles are regularly switched: first I am the speaker, communicating my experiences through stories, jokes, and other informal verbal modes, and you are the listener; in the next moment, you respond with your own stories, and I in turn become the listener. This is the dialogical element of communicative memory which I see at work in *The Trench*, and it takes place within and alters a social framework of group identity. Cultural memory, or official history, by contrast, is communicated only in one direction; the listeners receive the narratives communicated through official forms – history lessons, official rituals of commemoration on official dates, historical monuments. Communicative memory is typically expressed in a popular idiom, such as the ribald language of war stories. Cultural memory is expressed instead in an elevated idiom, including epic poetry and neoclassical history painting as well as

360 Jan Assmann and John Czaplicka, "Collective Memory and Cultural Identity," *New German Critique* 65 (Spring-Summer, 1995), 125–133.

361 Astrid Erll, *Memory in Culture* (London: Palgrave Macmillan, 2011), 30.

the authoritative and patriotic tones of history books. Because artists were highly trained in their specific métier, unlike their audiences, the roles of artist and audience were fixed. While most public monuments are examples of semi-official cultural memory, *The Trench* had more in common with the communicative memory of dialogical war stories, with their reliance on grotesque bodily humor and carnivalesque language.

Or rather, *The Trench* was a hybrid of the communicative and the cultural forms of memory. Unlike the dada collages, which debased the high diction of history painting with their form as well as their content, *The Trench* presented itself in the grand scale and elevated materials of history painting (figurative oil painting), if not in the handling of those materials (it was painted alla prima, unlike academic history paintings), and was hung in a public museum. At the same time, it continued to make use of elements of grotesque realism, with its excessively detailed recounting of all the ways the body could be wounded and violated, and with its emphasis on viscera and internal organs, as well as its ironic mixing of the high and low, what Bakhtin called the topographical shift from high (the rainbow in heaven) to the low (the brains, worms, and putrid water at the bottom of the trench). And this grotesque realism, like vulgar stories and jokes, invited viewers to respond in kind with their own jokes and stories, marking the painting as a form of *communicative*, rather than *cultural* memory. This is just what the art critic Schmits was concerned was happening, when he worried that viewers were responding to the painting by making "vulgar jokes" of their own. Despite the evident skill in the execution of the painting, its grotesque realism and vulgar jokes constituted a dialog, and a dialogic community of memory, which would keep the meaning of the war open for negotiation. Schmits seemed troubled by the painting's openness to dialog and negotiated meaning, to its ambiguity, and its refusal to speak in the diction of official culture which fixed the meaning of the war in reassuringly traditional terms such as "glory" and "patriotism."

Schmits decided that the meaning of the painting must therefore be one that he objected to: pacifism. He deplored the purchase of the work by the museum on the grounds that it was pacifist propaganda.[362] The notion that *The Trench* was *intended primarily* as a work of pacifist propaganda – rather than merely functioning to represent the war truthfully, took hold at this point in the growing public debate about the painting. Some readers of Schmits' essay confused the issue by defending Dix's supposed pacifism more than the painting itself. A long letter to the *Rheinische Zeitung* written by one F. Friedrich took exception to Schmits' statement that nobody needed reminding of the horrors of the war.[363] Friedrich worried that in fact Germans were already forgetting in 1923 how horrendous it had been, and were once again prey to manipulation by militarists and would-be war profiteers. The most important goal, he went on, was to educate the public, and especially youth, about the true nature of modern warfare, and to resist the continuing militarization of German culture, and he took *The Trench* to be well-suited to this purpose. Indeed, the letter reads like an attempt to enlist the painting and Dix himself for the radical pacifist movement. The author may well have been Ernst Friedrich (despite the *Rheinische Zeitung* giving his first initial as "F"), an anarchist-syndicalist organizer and tireless and prominent antiwar agitator. Ernst Friedrich was also the publisher of *War Against War* (1924), which was truly a work of pacifist propaganda that placed before the viewer photographs of the mutilated corpses of soldiers and the horrifically disfigured faces of wounded survivors.[364] Ernst Friedrich also founded the Anti-War-Museum in Berlin (1925). Dix went on to borrow some photographs from Friedrich as source material for watercolors of war cripples and for his *War* portfolio.

But the author of this letter – whether or not it was Ernst Friedrich – was by no means alone in late 1923 and 1924 in fearing that the spirit of

362 "Dennoch bedauern wir den Ankauf des Bildes. Man hat es als sittliche Tat gepriesen. Darunter kann hier nur pazifistische Propaganda verstanden werden." Schmits, "Ein Bild des Krieges."

363 *Rheinische Zeitung* (12 December 1923).

364 For an extended comparison of Friedrich's publishing activities and Dix's art about the war, see Dora Apel, "'Heroes' and 'Whores': The Politics of Gender in Weimar Antiwar Imagery," *The Art Bulletin* 79/3 (Sep. 1997), 366–384.

militarism was again abroad in the German public. In 1924, the left-liberal journal *Die Weltbühne* devoted an entire issue to addressing this concern, and the fear that the next war was already being prepared. For the most part these essays demonstrate a bitterness about the war, a sense of having been misled, lied too, thoughtlessly used. Although the various authors lightly caricature pacifists like Friedrich, the possibility that there might once again be a war in Europe, and soon, is taken seriously and regarded with horror. The German populace is blamed for having forgotten what it was like – even those who were there, and for continuing to glorify war and promote it as a personal adventure, a positive experience in a young man's life. One author describes with disgust a popular entertainment in Berlin, a fireworks display in Treptow park, which billed itself as "Five Minutes of Drumroll Fire at Verdun." The public is amused, the author complains, and has "completely forgotten what it was like back then, at Verdun; they've forgotten the mountains of dead and rivers of blood, and the filth and the slimy mud and the brutalization, and think instead on the good old army days, and wish that it could be like that again. Wish it in all innocence."[365] The special issue of *Die Weltbühne* also included a review of *The Trench*, by Paul Ferdinand Schmidt (who had written elsewhere about Dix and who had let Dix paint a portrait of him).

> Yes, this bath of steel, as it appears after a hundred-hour-long drumroll barrage of the familiar home of our frontline fighter; that's what Dix has documented for all future ages, with nerves of iron. Every square centimeter of this gigantic canvas (2 ½ by 2 ½ meters) piled high with horror, stench, and a feast for writhing maggots.[366]

365 "Da sitzen ein paar Tausend in Treptow, haben ganz vergessen, wie es damals vor Verdun war, haben die Totenberge vergessen und die Blutbäche und den Dreck und den Schlamm und die Vertierung, und denken statt dessen nur an die schöne Militärzeit, und dass es bald wieder so kommen möge. Denken in aller Harmlosigkeit daran. Heinz Pol, "Trommelfeur" *Die Weltbühne* 20/32 (7 August 1924), 236–237.

366 "Nun, dieses Stahlbad, wie es nach einem hundertstündigen Trommelfeuer über dem trauten Heim unsrer Frontkämpfer sich präsentierte: das hat Dix mit eisernen Nerven für all Zukunft dokumentiert; jeden Quadratzentimeter dieser Riesenleinwand (2 ½ mal 2 ½ Meter) angefüllt mit Grauen, Gestank und Beköstigung wimmelnder Maden." Paul Ferdinand Schmidt, "Der Schützengraben," *Die Weltbühne* 20/32 (7 August 1924), 235–236.

If the problem of representing the "truth" of the war, and the goal of emphasizing the eyewitness status of his own recorded memories of the war experience, came to preoccupy Dix after 1921 in ways that it had not preoccupied him before – even during the war itself – perhaps it is because it had become the frequent topic of heated, open debate, as evidenced by the reception of *The Trench* itself. And Dix seems to have approached the problem by identifying and speaking directly to a community of fellow veterans. This is not necessarily at the expense of communicating with art critics and insiders, many of whom were themselves also veterans. Rather, within the cloistered art world, he effectively drove a wedge between the veterans such as himself and the older generation, who clung to the outdated idiom of glory and heroism. Yet confronting a forgetful public with the reality of the war was not necessarily the same thing as proclaiming his opposition to all war, but may have had more to do with a widespread frustration with the public's misconceptions and with misrepresentations, and the desire to divide the viewing public between those who had experienced the front first hand and those – including older critics – who had not. We will see that in their responses to *The Trench*, it was the older critics who took it as an antiwar protest (and who objected to it on those terms), while fellow veterans emphasized its truthfulness, and welcomed it on those terms. What they agreed on was that its message – whether antiwar or truthfulness – was inseparable from the manner in which it was painted. I use the term "truthfulness" here not in a naïve way, but in recognition of the fact that, first, any representation of the war, even one by an eyewitness such as Dix, is necessarily constructed out of other images as well as out of actual memories which are themselves in turn socially constructed (as per Halbwachs), and second, that we now have no way of judging for ourselves the accuracy or objectivity of *any* representation of the war. Even eyewitness memories of the war were at some level fictions.[367] Paul Ferdinand Schmidt, a friend of Dix's but not a veteran, acknowledged both of these facts when he wrote,

367 Samuel Hynes, *A War Imagined: The First World War and English Culture* (New York: Atheneum, 1991).

> Nothing is exaggerated in this painting, it is just synthesized. What remained, not living, in ten different places in a destroyed trench, Dix has piled up in one spot. Project what is painted onto the reality from 1917, and the heart stops in hopeless terror. A man, a *Muschkote* [slang for a foot soldier, MM] among many, lay for four years in the trench and experienced that unnamable horror that the name "War" stands in for.[368]

Memories competed one with another in the discursive space of the Weimar Republic. The point of painting in the mode of grotesque realism, with its evident exaggerations, was to bring low the elevated tone – and therefore the falsity – of official modes of representation.

To return to the exchange between Schmits and F. (or Ernst) Friedrich: Schmits responded to Freiedrich's letter to the editors of the *Rheinische Zeitung* with a second essay on *The Trench*, this time situating it more directly within a discussion of pacifism generally, and what he perceived as the need for Germans to be prepared to defend themselves against military aggression (this was written during the Allies' military occupation of the Rhineland). His criticism of *The Trench* now focuses specifically on what Schmits takes to be its anti-war message, and its one-sided focus on a certain aspect of the reality of the war.

> We have nothing against it when somebody wants to enlighten the people about the nature of war. What we object to in Dix's picture, as a work of propaganda, is how one-sided, and thus false, it's lesson about war is.[369]

Schmit's objection is thus not that *The Trench* falsifies or even exaggerates the physical reality of the war, but that it presents *only* the physical reality,

368 "In diesem Bilde ist nichts übertrieben – es ist nur komprimiert. Was an zehn Stellen eines zertrümmerten Grabens an Nichtlebendigem übrig blieb, hat Dix auf einen Fleck zusammengehäuft. Denkt man sich das Gemalte in die Wirklichkeit von 1917 zurückübertragen, so erstarrt das Herz vor hoffnungslosem Grausen. Ein Mann, ein Muschkote unter vielen, lag vier Jahre im Schützengraben und erlebte das unnennbar Scheußliche, das der Name Krieg bedeckt." Paul Ferdinand Schmidt, "Der Schützengraben."

369 "Wir haben nichts einzuwenden, wenn man das Volk über die Natur des Krieges aufzuklären sucht. An dem Dixschen Bild als Tendenzbild tadeln wir, dass es das Volk einseitig, also falsch, über den Krieg unterrichtet." Walter Schmits, *Kölnische Zeitung* (14 December 1923, evening edition).

an objection traditionally raised against Naturalism, and is therefore, by virtue of only portraying physical, material reality, a falsification of a larger, presumably spiritual truth. And for Schmits, that deeper spiritual truth of the war was obviously a positive one.

Dix's fellow veterans in the Rhineland were having none of this, and they seem to have written letters to the editor critical of Schmit's position. He responded to their objections, too, in this second essay. Judging from what Schmits writes, the veterans hadn't praised Dix as a pacifist, but rather for memorializing their experience in a language that they could identify with. They accused Schmits of wanting to suppress the memory of the war and its sacrifice. Schmits in turn waves away this accusation; "Nothing could have been further from our desire," he writes. But for Schmits, any proper memorialization of the war had to aspire to the register of the classicizing and the heroic – to the idiom of official, *cultural* memory, rather than speak in the popular idiom of dialogical, *communicative* memory. Thus he deflects the veterans' criticism with such phrases as, "Our brave troops," and "warlike heroics."[370] This indirect evidence is a strong indication that, if Dix's purpose was indeed to tell the "truth" about the war – a truth that fellow veterans would recognize as truthful, and expressed in a manner that mimicked the soldier's own idiom, grotesquely realist, occasionally satirical and humorous, he had indeed achieved it.

The art critics who were also veterans were able to express their approval in print: "That's what it was like in the autumn days in the trenches, south of Soissons." wrote Alfred Salmony. He went on,

> The picture is not tendentious, but only a pedantically precise, objective depiction: This is what war is like. ... People don't understand his nerves of steel. Nobody else would be in a position to reproduce these piled-up cruelties in such detail, and to work up a picture out of them. That's a healthy countermeasure to both the nostalgia of veteran's organizations and salon painting.[371]

370 "Unseres tapfern Heeres" and "kriegerischen Heldentaten." Schmits, 14 December 1923.

371 So war es an Herbsttagen in den Gräben südlich von Soissons. Das Bild kennt keine Tendenz, nur peinlich genaue sachliche Schilderung: so ist Krieg. ... Diese Stahlnerven begreift man nicht. Keiner sonst wäre imstande gewesen, diese

A few months later, Max Liebermann asked to borrow the painting for the annual exhibition of the Berlin Art Academy in 1924. The well-known art critic and writer Julius Meier-Graefe was asked by Paul Fechter, the feuilleton editor of the culturally conservative *Deutsche Allgemeine Zeitung* to write about the exhibition, probably in the expectation that he would have something inflammatory to say about it, which he did.[372] Meier-Graefe was probably best known as the promoter of French Postimpressionist painting in Germany, and for his book on Vincent van Gogh; he had carried the banner of avant-garde art in his time, and was certainly no chauvinist of German culture; he had been on the side of international, especially French modernism against Carl Vinnen when the latter published his *Protest of German Artists* in 1911.[373] But in his essay on *The Trench*, he objected not so much to what it represented, as to the way that it was painted, which he felt was an "infamy," with an "offensive joy taken in the details."[374] And like Schmits, Meier-Graefe expressed his concern that the painting was both a work of pacifist propaganda and that it could have undesirable political consequences in the occupied Rhineland.

> Probably Herr Dix wanted in all simplicity to further the cause of pacifism, following the well-known deterrence theory. That's his private pleasure. But the picture has been put in a public place, and so become a German cultural document. That's the catch. In Cologne I saw a pair of officers from the other side [he means the occupying powers, the British, French, and Belgian armies, MM] standing in front

---

gehäuften Greuel in Einzelheiten zu geben, ein Bild damit zu bauen. Das ist gesunde Gegenwirkung gegen Vereinsromantik und Salonpeinture." Salmony, "Die neue Galerie," 6–11.

372 Crockett, "The Most Famous Painting." On Fechter, see Catherine Krahmer, ed., Julius Meier-Graefe, *Kunst ist nicht für Kunstgeschichte da. Briefe und Dokumente* (Göttingen: Wallstein, 2001), 523.

373 Carl Vinnen, *Ein Protest Deutscher Künstler* (Jena: Diedrichs, 1911). See Catherine Krahmer, ed., *Julius Meier-Graefe, Kunst ist nicht für Kunstgeschichte da. Briefe und Dokumente*, Göttingen, Wallstein Verlag, 2001, p. 523.

374 "Dieser Schützengraben ist nicht nur schlecht, sondern infam gemalt, mit einer penetranten Freude am Detail ... ." Julius Meier-Graefe, "Die Ausstellung in der Akademie," *Deutsche Allgemeine Zeitung* (2 July 1924, evening edition).

> of the picture, and I had to make myself scarce so as to avoid catching their critique, legitimated as it was by their professional expertise.[375]

The question of whether or not the work was one of pacifist propaganda was thus brought up in public again by Meier-Graefe, and his essay drew a variety of responses; it was clearly an important question for people. Max Liebermann, whom Meier-Graefe had attacked directly for including the painting in the show, defended it with a sort of metaphysical mystification, describing it as neither more nor less than an objective, unemotional depiction of the war itself, "the war as a terrible thing-in-itself," and as the artist's statement that "this is what a trench looks like."[376] But Liebermann, who was 77 years old, also spoke to the idea that Dix was entitled, even obligated, by his experiences to represent the truth of the front experience to those who had not been there.[377] Dix's artist colleagues (and fellow veterans) from the Rhineland, including Franz Wilhelm Seiwert, Heinirch Hoerle, and others, themselves outspoken pacifists and veterans, wrote to deny that Dix had in any way aimed to further the cause of pacifism, although they supported him nonetheless.[378] For Ernst Kállai, another art critic on the left who praised *The Trench*, it was an ambiguous work – the ambiguity

375 Wahrscheinlich hat Herr Dix in aller Einfalt für den Pazifismus wirken wollen, die bekannte Abschreckungs-Theorie. Das ist sein Privatvergnügen. Das Bild, an öffentliche Stelle gerückt, wird deutsches Kulturdokument. Das ist der Haken. Ich sah in Köln ein paar Offiziere von drüben vor dem Monstrum stehen und machte mich dünne, um nicht ihre fachberechtigte Kritik mitzunehmen. Meier-Graefe, "Die Ausstellung in der Akademie."

376 Max Liebermann, "… den Krieg als fürchterliches Ding an sich wollte der Künstler im Schützengrabenbilde veranschaulichen, ohne Pathos … Dix sagt: 'Seht euch mein bild an, so sieht's im Schützengraben aus." *Mannheimer Tageblatt* (10 October 1924), cited in Brigid S. Barton, "Die Entstehung eines Künstlerrufs: Otto Dix und *Der Schützengraben*," in Rainer Beck, *Otto Dix, 1891–1969: Zeit, Leben, Werk* (Konstanz: Stadler, 1993), 51.

377 Liebermann, "Und er hat nicht nur das Recht, sondern die Pflicht, es uns zu sagen, weil ihm ein Gott gab, zu sagen, was er gelitten und geduldet hat," *Mannheimer Tageblatt*.

378 F. W. Seiwert, Heinrich Hoerle, *et al.*, "Zunächst wissen wir, die wir Dix kennen, daß ihm nichts an einer pazifistischen Wirkung gelegen hat. …" "Zu dem Artikel

was essential to what Kállai called the work's "monumentality" – and could be read either as pacifist propaganda or as "highest praise of a fanatical worshiper of the god of war."[379]

Meier-Graefe's review took a bizarre rhetorical turn in a comparison with a painting by Rembrandt,

> Brains, blood, and guts can be painted in such a way as to make your mouth water. … Rembrandt's second Anatomy, with its belly opened up, makes you want to kiss it. This Dix painting makes you – pardon the ugly word – want to puke. Brains, blood, and guts are not so much painted as spread out before us in such a way that every animal reaction is pushed to the limit.[380]

He concluded by calling for its removal from the Wallraf-Richartz-Museum – indeed, he claimed to have already worked behind the scenes to get it removed from the museum's permanent collection, a move that many of the painting's supporters felt overstepped the bounds of art criticism.[381]

---

von Meier-Graefe: 'Die Ausstellung in der Akademie'," *Das Kunstblatt* 8 (October 1924), 317–318.

379 "[H]öchster Anbetung eines fanatischen Kriegsgottverehrers," Ernst Kállai, ""Dämonie der Satire." See also Heijo Klein, "Kállais Interpretation" des 'Schützengrabenbildes" von Otto Dix im Vergleich mit zeitgenössischen und gegenwärtigen Deutungen," *Acta Historiae Artium* 36 (1993), 180–88, and Peters, *Neue Sachlichkeit und Nationalsozialismus*, 197–199.

380 "Gehirn, Blut, Gedärm können so gemalt werden, dass einem das Wasser in Munde zusammenläuft. … Die zweite Anatomie Rembrandts mit dem offenen Bauch ist zum Küssen. Dieser Dix ist – verzeihen Sie das harte Wort – zum Kotzen. Gehirn, Blut, Gedärm werden so ausstaffiert, nicht etwa gemalt, dass alle animalische Reaktion zur Hochspannung getrieben wird." Meier-Graefe, "Die Ausstellung in der Akademie."

381 Paul Westheim wrote, in a letter to the editor of the *Deutsche Allgemeine Zeitung*, "Ich lese eben den Aufsatz von Meier-Graefe über die Akademie-Ausstellung. Dass Meier-Graefe das Kriegsbild von Dix 'zum Kotzen' findet … ist private Meinungsäußerung, die jeder so oder so nehmen kann. Aber Meier-Graefe übt nicht nur Kritik an dem Kriegsbild von Dix – in dem ich mit vielen anderen eine charakteristische Leistung eines jungen, unbedingt begabten und ehrlichen Talentes sehe. … eine Denunziation … wird hier zu einer behördlichen Zensurierung eines Museums und zur Unterdrückung eines Kunstwerks aufgefordert." *Deutsche Allgemeine Zeitung* (8 July 1924).

An anatomy painting, good enough to kiss? It did not take the defenders of *The Trench* long to mock the once esteemed and now somewhat old-fashioned Meier-Graefe. Willi Wolfradt in particular took aim at this comment in his defense of the painting, which was part of a much longer essay on Dix published in *Die Cicerone*.

> Truly it'll make you puke; it won't make you comfortable, and it's painted that way, it cries bloody murder, this still life of worms in split-open skulls, this insane landscape of bodies, skewered and pummeled to bits. ... That's just how a grunt [*Frontschwein*, slang for a frontline soldier, MM] paints, gentlemen: straightforward and unaesthetic![382]

Meier-Graefe and Wolfradt both responded to the grotesque realism of the painting, and their own responses are somewhat Rabelaisian. Even more so was the response of Carl Einstein, another supporter of Dix, who wrote that the best thing about the painting was how it gave the whole epoch, "a swift and technically sound kick in its swollen belly."[383] But Wolfradt, a fellow veteran as well as an art critic and author of a dissertation on the landscapes of Caspar David Friedrich, who had once described Dadaism as "an attempt to present to us for consideration the entrails of our time," explicitly praised the painting precisely because it was both true, in his estimation, and was expressed in the idiom of the soldier, the *Frontschwein*. Writers of the front generation recognized Dix's low, grotesque register as truthful, while older critics found it an inappropriate mode for a public monument. For members of Dix's own generation, fellow veterans as well as fellow members of the cultural avant-garde, the comically grotesque elements of the painting seemed an entirely appropriate visual language for a former infantryman to use.

382 "Wahrlich zum Kotzen und nicht zum Komfort ist das gemalt, dies himmelschreinde Stillleben der Würmer in aufgeschmetterten Schädeln, diese wahnsinnige Landschaft gespießter, wild zusammengestampfter Leiber. ... Wie halt so ein Frontschwein malt, meine Herren; es ist direct unästhetisch!" Willi Wolfradt, "Otto Dix," *Der Cicerone* 16/20 (1924), 943–954, and *Otto Dix* (Berlin: Jünge Kunst, 1924).

383 Carl Einstein, "Otto Dix," *Das Kunstblatt* 7/3 (March 1923), 97–102.

If, like the Dadaist "war cripples" series, the grotesque realism of *The Trench* was an attempt to create community around the memories of the front, built on a particular idiom which could be either verbal or visual, then Dix seems to have hit the mark. The painting clearly and forcefully separated those who found this idiom an appropriate, familiar, and perhaps the only adequate means to express the truth of their shared experiences, from those who were repelled by it and who refused to acknowledge its message as anything that they could find compelling or even acceptable.

In the wake of Meier-Graefe's politicization of the debate over *The Trench*, pressure was put on the museum's director Hans Secker to return the painting to Dix. It is not clear where the pressure came from; Dix himself thought that Konrad Adenauer, then mayor of Cologne and the future chancellor of West Germany, was involved.[384] By early 1925, *The Trench* was taken down from the walls of the Wallraf-Richartz Museum, and arrangements were made to sell the painting back to Nierendorf.[385] Forced to take the painting back, Nierendorf was even more aggressive in exhibiting it; he shipped it to an exhibition in Zurich in July of 1925, and dedicated an entire room to it in the retrospective of Dix's work he organized in his new gallery space in Berlin in February 1926, surrounded by prints from the portfolio *War*.[386] Nierendorf allowed it to be published in the album *Never Again War*, published by the radical antiwar movement, thereby furthering Dix's national fame but also lending credence to the

384 Dietrich Schubert has consistently held to this claim, most recently in, "Die Verfolgung des Gemäldes *Schützengraben* (1923) von Otto Dix," Rolf Kloepfer and Burckhard Dücker, eds., *Kritik und Geschichte der Intoleranz* (Heidelberg: Syncron, 2000), 351–370, here p. 358. Wolfgang Schröck-Schmidt, however, was unable to locate documentary evidence of such direct involvement. See Wolfgang Schröck-Schmidt, "Der Schicksalsweg des 'Schützengraben'" in Wulf Herzogenrath and Johann-Karl Schmidt, eds., *Otto Dix – zum 100. Geburtstag* (Stuttgart: Hatje-Cantz, 1991), 159–164.

385 Letter from Nierendorf to Dix, dated 30 January 1925, DKA, I, C, 524 g.

386 Undated letter from Nierendorf to Dix, late 1925 or early 1926, DKA I, C, 524 h.

mistaken idea that Dix himself was a radical antimilitarist.[387] Art critics continued to write about the painting. In 1926, Paul Westheim penned an essay on Dix for *Das Kunstblatt* in which he directly indicated that *The Trench* was, like the speech of soldiers, characterized by its brutal directness instead of the parables or allegories of, presumably, untruthful official histories. "To speak in parables doesn't make sense any longer; they learned that in 1914, too. That led to too many unscrupulous and shameless lies. Only one thing can compel conviction, can help now: the facts; the naked, brutal facts."[388] And in 1927, Ernst Kállai wrote his essay on Dix for the same journal, in which he assimilated Dix to the Baudelairian grotesque, and in which he suggested that it was impossible to tell if Dix rejected war or worshipped at its altar – and that it didn't matter.[389]

After Dix ended his contract with Nierendorf in May of 1927, when he left Berlin to take up his teaching post in Dresden, Nierendorf was still occupied with trying to find a museum to buy *The Trench*. He finally succeeded in getting Hans Posse, the young director of the Dresden Gemäldegalerie [Painting Gallery] to buy it in 1928 at the considerable asking price of 10,000 Reichsmarks, the year after Dix took up a teaching post in that city.[390] Posse was a nationalist, later a convinced Nazi who was commissioned by Hitler in 1939 to assemble what was to be the largest art collection ever for the so-called "Führer-Museum," planned for the city of Linz. But as director of the Gemäldegalerie Posse supported

387 Sozialistische Arbeiterjugend West-Sachsen, *Nie Wieder Krieg* (Leipzig: Roter Türmer, 1925), cited in Schröck-Schmidt, *Schicksalsweg*, footnote no. 24. It is not true that the painting was also in the exhibition by the same name that toured Germany in 1925.

388 "In Gleichnissen zu reden, auch das haben sie seit 1914 gelernt, hat keinen Sinn mehr; damit ist zu skrupellos und unverschämt geschwindelt worden. Nur eins kann noch überzeugen, kann besser helfen: die Tatsache, die nackte, brutalnackte Tatsache." Paul Westheim, "Dix," *Das Kunstblatt* 10 (1926), 142–146.

389 Kállai, "Dämonie der Satire."

390 Birgit Dalbajewa and Olaf Peters, "Die Auseinandersetzung mit dem Krieg," in Birgit Dalbajewa, Simone Fleischer, and Olaf Peters, *Otto Dix. Der Krieg – Das Dresdner Triptychon* (Dresden: Sandstein Verlag, 2014), 71–83.

avant-garde art and German Expressionism in particular, and conceived of the "Galerie Neue Meister." He was also a fellow veteran, and so perhaps had an understanding for *The Trench* that older critics lacked. Even with his support, there was serious concern that conservative members of the patrons committee, which covered half the cost of the purchase (the city of Dresden put up the remaining of 5,000 Reichsmarks), might resign in protest.[391] In this political environment, the painting was not put on display in the Gemäldegalerie in Dresden, but put into storage, from which it was retrieved only under the Nazi regime, in order to be exhibited as "degenerate art."

391 This from the director of the patrons committee, Heinrich Arnhold, as related in an undated letter from Nierendorf to Dix, October (?) 1928, DKA I, C 524 j. See also Dalbajewa and Peters, "Die Auseinandersetzung," 76.

CHAPTER 4

Dix and Other Veterans: The Print Portfolio *The War*, the *Reichsbanner*, and Social Democratic Memories of the War Experience

Soon after he had completed his large-scale painting of *The Trench*, Dix conceived of a project that would continue his engagement with the memory of the war, but in a very different format and scale: a series of etchings that would combine several different vignettes into one portfolio, one large, all-encompassing cycle that, like memory itself, would suggest an overwhelming, all-consuming experience through individual scenes without being chronological, narrative, or complete. Dix had already created two graphic portfolios, *Death and Resurrection* [Tod und Auferstehung] (1922) and *Circus* [Artisten und Zirkus] (1922), which Karl Nierendorf published, and before that he had published several in Dresden.[392] As with many artists in Germany at the time, graphic arts were an important part of his business strategy, and during the inflationary period they were extremely popular with collectors as a safe haven for monetary value, and more affordable than paintings. Early in the 1920s the pictures of war cripples had made use of avant-gardist formal strategies, and they used a complicated and unfamiliar formal language to convey equally unfamiliar messages about the war and the nature of the soldier's experience. His portfolio *The War* [Der Krieg], by contrast, would present a much more immediate formal vocabulary of realism, combined with an extraordinarily rich and varied range of techniques and with a striking display of technical mastery. It would convey the physical and psychological trials of trench warfare as seen from the perspective of a foot soldier, a perspective that was getting

392 Both portfolios are reproduced in their entirety in Olaf Peters, *Otto Dix* (Munich: Prestel, 2010).

increasing attention in the public, collective memory of the war in Weimar Germany in 1923 and 1924, and displacing other experiences, such as the years of hunger and privation for civilians or the loss of sons and husbands.

The *War* portfolio was a monumental work, comprising 50 prints done in a combination of etching, engraving, and aquatint, in an edition of 70. It was more monumental in its own way even than *The Trench*, despite the fact that the individual images were relatively small, ranging in size from 14 x 19.7 cm to 30 x 24.7 cm and printed on paper.[393] The eye-witness nature of the account is emphasized in many different ways. Dix made several compositional decisions in his etchings which made claims for their veracity, for their truth status as eye-witness records. Those compositional choices included point of view, scale, and the fragmentary nature of the overall cycle, as well as the dates and place names and other textual fragments used as titles. Dix mostly limited himself to the kinds of scenes which he himself might have witnessed, such as life in the trenches and the battlefield, as well as the occasional visit to a bar, brothel, or street in the occupied towns of the rear, and several of the individual titles name places where we know Dix himself fought. Yet the portfolio as a whole is not structured by a narrative arc or development as an autobiographical account would be. In contrast to the memoirs written by Ernst Jünger, Erich Maria Remarque, Ludwig Renn, and others, it does not progress from basic training to baptism by fire to the great battles and on to the end of the war. Nor is it marked by the itinerary of those great battles; there is no apparent chronological or thematic order at all. Rather, the individual scenes appear at random, in the manner of involuntary memories. It is a very selective view of the war.

It seems clear that Dix experienced what we would today not hesitate to label Post Traumatic Stress Disorder. Toward the end of his life he recounted how he had suffered from recurring nightmares in those postwar years, recalling that, "For years, for at least ten years, I had these

393 Verein August Macke Haus, *Otto Dix. "Der Krieg" Radierwerk, 1924* (Bonn: August Macke Haus, 1999) reproduces all 50 images, as does the exhibition catalog edited by Olaf Peters, *Otto Dix* (Munich: Prestel, 2010) and that of the exhibition *Otto Dix – The Evil Eye / Der Böse Blick* (Munich: Prestel, 2017).

dreams where I had to crawl through bombed out houses, through passageways that I could barely squeeze through. The rubble was always in my dreams."[394] Nonetheless, he did not create this cycle of images in the solitude of his personal memories and dreams. He created it at least partly in direct response to the public work of collective memory formation in Germany in 1923 and 1924, as well as the critical debate over his earlier, monumental painting *The Trench*. Today, Dix's cycle of etchings is routinely understood first and foremost as a warning against war and militarism. To this end the entire cycle is displayed in its own room in the First World War *Historial* in Peronne, France.[395] Dietrich Schubert in particular has repeatedly presented Dix and his *War* portfolio as strongly political, specifically leftist, and primarily antiwar.[396] Schubert sees in the portfolio the representation of an "imperialistic war ... in the interest of the Kaiser, weapons manufacturers, and generals."[397] But such indicators are in fact remarkably absent from the portfolio's 50 images. Otto Conzelmann, by contrast, attempted to decouple the work from any political context whatsoever, making the content of the work rather the artist's own sovereign individuality and the unique expression of his own very private experience of war as something elemental, beyond good

394 "Denn ich habe jahrelang, mindestens zehn Jahre lang immer diese Träume gehabt, in denen ich durch zertrümmerte Häuser kriechen mußte, durch Gänge, durch die ich kaum durchkam. Die Trümmer waren fortwährend in meinen Träumen." Interview with Maria Wetzel, "Professor Otto Dix – Ein harter Mann, dieser Maler," *Diplotamischer Kurier* 14 (1965), 731–745. Reprinted in Schmidt, *Otto Dix im Selbstbildnis*, 269–270.

395 An example of the French reception of this work is Philippe Dagen, "The Morality of Horror," in Annette Becker, ed., *Der Krieg / The War* (Peronne: Historial de la Grande Guerre, 2003), 9–23.

396 Dietrich Schubert, "Otto Dix und der Krieg," Dietrich Harth and Dietrich Schubert, eds., *Pazifismus zwischen den Weltkriegen: Deutscher Schriftsteller und Künstler gegen Krieg und Militarismus 1918–1933* (Heidelberg: HVA, 1985), 185–202; "Otto Dix: Die Radierungen Der Krieg (Berlin 1924) oder: das 'Yo lo vi'," in Verein August Macke Haus, *Otto Dix, Der Krieg*, 12–46.

397 Dietrich Schubert, "Otto Dix, Die Radierungen 'Der Krieg' von 1924," *Kunsthistorische Arbeitsblätter*, 9 (September 2002), 39–46. I wish to thank Dietrich Schubert himself for bringing this essay to my attention.

and evil, transformed by his Nietzschean artistic genius into a work of pure spirit.[398] What these two art historians have in common is a conception of Dix as an outsider, isolated either by his moral clarity or the aesthetic elitism of his creative spirit, either a Jeremiah or a Zarathustra. Annegret Jürgens-Kirchhoff has escaped this interpretive impasse by shifting her focus from the artist's intention to the effect of the work, which she argues is to create a strong negative depiction of the horrors of war [*Schreckensbilder*], and so to warn against further war.[399] Yet all three of these accounts share the assumption that the meaning of the portfolio came out of the artist's private, inner meditation on the war experience, even if it was intended to have a public effect. But to argue that the *War* portfolio was an isolated statement in the Weimar Republic amounts to a decontextualization of it. More recently, Linda McGreevy has done excellent work mapping the imagery of *The War* onto statistical realities, documentary military history, and other eyewitness accounts of the scenarios depicted – the specific battles or the situation in the trenches.[400] She reads them as first-person documents of the war which accord with the harrowing and often dehumanizing experiences of the common soldier so vividly presented in such studies as Eric Leed's *No Man's Land* and John Ellis' *Eye Deep in Hell*.[401] Essentially, she asks if they are truthful accounts, and finds that they are.

But here I am more interested in the *War* portfolio as a document of the evolving state of collective memory in Germany in the early 1920s than as a document of the war, or of Dix's individualistic integrity or his political acuity. I wish to return the work to the public context within which it was produced, to see that it was produced as expression of, rather than

398 Otto Conzelmann, *Der andere Dix – Sein Bild vom Menschen und vom Kriege* (Stuttgart: Hatje-Cantz, 1983).

399 Annegret Jürgens-Kirchhoff, *Schreckensbilder. Krieg und Kunst im 20. Jahrhundert* (Berlin: Reimer, 1993), 246 ff.

400 Linda McGreevy, *Bitter Witness* (Bern: Peter Lang, 2003), 292–324.

401 Eric Leed, *No Man's Land: Combat and Identity in World War One* (Cambridge: Cambridge University Press, 1979), and John Ellis, *Eye Deep in Hell: Trench Warfare in World War I* (New York, Pantheon Books, 1976).

in opposition to, a social discourse. I am guided here in part by Maurice Halbwach's model of history as a process of collective memory formation.[402] Rather than focusing on the question, Were the images in *The War* accurate and truthful representations of the front soldier's war experience? I will instead pose the questions: What and whose expectations of what counted as truthful first person accounts of the war experience did these images meet? What do they tell us about the process of collective memory of the war in Germany in 1924? Where did they fit into the spectrum of meaning-making about the war in 1923–1924? And perhaps the most difficult question: What attitude about the war did Dix express through these works, and where did that attitude fit into the public memory of and attitudes about the war? Whereas the existing literature on the *War* portfolio suggests that Dix intended it as a *rebuke* to the dominant discourse about the memory of the war in Weimar Germany, I will argue that, on the contrary, the attitudes and preoccupations which Dix expressed here were quite similar to those of a wide swath of his fellow former combatants. Those attitudes and preoccupations can be identified specifically with the veterans' groups affiliated with the Social Democratic Party, rather than with either the Communist Party or the reactionary nationalist parties. This means that a proper understanding of the *War* portfolio's message about the war will read it as a document of the evolving state of collective memory in Germany in the early 1920s, and not as a document of Dix's supposed exceptionalism. I will continue this project of finding the congruence, rather than the difference, between Dix's attitudes about the war and those of the society around him in the next chapter, where the next artwork Dix produced about the war, a large-scale triptych, will be viewed in its turn as a document of the public work of remembrance in Germany in the period 1927–1932. In this chapter and the next I will argue that these works had more to do with the situation in Germany in the 1920s than with an attempt to represent what the war was "really like." I will also look at the relationship between his work and the public discourse of mourning and memory which I think informed it, rather than treat it as though it had

402 Halbwachs, Maurice, *On Collective Memory* (Chicago: University of Chicago Press, 1992, Lewis A. Coser, ed. and translator).

been fashioned in the splendid isolation of the genius artist.[403] Another goal in this chapter will be to compare Dix's portfolio and similar cycles of prints made by others in Germany about the war.

The development of the *War* portfolio and the public reception of *The Trench*

During the course of 1923, while Karl Nierendorf was facilitating the sale of *The Trench* to the Wallraf-Richartz Museum in Cologne, he was also supporting Dix's latest efforts to represent the war experience. He provided 30 zinc plates in November for use in the portfolio (eventually, Dix would expand the portfolio to 50 plates). In December 1923 the Wallraf-Richartz Museum reopened to the public after rehanging the collection, now with *The Trench* prominently featured and so presenting it to the public for the first time. The debate about the painting and its appropriateness or inappropriateness as a public memorial of the war began in the press almost immediately, as discussed in the previous chapter. It is not often enough remembered that this was the context in which Dix worked on his cycle of prints in which he depicted the experiences of the front in minute detail.

As Dix turned his attention to the creation of this major print portfolio on the subject of the war, he studied printmaking technique with the Dresden Art Academy's graphic arts master, Wilhelm Herberholz.

403 On memory and remembrance see Bernd Ulrich and Benjamin Ziemann, eds., *Krieg im Frieden. Die umkämpfte Erinnerung an den Ersten Weltkrieg. Quellen und Dokumente* (Frankfurt: Fischer, 1997); Christian Saehrendt, *Der Stellungskrieg der Denkmäler im Berlin der Zwischenkriegszeit 1919–1939* (Bonn: Dietz, 2004); J. Dülffer and Gerd Krumeich, eds., *Der verlorene Frieden. Politik und Kriegskultur nach 1918*, Essen 2002; Michael Jeismann and Rolf Westheider, "'Wofür stirbt der Bürger?' Nationaler Totenkult und Staatsbürgertum in Deutschaland und Frankreich seit der Französischer Revolution," in Reinhart Koselleck, ed., *Der politische Totenkult. Kriegerdenkmäler der Moderne* (Munich: Fink, 1994), 23–49.

The preparatory sketches Dix made (many of which are held in the collection of the Kunstmuseum Albstadt and in the Zeppelin Museum in Friedrichshafen) were essentially of two kinds: relatively tight pencil sketches done in a small, oblong sketchbook, emphasizing expressive relationships between figures and compositional elements, and tonal sketches done with a brush and ink washes, which were much more concerned with a visual drama that combined strong contrasts between light and dark with energetic compositions and violent imagery. The ink wash compositions were dominated by action – troops crawling forward under barbed wire entanglements, for example, or running from an exploding shell – and the flashes of explosions signifying artillery bombardments. The skies are often indicated by unadulterated black ink, heightening the tension. Middle tones predominate. Dix was clearly imagining what the technique of aquatint could do for him, enabling him to convey emotional drama through painterly tenebrism. The pencil sketches, by contrast, indicate his intention to use aquatint by merely writing it in the margins. But as the conception of the portfolio evolved, Dix moved decisively away from these dramatic moments of combat, while retaining the visual idea of strong contrasts, inky black skies, and painterly middle tones. There are no exploding shells in the final portfolio, despite the ubiquity of that motif in the work of other artists.[404]

At the same time that Dix was working on the design and execution of the plates for *The War*, he was also occupied with consolidating his ascendance into the bourgeoisie, a move he had accomplished both through his success as an artist and through his marriage to the educated and well-to-do Martha Koch. In the winter of 1923–1924 his concern with his newfound status led to a preoccupation with, for example, skiing. This was more than just recreation; a skiing vacation was the practice and performance of bourgeois standing, and the sort of thing that Martha may well have been accustomed to. He was bitterly frustrated that a painter he knew from Düsseldorf, Arthur Kaufmann, who was less gifted (Dix pointed out) than he was, could afford to take his own

404 For example in works by Max Beckmann, Herman Max Pechstein, Theophile Steinlein, Felix Vallotton, and countless others.

family skiing while Dix could not. This envy became the occasion of one of his nastier spats over money with Nierendorf, whom he accused of holding out on him financially.[405] In the end Dix and Martha did go on an extended skiing vacation that winter, renting a farmhouse in the Black Forest. But Dix was also working on *The War*, bringing with him the metal plates and all of the materials needed to etch and engrave them.[406] In April of 1924 Nierendorf advanced Dix the money for a trip to Italy – a sort of Grand Tour, albeit one with a very eccentric itinerary, and a completion of his proper artistic education.[407] Nierendorf also suggested a trip to Paris, pointing out that the educated Martha spoke French.[408] In Italy Dix saw *The Three Living and Three Dead* in the fresco of the Camposanto in Pisa (c. 1360). The artist Max Niehauss had suggested to Dix a trip to Palermo, and had sent him a postcard the previous October from the catacombs, with a picture of a mummified, partly skeletal bodies dressed up as cardinals.[409] Dix took up the idea, and in Palermo he saw the *Triumph of Death* (c. 1360), and visited the catacombs of the Convento dei Cappuccini, where he drew the mummified heads (one such drawing of a *Mummified Death's Head* is in the Kunstmuseum Albstadt; see Figure 48).[410]

405 Letter from Dix to Nierendorf (undated, late December, 1923), Deutsches Kunstarchiv, Germanisches Nationalmuseum, Nuremberg, Otto Dix archive (hereafter DKA), I C 523. In the letter, Dix demands his due, brushes aside Nierendorf's own money worries (this was at the height of inflation), and complains that Kaufmann could afford, "samt Frau und Kinder wunderschöne Skiausrüstung und vergnügt sich den ganzen Tag während ich aber arbeite."

406 Recounted by Dix in an audio recording made in the 1960s; four decades later, the skiing trip still figured prominently in Dix's reminiscences. Otto Dix, *Ich folge lieber meinem Dämon: Originaltonaufnahmen* (Pforzheim: Brigade Commerz, 2009).

407 Letter from Nierendorf addressed to Dix in Italy, 3 April 1924, in which Nierendorf reminds Dix that the artist owes him some watercolors from the trip, in return for his having helped finance it. DKA I, C, 524 f.

408 Nierendorf, letter to Dix, February 1924, DKA I, C, 524 f.

409 Postcard from Max Niehaus to Dix, 10 October 1923, DKA I, C, 523.

410 Conzelmann, *Der Andere Dix*, 154 f.

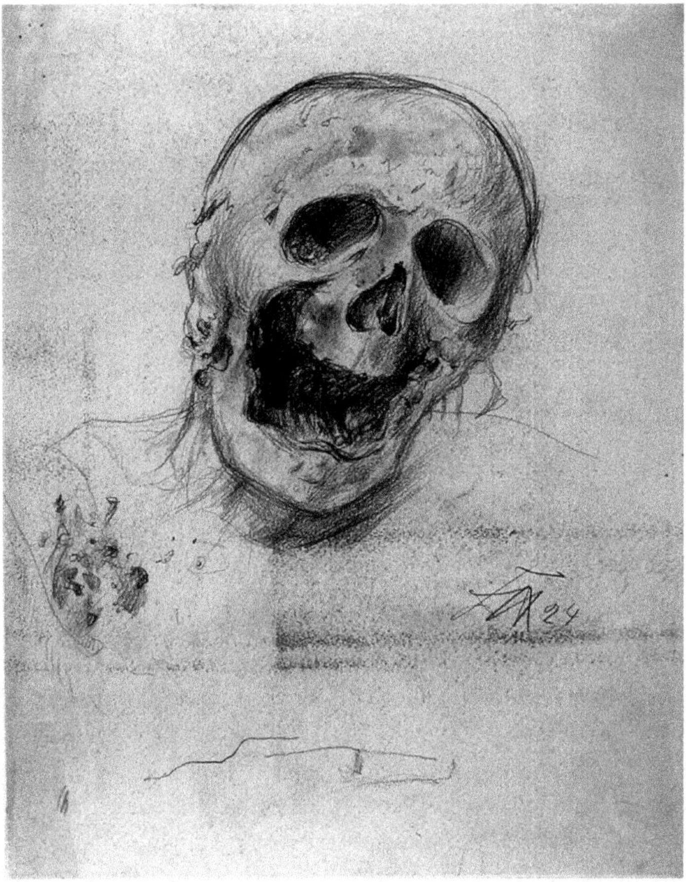

Figure 48. Otto Dix, *Mummified Death's Head*, pencil on paper, 1924, Kunstmuseum Albstadt 1999–0158-01GS. © Otto Dix / Artists Rights Society (ARS), New York / VG Bild-Kunst, Bonn. Photo © Kunstmuseum Albstadt, used with permission.

The images of death and decay which Dix was collecting would show up in several of the plates in *The War*. Besides the drawings from Palermo and the work of Goya, Dix had several photographs of cadavers which he used as source material for a number of images. Hugo Erfurth, a successful photographer in Dresden whose portrait Dix had painted, promised to make enlargements of two pictures of corpses for him, possibly provided by the anti-war activist Ernst Friedrich, and also to print a negative provided by

Max Roesberg, an industrialist whom Dix had also painted.[411] Dix knew how to make use of his expanding network within the bourgeoisie, and he probably intended to draw them into his project, perhaps in the hopes that these wealthy men would purchase sets of the prints once they were published. In early 1924 Nierendorf moved to Berlin to take over the gallery of I. B. Neumann, and he encouraged Dix to relocate to the capital, to further his own career. In June, Dix came to Berlin to have the plates he had already made printed by Otto Felsing, widely considered the best printer in Germany.[412] While he was there, he started looking for an apartment that would suit his new social station, and studio space to accommodate his large-format paintings. In the end it would take him more than a year to find a suitably elegant apartment, in the Kaiserdamm in Charlottenburg; Martha's father put up the money for the seven-year lease.[413] But in the summer of 1924 he was still alone in Berlin, and worked intensely on *The War*, writing with some pride to Martha in Düsseldorf that in a very short time he had managed to create compositions for an additional 26 plates.[414]

The War encompasses a wide variety of subjects, including:

- death and the decay of corpses, depicted with a maximum of objectivity (aided by some watercolor studies Dix had made in the morgue of brains and intestines);[415]
- the fatigue and resignation felt by the troops;
- the battlefield, either as an empty stage awaiting some sort of action or as the aftermath, the scene of some unimaginable violence that is, nonetheless, left to the viewer's imagination; the routines of the soldier's life;
- sexuality.

411 Schubert, *Otto Dix, Der Krieg*, p. 29 f.

412 Letter from Dix to Martha (June 1924), *Otto Dix, Briefe*, 80.

413 There is an extensive correspondence between Dix, Nierendorf, and the housing authority about the search for an apartment and studio, DKA, I. C. 524.

414 "Denk mal, ich habe mir schon wieder 26 neue Kriegsradierungen ausgedacht." *Otto Dix, Briefe*, p. 80.

415 Otto Dix Kunstsammlung, Zeppelin Museum, Friedrichshafen, Germany, reproduced in Olaf Peters, ed., *Otto Dix*, 90.

A surprisingly small number of the plates – just three – depict actual combat violence. Just as important are the themes which are conspicuously absent from the portfolio. Dramatic action is vanishingly rare. Instead we are frequently presented with moments of quiet, introspection, and even solitude. One might expect to find representations of such topics as the experience of women during the war, as mothers and wives who are left to grieve their men, or the relationship between the enlisted men and officers. Both of these subjects preoccupied Dix's contemporaries, but they do not appear here. Like most of his contemporaries, Dix focused exclusively on the Western Front to the exclusion of the war in Russia and in the Baltic, even though he had direct experience of the fighting there. But the subject of trench warfare, which had primarily been a factor on the Western Front, was already becoming mythologized in public memory even as the war in the East was quickly forgotten, and Dix's portfolio participated in this process of selection and mythologization.

In technical terms, *The War* is a masterwork of the printer's art, on a par with the greatest works of the German Renaissance. Over the course of 50 plates Dix explored the entire range of formal possibilities available to the intaglio artist. Some plates have a range of tonalities created by the varied use of different densities of aquatint, combined with reserved white areas, while still others are sharp, clear line drawings etched onto a plain white ground. Some compositions are dense with textures fashioned with the engraver's burin, different depths of etched lines, spattered aquatint, and hatching marks, while others are loose, open drawings of uniform line weight, either black etched lines on a white ground or, occasionally, dramatic compositions of white lines on an inky black field. Some compositions are simply line drawings on an otherwise white page, translated into an intaglio medium, while others are more painterly, almost Rembrandtesque, with lighter figures against a dark ground, again achieved through aquatint. There is also a range of drawing styles, from the precisely detailed renderings to which the steel tip of the burin lends itself, to surprisingly sketchy, rapidly done etchings. The sequence of images creates a rhythm made up out of this variety, and each of the five portfolios contains among its ten images examples of the widest possible variety of techniques. This variety, in turn, is used to create rich details and textures, which in turn convey with vividness the soldier's trying or extreme physical conditions.

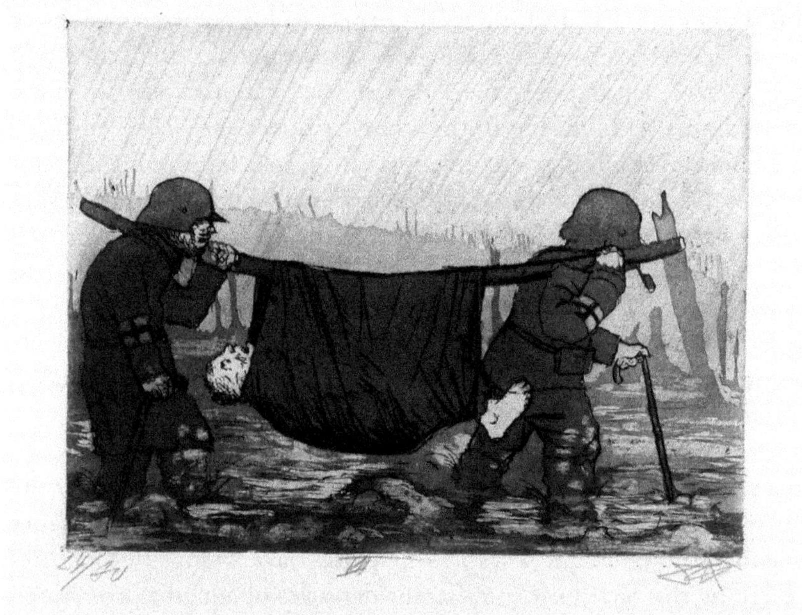

Figure 49. Otto Dix, *Stretcher Bearers in Houthulst Forest* [Verwundetentransport im Houthulster Wald] from *The War* [Der Krieg] (folio V, plate 47), etching, aquatint, and drypoint, 1924, Kunstmuseum Albstadt, Stiftung Sammlung Walther Groz SWG 1976–697. © Otto Dix / Artists Rights Society (ARS), New York / VG Bild-Kunst, Bonn. Photo © Kunstmuseum Albstadt, used with permission.

Each of the 50 images presents a small scale scene with just a handful of men or even just one, in small actions or private moments, going about the mostly tedious work of war, almost always featuring fatigue, grizzly wounds, hunger, fear, or some other form of bodily suffering and endurance. It is the single foot soldier's perspective of the war, which underscores sense that these are images recalled from personal, even private experience. For example, in *Stretcher Bearers in Houthulst Forest* [Verwundetentransport im Houthulster Wald] (folio V, plate 47) (see Figure 49), two soldiers at the front carry a wounded comrade away from the fighting near Ypres. This image combines many of the themes that Dix explores in the rest of the portfolio: the dreary, exhausting conditions of the fighting (the men have to carry the stretcher through the steady rain, but also through the mud and knee-deep standing water); the physical suffering of the wounded but also the profound fatigue and emotional detachment of the rest of the soldiers; the seemingly empty landscape that was not only inhospitable, but was also, as soldiers quickly learned, filled with myriad lethal dangers. Two different tones of aquatint are used, one for the stretcher bearers and their load, the second, lighter one for the wooded landscape in the background, dimmed by the rain. The steadily falling rain is also indicated by a light weight of etched lines, while the details of the figures and the folds of the stretcher canvas are indicated by a darker weight, achieved by leaving the plate in the acid bath longer. The contrast between the darker and lighter tones is used to convey the soaking rain and flooded fields, which were notorious features of the battlefield of Flanders. The composition is full of telling details: the walking canes which the bearers use to make their slow way to the dressing station; the pipe which one soldier smokes in silence, a sign of introspection maintained in spite of being soaked to the bone and the grimness of the job; the wounded man's pallor (conveyed by the reserve areas of his head and bare feet). His hanging head and open mouth suggest the possibility that he may in fact already be dead. In contrast to Dix's handling of materials in *The Trench*, nothing is exaggerated in this plate, everything is understated, and line and tone are handled with careful control. Rather than filling the composition up with as much texture and detail as the support can bear, as he had done in *The Trench*, Dix has instead used a judicious restraint that allows the viewer to fully take in the anecdotal details.

During the course of his work on the portfolio, the public debate over *The Trench* grew more heated and focused increasingly on the question of whether or not Dix's representation of the memory of the war in that painting was legitimate. The debate would end unhappily, with Hans Secker, the director of the Wallraf-Richartz, being forced to take the painting down and return it to Nierendorf. In the midst of these developments, Dix reprised elements of the composition of *The Trench* in two of the portfolio plates, *Collapsed Trench* [Zerfallender Kampfgraben] (folio I, plate 9) and *Abandoned Position Near Neuville* [Verlassene Stellung bei Neuville] (folio II, plate 11) (see Figure 50).

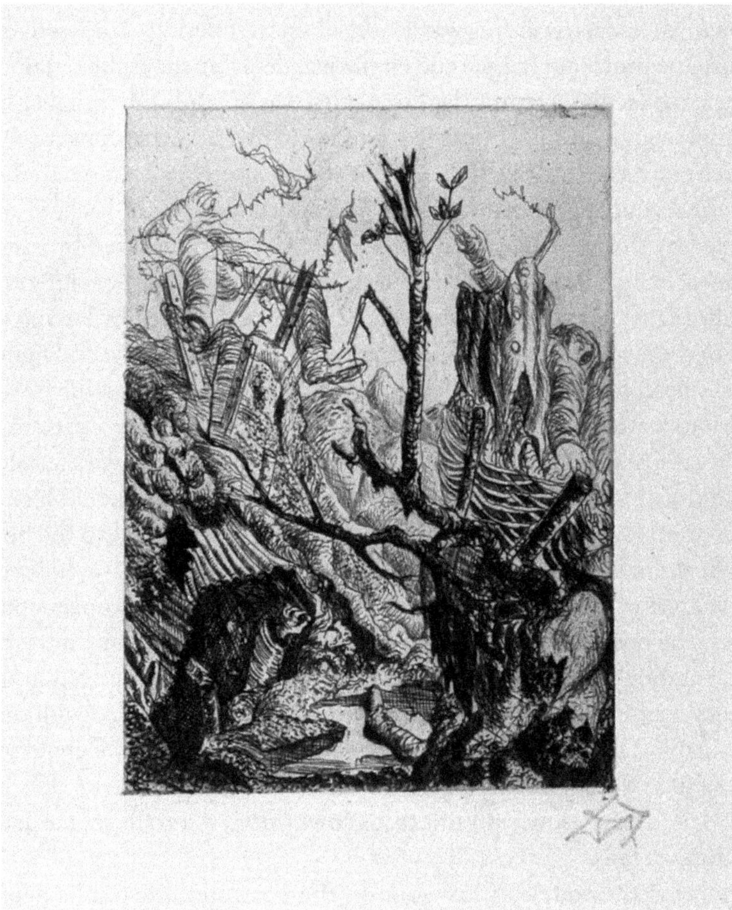

Figure 50. Otto Dix, *Abandoned Position Near Neuville* [Verlassene Stellung bei Neuville] from *The War* [Der Krieg] (folio II, plate 11), etching and drypoint, 1924, Kunstmuseum Albstadt, Stiftung Sammlung Walther Groz 1976–652. © Otto Dix / Artists Rights Society (ARS), New York / VG Bild-Kunst, Bonn. Photo © Kunstmuseum Albstadt, used with permission.

The latter plate even features the corpse of a soldier skewered on metal posts, silhouetted against a blank sky (but seen from a different angle). As in the painting, here, too, the bottom of the trench with its pools of stagnant water coincides with the bottom of the picture, while body parts emerge vaguely from collapsed walls and dugouts. In the center of the composition, a shattered branch in the foreground sprouts two leaves, a sign of the indomitable but vegetal life-force, reprising the theme of his earlier portfolio, *Death and Resurrection*. Like the drawings and gouaches made during the war, the landscape reveals the effects of the war and its modern, industrial means. Crater fields and ruined towns serve as indexical traces of the industrialized capacity for artillery production, and the fields of the dead serve as signs that killing has achieved an industrial scale, too. But the images do not depict the action of the conflict itself. Similarly, the battlefield is not seen from a commanding height; this is not the viewpoint of the officer who might survey and direct the action. Rather, it is the viewpoint of the foot soldier, who sees the war from within the trench, or peeking over its parapet – or even lower, from the entrance of a dugout. In the public debate over *The Trench*, Dix's defenders, and especially the fellow veterans among them, pinned the legitimacy of his representation of the front to his own battle experiences. If Dix emphasized the foot soldier's perspective when he revisited the themes of *The Trench* in these two plates, and throughout the portfolio, perhaps it was because this argument was so present in the public debate about his work.

There were other ways, too, in which Dix emphasized, even insisted on the eye-witness status of his account, of his memories. More than half of the 50 images in the portfolio include as part of their title a specific place name, and often specify a year and season, suggesting the eye-witness status of the memories represented here.[416] The use of place

416 Kira van Lil has noted the use of specific place names by Dix to insist on his eye-witness status, although she suggests that he might not have been at the site of some of the fighting he represents, such as Holthoust Forest. Kira van Lil, *Otto Dix und der Erste Weltkrieg. Die Natur des Menschen in der Ausnahmesituation* (Ludwig Maximillian University Munich, Dissertation, 2000).

names in these titles recalls Ernest Hemingway's condemnation in *A Farewell to Arms* (1929) of the hollow, heroic language in which the war was too often represented: "There were many words that you could not stand to hear and finally only the names of places had dignity." Some of the compositions bear the names of large, famous battles through which many German divisions moved (Champagne; the Somme; Flanders), while many more name smaller battles at which Dix was present, such as Vis-en-Artois, Neuville St. Vaast, and Monacu Farm. This last was the site of very heavy fighting between the Germans and the French, at a strategic point on a bend in the Somme river, on 30 and 31 July 1916.[417] Dix represented it as a nighttime scene lit by flares, *Flares Light Up the Monacu Farm* [Leuchtkugel Erhellt die Monacu-Ferme] (folio II, plate 17) (see Figure 51). The harsh illumination of the signal flare is indicated by white lines drawn on an inky black ground. It is suggestive of the moonlit scenes beloved by early nineteenth-century Romantic painters like Caspar David Friedrich or Johan Christian Dahl. The white lines would have been made by drawing with fluid asphaltum before covering the plate with a dense layer of resin to make the aquatint ground, creating a reverse drawing in which the stopped-out white lines indicate the jagged ruins of the farm house, wagon wheels, shattered tree stumps, barbed wire, a fresh corpse, and the bleached bones of an older one.

417 An account of this action from the French perspective can be found in *New York Times Current History: the European war*, 9 (October-December 1916) Volume 9, October-December 1916, 29.

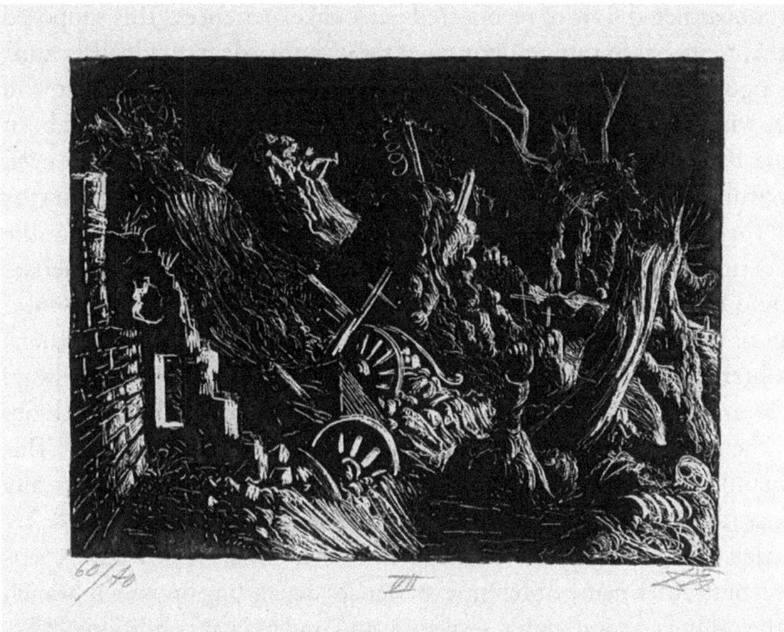

Figure 51. Otto Dix, *Flares Light Up the Monacu Farm* [Leuchtkugel Erhellt die Monacu-Ferme] from *The War* [Der Krieg] (folio II, plate 17), aquatint, 1924, Kunstmuseum Albstadt, Stiftung Sammlung Walther Groz SWG 1976–658. © Otto Dix / Artists Rights Society (ARS), New York / VG Bild-Kunst, Bonn. Photo © Kunstmuseum Albstadt, used with permission.

Dix has gone to great lengths to convince his viewers that the scenes he's depicted were his own first-hand experiences. The foot soldier's point of view, the place names of battles Dix had fought in himself, even the vividness of the images, and the richness of the details and textures, create the impression that the 50 scenes are accurate transcriptions of images seared indelibly into the artist's consciousness in moments of pain, horror, or spleen. The hallucinatory aspect of the plates suggests involuntary memory, years of trauma buried in the unconscious, reopening as disconnected fragments over and over in a private theater of recurring nightmares. And while the memories conveyed by these devices were undoubtedly authentic, these are also carefully calculated effects – they are not simply the result of an unobstructed flow of recollected personal experiences. This supposed authenticity has in turn underpinned the avant-garde individualism and/or oppositional politics that writers have ascribed to Dix, as the artist who bore witness, the isolated, almost prophetic voice of the one who had been there, had seen it, who remembered. But his choices might also have been shrewdly calculated to respond to the surrounding public discourse in 1923 and 1924. In literary reviews of writing about the war in Germany at the same time, there was a clear expectation that the recounted experiences should be those of the author.[418] The demand for a truthful representation of the war experience was explicitly formulated by, among others, the literary critic Wilhelm Pfeiler, who phrased the question this way: "Is it (any given novelistic narrative of the war) essentially truthful? Does he (the novelist) make the reader participate in the experience?"[419] This demand or expectation was not so much about what the war was really like as it was a statement about whose experience of the war counted. Yet as Alan Kramer has pointed out, there was no one, typical war experience, but rather many different experiences depending on which branch of the military an individual served in, and under what conditions.[420] So, for example, Dix's experience as a machine-gunner was undoubtedly very different from that of the soldiers who went over the top, or of artillery gunners who remained to the rear of the front line – but who were hardly out of danger. Correspondingly, there was not one "collective memory" in Germany after the war, but multiple collective memories, corresponding to the, "plural collectives, divided by class, confession, gender, generation,

418 Thomas F. Schneider, "The Weimar Republic and the Literature of the Great War," in Brian Murdoch, ed., *Critical Insights*. All Quiet on the Western Front *by Erich Maria Remarque* (Pasadena, CA: Salem Press, 2011), 23–37.

419 Wilhelm Pfeiler, *War and the German Mind: The Testimony of Men of Fiction Who Fought at the Front* (New York: Columbia University Press, 1941), 319. Cited by McGreevy, *Bitter Witness*, 292. McGreevy asks these same questions of Dix's pictures and is able to answer in the affirmative; there is no critical questioning of the demand itself, of its meaning within its own context, or of what it excludes.

420 Alan Kramer, "The First World War and German Memory," in Heather Jones, Jennifer O'Brien, and Christoph Schmidt-Supprian, eds., *Untold War: New Perspectives in First World War Studies* (Leiden: Brill, 2008), 385–415.

geography, milieu, and politics."[421] And yet the nearly exclusive focus on the experience of foot soldiers pushed out any interest in representing the experiences of those who had participated in the war in other ways. Artillery gunners, for example, who had been a favorite subject of official war artists, had not featured prominently in depictions of the war since it had ended. Likewise, the field hospital orderlies who saw their share of horror and whose experiences had featured in the artwork of older artists of the Expressionist generation, like Max Pechstein and Max Beckmann (who had themselves served in the role of orderlies), were no longer prominent by 1924. And the increasing focus on the enlisted man precluded any possible interest in the experience of, say, staff officers, to say nothing of the experience of women who were either near the front, as nurses, ambulance drivers, prostitutes, or in other capacities, or back home, as mourning mothers and wives.[422] This exclusionary emphasis on the experience of the foot soldier at the front reproduces what James Campbell has termed the ideology of combat Gnosticism, meaning that combat is presented as an experience that no non-combat veteran can understand – an idea to which I will return towards the end of this chapter.[423] Likewise, the fixation on the experience of the Western front with its stalemate, trench warfare, and otherworldly

421 Kramer, "First World War," 385.

422 On women at the front in the Austro-Hungarian army, see Christa Hämmerle, *Heimat/Front. Geschlechtergeschichte(n) des Ersten Weltkriegs in Österreich-Ungarn* (Vienna: Böhlau, 2014). In English readers at least have access to representations of the experience of women in medical roles, as nurses in the poetry of Vera Britten, and of women ambulance drivers in the fictionalized first person narrative of Helen Zenna Smith, *Not So Quiet …*, first published in 1930 and republished by The Feminist Press at CUNY (1993). Smith's novel shares with typical men's combat narratives the same harrowing scenes of combat, horrifying descriptions of mutilated male bodies, dead and dying, deprivations of the women's barracks life, sexuality, brutalization by (female) superior officers, incomprehension on the part of civilians back home, and even the violent deaths of (female) comrades as do the typical men's combat narratives. "Helen Zenna Smith" was also a pseudonym (for Evadne Price), and is the first-person narrator's name. For the experience of women back home, during and after the war, see Ute Daniel, *The War From Within: German Women in the First World War* (Oxford: Berg, 1997).

423 James Campbell, "Combat Gnosticism: The Ideology of First World War Poetry Criticism," *New Literary History* 30/1 (Winter, 1999), 203–215.

no-man's-land pushed aside any interest in the Eastern Front, despite the military successes and strategic gains which Germany had achieved there (this was true across the political spectrum, despite the postwar careers of the generals Paul von Hindenburg and Erich Ludendorf, whose military successes had been in the East). All of these preferences, as we will see, are mirrored in the choices of subject that Dix made in his portfolio.

Marketing efforts and critical reception

Meanwhile, Kal Nierendorf was already busy advertising and promoting the portfolio. He published the first 24 plates as offset prints in book form, in a run of 10,000 copies, priced at no more than one mark, and sent them to bookstores throughout Germany.[424] It may seem odd that Nierendorf printed a book of less than half the pictures, but his original presentation to Dix of 30 blank zinc plates suggests that he originally projected a portfolio of this scope – which was already quite extensive (up to this point, all of Dix's previous print portfolios had each contained fewer than ten sheets). Nierendorf may have considered the project essentially finished before Dix nearly doubled the size of the portfolio in those summer months of feverish work alone in Berlin. In any case, Nierendorf sent review copies of this inexpensive volume of lithograph reproductions to every major newspaper on the Left and many on the Right, and to writers, to local branches of the *Friedensgesellschaft* [Peace Society] to the League of Human Rights, and sent 1,500 copies to the labor unions for their celebration of the *Antikriegstag* [Anti-War Day]. By June Dix was already pulling a second set of proofs

424 If the portfolio was originally projected to have 30 plates, and Dix had already delivered 24 to Nierendorf before leaving Dusseldorf, he only needed to produce six more in Berlin. But he went on to produce 28 more images for a total of 52, of which two were edited out. The project had clearly gained a momentum of its own, as can be seen in the remarkable fertility and inventiveness of the imagery and anecdotal detail, and the formal variety of the technique.

of all 50 plates, working with Otto Felsing in Berlin. Dix made a quick self-portrait sketch in pen of himself as a soldier, with the legend written above it, "This is how I looked as a soldier" ["So sahe ich als Soldat aus"], and the inscription below, "I dedicate this 2nd proof of the War Portfolio to Karl Nierendorf in June 1924. Dix" (1924) (see Figure 52).

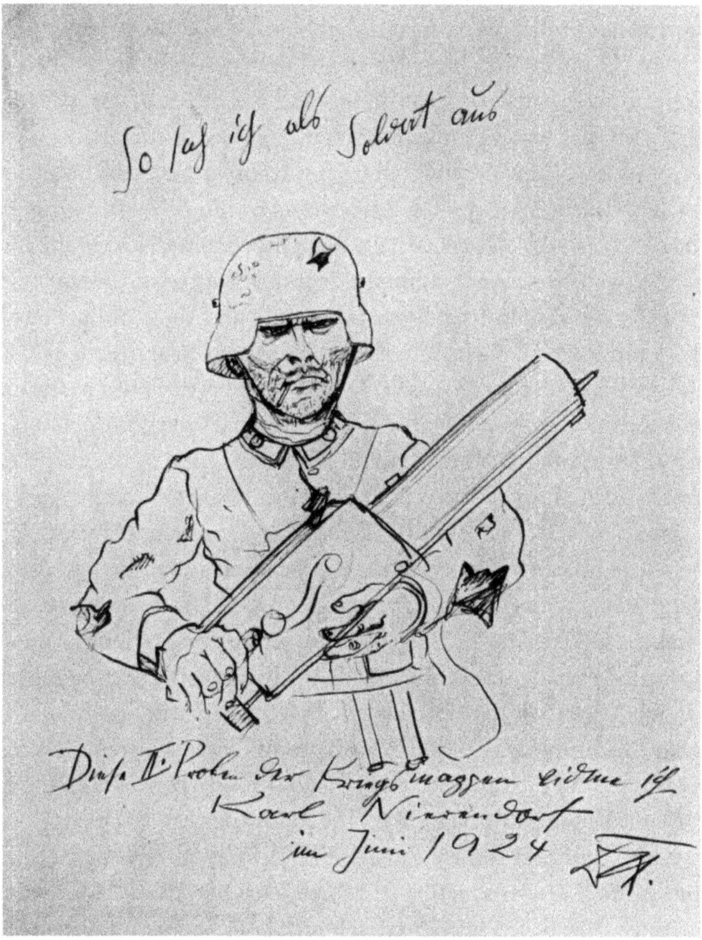

Figure 52. Otto Dix, *This is how I looked as a soldier* [So sah ich als Soldat aus], pen and ink on paper, 1924, Berlinische Galerie. © Otto Dix / Artists Rights Society (ARS), New York / VG Bild-Kunst, Bonn. Digital file: author's own scan.

The self-portrait is quite distinct in style from the actual plates: a quick and economically drawn sketch, without shading or texture, that emphasizes the torn uniform, the iconic *Stahlhelm* or steel helmet that frames and heightens the artist's penetrating gaze, and the machine gun cradled in his arms. It is above all a pointed reminder that Dix felt he had earned the right to represent the front experience through years of hard fighting which had left his face worn and his uniform torn, and that before the tools of his trade were the brush or the burin, they had been the Maxim gun and the hand grenade.

Nierendorf's marketing campaign had the effect of associating the portfolio with the antiwar movement, although the prints themselves lack the pathos of, say, Käthe Kollwitz's portfolio of woodcuts on the subject of the war, published in 1923, to say nothing of her lithograph poster for the "Nie wieder Krieg" [Never Again War] movement. Nor do the images address the subject of the complicity of industrialists and war profiteers in the war, or the link between warmongering and the conflicts between capitalists and the proletariat and the injustices of social inequality, as did the lithographs of George Grosz or the woodcuts of Franz Masareel, to name two examples. *The War* nonetheless became closely associated with the antiwar movement, which had a brief resurgence in 1924, the tenth anniversary of the start of the war. Nierendorf had deliberately worked to create this association as part of his marketing campaign. By autumn of 1925, he could boast to Dix that he had sold 15 copies of the portfolio.[425]

In the summer of 1924, Max Liebermann invited Dix to exhibit his already famous painting *The Trench* at the Academy exhibition in Berlin, where the critical reaction to it took a dramatic turn. The painting became the center of a national public controversy, especially thanks to the criticisms of Julius Meier-Graefe, and the responses to those criticisms by Willi Wolfradt and others. Pressure was put on the director of the Wallraf-Richartz Museum, Dr. Hans Secker, to return the painting to Dix. The following year, Nierendorf would prepare a second edition of the inexpensive book form of *The War*; for this one, he commissioned an introductory essay by Henri Barbusse.[426] The choice of Henri Barbusse to write an introduction for the book was significant on several

425 Letter from Nierendorf to Dix, no date (1925), DKA, I, C 524 h.

426 Letter from Nierendorf to Dix, 8 July 1925, DKA I, C 524 f.

levels. The well-known author of an important novel of the front, published during the war and translated into German shortly after, he was associated not only with the political Left in France, but had also founded an organization of former combatants, one which specifically emphasized the solidarity among the enlisted men, even those on both sides of no-man's-land, over solidarity between enlisted men and officers.[427] His veterans' organization only admitted men who had fought at the front. The choice of Barbusse was made by Nierendorf, it should be noted, although Dix does not seem to have voiced any objection. Barbusse's name on the book signaled that the viewer should expect the war to be represented here from the perspective of the common foot soldier, that its claim to legitimacy was also a claim to moral authority (as it was in Barbusse's novel), and that neither bitterness towards the former foe nor fondness for junior officers were part of the works' content. And indeed these expectations are met by the images themselves. Nierendorf was simultaneously trying to promote the portfolio by sending invitations to galleries to purchase it through subscription, but the growing notoriety of *The Trench* was working against Dix. Hermann Abels, who ran the art gallery *Centrale für graphische Kunst* in Cologne, referred disparagingly to *The Trench*, which was hanging in the same city, and to the idea of the "*Abschreckungsmethode*" [dissuasive effect], a term he had clearly picked up from the criticism of the painting in the paper. But worse yet, in his opinion, was Nierendorf's claim that the portfolio would be a "German monument to "The Unknown Soldier." For Abels, this constituted an offense to "every former frontline soldier."[428]

The association of the portfolio with pacifism and a strong anti-war sentiment was strengthened, too, by the project's similarity to Francisco Goya's *Disasters of War* (1810–1820). Dix's portfolio resembled that of the Spaniard's in format (a portfolio of a large number of thematically related prints), the handling of the theme (a matter-of-fact depiction of violence), and technique (in particular the extensive use of aquatint). Dix was actively encouraged to take Goya's work as a model by Nierendorf, who sent him several books on

427 Association républicaine des anciens combattants, or "Arac," founded in 1917 by Barbusse, Raymond Lefebvre, and others.

428 Letter from Abels to Nierendorf, 29 July 1924. Nierendorf sent the letter on to Dix, with his commentary written in the margins, DKA I, C 16.

the Spanish artist, as we have seen. At least one plate in *The War, A House Destroyed by Aerial Bombardment (Tournai)* [Durch Fliegerbomben zerstörtes Haus (Tournai)] contains direct quotations from one of Goya's images, *Ravages of War* [Estragos de la Guerra]. And the title of another plate, *Seen on the Escarpment at Cléry-sur-Somme* [Gesehen am Steilhang von Cléry-sur-Somme] (folio III, plate 28) (see Figure 53) directly recalls Goya's most famous title, "I Saw It" [Yo lo vi] (plate 44 of *Disasters of War*).

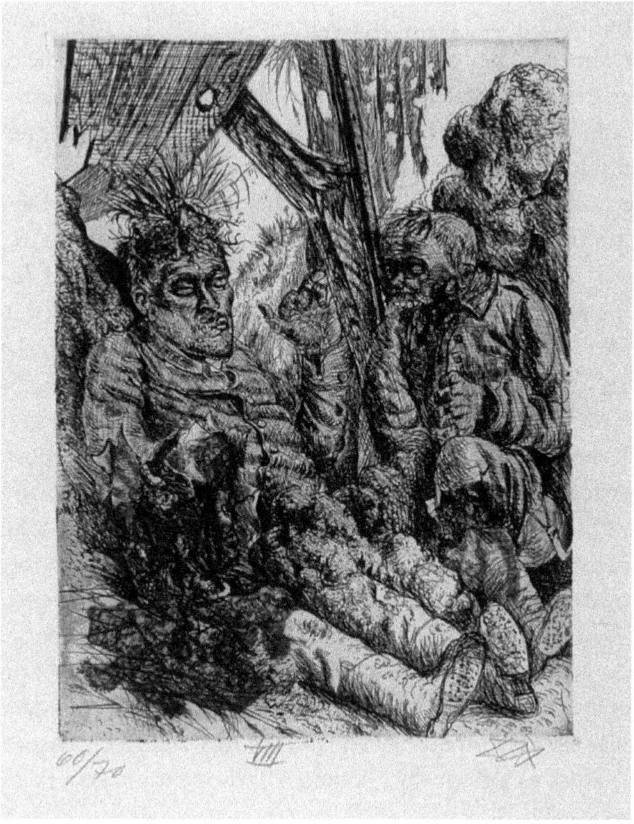

Figure 53. Otto Dix, *Seen on the Escarpment at Cléry-sur-Somme* [Gesehen am Steilhang von Cléry-sur-Somme] from *The War* [Der Krieg] (folio III, plate 28), etching, aquatint, and drypoint, 1924, Kunstmuseum Albstadt, Stiftung Sammlung Walther Groz SWG 1976–674. © Otto Dix / Artists Rights Society (ARS), New York / VG Bild-Kunst, Bonn. Photo © Kunstmuseum Albstadt, used with permission.

Like many of the plates in *The War*, this one examines the corpses of soldiers with a clinical, detailed observation, finely etched with a drypoint needle, of what torn-apart bodies actually look like. Nauseatingly indefinite masses of matter, represented by patches of aquatint roughly applied to make the shading stippled and uneven, spill out of rent openings or froth over in the process of putrefaction. But the detached observations are presented with a mordant sense of grotesque humor – these figures could have been taken from the earlier painting *The Trench*. The two bodies have been positioned by chance and violence in such a way that they could be idly sitting and gossiping, forgetful of the war (and by the war forgotten), except that one has had his lower jaw torn away, while grass grows from the top of the other's head, in a visual pun for hair (a joke that Dix repeated elsewhere). Like Goya before him, Dix indicates with his title that such cruel absurdity is not his invention, but typical of what he himself saw in wartime. Yet it must be pointed out that, while Dix certainly depicts the death and suffering German soldiers, he does not depict a cruel and violent enemy, as Goya had.

The critics did not fail to make the comparison with Goya, a comparison which they meant as praise. The critic from one newspaper, the *Rheinisch-Westfälische Zeitung*, wrote that *The War* was, "A work reminiscent of Goya's in its technical perfection and artistic, visionary power." Another stated that, "This totally realistic and at the same time exceptionally fantastical work presents a devastating document of our time, the equal of Goya's *Disasters of War*."[429] Once the second edition of the inexpensive bound version appeared, with its introductory essay by Henri Barbusse, the tenor of the discussion predictably shifted to an identification of an antiwar message. The critic for the *Börsenkurier* called it an, "objective depiction and a fearsome accusation," while another critic,

429 "Ein Werk, das an technischer Vollendung und künsterlischer visionärer Kraft unmittelbar an Goya denken läßt." "Ganz real und zugleich von unerhörter Phantastik stellt sich das Werk als erschütterndes Dokument unserer Zeit ebenbürtig neben Goyas Desastres de la Guerra" Both cited in Conzelmann, Otto, *Der andere Dix – Sein Bild vom Menschen und vom Kriege* (Stuttgart: Hatje-Cantz, 1983), 180.

writing in the *Essener Arbeiter-Zeitung* described it as "More fulsome than a thousand 'Nie wieder Krieg' manifestos.' The Berlin paper, the *B. Z. Am Mittag*, wrote that the viewer could hardly be called human who was not proud to call himself an opponent of all war [*Kriegsgegner*] to the core after seeing these images.[430] And one reviewer, speaking as a fellow veteran, praised the portfolio for its truthfulness to the suffering at the front; this was *Germania*, the newspaper of the German Center Party [Deutsche Zentrumspartei], which supported the Republic.[431] These were the responses of the socialist-oriented papers. In the right-leaning *DAZ*, the newspaper in which Meier-Graefe had attacked *The Trench* less than two months earlier, the assumption was still that the portfolio was broadly critical of the Great War, if not all war, although the judgment remains ambiguous. The critic wrote that

> of the two faces of the war, Dix has seen only the one, albeit from the ground up. The fanatical energy with which the artist here seeks to eliminate the last shreds of idealism from the depiction of that great conflict of the peoples, is too tendentious for the result to be truthful in any higher sense ... yet it must be admitted, that the horrors of war haven't been represented like this since Goya. The heart-stopping repugnance arising from the terrors amassed here seizes the viewer by the chest with an icy grip, and more than one of these terrible pages remains in the memory like a stone.[432]

430 "[S]achliche Schilderung und furchtbare Anklage" (*Börsenkurier*) and "Stürmischer als tausend 'Nie wieder Krieg' –Manifeste' (*Essener Arbeiter-Zeitung*) "Wer sich vor diesen Kriegsbildern nicht gelobt, Kriegsgegner bis ins Innerste zu werden, der ist wohl kaum mehr Mensch zu nennen." All cited in Conzelmann, *Der Andere Dix*, 181.

431 Ein furchtbares Dokument dessen, was wir im Felde erlitten haben." Conzelmann, *Der andere Dix*, 180.

432 "Von den zwei Gesichtern des Krieges hat Dix nur das eine gesehen, dieses allerdings aus dem Grunde. Die fanatische Energie, mit der hier versucht wird, vom Bilde des großen Völkerringens den letzten Fetzen von Idee herabzureißen, ist zu sehr Tendenz, als daß das Resultat in höherem Sinne noch wahr sein könnte. ... Im übrigen muß allerdings zugestanden werden, daß das Grauen des Krieges seit Goya nicht mehr so dargestellt worden ist. Das herzlähmende Entsetzen, das von diesen gehäuften Greueln ausgeht, greift dem Betrachter kalt an die Brust, und mehr als eines der fürchterlichen Blätter bleibt wie ein Stein in der Erinnerung

The themes of violence, dead bodies, and other portfolios

The most common theme in *The War*, by number of plates, and the one which perhaps more than any other emphasizes and even trades on the "objectivity" of the style (dispassionate, detailed, unflinching), is death and decay in all its various modes and forms. Along with the violence of direct, hand-to-hand combat (a theme which was, by contrast, only represented twice in the entire portfolio), the theme of the corpses of dead soldiers was very much in dialog with imagery of the war already present in the public discourse in Germany. Dix drew together images and types of depictions of death that were circulating in his world at the time: the photographs of the disfigured faces of dead soldiers published by Ernst Friedrich as pacifist propaganda as well as the updated memento mori imagery and the animal allegories of his colleagues and fellow-veterans in the German avant-garde such as Otto Schubert (1892–1970) and Adolf Uzarski (1885–1970), both of whom Dix knew well. Death and hand-to-hand fighting were two themes which had been made part of the visual vocabulary of the public memory of the war. Clearly if Otto Dix was going to make his own visual statement about the war, he was going to have to address these themes in his portfolio. In the course of the 50 plates one finds bodies disfigured by poison gas, caught in barbed wire, uncovered while digging trenches, and simply splayed on the ground, either in a trench or on the battlefield. There are also civilian victims, including an infant, and the cadaver of a horse. The latter could also be seen in photographs of the time, and could sometimes seem more poignant than images of the soldiers themselves; the poor beasts were conscripted into the army to pull field guns and do other drafting work, and could hardly have understood why they had been deliberately put in such danger. Dix's colleague Otto Schubert had in 1917 created an entire lithograph portfolio depicting the horse's suffering during the

liegen." *DAZ* (24 August 1924), signed D. R. D. Quoted in Conzelmann, *Der Andere Dix*, 181.

war, depicting terrified, wounded, and even dead animals. Schubert used horses to depict very basic forms of bodily suffering such as *Hunger, Heat, Thirst, Agony*, and *Labor*.[433] He had studied at the School of Arts and Crafts in Dresden before the war, immediately ahead of Dix, and had founded the Sezession Gruppe 1919 together with Dix after the war. During the war, Schubert sent home dozens of postcards he painted at the front, a few of which also featured frightened horses.[434] Schubert and Dix worked together in the Dresden Secession just two year later, on graphic arts specifically, and Dix must surely have known Schubert's lithograph portfolio. Dix's own image of a dead horse, *Horse Cadaver* [Pferdekadaver] (folio I, plate 5) (see Figure 54), its body swollen and its legs stretched stiffly upwards at awkward angles, recalls the cadaver in Schubert's print, *Death* [Tod] (lithograph, 1917) (Figure 23).[435] Dix fitted the upturned and outstretched legs of his horse cadaver tightly into the rectangular picture frame, and outlined it with deeply etched lines, for a strongly graphic effect. The composition originally included background details which Dix then scraped away, enhancing the starkness of the composition even more.

433 Otto Schubert, *Die Leiden der Pferde im Krieg*, lithograph portfolio, 1917, in The Robert Gore Rifkind Center for German Expressionist Studies, Los Angeles.

434 See *Horses Under Shrapnel Fire*, postcard dated 11 March 1916, private collection, show in the exhibition *Postcards from the Trenches*, and viewable on the exhibition website, <http://postcardsfromthetrenches.com/postcards> (accessed 16 August 2016).

435 From the lithograph portfolio, *Die Leiden der Pferde im Krieg*, 1917, plate 12.

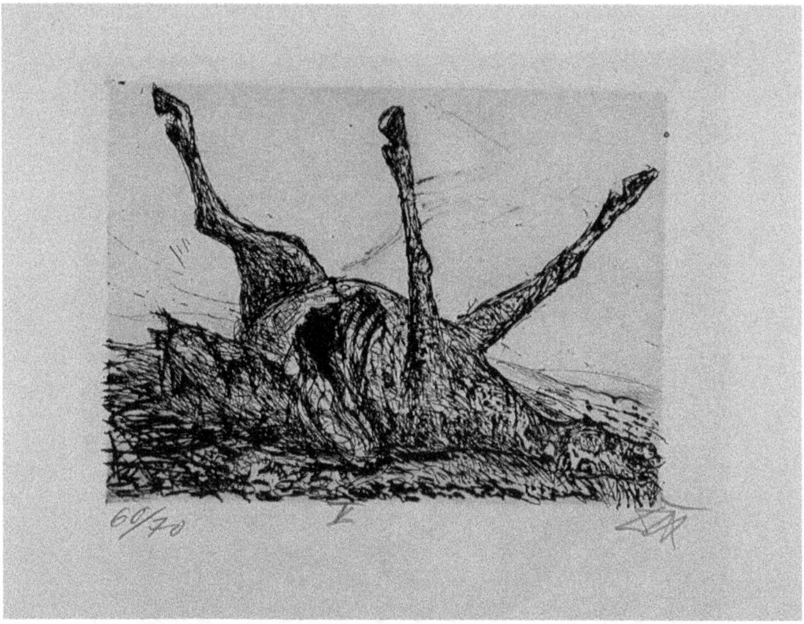

Figure 54. Otto Dix, *Horse Cadaver* [Pferdekadaver], from *The War* [Der Krieg] (folio I, plate 5), etching and drypoint, 1924, Kunstmuseum Albstadt, Stiftung Sammlung Walther Groz SWG 1976–644. © Otto Dix / Artists Rights Society (ARS), New York / VG Bild-Kunst, Bonn. Photo © Kunstmuseum Albstadt, used with permission.

Other images of death in *The War* are close studies – based on photographs borrowed from Ernst Friedrich – of the hideously damaged and disfigured faces and hands of dead soldiers, the festering wounds, lolling, swollen tongues, and exposed brains, images that had none of the quiet, dignified repose which was the norm in heroic battle paintings. Two such images are *Dying Soldier* [Sterbender Soldat] (folio III, plate 26), and *Dead Man (St. Clément)* [Toter (St. Clément)] (folio V, plate 42) (see Figure 55).

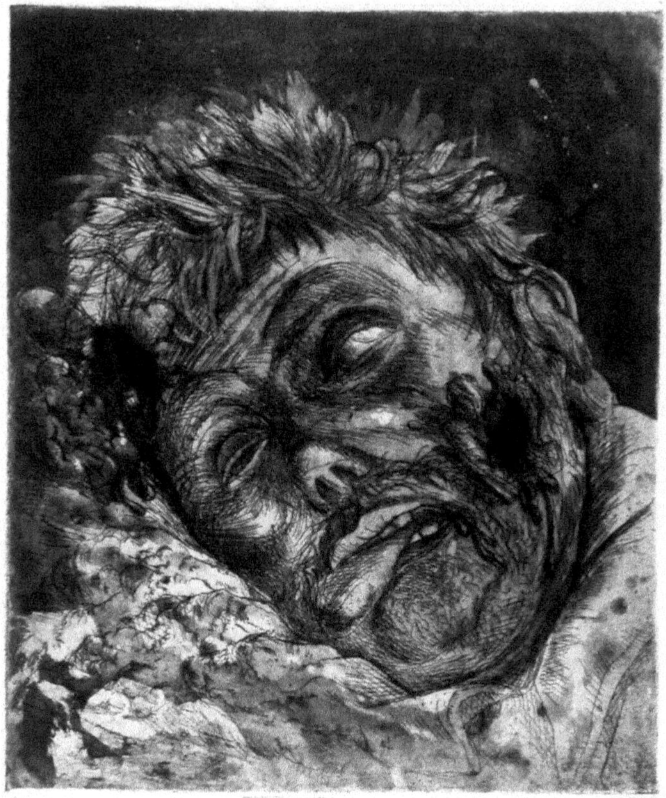

Figure 55. Otto Dix, *Dead Man (St. Clément)* [Toter (St. Clément)], from *The War* [Der Krieg] (folio V, plate 42]), Kunstmuseum Albstadt, Stiftung Sammlung Walther Groz SWG 1976–692. © Otto Dix / Artists Rights Society (ARS), New York / VG Bild-Kunst, Bonn. Photo © Kunstmuseum Albstadt, used with permission.

This is what men's bodies, killed by the violence of bullets, shrapnel, or bayonets look like, and their evident reliance on photographic documents, their rhetoric of veracity, is part of the point. This particular image, of a soldier killed by a bullet that had entered through his cheek and then pushed his brains out the back of his head, has also benefitted from Dix's careful study of a human brain done in the morgue in 1920 (*Human Brain* [Menschliches Gehirn] watercolor, 1920), and is a masterfully and painterly combination of shades of aquatint and different weights of etched lines.[436] Other images step into the realm of the allegorical and the memento mori, in caricatures of grinning, chattering death's heads and updated Dance of Death images, or the tradition of diablerie (a species of the grotesque; see previous chapter), in which skeletons put on the clothing and manners of the living in order to mock their vanity, such as *Dead Sentry* [Toter Sappenposten] (folio II, plate 18). Dix included not one but two versions of the Dance of Death theme, which was a popular memento mori image throughout early modern Europe, especially in German-speaking lands; the most well-known version was perhaps the series of woodcuts by Hans Holbein the Younger (c. 1525). In the nineteenth century, it had been updated by Alfred Rethel's woodcut cycle *Another Dance of Death from the Year 1848* [Auch ein Totentanz aus dem Jahr 1848] (1849), and during the war by Adolf Uzarski's set of lithographs, *Totentanz*.[437] Like Rethel, Uzarski pictured Death as a figure who not only participates in the war, but who actively instigates it, seducing young men to their destruction. Dix knew Uzarski from the artist's group Das Junge Rheinland in Düsseldorf, and painted his portrait in 1923.[438] In one of the two prints Dix did on this theme in *The War*, titled *Dance of Death Anno 17 (Dead Man's Hill)* [Totentanz Anno 17 (Höhe Toter Mann), folio II, plate 9], he was able to draw on one of his own works from the war, a gouache with the same title, translating the

436 This image was not reproduced in the book version, and so must have been one of the 20 plates Dix made later; suggesting both that the turn to the use of documentary photographs came later, as the project evolved, and that he got more sophisticated in his combination of aquatint and etching as he gained experience. *Human Brain*, private collection, reproduced in Olaf Peters, *Otto Dix*, 2010, 90.

437 Kirsten Fitzke, "Im Menschenschlachthaus hat der personifizierte Tod Konjunktur. Der industrialisierte Krieg in Totentanzzyklen aus dem Rheinland und Thüringen," in: Gertrude Cepl-Kaufmann, Gerd Krumeich, Ulla Sommers, eds., *Krieg und Utopie. Kunst, Literatur und Politik im Rheinland nach dem Ersten Weltkrieg* (Essen: Klartext, 2006), 234–250.

438 Otto Dix *Portrait of Adolf Uzarski* (1923), now in the Museum Kunstpalast in Dusseldorf.

spectral effect of colored phosphorescent light of flares lighting up no-man's-land at night into glaring black and white; the dead bodies caught in the barbed wire, seem to dance to a jig played by Death.[439]

By contrast with the theme of dead bodies, depictions of actual combat between soldiers are surprisingly few for a portfolio dedicated to representing the reality of the war. In fact, it contains only two. In the powerful, unsettling *Storm Troopers Advancing Under Gas* [Sturmtruppe geht unter Gas vor] (folio II, no. 12) (see Figure 27), a small team of German soldiers advances through a cloud of poison gas, masks and steel helmets obscuring their faces and transforming them into livid specters of death. The combination of iconic steel helmet, dehumanizing gasmask, and murky, apocalyptic atmosphere of poison gas make it an emblematic image for the entire war, which is undoubtedly why it has been reproduced so often, beginning with its service as the cover of Nierendorf's mass market offset print edition of the portfolio. But it is an ambiguous image, putting us, the viewer, on the receiving end of an assault of German soldiers, thus forcing Dix's original German audience into the position of the enemy. The plate reinterprets an earlier work, a gouache made while Dix was at the front, *Flooded Barbed Wire* [Überflutetes Drahtverhau] (1916) (see Figure 26), which depicted German soldiers advancing across a no-man's-land filled with mortal perils such as flooded trenches and shell holes and clouds of chlorine gas. But there the figures were more numerous and at a greater distance; it was an image of an army marching forward to engage another army in combat. These storm troopers are, on the other hand, the carriers of a new military doctrine developed by the German army relatively late in the war. It called for small groups of soldiers to move quickly and independently through the dangerous terrain of no-man's-land, killing a few defenders rather than attempting to seize and hold the entire line. It should be remembered that this was not Dix's experience of the war; he was a machine gunner, not a storm trooper, and his role was primarily defensive. These soldiers are clearly on the attack, and although the title reproduces the dry, impersonal language of the military dispatch, these troopers are

439 The gouache is in the collection of Kunstmuseum Albstadt, but frequently reproduced.

in the midst of combat; they throw their long-handled grenades (again, in the viewer's direction). Although the enemy is not shown (forcing the viewer into that role), it is clearly a depiction of German soldiers' aggression. Beneath those gasmasks are, presumably, faces distorted by bloodlust or set in grim determination, but they have been replaced by the uncanny, ghostly faces and hollow eyes of the stopped-out white masks, which fairly glow in the chemical murk of the aquatint foreground.

The second depiction of actual hand to hand fighting is the more direct and unambiguous, terribly violent *Surprise Attack of a Sentry by a Silent Patrol* [Überfall einer Schleichpatrouille auf einen Grabenposten] (folio V, no. 44) (see Figure 56). It depicts the most intimate and personal form of violence: one soldier (German), kills another soldier (nationality impossible to determine), not by shooting him from a distance, but grabbing him by the arm and stabbing him in the chest. Here the German soldier does indeed show his expression, and it is nothing but sadistic glee and the greedy pleasure of killing. The victim's features might have conveyed pain or dismay, but his face is obscured and cut off by the edge of the pictorial field. Unlike the previous image, both the killer and his victim are shown here. The composition is simple and forceful, dark except for the reserve area that highlights both men; presumably the German patrol has snuck up on this sentry at night. The crudely scrawled lines convey the forceful energy and wild mayhem of this sudden act of violence. It has been said that the soldiers of the war were always spoken of as the victims, as though they had been killed without themselves doing any killing.[440] Yet Dix was not the only one who depicted the act of killing, performed not reluctantly but with unbridled glee: Ernst Jünger, Blaise Cendrars, and lesser-known memoirists and letter writers did as well.[441] And this was not the first time that soldiers actually killing one another at close range, even hand-to-hand, had been depicted in a print cycle; Félix Vallotton, who had depicted the war as an official artist on the French side, had created a very similar image for his portfolio *C'est la Guerre*. Dix would surely have

440 Stephane Audoin-Rouzeau, and Annette Becker, *1914–1918: Understanding the Great War* (London: Profile Books, 2002), 39.

441 Audoin-Rouzeau and Becker, *14–18*, 40 ff.

known this portfolio by such a well-established graphic artist with a strong reputation in Germany.

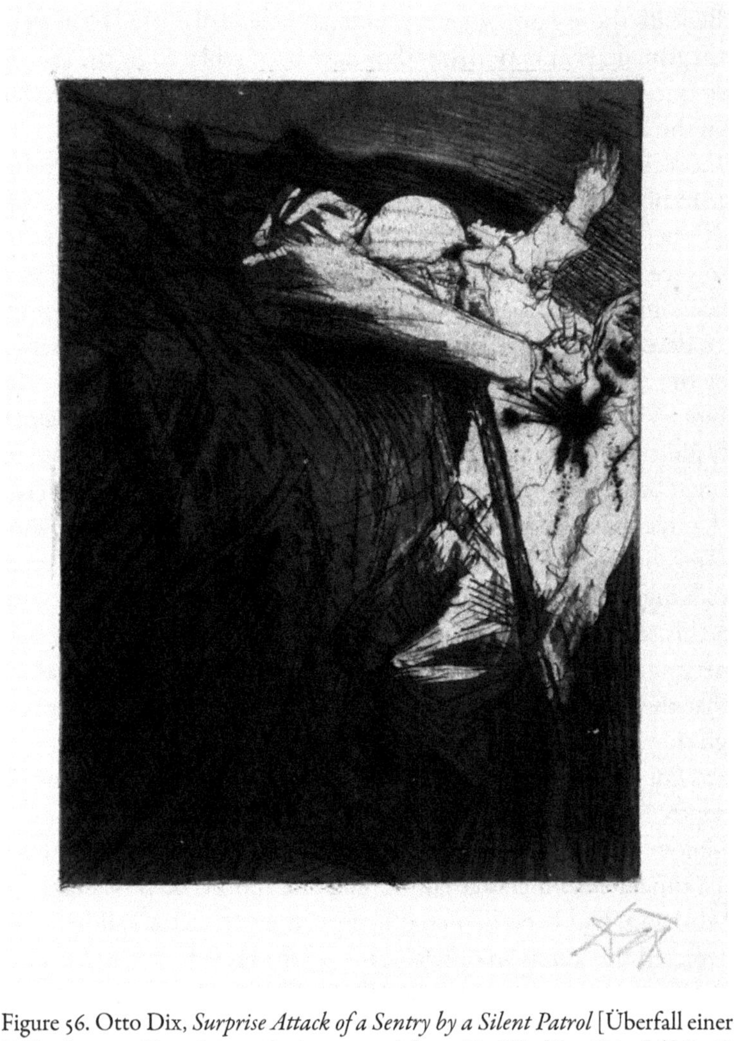

Figure 56. Otto Dix, *Surprise Attack of a Sentry by a Silent Patrol* [Überfall einer Schleichpatrouille auf einen Grabenposten] from *The War* [Der Krieg] (folio V, plate 44), etching and aquatint, 1924, Kunstmuseum Albstadt, Stiftung Sammlung Walther Groz SWG 1976–694. © Otto Dix / Artists Rights Society (ARS), New York / VG Bild-Kunst, Bonn. Photo © Kunstmuseum Albstadt, used with permission.

This scene of war as intimate murder is a marginal theme in a cycle of images that otherwise exclusively depicts the suffering and endurance of the German soldier. By contrast, a portfolio of lithographs published in 1915 by German artist and veteran Willi Jaeckel, entitled *Memento*, depicted much more brutal violence, including scenes of hand to hand fighting between German soldiers and their enemies.[442] Jaeckel also depicted German soldiers bayonetting the French defenders of a trench in his 1915 painting *Sturmangriff* [Attack], now lost (an ink drawing from 1914 depicts a similar action – seen from the point of view of the French defenders).[443] Jaeckel's figures are monumental, unlike Dix's more soberly proportioned compositions.[444] His imagery is more brutal, too: where Dix shows the cadaver of a dead horse, Jaeckel shows horses caught in barbed wire; where Dix has soldiers on leave cruising prostitutes, Jaeckel depicts them gang-raping a woman in occupied territory (in a composition borrowed from Goya's *Disasters of War*). Otto Schubert also included an atavistic scene of primitive hand-to-hand combat involving German and British troops armed with shovels as well as bayonets (*Hand-to-Hand Combat* [Nahkampf]) in his 1917 portfolio, *Twenty-Four Lithographs of the War in the West*.[445] But Jaeckel and Schubert had produced their respective portfolios during the war itself, at a time when, as we have seen, Dix was more interested in drawing from life, and therefore neglected scenes of combat, or, later in the war, drawing scenes of a war reduced to allegory, lacking the specificity of Jaeckel's and Schubert's violent encounters between real soldiers.[446]

442 Richard Cork, "'A Murderous Carnival': German Artists in the First World War," in Bernd-Rüdiger Hüppauf, ed., *War, Violence, and the Modern Condition* (Berlin: DeGruyter, 1997), 241–276.

443 See Schubert, *Künstler im Trommelfeuer des Krieges 1914–1918*, Heidelberg: Wunderhorn, 2013, p. 109.

444 See Dietrich Schubert, "Otto Dix, Die Radierungen 'Der Krieg' von 1924, in: *Kunsthistorische Arbeitsblätter*, Cologne: No. 9 (2002), pp. 39–46, with thanks to the author for bringing this essay to my attention.

445 In The Robert Gore Rifkind Center for German Expressionist Studies, Los Angeles.

446 Dix did draw a scene of brutal hand-to-hand fighting, *Handgemenge*, in 1917, but it was one of the allegorical representations typical for his work in those months. Reproduced in Schubert, *Künstler im Trommelfeuer*, p. 275.

The *Reichsbanner* and public memory

Thus far we have examined two important discourses to which Dix must certainly have been responding as he designed his compositions for *The War* in 1923 and 1924: the debate around his own painting *The Trench* and the work of his fellow artists, especially graphic artists who had already published print portfolios on the subject of the war before 1923 (there were others, too, in particular female artists, to whom we will turn at later in this chapter). There was another important discourse which Dix must have taken into account in those months, and that was the discussion about the meaning of the war, which might help us answer the question, posed above, What attitude about the war did Dix express through these works, and where did that attitude fit into the public memory work of the war? One way to answer this question might be to compare Dix's work to the attitudes and preoccupations of other veterans. This may seem like a problematic approach at first, because the historiography of the Weimar Republic has so long been dominated by the image of right-wing, militantly antidemocratic, uniformed groups like the *Stahlhelm* and, later, the Brown Shirts of the Nazi paramilitary group the SA. Since George Mosse's influential study *Fallen Soldiers*, the narrative has been that these right-wing nationalist groups were the only people who thought much about the war during the 1920s, and that their preoccupation with it led more or less directly to the rise of Nazism, the downfall of the Weimar Republic, and then to the Second World War.[447] Since Dix was clearly opposed to their nostalgia for the war and their evident desire to return to the battlefield, it has been difficult to see the portfolio – in relation to the public memory articulated by other veterans – as anything other than oppositional to the public memory espoused by other veterans. But the right-wing, nationalist veterans organizations were not the only voice in the Weimar Republic

447 George Mosse, *Fallen Soldiers. Reshaping the Memory of the World Wars* Oxford University Press, 1991

when it came to the memory of the war – the largest group was in fact the one associated with the Social Democratic party, the *Reichsbanner*, which was founded in 1924 by members of the Social Democrats and other center-left parties in order to defend the Weimar Republic against attacks from the far Left and, especially, the radical Right. Benjamin Ziemann has drawn the attention of historians to the central importance of this group in the Weimar period.[448]

The *Reichsbanner* continued the work of the Reich League of Disabled War Veterans, Ex-Servicemen, and War Dependents [Reichsbund für Kriegsbeschädigten, Kriegsteilnehmer, und Kriegerhinterbliebenen], begun already during the war, which aimed to establish control over the symbolic field of the war's meaning and memory, with the express purpose of providing an alternative to the nationalist and revanchist discourse of groups like the *Stahlhelm*. The very name of *Reichsbanner Schwarz-Rot-Gold*, which refers to the black, red and gold flag of the Republic, indicates the importance they placed on the symbolic order. Although Otto Dix never joined this group, or the parent Socialist Party (a move which would not have fit with his newly acquired bourgeois and academic status and would certainly have hampered his career prospects), his background matched the profile of their typical members, and his attitudes to the war and the republic seem to have been similar to theirs. Like them, Dix came from the industrial working class, and from a Protestant milieu. The Socialist Party had been strong in his industrial neighborhood in Gera, and his father was active in the party. The *Reichsbanner* represented the political sympathies closest to Dix's, as near as we can guess at them: left of center but not as far left as his communist friends like Conrad Felixmüller; socially critical of the results of rapacious capitalism, but with none of the outward signs of

448 I am indebted here to the work of Benjamin Ziemann, which is most fully set out in *Contested Commemorations, Republican War Veterans and Weimar Political Culture* (Cambridge: Cambridge University Press, 2012). See also Ziemann, "Republikanische Kriegserinnerung in einer polarisierten Öffentlichkeit. Das Reichsbanner Schwarz-Rot-Gold als Veteranenverband der sozialistischen Arbeiterschaft," *Historische Zeitschrift* 267/2 (October 1998), 357–398.

hostility to the Republic that we see for example in the art of his colleague George Grosz. It is perhaps therefore not a stretch to imagine that Dix's feelings about the war had much in common with the mass of veterans who belonged to the Social Democrat party. As Ziemann has said about the importance of the *Reichsbanner* to the public, their purpose was not only to turn the memory of the war into political capital, but also to win for like-minded veterans the moral authority to determine the meaning of the war, and the centrality to that meaning of the simple soldier's war experience.[449] At the center of their discourse was the notion that although the war had been senseless and the soldiers had suffered unimaginable privation and had been forced to witness a great deal of agony and death, *the war was nonetheless an important event in the veteran's biography*, and was formative for his identity; collectively the veterans were proud to have done their duty. This was the common foot soldier's truth of the war, and it was important for the members of the *Reichsbanner* to share that truth with the public. Theirs was what could be termed a "weak" antiwar statement; they did not flatly state that all armed conflict should be avoided at all cost (the message of the *Nie Wieder Krieg* movement, what could be termed by contrast a "strong" antiwar statement). The *Reichsbanner* did not claim that the Great War had been wholly without meaning, or had been nothing but a swindle. They were critical of the official "virtues" of heroism and self-sacrifice, and emphasized instead the trials of the front soldier, both physical and psychological.[450] They sought to commemorate the war without glorifying it; and they affirmed the legitimacy of the democratic Republic which issued out of it. The rightwing *Stahlhelm* by contrast, which was under the sway of the aristocratic officer class, promoted a mystical vision of a warrior race unified by the combat experience and transcending the individual, and nostalgia for the hierarchical, authoritarian Empire. Like the *Stahlhelm*, the *Reichsbanner* was also a paramilitary organization, with uniformed members marching in formation in the streets and holding ceremonies at war memorials on symbolically important dates.

449 Ziemann, "Repbulikanische Kriegserinnerung," 360.
450 Ziemann, "Repbulikanische Kriegserinnerung," 371 f.

Like the right-wing nationalists they obsessively kept the war present in memory and in the streets.

Dix, too, kept returning to the memory of the war, keeping it present in the public sphere, and the imagery of the *War* portfolio is remarkably congruent with the attitudes about the war espoused in the *Reichsbanner's* publications. While the imagery of *The War* is certainly anti-militarist and ought indeed to serve as a reminder of the realities of war, its spirit of memorial was not out of step with the attitudes espoused by the *Reichsbanner* in its publications and its public demonstrations, and by its predecessor before 1924, the *Reichsbund*. Those attitudes could be summed up as: adamantly opposed to the resumption of the war at any point in the future but also looking for a meaning for their own sacrifices and for the massive loss of life, to the point of being somewhat obsessively involved with the past; and generally supportive of the Republic, wary of a more radical communism and hostile to the conservative nationalist movement. In this respect Dietrich Schubert is mistaken when he writes that, "The true picture which Dix made of the front soldier and his agonizing death did not at all correspond to the ideology of the veterans' leagues."[451] Of course, Schubert has in mind here the reactionary, nationalist veterans' leagues, which have until recently dominated our view of the discourse of the war's memory in Germany between the world wars. But the mainstream organization, which represented the majority of party-affiliated veterans, was actually the *Reichsbanner*.

The *Reichsbanner* encouraged its members to share their memories and feelings about the war publicly.[452] It therefore provides a record of what other former fighters with backgrounds similar to Dix felt about and told themselves and each other about the war in 1924. Of course the imagery that Dix contributed to this collective memory work was not identical to the memory of the war constructed by the *Reichsbanner*. But it may be possible to map the differences between their version of the war and his, and so establish how close or distant to the mainstream

451 Schubert, "Otto Dix: Die Radierungen," 17.

452 Ziemann, *Contested Commemorations*, 5.

memory of the war his imagery actually was. In what follows I will attempt to answer the questions, To what extent and in what ways does the memory of the war constructed by Dix in his portfolio correspond to and harmonize with the memory of the war constructed and shared by other Germans in 1924, Germans with an outlook similar to his own? To what extent and in what ways does Dix's representation of the war experience contradict or undermine the memory of the war he shared with them?

To offer one example, let us consider the theme of the physical fatigue suffered by soldiers. The emotional tone of weary resignation conveyed by Dix was generally approved of in liberal circles. The tone preferred by conservative nationalist writers like Ernst Jünger, by contrast, was grim determination.[453] Take for example a passage from Jünger's memoir, *Storm of Steel*, that describes a scene, etched on the author's memory, of his men preparing for action in the midst of the Battle of the Somme.

> As the storm raged around us, I walked up and down my sector. The men had fixed bayonets. They stood stony and motionless, rifle in hand, on the front edge of the dip, gazing into the field. Now and then, by the light of a flare, I saw steel helmet by steel helmet, blade by glinting blade, and I was overcome by a feeling of invulnerability. We might be crushed, but surely we could not be conquered.[454]

453 The comparison between Jünger and Dix has often been made; with regard to the *War* portfolio, a recent sustained comparison which emphasizes the differences between the two memoirists, rather than their similarities, is Paul Fox. However, Fox emphasizes what he sees as the effects of trauma in their work, whereas I am attempting to emphasize Dix's calculated appeals to certain groups of veterans. Paul Fox, "Confronting Postwar Shame in Weimar Germany: Trauma, Heroism, and the War Art of Otto Dix," *Oxford Art Journal*, 29/2 (2006), 247–267.

454 Ernst Jünger, *Storm of Steel* (New York: Penguin Books, 2004, Michael Hoffmann, translator), 99. "Während des uns umbrausenden Orkans ging ich den Abschnitt meines Zuges ab. Die Männer hatten die Bajonette aufgepflanzt. Sie standen in steinerner Unbeweglichkeit, das Gewehr in der Hand, am vorderen Hange des Hohlwegs und starrten in das Vorgelände. Ab und zu, beim Schein einer Leuchtkugel, sah ich Stahlhelm an Stahlhelm, Klinge an Klinge blinken und wurde von einem Gefühl der Unverletzbarkeit erfüllt. Wir konnten zermalmt,

In the original version of the text, published immediately after the war and republished in 1922, this passage continued, "In such moments the human spirit triumphs over the mighty expressions of matter, the fragile body steeled by will poses itself before the most fearsome tempest."[455]

Contrast this image with the very human exhaustion of soldiers in Dix's portfolio, resting as they wait to be relieved or on their way back to the rear, the subject of no less than three plates in *The War*, each depicting a group of men small enough to have been those under Dix's own command: *The Second Company Will Be Relieved Tonight* [Die II. Kompagnie wird heute Nacht abgelöst] (folio II, plate 20); *Battle-Weary Troops Retreat (Battle of the Somme)* [Abgekämpfte Truppe geht zurück (Sommeschlacht)] (folio III, plate 21); and above all *Resting Company* [Ruhende Kompagnie] (folio II, no. 14) (see Figure 57).[456]

---

aber nicht besiegt werden." Ernst Jünger, *In Stahlgewittern*, Stuttgart: Klett-Cotta, 1978), 113.

455 Translation from Thomas Nevin, *Ernst Jünger and Germany. Into the Abyss, 1914–1945* (Durham, NC: Duke University Press, 1996), 51. After the Second World War, Jünger revised the text, and this last line was cut. Michael Hoffmann's translation is based on the 1978 version of the text, and so does not include this line. The original German reads, "In solchen Augenblicken triumphiert der menschliche Geist über die gewaltigsten Äußerungen der Materie, der gebrechliche Körper stellt sich, vom Willen gestählt, dem furchtbarsten Gewitter entgegen." Ernst Jünger, *In Stahlgewittern* (Berlin: E. S. Mittler und Sohn, 1922), 74.

456 Olaf Peters, "War 1924," in Olaf Peters, ed., *Otto Dix* (Munich: Prestel, 2010), 65.

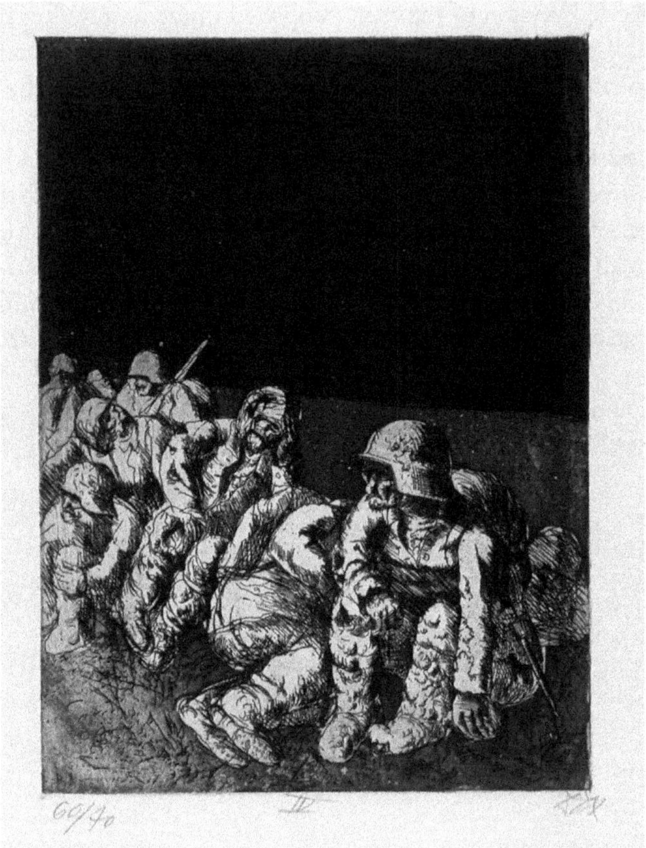

Figure 57. Otto Dix, *Resting Company* [Ruhende Kompagnie], from *The War* [Der Krieg] (folio II, plate 14), etching and aquatint, 1924, Kunstmuseum Albstadt, Stiftung Sammlung Walther Groz SWG 1976–655. © Otto Dix / Artists Rights Society (ARS), New York / VG Bild-Kunst, Bonn. Photo © Kunstmuseum Albstadt, used with permission.

Nowhere in all of the art depicting the First World War has an artist represented a more profound fatigue, an exhaustion that reaches so deeply into the depths of the soldiers' souls. Both Dix and Jünger utilized the hallucinatory effect of figures sharply illuminated against the impenetrable chaos of war by the glaring chemical light of a flare. That sudden, brief spectral light was a metaphor for the indelible outline of a vivid moment burned into the memory like a photographic exposure, a haunting image which, already by the early 1920s, belonged inalienably to every representation of the war. No text and no film neglected to include it (and we've already seen it before in this portfolio, in the image of Monacu Farm, Figure 51, discussed above). But there the similarity ends between Dix's recollection and Jünger's. Dix's men – and they are merely men, no longer warriors – do not display anything like invulnerability, but rather bone-weariness. In Jünger's description, in the passage excised after the Second World War, his men are steeled by an inner will. But in Dix's depiction the men are utterly drained by the battle that has clearly been raging around them for many days and nights (in one instance Dix specifies in the title that the battle was the Somme). Whereas Jünger fashions an image of impersonal, identical figures marked by unvarying steel helmets, Dix has individuated each soldier, introduced the maximum pictorial variety into their tattered uniforms, and created almost an atlas of all the ways that a man's body can express total exhaustion. How do such depictions of weary soldiers, as opposed to Jünger's serried ranks of indomitable warriors, accord with ideas held about the fighting man in Germany in 1924? Among former combatants in socialist democratic circles it was acceptable in the 1920s to acknowledge that combat had often resulted in exhaustion and feelings of isolation; in conservative nationalist circles it was not acceptable to acknowledge this.[457] The point is not merely that Jünger remembered his men as a unified rank of warriors devoid of human weakness while Dix remembered his as profoundly weary. More importantly, the differences in their depictions reflected two different notions of what it meant to say that the German soldiers could be "crushed but not defeated," notions declaimed by two different political world views. On the Right the myth of the undefeated German army meant that a new kind of German warrior had been smelted in the crucible of the

457 Ziemann, *Contested Commemorations*, 88–89; Daniel Morat, "Kalte Männlichkeit? Weimarer Verhaltenslehren im Spannungsfeld von Emotionen- und Geschlechtergeschichte," in Manuel Borutta and Nina Verheyen, eds., *Die Präsenz der Gefühle. Männlichkeit und Emotion im 19. und 20. Jahrhundert* (Bielefeld: Transcript, 2010), 153–177.

war, formed into an unbending group identity by a hard, fell will. But on the Left it meant rather that the men had stuck it out and done their duty *despite* being hopelessly and pointlessly exhausted by their ordeal. And indeed, morale had remained remarkably high in the German ranks right up to the very end of the war.[458] Soon after the scene that Jünger describes, all of his men were annihilated together in the Battle of the Somme, a fate Jünger himself escaped only because he had already been wounded and sent to the rear. So "invulnerability" must be understood already by this early date as a metaphor for some mystical unity and self-identity, the existence of an ideal nation and race unbounded by time or circumstance, an ideal to which actual flesh-and-blood bodies must be sacrificed without complaint or sorrow. His recollection of his men is transformed by metaphors of inner steel will and outer steel unity into a pitiless code of masculinity, a code that would foster the cruelty and inhumanity of fascism.[459] This is no doubt why Jünger redacted the passage in the decades of the Bonn Republic. But Dix remembers his men with altogether more empathy and humanity. And in these three prints Dix represents groups of men who correspond to the social democratic conception of the German soldiers who were "crushed but not defeated." They are crushed spiritually, but they have at least survived, and have not broken ranks; the position is not abandoned and the integrity – but not the uniformity – of the group is maintained.

Throughout the portfolio, the German soldier is repeatedly shown as the passive victim of the impersonal horrors of war such as rain and cold, hunger, fear, fatigue, vermin, and life in the trenches, as well as bullets and artillery shells. We have already seen that Dix minimized

458 Alexander Watson, *Enduring the Great War. Combat, Morale, and Collapse in the German and British Armies, 1914–1918* (Cambridge: Cambridge University Press, 2008), 57–72.

459 Klaus Theweleit, *Male Fantasies, Vol. 2: Male Bodies: Psychoanalyzing the White Terror* (Minneapolis: University of Minnesota Press, 1989, Erica Carter, translator); George Mosse, *Fallen Soldiers. Reshaping the Memory of the World Wars* (Oxford: Oxford University Press, 1991); Bernd Hüppauf, "Langemarck, Verdun, and the Myth of a New Man in Germany after the First World War," *War and Society* 6/2 (1988), 70–103; and Morat, "Kalte Männlichkeit?," 153–177.

the place of combat relative to the art of his colleagues Otto Schubert and Willi Jaeckel, who had published their own portfolios during the war. This move away from the depiction of violence perpetrated *by* German soldiers to the German soldier *as victim* was itself symptomatic of a move in Germany generally away from a memory of the war that centered on combat to one which, by 1924, was centered squarely on the German soldier's suffering. In the intervening years the veterans associated with the Social Democrats had moved the public memory of the war away from an emphasis on combat, in which Germans were necessarily perpetrators as well as victims, and towards an emphasis on the soldier's suffering and hardship. But at the same time, Dix did depart from the orthodoxy that was being established in the public memory of the war, and that would dominate the publications of the Social Democrat veterans; in *Storm Troopers Advancing Under Gas*, and especially in *Surprise Attack of a Sentry by a Silent Patrol*, Dix acknowledge very forcefully that German soldiers had not only suffered and died, but had also killed. The memory conveyed by Dix in *The War* is not identical to that of the *Reichsbanner*.

Another theme which Dix's portfolio shared with the discourse of the *Reichsbanner* was that of the routines of army life. This topic was important to the representation of the front soldier's experience, and especially life at the front and in the trenches. Most of a soldier's time, after all, was not spent in fighting, but in waiting, working, eating, and of course marching. These motifs are in fact the subject of 11 of the 50 plates. The scenes include the tedium of spending cramped hours trapped in a dugout (presumably while an artillery bombardment, which might last days, pummels the trenches overhead), playing skat, hunting lice, or just sleeping (*Dugout* [Unterstand] folio V, plate 45), as well as isolated soldiers huddled alone in trenches, keeping watch. *In Machine-Gun Squad Advances (Somme, November 1916)* [Maschinengewehrzug geht vor (Somme, November 1916)] (folio V, plate 41), a machine gun squad carrying their heavy burdens of machine guns and ammunition crates clambers down a steep slope. They struggle to find their footing in what at first appears to be deep mud, but which on closer inspection turns out to be an endless field of bloating, decaying corpses.[460] This image in particular depicts Dix's own daily experience, carrying the heavy machine gun and ammunition through a landscape of mud and death (the commanding officer bears a distinct resemblance to Dix himself), rendered as a grotesque joke, shared between survivors.

Stories of sexual encounters between soldiers and civilians were perhaps just as important for the communal formation of memories of the war, in particular within communities of veterans, as were themes of violence and combat. Stories shared between men about sexual adventures during the war, typically in towns near the front, served as a form of community building, establishing bonds not only of gender, but also of combat experience. Sex with prostitutes in the occupied towns of France and Belgium had been the subject of several works Dix made in the early 1920s, and he revisited those motifs in three of the plates in *The War*. A fourth plate depicting a soldier raping a nun, who struggles furiously against her attacker, one of the most violent images in the whole suite, was left out of the final selection for the portfolio. *Sailors in Antwerp* [Matrosen in Antwerpen] (folio IV, no. 32), reworks one of Dix's favorite themes to explore in both lithographs and in watercolor, a medium in which he produced a prodigious amount of quasi-pornographic work for private collectors in the years 1920–1923. In those works the sailor had become a specific type: enormous; sexually aggressive; animalistic.[461] In this plate the women are fleshy, the sailors are burly and blunt-nosed, with big, meaty hands that grip the brothel women as they go through their prefatory ritual of drinking a glass of champagne and dancing in a parlor of overstuffed furniture, harshly lit by the glare of an oil lamp.

460 Peter Paret discusses this plate in great depth; "Machine-gun Section Advancing," in Peter Paret, *Imagined Battles. Reflections of War in European Art* (Chapel Hill: University of North Carolina Press, 1997), 99–115.

461 Michael Mackenzie, catalog entry for *Sailor and Prostitute* [*Matrose und Mädchen*] (1923), in Reinhold Heller, ed., *Stark Impressions: Graphic Production in Germany, 1918–1933* (Evanston, IL: Northwestern University, 1993), 278.

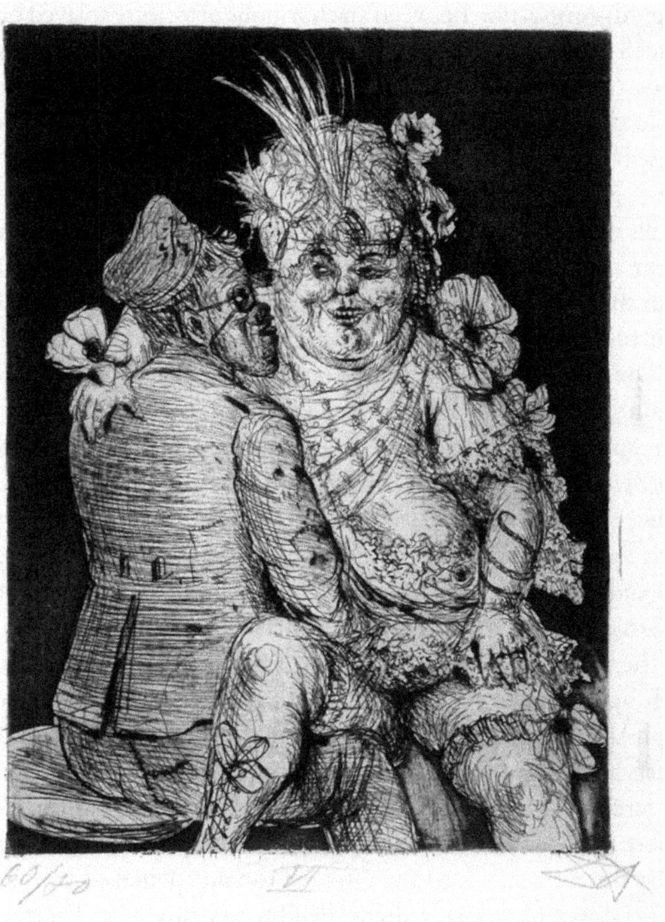

Figure 58. Otto Dix, *A Visit to Madame Germaine's in Mèricourt* [Besuch bei Madame Germaine in Mèricourt] from *The War* [Der Krieg] (folio IV, plate 36), etching, aquatint, and drypoint, 1924, Kunstmuseum Albstadt, Stiftung Sammlung Walther Groz SWG 1976–684. © Otto Dix / Artists Rights Society (ARS), New York / VG Bild-Kunst, Bonn. Photo © Kunstmuseum Albstadt, used with permission.

A Visit to Madame Germaine's in Mèricourt [Besuch bei Madame Germaine in Mèricourt] (folio IV, no. 36) (see Figure 58) is essentially a revision of the motif in *Memory of the Hall of Mirrors in Brussels* (see Figure 40), with the same disproportion between an enormous prostitute splayed on the lap of a much smaller man. But in *The War*, he reworked that image as *Visit to Madame Germaine's in Méricourt*, and the officer has been transformed into a simple, threadbare foot soldier, while the trappings of material privilege and tawdry glamour have been left out. Dix has again used the drypoint needle to add not only texture to the two figures but telling details, like the lacy frills of her clothes and the many crudely stitched repairs in his worn uniform, the traces of his time spent at the front – this is no deskbound clerk in the rear town of Mèricourt or nearby Lens, but a soldier taking his short leave or, perhaps, convalescing. Mèricourt was, in fact, the town where Dix spent time convalescing from an illness in late 1916. Was Madame Germaine's a real brothel there? If so, then this picture has a more direct connection to Dix's own wartime experience in occupied territory than does *Hall of Mirrors*. Likewise, the third plate in this group, *Frontline Soldier in Brussels* [Frontsoldat in Brüssel] (folio IV, no. 34), in which the soldier of the title leers with obviously carnal intent at a parade of prostitutes walking up and down a Brussels street in front of a café, reworks a watercolor composition that was explicitly a self-portrait. Dix changed little in translating the watercolor, *Me in Brussels* [Ich in Brüssel] (see Figure 34), into an etching, except to replace himself with a lower-ranked soldier and to multiply the streetwalkers from one to several (four are visible full-figure, with at least two more in the background). Where the single woman in the watercolor entices our protagonist, Dix the soldier, by lifting her skirts to expose her bare, and large, buttocks, here the women are fully clothed. But Dix the artist has used the range of tonality achieved with aquatint, and areas stopped out to highlight their breasts, thighs, and buttock, all of which are very large. He has also used his drypoint needle again to rework the area of their pubis, to the point of suggesting the pubic hair hidden by the clothing, as well as their cleavage and their heavily made-up mouths and eyes, and even their feather hats and boas – all the fetish markers of a commodified sexuality. Dix also used the drypoint needle to darken his soldier, creating a strong contrast between him and the women he is cruising, a contrast which is echoed by the bright, reserved rectangle of the café window, illuminated from within, set against the silken darks of the nighttime street in occupied Brussels.

In *Madame Germaine's*, the lace of the woman's loose undergarments is similarly enhanced by the etching needle, setting up a parallel and opposition between the two which borders again on the allegorical, a sort of "mismatched couple," a theme popular in the art of the German Renaissance, and one which Dix would revisit again and again in paintings like *Mismatched Couple* [Ungleiches Liebespaar] (1925, Galerie der Stadt Stuttgart). Like many early modern allegorical themes, the "mismatched couple" could simultaneously insist on the sanctity and virtue of a well-considered marriage, through depicting a negative example, and subvert that sanctity by reveling in the imperfect, decaying, or overly abundant, grotesque body.[462] Dix of course pushes the theme here fully in the direction of the Rabelasian in its grotesque humor.[463] Humor and humorous stories about sex with grotesque bodies were, like humorous stories about encounters with the grotesque bodies of the dead, the capital that circulated in an economy of male comradeship among former front line soldiers, an economy that functioned, by 1924, to exclude women as well as others who hadn't seen the fighting at the front, as we will see.

The pamphleteer Heinrich Wandt depicted the town of Ghent, turned into a garrison town by the German Army, as a "moral swamp" in his work *Etappe Gent*, published in 1920 and republished in 1926 – but a moral swamp specifically for the officers.[464] Dix, by contrast, participated in a much more celebratory, ribald memory of the staging towns, depicting them as sites of lively sexual congress, fraternization, and prostitution, specifically for the enlisted man, without the moralizing tone. In keeping with the prominent place that sex, and especially sordid commercial transactions around sex, held in his other work, Dix rather celebrated the opportunities

462 W. A. Coupe, "Ungleiche Liebe: A Sixteenth-Century Topos," *The Modern Language Review* 62/4 (October 1967), 661–671.

463 James van Dyke, "On the Grotesque Body in a Double-Sided Drawing by Otto Dix," Bettina Matthias, Eliza Garrison, and James van Dyke, eds., *Naked Truth. Approaches to the Body in Early-Twentieth-Century German-Austrian Art*, Middlebury: Middlebury College Museum of Art, 2015), 61–77; Michael Mackenzie, "'Wie ein Frontschwein malt': Otto Dix, Grotesque Realism, and the Language of the Trenches," presentation delivered at German Studies Association annual conference in St. Paul, 2008.

464 Ziemann, *Contested Commemorations*, 44–49.

for sex that the reserve town presented to the enlisted man such as himself. Here bawdy stories of sex during the war function as the stuff which binds men together in their camaraderie, founded on their collective memories of the war. The theme of the garrison town was controversial enough in 1924 that Nierendorf worried the pictures of this theme would result in the entire run of the portfolio being confiscated by the police. He suggested creating a separate portfolio of just these scenes. But Dix refused to take it out, saying that the plate *A Visit to Madame Germaine's* would be a, "slap in the face for anybody with a bourgeois idea about the frontline soldier."[465]

The difference between how enlisted men and officers experienced the erotic opportunities thrown up by the war brings us to the topic of the conflict between officers and enlisted men more generally. One of the central tropes around which the former enlisted men constructed their memories of the war – at least as represented by the membership of the *Reichsbanner* – was their resentment of the officer class. The privilege and relative comfort enjoyed the officers during the war, and the myriad mean spirited ways in which they lorded their authority over the enlisted men, was a topic which was dwelt on in the pages of the *Reichsbanner* publication from 1924 onward, expressing a lasting hostility and enmity. One of the main ideological differences between the leftist, socialist veteran's organizations like the *Reichsbanner*, and rightwing, nationalist groups was that the latter claimed to remember and cherish a camaraderie between enlisted men and officers (especially in essays written by former officers), whereas the enlisted men in the *Reichsbanner* nursed a grudge against an officer class that they remembered as arrogant and callous. Dix, however, avoided this topic entirely, and included no identifiable officers (some soldiers leading marching troops may be NCOs or field officers, but they are not depicted in those moments enjoying or abusing their authority). This is all the more surprising in that the officer class was firmly identified with the wealthy industrialists and other capitalists in the work of Dix's contemporaries like George Grosz. Of the three kinds of people that the enlisted men developed their communal identity in opposition to – the enemy, women, and officers – only women are represented in *The War*.

465 "… Schlag ins Gesicht für alle, die eine bürgerliche Vorstellung vom Frontsoldaten hatten." Letter from Dix to Nierendorf, 17 July 1924, DKA I, C, 524 f.

And yet the officer class did figure in Dix's work earlier in the 1920s. The Dada collages heaped contempt on former officers as well as war invalids, especially in *Skat Players* (see Figure 30). The painting *Memory of the Hall of Mirrors in Brussels* depicts both an officer and a woman together, in a brothel, as we have already noted, but when Dix reworked this image as *Visit to Madame Germaine's in Méricourt*, he transformed the ridiculous, red-faced officer into an enlisted man, a simple, threadbare soldier exchanging his meager pay for a brief sexual encounter, and eliminated the mirrored surroundings and bottle of champagne which had earlier indicated the officer's privileges. Perhaps this choice must also be seen as part of a larger pattern in Dix's work: by 1924, he had to a great extent moved away from the socially critical subjects of his earlier *Neue Sachlichkeit* paintings, the working-class women and children in tenement neighborhoods, and was increasingly occupied with his growing practice as a portraitist of the wealthy professional class of the Weimar Republic. The members of the *Reichsbanner* attacked the officer class – which overlapped with the postwar professional class and the bourgeoisie, the class of Dix's patrons and portraiture clientele. But as Dix himself by now entertained ambitions of entering that class, he no longer participated in those attacks.

Women's grief

Women's experiences of the war are represented among the 50 prints and, importantly, in a fifty-first print, not included in the final, published portfolio, But they are represented in very particular ways. Women appear only as prostitutes and, in one instance, as a mother of a dead infant, evidently killed by a falling bomb or perhaps the shelling of her home. The mother is literally driven mad by her grief, in a moment once again reminiscent of the Belgian artist Antoine Wiertz (specifically *Hunger, Madness, Crime* [Faim, Folie et Crime] 1853, Wiertz Museum, Brussels). In the print that was not included, a nun is raped by a soldier. It is a violent and sexually graphic image in which the woman desperately but futilely struggles against her attacker, and she is positioned so that we can see her face; her splayed, foreshortened legs are opened towards us, while the soldier who rapes her has his back to us, a *Ruckenfigur* who, it is not too far-fetched to suggest, serves as the viewer's proxy. Grotesque, cynical whores, maddened young mothers with the damaged little corpses of their babies, and nuns being violated and sexualized against their will; these are the war experiences afforded to women in Dix's imaginary. It is a narrow range of grotesque, Rabelasian images. What Dix does not seem to have any interest in are images of women who experience the pain and loss of the death of a soldier son or husband. Yet this particular experience of the war was one in fact shared by millions of women in every nation. The pressing need that these women had to give meaning to their loss was one of the driving social forces behind the collective memory work of the war, and the creation of public memorials across Europe and the world. For every former combatant who had lost a comrade was a mother or a wife who had lost a son or husband. Yet the veteran's leagues – the democratic *Reichsbanner* as well as the conservative nationalist *Stahlhelm*, all disregarded or denigrated those women's experiences.

There were in fact women artists who created images of women's grief at the loss of men in uniform. In the medium of the graphic arts in particular, and especially in the woodcuts which were so important to German Expressionism before, during, and immediately after the war, several women artists depicted other women grieving over the sight of uniformed dead male bodies. Claudia Siebrecht has turned the attention of art historians to the work of avant-garde German women artists working in woodcuts, especially, creating emotionally complex, affective images of mothers in particular, mourning the loss of their soldier sons.[466] Between 1916 and 1918 these took the form of an Expressionist vocabulary. Sella Hasse published a series of woodcuts during the war, filled with Marin imagery; one of these, *Mater Dolorosa on the Battlefield* [Mater Dolorosa auf den Schlachtfeldern] (1916) (see Figure 59) depicts a woman (Mary), walking among the corpses of a battlefield, strewing them with flowers. In an image that recalls the Marin tradition of *imitatio Christi*, her feet are pierced by the bladed weapons bristling from the field of dead soldiers upon which she treads, barefoot. As

466 Claudia Siebrecht, *The Aesthetics of Loss. German Women's Art of the First World War* (Oxford: Oxford University Press, 2013).

Siebrecht observes, the dead are peaceful, and appear to be sleeping (a conceit that would continue after the war to appear in monuments that sought to associate the dead with medieval, quasi-religious imagery); they are neither distorted nor disfigured by their violent deaths.[467]

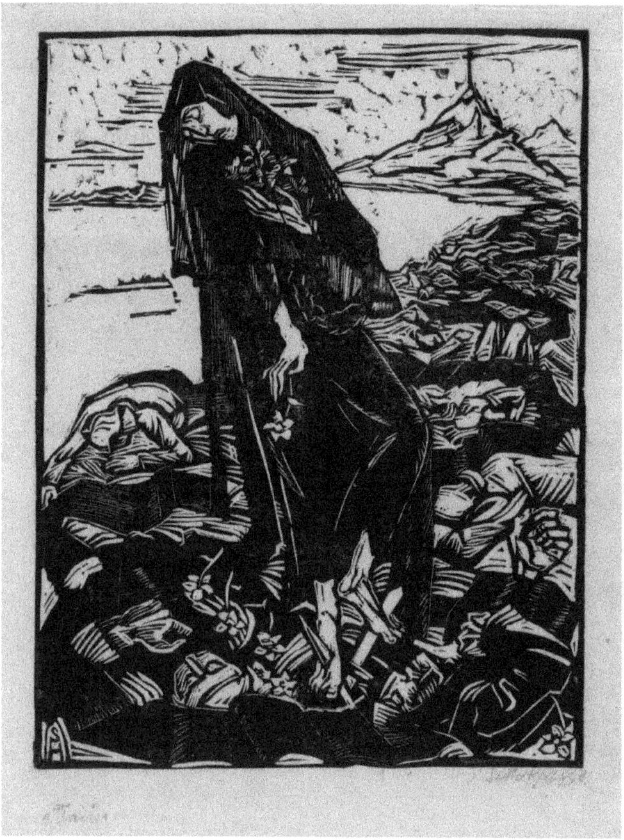

Figure 59. Sella Hasse, *Mater Dolorosa on the Battlefield* [Trauer (Die Schmerzensmutter auf den Schlachtfeldern)], woodcut, from *War Pages* [Kriegsblätter] (plate 4), 1914–1916, Kupferstichkabinett, Berlin.

467 Claudia Siebrecht, "The *Mater Dolorosa* on the Battlefield – Mourning Mothers in German Women's Art of the First World War," *History of Warfare* 49 (2008), 259–291, and *Aesthetics of Loss*, 121–129.

By contrast, when Dix represented the corpses of dead soldiers, which he did in more than a dozen images in *The War*, either in small groups or, as here in Hasse's woodcut, in fields strewn with bodies, they are shown contorted and disfigured by death, maimed or mutilated by the violence that killed them, and bloated and decaying because they lie on the ground unburied, exposed to the elements. In *Evening on the Wijtschaete Plain* [Abend in der Wijtschaete-Ebene (November 1917)] (folio 3, no. 27) (see Figure 60), the low, flat, featureless landscape of Flanders is emphasized; it stretches to the distant horizon, covered with bodies as far as the eye can see.[468]

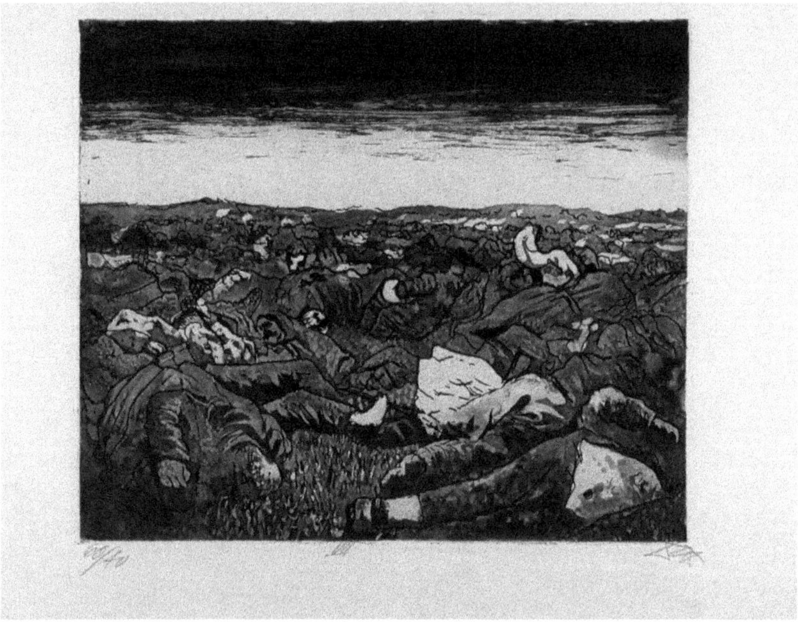

Figure 60. Otto Dix, *Evening on the Wijtschaete Plain* [Abend in der Wijtschaete-Ebene (November 1917)] from *The War* [Der Krieg] (folio III, plate 27), etching and aquatint, 1924, Kunstmuseum Albstadt, Stiftung Sammlung Walther Groz SWG 1976–673. © Otto Dix / Artists Rights Society (ARS), New York / VG Bild-Kunst, Bonn. Photo © Kunstmuseum Albstadt, used with permission.

468 Michael Mackenzie, catalog entry, Heller, ed., *Stark Impressions*, 48–49.

It is a masterpiece of the use of aquatint, which Dix has used in two tones to depict the field-gray uniforms of the countless German dead, while stopping out areas to represent the pallid skin of their corpses, revealed where uniforms have been haphazardly stripped away by the violence: a belly here, the back of a torso there. Only these random patches of white relieve the gray field of the dead beneath a darkening November sky. Hasse's woodcut depicts an upright female figure contrasted with the prone bodies of the dead (and the vertical format of the print accommodates her); posture, gestures, facial features, and the Christ-like wounds of her feet, are all expressive of emotional and spiritual meaning. The woodcut technique harmonizes with the late medievalism of the theological concepts of the *mater dolorosa* and the *imitatio Christi*. Dix, by contrast, does not express sorrow for his fallen comrades, but rather emphasizes what unburied bodies exposed to the elements actually look like. Again, the emphasis is on eyewitness truthfulness. The deaths of his soldiers does not redeem or dignify the war's losses, but rather emphasize the brutality and profanity of mechanized killing.

In March of 1918, Franz Pfemfert's periodical *Die Aktion* published a special issue that carried the theme "Golgotha" (vol. 8, no. 11/12, 23 March 1918), which featured several woodcuts, in particular by women Expressionist artists, that combined women's mourning for their dead with Christological imagery, and the formal pathos of what would come to be dubbed "O Mensch" Expressionism.[469] At the same time Otto Dix, who was engaged at that moment with an Expressionist vocabulary, tried his own hand at the theme of the Mater Dolorosa in several drawings with that title (1918) (see Figure 61).

469 Siebrecht, *Aesthetics of Loss*, 135.

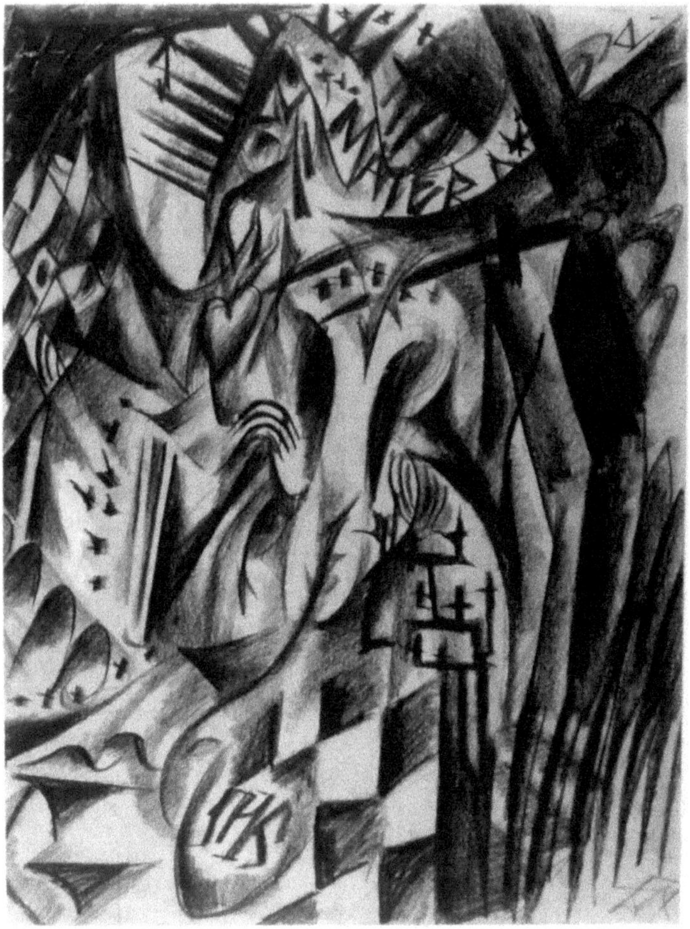

Figure 61. Otto Dix, *Mater Dolorosa*, 1918, Kunstmuseum Albstadt, Stiftung Sammlung Walther Groz SWG 1983–72. © Otto Dix / Artists Rights Society (ARS), New York / VG Bild-Kunst, Bonn. Photo © Kunstmuseum Albstadt, used with permission.

These, too, included images of a mourning Marin figure, barely recognizable but helpfully labeled with the legend "Mater Dolorosa" worked into the image itself, in a manner popular in early post-war Expressionism, and a pair of images of Christ. One depicts his body on the cross, the other is in the form of Veronica's veil, perhaps surrounded by a crown of thorns. The

Veronica image was a motif to which Dix would return after the Second World War. These motifs are worked into a bold, bristling Cubo-Futurist composition of checkerboard and spikes. Is this drawing Dix's own response to the spate of images of the mourning mother made by women, a motif which had come to represent specifically women's grief for their sons, victims/sacrifices of the war? The elevation of the war experience into religious, or at least cosmological, themes, fits with other work which he was doing at the time, as we have seen in Chapter 2, as was the division of the cosmological into male and female aspects, here represented by Christ and Mary/Veronica.[470] Siebrecht observes that in his own version of the Mater Dolorosa theme, Dix does not seem concerned with representing "the pain of losing a son."[471] I think that the gendered difference between the popularity of the Mater Dolorosa theme among female German Expressionist artists and Dix's own handling of the same theme also exhibits an increasing emphasis after the war among ex-servicemen on their own experience of combat as the one and only valid truth of the war, the only pain or suffering worth representing. With time, this attitude spread throughout the culture, as we saw in the previous chapter with the reception history of Beno Elkan's memorial sculpture of a mourning mother kneeling and clutching her breast with one hand, covering her face with the other (see Figure 46). In 1920, the same year that Willy Jaeckel published a lithograph of a *Grieving Mother* [Klagende Mutter] on her knees and surrounded by the corpses of slain soldiers, her arms thrown up to heaven in bitter rebuke, Elkan's sculptural depiction of maternal grief was lauded in *Der Cicerone* for the unique perspective it brought to the mass death of the war, beyond misguided notions of glory and honor. But by 1930 it was disparaged in *Das Kunstblatt* specifically because it was only concerned with women's grief, and specifically a mother's.[472]

470 See Siebrecht, *Aesthetics of Loss*, 127–128. Siebrecht does not mention the Veronica Veil in this picture by Dix, although she includes a discussion of the motif by other women artists done the same year.

471 Siebrecht, "*Mater Dolorosa*," 288.

472 See Kathrin Hoffmann-Curtius, Sieg ohne Trauer – Trauer ohne Sieg: Totenklage auf Kriegsdenkmälern des Ersten Weltkrieges," in Gisela Ecker and Maria Kublik-Kramer,

The depiction by women artists of women's grief culminated in a monumental portfolio of woodcuts by Käthe Kollwitz, published in 1923 and simply titled *War* (Krieg), much as Dix would title his own, much larger set the following year.[473] As Annegret Jürgens-Kirchhoff has pointed out, Kollwitz never fully gave herself over to the sentiments of pacifism and the "Nie-Wieder-Krieg" movement, despite having created the poster which immortalized that very phrase. Early in the war she made images for the nationalistic publication *Kriegszeit*, as did her friend and fellow-artist Ernst Barlach. Her own son Peter was killed at the front in 1914, and she needed to hang on to some feeling that the war had been justified, as a defense of the nation, in order to give some meaning to his death.[474] In this she was like the grieving civilians whom she depicted. By 1919 she was making images of bereft mothers specifically, as in the lithograph *Mothers* [Die Mütter] (1919), which depicts women of varying ages, all of them facing the viewer, some grasping their young children while others hide their faces in lachrymose grief. The woodcut portfolio *War* treats the theme of women's grief in a more multifaceted but also more monumental and powerful way. The prints in this portfolio do not depict any battlefields or fighting; there are no dead soldiers and, indeed, no uniformed men at all. Instead, Kollwitz depicts bereaved parents, widows left with infants to care for, groups of sorrowing mothers, and "The People," which is the title of a print depicting older men, women, and children, clearly seized by grief and loss. Kollwitz created monumental graphic images, roughly cut into the wooden plates, with figures or figure groups gathered together in a compact mass and isolated against a blank background, as if hewn from a single, massive block of wood. They are like proposals for monumental sculptures, memorials to the sacrifice of the men and women who had lost their sons. Only one print, *The Volunteers*, depicts the young men who, we understand, are foredoomed to die, but in keeping with the guiding concept, they are still civilians; the point in every image is the way in which the emotional lives and attachments of civilians are torn

---

Trauer Tragen – Trauer Zeigen: Inszenierungen der Geschlechter (Munich: Wilhelm Fink, 1999), 259–286, here 275 ff.

473 Erin Hogan, catalog entries, Heller, ed., *Stark Impressions*, 60–69.

474 Anagrett Jürgens-Kirchhoff, *Schreckensbilder*, 291 ff.

asunder by war, and the death it brings. In *The Volunteers*, Death in fact makes an appearance in allegorical form, as a skeleton leading the young men – who appear to be wracked with an almost agonizing ecstasy – with his recruiting drum. One plate in particular, again titled *Mothers* [Die Mütter], reworks the idea of the earlier lithograph (see Figure 62). But now the women are gathered together in a defensive circle, facing inwards; none of them looks out at the viewer. They wrap their arms around one another protectively, locking hands on wrists, and though some have been crying, none hide their faces now, gazing out instead in all directions, watchful and ready. The group forms a solid, impenetrable mass, from which peek out small children, as wary as their mothers; this is what the women are protecting. One woman holds an infant close, and another appears to be pregnant. But they have no intention of letting these children provide more fodder for the cannons.

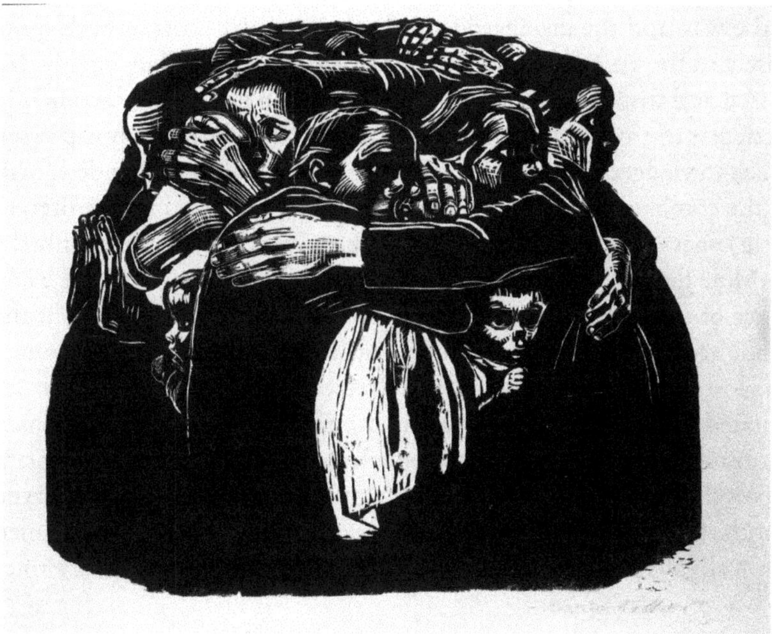

Figure 62. Käthe Kollwitz, *The Mothers* [Die Mütter], woodcut, 1921–1922, from *War* [Krieg] (plate 6), 1923, Philadelphia Museum of Art, given by Dr. and Mrs. William Wolgin. © Käthe Kollwitz / Artists Rights Society (ARS), New York / VG Bild-Kunst, Bonn. Photo © The Philadelphia Museum of Art / Art Resource, NY.

"War," as a title, meant something very different for Dix. In his own cycle of prints, he displayed a complete disinterest in what the war had meant for women back home, for mothers and wives, or in their own postwar community of memory. The grief of loss, an experience shared by as many people as the experience of the front itself, was not Dix's subject, in contrast to Käthe Kollwitz, Sella Hasse, and others. The only civilian experiences that Dix represented were those of the French and Belgian cities occupied by the German army, which were bombed by the Allies and cruised by sexually predatory German troops. Dix's representation of the war experience in his own graphics portfolio is quite gendered, is a specifically male perspective on the war's memory, and as such is overtly opposed to the female experience pictured by Käthe Kollwitz, Sella Hasse, or other German women artists.[475] Dix's single-minded emphasis on the soldier's personal experience of the front as the only legitimate memory of the war, and the disregard for other perspectives corresponds quite closely to the attitude expressed by the *Reichsbanner*. They openly dismissed and disparaged the claim of civilians in general and women in particular to any communal memory which could be publicly expressed or acknowledged. The *Reichsbanner* maintained a single-minded focus on the combat soldier's experience. This is an example of what literary critic James Campbell has termed "combat Gnosticism." Where only the frontline fighter's experience counts as the truth of war, there the experience of others has no place. This ideology effectively shuts out of the public arena of memory and meaning the grief and suffering of women who lost the men of their families.[476] Indeed, when the *Reichsbanner* was founded in 1924, the year Otto Dix brought out his portfolio, women were excluded from membership, much to the irritation of female members of the parent German Socialist Party.[477] Nadine Rossol has observed that the imagery on the covers of the Reichsbanner journal featured men heroically defending the republic, often violently, while women's roles

475 Siebrecht also discusses Katharina Heise and Mizi Otten-Friedmann, *Aesthetics of Loss*.
476 Campbell, "Combat Gnosticism."
477 Ziemann, *Contested Commemorations*, 78.

were minimized.[478] At the same time, the *Reichsbanner* magazine emphasized, in regular features, an element which we do find represented in Dix's art about the war: low, humorous anecdotes which functioned as "the glue that bound together the ... members who had served at the front," in Ziemann's words.[479] Anecdotal memories of combat experiences in the form of short, personal remembrances of various aspects of the fighting submitted by readers were selected for their "truth value," and were well received by the membership. The publication of these anecdotes fulfilled what the editorial staff considered it to be the duty of the journal to do, which was to, "conjure up the true face of the war incessantly, without doing that in the black-and-white manner of the radical pacifists."[480] Again, I am not suggesting that this organization and its publication (which only began appearing in 1924) had a direct influence on Dix. But he did share a background with its membership, and judging by what he emphasized in his art, and by which subjects he left out, he seems to have shared their attitudes and dispositions which were, in many important respects, not dissimilar to those of their counterparts in the conservative veteran's leagues, despite their political enmity.

478 Nadine Rossol, *Performing the Nation in Interwar Germany. Sport, Spectacle, and Political Symbolism, 1926–1936* (London: Palgrave Macmillan, 2010), 32.

479 Ziemann, *Contested Commemorations*, 77.

480 Franz Osterroth, "Errinerungen 1900–1924," 192, cited and translated in Ziemann, *Contested Commemorations*, 80.

CHAPTER 5

Dix in the Late Weimar Era: The Triptych *The War*, *All Quiet on the Western Front*, and the Contest over the Memory of the War

Otto Dix moved to Berlin in the autumn of 1925, together with his wife, Martha, and their baby daughter, Nelly. In the German capital he built a career as a private portrait painter, and his work was in high demand with its combination of precisely rendered details and sharply observed, unflatteringly caricatured features. Both qualities were heightened by his increasingly pronounced use of an old-masters-like smooth, glossy surface and minute brushwork, a painstaking method of layered oil and tempera, incorporating what had been presented in an influential book on technique as the methods of the German Renaissance masters.[481] Combined with frequent borrowings from German Renaissance painters like Albrecht Dürer and Hans Baldung Grien, the conspicuously high craft of his paintings helped to establish his reputation in the German art world. Besides his commissioned portraits, Dix also painted some of the figures around him who were in one way or another representative of the sophisticated, self-consciously modern metropolis: the dancer and social sensation Anita Berber; the journalist and quintessential "New Woman" Sylvia von Harden; the dealer in avant-garde art Alfred Flechtheim. In 1925, when Gustav Hartlaub organized the epochal exhibition *Neue Sachlichkeit* in Mannheim, he featured Dix prominently, but avoided any "war pictures."[482] In

481 Max Doerner, *The Materials of the Artist and Their Use in Painting* (New York: Harcourt, Brace and World, Inc., 1934, Eugen Neuhaus, translator), originally published as *Malmaterial und seine Verwendung im Bilde* (Munich: Verlag für praktische Kunstwissenschaft, 1921).

482 Nierendorf had offered to lend him the controversial *The Trench*, which he was aggressively trying to show; Hartlaub dodged the overture with the quick note, "War

February of 1926, Nierendorf held a retrospective of his work, including *The Trench*, and later that same year, Dix had six paintings, all but one portraits, in the *Internationale Kunstausstellung* [International Art Exhibition] in Dresden. During this period in Berlin, Dix seems to have neglected the war as a subject, and gained a reputation apart from the notoriety of *The Trench*. His evident technical mastery and his increasingly high profile, especially after the international exhibition in Dresden, led to his appointment in the autumn of 1926 as a professor at the Dresden Art Academy, where he had once been a student. Dix was hired to replace his former professor Otto Gussmann, who was recently deceased. And recently retired from the Academy was Oskar Kokoschka, the same artist whom Dix had earlier mocked in his painting *The Matchbook Seller*.

Once relocated in Dresden, where he took up his teaching responsibilities in May of 1927 (having first taken a semester's leave to complete portrait commissions), and where he was granted a large studio and the freedom to paint something other than society portraits, Dix began to work on what were essentially large-scale history paintings, but with contemporary life as their subjects, much as Edouard Manet had done in the nineteenth century. Dix revisited the themes of his earlier works, transforming them into ambitious salon pieces. This was certainly true of the work which will be the main subject of this chapter, *The War*, which transformed *The Trench* into a carefully composed and skillfully executed multi-panel altarpiece. The project also included *Street Battle* [Strassenkampf] (1927, lost), which was a reworking of one of his own earlier painting, *Barricade* (1920), but this time based on the composition of Francisco Goya's *Third of May 1808* (1814).[483] It also includes *Three Women* [Drei Weiber] (1926), a life-size reworking of the classical "Three Graces" motif but with prostitutes. *Three Women* is another exercise in grotesque humor, with its women of Rabelasian proportions degrading the classical ideal typically exemplified by the three graces. Dix had already begun *Metropolis* [Großstadt] (1927–1928) in Berlin, and he now expanded it in his new, spacious Dresden studio to a triptych, that quintessential German Renaissance

---

painting in this exhibition unfortunately impossible." Cited in Crockett, *German Post-Expressionism*, 151.

483 James van Dyke, "Otto Dix's *Streetbattle* and the Limits of Satire in Dusseldorf, 1928," *Oxford Art Journal* 32/1 (2009), 37–65.

format. The central panel reworks the themes of his earlier self-portrait-as-dandy, *Ode to Beauty* [An die Schönheit] (1922), and explores elements of the sophisticated Berlin society which he had just left behind: jazz bands; American dances; and fashionable dresses and cocktails. Dix is reveling in his extraordinary rise from proletariat to well-dressed man-about-town. His place is now in the center of the action (even though he omits his own self-portrait from this version), with the well-dressed society types depicted here in the central panel, including several people prominent in local Dresden society and politics as well as Dix's own social circle.[484] In the wings of this triptych, however, Dix returned to the theme of war invalids reduced to begging, who appear like forgotten remnants of the past to haunt the phantasmagorical streets of Berlin (see Figure 1).[485] These disabled veterans crowd the streets in the side panels together with lines of prostitutes. It has often been argued that Dix would combine prostitutes and war invalids in the same pictures in order to suggest that both are proletarians, forced to sacrifice their bodies to a society that then casts them aside (see the discussion of *Prostitute and War Wounded* [Dirne und Kriegskrüppel] in Chapter 2).[486] But the prostitutes in *Metropolis* are simply reminders of the militarized sexual instinct which the crippled veterans in the painting can no longer satisfy – but which Dix can. This is a return to Dix's theme of his own intact sexual potency, contrasted with the supposed impotence of disabled veterans (see Chapter 2). There is little sympathy or pity expressed here, let alone class analysis. The juxtaposition in the left panel of *Metropolis* is nothing short of cruel: the whores especially flaunt their legs while the crippled veterans are barely able to walk or stand. Two of the three are missing both legs; the third is collapsed on the ground, presumably inebriated, dependent on alcohol in his miserable social condition and "too drunk to fuck," as the saying goes.[487] Meanwhile, in the center panel,

484 See Birgit Schwarz, *Otto Dix. Großstadt*. Frankfurt am Main and Leipzig, 1993.

485 See James van Dyke on the phantasmagorical qualities of this monumental work, "Otto Dix's philosophical metropolis," in Olaf Peters, ed., *Otto Dix* (Munich: Prestel, 2010), 178–197.

486 See Dietrich Schubert especially.

487 Dietrich Schubert interprets these disabled and pathetic veterans as figures of melancholy, and therefore as signs of the artist's sarcasm or criticism; for if Dix's pictures

legs seem to be everywhere, and a couple dances the Foxtrot, a dance which especially emphasizes movement below the knees.[488] Try doing *that* with two wooden legs! – or so the painting seems to say. The male dancer is a stand-in for the artist, who had once considered dancing competitively with his wife Martha, and who appeared as himself in the earlier version of this scene in *Ode to Beauty*. Here he and his red haired dance partner (identifiable as one of the models in *Three Women*) swing their legs with gusto. Dix has replaced the erotic glamor of the soldier's uniform, discussed earlier, with that of the tuxedo, and made the common equation of sexual vigor with proficiency on the dancefloor (contrasted with the inebriated, invalided, and impotent condition of the less fortunate veterans in the street). Women continued to occupy the purely instrumentalized role of prostitutes in Dix's memory work of the war, as it had in the *War* portfolio. Meanwhile, in France the artist André Devambez had exhibited a triptych in Paris in 1924, with predella, which featured three women – whether they're mourning or only pining is ambiguous – in the central panel, long-suffering soldiers at the front in both side panels, and a row of wooden crosses in the predella.[489]

Despite the display of skillful, traditional technique, and the large, public scale of the paintings, this whole body of work, the large format paintings begun by Dix in his new studio in Dresden, indicates a return to the themes

of war cripples were to lack this quality, he argues, they would lack empathy, and would exhibit nothing but cynicism. Schubert, "Krüppeldarstellungen im Werk von Otto Dix nach 1920: Zynismus oder Sarkasmus?," in Gertrude Cepl-Kaufmann and Gerd Krumeich, eds., *Krieg und Utopie. Kunst, Literatur und Politik im Rheinland nach dem Ersten Weltkrieg* (Essen: Klartext, 2006), 293–308. I am suggesting that the interpretation Schubert goes out of his way to reject is in fact the correct one.

488 Karsten Müller, "The Charleston and the Prosthetic Leg: Otto Dix and the Art of the Balancing Act," in Olaf Peters, ed., *Otto Dix* (Munich: Prestel, 2010), 164–178.

489 Paul Devambez, *La Pensées aux absents* (second, smaller version, 1927, Musée Saint-Quentin). The three women, of three generations, are dressed in mourning; the crosses below them indicate a permanent "absence." Significantly, the format of the frame and arrangement of the panels is more in keeping with an Art Nouveau decorative ensemble than an actual altarpiece, whereas the proportions of the side panels in *The War* is exactly half of the center panel, as though they could be closed over it as in a late medieval altarpiece.

of grotesque humor and the overabundant female body, the lower bodily stratum, and the openings of wounds and orifices, as well as a grotesquely humorous violence (specifically of soldiers against civilians) – the carnivalesque, degrading, and humorous speech of the soldier, now uneasily haunting the civilian life of the Weimar-era metropolis. It is dismaying to see Dix relishing yet again with uncharitable satisfaction his own good fortune in returning from the war whole and sexually potent, able to frequent brothels, while other soldiers did not. Yet such callousness towards the plight of his fellow veterans was not peculiar to Dix, but might have been shared by the rank-and-file membership of the *Reichsbanner*, with whom I have argued Dix shared a class and cultural background. The *Reichsbanner* was preceded by the Reich League of Disabled War Veterans, or *Reichsbund*, which staged the sorts of parades of disabled veterans that Dix mocked in *War Cripples* in 1920.[490] Although non-disabled veterans were invited to join the *Reichsbund*, few were moved to do so. This lack of interest in or solidarity with disabled veterans led by 1924 to the founding of the *Reichsbanner*, aimed at non-disabled vets who were Social Democrats. The new organization was much more popular, and its membership eventually expanded to include non-veterans.[491]

In 1928, Dix continued his practice of reworking his earlier motifs as large-scale museum pieces, by beginning work on a design for a monumental painting based on *The Trench*. The new version would eventually be a triptych with a predella, simply titled *The War* [Der Krieg] (1928–1932) (see Figure 3). The central panel is similar to *The Trench* in its subject matter, in its emphasis on grisly detail, and in its square format. Dix also retained from the earlier painting the organization around a trench with a formless, visceral center and a periphery of corpses flung into unnatural positions.[492]

490 Christian Weiß, "'Soldaten des Friedens'. Die pazifistischen Veteranen und Kriegsopfer des 'Reichsbundes' und ihre Kontakte zu den französischen *anciens combatants* 1919–1933" in Wolfgang Hardtwig, ed., *Politische Kulturgeschichte der Zwischenkriegszeit 1918–1939* (Göttingen: Vandenhoeck & Ruprecht, 2005), 183–204.

491 Benjamin Ziemann, *Contested Commemorations, Republican War Veterans and Weimar Political Culture* (Cambridge: Cambridge University Press, 2012), 35 f.

492 Birgit Dalbajewa, Simone Fleischer, and Olaf Peters, *Otto Dix. Der Krieg – Das Dresdner Triptychon* (Dresden: Verlag, 2014), 42–45. The painting is commonly referred to as a triptych, although it also has a predella.

If the print portfolio was created in the context of – and partly in response to – the controversial reception of *The Trench*, then this was also the case for *The War*. Additionally, in 1928 the subject of the war returned dramatically to public life in Germany. Erich Maria Remarque's novel *All Quiet on the Western Front* was only one of the many war novels and memoirs to appear that year, although it was by far the best seller. At just this moment *The Trench*, which Nierendorf had been regularly exhibiting, was finally purchased, by the Dresden art museum, only to disappear into storage for good, or so it seemed. The museum had been persuaded to purchase it in the wake of Dix's appointment to the faculty of the Dresden Art Academy, but they clearly had no intention of exhibiting this troublesome object from the past. If Otto Dix, the painter of the most notorious public representation of the war, wanted to continue to be relevant to this public memory work, he would have to paint another major work on the subject.

It would take him until 1932 to complete it. Judging by its vast scale, Dix clearly intended *The War* for a public venue, and it would have been reasonable for Dix, who by now had several works in prominent museums and who was a professor of painting at one of Germany's most prestigious art academies, to expect that it would find a home in a major German museum, as *The Trench* had in its day, and as *Metropolis* did. Ludwig Justi, the director of the National Gallery in Berlin, felt pressured to purchase the painting, or at least to borrow it on a permanent basis for exhibition, although he refused.[493] But just a few short months after the painting was completed, Hitler's National Socialist party would seize power, and as a direct result Dix's works, especially *The Trench*, would be prominently featured in their various exhibitions of "degenerate art." *The War* was exhibited only once before the end of the Weimar Republic, at the annual Berlin Art Academy exhibition (a venue where *The Trench* had also been shown in the early 1920s), after which Dix packed it up and put it into storage, in effect hiding it from the Nazis.[494] The painting was shown again only after

493 Letter from Ludwig Justi to Otto Dix, 26 April 1933, Deutsches Kunstarchiv, Germanisches Nationalmuseum, Nuremberg, Otto Dix archive (hereafter DKA) I, B 12e.

494 See Fritz Loeffler, *Otto Dix und der Krieg* (Leipzig: Reclam, 1986).

the Second World War, in 1946, in the General German Art Exhibition [*Allgemeine Deutsche Kunstausstellung*] in Dresden, where artwork from all zones of occupied Germany, East and West, was shown.[495] A decade later the triptych was lent to the city of Dresden's art collection where it was exhibited in various museums, always dramatically displayed, sometimes as the sole painting in a room of sculpture, sometimes hung between paintings by Dürer and Cranach. It was finally purchased by the GDR for the Galerie Neue Meister in Dresden in 1968.[496]

The War in the context of public memory work

The contest over the commemoration of the front experience in the Weimar era turned to a large extent, in the second half of the 1920s, on the degree to which the war experience was heroicized, or the extent to which such heroicization was actively resisted. In the flood of literary representation of the war the heroic perspective dominated, and was even present to some degree in Remarque's *All Quiet on the Western Front*. But the *Reichsbanner* worked to counter the heroic image of the front experience.[497] On the cover of its illustrated weekly paper, the *Illustrierte Reichsbanner-Zeitung*, the group often published artworks depicting the emphatically unheroic, contorted corpses of dead German soldiers lying abandoned in no-man's-land or caught in the barbed wire entanglements. Even if Dix was not himself one of the 90,000 subscribers to the *Reichsbanner's* illustrated paper, he would have seen the covers at newsstands. One of these covers was a painting by his old friend Otto Griebel, a fellow veteran, fellow classmate at the Arts and Crafts School in Dresden before the war, and fellow member of the Dresden Secession

495 Dietrich Schubert, *Otto Dix* (Reinbek: Rowohlt, 1980, revised edition, 2001), 122.

496 Birgit Dalbajewa, *Otto Dix in der Dresdener Galerie* (Dresden: Sandstein, 2007), 15 f.

497 Ziemann, *Contested Commemorations*, 268.

Group 1919 after the war. The painting reproduced on the front page of 31 July 1926 issue was leant by Karl Nierendorf's gallery, another reason Dix might have been aware of it.[498] The *Reichsbanner* continued to publish such works on the front page of its illustrated weekly throughout the second half of the 1920s. During the four years that Dix was working on *The War*, from 1928 to 1932, the discourse about the memory of the war and its meaning was ever more violently pulled between different poles, shaped and reshaped by the shifting force fields of political conflict. This discourse also took the form of competing parades and demonstrations held by different movements, including the Stahlhelm and other nationalist groups, and the *Reichsbanner*, at memorials and in the streets of numerous German cities.[499] My goal in this chapter will be to map the changing image of Dix's triptych onto this convulsed field, without reducing the artwork to the political discourse and collective memory work which informed it. The emphasis here will be once again less on Dix's private psychological experience and more on *The War* as part of a public process of memory work. My task will be to locate *The War* within a larger pattern of public meanings, and to map out the tensions and polarities which made up that pattern.

In what follows, I will investigate the iconography of the painting, alongside what little written criticism there was (because it was only exhibited once before the Nazi seizure of power, for a few weeks in the Exhibition of the Berlin Fine Arts Academy in 1932, the critical reception of this painting in the press was nothing comparable to that of the earlier *The Trench*).[500] I will investigate its many and complex art historical refer-

498 Otto Griebel, "Gedenkblatt" *Illustrierter Reichsbanner Zeitung* (31 July 1926), front page, reproduced in Nadine Rossol, "Commemoration of the Fallen (Germany)," *1914–1918-online. International Encyclopedia of the First World War.* <https://encyclopedia.1914-1918-online.net/article/commemoration_cult_of_the_fallen_germany> (updated 8 October 2014).

499 Nadine Rossol, *Performing the Nation in Interwar Germany. Sport, Spectacle, and Political Symbolism, 1926–1936* (London: Palgrave Macmillan, 2010).

500 James van Dyke lists several items in the Berlin daily press in "Dix Petrified," in Deborah Ascher Barnstone and Barbara McCloskey, eds., *The Art of War* (Oxford: Peter Lang, 2017), 103–127. See also the items from the specialized art press below.

ences as well as motifs which need to be compared with concepts circulating widely in the public sphere in Germany at the end of the Weimar period. These motifs, I will argue, suggest that the painting was in a dialog with politicized debates about the memory and the meaning of the war, a dialog which was much more detailed and specific than has been recognized.[501] The painting is much more about the way the war was remembered in the late 1920s than it is about the war itself. As with *The Trench* and the portfolio *The War*, I will discuss this painting – which I will argue was essentially intended as another public memorial and an intervention in the public discourse about the memory and the meaning of the war – in conjunction with other, similar monuments.

As with the portfolio *The War*, discussed in the previous chapter, the modern reception of the triptych by the same title has been partly shaped by the assumption that Otto Dix was a vehemently antiwar artist, and that his depictions of the front experience were above all condemnations of the war, its inhumanity and stupidity, and of its wasteful sacrifice of human life.[502] As in the previous chapter, I will seek here to establish a more complicated and ambivalent reading, related to the complex and evolving contemporary debate about the meaning and value of the war and its sacrifices for Dix's contemporaries, about the public memory of the war experience, and to discussions of the proper way to commemorate those experiences and sacrifices. It is clear that Dix was ambivalent about

501 The mainstream interpretation of the painting is best represented by Dietrich Schubert, "Otto Dix – das Triptychon 'Der Krieg' 1929–1932," in *Heidelberger Jahrbücher* 48 (2004), 311–331, and Jorg Martin Merz, "Otto Dix' Kriegsbilder. Motivationen – Intentionen – Rezeptionen," *Marburger Jahrbuch für Kunstwissenschaft* 26 (1999), 189–226. Most recently see Olaf Peters, "Eine Summe des Krieges. Otto Dix' Triptychon 'Der Krieg' (1929–1932)," in Dalbajewa Birgit, Simone Fleischer, and Olaf Peters, *Otto Dix. Der Krieg – Das Dresdner Triptychon* (Dresden: Sandstein, 2014), 139–159.

502 For example Dietrich Schubert, "Das Triptychon." Jay Winter in his book *Sites of Memory, Sites of Mourning* – a book which is otherwise very informative for the present study – reads Dix as an antiwar artist, pure and simple. *Sites of Memory, Sites of Mourning: The Great War in European Cultural History* (Cambridge: Cambridge University Press, 1995), 159–164.

the war, and about its meaning, and this has become widely – though not universally – accepted among art historians at least.[503] Other interpretations have used Dix's enthusiasm for Nietzsche to read this complex work as a celebration of life's amoral will to express itself through destruction.[504] But this has led to an exaggerated emphasis on the individual creativity, liberty, and spiritual integrity of the artist, and to the decontextualization of his work from the larger society of which he was, after all, a part. Both of these standard readings – of Dix the antiwar artist and Dix the Nietzsche disciple – make the painting too much a personal affair of the artist's private engagement with his own memories, his presumed opposition to public culture, and speculations about his personal psychological processes of trauma. By the late 1920s in Germany the veterans of the war had begun to carry out their conflicts over the war's meaning in public, and it is reasonable to suppose that Dix was responding to these conflicts.

The conflicts among Dix's fellow veterans, their contest over the meaning of the war and its memory, often happened around the many conventional monuments built across Germany, at the feet of which those veterans regularly laid their wreaths, made their speeches, and gave ritualized and ceremonial expression to their understanding of the war and its sacrifices.[505] Dix himself acknowledged that this large-scale triptych was intended as a kind of public monument, or perhaps as a riposte to the many public monuments which dotted the landscape of Weimar Germany. Dix even spoke half-jokingly of

503 Linda McGreevy, *Bitter Witness: Otto Dix and the Great War* (Bern: Peter Lang, 2003), and Olaf Peters, "Intransigent Realism. Otto Dix between the World Wars," in Olaf Peters, ed., *Otto Dix* (Munich: Prestel, 2010), 13–31.

504 Otto Conzelmann, *Der andere Dix – Sein Bild vom Menschen und vom Kriege* (Stuttgart: Hatje-Cantz, 1983), and Mathias Eberle, *World War I and the Weimar Artists. Dix, Grosz, Beckmann, Schlemmer* (New Haven, CT: Yale University Press, 1985).

505 Ludwig Linsmayer, *Politische Kultur im Saargebiet 1920–1932. Symbolische Politik, verhinderte Demokratisierung, nationalisiertes Kulturleben in einer abgetrennten Region* (St. Ingebert: Röhrig, 1992), 50–60; Michael Jeismann, Rolf Westheider, "'Wofür stirbt der Bürger?' Nationaler Totenkult und Staatsbürgertum in Deutschaland und Frankreich seit der Französischer Revolution," in Reinhart Koselleck, ed., *Der politische Totenkult. Kriegerdenkmäler der Moderne* (Munich: Fink, 1994), 23–49.

displaying it in a special bunker that viewers would have to go down into, like a dugout, which would have made of it part public memorial, part refusé pavilion in the tradition of painters denied a proper public venue (like Gustave Courbet), and part commercial waxworks spectacle.[506]

As with the graphic portfolio which Dix had made earlier in the decade, this painting didn't so much counter the tropes and the received images of the war as reproduce them, just with greater vehemence and harsher imagery than people were used to or comfortable with. At the same time, the painting represents something dramatically new, something which had not before been seen or contemplated in representations of the war, with the exception of his own earlier work, *The Trench*: a visual depiction in high art of grotesquely mutilated corpses, on the scale of a public memorial. This reality of the war, the destruction of the soldiers' bodies on a vast scale was represented in many forms and in many ways: in literary texts; in films; in monumental architecture covered with names of the legion missing dead and even the display of piles of their bare and unidentified bones in the case of the ossuary at Douamont, in Picardy, France. But commissioned monuments which gave visual representation to the memory of mass death in high art, typically in bronze or stone, always hid the physical appearance of bodies torn apart by industrial warfare. For those who made public memorials there was a taboo against representing mutilation. Although Dix was once again working without a commission, and in painting rather than sculpture, this new work was once again conceived as a kind of response to the visual language of public memorials, and in that sense he once again broke this taboo. Why did he do so?

In the 1960s, after the atrocities and genocide perpetrated by the German nation in a second world war, Dix claimed that he had painted this triptych because he wanted to tell the truth about what the war had been like in the face of renewed war-mongering.

506 He told his friend the art historian Fritz Löffler that he thought to exhibit *The War* "als Pro-Memoria des Krieges und als Warnung für künftige Geschlechter in einem Betonbunker an einem öffentlichen Platz aufzustellen." Fritz Löffler, "Otto Dix," *Zeitschrift fur Kunst* 3 (1949), 173–93, here 176, cited in Jorg Merz, "Otto Dix' Kriegsbilder," 199.

> The picture was created ten years after the First World War. During these years I had made many studies, in order to develop the war experience artistically. In 1928 I felt ready to take on this huge theme. … At that time, incidentally, many books were once again propagating without restraint in the Weimar Republic a heroism and a heroic ideal, which had long since been made absurd in the trenches of the First World War. People were already beginning to forget what terrible suffering the war had brought them. Out of this situation was created the triptych. I simply wanted to show – almost in the fashion of a reportage – my experiences of the years 1914–1918 concisely and objectively.[507]

While undoubtedly sincere this answer is another repetition of a trope of war representation. Nearly everybody who represented the war, in any medium, claimed to be telling the "truth" about it, presumably in the face of others' "untruthful" – or at least insufficiently truthful representations.[508] And the triptych *The War* contains much else besides mutilated bodies; the "truth" represented in this painting also contains much that was common in all kinds of representations of the war experience, in Germany and also in France and England: not only the vast destruction of town and landscape, not only the privations, filth and exhaustion of life in the trenches, but also

507 Das Bild entstand zehn Jahre nach dem 1. Weltkrieg. Ich hatte während dieser Jahre viele Studien gemacht, um das Kriegserlebnis künstlerisch zu verarbeiten. 1928 fühlte ich mich reif, das große Thema anzupacken … In dieser Zeit übrigens propagierten viele Bücher ungehindert in der Weimarer Republik erneut ein Heldentum und einen Heldenbegriff, die in den Schützengraben des 1. Weltkrieges längst ad absurdum geführt worden waren. Die Menschen begannen schon zu vergessen, was für entsetzliches Leid der Krieg ihnen gebracht hatte. Aus dieser Situation heraus entstand das Triptychon. Ich wollte ganz einfach – fast reportagemäßig – meine Erlebnisse der Jahre 1914–1918 zusammenfassend sachlich schildern …" Interview in *Neues Deutschland*, East Berlin, December 1964. Cited in Diether Schmidt, *Otto Dix im Selbstbildnis* (East Berlin: Henschel, 1981), and in Jorg Merz, "Otto Dix' Kriegsbilder. 189–226.

508 The most salient example of this logic is Norton Cru, *Temoins. Essai d'analyse et de critique des souvenirs de combattants édités en français de 1915 à 1928* (Paris: Gallimard, 1930; 3rd edn. Nancy: Presses Universitaires de Nancy, 2006). Jay Winter, *Remembering War. The Great War Between Memory and History in the Twentieth Century* (New Haven, CT and London: Yale University Press, 2006), 242–251; Jay Winter, *Sites of Memory, Sites of Mourning: The Great War in European Cultural History* (Cambridge: Cambridge University Press, 1995), 183–186.

camaraderie; duty and sacrifice; and not least of all the grievously tested but unbroken fighting spirit of the soldiers. Some of these "truths" were objective facts, substantiated in modern times by historians working with documentary evidence. Others were clearly distortion and compensation, nostalgia, amplification, and wishful thinking. But in 1928 these truths were all first and last collective memories, produced by discourse, subjective in nature, and shaped by the pressures of public political conflict and by private grief and psychological needs of varying kinds.[509] These "truths" were repeated endlessly in the public sphere: the misery and horror of trench life; the camaraderie of the soldiers; their unbroken determination regardless of the futility of the cause. But the double bind for each eyewitness was the condition that it was only by reproducing the common tropes and clichés that their own uniquely truthful narratives or memories could be made legible – perhaps even to themselves. This is the dynamic at work in Otto Dix's monumental triptych *The War*. Perhaps the most important and oft-repeated "truth," of central importance to this triptych was the apotheosis of the dead, their quasi-religious, even salvific role in post-war European memory, and their continued public life after death. The master narrative of this myth is of course the Christian narrative of salvation, and this relationship is clearly acknowledged by the altar-like triptych format of Dix's painting.[510]

Many of the images in the triptych *The War* were by this time conventional. They were familiar from the many novels and films and war memorials produced in Weimar Germany. And those public works were in turn commented on in published criticism of novels and memorials, and essays published in the newspapers and journals of various veterans' groups. What was the relationship between this sprawling cultural production, this public

509 Winter, *Remembering War*, 135–153; Joanna Bourke, "Introduction: 'Remembering' War," *Journal of Contemporary History* 39/4 (October 2004), 473–485; Sean A. Forner, "War Commemoration and the Republic in Crisis: Weimar Germany and the Neue Wache," *Central European History* 35/4 (2002), 513–549.

510 Klaus Lankheit, *Das Triptychon als Pathosformel* (Heidelberg: Winter, 1959), 68, cited in Olaf Peters, *Neue Sachlichkeit und Nationalsozialismus. Affirmation und Kritik 1931–1947* (Berlin: Reimer, 1998), 210.

memory work, and the individual artwork made by a well-known, even notorious painter and veteran? What would his painting have meant to a broad audience that included not only arts cognoscenti but also average, middle-class museum-goers, including veterans? As we saw in the previous chapter, by 1924 and the founding of the *Reichsbanner Schwartz-Rot-Gold*, the discussion of the war and the meaning of its memory centered around questions of nostalgia for the front experience, and resentment, whether of the enemy, the officer and political class, or the outcome of the war. These debates became much more fluid and dynamic during the late years of the Weimar Republic, the years during which Dix worked on the triptych, especially after the publication of a flood of memoiristic war novels that began with Remarque's *All Quiet on the Western Front* in 1928.[511] We will see that, partly as a result of this fluidity, the direction of Dix's project and his imagery changed under his brush. The fund of images being reproduced in the wider culture pulled the meaning of the triptych this way and that, rendering it conflicted, incoherent.

Preliminary analysis of *The War*

The triptych *The War* is structured in a complicated pattern, arranged around a loose narrative of a battle, although the battle itself is not directly depicted. Instead, the narrative appears to move episodically through a full day, beginning on the left with the march towards the front in the

511 See Thomas F. Schneider's study of the reception of *All Quiet on the Western Front*, which tracks the novel's dramatically volatile critical reception month to month from 1928 to 1931, "Die Meute hinter Remarque. Zur Diskussion um *Im Westen nichts Neues* 1928–1930," *Jahrbuch zur Literatur der Weimarer Republik*, 1 (1995), 143–170; Schneider, "'Sie werden auferstehen!' Otto Dix' Triptychon 'Der Krieg' im Kontext zeitgenössischer visueller und literarischer Repräsentationen des Ersten Weltkrieges," in Birgit Dalbajewa, Simone Fleischer, and Olaf Peters, eds., *Otto Dix. Der Krieg – Das Dresdner Triptychon* (Dresden: Sandstein, 2014), 125–135.

fog-bound early morning hours. The panel on the right wing depicts a scene behind the lines, with the flames of battle in the distance. Wounded soldiers flee this inferno as best they can; some crawl, others are carried by their comrades, and some lie dead on the ground. Between these two, in the square-format panel of the center, is the aftermath. Nothing moves, no column of smoke rises from the ruined village in the distance, which one would expect to see as the time-honored sign in history painting that a battle has just been concluded. The silent stillness after the battle was the moment which preoccupied Dix in all three of his monumental war paintings, *The Trench* and the later *Flanders* as well as *The War*, and this center panel reworks the same scene as that depicted in *The Trench*. The immobility of everything – including the figure in a gasmask, wearing the German steel helmet, who may even still be alive, provides the viewer with the pause needed to make sense of the composition, and to savor every grisly detail of the wrack, ruin, and gore spread out beneath the gaze. Below this central panel is a predella, a compositional element often seen in large-scale multi-panel altarpieces depicting Christ's Passion, such as Matthias Grünewald's *Isenheim Altarpiece* (1512–1516). In such works the body of Christ in the tomb was represented in this low horizontal panel. In *The War*, three soldiers are stretched out in place of the body of Christ – whether in death or in sleep is not immediately clear. The predella is of a different visual order from the three panels above it. Through perspective and tromp-l'oeil techniques, it seems more directly connected to the viewer's own space. The tarp stretched out over the bodies of the men in the cramped space appears to have one corner tacked to the bottom edge of the panel above. The lower panel presents itself as a rough wooden box set beneath the frame-and-canvas artwork above it, not unlike a rude coffin, with the front face removed, affording the viewer a glimpse within. But this is a dugout, not a burial chamber; the figures are in fact sleeping, and the cloth is not a pall or a shroud but is actually there to keep soil shaken loose by the bombardments above from sifting between the boards onto the sleeping men below. Yet it seems hidden like a reliquary chamber in the foundation of the allegorical image cycle erected upon it, containing in its crypt-like interior the ultimate meaning of that cycle in the form of the bodily remains of its martyrs.

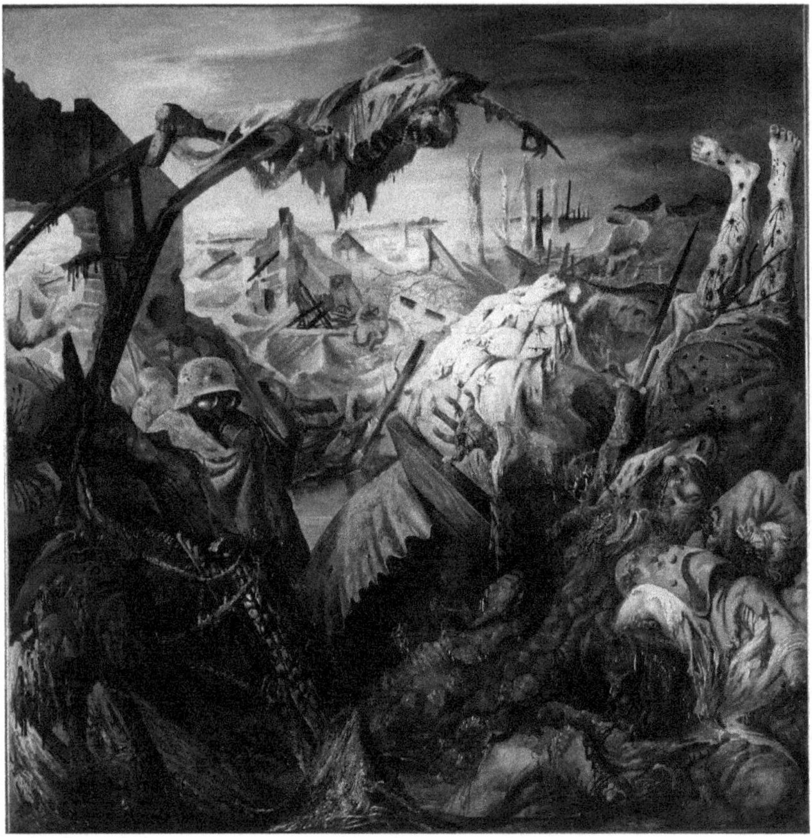

Figure 63. Otto Dix, *The War*, central panel, oil and tempera on wood panel, 1928–1932, Staatliche Kunstsammlungen, Dresden, Galerie Neue Meister. © Otto Dix / Artists Rights Society (ARS), New York / VG Bild-Kunst, Bonn. Photo Art Resource, NY / Erich Lessing, used with permission.

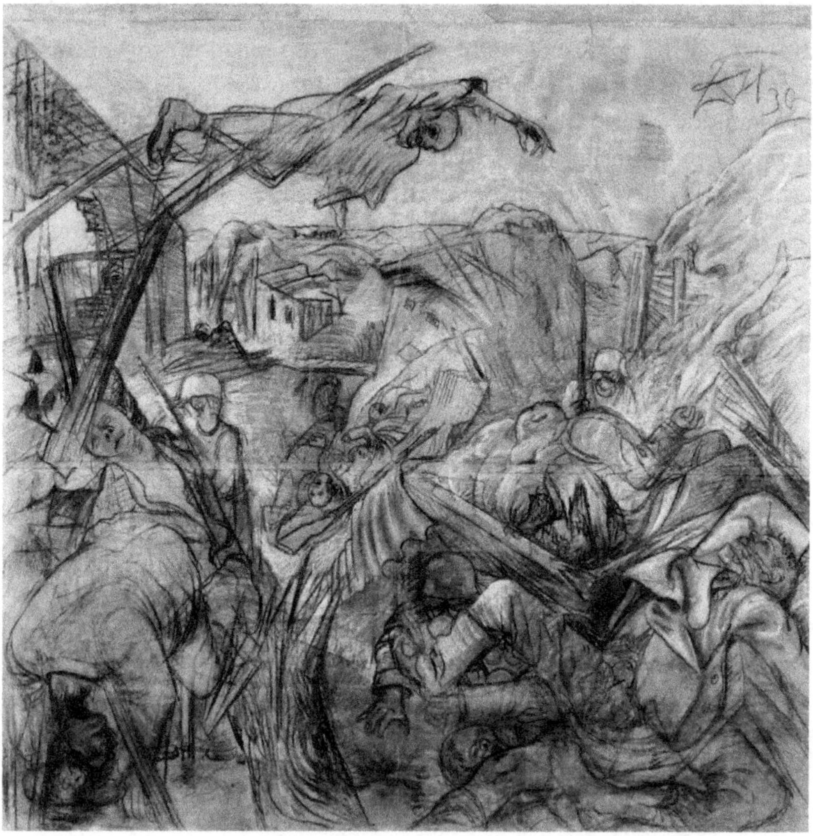

Figure 64. Otto Dix, cartoon of *The War*, central panel, charcoal, white and colored chalks, gouache, pencil on gray cardboard, laid down on canvas and stretcher, 1929–1930, Hamburger Kunsthalle, Hamburg. © Otto Dix / Artists Rights Society (ARS), New York / VG Bild-Kunst, Bonn. Digital file: author's own scan.

All of these panels are not only overwhelming in their wealth of anecdote and pictorial incident, but are also thick with a combination of art historical references, most of which have already been discussed in the literature on this complex work.[512] But they are also built around references to themes that were circulating in the vernacular culture of Weimar Germany, themes having to do directly with issues of the memorialization of the war and a construction of meaning for the war experience. As I have argued in previous chapters, Dix could simultaneously speak to an audience of sophisticated and knowledgeable viewers of painting and at the same time to a broader audience of veterans. But whereas in the chapter on *The Trench*, that audience of veterans could have been relied upon to respond to the "truthfulness" of a humorously grotesque realism, in *The War* those veterans were being addressed through a vocabulary of motifs and images which had emerged in the discourse about the meaning of the war, a discourse which took on a new and distinctive shape after 1925.

The central panel (see Figures 63 and 64) is at first glance a chaos of mud, gore, violated bodies and ruined houses, with charred tree stumps and wreckage littering the battlefield in the foreground, matched by the craters and ruined houses of the background. The seemingly shapeless, oozing chaos is in fact divided like a baroque landscape painting into clearly staged areas of fore, middle and background, each progressively cooler in hue and lighter in value. The darkest tonalities are given to the sagging formless shapes closest to the foreground, along the bottom edge of the

512 Some of the art historical references are plausible, for example Dieter Scholz's identification of the wagon wheel, a late addition to the iconography of the painting, with the symbol of the martyrdom of St. Catherine (and thus to the "martyrdom" of the soldiers), specifically as represented in Lucas Cranach's *Altar of St. Catherine* in Dresden (1506), Dieter Scholz, "Das Triptychon der Krieg," in Wulf Herzogenrath and Johann-Karl Schmidt, eds., *Otto Dix – zum 100. Geburtstag* (Stuttgart: Hatje-Cantz, 1991), 261–267. Others seem less plausible, for example Olaf Peters identifies the shape of the blade of Death's sickle, suggested by the hovering dead soldier and the bent iron beams holding him aloft, and relates it to Nicholas Poussin's *Et in arcadia ego*, which Erwin Panofsky once argued might also contain a more or less hidden image of Death's sickle. Peters, *Neue Sachlichkeit und Nationalsozialismus*, 206 ff.

panel, anchored by the charred stump in the center. The lightest tones are used for the cratered moonscape which makes up the distant background. The piled-up rubble, wreckage, spilled sandbags and bodily remains are arranged into a neatly circular composition. The ruins of a house rise up on the left, in a motion continued by the dramatic, spectral figure of a badly decomposed corpse, held aloft like an angel of death which gestures back down to the realm of corpses on the right. These in turn pull the composition further downwards to a dense substratum of livid decomposing flesh, torn uniforms and a murky, inchoate mass of mud, glistening innards, thick blood, and slimy pools of water painted in sticky, viscous earth tones.

The Trench had already featured the body of a dead soldier grotesquely skewered on the bent steel beams that had once reinforced a dugout. This figure in its ridiculous pose had made up part of the grotesque humor which I argued in a previous chapter was part of that painting's address to fellow veterans, and which had offended the sensibilities of older, non-veteran commentators. Now, in *The War*, that figure is allegorical rather than grotesque, thus partaking of a more dignified pictorial language. What the figure points to is another body, this one inverted, its exposed legs and feet covered over in bullet wounds. The blood dripping from these wounds coagulated and dried while running downwards. This figure is a parody of the tormented figure of Christ on the Cross from Grünewald's *Isenheim Altarpiece* in Colmar. Every army had its persistent legend of a fellow soldier crucified in no-man's-land by the enemy, thus exposing what was supposed to be the enemy's blasphemous sadism. But here the figure seems to have been thrown up by the bursting artillery shells, which is to say by the war itself. Therefore the closest parallel to this crucified soldier can be found in Ernst Jünger's *Storm of Steel*, in the chapter "Guillemont," one of the most riveting chapters in Jünger's vivid description of the war. Lost in the battlefield, trying to find their position, Lieutenant Jünger's platoon finally finds, "a strangely constellated group of corpses serving as a landmark. One of the dead lay there as if crucified on the chalk slope. It was impossible to imagine a more appropriate landmark."[513]

513 Ernst Jünger, *Storm of Steel* (New York: Penguin Books, 2004, Michael Hoffmann, translator), 96.

The figure of Death is also of course a parody of John the Baptist, who points in Grünewald's Crucifixion to the hideously suffering body of Christ.[514] Grünewald, about whom little was really known at the time, was considered by Germans to be a quintessentially German artist, and the *Isenheim Altarpiece* was recognized as his masterpiece. It was located in Colmar, in Alsace, which had been German territory from the Franco-Prussian War of 1870 to the end of the world war; it had been removed by German authorities from that city, taken to Munich for safekeeping and restoration. In Munich it was exhibited to great fanfare and large crowds, including wounded veterans. After the war, when Alsace was returned to France under the terms of the hated Treaty of Versailles, the painting was repatriated to France and restored to the city of Colmar, now once again a French city.[515] In an ironic twist of fate, Otto Dix would be held by the French as a POW in Colmar at the end of the Second World War, where he would be allowed to see it.[516] For Germans between the wars the *Isenheim Altarpiece* was a significant piece of their own artistic patrimony and represented what was especially German about German art, but it also embodied the humiliation of the loss of Alsace to France, and became a cult object for German nationalism and revanchist sentiment.[517] Dix greatly admired Grünewald, but the quotation of this specific painting in this period could hardly avoid conjuring up tensions with and resentments against France; a reference to it inserted into a painting about the war itself necessarily recalled rivalries between French and German culture. And as we saw in Chapter 2, in

514 Sylvie Lecoq-Ramond, "Un Maitre ancien du XXe siècle: Otto Dix et l'art de Grünewald," in Sylvie Lecoq-Ramond, Rainer Beck, *et al., Otto Dix et les maîtres anciens* (Colmar: Musée d'Unterlinden, 1996), 66–94, here 83.

515 Ann Stieglitz, "The Reproduction of Agony: Toward a Reception-History of Grünewald's Isenheim Altar after the First World War," *Oxford Art Journal* 12 (1989), 87–103; Aude Briau, "Otto Dix face à la 'plus grande icône de l'art allemand', 1900–1924," in Frédérique Goerig-Hergott, ed., *Otto Dix – le Retable d'Isenheim* (Paris: Hazan, 2016), 29–41.

516 Frédérique Goerig-Hergott, ed., *Otto Dix. Le Retable d'Issenheim* (Paris: Editions Hazan, 2016).

517 Keith Moxey, "Impossible Distance: Past and Present in the Study of Dürer and Grünewald," in Larry Silver and Jeffrey Chipps Smith, eds., *The Essential Dürer* (Philadelphia: University of Pennsylvania Press, 2010), 206–226, here 211.

the discussion of the *Memory of the Hall of Mirrors in Brussels* (see Figure 40), Dix often made the marketing of French art (specifically Cubism) in Germany a target of his satiric wit. In his portrait of Alfred Flechtheim done in 1926, Dix included his own pastiche of a Cubist painting on the wall behind the Berlin art dealer, and in an act of artistic one-upmanship he signed his own name on this painting-within-the-painting! Now, in the late 1920s, a reference to Grünewald's most famous work, one which it was widely felt the French unfairly possessed, would have represented the counterweight to the incursions of the French avant-garde into the German art market.

In the panel on the left (see Figures 65 and 66), German soldiers march through the early morning mist, presumably in the direction of the front. Emerging from the dense fog is another column of visibly weary soldiers, returning from the trenches. The last two figures in the outward bound column turn their backs to us, so that we can only see their heavy packs, the equipment and weapons of the front soldier; their rifles are hoisted on their shoulders. The figure on the left turns his head slightly, so that we see the distinctive outline of his steel helmet – the iconic steel helmet or *Stahlhelm*, which replaced the old-fashioned spiked helmet beginning with Verdun. The figure to his right seems to carry an extra pair of boots in his pack, and the hobnailed sole of one is visible. Ahead, one soldier hoists a heavy machine-gun on his shoulder, the very weapon that Dix had carried. Ahead of these soldiers the entire column is reduced to long rows of steel helmets, each glinting dully in the dim light, matching the color of the banks of fog. To the left the column of weary returning soldiers is reduced to rows of glinting helmets and a picket of shouldered rifles barely emerging from the fog, stretching endlessly into the landscape. It is an effective image of the modern mass army of anonymous foot soldiers, and of the weariness of the regular rotation: up to the front lines and the endless artillery fire, then back to the rear lines for the survivors to rest, before going up to the front again. Dieter Scholz among others has read this panel as a critical representation of the endless and futile round of fighting and exhaustion, its cyclical nature symbolized allegorically by the wagon wheel in the foreground.[518]

518 Scholz, "Das Triptychon der Krieg."

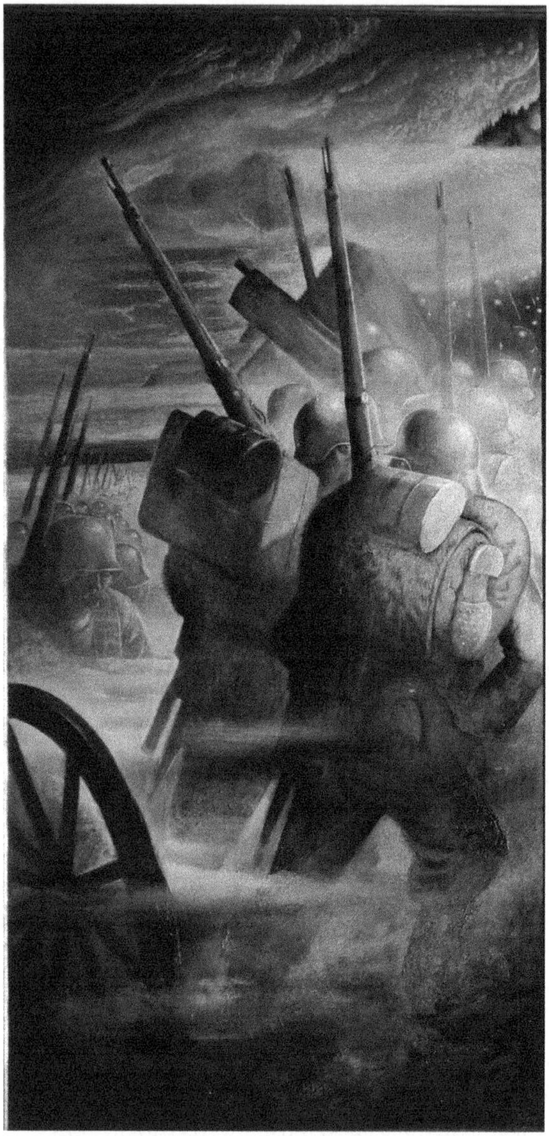

Figure 65. Otto Dix, *The War*, left panel, oil and tempera on wood panel, 1928–1932, Staatliche Kunstsammlungen, Dresden, Galerie Neue Meister. © Otto Dix / Artists Rights Society (ARS), New York / VG Bild-Kunst, Bonn. Photo Art Resource, NY / Erich Lessing, used with permission.

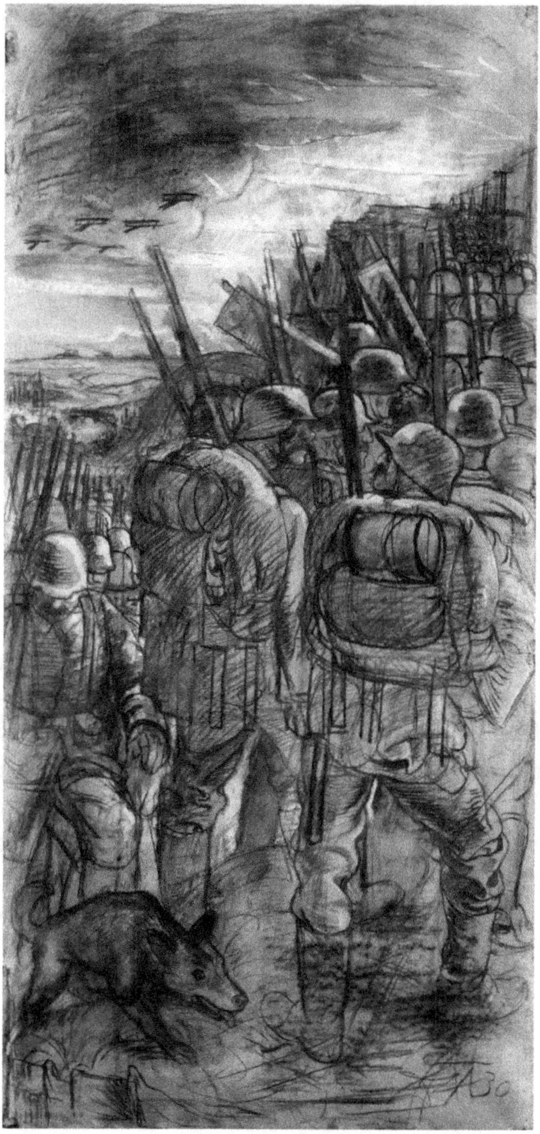

Figure 66. Otto Dix, cartoon of *The War*, left panel, charcoal, white and colored chalks, gouache, pencil on gray cardboard, laid down on canvas and stretcher, 1929–1930, Hamburger Kunsthalle, Hamburg. © Otto Dix / Artists Rights Society (ARS), New York / VG Bild-Kunst, Bonn. Digital file: author's own scan.

The twin columns of soldiers depict a tight formation, even in their exhaustion. When the French sociologist Marcel Mauss developed his idea of "bodily technique," published the same year this painting was finished in a paper titled "Les techniques du corps," he drew his primary examples from the world war, especially the distinctive rhythm that the soldiers of different nationalities had for marching. It was possible, he claimed, to know from a distance which country a passing column was from, without even seeing their uniforms.[519] Dix's image of marching soldiers depicts a bodily practice, one specific to a generation, uniting them in their lived experience. The motif of the marching column of soldiers, going either to the front or returning, is one that also appears more than once in Dix's etching portfolio, *The War*. Curiously, the motif strongly recalls two paintings by nineteenth-century realists, both also triptychs, and both in Brussels.[520] *The Chalk Handler* [Les Marchands de craie] (1882), by Leon Frederic (Brussels, Musée de l'Art Moderne), depicts an itinerant merchant and his threadbare family, as they trudge barefoot first from one village along a muddy road, in the left panel, and then towards the next in the right panel. In the center they share a meager meal in open country, aesthetic and programmatic heirs to Courbet's *Stonebreakers*. An even closer match is *Triptych of the Mine* [Triptyque de la mine] by Constantin Meunier (1902, Brussels, Musée Constantin Meunier). Here is depicted in one panel, the left, both a row of workers coming from the mine, towards the viewer, and the next shift marching away towards the pit in the distance. In the center panel is the blasted and smoking landscape of the coal fields, with a row of weary miners returning home at the end of their day. The right-hand panel shows the scene down in the mine itself, emphasizing the hunched but heroic, half naked bodies of the miners in their daily purgatory. The two triptychs anticipate Dix's own so closely that one wonders if, as a soldier Dix didn't after all visit someplace other than the brothels while taking his R&R in Brussels. In any case, the similarity signals a connection between the wearying work of war depicted by Dix and the larger, Realist tradition of representing a weary

519 Marcel Mauss, "Les techniques du corps," *Journal de Psychologie* 32/3–4 (15 March-15 April 1936), n. p.

520 Both are reproduced in Monika Potztal, *Ludwig Dettmann: Zwischen Avantgarde und Anpassung* (Heide: Boyens, 2008), 49 and 56.

but also noble and proud working class. In a larger sense, the similarity suggests the socialist idea that, for the working class, war was so to speak labor by other means, done by long-suffering yet proud men, and dignified and sacralized not by patriotism, but by their sense of solidarity and duty to class.

Certainly the cycle of a tour at the front and relief and rest in the back structured the lives of soldiers for years, judging by the novels of the war. Henri Barbusse represented it in his novel *Under Fire*, which was a best-seller in translation in Germany and which Dix had read.

> This stay in the trenches has been frightful. The 18th Company was in the vanguard: eighteen killed and some fifty wounded – at least one man out of three in four days. And that was without any attack, just from shelling.
> We know this and as the battalion comes towards us and our paths cross, trampling the mud of the field, we recognize familiar faces [...].

Here the motif of two columns of soldiers marching past each other closely matches the left panel of Dix's triptych; one column is going up, the other coming back. As the passage in Barbusse's novel continues, it begins to suggest something other than the misery of the front. It represents an unexpected side of the war, a camaraderie and, beyond that, an ebullience which at first seems implausible until the narrator explains it:

> Arising from among these soldiers returning from the frightfulness of the lower depths, is a deafening din. They are all speaking at once, very loudly, waving their hands, laughing and singing. [...]
> These men are happy, despite everything, as they emerge from hell – for the very reason that they are emerging. They are coming back, they are saved. Once again death was there, but spared them. ... Today, each of these men is sure that he will live a little while longer.[521]

Each will live, as Barbusse explains, for at least six more weeks, the duration of the rest period in the rear. And six more weeks of life is reason enough for these tired soldiers to delight in each other. Although this side of the war appears at first glance to have little in common with the grim scene depicted in the left panel, the regular rotation might have suggested to Dix's fellow veterans at least another kind of experience.

521 Henri Barbusse, *Under Fire*, 44–47.

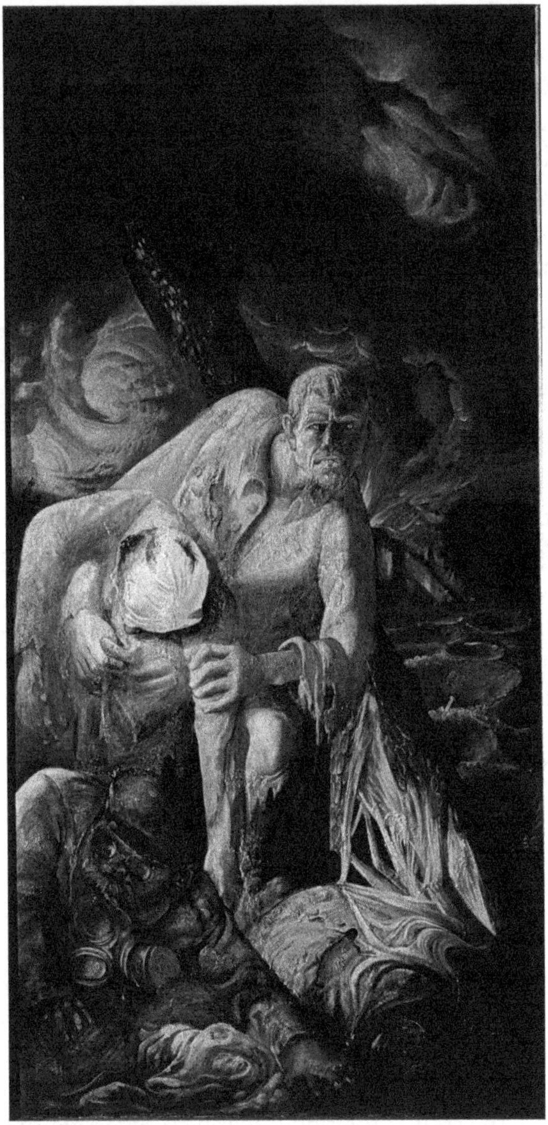

Figure 67. Otto Dix, *The War*, right panel, oil and tempera on wood panel, 1928–1932, Staatliche Kunstsammlungen, Dresden, Galerie Neue Meister. © Otto Dix / Artists Rights Society (ARS), New York / VG Bild-Kunst, Bonn. Photo Art Resource, NY / Erich Lessing, used with permission.

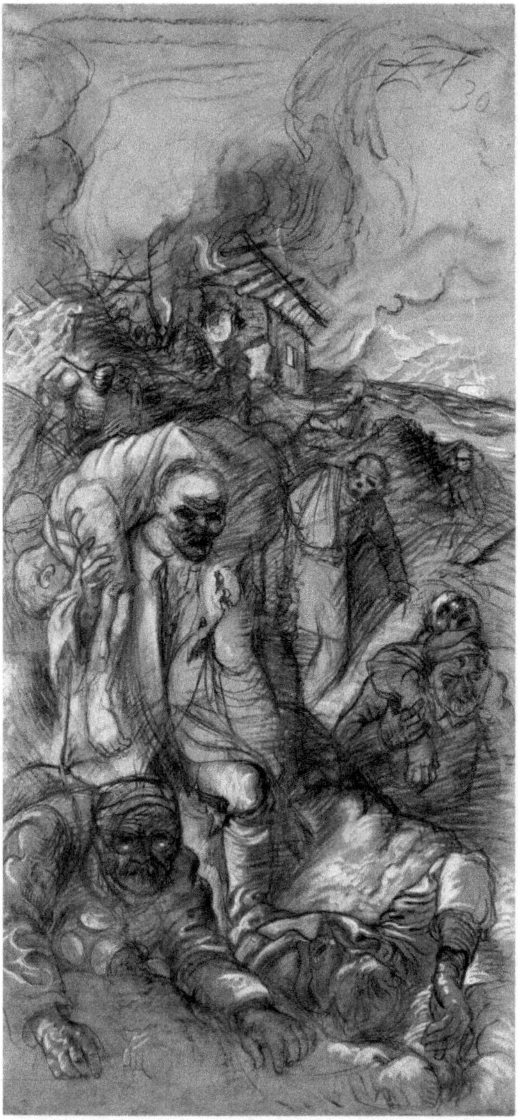

Figure 68. Otto Dix, cartoon of right panel, earlier version, charcoal, white and colored chalks, gouache, pencil on gray cardboard, laid down on canvas and stretcher, 1929–1930, Hamburger Kunsthalle, Hamburg. © Otto Dix / Artists Rights Society (ARS), New York / VG Bild-Kunst, Bonn. Digital file: author's own scan.

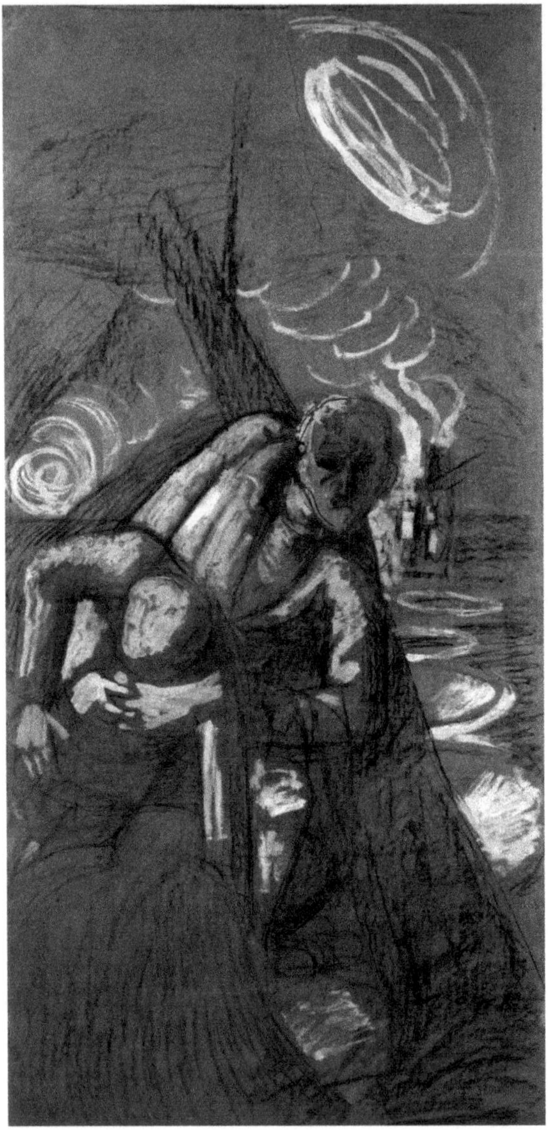

Figure 69. Otto Dix, cartoon of right panel, later version, charcoal, white and colored chalks, gouache, pencil on gray cardboard, laid down on canvas and stretcher, 1929–1930, Hamburger Kunsthalle, Hamburg. © Otto Dix / Artists Rights Society (ARS), New York / VG Bild-Kunst, Bonn. Digital file: author's own scan.

The image of the marching soldiers on the left is answered, in the right-hand panel, by a soldier carrying a wounded comrade from the dangers of the battlefield – represented by the inferno in the background, the violence of battle rendered as a storm, a natural, even meteorological phenomenon (see Figures 67, 68, and 69). The figure group, pale, even grisaille against the fiery backdrop, are rendered almost as a monumental sculptural group themselves, in the manner of the depictions of saints in the outer wings of Jan van Eyck's fifteenth-century *Ghent Altarpiece*.[522] While several early Netherlandish altarpieces feature grisaille figures of saints on their outer wings, van Eyck's was by the 1920s the most famous example, and the wings specifically had been prominently displayed in Berlin until 1920. Similarly to the *Isenheim Altarpiece*, the *Ghent Altarpiece* had become a reminder of the supposed victimization of Germany by the terms of the Treaty of Versailles.[523] That treaty had commanded that the six outer panels of this multi-panel Flemish work – including those with the grisaille depictions of saints – which had been legally purchased by the King of Prussia in 1821 and given by him to the Berlin *Gemäldegalerie*, be brought to Belgium after a century in a Berlin museum, a penalty duly carried out in 1920.[524] The *Ghent Altarpiece* was thus another emblem of German defeat and humiliation – the more so because a plan had been publicly discussed in Germany to bring the remaining central panels from St. Bavo Cathedral

522 James van Dyke discusses this "grisaille" effect at length, relating it to the debates about trauma and war neuroses. Van Dyke, "Dix Petrified."

523 "Germany undertakes to deliver to Belgium, through the Reparation Commission, within six months of the coming into force of the present Treaty, in order to enable Belgium to reconstitute two great artistic works: (1) The leaves of the triptych of the Mystic Lamb painted by the Van Eyck brothers, formerly in the Church of St. Bavo at Ghent, now in the Berlin Museum." Versailles Treaty, Article 247. The other "great artistic work" referred to the wings of the *Last Supper* triptych by Dieric Bouts, in Munich.

524 Till-Holger Borchert, "Collecting Early Netherlandish Paintings," in Bernhard Ridderbos, Anne van Buren, and Henk van Veen, *Early Netherlandish Paintings. Rediscovery, Reception, and Research* (Los Angeles, CA: J. Paul Getty Museum, 2005), 173–216, here 42 and 185 f; Bernhard Ridderbos, "Objects and Questions," in *Early Netherlandish Paintings*, 4–172, here p. 42.

in Ghent to Berlin if and when Germany won the war, reuniting the work in Germany, not Belgium.[525] In English-language art history (not least of all Erwin Panofsky's) fifteenth-century Flemish painting has always been considered a distinctive tradition, somewhat apart from the rest of European art history. But German art historians considered it very much a German affair.[526] Like Grünewald, van Eyck was considered by Germans to be a German artist, an exemplar of a brand of realism, including its typical grisaille representations of saint statues, that was specifically theirs, a claim which had just recently been reiterated by the influential art historian Max Friedländer, in 1924.[527] Having been in Berlin for a century, the van Eyck panels were now back in Belgium – the site of Dix's rapacious dealings with Belgian prostitutes in his self-portrait *Me in Brussels* from 1922 (see Figure 34). As with the overt reference to Grünewald's altarpiece, this specific art historical reference may function as a marker of revanchism and resentment – not necessarily Dix's own, but within the wider discourse of memorialization and interpretation of the war and its sacrifices.

The pale figure group dominating the right panel is a dramatic motif, and Dix has given his own features to the soldier who heroically carries his wounded comrade away from danger. One soldier carrying another, wounded one is an iconic image of *Kameradschaft*, which emerged in

525 Johannes Rößler, "Zwischen den Fronten. Der Genter Altar im Ersten Weltkrieg und im Friedensvertrag von Versailles," in Stephan Kemperdick and Johannes Rößler, eds., *Der Genter Altar der Brüder van Eyck, Geschichte und Würdigung* (Petersberg: Michael Imhof, 2014), 101–111. Only six of the eight outer panels were purchased in 1820; the panels with Adam and Eve remained in St. Bavo Cathedral. The six panels in Berlin, which were painted on both sides, were split in 1894 so that both sides could be displayed on the wall simultaneously. All 12 resulting panels were returned to Belgium after 1919, to great fanfare.

526 Wessel Krul, "Realism, Renaissance and Nationalism," in Bernhard Ridderbos *et al., Early Netherlandish Paintings*, 252–289, here p. 256.

527 The first volume of Max Friedländer's *Altniederländische Malerei*, which handled the van Eycks and Petrus Christus specifically, appeared in 1924. Friedländer was at the time the head of the Kupferstichkabinett of the Berlin museum. Bernhard Ridderbos, "From Waagen to Friedländer," in Bernhard Ridderbos *et al., Early Netherlandish Paintings*, 218–251.

the 1920s as a complex concept, the gravitas of which is not conveyed by the English cognate "camaraderie." As Thomas Kühne has shown, *Kameradschaft* evolved over the course of the interwar period into a virtue which redeemed the war experience, which rendered the war's sacrifices worthwhile and meaningful, and not only for those on the political Right. The term *Kameradschaft* signified the willingness of the German soldier to sacrifice – a drink of water, a cigarette, his own life – for another soldier.[528] It was, in Kühne's analysis, elevated to a panacea for the pervasive sense of crisis in the Weimar Republic and at the very center of a struggle over the memory of the war and its meaning.[529] Indeed, it was an antidote to the fear that the war and its millions of deaths might actually have been meaningless. This virtue was nothing less than the transfiguration of the pointless mass death of the war into a sacred trust. The concept of the virtue of *Kameradschaft* circulated not only as an image in the visual language of public memorials, but in the pages of newspapers of conservative, centrist, and liberal editorial leaning, in the journals of veterans' organizations, and in the flood of novels published at the end of the decade which depicted the experiences of the (educated and literate) German soldier.[530] According to at least one popular book of moral instruction, supposedly based on the first-person accounts of hundreds of veterans, the *Kameradschaft* of the front soldier ought to be the central lesson drawn from the war, and form the moral compass of future generations.[531] This quality and virtue was by no means limited to the discourse of conservative and nationalist veterans' groups like the *Stahlhelm*, although what, precisely, it represented differed significantly between the nationalist Right and the liberal Left.

528 Thomas Kühne, *Kameradschaft. Die Soldaten des nationalsozialistischen Krieges 20. Jahrhundert* (Göttingen: Vandenhoeck and Ruprecht, 2006); Thomas Kühne, *The Rise and Fall of Comradeship. Hitler's Soldiers, Male Bonding and Mass Violence in the Twentieth Century* (Cambridge: Cambridge University Press, 2017), 45–70.

529 Kühne, *Kameradschaft*, 38.

530 On the explosion of literary representations in Germany, Michael Gollbach, *Die Wiederkehr des Weltkrieges in der Literatur. Zu den Frontromanen der späten Zwanziger Jahre* (Kronberg: Scriptor, 1978).

531 J. Schneider, *Lebensweisheit für Deutsche, besonders Reichswehr und Polizei* (Berlin: Offenen Worte, 1926), cited in Kühne, *Kameradschaft*, 50.

If art historians writing on *The War* – and on Dix's images of the war in general – have missed what he could have valued in the front experience, and have thus mistaken his pictures for straightforwardly antimilitarist condemnations of the war, it is because they have overlooked the central importance of *Kameradschaft* in Germany in the 1920s. Dix's preoccupation with *Kameradschaft*, far from isolating him, actually put him in the mainstream of the wider public discourse of the late 1920s. The figure in the right panel, a soldier risking his own life to drag a comrade to safety, is a direct expression of this virtue, painted at a moment when the discourse of *Kameradschaft* came to a head in Germany.

Perhaps the most poignant representation of *Kameradschaft* was towards the end of the Hollywood film of *All Quiet on the Western Front*, when the protagonist Paul carries his wounded comrade, Kat over his shoulders like a sack all the way to a field hospital. In the original novel, Erich Maria Remarque incorporates into this scene all of the sub-themes of *Kameradschaft*: the recitation of the adventures had together, many of them humorous and turning on the simple pleasures of the body; the older soldier's almost maternal care for the younger; the mutual nature of sacrifice; the shared danger and privation; the sharing of a drink and a smoke. In keeping with the novel's stylistic rhetoric of objectivity, the first-person narrator does not dwell on his own sacrifice; it is communicated to the reader rather by outward physical signs of Paul's extreme exertion as he carries Kat piggy-back (not over his shoulders, as Lewis Milestone would film it).

> Kat is not very heavy; so I take him up on my back and start off to the dressing station with him. He suffers acutely on the way. We do not speak much. I have opened the collar on my tunic and breathe heavily, I sweat and my face is swollen with the strain of carrying. All the same I urge him to let us go on, for the place is dangerous.
> "Shall we go on again Kat?"
> "Must, Paul."
> "Then come."
> I raise him up, he stands on the uninjured leg and supports himself against a tree. I take up the wounded leg carefully, then he gives a jump and I take the knee of the sound leg also under my arm. …
> We lie down in a small hole to wait till the shelling is over. I give Kat some tea from my water bottle. We smoke a cigarette. …

> "Do you remember, Kat, how we commandeered the goose? And how you brought me out of the barrage when I was still a young recruit and wounded for the first time? I cried then. Kat, that is almost three years ago."[532]

By the time they get to the dressing station, Kat is dead. The loss of the first-person narrator's comrade puts an end to the last vestiges of boyish fun which the novel depicts with undeniable relish. But for German readers in 1929, this scene represented the value and the meaning that the war supposedly brought forth into the world.[533]

Another novel of the war, Ludwig Renn's *Krieg* [*War*], published in 1929, also included the motif of one soldier carrying another from the battlefield. In the midst of the confusion of his first battle, the fictionalized private Renn struggles to locate the direction from which shots are being fired by Belgian snipers; he is uncertain whether he should take cover or advance, and his Lieutenant knows little better what to do. "Take me with, comrade! Grab me by the shoulder," cries another soldier, and the first-person narrator struggles to carry him from danger. "I toss my gun into my left hand and grab round his body. Shots ring against the wall. He steps with his left foot but sinks to the ground again. ... Something tears at my cap. My head is singing. I drag him forward. He groans. ... He starts to slip from my arms. His thigh is soft. I grasp around in his shirt."[534] Ernst Jünger didn't neglect to include this motif in his first-person account of the war, either, and like Renn, whose political stance in the late 1920s could hardly have been more different, Jünger represents himself as the hero who carries a wounded comrade away from danger and saves him from a long, slow death lying wounded on the battlefield.

532 Remarque, *All Quiet*, 242–243.

533 Kühne, *Kameradschaft*, 60–62.

534 "Nim mich mit, Kamerad,' schreit einer. 'Faß mich unter der Schulter!" Ich werfe das Gewehr in die linke Hand und packe ihn um den Leib. Ob es ihm wehtut, ist jetzt gleich! Er ist schwer. Es knallt gegen den Hauswand. Er tritt mit dem linken Fuß auf und sinkt wieder ein. Zwischen Haus und Wagen ist nur ein schmaler Gang. Etwas reißt an meiner Mütze. Der Kopf summt mir. Ich zerre ihn vorwärts. Er stöhnt. Wir sind schon am ersten Fenster vorbei. Er beginnt mir aus dem Arm zu rutschen. Seine Hüfte ist weich. Ich kralle mich in seinem Rock." Ludwig Renn, *Krieg* (Frankfurt: Societäts-Verlag, 1932 edition), 35.

> But no sooner had we reached the shallow communication trench than a first clutch of shrapnels blew up in our midst. One ball smashed the wrist of a man in front of me, sending the arterial blood spurting everywhere. He reeled, and made to lie down on his side. I took him by the arm, pulled him to his feet in spite of his complaints, and only let go of him when we'd reached the dressing-station next to battle headquarters.[535]

It is this same image – of one soldier carrying a wounded comrade away from danger, at risk to his own life, which is depicted in the right hand panel of *The War*. The face of the soldier doing the carrying – the protagonist, as it were, of the story, is that of Dix himself.[536] The painting is thus, like each of these three literary representations, a first-person narrative in which the author himself (or his persona) displays the prime virtue of the "spirit of the front," the very thing which gave the war and its experience meaning and value. The passages from these three books by three very different German authors with three very different projects and political sympathies indicates the spectrum of possible associations that the motif could have, even in literary representations.

Eric Leed, in his study of the experience of the war and its effects on individual identity, as read through works of literature, has pointed to a "fixation" on the dead, "reinforced in the pageants, memorials, rituals, and songs of veteran's groups. … The casualties of war became the central figures in a cult of suffering and self-sacrifice."[537] And Jason Crouthamel has recently suggested that the idealization of their own sacrifice was itself a symptom of trauma, that this is why veterans "obsessively" celebrated their heroism and the ideals of comradeship.[538] But I wish to avoid a psychological reading of Dix's painting which would take it to be

535 Jünger, *Storm of Steel*, 101. This passage also comes from the central chapter "Guillemont."

536 Many have pointed this fact out. See for example Schubert, *Otto Dix im Selbstzeugnissen*, 102.

537 Eric J. Leed, *No Man's Land: Combat and Identity in World War One* (Cambridge: Cambridge University Press, 1979), 212.

538 Jason Crouthamel, *The Great War and German Memory, Society, Politics and Psychological Trauma, 1914–1945* (Exeter: University of Exeter Press, 2009).

merely symptomatic. Rather, I would emphasize a more deliberate effort at memorialization, with the intention of directly and fully reaching the community of veterans and mourners, rather than therapeutically exploring his own psychic trauma. Dix is here telling a story of his own experience in the war – whether the anecdote happened to him or to another man is beside the point, as it often is in war stories. It was a typical story, told over and over, to convey a "deeper truth" about the war. Thomas Kühne has demonstrated that *Kameradschaft* had come by the late 1920s to dominate the discourse of remembrance of the war, giving it a meaning that was often distinct from nationalist claims. Dix fully participates in this discourse, identifying himself and by extension his art, in the public sphere, with this particular and central redemptive virtue. At the same time, as Kühne has shown, the image of *Kameradschaft* is itself ambiguous, politically multivalent.

The concept of a redemptive meaning to the war and its sacrifices is suggested by the very format of the work – that of an altarpiece such as one would find in a church or cathedral chapel, where services would be held for the dead in perpetuity. This salvific function and format is continued by the predella below (see Figures 70 and 71). The predella depicts what appear to be several soldiers sleeping in a dugout, which is perhaps reached via the collapsed entrance we see in the middle of the central panel. At the same time, these men sleeping beneath their tarp could easily be mistaken for dead soldiers buried in a grave, covered by a shroud; the paleness of their skin and the very format of the predella – typically reserved in late medieval German altarpieces for the image of Christ entombed, strengthens this connotation. Stephen Goebel has recently shown that the image of the dead soldier who is presented as though he were in a state of restful sleep was one of the central images of those war monuments that sought to establish a meaningful continuity between the war and a distant, often medieval past. It emerged during the 1920s as a central discursive figure which, alongside that of *Kameradschaft*, suggested that the sacrifices of the war had been meaningful.

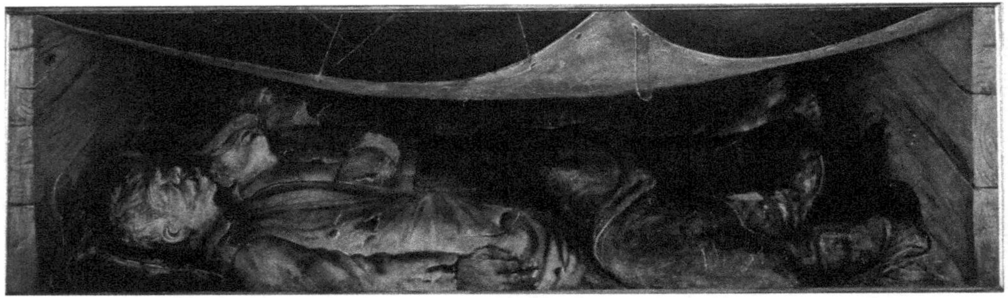

Figure 70. Otto Dix, *The War*, predella, oil and tempera on wood panel, 1928–1932 Staatliche Kunstsammlungen, Dresden, Galerie Neue Meister. © Otto Dix / Artists Rights Society (ARS), New York / VG Bild-Kunst, Bonn. Photo Art Resource, NY / Erich Lessing, used with permission; Digital file: author's own scan.

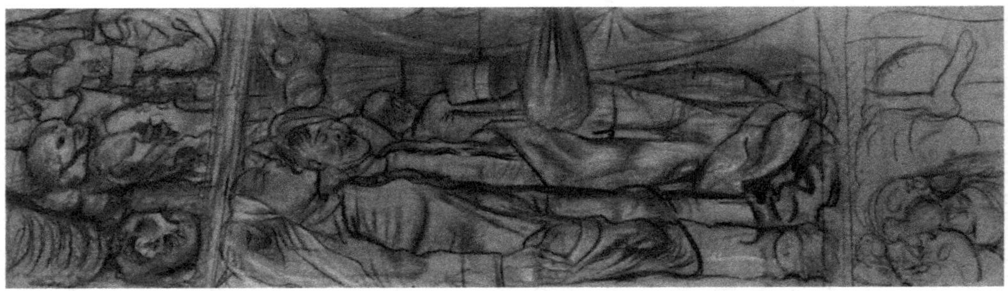

Figure 71. Otto Dix, cartoon of *The War*, predella, charcoal, white and colored chalks, gouache, pencil on gray cardboard, laid down on canvas and stretcher, 1929–1930, Hamburger Kunsthalle, Hamburg. © Otto Dix / Artists Rights Society (ARS), New York / VG Bild-Kunst, Bonn; Photo: bpk Bildagentur / Hamburger Kunsthalle / Elke Walford / Art Resource, NY.

The figure of the dead soldier displayed as though in a restful sleep was especially prevalent in Germany, beginning in 1925 and continuing into the early 1930s. A model for a proposed sculptural memorial, shown at the same Berlin Art Academy exhibition as *The War* in 1932, for example, features just such a figure of the "sleeping dead," and Dix's monumental painting clearly participates in this emerging vocabulary of memorial sculpture.[539] Laid out on a tomb, positioned in a chapel-like space, the simple soldier who reclines in repose in so many German memorials, waiting to rise again in a narrative of redemption, held out the promise of meaning for a grieving German public. With this image, sculptors or those who commissioned them sought to overcome the gap between the present and the past, whether the immediate prewar past or a more distantly historical one, and to overcome the loss of individuals or, more abstractly, of the millions of war dead.[540] The medievalism of the format chosen by Dix here as part of the evolution of his memorial monuments from *The Trench* to *The War* is of a piece with the broader medievalizing discourse in which this redemptive image circulated.

According to Goebel's analysis, revanchism and resentment are not necessarily part of the message of such monuments, but they are not ruled out, either. The historian of the German welfare system, Greg Eghigian, has suggested that resentment was a particularly powerful and even politically influential affect in Germany between the wars, but that this emotion did not *necessarily* involve fantasies of vengeance or the revanchist politics specific to revolutionary conservative political movements such as National Socialism.[541] If Eghigian is right about this, then it may be that Dix was here expressing a resentment about the war, without necessarily expressing either a strong antiwar sentiment or, conversely, an overt desire for vengeance against

539 The proposed sculptural monument was by Paul Merling. A photograph of the model was printed in the *Berliner Illustrierte Zeitung*, 41/43 (30 October 1932), reproduced in van Dyke, "Dix Petrified," 118. It was compared directly to Dix's triptych by the art critic Bruno Werner in *Die Kunst für Alle*; see below.

540 Stefan Goebel, *Great War and Medieval Memory*, 254–262.

541 Greg Eghigian, "Injury, Fate, Resentment, and Sacrifice in German Political Culture, 1914–1939," in Greg Eghigian and Matthew Paul Berg, eds., *Sacrifice and National Belonging in Twentieth Century Germany* (College Station: Texas A&M University Press, 2002), 90–117.

the Allies. If the resentment expressed by Dix was similar to the resentment shared by other Germans, in this narrative, then it was a generalized resentment, directed at the fate of Germany in and after the war – resentment as a form of national identity and belonging to a *Schicksalsgemeinschaft* [a community united by a common fate] – rather than being directed at those actually responsible for the war. And it should be remembered that, during the war, Dix had viewed the industrialized destruction as a kind of natural occurrence, a natural law or force, rather than the result of political decisions, political will or lack thereof.[542] Monuments that featured dead soldiers as though they were only peacefully sleeping were politically ambiguous; the trope of the sleeping dead could be and was deployed by those on the left, center, or right; resentment shaded imperceptibly into mourning, and the recumbent figure of the sleeping/dead soldier inhabited just this indeterminate zone of ambiguous meaning.[543]

The development of *The War*: An evolving meaning

The triptych *The War* did not spring directly from Dix's memories of his own experiences, fully formed with all of its freighted motifs and ambiguities. Dix labored for years on this work, beginning in 1928 and not completing it until 1932. Max Sauerlandt, the director of the Hamburg art museum, paid Dix a visit in his studio at the Academy in Dresden on 25 November 1929, and wrote in his journal afterward that he had the impression "that in the *year and a half* that he has been working on this large work, Dix has made a decisive stride forwards in the artistic expression of his intentions, and that his whole art must achieve a new level through the passionate labor on this one work" [my emphasis].[544] Besides the indication that Sauerlandt – a

542 Otto Dix Field Notebook, held in Kunstmuseum Albstadt.

543 Goebel, "Re-membered and re-mobilized," 248–249.

544 "Dix in der eineinhalbjährigen Arbeit an diesem großen Werk innerlich und in der künstlerischen Darstellung seiner Absichten einen entscheidenden Schritt vorwärts

fellow veteran – was impressed by this work, his comments clearly indicate a starting point in 1928, despite the fact that Dix signed the painting with the dates 1929–1932 (Sauerlandt stated that the work was nearly complete at the time of his visit, although Dix would labor over it for two more years; see below). A close examination of the sketches he made and the full-scale cartoons he prepared – and of the quite significant changes that he made to the composition even after the drawings in the cartoons had been transferred to the panels and painted in – reveal an artist whose ideas were indeed undergoing a transformation. I will argue that those ideas were changing in response to a dramatically shifting situation of memory work taking place outside of Dix's studio walls, and outside of his own memories of the war, taking place in the streets, in front of public war memorials, in movie theaters, and in the pages of newspapers and magazines and novels of the war. The result of this process may have been an artwork that was even more ambiguous than it had been at the outset, but it was also an artwork fully in dialog with the wider, messy work of remembrance.

In 1929 Dix had drawn the quite detailed and highly finished full-scale cartoons now held by the Hamburg Art Museum, as part of his Old Masterish working process.[545] Dix was essentially following a method that he had adopted by 1925 out of Max Doerner's influential book on traditional painting technique and materials.[546] Working with a combination of tempera and oil paint, with solid outlines, great detail, and the even tonal transitions made possible by multiple transparent color glazes, he felt that he needed the composition to be worked out in as much detail and precision as possible.[547]

getan hat und daß seine ganze Kunst durch die leidenschaftliche Arbeit an diesem einen Werk ein neues Niveau gewinnen muß." Max Sauerlandt, Direktor des Museums für Kunst und Gewerbe in Hamburg, *Ausgewählte Schriften*, Heinz Spielmann, ed., vol. 1, "Reiseberichte 1925–1932" (Hamburg: Christians, 1971), 131 ff., cited in Jorg Merz, ""Otto Dix' Kriegsbilder. 198.

545 Olaf Simon, "Wege zum Bild – die Kartons," in, Birgit Dalbajewa, Simone Fleischer, and Olaf Peters, *Otto Dix. Der Krieg – Das Dresdner Triptychon* (Dresden: Sandstein, 2014), 169–172.

546 Doerner, *Materials of the Artist.*

547 See for example the underdrawing of the *Fritz Glaser Family Portrait* [*Familienbildnis*] (1925) reproduced in Maria Körber, "Studien zur Maltechnik der Neuen Sachlichkeit

This also included the distribution of lights and darks, and shading and highlights are clearly indicated in the cartoons – light areas being indicated by white paint, in the way that white chalk was used by the Old Masters in pencil drawings on colored paper. The next step would be to transfer the drawings to the carefully prepared painting support – in this case hardwood panels built by a professional carpenter, then sized and sanded. After covering this underdrawing with a somewhat transparent greenish-yellow ochre imprimatur, he painted a thick, textured layer of egg tempera, giving the lighter or darker tones and modeling.[548] This underpainting would have closely followed the compositions of the cartoons. But then in the course of 1929 he made significant changes to these compositions, despite their high degree of detail and finish. Dix painted over much of the original designs in a second underpainting, carried out with loose brushstrokes and even a palette knife, indicating that he had changed his mind in significant ways about what he wanted these images to convey. When Sauerlandt visited Dix's studio, he wrote that "It was most interesting for me to see the earlier versions, retained in tracings [he certainly means the cartoons, which were transferred directly to the panels by tracing, MM], and to compare them with the new compositions which are now nearly completed. Only the left wing of the triptych stands now in the form of the earlier design."[549] Thus,

---

in Dresden," in Birgit Dalbajewa, ed., *Neue Sachlichkeit in Dresden* (Dresden: Sandstein, 2011), 144–169, fig. 8, and in Sabine Rewald, Ian Baruma, and Matthias Eberle, *Glitter and Doom. German Portraits From the 1920s* (New York: Metropolitan Museum of Art, 2006), 107, plate 25.

548 Anna Barbara Lorenzer, "Studien zur Maltechnik von Otto Dix von 1910–1933," *Zeitschrift für Kunsttechnologie und Konservierung* 3 (1989), 113–148. The several paint layers and changes have been more thoroughly investigated on the occasion of an exhibition in Dresden in 2014, and are thoroughly documented and discussed in the catalog, Marlies Giebe and Maria Körber, "'… weil Dix hier malt wie ein Alter Meister und dabei doch ganz er selbst geblieben ist.' Maltechnische Studien zum Triptychon 'Der Krieg' von Otto Dix," in Birgit Dalbajewa, Simone Fleischer, and Olaf Peters, eds., *Otto Dix. Der Krieg – Das Dresdner Triptychon* (Dresden: Sandstein, 2014), 219–251.

549 "Es war für mich von dem höchsten Interesse, die in Pausen noch erhaltene erste Fassung mit der jetzt gefundenen Lösung zu vergleichen, die schon fast fertig durchgeführt ist. Nur der linke Flügel des Triptychons steht noch in der Form des früheren Entwurfes." Max Sauerlandt, *Ausgewählte Schriften*, 131 f.

by late November 1929, Dix had not only completed the transfer of the cartoons to the panels and the first underpainting, he had also heavily revised the compositions with the second underpainting. This second underpainting was documented in a set of professional photographs that Dix himself commissioned, and which show this thick layer of tempera, applied loosely and in places almost willy-nilly, sometimes with a palette knife, the better to cover over parts of the composition that Dix now rejected.[550] And Sauerlandt was right: it is fascinating, and informative, to compare the finished compositions to the original designs preserved in the cartoons.

Although there are several extant sketches from Dix documenting the early process of designing the overall composition, I will concentrate in what follows on the differences between the much more finished and detailed cartoons and the final painting. There are several things to keep in mind as we undertake this comparison, and attempt to retrace as best we can the development of the rich imagery of this monumental work. First, the revisions Dix undertook were carried out between late 1928 and early 1930, at a time when the public work of the memory of the war had irrupted into public discourse and open conflict. Second, in trying to reconstruct a timeline for the whole work, one that incorporates the cartoons, it should be noted that the date Dix wrote on them, 1930, cannot be correct, because Dix had already substantially changed the compositions by the time Sauerlandt saw the painted panels in Dix's studio in late 1929; the drawings must have therefore been completed and transferred well before this moment. It is impossible to say for certain why Dix gave them later dates, but one possibility would be that, at some point in the course of 1930, feeling that he had moved definitively beyond them, he signed and dated them (as was his practice) in order to put them, as it were, into the archive of the work. It being 1930 when he signed them, he dated them "1930." Some evidence that speaks for this theory is the fact that he signed what appears to be an early sketch for the central panel with the legend, "Skizze zum Kriegsbild" [sketch for the war picture] (no date), assigning to the sketch an essentially archival significance which had only emerged

550 These photographs are reproduced in Dalbajewa, *Otto Dix, Triptychon Der Krieg*, 180, 189, and 212–213. There is no photograph of the right-hand panel.

with the development of the project over time.[551] Even more significant is the fact that he hired a professional photographer to document the work in progress with glass plate negatives. The archival photographic documentation must have taken place at a point when Dix felt that he was ready to begin the final stage, the application of glazes in oil, after which any further alteration of the underpainting would essentially be impossible. It seems very likely, therefore, that the evolution of the work and its meaning which I will next trace took place between mid 1928 and sometime late in 1931; by 1932 the work would have progressed to the point where color harmonies could still be altered and small details added, but alteration of the imagery could only be minimal.

The period from 1928 to 1931 was an important time in the public memory work of the war in Germany. During this period, to point to just one manifestation of that memory work, the competing parades and demonstrations of the *Stahlhelm* and similar organizations and of the *Reichsbanner* turned increasingly into violent confrontations between the groups. And, as Nadine Rossol has shown, the central political parties, including the Social Democrats, held ever-larger parades and demonstrations during just these years to mark Constitution Day – 11 August, the day the Weimar Constitution had been ratified in 1919 – events which prominently featured the *Reichsbanner* in the form of veterans in uniform and steel helmet marching in formation, but which by 1929 had also taken on a quality of mass spectacle with thousands of other participants and even more spectators.[552] During the festivities in Berlin in August 1929 (held in part in the Berlin stadium), the *Reichsbanner* erected in front of the Brandenburg Gate an enormous temporary monument to the dead of the world war, 17 meters high; it took four hours for 150,000 *Reichsbanner* men to march past it.[553]

In the central panel, the most important change between the cartoon and the finished painting is the addition of the inverted figure, covered in bullet holes that resemble the pustulating sores of the crucified Christ in

551 Ulm Museum, reproduced in Dalbajewa, *Otto Dix, Triptychon Der Krieg*, p. 187.

552 Nadine Rossol, *Performing the Nation in Interwar Germany. Sport, Spectacle, and Political Symbolism, 1926–1936* (London: Palgrave Macmillan, 2010), 18–19 and 71 ff.

553 Rossol, *Performing the Nation*, 69–70.

Grünewald's *Isenheim Altarpiece*. He is nowhere to be seen in the cartoon (or in the earlier sketches); only two dead soldiers are splayed on either side of the devastated trench. Dix also made the overall effect much more grisly, cutting off the legs and lower torso of the dead soldier on the right, letting his innards spill out onto the ground, and decapitating the one caught on the barbed wire on the left, allowing the head to roll down to the bottom of the frame. But it is the inverted figure which is the most riveting motif, and which unifies, in its own horrific way, the entire work. The decomposing corpse floating like an image of Death above the scene now points toward it, just as John the Baptist points to Christ in the Grünewald's own triptych, and the composition becomes a parody of that earlier Crucifixion. In the cartoon, the right half of the composition had featured instead details of trench construction; these have now been painted over with white sandbags, maintaining the overall tonal composition. The original hill or mound of earth raised over the edge of the trench has been painted out, so that the feet of the inverted figure rise up over the horizon, with only a rose-colored band of sky behind them. Dix also raised the horizon line and filled in the cratered landscape of no-man's-land.

The decision to include a parody of Grünewald's Christ must be seen in the context of what has been characterized by Anne Stieglitz as a flood of popular books about the *Isenheim Altarpiece*, including many portfolios with photographic details of the gruesome painting, and texts which sought to highlight that gruesomeness.[554] These publications range in quality and cultural ambition from Wilhelm Worringer's, in the 1920 reissue of his art historical study *Formprobleme der Gotik*, now enriched with detailed close-ups of Grünewald's masterpiece, to Wilhelm Niemeyer's more popular book *Matthias Grünewald – der Maler des Isenheimer Altars* of 1921, to Oskar Hagen and Reinhard Piper's monograph *Matthias Grünewald* of 1923.[555] Niemeyer wrote, rather luridly,

554 Stieglitz, "Reproduction of Agony," 87–103.

555 Oskar Hagen and Reinhard Piper, *Matthias Grünewald* (Munich: R. Piper, 1923); Wilhelm Niemeyer, *Matthias Grünewald – der Maler des Isenheimer Altars* (Berlin: Furche, 1921); Wilhelm Worringer, *Formprobleme der Gotik* (Munich: Piper,

> And blood! As we look at these corpse-green bloody feet of Grünewald's Christ, drilled through by those 'steel' blue nails, it is as though no painter before has ever been able to represent blood, real blood! Blood, how it streams like threads in glutinous, slow-moving droplets![556]

This passage, and others like it, have been characterized by Ann Stieglitz as catering to a "'Schaulust,' a morbid gaze," connected to the sense of loss of cultural heritage when the *Isenheim Altarpiece* was returned to Colmar, in Alsace, itself now lost to the ancient enemy, France. The names "Grünewald" and "Isenheim Altarpiece" were thus not neutral terms, with merely art historical connotations. It was impossible in the 1920s to say "Grünewald" and not also say "blood!" and "wound" but also "archenemy," impossible not to hear the echoes of sermons on both resurrection and irredentism delivered to veterans of the Front. It should be remembered that, during the Constitution Day festivities in Berlin in August of 1929, the *Reichsbanner* parade, like many of its other public events, prominently featured reminders of territories "lost" or occupied as a result of the loss of the war; the centrist, largely Social Democrat and pro-republican group did not shy away from displays of irredentism.[557] It would not, therefore, necessarily seem strange for an artist who was, like the members of the *Reichsbanner*, preoccupied with the work of publicly remembering the war and its sacrifices, to include references to the loss of cultural patrimony.

The predella – with its medieval overtones and salvific associations – also underwent significant changes between the cartoon and the actual, painted version. In the cartoon, it had been much clearer that these are men sleeping soundly in their dugout. One figure even sleeps on his side. What could be called genre details were included: bags and parcels hung by cords from the ceiling, to keep them away from the rats; gasmasks hung there, too. *All Quiet on the Western Front* has been pointed to as a source for the

---

republished with 50 plates in 1919; a new edition was brought out in December 1926). Ann Stieglitz, "Reproduction of Agony," 101, footnote 5.

556 Niemeyer, *Matthias Grünewald*, 18, cited and translated by Stieglitz, "Reproduction of Agony," p. 95.

557 Rossol, *Performing the Nation*, 70.

rats, but Ludwig Renn's novel, *Krieg*, has a description of similar details.[558] Death was vividly present in the earlier versions of the painting, but in the form of bones segregated into subterranean compartments like ossuaries on either side of the dugout. Dix altered the composition so that the ambiguity of the recumbent figures was heightened; they are now much more readily mistaken for corpses in a tomb. This in turn recalls all the more forcefully the trope of the enchanted sleep of the fallen. Stephen Goebel writes that the many examples of recumbent figures in German war memorials were presented with deliberate ambivalence as both dead corpses awaiting resurrection and as sleeping figures who will soon reawaken. The image of the 'sleeping dead' is explicitly Christological and redemptive.[559] The recumbent soldier, and the confusion of death and "enchanted sleep" in so many memorials from the mid-1920s on in Germany, was in Goebel's analysis part of a wider trend in Europe towards the use of specifically Christian language of redemptive sacrifice to create a sense that the mass death of the war had served some greater purpose.[560] And Jay Winter has pointed out that the trope of the dead who come back to life in order to admonish the post-war living, survivors and civilians alike, demanding vindication or revenge, was a prevalent one.[561] Dix's use of the image of the sleeping dead in his own quasi-religious monument must be seen in the same context as other memorials that represented the uniformed First World War soldier in enchanted sleep, such as Ewald Mataré's war memorial in Kleve, near Düsseldorf (1933–1934, destroyed),[562] and Bernhard Bleeker's figure,

558 "Unser Unterstand wurde immer vollkommener mit ... Nägeln an der Decke, um die Wurst und das Brot so aufzuhängen, daß die Ratten nicht daran käme." Renn, *Krieg*, 1932, 136. References to Remarque in Dieter Scholz, "Das Triptychon *Der Krieg*, 263, among others.

559 Stephen Goebel, "Re-membered and re-mobilized: The 'Sleeping Dead' in Interwar Germany and Britain," *Journal of Contemporary History*, 39/4 (October 2004), 487–501.

560 Stephen Goebel, *The Great War and Medieval Memory: War, Remembrance, and Medievalism in Britain and Germany, 1914–1940* (Cambridge: Cambridge University Press, 2007), 232.

561 Jay Winter, *Sites of Memory, Sites of Mourning*, 15–28.

562 Inge Zacher, *Ewald Mataré: Der 'Tote Krieger' in Kleve* (Kleve: Boss, 1985).

The Sleeping Warrior [Der Schlafende Krieger], who still lies peacefully in a crypt beneath the war memorial in the Munich Hofgarten (1925).[563]

In the cartoon for the left-hand panel there are two columns of soldiers, one coming and one going; the returning soldiers are accompanied by a dog; in earlier sketches this space had been anchored by a dead horse and wagon wheel (presumably both had been used to pull an artillery piece). Was the dog an emblem of loyalty? A medievalizing image of the "dogs of war?" Or did it recall another emotional bond of the front, that between soldiers and the dogs who went with them to the front to be employed as message carriers? There is even a dog featured in the film *Westfront 1918*. The column of men going to the front is endless, an effect heightened in the cartoon by a rise in the road and a forced perspective device. The last two men at the back chat amiably.[564] They are passing the time – not unpleasantly – in conversation as they march off to the front lines (see Figure 66). The *Gemütlichkeit* of this scene is underscored by the pipe smoked by the taller figure on the left, a soldier's pipe (commonly called a *Reservistenpfeife* – a "reservist's pipe"). Their wearisome march is made tolerable by the simple, earthy pleasures of military life: a pipe and comradeship formed out of shared privation and witty banter. Anybody in Dix's audience who had served in the war could have counted off the range of well-worn topics of conversation, and recalled the humorously grotesque slang in which it would have been spoken.[565] In the final painting, the original wagon wheel

563 Goebel, *The Great War and Medieval Memory*, 262; and Gavriel D. Rosenfeld, *Munich and Memory: Architecture, Monuments, and the Legacy of the Third Reich* (Oakland: University of California Press, 2000), 114–115.

564 The same motif of one receding figure turning to speak to another, affording the viewer a glimpse of his profile, can also be seen in the central panel of Meunier's *The Mine*, discussed above, in the two stragglers who are closest to the viewer. This strengthens the suspicion that Dix may have seen and dimly remembered the composition of this triptych while in Brussels during the war, if not subsequently.

565 Joanna Bourke speaks of "the joyous celebration of the 'material bodily principle'" in stories of the war, stories that often mixed death with sex and the scatological, "this carnivalesque inversion of what was sacred," as well as a whole section on "storytelling," that focuses on stories, often exaggerated, of killing. *An Intimate History of Killing*, 3 and 21 ff.

reappears to replace the dog. This wheel has sometimes been treated as a key to an entire iconographic program, supposedly elevating the endless cycle of the soldier's movements – up to the front and then back for rest and then up to the front again – to a meditation on Nietzsche's idea of the "eternal return."[566] The more significant change in the final painting, I think, is that the two soldiers no longer chat, and we no longer see their facial features, or just barely. The effect is much more lugubrious, eliminating genre and anecdote despite the details of gear and equipage. We are no longer encouraged to forget that the soldiers are marching off to the front and to what we know, from the opposite panel, will be an inferno, ending in devastation and then rest, eternal or otherwise.

The left panel had not yet been revised by the time of Sauerlandt's visit in late 1929, according to his account. Given how much work would still have been left to do on the panel before it could be exhibited in October 1932, it must have been revised at some point in the course of 1930 or 1931, early 1932 at the latest, and the photographs of the second underpainting must therefore also date to this period.[567] The reworking of the left panel was a complicated process, with several intermediary stages revealed by the x-ray and fluoroscopic images made of it in preparation for the exhibition in Dresden of 2014.[568] Some changed elements are covered over with the usual thick and opaque tempera paint layer, while others are done with thinner oil layers, that is, at a relatively late stage in the process. The outlines of the original profiles of the two chatting soldiers, for example, were not so heavily covered over, and so can be seen as pentimenti in the raking light, indicating that these faces were changed late in the process (as late as 1931?).

566 Schubert, *Triptychon Der Krieg*, 321 f.

567 The date given by Giebe and Körber for the photographs is 1929, but there is little documentary evidence for an exact date. The name of the photographer is not known, and the only written reference to them is dated to October 1932, in connection with the exhibition of the Berlin Academy. Giebe and Körber, "Maltechnische Studien," footnote 56.

568 Marlies Giebe and Maria Körber, "'… weil Dix hier malt wie ein Alter Meister und dabei doch ganz er selbst geblieben ist.' Maltechnische Studien zum Triptychon 'Der Krieg' von Otto Dix," in Birgit Dalbajewa, Simone Fleischer, and Olaf Peters, eds., *Otto Dix. Der Krieg – Das Dresdner Triptychon* (Dresden: Sandstein, 2014), 219–251.

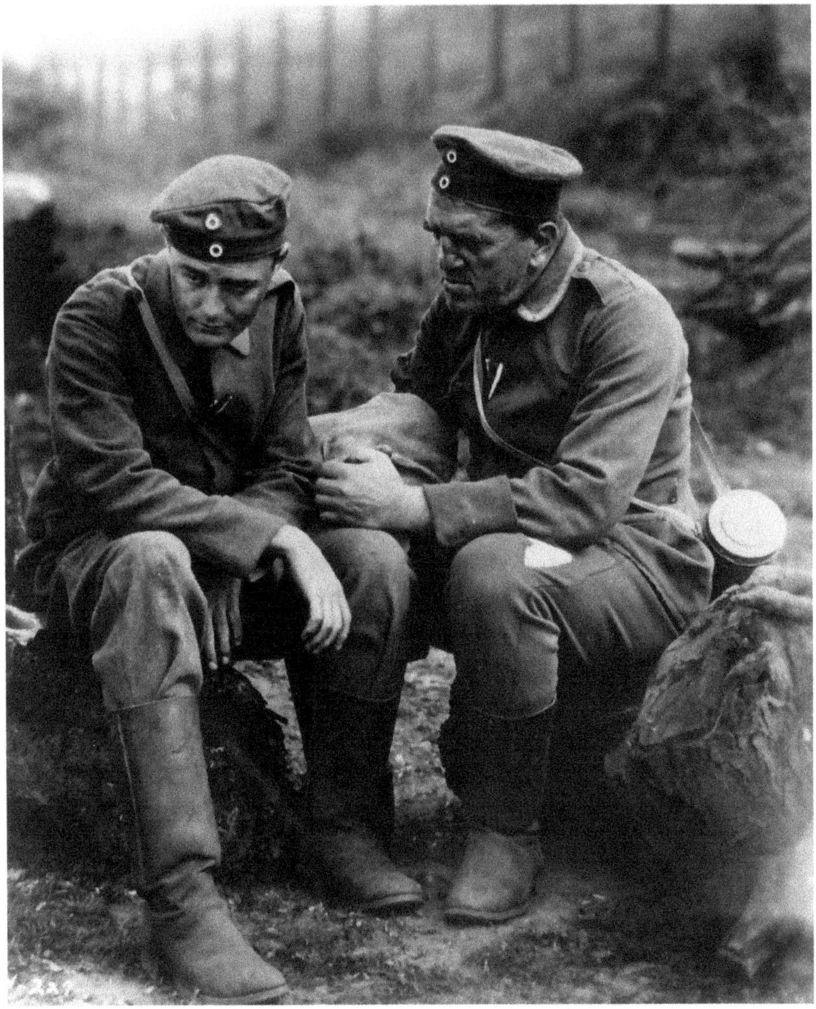

Figure 72. Photo from *All Quiet on the Western Front*, film by Louis Milestone, Universal Studios, 1930.

It has been pointed out by scholars that *The War* draws on *All Quiet on the Western Front*, published in 1928, and that Dix had sent Erich Maria Remarque a copy of his etching portfolio that same year – the year he began working on the triptych.[569] The imagery of the left-hand panel in particular has been compared to specific passages in the novel.[570] In the cartoon, the shorter of the two soldiers bore a striking resemblance to the distinctive features of the short and almost comically ugly Louis Wolheim, the American actor who played the role of Kat in the Hollywood film of *All Quiet on the Western Front* (see Figure 72). The resemblance is purely coincidental; the movie premiered in Germany on 4 December 1930 and the cartoons must have been completed well before Sauerlandt's visit to Dix's studio in on 25 November 1929, more than a year earlier. But the film was banned a few days after it opened, not because of its pacifist message, but because Josef Goebbel's thugs relentlessly disrupted screenings of it. It was released again on 2 September 1931. When viewers saw Dix's triptych in the annual exhibition of the Berlin Academy a year later, they would have not only the text of Remarque's novel in mind, but also the film version. If Dix altered this panel as late as 1931, as I suggested above, then perhaps it was in order to avoid any discussion of the unintentional resemblance between his front soldier and Kat from Milestone's film. The faces in profile seem to have been altered very late in the process, and only in oil. The earlier outlines of the faces are visible beneath the colors of the new design, indicating that they were not covered over in impasto tempera the way that other rejected compositional elements were, and Dix had to resort to the somewhat awkward expansion of their haversacks to cover over the faces. If he made these changes so late in the process, they may well have come after the initial release of the film in Germany.

569 Merz, "Dix' Kriegsbilder," 199.

570 Lothar Fischer, *Otto Dix, Ein Malerleben in Deutschland* (Berlin: Nicolaische Verlagsbuchhandlung, 1981), 17. Fischer cites a specific passage from the novel describing the emergence of a column of soldiers from a moonlit fog, "Die Köpfe wurden hier zu Gestalten; – Röcke, Hosen und Stiefel kommen aus dem Nebel wie aus einem Milchteich. ... eine Kolonne – keine Menschen" (n.p). Fischer states that it is the final version of the triptych which is influenced by the novel. Fischer, *Ein Malerleben*, 17.

The right-hand panel has a more complicated history. In the original cartoon (see Figure 68), several soldiers are carrying their comrades to safety – Dix would later reduce this to a single pair (see Figures 67 and 69). The changes made to the composition were significant enough that Dix seems to have felt the need to start from scratch, with a new cartoon (there is even a third cartoon, of the same dimensions but with a very different composition – a single soldier standing beneath a rainbow – and a completed painting based on this cartoon, now in Stuttgart). This second cartoon is less detailed, as if Dix were by this point impatient to get on with painting the panel itself. By the time the new underpainting was photographed this panel had been repainted following the design of the second cartoon. Even still, the face in the second cartoon is not yet Dix's own. In fact, he seems to have struggled with the face quite a bit, and the decision to make the figure a self-portrait must have come even later, in the execution of the panel itself.[571] In earlier sketches for this panel, the soldier always carried his comrade piggyback, much as Paul is described carrying Kat to the bandaging station (see above) toward the end of *All Quiet on the Western Front*. In the first cartoon, Dix changed this to show the wounded soldier being carried lengthwise over his comrade's shoulders. Now, in the newer cartoon, and in the final work, the arrangement of the two soldiers closely matches that of the famous Pasquino sculpture group, believed to represent Menelaus supporting the body of the dying Patroclus.[572] A copy of this ancient work was in Dresden (now in Leipzig), and it was also reproduced in the *Meyer's Lexicon* of 1888. Here again Dix speaks at one and the same time to an audience of fellow veterans, and to art cognoscenti – critics and even museum directors. But art historians have not pursued the complex web of intertextual meanings, both high and low, that the *Pasquino Group* would have opened out onto for Dix's peers. To begin with, the closely related term "Pasquinade" was once a current term

571 Olaf Peters claims that the face of this soldier originally resembled Hitler's, which he interprets as an iconographic connection with the large-scale painting *Sieben Todessünden* of 1933. Peters, *Neue Sachlichkeit und Nationalsozialismus*, 217.

572 First-century CE Roman copy of a Hellenistic sculpture. Schubert, "das Triptychon," 322.

for a lampoon.[573] But for an educated audience the *Pasquino Group* reference with its erudite evocation of Menelaus and Patroclus and the Trojan War would have actually pointed downwards to the lower cultural register of satire, specifically to the best-known and most widely read of the many parodies of Remarque's novel of the war, *Vor Troja Nichts Neues* ("All Quiet in the Trojan War") by one Emil Marius Requark.[574] Although this, too, is a recondite satire, it was a satire nonetheless (the "*Quark*" within the pseudonym "Requark" is somewhat childish German slang for 'nonsense'), and its target was the supposed cynicism with which Remarque and the Ullstein publishing house marketed the book as the truthful reportage of an eye witness, of a veteran who lived through and suffered the front experience when, it seemed, this was not in fact the case.[575] When in the course of 1929 Dix changed the figure group from his original conception of a soldier carrying his comrade piggyback to, eventually, the Pasquinade design, he must have known that he was deserting Remarque's text for a doubled reference to satires of it.

One reason Dix might have wished to avoid any obvious references to *All Quiet on the Western Front*, except for parodic ones, was the fact that the reception of the novel had swung quickly from overwhelmingly positive in 1929 to largely negative by late 1930. It was the most spectacular best-seller in German publishing history when it was published by Ullstein in 1929 (after having first been serialized in 1928 in newspapers owned by the Ullstein company). It was and is credited with unleashing a wave of books about the war, especially novels in the form of first-person memoirs,

573 Although perhaps erudite and already falling out of use, this term and its associations with the statue were still well-known enough in the early 1930s to appear in the *Brockhaus* encyclopedia under the entry "Pasquino."*Der Grosse Brockhaus*, 14, 1933, 214 f.

574 "Requark" was the pseudonym of Max Joseph Wolff, 1868–1941, a Berlin author and philologist, and a respected translator of Shakespeare. Erhard Schütz, "Romantik der Sachlichkeit. Die Marke Remarque, Ernst Jüngers Lehren und die rechten Konsequenzen daraus," in Edward Bialek, Manfred Durzak, eds., *Literatur im Zeugenstand; Beiträge zur deutschsprachigen Literatur- und Kulturgeschichte* (Bern: Peter Lang, 2002), 283–302.

575 Erhard Schütz, "Romantik der Sachlichkeit," 287 ff.

most but not all of which were explicitly positive about the experience. It is certainly this literary fashion which Dix had in mind when he later remembered how "in those days in the Weimar Republic also a lot of books were free to propagate once again heroism and a heroic image."[576] But in the period March through June 1929, a lively discussion sprang up about whether or not, and to what degree, the depiction of the front experience in *All Quiet on the Western Front* was "true."[577]

Thomas Schneider, the Remarque scholar, has drawn a useful distinction between two related concerns about the truthfulness of *All Quiet on the Western Front* in the criticism. Some critics were concerned with "facticity" – with the accuracy of objective, factual details such as the dates of certain battles, the numbers of participants, details of uniforms, weapons, techniques, material, etc. Others were more concerned with "authenticity," the truthful depiction of what the war was like, of the reaction of the soldiers to the war of materiel, of the soldiers' speech – and of their understanding of the war's "meaning."[578] Certainly it was the latter sort of "truthfulness," and a concern with the war's meaning, that Dix's triptych also aimed at. The critics increasingly came to the general conclusion in the summer of 1929 that Remarque's book was "literature," rather than a genuine first-hand account or unadorned diary. The original book jacket did not carry the word "novel" anywhere on it, and the publisher nowhere acknowledged that it was a work of fiction; it was not widely known at the time that "Erich Maria Remarque" was a pseudonym, or that the author was already a published novelist and occasional writer of frivolous style pieces in fashionable magazines. The dawning realization among the public that it was a work of literature undermined enthusiasm for the book as a "truthful" account. By the end of 1929 opinion on the book was divided.[579]

576 "In dieser Zeit übrigens propagierten viele Bücher ungehindert in der Weimarer Republik erneut ein Heldentum und einen Heldenbegriff …," cited in Wetzel, "Ein harter Mann, dieser Maler."

577 Hubert Rüter, *Remarque. 'Im Westen nichts Neues.' Ein Bestseller der Kriegsliteratur im Kontext* (Paderborn: Schöningh, 1980), 150–173.

578 Schneider, "Die Meute hinter Remarque," 147 f.

579 Schneider, "Die Meute hinter Remarque," 153 ff.

Otto Dix was clearly responding to this very public debate, carried out in the press, and in pamphlets, satires, and of course further novels, when he described his goal in painting his triptych. "I wanted to show very simply, concisely and objectively – almost like a reporter – my experiences in the years 1914–1918, and show that real human heroism consisted in surviving all that senseless death. I didn't want to foster angst and panic, but rather share knowledge about the horribleness of war, and so awaken the power of resistance."[580]

If the concept of *Kameradschaft* was increasingly important in the discourse of veterans' groups, the pose which Dix utilized to express it was also well established in the art of his contemporaries. Sculptural war memorials which had used a similar pose included Jakob Wilhelm Fehrle (1884–1974) for a monument to the fallen titled simply, *Pieta* (1920), in the cemetery of Göppingen, near Stuttgart, and Ernst Paul Hinckeldey's sculpture *Sacrificial Death* [Opfertod], erected in the city of Herford (Westphalia).[581] The former depicted a mother supporting the dead body of her son.[582] The latter however depicted two men, both soldiers, and carried as inscription on its pedestal a verse from the Gospel of John, "Greater love hath no man than this, that a man lay down his life for his friends."[583] Both sculptures were eventually removed during the Nazi period, Hinckeldey's undoubtedly due to the angular modernity of its formal vocabulary, and Fehrle's because, it has been suggested, the mother's mercy is unconditional, and thus at odds with a National Socialist racial doctrine

580 "Ich wollte ganz einfach – fast reportagemäßig – meine Erlebnisse der Jahre 1914–1918 zusammenfassend sachlich schildern und zeigen, daß echtes menschliches Heldentum in der Überwindung des sinnlosen Sterbens besteht. Ich wollte also nicht Angst und Panik auslösen, sondern Wissen um die Furchtbarkeit eines Krieges vermitteln und damit die Kräfte der Abwehr wecken." Interview in *Neues Deutschland*, East Berlin (December 1964). Diether Schmidt, *Otto Dix im Selbstbildnis*, 198.

581 Reproduced in Volker G. Probst, *Bilder vom Tode. Eine Studie zum deutschen Kriegerdenkmal in der Weimarer Republik am Beispiel des Pièta-Motives und seiner profanierten Varianten* (Hamburg: Wayasbah, 1986), 132.

582 Probst, *Bilder vom Tode*, 347.

583 King James Bible (John 15:13). In Martin Luther's German the verse reads, "Niemand hat größere Liebe den die, daß er sein Leben läßt für seine Freunde."

of mercilessness.[584] The *Kameradschaft*/pieta pose would receive its final expression at the hands of the sculptor most successful under the Nazi regime, Arno Breker (1900–1991), in a design for a sculpture to be called, simply, *Kameradschaft*.[585] Breker's overweening, monumental warriors defined the "Fascist aesthetic" in the 1930s, at least in figurative sculpture. But in the 1920s he had flirted with modernism, and his path crossed Dix's at a number of points: both had studied at the Düsseldorf Art Academy at the same time, and Breker briefly had contact with the avant-garde group Das junge Rheinland. Later in the decade they shared the same art dealer, Alfred Flechtheim, and in 1927 Breker apparently made a portrait bust of Dix.[586] The pose has its art historical source – certainly known to all these artists – in Michelangelo's final, unfinished sculpture, the *Rodanini Pieta* in Milan (1550s–1564). In 1932, Breker was in Milan, working on a bronze reconstruction of the *Rodanini Pieta*. In Breker's own *Kameradschaft* of 1938, two male figures are shown in a similar pose to the *Rodanini Pieta*. The figures are nude rather than uniformed soldiers, but the thirst for violence is clear, and the one figure seems to look back in anguish at the sacrifices of the previous war while striding forward to seek his vengeance in the next. The hyper-muscularity and aggression of both bodies redirects the viewer's attention away from the homoeroticism of their overlapping frontal nudity, in an overcompensation that can only be characterized as male hysteria.

The figure of Patroclus himself was one half of a duo with Achilles, one of the greatest warriors of Western literature and myth; the two together are not only the ideal type of every front soldier's *Kameradschaft*, they also bring to the surface the homoeroticism latent in the all-male Pieta motif,

584 Birgit Bressa, *Nach-Leben der Antike, Klassische Bilder des Körpers in der NS Skulptur Arno Brekers* (University of Tübingen, dissertation, 2001), 347. Hinckeldey went on to have a career as a prominent Nazi sculptor, with a minor specialty in monuments to Horst Wessel.

585 Volker G. Probst, *Das Pietà-Motiv bei Arno Breker* Bonn: Marco, 1985).

586 Jonathan Petropoulos, *The Faustian Bargain: The Art World in Nazi Germany* (Oxford: Oxford University Press), 220 ff.

and which later surfaced as kitsch in Breker's sculpture design.[587] Here is another moment of ambivalence in *The War*: It depicts a moment of physical care, even tenderness, between two men, arising out of an emotional bond which was cherished and idealized after the war, but which must have had an unpredictable character in reality. Magnus Hirschfeld wrote extensively about homoerotic bonds and activity in the trenches.[588] But Dix himself had on occasion used his art to express his own hostility towards homosexuals, caricaturing them in such watercolors as *The God of the Hairdressers* [Der Gott der Friseure] (see Figure 43). Watercolor in the early 1920s was the medium through which Dix explored myriad themes of sexuality. Yet in the right panel of *The War* he places himself in the role of the soldier who grasps and handles and pulls close the body of a weakened fellow soldier, a physical expression of *Kameradschaft*, of a particularly intense emotional bond between two soldiers.[589] Perhaps this ambiguity reproduced a larger ambivalence in the discourse of many veterans, like the tensions and ambivalences around the issues of pacifism, resentment, and nationalism. The text of the lament, "Ich hatt' einen Kamerade," (written by Ludwig Uhland during the Napoleonic Wars), sung by veterans of all political stripes at countless ceremonies in front of memorials between the wars, includes the lines, "Er liegt zu meinen Füßen / als wär's ein Stück von mir" [He lies there at my feet / as if he were a part of me], blurring the line between violence and tenderness, homosocial and homoerotic, self and other, subject and object. Just as part of the experience of the front was, at least in memory, the lifting of taboos on certain kinds of heterosexual activity, in the brothels and bedrooms of occupied towns, so too it seems to have made possible a wider range of physical intimacy between men, not exclusively sex, per se, but nonetheless a physical intimacy normally beyond the socially acceptable range of gender boundaries. In the war, as Santanu Das has pointed out,

587 Kühne, *Kameradschaft*, 233 f.

588 Magnus Hirschfeld, *Sittengeschichte des Weltkrieges* (Berlin: Verlag für Sexualwissenschaft Schneider & Co.), 1930.

589 Claudia Bruns, "The Politics of Masculinity in the (Homo-)Sexual Discourse (1880–1920)," *German History* 23/3 (August 2005), 306–320.

the male body was an object of pain, not desire, but also the site of a non-genital "tactile tenderness."[590]

The critical reception of *The War* in 1932

The War was exhibited in the annual exhibition of the Berlin Fine Arts Academy in 1932. The exhibition was reviewed by Paul Westheim in *Das Kunstblatt*, in an essay in which the critic mentions only two other works: Ernst Barlach's sculptures for the façade of the Lübeck cathedral, and Ernst Ludwig Kirchner's Varieté from 1908 (as well as Kirchner's latest work, done in the solitude of his studio in the Swiss Alps).[591] Turning to Dix's triptych, Westheim summed up its content as follows, "The experience of the war: the streams of blood; the shredded bodies; the senselessness won't let this '*Frontkämpfer*' rest."[592] Westheim framed the work in terms of Dix's experience of the war, his status and legitimacy as a veteran of the front, and as the result of the trauma of the experience. And then he went on to give it another framework, one that spoke specifically to the literate readership of *Das Kunstblatt*, and its knowledge of art history. "He paints a *mene tekel* on the wall; the word that Goya wrote on one of his war etchings, '*hé visto*,' 'I saw it,' could be written on this tableau, too." "Mene tekel" was the famous "writing on the wall" seen by the prophet Daniel in Belshazzar's palace,

590 Santanu Das, *Touch and Intimacy in First World War Literature* (Cambridge: Cambridge University Press, 2005), 119.

591 Paul Westheim, "Die Akademie-Ausstellung" *Das Kunstblatt*, 16 (November 1932), reprint (Lichtenstein: Kraus Reprint, 1978), 83.

592 "Im nächsten Saal das große Kriegs-Tryptichon von Dix, Variante jenes einzigartigen Kriegsbildes, das Dix vor zehn Jahren malte. Das Erlebnis des Krieges: die Blutschwaden, die zerfetzten Leiber, die Sinnlosigkeit, läßt diesen 'Frontkämpfer' nicht zur Ruhe kommen. Ein Mene Tekel malt er an die Wand; das Wort, das Goya auf eine seiner Kriegsradierungen setzte, 'hé visto' – 'ich habs gesehen' könnte auch auf dieser Tafel stehen," 83. The actual title of the print from Goya's *Disasters of War* that the author had in mind was "Yo lo vi."

and which only Daniel was able to decipher as: "God has numbered the kingdom and brought it to an end; the king has been weighed and found wanting" (Daniel 1: 28). *Hé visto* and *mene tekel.* Westheim combines the eye-witness' claim to the truth of his memories, and of his representation of them, with the Biblical prophet's rhetoric of condemnation.[593] Westheim here bestows upon Dix just that status which Jay Winter terms the "moral witness," whose outraged presentation of the truth, a truth experienced first-hand ("*hé visto*"), demands to be acknowledged, and gives the lie to what the witness sees as widely circulating false memories.[594]

Another review, this one by Bruno Werner, also compared it to Dix's earlier painting, *The Trench*:

> Otto Dix presents a triptych, in a certain sense a new version of his original trench picture, this one named *The War*. Presumably he sensed what a bad impression his first picture made in terms of painting. This time he has proceeded with the purely legitimate methods of painting, and painted in blood and horror the shredded men who, vegetating, sink into the landscape.

Like many critics, Werner made the obvious comparison with Dix's own earlier painting *The Trench*. As with that earlier work, the critics were curiously divided over whether this one was well painted or not – the critic Max Osborn, for example, writing in the Social Democrat-friendly *Vossische Zeitung* (for which paper he had also been a war correspondent, as well as the regular art critic), stated confidently that the new work, in its depictions of the horrors of the trenches, did not overshadow the earlier version, and that it was in fact a failure as a painting. "Who would have believed that Dix could be capable of such disastrous color harmonies?"[595] The politically

593 It was a scene that had, in the history of art, been most famously painted by Rembrandt (c. 1638, London, National Gallery of Art).

594 This is similar to the anger that Jay Winter identifies in the writings of those who felt that conventional representations of the war experience falsified it for venal reasons of political expediency and personal success. Winter, *Remembering War*, 269.

595 "Otto Dix' große Phantasie über den Krieg, wie ein Altarwerk mit Seitenflügel und Predelle aufgebaut … obwohl die ältere ähnliche Arbeit dadurch nicht übertroffen wird – , ist als malerisches Werk verfehlt. So fatale Farbigkeit hätte man

more nationalist-oriented Werner went on to fault the grotesque realism of Dix's mutilated bodies, merging into the formless muck of the earth, for being in his estimation a one-sided depiction of that war experience, lacking spiritual transcendence.

> This is certainly one side of the war. But as one can recognize on the left panel, with the marching soldiers, he always comes dangerously close to the line where actual art ends. Because this painting remains at bottom unspiritual. But there certainly breathes here an elemental experience, one that concerns us all, and which chills us once again when we stand before this picture.[596]

This critic compared *The War* not only to Ernst Barlach's drawings and copies of his new sculptures for the cathedral in Lübeck, but also to a model of a proposed design for a war memorial by Paul Merling, about which he wrote,

> The five soldiers stand quiet and still, differentiated only by their gesture and by their haircut. With their motionless earnestness and their standardized form they have something of the nature of old apostle shrines. This sculpture group should be carried out, to demonstrate that it is indeed possible in our times to dedicate a figurative monument to the Great War.[597]

Dix nicht zugetraut." Max Osborn, "Akademie in großer Form. Die Eröffnung der Herbstausstellung," *Vossische Zeitung* (15 October 1932, evening edition).

596 "Otto Dix hat ebenfalls ein Triptychon und gewissermaßen einen Neufassung seines ursprünglichen Schützengrabenbildes ‚Der Krieg' genannt. Vermutlich hat er gespürt, welchen schlechten malerischen Niederschlag in seinem ersten Bild ein starkes Erlebnis gefunden hatte. Er ist diesmal mit den rein legitimen Mitteln der Malerei vorgegangen und hat in Blut und Grauen den zerfetzten Menschen, der vegetativ mit der Landschaft verwächst, gemalt, und damit gewiß eine Seite des Krieges. Aber wie man an dem linken Flügel mit den marschierenden Soldaten erkennt, streift er immer gefährlich die Grenze, an der die eigentliche Kunst aufhört, denn diese Malerei bleibt in Grunde ungeistig. Aber sichtbar atmet hier ein elementares Erlebnis, das uns alle angeht, und von dessen Schauder wir heute angesichts dieses Bildes wieder betroffen werden." Bruno E. Werner, "Herbstausstellung der Preußischen Akademie," *Die Kunst für Alle* 48/3 (December 1932), 91–96.

597 "Die fünf Soldaten, die um einen toten sechsten still und unbewegt stehen und sich nur durch Gebärde und Haartracht voneinander zu unterscheiden scheinen, haben mit ihrem unbewegten Ernst und ihrer Gleichform etwas vom Wesen alter

It seemed appropriate to this critic to compare Dix's monumental painting to a war memorial, one that considers specifically the subjects of death, grief, and *Kameradschaft*. However, it's the figurative sculpture, rather than Dix's painting, which demonstrated for Werner that figurative art can serve as a memorial, "in our times." It is specifically in the left panel, with its marching troops, where the painting seemed insufficient to Werner, where a sculptural monument was better suited to the work of memorial and representation. But an article which appeared in the *Deutsche Frauen-Zeitung* in November 1934 praised the left panel in particular, and the triptych in general, precisely for its "truthfulness." Under the title, "Art and *Volk*," the article attempts to salvage some of Neue Sachlichkeit for German art under National Socialism, with illustrations of works by Schrimpf, Lenk, and Kanoldt. It included a detail of the left panel of the *War* triptych.

> To this eternal and inexhaustible theme of Homeland is added a new one: the War. This deepest experience of our *Volk* had not until now found a worthy artistic expression, but only banal, incidental, photojournalistic excerpts or representations distorted by hollow pathos. Otto Dix is the first, as seen in this panel from a multipanel, altar-like painting, the march towards the battle through the gun smoke, which depicts just as much the heavy tread of fate. … And so there is today once again painting that we can rejoice in, the future of which we can hope for. It has once again intelligible content, is once again popular, forming a bridge to the *Volk*. It has a beautiful, clear form and an unsoiled craft that the next generation can build on. It mirrors the ethos that lives in the new Germany, the love of Homeland and the pride in the glorious deeds of our *Volk*.[598]

Apostelschreine. Man sollte diese Gruppe ausführen, um zu zeigen, ob es nicht in unserer Zeit doch möglich ist, dem großen Krieg ein figürliches Ehrenmal zu weihen." Werner, "Herbstausstellung."

598 "Zu diesem ewigen und unerschöpflichen Thema der Heimat kommt ein neues: der Krieg. Dieses tiefste Erlebnis unseres Volkes hat bisher in der Malerei, von belanglosen, Zufälliges fotographieartig herausschneidenden oder in hohlem Pathos entstellenden Darstellungen noch keine würdige Verdichtung gefunden. Als erster hat Otto Dix in dem hier gezeigten Teils eines mehrflügeligen, altarhaften Bildes den Marsch in die Schlacht durch den Pulverqualm, gleichsam den schweren Schritt des Schicksals selbst geschildert … So gibt es heute wieder eine Malerei, deren wir froh werden können, auf deren Zukunft wir hoffen dürfen. Sie hat wieder verständliche Inhalte gefunden, die eine Brücke zum Volk schlagen und wieder volkstümlich sind.

Thus in a women's magazine published under the Nazi dictatorship – in an essay already characterized by loud declarations of glorious future for Homeland and *Volk* – it was possible to see in the left panel of the triptych a hopeful sign of the renewal of German art, but also the claim that the work was intelligible to the general public.

Like many writers who wished to represent the "truth" of the war experience, in contrast to the many "false" misrepresentations, Dix was subject to a double bind: to publicly give meaning to the war experience in 1929 or 1931, to claim the moral authority to do so, seemed to require him to represent that experience with a certain emphasis on realism, but also within a certain predetermined range of recognizable images. The realistic representation of the horrors of the war were the guarantee that he had witnessed it with his own eyes, and that he thus spoke the truth. No wonder Dix's triptych seems ambivalent. Even the leftist, republican veterans' organization the *Reichsbanner* was ambivalent, in many ways, about the core myth of the war, the "front experience" with all of its connoted values, affects, and symbolism, and about the cult of the dead which was the emotional core of the memory of the war.

Thus the painting is structured by deep internal conflicts and sets up an endless cycle of deferral of final meaning, from the horrifying image of soldiers – friends and comrades – pulped beyond form, let alone recognition, to the recuperative image of the "sleeping dead" in their tomb below (albeit actually just sleeping), to the redemptive virtues of comradeship and soldierly fortitude in the side panels, back to the undeniable truth of modern industrialized warfare, all contained within the sanctifying and overtly Germanic format of the multi-paneled altarpiece. It is not merely an ambiguous image, it is deeply ambivalent and complex, oscillating between horror and hope, while cycling through the affective states of resentment, both against the war and against Germany's enemies, then buoyed by sustaining tropes of national identity and myth.

Sie hat eine schöne, klare Form und ein sauberes Handwerk, worauf Kommende aufbauen können. Sie spiegelt das Ethos, das im jungen Deutschland lebt, die Liebe zur Heimat und den Stolz auf die Großtaten unseres Volkes." "Kunst und Volk," cited in Lothar Fischer, *Ein Malerleben*, 102 f.

CHAPTER 6

Dix in Nazi Germany and "Inner Emigration": *Flanders* and the End of the Contest over the Memory of the War

When the Nazis came to power in early 1933, they and their camp followers brought with them a long list of resentments. There was a disgust (real or feigned) for the urban modernity and demimondaine night life which Otto Dix had once depicted in his art. There was a bitter and implacable resentment of the way the war and Germany's loss of it had been represented – from the Versailles Treaty to Dix's infamous painting *The Trench*. And in some quarters there was an abhorrence of modern art as such, which was viewed as a symptom of cultural decay. Dix's paintings of that decay, which had made him notorious, were themselves viewed as a symptom, and so much the worse because he had been recognized and rewarded with an official position. Richard Müller, a former teacher and colleague of Dix at the Dresden Art Academy, wrote in the newspaper in September of 1933, "What a heavy burden of guilt is carried by those who appointed this man, of all people, as painting professor in the Art Academy."[599]

Three months after Hitler's election, Dix was summarily dismissed from his teaching post, an administrative act carried out by Müller himself, and was left to paint portraits to earn his living, to retreat to a rural setting and make landscapes, and to pursue large-scale historical and allegorical paintings in his slow and painstaking technique. Back in Dresden, Nazi arts officials hauled *The Trench* back out of storage to display it, in an exhibition of what would soon come to be called "degenerate" art, as

599 "Welch schwere Schuld haben manche Leute auf sich geladen, als sie ausgerechnet diesen Mann als Lehrer an die Kunstakademie beriefen ..." Richard Müller, "Spiegelbilder des Verfalls in der Kunst," *Dresdner Anzeiger* (23 September 1933).

an example of un-German cultural excrescence and the sabotage of the German military spirit. Extraordinarily, Dix chose at this moment to begin working on yet another large-scale depiction of the front experience, a painting which he titled *Flanders* [Flandern] (1934–1936) (see Figure 4), and which he dedicated to the French novelist of the war and leftist veterans organizer, Henri Barbusse.

It had been more than 14 years since the world war had ended, and much had changed. Dix was no longer the radical artist, eager to antagonize bourgeois sensibilities. He wasn't really a "difficult" painter any longer, although his newest painting of the war still refused to heroicize the experience in any way. German soldiers were still represented here exclusively as victims. But neither did this painting feature the frank depictions of gore and dismemberment, the pornographic wounds, of *The Trench*, or the grotesquely, comically deformed veterans of *War Cripples*, which was also on display in that early, 1933 iteration of a "degenerate art" exhibition.[600]

Something else important had changed as well, something that had to do with the context in which Dix made this last monumental war painting. A public debate had raged for the entire duration of the Weimar Republic over the meaning of the war experience and its sacrifices, and I have endeavored to show throughout this book that, at every stage and with each new artwork about the war, Dix sought to participate in, even intervene in that public debate. He had something to say about it, and claimed his authority to speak on the subject by virtue of having suffered and survived as an eye witness. Increasingly, over the decade of the 1920s, his public statements in the form of artworks were congruent with the positions taken by the Social Democratic groups of veterans – groups with which Dix shared a background and an outlook, even if he never would have paid up a membership in such a group. But by the end of the Weimar era, the debate had taken on the form of street fighting and rival demonstrations by opposing uniformed, paramilitary bands, one conservative, nationalist, anti-democratic and militaristic, now organized in

600 Olaf Peters, *Otto Dix. Der unerschrockene Blick* (Stuttgart: Reclam, 2013), 180 f.

the brown uniforms and under the swastika banners of the SA, the other socialist, supportive of the democratic republic, and anti-militaristic – also marching in uniforms, under the black, red, and gold flag of the Republic.[601] But when the National Socialists came to power, they quickly monopolized the production of meaning about the war and its memory, effectively ending the public debate. This control over the production of meaning about the war was part of their core political mission. In this context, it was in a sense an act of profound defiance for Dix to have painted *Flanders*, however mild it may have been compared to his earlier paintings, and to have dedicated it to Henri Barbusse, however ambiguous the meaning of the dedication was, and to have exhibited it in public, even if it was only exhibited in Switzerland. But the painting was a unilateral act of communication, as there was no longer a public *debate* about the meaning of the war for Dix to participate in.

Instead of a public debate about the meaning of the war and its enormous sacrifices, there was now only a dispute about modern art within the Nazi party. Dix was caught up as a pawn in this intraparty struggle. At the beginning, the question remained open whether modern artists (and the business of modern art) would be allowed to continue, or would perhaps even be promoted within a regime that, in places, embraced modernity and rejected bourgeois conventions. One knew very well that Hitler hated modern art; he frequently railed against it in his speeches, whipping up populist resentment. But would he actually trouble himself to intervene in the business of exhibitions, as the Kaiser had once done? Would the fanatical anti-modernist cultural warriors in the party, foremost among them Alfred Rosenberg, be given free rein to persecute modern artists and eliminate modern art from public venues, or would the party be too preoccupied with governing a complex modern state in precarious circumstances to pursue such pet projects? Art professionals obviously hoped it would be the latter, and not implausibly. But the activist cultural pressure groups, such as Rosenberg's *Kampfbund für deutsche Kultur* [Combat League for

601 Benjamin Ziemann, *Contested Commemorations, Republican War Veterans and Weimar Political Culture* (Cambridge: Cambridge University Press, 2012).

German Culture] also saw this as their long-awaited moment, and they were not about to let it slip away from them.

For the time being – in 1933 and 1934, the time when Dix was working on *Flanders* – things were left undecided, or were left in the hands of local officials (in Dresden and Saxony, in our case). In a regime guided by an ethos of authoritarianism, brutality, resentment, and disregard for the rule of law (though mostly punctilious about bureaucratic niceties), local officials were free or even encouraged to wield their authority arbitrarily, even while they were usually locked into rivalry with other officials in a rapidly expanding bureaucracy of overlapping and competing jurisdictions.[602] It is indicative of the chaos attending the Nazi seizure of the state apparatus that, by the time Dix began painting *Flanders*, both of the officials involved in firing him had in turn lost their own posts.

Although Dix later spoke of this time as an "inner emigration" he was in fact very actively trying to maintain his career as an artist in reduced circumstances and in a very delicate – but in his opinion and the opinion of his dealer by no means impossible – situation. And his attempt to maintain a career exhibiting his work centered on his overt adoption of recognizably Germanic forms and art historical references, including the landscape forms of the *Donauschule* [Danube School] of painters. *Flanders* overtly utilizes just these forms, even while it continued to emphasize the qualities of the front experience valorized by center-left veterans' groups. It is, therefore, a highly ambivalent painting, but one which Dix perhaps believed he could exhibit in 1936. That hope would have been dashed once and for all in the course of 1937, when his work was featured prominently in the best-known of the Degenerate Art exhibitions. *Flanders* celebrates the virtues lauded by center-left veterans but in the formal language of German artists valorized by conservative and nationalist art writers, without the gruesome and grotesque realism and aggressive emphasis on mangled bodies that continued to make his earlier representations of the war so controversial.

602 Gordon Craig, *Germany, 1866–1945* (London: Oxford University Press, 1978), 595, and Martin Broszat, *The Hitler State: The Foundation and Development of the Internal Structure of the Third Reich* (London: Longman, 1981), xiii.

The accession of the National Socialist party to power and the end of the Weimar Republic

On 30 January 1933, the aging Field Marshall Paul von Hindenburg, a faded figure from the Great War and now the ageing president of the German Republic, appointed the leader of the National Socialist German Worker's Party (NSDAP), Adolf Hitler, as Chancellor of Germany in an effort to bring that movement into the political mainstream and either dissipate or harness its energy. This was a catastrophic miscalculation. One month later the Reichstag had been disbanded and then the building set ablaze (an act for which an obscure communist agitator was blamed); Hitler had been granted emergency powers; and his circle began the process of *Gleichschaltung*, of bringing all government offices and, eventually, all areas of public and civic life into line with the ideas and goals of National Socialism.[603] From the start it had been their intention to include institutions of higher education and the arts under this ideological control, a project spearheaded by the *Kampfbund für deutsche Kultur* [the Fighting League for German Culture], an anti-modernist pressure group. By the end of March – just eight weeks after Hitler's appointment as Chancellor – the Enabling Act gave him the authority to pass laws by fiat, without either a vote from the Reichstag or respect for the constitution of 1919, and the first concentration camps for political prisoners were opened. In late September of 1933, the *Reichskulturkammer* [Reich Chamber of Culture] was organized under Propaganda Minister Joseph Goebbels, providing the Nazi party with a bureaucratic structure to manage every arts professional in Germany.

The National Socialist ascension to power was the triumph of an alliance of many different groups who had nursed their resentments against various aspects of modern culture for many years – in some cases since before the war. The *Stahlhelm* and other organizations of far-right and anti-democratic figures had always characterized the Weimar Republic

603 A concise historical overview is Richard J. Evans, *The Coming of the Third Reich* (London: A. Lane, 2003).

as illegitimate, a soulless bureaucratic "system" run by the "November Criminals" (a moniker that referred to the month of the Republic's founding). One of their most cherished myths was the "Stab-in-the-Back Legend" which held that it had been above all Jewish war profiteers and saboteurs who had deliberately lost the war while the German army had still been within striking distance of Paris. For others the cause of their resentment was cultural. While many embraced the possibilities of technological and social dynamism for an ascendant German nation, many more resented the dislocating effects of modern culture: the loosening morals; the sexual liberation of the cities, especially Berlin; and the luridness of modern entertainment, films, popular music – and of course the supposed deleterious influence of all things Jewish. Their slogans and catchphrases were many, such as "Kurfurstendamm" – the glamorous boulevard in Berlin that became a synecdoche for everything the conservatives hated about jazz-age Germany. Still others were repulsed by the modern artists who enshrined this lurid, conflict-ridden culture in their art – instead of offering as an alternative an idealized, nostalgic image of the past, either classicizing or *völkisch* and rural. The drive against modern art was led by Bettina Feistel-Rohmeder, founder of the *Deutsche Kunstgesellschaft* (German Art Society), founded in Dresden in 1920, which nurtured the *völkisch*, anti-modernist flame through the years of the Weimar Republic.[604]

The weakened social order and open sexuality of modern urban culture, an art that celebrated lurid sexuality and immorality, an image of the war that emphasized loss and death instead of bravery and heroism; Dix seemed to unify so many of the preoccupations of the revolutionary right. The *Reichskommisar* of Police for the state of Saxony, a vicious and violent Nazi by the name of Manfred Freiherr von Killinger, working together with the rector of the Dresden Art Academy, Richard Müller, utilized

604 The conflict between the dynamic and ascendant modern culture of Weimar Germany and its conservative enemies constitutes an entire academic sub-discipline with a flourishing literature. On the undercurrent of racist and *völkisch* artists who expected to have their day after the Nazi seizure of power, and especially the figure of Bettina Feistel-Rohmeder, see Joan L. Clinefelter, *Artists for the Reich. Culture and Race from Weimar to Nazi Germany* (Oxford: Berg, 2005).

the Law for the Protection of a Professional Civil Service [Gesetz zur Wiederherstellung des Berufsbeamtentums], promulgated on 7 April 1933 to dismiss Dix, despite the fact that Dix already had tenure.[605] The law had been promulgated to enable the immediate dismissal of Jews and political opponents from tenured positions in the civil service, including professors and judges, and von Killinger presumably imagined that this was just how he was using it in this instance.

Manfred von Killinger was no faceless bureaucrat. He was born of the hereditary aristocracy and raised in privileged circumstances. He had been a naval officer in the war, and after the war he was a member of a Freikorps unit and then the *Stahlhelm* as well as the *Wiking Bund*, with the goals of a military coup in Germany and the nullification of the Versailles Treaty, through renewed warfare if necessary. A high-ranking leader in the SA and the NSDAP, he was elected to the Saxony *Landtag* as leader of the NSDAP fraction, and in 1932 he went to the Reichstag as the Nazi representative for Dresden. After Hitler was named chancellor in early 1933, von Killinger was appointed *Reichskommisar* for Saxony on 10 March. The elected government of Saxony resigned soon thereafter, and von Killinger became acting governor. He only retained the office of Commissar for two months before his political rival, Martin Mutschmann, who was *Gauleiter* for the region, demoted him to the role of Minister President of Saxony.[606] But during that brief period, von Killinger found time to see to it that Otto Dix was removed from his teaching post at the Academy. Immediately upon the promulgation of the Law for the Protection of a Professional Civil Service von Killinger telephoned the rector of the Academy in Dresden, Richard Müller, and instructed him to fire Dix, who had once been one of Müller's own students. Müller, a symbolist in the vein of Max Klinger, producing highly erotic, bizarre, and often kitschy paintings and etchings, had been

605 Rainer Beck, "'Flucht ist immer falsch' – Inneres Exil als Emigration. Otto Dix im Dritten Reich" in Moshe Zuckermann, ed., *Geschichte und Bildende Kunst* (Göttingen: Wallstein, 2006), 149–178.

606 Andreas Wagner, *Mutschmann gegen von Killinger. Konfliktlinien zwischen Gauleiter und SA-Führer während des Aufstiegs der NSDAP und der „Machtergreifung" im Freistaat Sachsen* (Beucha: Sax, 2001, dissertation).

elected rector less than three weeks prior to this, by a unanimous vote of the faculty, including Dix.[607] Shortly thereafter Müller joined the Nazi party, but by January of 1935 would himself be cashiered from his post, under the same Law for the Protection of a Professional Civil Service that had been used to fire Dix. Müller dutifully carried out his instructions to fire his colleague and former student.[608] Müller wrote a note to von Killinger dated 6 April in which he informed the Commissar that he had moved to dismiss Dix, in accordance with von Killinger's wishes, but that Dix was at just that moment in Gera (presumably visiting his parents).[609] Von Killinger merely wrote in the margin, "Is that swine still alive?" This was not necessarily idle talk from a man who had in the early 1920s been a member of a Freikorps assassination squad, conspiring to murder the Minister of Finance of the Weimar Republic, Mathias Erzberger, for the "crime" of signing the Versailles Treaty, and possibly even Walther Rathenau.

Unfortunately for Dix, von Killinger had his own ideas about how to remember and commemorate the war (which for him included the years spent fighting in the Freikorps, in the Marinebrigade Erhardt, in 1919–1921), and had also made his own work of remembrance public, in the form of published memoirs. He and Dix were, in this regard, rivals of a sort. Von Killinger had written a small book of his reminiscences of combating Bolshevik revolutionaries in Munich in 1919, during the Bavarian Soviet Republic, a book reprinted shortly after he was made Commissar of Saxony. When he fired Dix he was also writing another volume of first-person narratives, this one about fighting Polish nationalists in Upper Silesia in 1921. It carried the dedication, "Den Toten Kameraden zum Gedächtnis" [To the memory of the dead comrades].[610] The Marinebrigade Erhardt also marched on Berlin during the Kapp Putsch of 1920, swastikas hastily painted on

607 The typewritten protocol of the meeting of 22 March 1933, <http://www.saxonia.com/jpg/wahl_rm_rektor_bes.jpg>.

608 Müller, "Spiegelbilder des Verfalls.

609 Reproduced in Rainer Beck, *Otto Dix 1891–1969. Zeit, Leben, Werk* (Konstanz: Stadler, 1993), 144, and on line at <http://www.saxonia.com/jpg/dix_notiz.jpg>.

610 Manfred von Killinger, *Ernste und Heiteres aus dem Putschleben*, and *Kampf um Oberschlesien 1921* (Leipzig: K. F. Koehler, 1934).

their helmets and vehicles to identify which side of the fighting they were on. When the putsch failed and the brigade was forcibly disbanded, von Killinger and many of his "comrades" formed the *Organisation Consul*, a secret group dedicated to militarism, ultra-nationalism, and political violence – in order to keep the "spirit of the front" alive within the democratic republic which they loathed. His written narratives depict life and fighting in the Wiking and the Freikorps as good fun and adventure combined with military discipline and skill in combat. But von Killinger also relishes the extreme violence as well as the contempt of – and occasional sadism towards – women. The men under his command are portrayed as having a simple nobility, decisiveness and readiness for violence, and respect for hierarchy. They are depicted as an isolated subculture, an all-male band apart, with little use for, or place in, civil society. But they are obedient to von Killinger, their commanding officer, patriotic, and race-conscious – the books are filled with an aggressive anti-Semitism. Every page reiterates the affection between the ranks, within a clear hierarchy – precisely the right-wing officer's notion of *Kameradschaft* which we encountered in the previous chapter in the discussion of the triptych *The War*.[611] Nowhere in von Killinger's texts is the German soldier portrayed as a victim in any way. When Dix protested to von Killinger over his dismissal, the *Reichskommisar* scorned his petition with the comment that Dix had been guilty of making art that, "aimed to undermine the will to fight."[612] This judgment was not simply reflexive. The two men had for more than a decade, each in his own chosen medium, professed essentially opposite conceptions of what it meant to honor the memory of the war. Von Killinger's published first-person narratives made the implicit claim that the near civil-war fought

611 Thomas Kühne, *Kameradschaft. Die Soldaten des nationalsozialistischen Krieges 20. Jahrhundert* (Göttingen: Vandenhoeck and Ruprecht, 2006); Henning Pietzsch, *Die Fronterfahrungen der deutschen Soldaten im Ersten Weltkrieg und ihre Ideologisierung zum ‚Fronterlebnis' in den zwanziger Jahren* (Stuttgart: Ibidem, 2005).

612 "... haben Sie bilder gemalt, die geignet sind, den Wehrwillen zu beinträchtigen." Typewritten letter from Reichskommisar von Killinger to Dix (15 April 1933), <http://www.saxonia.com/jpg/dix_killinger.jpg>. The correspondence is in the Germanisches National Museum archive, Nuremberg.

by the Freikorps had been a continuation of the actual war and of the all-male life of soldiers at the front. Republished in 1934, these books were meant to form a bridge between those weeks of political violence and the ascension to power of the National Socialists. There is little doubt that von Killinger dismissed Dix from his teaching post in order to punish and marginalize him because of the artist's own memorialization of the war, which was identifiably close to the social-democratic position. When Dix went on to paint *Flanders*, the figure group he placed in the center foreground was the exact opposite of von Killinger's conception of the community of German soldiers: the figures are passive, victimized, and display an altogether different conception of *Kameradschaft*. But this painting would never be shown in National Socialist Germany; von Killinger and his ilk had succeeded in monopolizing the public discussion about the memory of the war. Nonetheless, by the time both the painting and von Killinger's latest book were finished, the former Freikorps commander had already been pushed out of his own administrative post, barely surviving the purge of SA leadership with his life, and would be serving as the German Consul General in San Francisco.[613]

In late September of 1933 the anti-modernists in Dresden organized an exhibition of "degenerate" art, one of the many precursors to the famous exhibition by that name held in Munich in 1937.[614] Shown in the courtyard of the Neue Rathaus, the exhibition featured two large works by Otto Dix, both representations of the war and its effects: *The Trench* and *War*

613 Claus-Christian W. Szejnmann, *Nazism in Central Germany: The Brownshirts in 'Red' Saxony* (New York: Berghahn Books, 1999). Von Killinger was not neutered, however; he would go on to play an active role in the Holocaust in Romania. Wolfgang Benz, Brigitte Mihok, eds., *Holocaust an der Peripherie. Judenpolitik und Judenmord in Rumänien und Transnistrien 1940–1944* (Berlin: Metropol, 2009).

614 There is some disagreement about whether the Dresden exhibition held in the autumn of 1933 was titled "Entartete Kunst" [Degenerate Art] or "Spiegelbilder des Verfalls in der Kunst" [Reflections of Degeneration in Art]. Jonathan Petropoulos, *Art as Politics in the Third Reich* (Chapel Hill: University of North Carolina Press, 1996), 33; Dietrich Schubert, "Die Verfolgung des Gemäldes *Schützengraben* (1923) von Otto Dix," in Rolf Kloepfer and Burckhard Dücker, eds., *Kritik und Geschichte der Intoleranz* (Heidelberg: Syncron, 2000), 352.

Cripples (45% Employable), neither of which had been seen in public for several years by that point. The exhibition was organized by the academicians (and soon to be Nazi propaganda artists) Walther Gasch and Willy Waldapfel.[615] It is often stated in the literature that it was Müller who had organized the exhibition, but after the war, at Müller's denazification hearings, Fritz Löffler (who was working as an assistant in the Dresden City Art Collections at the time and was an eyewitness to the preparations for the exhibition) stated that Müller hadn't played any role in it.[616] But he did publish a screed in a local paper, the *Dresdner Anzeiger*, entitled "Spiegelbilder des Verfalls in der Kunst" [Reflections of the Decay in Art], which shared many of Bettina Feistel-Rohmeder's themes, and in which Müller wrote that his colleagues at the Academy had heaped shame upon themselves when they hired Dix.[617]

Meanwhile, deprived of his job and his pension, Dix entered a difficult period in his life and career. From this point forward, the artist would once again have to rely on portrait commissions to earn his living – and to maintain the bourgeois standing of his family. At the age of 41, Dix moved his family – which now included three children – to a picturesque area of southern Germany, near the shore of Lake Constance, where Martha's ex-husband and current brother-in-law Hans Koch owned a drafty sixteenth-century castle he had purchased in the early 1920s. The family lived there until 1936. In 1935, Martha's father died and the Dix family used her substantial inheritance to build a proper bourgeois villa near the village of Hemmenhofen, on the eastern end of Lake Constance and very near the Swiss border.[618] Besides a spacious and well-lit studio, the new house had all of the requisite bourgeois amenities, including a wrap-around balcony,

615 Peters, *Otto Dix*, 180 f.

616 Dietrich Schubert states that Müller was one of the organizers, *Otto Dix*, 107. Löffler's testimony can be viewed on line at <http://www.saxonia.com/loeffler/images/Vern_Dr.Loeffler.jpg>.

617 Richard Müller, "Spiegelbilder des Verfalls in der Kunst," *Dresdner Anzeiger* (23 September 1933), cited in Olaf Peters, *Otto Dix*, 182, and in Schubert, "Die Verfolgung," 361.

618 Bernd Erhard Fischer, *Otto Dix in Hemmenhofen* (Berlin: Edition A B Fischer, 2010), 12.

an elegant staircase, and a grand piano for Martha to play. They would continue to live in the house the rest of their lives, although Dix maintained a private studio in Dresden even into the postwar period (after the war he would split his time between East and West Germany). And so, despite his considerable professional difficulties, including loss of teaching post and the public defamation of his work, and the dramatic political situation in general, Otto Dix also achieved his class ambitions. At the same time, he reestablished his relationship with Karl Nierendorf, after having ended their business partnership some years before. He would need a loyal friend and energetic advocate like Nierendorf to help him navigate the cultural bureaucracy of the National Socialist state cultural apparatus, and to help him make a living exclusively from the sale of his art again.[619]

Dix's reputation and professional standing after 1933

This is the period which was later called his "inner emigration," although it is clear that Dix never gave up his efforts to exhibit and sell his work, and that he acquired, with considerable help from friends, the certifications from the Nazi cultural bureaucracy required to maintain his professional status as a painter. His sustained efforts at exhibiting his landscape paintings, both in Germany and internationally, suggests a conscious effort to reach some accommodation with the new political reality and the cultural expectations of the new regime. Dix was hardly unique in this, as Jonathan Petropoulos has shown in his most recent study of modernist artists in the Third Reich.[620] In the previous chapter, we saw that, already in 1933, Dix's monumental, multi-panel painting of the war experience could be recommended by some National Socialist-aligned critics as a representation fit for the public within a conception of Homeland and *Volk* (what was and

619 Letter from Nierendorf to Dix (8 May 1933). Galerie Nierendorf archive.

620 Jonathan Petropoulos, *Artists Under Hitler. Collaboration and Survival in Nazi Germany* (New Haven, CT: Yale University Press), 2014.

was not acceptable was notoriously unclear at this stage) – and that its high level of craft and representational clarity could also serve as a model for future artists. Not every official voice rejected his previous work.

Dix was no longer producing and exhibiting such difficult work as he had in the past. His most biting social commentaries were already several years behind him. The side panels of the *Metropolis* triptych, with its disabled veterans and aggressive, derelict whores, or the three grotesque "graces" of 1928 were six years in the past – six years that Dix had spent perfecting his old master's technique and teaching it to students. But more than that, it was twice as long since he had built his reputation as a provocative artist of grim urban realism, wickedly caricatured portraits, and lewd sex and murder scenes. His portraits, which were very much in demand and from which he primarily earned his living with the brush, were now relatively tame. Dix himself was generally worried that he had lost the trenchant quality that was the strength and individuality of his art, and his touchiness on this subject led to another sharp conflict between him and Nierendorf. Dix complained bitterly that Nierendorf had said to others that Dix's work was no longer difficult enough. Nierendorf defended himself by saying that he, Nierendorf, always came to the defense of Dix when others said his work was no longer as intense as it had been. Even so, Nierendorf had to admit that Dix's "neoclassical" paintings and his "Renaissance quotations" were not really his thing.[621]

It was not the case that Dix was officially forbidden from exhibiting his work, as has often been repeated in the literature, although it became

621 Letter from Nierendorf to Dix (21 October 1933), Galerie Nierendorf. "Dass unser Gespräch bei Lenk solche Schärfe bekam, war wirklich äusserst unangenehm. […] Niemals kann ich gesagt haben, Du seist nicht 'wüst' genug. Ich finde viele Deiner sogenannten 'klassizistischen' Bilder hervorragend, nur sind nicht alle so …… eindringlich wie andere. Dass aber kein Mensch von einem Künstler immer die gleiche Intensität verlangen kann, habe ich tausendmal betont, wenn an Dir herumgetadelt wurde. […] Ich weiss genau, dass gewisse Renaissance-Zutaten (die Du gar nicht nötig hast) den künstlerischen Charakter Deiner Bilder nicht wesentlich mindern, wenn sie auch mir nicht liegen. Trotzdem ist die innere Kraft Deiner Gestaltung unmittelbar und von keinem anderen deutschen Maler erreicht. Und auf die eigentliche Potenz und den Grad der geistigen Realisierung allein kommt ja alles an.

increasingly difficult for him to do so after about 1936.[622] In order to pursue professional activities as a painter, it was necessary for him to join the newly organized Reich Chamber of Culture, as membership in this newly created professional organization had been made a precondition for artists, writers, actors, architects, and musicians to pursuing professional activities – such as publicly exhibiting artwork or accepting architecture and design commissions – in the new Germany. The creation of this Chamber, which was headed by a convinced Nazi, was one of the ways in which the National Socialists sought to establish ideological control over the culture. Jewish cultural professionals were shut out of the Chamber, although for a time they had their own parallel organization which allowed them to pursue their careers within segregated venues.[623] This effectively made them into second-class citizens, which was unprecedented in the more than 60-year history of the unified German state. But the Chamber quickly became an arena in which competing figures jockeyed for professional advantage because different bureaucratic bodies had overlapping jurisdictions. Thus, the Reich Chamber of Culture provided the opportunity for ideological *control*, but tended not to provide ideological *clarity*.

We know that attitudes about modernism and modern art within the Nazi Party were not monolithic in 1933, but were split into two camps by the rivalry between two influential and energetic figures, Joseph Goebbels and Alfred Rosenberg.[624] If Rosenberg hated modernism as un-German and alien, racially inferior, then Goebbels was among those – and there were many – who thought that Expressionism in particular expressed an essentially "Nordic" spirit (an idea that did not originate with National

---

Dass Du nicht grösseren Erfolg hast, liegt allein daran, dass die Menschen nicht die Kraft aufbringen, die Deinen Arbeiten gegenüber erforderlich ist. Da versagen viele, die angeblich 'Kunstverständnis' haben, vor allem Kunsthistoriker."

622 According to Olaf Peters, the "legend" that Dix was forbidden from exhibiting originated with Löffler, who certainly knew better. *Neue Sachlichkeit und Nationalsozialismus. Affirmation und Kritik 1931–1947* (Berlin: Reimer, 1998), 126 ff.

623 Alan E. Steinweis, *Art, Ideology, and Economics in Nazi Germany. The Reich Chambers of Music, Theater, and the Visual Arts* (Chapel Hill: The University of North Carolina Press, 1993), 120–121.

624 Petropoulos, *Art as Politics*, 19–50.

Socialism). Rosenberg by contrast embraced a *völkish* (populist, anti-elitist, nationalist and racist) view of culture, and had built an influential cultural infrastructure – the Fighting League for German Culture. But he had no bureaucratic authority in the new state, at least not in 1933. Goebbels by contrast wielded significant but as yet poorly defined bureaucratic power, but turned out to be ready to set his own preferences aside in deference to the provincial tastes and resentments of his Führer, with a view to furthering his own career and boundless professional ambition. Goebbels was personally sympathetic to modern artists, but was not a staunch ally, looking only to advance himself. Rosenberg on the other hand was an implacable enemy of modern art. As Rosenberg gained real political power, Goebbels outmaneuvered him, and maintained his closer proximity to Hitler, by adopting Rosenberg's own anti-modernist posture.[625] Like many other high-ranking Nazi officials, many of whom came from an educated and cosmopolitan milieu in which modern art, French as well as German, had come to be widely if not universally accepted over the course of the previous three decades, Goebbels continued to admire and even collect art with mild modernist tendencies (he owned and privately displayed works by Emil Nolde, Ernst Barlach, and even Käthe Kollwitz). But he made the shrewd – if deeply cynical – career move of giving his full-throated support to the *völkish* position and the populist politics of anti-modernist resentment which had raised Hitler up.

In this fluid situation – before the Nazi party had fully radicalized itself – a modernist artist like Dix might hope to continue a public artistic career. Many who ended by emigrating began by joining the newly created Reich Chamber of Culture. For some, such as Walter Gropius and Mies van der Rohe as well as visual artists such as Oskar Schlemmer, Max Pechstein, Erich Heckel, and Karl Schmidt-Rottluff or Ernst Barlach, enrolling in the new Reich Chamber of Culture may have simply seemed like a new layer of bureaucracy regulating their professional standing; it was not yet clear that Hitler's personal tastes – however aggressively professed – would become state policy.

625 This is a well-known history. Jonathan Petropoulos has most recently emphasized the extent to which some among the Nazi elite supported modern art, music, and even architecture, at least during these early years. Petropoulos, *Artists Under Hitler*.

Most artists probably hoped that cultural life in Germany would soon enough return to normal. In the event, just four years later – in 1937 – the modernists would be forced out of the Chamber, and the Jewish cultural organization would be dissolved by Goebbels. As of 1933, Dix applied for acceptance into the Chamber; he was eventually accepted; Max Beckmann never was, and Käthe Kollwitz was expelled for her criticism of the regime within the year.

In the summer of 1933 Nierendorf put on an exhibition of German modernists in his Berlin gallery, including Nolde, Rottluf, Heckel, Christian Rohlfs, Paul Klee, Lyonel Feininger, Oskar Schlemmer, Georg Schrimpf, and Franz Lenk – as well as Dix. Nierendorf wrote Dix that the exhibition had been well received, especially his portrait of the actor Heinrich George (1932).[626] Nierendorf wanted to put on a one-person show of Dix, but needed to convince the people at the *preußisches Kultusministerium* [Prussian Cultural Ministry]. He worked tirelessly in the halls of power of the new Reich, speaking with, among others, Hans Werner von Oppen, the Prussian Culture Ministry's liaison for museums – a staunch supporter of German avant-garde art, so long as it was identifiably "Nordic."[627] Nierendorf – ever optimistic in his letters to Dix – assured him that he would soon be "rehabilitated."[628] He brought with him on these excursions publications on Dix and reproductions of his work, being careful not to show the "crass" and "disruptive" [*zersetzenden*] pictures. "The prejudice against you is still enormous," he wrote, "but I'm certain that we'll be able to put on an exhibition soon."[629] Nierendorf was also showing Dix's work to

626 Letter from Nierendorf to Dix, 7 August 1933, Galerie Nierendorf. The artists for the exhibition were listed in a letter to Dix from 8 May 1933.

627 Timo Saalmann, *Kunstpolitik der Berliner Museen 1919–1959* (Berlin: de Gruyter, 2013), 170.

628 "Vorige Woche habe ich im Preussischen Kultus-Ministerium wieder einmal Deinen 'Fall' zur Sprache gebracht und bei dem Referenten, Dr. von Oppen gutes Verständnis für Dich gefunden. Ich bin überzeugt, dass die Rehabilitierung bald kommen wird, das ist eine Frage der Zeit." Letter from Nierendorf to Dix, 26 February 1934, Galerie Nierendorf.

629 "Das Vorurteil gegen Dich ist noch immer gross, aber ich bin fest überzeugt davon, dass wir bald eine Ausstellung veranstalten können." Letter from Nierendorf to Dix, 26 February 1934, Galerie Nierendorf.

the new director of the National Gallery in Berlin, Eberhard Hanfstaengel, who expressed interest in collecting drawings Dix was making in Randegg.[630] Eventually Nierendorf succeeded in getting Dix his membership in the *Reichskammer der Bildenden Künste* of the *Reichskulturkammer* [Reich Chamber for the Visual Arts], dated 1 January 1934.

But in the end the exhibition would not be of Dix's work alone, doubtless because that would have been too risky politically. Instead, Nierendorf suggested an exhibition of the landscapes that Dix and Franz Lenk made side-by-side in the hills around Randegg. Franz Lenk, who had always practiced a precisely observational painting using, much like Dix, traditional materials and methods (but without the touches of irony or caricature), had himself become a functionary in the Nazi cultural bureaucracy, and was a member of the Presidium of the Reich Chamber of Culture.[631] Dix and Lenk painted together throughout 1934, and the fruits of their labors were exhibited by Nierendorf in his Berlin gallery in January of 1935, despite the fact that Nierendorf was hospitalized for several months after a bad heart attack. In keeping with Nierendorf's policy of emphasizing German art, the exhibition was titled "Two German Painters." The landscape paintings that Dix was making in the hills around Randegg strongly recalled the sixteenth-century painters of the *Donauschule* [Danube School] and to some extent German Romantics like Caspar David Friedrich and Philip Otto Runge. Many of Dix's paintings of the villages around Randegg and, later, Hemenhoffen, resemble those of Flemish painters such as Joachim Patinir (1480–1524) and Lucas van Valckenborch (1535–1597, who was also associated with the Danube School). Besides the old-master techniques, materials and surfaces – to which he now added the challenging medium of silverpoint – Dix also pursued his interest in art historical motifs and compositional devices borrowed from his "Germanic" forebears. While he had already been pursuing his interest in these qualities before the Nazi seizure of power, it certainly made it easier for Nierendorf to enable him to continue his public career, in however limited a fashion. Efforts on the

630 Letters from Nierendorf to Dix, 26 February 1934, and 19 September 1934, Galerie Nierendorf.

631 Olaf Peters, *Neue Sachlichkeit und Nationalsozialismus*, 131 ff.

part of art historians to see a veiled objection to the Nazi persecution of the Jews in his painting of the *Jewish Cemetery in Randegg* (1935) is probably wishful thinking.[632] Dix often painted landscapes in the region in the winter in these years, and the motif of a cemetery in the snow fit well with his interest in motifs reminiscent of Caspar David Friedrich and the German Romantics generally, as well as earlier, "Germanic" artists, such as Valckenborch.[633] One of the compositional devices which Dix borrowed from his forebears, the so-called *Weltlandschaft*, or "world landscape," would feature prominently in *Flanders*.

Exhibiting Dix together with Lenk would have reminded viewers that Dix had a friendship and working relationship with another artist who had standing in the ranks of the new bureaucracy. Nierendorf and Dix were clearly making a calculated attempt to, as the canny businessman said, "rehabilitate" Dix, much as he had once utilized the antiwar movement to exhibit and promote Dix's representations of the war.[634] The painting that most emblematically displayed this new side of Dix was his self-portrait with his older son Ursus standing close in front of him and his younger son Jan riding on his shoulders, *Self-Portrait With Jan and Ursus*.[635] The painting combines his role as father with his newfound devotion to the

632 The claim that this landscape was intended as a veiled criticism of the regime remains something of a truism in the literature on Dix, but was disputed already by Birgit Schwarz, *Werke von Otto Dix* (Karlsruhe: Saatliche Kunsthalle Karlsruhe, 1986), 16. The most thorough argument in favor of this interpretation can be found in Peters, *Neue Sachlichkeit und Nationalsozialismus*, 135–144.

633 Dix painted a picture of Hemmenhofen in Winter in 1940 which strongly resembles Valckenborch's *Massacre of the Innocents* (1586), not only in terms of the arrangement of the town and the perspective construction, or in the motif of a village of pitched and step-gabled roofs under a heavy blanket of snow, but also in the handling of the low winter sky and the bare, gnarled, snowy branches of trees. Reproduced in Christoph Bauer, ed., *Otto Dix. Werke von 1933 bis 1969* (Cologne: Wienand, 2003), 42. What Dix leaves out, significantly, is the violent action that served Valckenborch as a pretext for his winter landscape.

634 Olaf Peters, *Otto Dix*, 188.

635 Destroyed, reproduced in Diether Schmidt, *Otto Dix im Selbstbildnis* (East Berlin: Henschel, 1981), 133.

German landscape and his longstanding fealty to German old masters, and it attracted a good deal of the critics' attention.

Nierendorf, as always, reported to Dix that the show was received with great enthusiasm.[636] The Ministerial Director of the Art Section of the *Reichserziehungsministerium* [Reich Ministry of Science, Education, and Culture], Wolfgang von Staa, another arts functionary who supported modern art, even visited Nierendorf in his gallery to praise the exhibition, but did not think the time was right to purchase a work by Dix with public money for a museum.[637] Meanwhile, Nierendorf kept up his lobbying campaign on Dix's behalf in the Prussian Culture Ministry, showing photos of Dix's latest work to von Oppen again, who he hoped would then show them to the Prussian Cultural Minister, Bernhard Rust.[638] There were some art journals between 1933 and 1935 with critical positions that imagined a place for modern art in the new, nationalist state, journals like *Zukunft* and *Kunst der Nation*. Critics writing in these publications consistently praised Dix's work for its references to the Danube School, Altdorfer, Baldung Grien, and Cranach.[639] Fritz Hellwag, for example, writing in *Die Kunst*, compared the *Self-Portrait With Jan and Ursus* to Philip Otto Runge. Such critics were prepared to abet Dix's rehabilitation. This was also thanks in part to Nierendorf's efforts, meeting with art critics one by one to explain the sense of the work to them.[640] Hellwag wrote in *Die Kunst*,

> It was before now difficult to imagine the painter Otto Dix face-to-face with the grand tranquility of nature, he who struggled in wild fury with those problems that spilled forth out of the chaos of the all-too-human, problems which nearly threatened

636 Letter from Nierendorf to Dix, 2 February 1935, Galerie Nierendorf.

637 Letter from Nierendorf to Dix, 18 February 1935, Galerie Nierendorf. On von Staa, Saalmann, *Kunstpolitik der Berliner Museen*, 170.

638 Letter from Nierendorf to Dix, 16 February 1935, Galerie Nierendorf. It is hard to imagine that Rust – who was also *Reichserziehungsminister*, would have had much sympathy; a cultural reactionary (and *Stahlhelm* member), his cultural outlook was very much opposed to that of von Oppen and von Staa.

639 Paul Fechter, *Deutsche Zukunft* (10 February 1935), 15, and F. Paul (pseudonym for Paul Ferdinand Schmidt), *Kunst der Nation*, n. d., n. p.

640 Letter of 30 January 1935, Galerie Nierendorf archive.

> to overwhelm him. It wasn't he who was responsible for such difficulties, but rather the times in which he was forced to live …[641]

Unfortunately for Dix, there were much more hostile critical voices as well, who viewed these formal and marketing strategies as sheer bad faith. The anonymous art critic writing in the official newspaper of the SS, *Das Schwarze Korps*, suggested mockingly that, having been "healed," Dix would soon no doubt be declared "*the most important painter in the era of National Socialism*. And why not?"[642] In keeping with an apparent editorial policy of denouncing with extreme hostility just such attempts to rehabilitate modern artists in the Nazi state, the nameless SS writer attacked the sympathetic critic, Fritz Hellwag, as much as he attacked Dix.[643] This was but one skirmish in a battle over the direction which art was to take in National Socialist Germany. Hellwag spoke for those who, like Goebbels, Emil Nolde, and Otto Andreas Schreiber (director of *Kunst der Nation*), were convinced that German modernist art was the authentic expression of a "Nordic" cultural spirit. He also was typical of those arts professionals who naively hoped that the initial surge of combative cultural resentment coming from Rosenberg and the Fighting League for German Culture would soon subside, and that they would be able to continue with business as usual: museum directors, cultural officials like von Oppen and von Staa, and of course art dealers like Nierendorf.

641 "Es war bisher schwer, sich den Maler Otto Dix vor der großen stillen Natur zu denken, ihn, der unter heftigsten Temperamentsausbrüchen mit Problemen gerungen hat, die aus dem Chaos des Allzumenschlichen herausquollen und ihn fast zu überwältigen drohten. Nicht er ist für dies Problematische verantwortlich gewesen, sondern die Zeit, in der er zu leben gezwungen war …" Fritz Helllwag, "Otto Dix. Bilder aus dem Hegau," *Die Kunst* 71 (1934–1935), 272, cited in Christoph Bauer, "Das altmeisterliche und spätexpressionistische Werk von Otto Dix," in Bauer, ed., *Otto Dix*, 11.

642 "… es wird sicher nicht mehr lange dauern, dann werden wir von dienstfertigen Kritikern hören, dass Otto Dix *der bedeutendste Maler im Zeite des Nationalsozialismus* ist. Warum auch nicht?" Emphasis in the original. *Das Schwarze Korps* (26 June 1935), n. p.

643 Christian Saehrendt, *„Die Brücke" zwischen Staatskunst und Verfemung: expressionistische Kunst als Politikum in der Weimarer Republik, im „Dritten Reich" und im Kalten Krieg* (Stuttgart: Franz Steiner, 2005), 71.

The editorial staff of the SS newspaper was by contrast on the side of the ideologues of who had brought their anti-modernist cultural resentment and implacable hatred of Weimar, the so-called "Era of the System," with them into power. The anti-modernists soon prevailed, not least because Goebbels decided to abandon the modernists and outflank his bureaucratic rival Rosenberg by swinging to the antimodernist side. *Kunst der Nation* was shut down, and artists closely associated with German modernism like Otto Dix found it increasingly difficult to exhibit their work. Nonetheless, Dix continued to show work in various exhibitions, including one in the Cologne Kunstverein in 1940.[644] As late as 1944 he had work in the annual exhibition of the Kunsthalle in his home town of Gera.

The anonymous SS art critic made no bones about the nature of the objection to Dix. Not only was he a "cultural Bolshevik" and a painter from the "Kurfürstendamm," he was an "antiwar painter," who "mocked the German front soldier and the German victims of the war."[645] Alongside the self-portrait with his sons, which was representative of the artist's supposed "rehabilitation," the *Schwarze Korps* printed a detail of *War Cripples (45% Employable)*, which was presented here as the "authentic" – which is to say, antisocial Dix. Although the enormous collage was at that point 15 years old, it was currently being exhibited as part of the traveling exhibition of "Degenerate" art, along with, of course, *The Trench*. This was an oversimplification of the actual meaning of these works in their original context – as I have been arguing all along. But this oversimplification fit the editors' purposes of combining cultural resentment against the Weimar era and a specifically irredentist celebration of the myth of the German front soldier. It was part of a regular drum beat of willfully one-sided interpretations of Dix's large-scale paintings of the war: that it constituted *Wehrsabotage* [sabotage of the military spirit], and that it aimed to discredit the front experience and nullify the sacrifices made in the war. To a great extent it is because of this co-ordinated campaign of slander that these particular works were understood after the Second World War as simply antiwar

644 See Peters, *Neue Sachlichkeit und Nationalsozialismus*, p. 125.

645 "... er malte *Antikriegsbilder* und verhöhnte den deutschen Frontsoldaten, die deutschen Kriegsopfer ... ." *Das Schwarze Korps* (26 June 1935), n. p.

and even antifascist works, which in turn strengthened Dix's reputation in both East and West Germany.

The attack had its intended results. While the director of the museum in Danzig purchased a painting from the joint Dix and Lenk exhibition, *Pine and Acacia Trees* [Fichte und Akazie], and planned to include it in an exhibition to open in May, the exhibition itself was cancelled due to pressure from the N. S. Kulturgemeinde in Berlin, with particular reference to the "cultural Bolshevism" of Dix.[646] And although Nierendorf originally hoped to have a second exhibition of Lenk and Dix together after the relative success of their first exhibition, by August of 1935 Lenk no longer felt that he could be associated with Dix in the public sphere. Nierendorf was left to reassure Dix that he would continue to show his work in his gallery.[647]

It is in the context of this campaign of defamation, focused above all on *The Trench*, that Dix went to work on another larger-scale painting of the war experience. Once again, the public dialog around *The Trench* was an impetus for Dix to start working on another monumental representation of the front experience, but this time, one that drew on his increasing preoccupation with landscape painting. There can be little doubt, given the size of the work, that this was once again intended for public exhibition. He worked on this painting in his studio in Dresden, where he also worked on other large paintings like *Triumph of Death* and *The Seven Deadly Sins*. Dix had made enough progress on it by March 1934 that Nierendorf wrote, after visiting Dix in Dresden, "Also the new war picture, in its simple grandeur makes such a powerful impression, that one won't forget it."[648] But Dix could only work on these projects intermittently, when he was in Dresden. The work on *Flanders* was interrupted – by portrait work, a mural project in Chemnitz, and by life in Randegg with three young children, landscape painting, and again taking up pastimes proper to a bourgeois gentleman,

646 Letters from Nierendorf to Dix, 30 January and 31 May 1935, Galerie Nierendorf.

647 Letter of 3 August 1935, Galerie Nierendorf archive. Nierendorf wrote that Lenk had called him on the phone to tell him he couldn't be in any more shows with Dix.

648 "Auch das neue Kriegsbild in seiner einfachen Grösse wirkt schon jetzt so mächtig, dass man es nicht vergisst." Letter from Nierendorf to Dix, 26 March 1934, Galerie Nierendorf.

like learning to hunt. By early 1936 he had already suspended work on it long enough that, on his return to his studio in Dresden, he wrote to Martha that he was "returning to work on the large war picture which I've started."[649]

Flanders

In a shattered and flooded landscape a group of German soldiers barely emerges from the mud, or perhaps they are subsiding into it. They are silent, monumental, silhouetted against a cloud-clotted sky lit by both flaming sun and phosphorescent moon. The landscape has been destroyed by a bombardment that must have lasted days, and no assault can cross the flooded and cratered no-man's-land. The soldiers don't seem to be dead, only resting, huddling against one another.[650] The overwhelming impression of the painting is one of exhaustion. The soldiers are exhausted; the ground is exhausted; the war is exhausted. In contrast to the earlier triptych *The War*, the present composition lacks any display of martial virtues; It also lacks the emphasis on gore and innards that *The War* had carried over from *The Trench* of 1924. What is left is exhaustion, and a certain formlessness as figures sink into and become one with the shapeless, sodden earth. In contrast to the earlier works there are no split-open skulls or disemboweled figures; there may be blood soaking into the already-saturated ground, but no decaying bodies seething with worms. One bloated body floats face up in the water in the middle distance (and closer inspection reveals a couple more corpses in the distance), but compared to earlier works, this one is relatively restrained. Given the emphasis Dix had earlier placed on the awful

649 Letter from Otto Dix to Martha, written before 11 March 1936, *Otto Dix, Briefe*, 126. In other letters from the same year Dix mentions hunting pheasant, hares, and deer with patron, *Otto Dix, Briefe*, 126 and 135.

650 Dieter Honisch, *Bilder vom Menschen in der Kunst des Abendlandes* (Berlin: Mann, 1980), 362, and Otto Karl Werckmeister, "Radical Art History" *Art Journal* 42/4 (Winter 1982), 284–291, here 287.

details of mutilation and decomposition, and the attention paid to that emphasis by the critics, this new understatement is of central importance.

The painting is split between a dark lower half rendered almost exclusively in umber and sienna, and an upper half dominated by a dramatic sky filled with complicated, intricately structured cirrus clouds mingling with the smoke rising from the vast battlefield. The deep blue of the sky on the right, where the full moon is setting, contrasts in a kind of cosmic battle with the flaming red on the left where the sky is set on fire by the rising sun (even the moon itself is, impossibly, tinted red). A realm of mud, slime, and war below, and in the heavens above a struggle between sun and moon, suggesting, presumably, the storm of steel as well as the actual weather, or even life and death, terror and hope, beneath all of which the simple front soldier is helplessly exposed. The foreground consists entirely of the three figures huddled together, the central one with a dully glinting steel helmet which forms the center of the composition, while the other two cower against him, seeking some comfort from the wet and the cold and, of course, the trauma of the artillery barrage which, though now silent, has left these men emotionally and psychically shattered. The men do not so much sink into the mud as become one with it. Between the foreground and the horizon is a distant background – there is no real middle ground – which begins in the distance and stretches seemingly to infinity, a vast destroyed and watery landscape of flooded shell holes and trenches, and in the far, far distance tiny silhouettes of destroyed towns, wooded copses turned to a stubble of tree stumps, and a burning town adding its plume of smoke to the complicated and fantastic meteorological phenomena above. All of the requisite iconography of the world war is here in the background, in miniature: the barbed wire and the ruins; the shattered tree stumps and the bloated corpses. Slowly, with patient looking, increasing numbers of shell-shocked German soldiers appear, cowering beneath tarps at the edge of the water, like terrified animals sheltering in the banks of some primordial river. They have been driven from their trenches and craters by the rising flood waters. The dramatic spectacle in the sky, with sun and moon and their gathered clouds opposed like two armies, is of course an overt reference to the most famous work of the German Renaissance painter Albrecht Altdorfer, *The Battle of Alexander*, of 1529 (Munich, Pinakothek).

Altdorfer, too, paints a vast panorama of a landscape of mountains and sea that stretches seemingly to the very ends of the Earth. The difference is that Altdorfer actually depicts the innumerable hosts of his armies in boggling miniature detail.

The composition of *Flanders*, which at first blush seems to be a formless chaos, is actually a tightly organized depiction of diluvial pools and inlets. The unbroken silhouette of the three foreground figures culminates in the clearly modeled dome of the iconic steel helmet, and the charred tree stump wreathed in barbed wire rises up behind this shape to break the horizon line at the center – just where the smoke of the distant burning town billows up to join the clouds in the sky. These clouds in turn arc and point towards the center of the painting, drawing our attention insistently back to this central knot of symbols: *Stahlhelm*; barbed wire; tree stump, the relics of the martyrdom of the front soldier, like a Great War *Man of Sorrows*.[651] Everything in the painting is wrenched towards this center. The simultaneous appearance of the sun and moon, flanking this mound with a body at the foot of a tree, calls to mind the scene at Golgotha, when the midday sky darkened while Christ hung on the cross (a very old iconographic tradition also features sun and moon flanking the cross). Behind this compositional center the stagnant water in the middle ground wends its way, reflecting the brighter colors of the sky and tightly knitting the top and bottom halves of the picture plane together. Everywhere the sodden shreds of cloth (tarps? uniforms?) hang down like moss from shattered branches and poles, heightening the effect of wet, mud, decay, and return to the earth. The shaggy effect of these hanging, dripping tatters is a very particular device borrowed from the Danube School painters, in particular Altdorfer, Cranach, and especially Wolf Huber.

On the plain in Flanders that stretches from a ridge line running between the towns of Wijtschate and Passchendaele to the Atlantic coast

651 Britta Schmitz also sees here a reference to Golgotha, as well as to the theological implications of the Biblical Flood narrative, namely man's loss of control over and even refuge in God's creation. Britta Schmitz, "Otto Dix' 'Flandern' 1934–1936," in Wulf Herzogenrath and Johann-Karl Schmidt, eds., Wulf Herzogenrath and Johann-Karl Schmidt, eds., *Otto Dix – zum 100. Geburtstag* (Stuttgart: Hatje-Cantz, 1991), 268–271.

the ground is low and the water table close to the surface, drained by a vast and intricate system of canals, channels, and ditches in order to make the country arable. But the intensive shelling of the region, including the city of Ypres, had destroyed this intricate system of drainage, and as a result the frequently heavy rains flooded the entire battlefield.[652] The artillery barrages – some of the heaviest in the war – reduced the landscape and the trench system to little more than a field of craters. It was another long, grim battle of attrition that dragged on for years in the most horrid conditions of flooded trenches and mud. In the years after the war, the image of soldiers in both British and German uniforms picking their way between flooded shell holes, scuttling along on duckboards trying not to slip and fall into the morass – which meant death by drowning in the mud – and sheltering in the flooded craters, became the fixed iconography of Flanders. The paintings of the official British war artists Paul Nash (*The Menin Road*, 1918) and C. R. W. Nevinson (*The Harvest of Battle*, 1919) incorporated this iconography into their monumental depictions of the theater. During the war Dix himself had painted the flooded trenches – with soldiers drowning in them, in *Flooded Barbed Wire* [Überflutetes Drahtverhau] in 1917 (see Figure 26). Looking at Dix's sky, lit up like fire above the watery landscape, it's impossible not to mention a passage from *The Great War and Modern Memory*, Paul Fussel's classic study of the death of a sincere Georgian diction, and the birth of an ironic modernist one, from the trenches of the war. "If Flanders was flat and wet, it had the distinction of offering terrain and weather productive of superb dawns and dusks."[653] Fussel goes on to quote from Hugh Quigley's diary of Passchendaele, published in 1928, "Its flatness gathers up everything to the world overhead and adds a great depth and shimmering distance to the gold, rose, and green, touching them finely to a delicate gleam."[654] Fussel's point is that such painterly and elevated language, rich in pastoral tradition, could no longer be sustained after the

652 John Keegan, *The First World War* (New York: Vintage, 2000), 358.

653 Paul Fussel, *The Great War and Modern Memory* (New York: Oxford University Press, 1975), 56.

654 Hugh Quigley, *Paschendaele and the Somme. A Diary of 1917*, 1928, 87–88, cited in *Fussel, The Great War*, 56.

war. That may have been the case for English poetry, but Dix certainly returned to the pastoral, touched with rose and gold, in the early 1930s as he explored the landscape of the northern bank of Lake Constance, and he drew on it when he returned to the subject of Flanders.

World painting

Flanders is dedicated to the French novelist Henri Barbusse, who wrote his novel *Under Fire* while the war was still raging, a novel Dix admired greatly.[655] This has suggested to art historians a comparison with the following passage from *Under Fire*, which comes near the very end of the book:

> We waited for daylight at the place where we had stopped and slumped to the ground. It came little by little, icy, dark, and sinister, spreading over the livid expanse.
>
> The rain stopped. There was none left in the sky. The leaden plain, with its tarnished mirrors of water, seems to be emerging not only from night, but from the sea.
>
> Half drowsing, half asleep, sometimes opening our eyes only to shut them again, paralysed, exhausted and cold, we experience the incredible renewal of light.
>
> Where are the trenches?
>
> We can see lakes and between them lines of stagnant, milky water.
>
> There is even more water than we thought. The water has got everywhere, spreading all around, and the prediction of the men last night has been realized: there are no trenches – the trenches are under those canals. The world is flooded. The battlefield is not asleep, it is dead. Somewhere over there life may go on, but we cannot see that far.
>
> I half get up, painfully, swaying like an invalid, to look around. My coat weighs me down with its dreadful burden. Beside me are three monstrously shapeless forms. One of them – Paradis [a member of the narrator's squad, MM], under an extraordinary

655 Löffler, *Otto Dix und Der Krieg*, 39.

> crust of mud, with a swelling around his waist in place of his cartridge belt – also rises. The others are asleep and motionless.
>
> And then what is this silence? It is prodigious. There is no noise, except from time to time the falling of a sod of earth into the water, in the midst of this fantastic paralysis of the world. No one is shooting: no shells, because they would not explode; no bullets, because the men …
>
> The men! Where are the men?
>
> Bit by bit we start to see them. There are some not far from us, spread out, asleep, caked in mud from head to foot, changed almost into things.
>
> Some distance away I can make out others, curled up and stuck like snails along a rounded embankment half covered in water – a motionless line of crude shapes, parcels next to one another, dripping with mud and water, the color of the earth that surrounds them.[656]

Not only does the painting *Flanders* follow this text closely, but even the carefully achieved effect of revealing only gradually to the attentive viewer the presence of living men sheltering in the embankments along the water's edge corresponds to it. So does the relative quiet, incongruous as it is in relation to the catastrophic destruction of battle which is everywhere in evidence, and the obvious exhaustion of the soldiers. Dix was – as I have noted previously – unsurpassed in his depiction of a soldier's exhaustion. Yet the most important passage of this text, from a pictorial point of view, is perhaps the sentence, "The *world* is flooded." Because Dix has here combined the notorious flooding of the battlefield in Flanders with the device of the *Weltlandschaft* [world landscape] in the paintings of artists such as Joachim Patinir and others of the Danube School. The central feature of

656 Henri Barbusse, *Under Fire*, Chapter 24, "The Dawn" (London: Penguin, 2003, Robin Buss, translator), 296–297. Original *Le Feu*, 1916. This passage has been presented as the reference point for Dix's painting often, including Löffler, *Otto Dix und der Krieg*, 39, and *Otto Dix*, 97, Britta Schmitz, "Otto Dix 'Flandern' 1934–1936," in Herzogenrath and Schmidt, eds., *Otto Dix – Zum 100. Geburtstag*, 268–271, and Jorg Martin Merz, "Otto Dix' Kriegsbilder. Motivationen – Intentionen – Rezeptionen," *Marburger Jahrbuch für Kunstwissenschaft* 26 (1999), 189–226, here 214.

this device is a landscape seen from a high vantage point that stretches out to the edges of the Earth, affording the viewer a glimpse of distant rivers, lakes, forests and mountain ranges, painted in exacting and miniscule detail; not just a landscape, but seemingly all possible landscapes, as though all of creation could be encompassed and examined with the scene. Extensive waterways typically unify both the spatial and the color composition. Barbusse himself imitates this effect in his text at the very beginning of the novel, in a kind of prologue in which the world at war is viewed by convalescents taking their cures in a *Magic Mountain*-like sanatorium in neutral Switzerland. They have just heard the news that the war has broken out, and are gripped by a collective vision from their Olympian heights:

> The calm expanses of the valley dotted with villages pink as roses and soft pastures, the splendid outlines of the mountains, the black lace of the pine trees and the white lace of the eternal snows, are filled with the bustling of mankind.
>
> Multitudes teem in clearly defined masses. On fields attacks sweep forward, wave after wave, then come to a standstill; houses are gutted like men and towns like houses; villages appear in crumpled white as though they had fallen onto the earth from the sky; frightful loads of dead and wounded men alter the shape of the plains.
>
> You can see every country where the borders are eaten away with massacres constantly tearing new soldiers from its heart, full of strength, full of blood; your gaze follows these living tributaries for the river of the dead.
>
> North, south and west, battles rage, on all sides, in the distance. You can turn this way or that; there is not a single horizon on which there is no war.[657]

This ekphrastic text seems to both recall Altdorfer's *Battle of Alexander* and anticipate Dix's *Flanders*; it is the link between the two paintings.[658] If Dix

657 Barbusse, *Under Fire*, Chapter 1, "The Vision," 3–4. Werckmeister also cites this passage, but without comment, in "Radical Art History," 287. It should be noted that Barbusse wrote this in 1916, and so his reference would be the *First* Battle of Flanders, in the autumn of 1914, although Dix had lived through the Third, in 1917.

658 The *Weltlandschaft* device had gained some currency among Neue Sachlichkeit painters, in particular the Viennese painter Herbert von Reyl-Hanisch 1898–1937), who was, like Dix, a society portraitist, and who used the *Weltlandschaft* motif as the

had recently reread Barbusse's novel, this passage at the beginning may well have suggested to him a link between his own intense interest at the time in the Northern Renaissance landscape device of the *Weltlandschaft* and his ongoing preoccupation with depicting the war experience, while the book's final descriptive passage on the flooded trenches of Flanders provided the ideal motif, with its 'tarnished mirrors of water" and its soldiers caked with mud and sheltering like snails in the embankments.

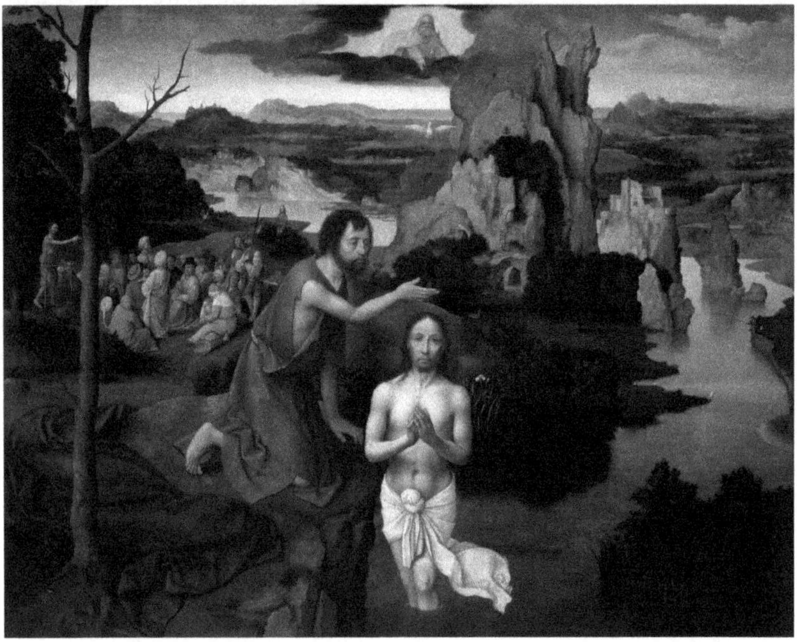

Figure 73. Joachim Patinir, *The Baptism of Christ*, oil on oak panel, 1510–1520, Kunsthistorisches Museum, Vienna. Digital file: Google Cultural Institute online.

In *Weltlandschaft* paintings, the narrative action in the foreground – typically Biblical in nature – can seem a mere pretext for the depiction of extensive and often fantastical landscapes, as for example in Patinir's painting

background to several of his portraits as well as, most fully, *Die Großen Hafenstadt*, 1928, and Franz Seclacek (1891–1945).

of *The Baptism of Christ* (1510–1520) (see Figure 73) or Albrecht Altdorfer's *Christ on the Cross Between Mary and John* (c. 1512). *Weltlandschaft* also featured ominous weather, cloud formations, and occasionally, as in Patinir's *Baptism*, a heavenly omen. The extensive waterways unify the color compositions by reflecting the light of the sky in the lower half of the painting, while the foreground is often painted in a nearly monochrome umber or sienna. Dix systematically acquired and incorporated this set of devices in his landscapes around Randegg between 1934 and 1938.[659] In his landscape *Waldrand mit Buche*, 1935, for example, Dix borrows the entire composition – trees on either side, roadway leading from foreground over hill and dale into the a blue-tinted peak and bay in the far distance, with emphasis on precisely textured foliage and sharply drawn cirrus clouds in a cerulean sky – from Albrecht Altdorfer's well-known painting *Danube Landscape Near Regensburg with Scheuchenberg* (c. 1528), in the Alte Pinakothek, Munich.[660] What's more, Patinir painted a version of a narrative scene which was to become one of Dix's favorites in the 1930s: St. Christopher carrying the Christ Child on his shoulder across a river (c. 1520).

The choice of Flanders as subject

Why did Dix specify the flooded trenches of Flanders, of all the possible motifs that he might have selected for such a painting? Neither *The Trench* nor the triptych *The War* specify a particular battle or location – although many of the 50 prints from the portfolio *The War* do (and the incessant rain in Flanders is depicted in *Stretcher Bearers in Houthulst Forest*; see Figure 49). The Germans fought major battles against the British, the Canadians, and the French in Flanders in the autumn of 1914, in the spring

659 Several examples are reproduced in Bauer, ed., *Otto Dix. Werke*; the painter's progress in his efforts can be seen in: *Randegg bei Gewitter* (1934), 41; *Randegg mit Vögeli* (1936), 45; and *Allensbach und Reichenau* (1938), 40.

660 *Waldrand mit Buche* (1935) reproduced in Bauer, ed., *Otto Dix. Werke*, 39.

of 1915, and again in the summer and autumn of 1917. The two sides fought repeatedly over the same stretch of ground, including the once important market towns of Ypres and Cambrai, the town of Passchendaele, the Wijtschate plain and Pilckem ridge, and the rivers Yser and Lys. They fought two more battles over the same territory in 1918. Dix himself participated in the long battle of 1917, the so-called "Third Battle of Flanders" ("Third Battle of Ypres" in English, also sometimes simply called "Passchendaele"), alternating between fighting on the front line and quieter guard duty in Brussels.

Over time, the iconography of Flanders, rain and flooding and mud, increasingly stood in for the entire Western Front which, in turn, represented the entirety of the war, displacing the other theaters, for Germans as well as the British and, especially, Canadians. In 1927 Franz Schauwecker (1890–1964) edited and published an album of photographs, *So war der Krieg* [The War Was Like This] (it went through several subsequent editions), which was as influential as Ernst Jünger's memoir *Storm of Steel* or the publications of the *Reichsbanner*.[661] The book includes photos from every theater and of every aspect of the fighting, but Schauwecker nonetheless describes in his foreword a landscape that is unmistakably that of Flanders,

> flooded by water and mud or frozen into a devastated and shattered sea of earth, barbed wire, wooden beams, sand bags and shredded iron […] a land which has sucked in the dead and the fallen, turned them to earth and reincorporated them – in this territory sanctified by blood, and beneath explosions of steel, howling storms and claps of thundering detonations ….[662]

661 Franz Schauwecker also published a novel about the war experience, *Im Todesrachen. Die deutsche Seele im Weltkriege* (1919), and was later an editor, along with Jünger, of *Die Standarte*, the official publication of the *Stahlhelm*. Nadja Bengsch, "Franz Schauwecker – der 'Dichter des heldischen Lebens'," in Rolf Düsterberg, ed., *Dichter für das „Dritte Reich,"* Vol. 2, *Biografische Studien zum Verhältnis von Literatur und Ideologie* (Bielefeld: Aisthesis, 2011), 175–205, and Bernd Hüppauf, "Zwischen Metaphysik und visuellem Essayismus. Franz Schauwecker: *So war der Krieg* (1928)," in Thomas F. Schneider, ed., *Von Richthofen bis Remarque* (Amsterdam: Rodopi, 2003), 233–248.

662 "In diesen Trichtergeländen voll Schlamm und Wasser oder erstarrt zu einem wüst zersplitterten Meer von Erde und Draht, Balken, Sandsäcken und Eisengefetz

Schauwecker's own interpretation of the meaning aligned with the *Stahlhelm* rather than the *Reichsbanner* or Barbusse. But for Schauwecker, too, the war was the Western Front, and specifically the flooded, shattered landscape of Flanders, "sanctified by blood," and for him this muddy, sucking morass that reincorporated the dead into itself also birthed a heroic nationalist consciousness, just as, for Barbusse and the *Reichsbanner*, it had birthed a heroic class solidarity. For Dix it clearly remained, after 1933, the territory over which the struggle for the meaning of the war continued to unfold.

However, as we noted at the outset of this chapter, by 1936 there was no chance for Dix to actually participate in a such a public struggle; Schauwecker, von Killinger, and their ideological ilk had triumphed, and monopolized the public discussion of the war's meaning. *Flanders* would not be exhibited in Germany until it was bought from the artist by the West Berlin Galerie des 20. Jahrhunderts in 1963 (from which it passed in 1968 into the Neue Nationalgalerie, West Berlin). Dix did exhibit the painting in Zurich in 1938, as part of a one-man exhibition of more than 40 paintings and 24 graphic works held by the Galerie Wolfsberg, his second in that space in the 1930s (the retrospective that was originally planned to travel to Vienna as well, but this station had to be cancelled when Austria was annexed by Nazi Germany).[663] But the Swiss critics were more interested in comparing the work to the artist's own earlier, notorious war paintings, specifically *The Trench*, which had been shown in the same gallery two years earlier, than in discussing the meaning of the battlefields of Flanders or of the war generally. The critic for the *Zuricher Kunstchronik* wrote,

---

[...] auf dieser Erde, die die Toten in sich aufgesogen und die Gefallenen, zu Erde verwandelt, sich wieder einverleibt hat – in diesem durch das Blut geheiligten Erdreich ist unter Krämpfen von Stahl und Explosion und unter den rasenden Stürmen und Ausbrüchen donnernder Sprengungen der Nationalismus geboren worden." Franz Schauwecker, *So war der Krieg. 200 Kampfaufnahmen aus der Front* (Berlin: Frundsberg, 1927), 3.

663 Felix Graf, "Otto Dix im Kunstsalon Wolfsberg," *Journal of Swiss Archaeology and Art History* 70/4 (2013), 259–265. My gratitude goes to Benni Wolfensberger for drawing my attention to this essay. Also *Neue Züricher Zeitung* 8 May 1938, e1.

> If once a terrifying barbed wire image from the world war had a tumultuous effect, the artist now has considerably more distance to his motif in his monumental picture "Flanders Battlefield," which now hangs in the Wolfsberg gallery. The soldiers' corpses are here again piled up until they meld into the glaciers of a grisly landscape.[664]

And the reviewer for the *Neue Züricher Zeitung* stressed the tension between the aggressively critical subject matter and the outwardly polite old master technique, despite its "devastating power of documentation." But he, too, returned to dwell on his memory of *The Trench*, which in his opinion had been skillfully painted but exhibited a "horrible realism that would make any old German depiction of the legendary Ten Thousand Martyrs look like a kindergarten picture."[665]

The dedication to Barbusse

In the remainder of this chapter, I would like to explore just what that dedication might have suggested to Dix and his audience, and then turn to some of the specific imagery in the painting which has gone unremarked upon, namely the gestures and physical interaction between the three soldiers.

The dedication to Barbusse indicates not only an overt connection between the painting and the novel which it closely matches, but also that Dix shared Barbusse's humanism and valorization of an international solidarity between former front soldiers. Barbusse's novel, translated into German already before the end of the war, represented the humanist, liberal interpretation, including the view that the front soldier was primarily

664 "Hatte einst eine schreckhafte Stacheldrahtszene aus dem Weltkrieg aufwühlend gewirkt, so stand dann der Maler dem Motiv seines Riesenbildes 'Flandrisches Schlachtfeld', das jetzt im 'Wolfsberg' hängt, schon mit grösserer Distanz gegenüber. Die Soldatenleichen häufen sich zu einer gleichsam vergletscherten Landschaft des Grausens." "Otto Dix im 'Wolfsberg'," *Das Werk*, 25/6 (June 1938), 20.

665 *Neue Züricher Zeitung*, 8 May 1938, p. e1.

a victim of the war and the ruling and officer class that made it, an interpretation which the *Reichsbanner* shared.[666] And if the *Reichsbanner* saw the frontline soldier as a victim, this was a sentiment also emphasized by Dix in *Flanders*. The *Reichsbanner* also shared one of their most significant commitments with Barbusse: an international brotherhood among the former enlisted men, who were drawn, like Dix, from the working class. The author of an article in the journal of the *Reichsbanner* wrote, in 1932,

> The *Stahlhelm* always emphasizes the Front Experience that binds its members. Now, we republicans [i.e. supporters of the Weimar Republic, MM] in the *Reichsbanner*, which certainly counts as many front soldiers in its ranks as the *Stahlhelm*, are also unified by a Front Experience. Only, we understand something very different by that term. For us, the Front Experience doesn't just mean a martial esprit de corps and its continued cultivation in the postwar period. And the Front Experience doesn't mean seeing a higher being in the person of the officer who marches in our ranks – he can only be our equal as a comrade in arms. ... No, for us the Front Experience means maintaining the solidarity of the men who supported each other through life and death in the trenches, out of which can be formed the equality of the whole of the people.[667]

Otto Dix emphasizes just this quality of *Kameradschaft* among the simple foot soldiers who are doing their best just to survive, and it was also the virtue that Barbusse celebrated. We have seen throughout this book that Dix was consistently focused on the issue of *Kameradschaft*, which remained into the 1930s the central concept around which the contest over the meaning of the war and its public memory was focused. If on the one side, nationalist reactionaries imagined and celebrated a fighting spirit in the German soldier, and solidarity between enlisted men and

666 Ziemann, *Contested Commemorations*, 273. Where the Reichsbanner differed from Barbusse on this issue was that the French novelist actively promoted the revolutionary communist cause, whereas the Reichsbanner, in its many publications and rituals, saw the front experience as the foundation and legitimacy of the democratic republic. Dix, too, had refused to embrace the cause of communism over and against the republic, a refusal in the face of the pressure of friends like Conrad Felixmüller.

667 Ulrich and Ziemann, *Krieg im Frieden*. 112.

frontline officers (a solidarity kept alive after the war), then Barbusse – like the socialist membership of the *Reichsbanner* – imagined and celebrated an international working-class consciousness among former front soldiers, a solidarity between enlisted soldiers on both sides of the front (also kept alive after the war). Barbusse's was a lateral rather than a vertical solidarity. However, by the time Dix painted *Flanders*, the *Reichsbanner* had already lost the contest over the meaning of the commemoration of the war in the early 1930s. In March of 1933 the *Reichsbanner* was banned, and its publications ceased. They were accused throughout the early 1930s of undermining German *Wehrhaftigkeit* the readiness for defense – the same thing that Dix's painting *The Trench* was accused of.[668]

And yet victimhood – or sacrifice, also had its positive value, if it was willingly endured. Victimhood then became heroic. The novel *Under Fire* expressed this sentiment about the French fighting man,

> One can see what vision and what fear and what farewells are in their silence, their immobility, the mask of calm that inhumanly grasps their faces. They are not the sort of heroes that people think they are, but their sacrifice has greater value than those who have not seen them will ever be able to understand.[669]

The final line hits almost exactly the same note as many of the statements by the *Reichsbanner*: mass death was a tragedy, but self-sacrifice was a virtue. It was dignified and made sacred by the clear-eyed determination with which it was offered by those who were willing to make it. Tightly linked to this homily was the sense that the great sacrifice of the war must be both obsessively reiterated, and can only be truthfully enunciated by those who were there, in the trenches. Dix himself insisted vehemently, even years later, on the principle that only the *authentic and uncomplaining* veteran of the front could bear witness to the truth of the war, which truth was quite explicitly a heroic victimhood (an exclusionary idea which I related in Chapter 4 to the idea of the "Gnosticism of the front"),

668 Ziemann, *Contested Commemorations*, 271.
669 Barbusse, *Under Fire*, 223.

> If you want to be heroes, you have to embrace these disgusting conditions. You have to have been there. And not "fresh-faced and eager and glad," but really, really experienced it all. Only then are you heroes. When you've really gone to the lowest depths, the lice and the filth, the hunger, the fear, the shit in your pants, then you're heroes.[670]

By "heroes" here, Dix seems to have meant not so much valor as belonging to the community of the front. Thus, the decision to dedicate the painting to Barbusse and his novel can be seen, not as a rejection of the war as meaningless suffering, but rather the identification of a specific meaning of that suffering: the virtue of a victimhood willingly embraced, in class solidarity with all frontline soldiers, the men on both sides. At the same time, it can be seen as a rebuke to those, like von Killinger and others, who claimed instead that the meaning of the war was nationalist solidarity between men within a reactionary social hierarchy.

Tenderness and touch

The three soldiers in the foreground of *Flanders* huddle close, for warmth and, clearly, for comfort. The two flanking figures both reach out and touch the soldier who sits slumped between them, seeking reassurance in his massive form. His monumentality is emphasized by the steel helmet, which carried so much significance, and by the combination of trench coat and cloak which covers most of his body. The contour of his helmet is continued by his slumped shoulders, and then by the shapes of the other two

670 "Wenn ihr Helden sein wollt, so müßt ihr diese Schweinerei, müßt ihr auch bejahen. Da müßt ihr auch dabei gewesen sein. Und nicht frisch – fromm – fröhlich, sondern alles, alles erleben: erst dann seid ihr Helden. Wenn ihr in die niedrigsten Tiefen gegangen seid, die Läuse und Dreck, den Hunger, die Angst, die Hosenscheißerei, dann seid ihr Helden." Cited in Schmidt, *Otto Dix im Selbstbildnis*, 204.

figures huddled against him.[671] His head is sunken into his shoulders, his face mostly hidden by the visor of the helmet, and by the bushy mustache which hides his mouth; he has no discernable expression. He reaches out with his left hand (although it seems clear that his left hand originally rested in his own lap), and grasps – what? A knee? But not his own, because they are elsewhere, and the figure to his proper left has both of his knees tucked up under him. Yet this flanking figure, too, may have been moved – he seems to have originally sat more upright. In any case, the figures touch, seek and give comfort. This is the physical expression that Dix gives here to the ideal of *Kameradschaft*.

Dix was not unique in depicting *Kameradschaft* through the comforting tenderness of a touch. A similar display of physical tenderness could be seen in a public sculpture by his colleague from his younger days in Düsseldorf, Jupp Rübsam, the memorial to the 39th Fusiliers Regiment [Denkmal der 39er] (see Figure 74), dedicated in 1928, which had been the target of right-wing activism in the late 1920s. In 1933, it was one of the first artworks which the Nazis dismantled – it was even higher on their list of scores to settle than *The Trench*. Heavily monumental, it depicted two soldiers lying flat on their stomachs, propped up on their elbows, their heads raised and gazing forward, resembling a kind of double sphinx. One figure wore the *Stahlhelm*, the other had his head bandaged. The soldiers lay prone and unarmed, wounded; they were strikingly unheroic even though the monumentality of the work was emphasized. At the front of the sculpture as the viewer faces it, and immediately above the dedication plaque, the two men hold hands. Or rather, the soldier wearing the steel helmet puts his hand gently on the hand of his wounded comrade. Although the two men are identical in size, there is nonetheless a distinct difference between the two, with the stronger man giving comfort to the weaker. Neither figure looks down at their joined hands; both look straight ahead, sphinx-like. But the tender gesture is the center of the composition and the emotional center of the monument.

671 His pose resembles that of the central figure in Ernst Barlach's *War Memorial* made for Magdeburg Cathedral in 1928, as noted by Otto Karl Werckmeister, "Radical Art History" *Art Journal* 42/4 (Winter 1982), 284–291.

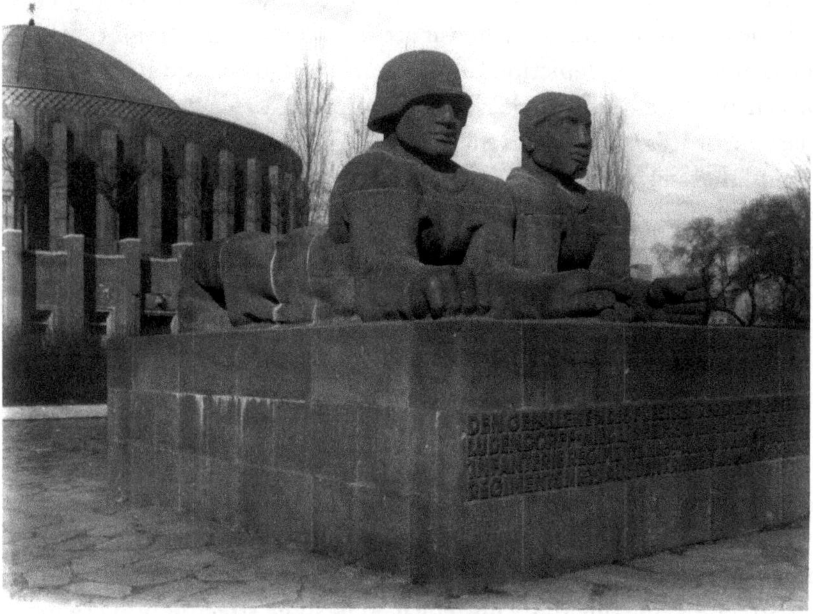

Figure 74. Jupp Rübsam, *Monument to the 39th Fusiliers Regiment*, granite, 1928, Düsseldorf. Photo: Julius Söhn, 1934 / Stadtarchiv Düsseldorf 209–802-004, used with permission.

By contrast, in Wilhelm Sauter's 1934 painting *The Good Comrade* [Der gute Kamerad], a soldier pauses only briefly from firing his rifle to gaze with sadness upon the body of his dead comrade, who lies at the bottom of the shell hole they have taken shelter in (exhibited at the Heroische Kunst exhibition in Berlin in 1935). And in Elk Eber's *The Last Hand Grenade* [Die letzte Handgranate], a lithograph related to the painting of the same title, 1936, another hero in a flooded crater spares no notice for his dead comrade as throws his last grenade, expressing instead a determined resistance even as the British troops overrun him. These are overt expressions of grim determination and foredoomed valor (increasingly symbolized in nationalist-minded imagery by the long-handled grenade), and not of tenderness. This quality – and their kitschy, illustrational and heavily bathetic style – endeared them to National Socialist art functionaries, and to the Nazi art critic Wilhelm Westecker, who included both in his volume of appropriate German war art, *Krieg und Kunst*, in 1940.[672] The most monumental depiction of *Kameradschaft*, discussed in the previous chapter, was Arno Breker's relief sculpture *Kameraden*, of which a plaster cast was exhibited in the Great German Art Exhibition in 1940. Again, there is no glimmer of tenderness between the two naked warriors, one dead, the other holding his limp body; there is only defiant rage, physical strength, and the unmistakable theme of revanchism, as the living warrior looks back over his shoulder to express his anger. Perhaps the most telling work on this theme is Wilhelm Sauter's *Heroes' Shrine* [Heldenschrein], a triptych, published in *Das Bild* in 1936. Its format – a triptych plus predella with dead soldiers – so clearly recalls Dix's *The War* that it's hard to imagine that it wasn't a direct riposte. It shows both front soldiers from the world war and Brown Shirts engaged in street battles against an unseen enemy. Dead men in both uniforms are laid side by side in the predella. It is a piece of shameless kitsch and mythmaking, but the central image is one of solidarity and comradeship. Five SA men stand in the street, having obviously just engaged in some street fighting (which could have either been with communists or just as likely with uniformed members of the Reichsbanner). The central figure has been beaten up; his shirt is torn, and he is being physically supported between two of his comrades. This group of three is guarded in turn by two more flanking figures, who look off belligerently in either direction, fists clenched and jaws set. There is a strong undercurrent of fetishism in their jackboots and uniforms, but there is no hint of tenderness between the figures, even as the grapple with their wounded comrade's body. It is clear that such physical tenderness would only undermine their *Wehrhaftigkeit*. The emotional contrast with the *Monument to the 39th Fusiliers* and *Flanders* could hardly be more striking.

Rübsam was a veteran, himself a member of the 39th Fusiliers Regiment which had seen heavy fighting and heavy losses. Together with Dix he had been a member in the early 1920s of the group Das

672 Wilhelm Westecker, *Krieg und Kunst. Das Erlebnis des Weltkrieges und des Großdeutschen Freiheitskrieges* (Vienna and Leipzig: Luser, 1940), 65 and 83.

junge Rheinland around the legendary Düsseldorf modern art dealer Johanna Ey. Rübsam had been introduced to the group in 1920 by none other than the slightly younger Arno Breker. It is not hard to imagine that Dix would have been aware of Rübsam's monument in the late 1920s or early 1930s. The two days of dedication ceremony and speeches for it in 1928 were covered extensively by the local papers, attempting to fix the meaning of what proved to be a troublingly ambiguous sculpture.[673] Later, the controversy surrounding it achieved national attention. Rübsam himself stated publicly, in the 39th's own newsletter that it was supposed to remind its intended audience – other veterans of the regiment – of the war, and of "need, death, and comradeship, and ... hope."[674] But the monument failed in various ways to fulfill the expectations and representational needs of one segment of its immediate audience – the conservative managing committee of the regiment's veterans association. The figures were not sufficiently heroic, it was felt, and their features were not sufficiently Germanic or even European; it did not do honor to the 7,000 fallen soldiers of the regiment.[675]

For the monument's defenders the ambiguity which troubled many was a positive quality.[676] An art critic writing in *Das Kunstblatt* – who at first emphasized the work's unusual and even alienating features – made the distinction between the contemporary audience, which had the benefit and the burden of collective memory, and the audience of future generations. The contemporary audience seeks liberation from painful memories

673 The history of the commission and reception of this monument is richly documented in Jutta Pitzen, *Jupp Rübsam, 1896–1976* (Krefeld: Kühlen, 1991).

674 "Da habt Ihr ein Mal zum Gedächtnis an den Krieg, an Not, an Tod und Kameradschaft und ein Mal zum Gedächtnis zugleich." Jupp Rübsam, "Unser Denkmal. Das Urteil eines Architekten," *Der 39er*, 3/11 (1928), 82, cited in Brandt, Susanne, "Trauer und fortgesetzter Krieg. Totengedanken zwischen Trauer und Kriegsverherrlichung in Düsseldorf nach dem Ersten Weltkrieg," in Jost Dülffer and Gerd Krumeich, eds., *Der verlorene Frieden. Politik und Kriegskultur nach 1918* (Essen: Klartext, 2002), 243–260, here 258.

675 Erweiterte Vorstandssitzung des Verbandes ehem. 39er, 10 March 1929, cited in Brandt, *Düsseldorf*, 258.

676 Pitzen, *Jupp Rübsam*, 60–61.

through an idealized image – at remembrance ceremonies and from memorial monuments. But the artist must aim higher, must address himself to future generations.

> These later audiences will no longer remember either the regiment number or the uniform, or anybody from the old *Kameradschaft*. But they will grasp from the unusual form of the *Memorial to the 39th* that there was an extraordinary experience behind it, and from the exceptional tension of both figures they will gather something of the monumentality of the accomplishment of that time.[677]

This is nothing less than an intuition of Maurice Halbwach's theory of collective memory, which makes the central distinction between a living, social memory that is primarily dialogic and fluid, held in common by those who experienced events first hand, and the passing of that social, discursive memory into a fixed, official culture in the form of monuments, both textual and sculptural, beheld by later generations.[678]

The outrage of the conservative, *völkisch* officer's association of the 39th Fusiliers reached all the way to Erich Luddendorf, the second in command of all German forces during the war and a leader of the conservative nationalist movement, who had also served at one time as the commanding officer of the 39th Fusiliers, and whose name was thus prominently featured in the inscription. Ludendorff's contributions to the debate, and his wife's, were characterized by anti-Semitic slurs and

677 "Man wünscht eben ganz allgemein bei der Erinnerungsfeier und angesichts eines Gefallenendenkmals Befreiung durch idealisierte Vorstellung ... Diese Beziehung liegt für den Künstler ausschließlich im Überzeitlichen, denn er selbst und seine ganze Umwelt vergeht, sein Werk aber bleibt für spätere Geschlechter. Diese späteren kennen weder die Regimentsnummer mehr noch Uniform noch irgendeinen aus der ehemaligen Kameradschaft, sie begreifen aber in der ungewöhnliche Erlebnis und in der außergewöhnlichen Form des 39er-Denkmals das dahinterliegende ungewöhnliche Erlebnis und in der außergewöhnlichen Spannung beider Figuren etwas von der Monumentalität der Leistung jener Zeit." Georg Kutzke, "Denkmal des Füsiliers-Regiments Nr. 39, Düsseldorf," *Das Kunstblatt* 14, 180–181.

678 Maurice Halbwachs, *On Collective Memory* (Chicago: University of Chicago Press, 1992, Lewis A. Coser, editor and translator).

complaints about the supposedly Semitic and "oriental" facial features of the figures, and implications of a Jewish plot involving the city council and Rübsam himself (the artist was not Jewish, but several commentators implied that he, and certain supporters of the monument in the Düsseldorf city government, were). As the debate over the sculpture and the nationalist rhetoric heated up, the monument was repeatedly vandalized; saboteurs even attempted and failed in 1930 to blow it up. The officer's association of the 39th Fusiliers demanded that it be removed, or that at the very least changes be made to the sculpture, specifically that the facial features be made more "Germanic."[679] In the end, a competition was held for a new design for the monument, with a winner selected in 1932: the Hamburg sculptor Richard Kuöhl (1880–1961), once an avant-gardist who, like Breker, would successfully adapt his style to the expectations of the National Socialist regime.[680] His new design, like his other memorial sculptures, features serried ranks of soldiers marching in lock step. Even when fallen, Kuöhl's heroes look upright, displaying their steel helmets and long-handled grenades for future generations to gaze upon with solemn gratitude.[681] The new monument wasn't unveiled until 1939, just in time for the next war.[682] The remaining fragments of Rübsam's monument were returned to their original location, in front of the Tonhall in Düsseldorf, in 1978. Dix may well have been aware of this dispute, unfolding on the national stage and pitting high-profile reactionary nationalists against the memorial of his old friend and colleague back in Düsseldorf, and he may have taken note of the decision to commission a new monument with more *Stahlhelm*-oriented nationalist imagery to replace the unheroic but tender and comforting imagery of *Reichsbanner* – oriented *Kameradschaft*.

679 Pitzen, *Jupp Rübsam*, 68.

680 Rudolf Schmidt, *Architekturplastik. Bildhauer Richard Kuöhl* (Berlin, Gebr. Mann, 1997).

681 See for example Kuöhl's Denkmal für die Rendsburger 85er in Rendsburg, Schleswig-Holstein (1922), and his 76er Denkmal Dammtor in Hamburg (1936).

682 Brandt, *Düsseldorf*, 259.

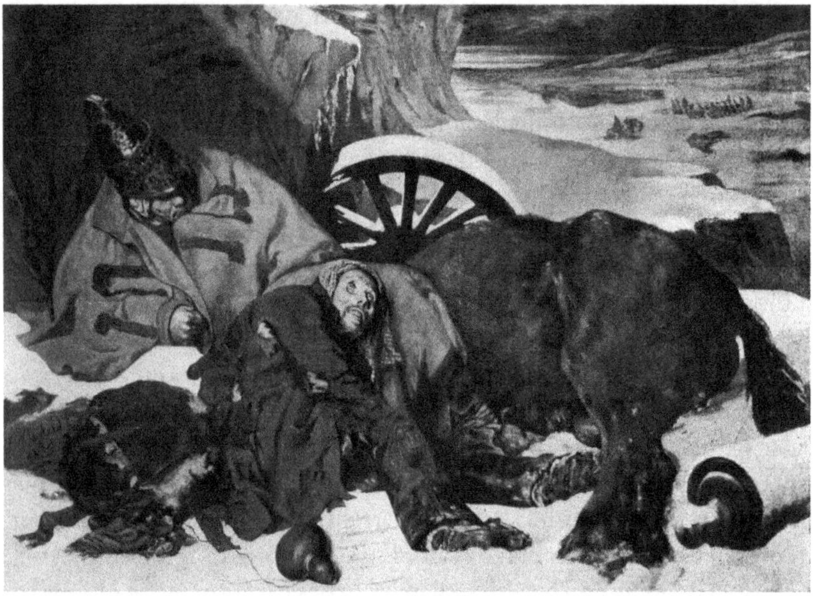

Figure 75. Joseph-Fernand Boissard de Boisdenier, *Episode de la Retraite de Moscou*, 1835, Musée des Beaux-Arts, Rouen.

There is a small tradition of artworks depicting such tender gestures between weary, suffering soldiers. A painting of the Napoleonic wars, *Episode from the Retreat from Moscow* [Episode de la Retraite de Moscou] (1835) (see Figure 75), by the Frenchman Joseph-Fernand Boissard de Boisdenier bears a certain resemblance to *Flanders* (Dix could have seen it reproduced in a book published by the art historian Henri Focillon in 1927).[683] Dix's composition has at least as much in common with Boissard's early nineteenth-century history painting as with Ernst Barlach's *War Memorial* in Magdeburg Cathedral (1928), which Otto Werckmeister identified as a

683 Henri Focillon, *La peinture au XIXe siècle. Le retour à l'antique. Le romantisme* (Évreux: Hérissey, 1927), 249. Focillon described the painting's "... neige digne de la neige d'Eylau, cadavres peints avec des dons de coloristes tragique qui font regretter une production trop rare," 250 f. But the painting was reproduced in black and white in the book.

source for *Flanders*.[684] In both Dix's and Boissard's paintings two figures, one much larger than the other, huddle together, wrapped in well-worn heavy campaign coats. In Boissard's painting, the larger man belongs to the Dragoon Imperial Guard (the so-called "Empress Dragoons"), readily identifiable by the (artificial) panther-print turban around his helmet, while the smaller man is merely a soldier of the line.[685] In both paintings the smaller figure, tattered cloak pulled tight round himself, looks desperately to the larger man for comfort, while the larger soldier's features are hidden by a helmet pulled low and by his bushy mustache. The similarities are striking. Even the rump of the dead horse to the right of Boissard's pair corresponds to a nearly identical shape in *Flanders*, where a third figure, darker than the others, huddles beneath a tarp. Behind Boissard's two freezing troopers is the half circle of a wagon wheel – a favorite motif of Dix's – covered in snow and unifying the contours of the foreground group, and behind that is a frozen, inhospitable landscape. In the snowy distance can be seen smaller groups and columns of Napoleon's army retreating towards the rapidly fading pallor of daylight at the far edge of a black winter sky. The soldiers in the foreground are forgotten, and for them all hope is lost.

Although Boissard's painting had gained some currency in 1935–1936, I am certainly not suggesting that Dix copied the composition, if he even knew it, and perhaps the many similarities are merely coincidental, stemming from the shared theme of half-dead soldiers awaiting their fate in a wasteland, left behind by a defeated and abandoned army.[686] But Boissard's painting with its themes of stoical suffering and victimization, without the least gesture of violent glory, was closer to the mood that Dix sought than were the sorts of heroic combat paintings and regimental monuments

684 Werckmeister, "Radical Art History," 288.

685 Ronald Pawly, *Napoleon's Dragoons of the Imperial Guard* (Oxford: Osprey, 2012).

686 It was exhibited in Rouen in 1934 in a benefit exhibition for the aid of families with numerous children, at the Bibliotheque Nationale in Paris in 1935, and at the Petit Palais in Paris in 1936, in the exhibition "Gros, ses amis, ses élèves: exposition Petit Palais." It was being shown in an exhibition in Copenhagen in 1914 when the war broke out, and it couldn't be repatriated to France until 1920. Information courtesy of the staff of the Musée des Beaux-Arts, Rouen.

then being produced, and finding official favor, in Germany under the National Socialists.

Boissard's painting and Rübsam's monument can help us to better recognize in *Flanders* the themes of physical tenderness offered as comfort between miserable and suffering soldiers. The men not only huddle against one another for warmth and comfort, but they reach out and touch one another. This physical tenderness and intimacy exceeded the bounds of the socially acceptable intimacy between men in civilian life.[687] For Boissard, painting a large-scale public history painting 23 years after Napoleon's retreat from Moscow, this physical intimacy between men was *the* truth that gave spiritual meaning to that national catastrophe, and was the element worthy of public memory.[688] For Dix, painting 16 years after Germany's own catastrophe, the constellation of public memory was quite similar. Mutual care among the foot soldiers, as an expression of *Kameradscahft*, had been held up – in this case by center-left veterans – as one of the cardinal virtues giving meaning to mass death and defeat. In his monumental painting, scaled for public exhibition, Dix represented a moment of physical tenderness that exceeded the limits of physical expression that men could share in civilian life. In both paintings the difference in size between the two men conveys the unmistakable sense that comfort is not actually so much mutual as offered by one man, who is visibly stronger, calmer, and more stoical, to the other, smaller and more frightened man. This difference in size between the two men is subtly substituted for a difference in gender, corresponding to a distinction between one who provides comfort and one who seeks it, and so an intimate gesture verges towards the erotic. This act of tender comfort may be understated and reserved – we have seen that Dix would not have wanted to suggest homoeroticism among soldiers – but it is essentially

687 Santanu Das, *Touch and Intimacy in First World War Literature* (Cambridge: Cambridge University Press, 2005).

688 It is worth remembering that Boissard's teacher at the Academy was Antoine-Jean Gros, who once represented Napoleon compassionately and fearlessly touching the open wound of one of his soldiers suffering from plague in the *Plague House at Jaffa* (1804).

one half of the theme of the painting, where the other half is their Calvary in the flooded, shattered plains of Flanders.

And what would those in the right-wing veterans' movements have said about such a gesture of tenderness between two suffering German soldiers – had Dix but had a chance to exhibit *Flanders* in Germany? One indication could be gathered from the reception of the *Monument to the 39th Fusiliers Regiment* in 1928. When the National Socialists came to power in 1933, they immediately dismantled Rübsam's monument. Nine months later, they took *The Trench* out of storage and included it in the first exhibition of so-called "Degenerate Art."

Conclusion

Although it appears at first to be simpler than the earlier paintings and representations of the war, *Flanders* is a nuanced and layered painting that welds together a monumental depiction of the exhausted front line soldier and a vast, panoramic view of the world as a great, diluvian battlefield. Dix has once again borrowed from a number of art historical sources to give nuance to the composition, from the *Weltmalerei* of Albrecth Altdorfer, Joachim Patinir, and possibly Rubens, to the Napoleon's-retreat-from-Moscow painting of Fernand Boissard. This time, Dix even included references to a textual representation of the war, Henri Barbusse's *Under Fire*. The main themes of the painting were the exhaustion and victimization of the front soldiers, who were abandoned in an endless and uninhabitable landscape of destruction, and the tenderness and physical comfort which they shared with each other so that they might survive. Once again, the painting emphasized a specific virtue which the war had forced upon these soldiers, which gave meaning to the war, and which was identifiably a virtue embraced on the left, by working-class and middle-class veterans who had been supporters of the Republic while it had endured. Like the works before it, this last painting of the front experience was not a strongly antiwar painting, so much as it was a public embrace of these specific virtues, and a rejection of the nationalist myth of a mystical brotherhood of the front that transcended class antagonisms. Unfortunately for Dix, his conception of the meaning of the war was no longer tolerated in Germany, where the National Socialists, embodied by the likes of Manfred von Killinger, had achieved a monopoly on the public discourse about that meaning.

Epilogue

In 1937, the year after Dix finished *Flanders*, he was still able to exhibit works in, for example, the *Jubiläumsausstellung* [Anniversary Exhibition] in the Gera *Kunstverein* [Gera Art Society]. He exhibited a Hegau landscape and a portrait of his mother (Letter to Franz Lenk, 1937, original in the Dix Haus in Gera). In the same year, his work was exhibited in the Degenerate Art exhibition in Munich, and soon the Gera Art Society was informed by the Reich Cultural Chamber of Visual Arts [Reichskulturkammer der bildende Künste] in Berlin that his works had to be taken down. Dix wrote to his friend Lenk, a member of the Reich Cultural Chamber, and asked if this was how he was going to be treated in the future; if so, he would seriously consider emigrating, rather than give "these people" the pleasure of watching him starve. In his opinion, "it would be impossible to characterize either of these two pictures as 'degenerate'."[689] Having built his new villa in Hemmenhofen in 1936, he retreated more fully into landscape painting

689 "Ich habe anläßlich der Jubiläumsausstellung im Geraer Kunstverein 2 Bilder ausgestellt – eine Hegaulandschaft und ein Porträt meiner Mutter. Gestern erhielt ich die Nachricht vom G. K. V. das beide Bilder auf Anweisung der Reichskulturkammer d. b. Künste Berlin abgehängt werden mußten. Vielleicht können Sie sich gelegentlich mal erkundigen, wer dahinter steckt und ob diese Methode gegen mich weiter fortgesetzt werden soll. Ich würde mich, sollte letzteres der Fall sein, bald bemühen ins Ausland zu gehen … Beide Bilder sind unmöglich als entartet zu bezeichnen … Schließlich will ich ja den Leute nicht den Spaß machen, vor ihren Augen zu verhungern." Letter from Dix to Franz Lenk (n.d., 1937), *Otto Dix, Briefe*, 488.

and, increasingly, religious themes such as St. Christopher and the Virgin Mary holding the Christ Child on her lap. He also continued to carry out portrait commissions, now fully devoid of critical or caricatural elements.

Like other men his age Dix was mustered into the *Volkssturm* (a militia force made up of men too old and boys too young to have been conscripted yet) in December of 1943.[690] During the late months of the war, in March 1945, he was sent out to fight, and was in short order captured by the French.[691] They brought him to a POW camp at, of all places, Colmar, a city known to art historians as the home of Grünewald's *Isenheim Altarpiece*. The commandant of the camp, realizing that Dix was a famous artist, allowed him to go view the painting, and then to set up in the studio of a local artist, Robert Gall. He then gave Dix the commission of painting an altarpiece for the chapel of the camp – the first painting Dix made for an actual religious function, or, as he stressed in his letters home, an altar for his fellow prisoners.[692] The triptych, a little more than a meter high and half again as wide, was carried out in his old technique of mixed oil and tempera, between June and October of 1945; Dix even made a complete set of cartoons for the work.[693] At the center is the Madonna and Child, bearing a strong resemblance to his neighbor in Hemmenhofen (and possibly his mistress), Irmgard Bahle, who had sat as a model for his Madonna paintings before, though Dix must have painted her from memory or

690 Military pass, Deutsches Kunstarchiv, Germanisches Nationalmuseum, Nuremberg, Otto Dix archive, I, A 2.

691 Dix wrote a postcard from a French POW camp to his family informing them that he'd been in captivity since 18 April. POW postcard (15 June 1945), *Otto Dix, Briefe*, 268.

692 See Erdmuthe Mouchet, lecture delivered at the Museum Haus Dix, Hemmenhofen-Gaienhofen, 30 April 2016, text available on line at <http://wintzenheim3945.free.fr/D42F_Otto-Dix/D42F_Otto-Dix.htm> (accessed 27 November 2017). In the event the altarpiece was never installed in the makeshift chapel, but was sold by the commandant to local art collectors for his own profit. It did not resurface in the artist's lifetime.

693 The painting is now in the Pilgrimage Church of Maria Frieden in Berlin Mariendorf – it is in fact the pilgrimage icon. See the website, <http://www.maria-frieden-berlin.de/wallfahrt-bild.html> (accessed 27 November 2017).

perhaps a photograph.[694] She is flanked in the two panels by Saints Peter and Paul – both in chains, before a crowd of fellow prisoners, the ruins of the nearby town, and the barbed wire enclosure of the camp. The barbed wire – taken up in the title, *Madonna Before Barbed Wire* – becomes a kind of grim red thread connecting the First World War, for which it was a symbol, to the POW camp which constituted Dix's primary experience of the Second World War.

For two decades, from 1919 to 1938, Otto Dix had sought to guide the public discussion of the memory of the Great War and its meaning, all the while painting in the shadow of the old German masters (and emphasizing at every turn his own eyewitness status and also his aggressive, heteronormative masculinity). For two decades he had with determination sought to remind the public that, whatever virtue might be ascribed to the front soldier's suffering, it was nonetheless suffering first and foremost. After all his efforts, he had had to watch the fanatical nationalists and revanchists seize hold of the public discourse and turn it mercilessly toward their twisted dream – and everybody else's nightmare – of a resumption of the war. And now, in the ruins of their vainglorious dream, Dix found himself at one and the same time an aging prisoner of war and an artist working in the presence of his beloved Grünewald's greatest masterpiece, painting a monumental public work for his captors, a prayer lifted up by POWs everywhere to the Madonna of Barbed Wire, a Virgin Mary with the features of his mistress back home.

694 See *Mutter mit Kind (Frau Irmgard Bahle)* [Mother and Child], 1942, and *Der Heilige Lukas malt die Madonna (Selbstbildnis)* [Saint Luke Paints the Madonna (Self-Portrait)], 1943. Frau Bahle was the wife of the psychologist Julius Bahle, who also lived in Hemmenhofen; she was purported to be Dix's mistress, and also appears to play the role of one of Lot's daughters, exposing herself to the viewer – *Lot and His Daughters* (1939).

Bibliography

Adkins, Helen, "Erste Internationale Dada-Messe," in *Stationen der Moderne: Die bedeutenden Kunstausstellungen des 20. Jahrhunderts in Deutschland* (Berlin: Berlinische Galerie, 1988), 157–183.

Alexander, Caroline, "Faces of War," *Smithsonian Magazine* (Feb. 2007).

Apel, Dora, *Cultural Battlegrounds: Visual Imagery and the Tenth Anniversary of the First World War in Weimar Germany* (dissertation, University of Pittsburgh, 1995).

Apel, Dora, "'Heroes' and 'Whores': The Politics of Gender in Weimar Antiwar Imagery," *The Art Bulletin* 79/3 (September 1997), 366–384.

Ashplant, Timothy G., Graham Dawson, Michael Roper, *The Politics of War Memory and Commemoration* (Abingdon, UK: Routledge, 2000).

Assmann, Jan, *Cultural Meaning and Early Civilization: Writing, Remembrance, and Political Imagination* (Cambridge: Cambridge University Press, 2011),

Assmann, Jan, and John Czaplicka, "Collective Memory and Cultural Identity," *New German Critique* 65 (Spring-Summer, 1995), 125–133.

Audoin-Rouzeau, Stéphane, *Men at War 1914–1918: National Sentiment and Trench Journalism in France During the First World War* (Oxford: Berg, 1992).

Audoin-Rouzeau, Stéphane, and Annette Becker, *1914–1918: Understanding the Great War* (London: Profile Books, 2002).

Bakhtin, Mikhail, *Rabelais and His World*, trans. Hélène Iswolsky (Bloomington: Indiana University Press, reprint edition 1984).

Barron, Stephanie, ed., *Degenerate Art. The Fate of the Avant-Garde in Nazi Germany* (Los Angeles, CA: Los Angeles County Museum of Art, 1991).

Barton, Brigid S., "Die Entstehung eines Künstlerrufs: Otto Dix und *Der Schützengraben*," in Rainer Beck, *Otto Dix, 1891–1969: Zeit, Leben, Werk* (Konstanz: Stadler, 1993).

Bauer, Christoph, ed., *Otto Dix. Werke von 1933 bis 1969* (Cologne: Wienand, 2003).

Baumgarten-Crusius, Artur, *Sachsen in großer Zeit. Geschichte der Sachsen im Weltkrieg*, Vol. II (Leipzig: Minerva, 1920).

Beck, Rainer, "'Flucht ist immer falsch' – Inneres Exil als Emigration. Otto Dix im Dritten Reich" in Moshe Zuckermann, ed., *Geschichte und Bildende Kunst* (Göttingen: Wallstein, 2006), 149–178.

——, *Otto Dix, 1891–1969: Zeit, Leben, Werk* (Konstanz: Stadler, 1993).

Bengsch, Nadja, "Franz Schauwecker – der 'Dichter des heldischen Lebens'," in Rolf Düsterberg, ed., *Dichter für das "Dritte Reich,"* Vol. 2, *Biografische Studien zum Verhältnis von Literatur und Ideologie* (Bielefeld: Aisthesis, 2011), 175–205.

Benz, Wolfgang, Brigitte Mihok, eds., *Holocaust an der Peripherie. Judenpolitik und Judenmord in Rumänien und Transnistrien 1940–1944* (Berlin: Metropol, 2009).

Bergius, Hanne, "Dada Grotesque," in Pamela Kort, *Comic Grotesque: Wit and Mockery in German Art, 1870–1940* (Munich: Prestell, 2004), 155–170.

Berman, Patricia, "Edvard Munch's Self-Portrait with Cigarette: Smoking and the Bohemian Persona," *The Art Bulletin* 75/4 (December 1993), 627–646.

Böhme, Ulrich, *Fassungen bei Ernst Jünger* (Meisneheim am Glan: Hain, 1972).

Boraston, J. H., *Sir Douglas Haig's Despatches* (London: Dent, 1920).

Borchert, Till-Holger, "Collecting Early Netherlandish Paintings," in Bernhard Ridderbos, Anne van Buren, and Henk van Veen, *Early Netherlandish Paintings. Rediscovery, Reception, and Research* (Los Angeles, CA: J. Paul Getty Museum, 2005), 173–216.

Bourke, Joanna, "Introduction: 'Remembering' War," *Journal of Contemporary History* 39/4 (October 2004), 473–485.

Brandt, Susanne, "Trauer und fortgesetzter Krieg. Totengedanken zwischen Trauer und Kriegsverherrlichung in Düsseldorf nach dem Ersten Weltkrieg," in Jost Dülffer, and Gerd Krumeich, eds., *Der verlorene Frieden. Politik und Kriegskultur nach 1918* (Essen: Klartext, 2002), 243–260.

Bressa, Birgit, *Nach-Leben der Antike, Klassische Bilder des Körpers in der NS Skulptur Arno Brekers* (University of Tübingen, dissertation, 2001).

Briau, Aude, "Otto Dix face à la 'plus grande icône de l'art allemand', 1900–1924," in Frédérique Goerig-Hergott, ed., *Otto Dix – le Retable d'Isenheim* (Paris: Hazan, 2016), 29–41.

Broszat, Martin, *The Hitler State: The Foundation and Development of the Internal Structure of the Third Reich* (London: Longman, 1981), xiii.

Bruns, Claudia, The Politics of Masculinity in the (Homo-)Sexual Discourse (1880–1920)," *German History* 23/3 (August 2005).

Buderer, Hans-Jurgen, "Die Geschichte einer Ausstellung, 1923, 1925, 1933" in Manfred Fath, ed., *Neue Sachlichkeit: Bilder auf der Suche nach der Wirklichkeit: Figurative Malerei der zwanziger Jahre* (Munich: Prestel, 1994), 15–37.

Campbell, James, "Combat Gnosticism: The Ideology of First World War Poetry Criticism," *New Literary History* 30/1 (Winter 1999), 203–215.

Cassou, Jean, "Otto Dix," in Galerie "Im Erker," *Otto Dix: Der Krieg* (St. Gallen: Galerie "Im Erker," 1962), 12.

Clinefelter, Joan L., *Artists for the Reich. Culture and Race from Weimar to Nazi Germany* (Oxford: Berg, 2005).

Cohen, Deborah, *The War Come Home. Disabled Veterans in Britain and Germany, 1914–1939* (Berkeley: University of California Press, 2001).

Connelly, Frances S., *The Grotesque in Western Art and Culture. The Image at Play* (Cambridge: Cambridge University Press, 2012).

——, "Profound Play: The Image Tradition of the Comic Grotesque," in Pamela Kort, ed., *Comic Grotesque: Wit and Mockery in German Art, 1870–1940* (Munich: Prestell, 2004), 195–209.

——, ed., *Modern Art and the Grotesque* (Cambridge University Press, 2009).

Conzelmann, Otto, *Der andere Dix – Sein Bild vom Menschen und vom Kriege* (Stuttgart: Hatje-Cantz, 1983).

——, *Otto Dix* (Hannover: Fackelträger, 1959).

Cork, Richard, *A Bitter Truth. Avant-garde and the Great War* (New Haven, CT: Yale, 1994).

——, "'A Murderous Carnival': German Artists in the First World War," in Bernd-Rüdiger Hüppauf, ed., *War, Violence, and the Modern Condition* (Berlin: DeGruyter, 1997), 241–276.

Coupe, W. A., "Ungleiche Liebe: A Sixteenth-Century Topos," *The Modern Language Review* 62/4 (October 1967), 661–671.

Craig, Gordon, *Germany, 1866–1945* (London: Oxford University Press, 1978).

Crockett, Dennis, *German Post-Expressionism. The Art of the Great Disorder 1918–1924* (University Park: Pennsylvania State University Press, 1999).

——, "The Most Famous Painting of the 'Golden Twenties'?," *Art Journal* 51/1 (Spring 1992), 72–80.

Cron, Hermann, *Imperial German Army 1914–1918: Organisation, Structure, Orders-of-Battle* (Gliwice: Helion & Co., 2002, reprint of 1937 edn.).

Crouthamel, Jason, *The Great War and German Memory, Society, Politics and Psychological Trauma, 1914–1945* (Exeter: University of Exeter Press, 2009).

Cru, Norton, *Temoins. Essai d'analyse et de critique des souvenirs de combattants édités en français de 1915 à 1928* (Paris: Gallimard, 1930; 3rd edn. Nancy: Presses Universitaires de Nancy, 2006).

Dagen, Philippe, *Le Silence Des Peintres* (Paris: Fayard, 1996, reprint Paris: Éditions Hazan, 2012).

——, "The Morality of Horror," in Annette Becker, ed., *Der Krieg / The War* (Peronne: Historial de la Grande Guerre, 2003), 9–23.

Dalbajewa, Birgit, *Otto Dix in der Dresdener Galerie* (Dresden: Sandstein, 2007), 15 f.

——, Simone Fleischer, and Olaf Peters, *Otto Dix. Der Krieg – Das Dresdner Triptychon* (Dresden: Sandstein, 2014).

——, and Olaf Peters, "Die Auseinandersetzung mit dem Krieg," in Birgit Dalbajewa, Simone Fleischer, and Olaf Peters, *Otto Dix. Der Krieg – Das Dresdner Triptychon* (Dresden: Sandstein, 2014), 71–83.

Dalzell, Tom, *Vietnam War Slang. A Dictionary on Historical Principles* (London: Routledge, 2014).
Daniel, Ute, *The War From Within: German Women in the First World War* (Oxford: Berg, 1997).
Das, Santanu, *Touch and Intimacy in First World War Literature* (Cambridge: Cambridge University Press, 2005).
——, "Wilfred Owen and the sense of touch," in Santanu Das, *Touch and Intimacy in First World War Literature* (Cambridge: Cambridge University Press, 2005), 137–174.
Das Werk (unsigned), "Otto Dix im 'Wolfsberg'," 25/6 (June 1938), 20.
de La Sizeranne, Robert, *L'Art pendant la guerre 1914–1918* (Paris: Hachette, 1919).
Déchelette, François, *L'Argot des Poilus. Dictionnaire humoristique et philologique* (Paris: Editions de Paris, 2004).
Delaporte, Sophie, *Les Guelles Cassés. Les blesées de la face de la Grade Guerre* (Paris: Éditions Noêsis, 1996).
Dix, Otto, *Ich folge liber meinem Dämon: Origanaltonaufnahmen* (Pforzheim: Brigade Commerz, 2009)
Doerner, Max, *Malmaterial und seine Verwendung im Bilde* (Munich: Verlag für praktische Kunstwissenschaft, 1921).
——, *The Materials of the Artist and Their Use in Painting*, trans. Eugen Neuhaus (New York: Harcourt, Brace and World, 1934).
Doherty, Brigid, "'See, We Are All Neurasthenics!' or, the Trauma of Dada Montage," *Critical Inquiry* 24/1 (Autumn 1997), 82–132.
——, "The Work of Art and the Problem of Politics in Berlin Dada," *October* 105 (Summer 2003), 73–92.
Domeier, Norman, *The Eulenburg Affair. A Cultural History of Politics in the German Empire* (Rochester, NY: Camden House, 2015).
Dülffer, Jost, and Gerd Krumeich, eds., *Der verlorene Frieden. Politik und Kriegskultur nach 1918* (Essen: Klartext, 2002).
Eberle, Mathias, *World War I and the Weimar Artists. Dix, Grosz, Beckmann, Schlemmer* (New Haven, CT: Yale University Press, 1985).
Eghigian, Greg, "Injury, Fate, Resentment, and Sacrifice in German Political Culture, 1914–1939," in Greg Eghigian and Matthew Paul Berg, eds., *Sacrifice and National Belonging in Twentieth Century Germany* (College Station: Texas A&M University Press, 2002), 90–117.
Einstein, Carl, "Otto Dix," *Das Kunstblatt* 7/3 (March 1923), 97–102.
Ellis, John, *Eye Deep in Hell: Trench Warfare in World War I* (New York, Pantheon Books, 1976).
——, *The Social History of the Machine Gun* (Manchester, NH: Ayer, 1975).

Emerson, Caryl, "The Outer Word and Inner Speech: Bakhtin, Vygotsky, and the Internalization of Language," *Critical Inquiry* 10/2 (Dec. 1983) 254–264.

Erll, Astrid, *Memory in Culture* (London: Palgrave Macmillan, 2011).

Evans, Richard J., *The Coming of the Third Reich* (London: A. Lane, 2003).

Fischer, Bernd Erhard, *Otto Dix in Hemmenhofen* (Berlin: Edition A B Fischer, 2010).

Fischer, Lothar, *Otto Dix, Ein Malerleben in Deutschland* (Berlin: Nicolaische Verlagsbuchhandlung, 1981).

Fitzke, Kirsten, "Im Menschenschlachthaus hat der personifizierte Tod Konjunktur. Der industrialisierte Krieg in Totentanzzyklen aus dem Rheinland und Thüringen," in Gertrude Cepl-Kaufmann, Gerd Krumeich, Ulla Sommers, eds., *Krieg und Utopie. Kunst, Literatur und Politik im Rheinland nach dem Ersten Weltkrieg* (Essen: Klartext, 2006), 234–250.

Fleischer, Simone, "Der Künstler und der Krieg" in Birgit Dalbajewa, Simone Fleischer, and Olaf Peters, eds., *Otto Dix. Der Krieg – Das Dresdner Triptychon* (Dresden: Sandstein, 2014), 14–33.

Focillon, Henri, *La peinture au XIXe siècle. Le retour à l'antique. Le romantisme* (Évreux: Hérissey, 1927).

Forner, Sean A., "War Commemoration and the Republic in Crisis: Weimar Germany and the Neue Wache," *Central European History* 35/4 (2002), 513–549.

Fox, Paul, "Confronting Postwar Shame in Weimar Germany: Trauma, Heroism, and the War Art of Otto Dix," *Oxford Art Journal*, 29/2 (2006), 247–267.

Frantzen, Allen, *Bloody Good. Chivalry, Sacrifice, and the Great War* (Chicago: University of Chicago Press, 2004).

Friedländer, Salomo ("Mynona"), "Grotesk," *Der Einzige* (1919), and *Der Querschnitt* (1921), cited in Thomas O. Haakenson, "'The Merely Illusory Paradise of Habits': Salomo Friedländer, Walter Benjamin, and the Grotesque," *New German Critique*, 36/1 (106) (Winter 2009), 119–147.

Funkenstein, Susan Laikin, "Anita Berber: Imaging a Weimar Performance Artist," *Woman's Art Journal*, 26/1 (2005), 26–31.

Fuß, Peter, *Das Groteske. Ein Medium des kulturellen Wandels* (Cologne: Böhlau, 2001).

Fussell, Paul, *The Great War and Modern Memory* (New York: Oxford University Press, 1975).

Galerie Arnold, *Zweite Ausstellung Dresdener Künstler, die im Heeresdienste Stehen. Galerie Arnold, Sept. 27 – Oct. 29, 1916* (Dresden: Galerie Arnold, 1916).

Gaughan, Martin, *German Art 1907–1937: Modernism and Modernization* (Oxford: Peter Lang, 2007).

Gay, Peter, *Weimar Culture. The Outsider as Insider* (New York: Harper and Row, 1968).

Geyer, Michael, "Ein Vorbote des Wohlfahrtsstaates," *Geschichte und Gesellschaft*, 9/2 Vol. 9 (1983), 230–277.

Giebe, Marlies, and Maria Körber, "'... weil Dix hier malt wie ein Alter Meister und dabei doch ganz er selbst geblieben ist.' Maltechnische Studien zum Triptychon 'Der Krieg' von Otto Dix," in Birgit Dalbajewa, Simone Fleischer, and Olaf Peters, eds., *Otto Dix. Der Krieg – Das Dresdner Triptychon* (Dresden: Sandstein, 2014), 219–251.

Giloi, Eva, *Monarchy, Myth, and Material Culture in Germany 1750–1950* (Cambridge: Cambridge University Press, 2011).

Goebel, Stephen, *The Great War and Medieval Memory: War, Remembrance, and Medievalism in Britain and Germany, 1914–1940* (Cambridge: Cambridge University Press, 2007).

——, "Re-membered and re-mobilized: The 'Sleeping Dead' in Interwar Germany and Britain," *Journal of Contemporary History*, 39/4 (October 2004), 487–501.

Goerig-Hergott, Frédérique, ed., *Otto Dix. Le Retable d'Issenheim* (Paris: Editions Hazan, 2016).

Goldstein, Joshua, *War and Gender: How Gender Shapes the War System and Vice Versa* (Cambridge, Cambridge University Press, 2001).

Gollbach, Michael, *Die Wiederkehr des Weltkrieges in der Literatur. Zu den Frontromanen der späten Zwanziger Jahre* (Kronberg: Scriptor, 1978).

Gordon, Donald, *Ernst Ludwig Kirchner* (Cambridge: Cambridge University Press, 1968).

Gough, Paul, "'Calculating the Future'. Panoramic sketching, reconnaissance drawing and the material trace of war," in Nicholas J. Saunders and Paul Cornish, eds., *Contested Objects. Material Memories of the Great War* (Abingdon: Routledge, 2009), 237–250.

Graf, Felix, "Otto Dix im Kunstsalon Wolfsberg," *Journal of Swiss Archaeology and Art History* 70/4 (2013), 259–265.

Grayzel, Susan R., "Women and Men," in John Horne, ed., *A Companion to World War I* (Oxford: Wiley & Blackwell, 2010), 263–278.

Griebel, Otto, "Erlebnis und Vorbild – Otto Dix," *Bildende Kunst* 11 (1966), 581–586.

——, *Ich war ein Mann der Straße. Lebenserinnerungen eines Dresdner Malers* (Altenburg: DZA, 1995, 2nd edn.).

Grosz, George, and John Heartfield, "Der Kunstlump," *Der Gegner* 1/10–12 (Berlin: Malik, 1920), 48–56. Translated as "The Art Scab," in Anton Kaes, Martin Jay, Edward Dimendberg, eds., *The Weimar Republic Sourcebook* (Berkeley: University of California Press, 1994), 483–486.

Gutbrod, Philipp, *Otto Dix, The Art of Life* (Stuttgart: Hatje Cantz, 2010).

Haakenson, Thomas O., "'The Merely Illusory Paradise of Habits': Salomo Friedländer, Walter Benjamin, and the Grotesque," *New German Critique*, 36/1 (106) (Winter 2009), 119–147.

Hagen, Oskar, and Reinhard Piper, *Matthias Grünewald* (Munich: R. Piper, 1923).

Halbwachs, Maurice, *On Collective Memory* (Chicago: University of Chicago Press, 1992, Lewis A. Coser, ed. and translator).

Hämmerle, Christa, *Heimat/Front. Geschlechtergeschichte(n) des Ersten Weltkriegs in Österreich-Ungarn* (Vienna: Böhlau, 2014).

Hannoosh, Michele, *Baudelaire and Caricature. From the Comic to an Art of Modernity* (University Park: Pennsylvania State University Press, 1992).

Hartlaub, Gustav, "Der Zynismus als Kunstrichtung?," *Frankfurter Zeitung* (13 September 1924).

Hartley, Keith, and Sarah O'Brien Twohig, eds., *Otto Dix, 1891–1969* (London: Tate Gallery, 1992).

Heller, Reinhold, ed., *Stark Impressions: Graphic Production in Germany*, 1918–1933 (Evanston, IL: Northwestern University, 1993).

Henze, Wolfgang, ed., *Ernst Ludwig Kirchner – Gustav Schiefler, Briefwechsel 1910–1935/38* (Stuttgart: Belser, 1990).

Hermans, G., *Musée Wiertz, Album Illustré* (Antwerp: Hermans, c. 1900).

Herzogenrath, Wulf, "Die Mappe *Der Krieg* 1923/24," in Wulf Herzogenrath and Johann-Karl Schmidt, eds., *Otto Dix – zum 100. Geburtstag* (Stuttgart: Hatje-Cantz, 1991), 167–192.

Herzogenrath, Wulf, and Johann-Karl Schmidt, eds., *Otto Dix – zum 100. Geburtstag* (Stuttgart: Hatje-Cantz, 1991).

Hirschfeld, Magnus, *Sittengeschichte des Weltkrieges* (Berlin: Verlag für Sexualwissenschaft Schneider & Co.), 1930.

Hofer, Hans Georg, *Nervenschwäche und Krieg. Modernitätskritik und Krisenbewältigung in der österreichischen Psychiatrie (1880–1920)* (Vienna: Böhlau, 2004).

Hoffmann-Curtius, Kathrin, "Sieg ohne Trauer – Trauer ohne Sieg: Totenklage auf Kriegsdenkmälern des Ersten Weltkrieges," in Gisela Ecker and Maria Kublik-Kramer, *Trauer Tragen – Trauer Zeigen: Inszenierungen der Geschlechter* (Munich: Wilhelm Fink, 1999), 259–286.

Honisch, Dieter, *Bilder vom Menschen in der Kunst des Abendlandes* (Berlin: Mann, 1980).

Horn, *Die deutsche Soldatensprache* (Giessen: Töpelmann, 2nd edn., 1905).

Hüppauf, Bernd-Rüdiger, "Langemarck, Verdun, and the Myth of a New Man in Germany after the First World War," *War and Society* 6/2 (1988), 70–103.

——, "Zwischen Metaphysik und visuellem Essayismus. Franz Schauwecker: *So war der Krieg* (1928)," in Thomas F. Schneider, ed., *Von Richthofen bis Remarque* (Amsterdam: Rodopi, 2003), 233–248.

Hynes, Samuel, *A War Imagined: The First World War and English Culture* (New York: Atheneum, 1991).

Imme, Theodor, *Die deutsche Soldatensprache der Gegenwart und ihr Humor* (Dortmund: Ruhfus, 1918).

Jähner, Horst, "Vor dem wie steht das was: Zu den Bildern über den Krieg von Otto Dix," *Bildende Kunst*, 6 (1957), 370–375.

Jaspert, Bruno, "Benno Elkan: Den Opfern," *Das Kunstblatt* 14 (1930), 178–180.

Jeismann, Michael, and Rolf Westheider, "'Wofür stirbt der Bürger?' Nationaler Totenkult und Staatsbürgertum in Deutschaland und Frankreich seit der Französischer Revolution," in Reinhart Koselleck, ed., *Der politische Totenkult. Kriegerdenkmäler der Moderne* (Munich: Fink, 1994), 23–49.

Jelavich, Peter, "Grotesque and Carnivalesque: Negation and Renewal around 1900," in Pamela Kort, *Comic Grotesque: Wit and Mockery in German Art, 1870–1940* (Munich: Prestell, 2004), 89–129.

Jünger, Ernst, *In Stahlgewittern* (Berlin: E. S. Mittler und Sohn, 1922).

——, *In Stahlgewittern*, Stuttgart: Klett-Cotta, 1978).

——, *Kriegstagebuch 1914–1918* (Stuttgart: Klett-Cotta, 2014).

——, *Storm of Steel*, trans. Michael Hoffmann (New York: Penguin Books, 2004).

Jürgens-Kirchhoff, Annegret, *Schreckensbilder. Krieg und Kunst im 20. Jahrhundert* (Berlin: Reimer, 1993).

Kállai, Ernst, "Dämonie der Satire," *Das Kunstblatt* 11 (1927), 97–104.

Karcher, Eva, *Eros und Tod im Werk von Otto Dix* (Munster: Lit, 1984).

Keegan, John, *The First World War* (New York: Vintage, 2000).

Kessel, Martina, "Gewalt Schreiben. 'Deutscher Humor' in den Weltkriegen," in Wolfgang Hardtwig, ed., *Ordnungen in der Krise; Zur Politischen Kulturgeschichte Deutschlands 1900–1933* (Munich: Oldenbourg, 2007), 229–258.

Kienitz, Sabine, "Beschädigte Helden. Zur Politisierung des kriegsinvaliden Soldatenkörpers in der Weimarer Republik," in Jost Dülffer and Gerd Krumeich, eds., *Der verlorene Frieden. Politik und Kriegskultur nach 1918* (Essen: Klartext, 2002), 199–214.

Kiesling Scott F., "Playing the Straight Man: Displaying and Maintaining Male Heterosexuality in Discourse," in Kathryn Campbell-Kibler, Robert J. Podesva, Sarah J. Roberts, *et al.*, eds., *Language and Sexuality. Contesting Meaning in Theory and Practice* (Stanford, CA: CSLI Publications, 2002), 249–267.

Killen, Andreas, *Berlin Electropolis: Shock, Nerves, and German Modernity* (Berkeley: University of California Press, 2006).

Klein, Heijo, "'Kállais Interpretation' des 'Schützengrabenbildes' von Otto Dix im Vergleich mit zeitgenössischen und gegenwärtigen Deutungen," *Acta Historiae Artium* 36 (1993), 180–88.

Kohlrausch, Martin, *Der Monarch im Skandal: Die Logik der Massenmedien und die Transformation der wilhelminischen Monarchie* (Berlin: DeGruyter, 2005).

Kölner Stadtanzeiger (unsigned), "Zur Neuordnung des Wallraf-Richartz-Museums," *Unterhaltungsbeilage der Stadt-Anzeigers für Köln und Umgebung* (2 December 1923).

Körber, Maria, "Studien zur Maltechnik der Neuen Sachlichkeit in Dresden," in Birgit Dalbajewa, ed., *Neue Sachlichkeit in Dresden* (Dresden: Sandstein, 2011), 144–169.

Kort, Pamela, *Comic Grotesque: Wit and Mockery in German Art, 1870–1940* (Munich: Prestell, 2004).

Koselleck, Reinhart, and Michael Jeismann, eds., *Der politische Totenkult: Kriegerdenmäler in der Moderne* (Munich: Fink, 1994).

Krahmer, Catherine, ed., Julius Meier-Graefe, *Kunst ist nicht für Kunstgeschichte da. Briefe und Dokumente* (Göttingen: Wallstein, 2001).

Kramer, Alan, "The First World War and German Memory," in Heather Jones, Jennifer O'Brien, and Christoph Schmidt-Supprian, eds., *Untold War: New Perspectives in First World War Studies* (Leiden: Brill, 2008), 385–415.

Krul, Wessel, "Realism, Renaissance and Nationalism," in Bernhard Ridderbos, Anne van Buren, and Henk van Veen, *Early Netherlandish Paintings. Rediscovery, Reception, and Research* (Los Angeles, CA: J. Paul Getty Museum, 2005), 252–289.

Kühne, Thomas, *Kameradschaft. Die Soldaten des nationalsozialistischen Krieges 20. Jahrhundert* (Göttingen: Vandenhoeck and Ruprecht, 2006).

——, *The Rise and Fall of Comradeship. Hitler's Soldiers, Male Bonding and Mass Violence in the Twentieth Century* (Cambridge: Cambridge University Press, 2017).

Kunstmuseum Stuttgart, *Otto Dix and the New Objectivity* (Stuttgart: Hatje Cantz, 2012).

Kunstsammlung Nordrhein-Westfalen, *Otto Dix – The Evil Eye / Der Böse Blick* (Munich: Prestel, 2017).

La Veleye, Émile de, *Catalogue du Musée Wiertz, précédé d'une Notice Biographique extraite de la 'Revue des Deux Mondes* (Bruxelles: Weissenbruch, 1875).

Lais, Otto, *Maschinengewehr im Eisernen Regiment (8. Badisches Infanterie-Regiment No. 169)* (Karlsruhe: G. Braun, 1935).

Lankheit, Klaus, *Das Triptychon als Pathosformel* (Heidelberg: Winter, 1959).

Lecoq-Ramond, Sylvie, "Un Maitre ancien du XXe siècle: Otto Dix et l'art de Grünewald," in Sylvie Lecoq-Ramond, Rainer Beck, *et al.*, *Otto Dix et les maîtres anciens* (Colmar: Musée d'Unterlinden, 1996), 66–94.

Leed, Eric, *No Man's Land: Combat and Identity in World War One* (Cambridge: Cambridge University Press, 1979)

Lehmann, Hans-Ulrich, *Otto Dix: Die Zeichnungen im Dresdner Kupferstich-Kabinett: Katalog des Bestandes* (Dresden: Kupferstich-Kabinett, 1991).

Leighten, Patricia, *Re-Ordering the Universe: Picasso and Anarchism, 1897–1914* (Princeton, NJ: Princeton University Press, 1989).
Lerner, Paul, *Hysterical Men. War, Psychiatry, and the Politics of Trauma in Germany, 1890–1930* (Ithaca, NY: Cornell University Press, 2003).
Lewis, Beth Irwin, *George Grosz. Art and Politics in the Weimar Republic* (Princeton, NJ: Princeton University Press, 1991).
Linsmayer, Ludwig, *Politische Kultur im Saargebiet 1920–1932. Symbolische Politik, verhinderte Demokratisierung, nationalisiertes Kulturleben in einer abgetrennten Region* (St. Ingebert: Röhrig, 1992).
Lloyd, David, *Battlefield Tourism: Pilgrimage and the Commemoration of the Great War in Britain, Australia, and Canada, 1919–1939* (London: Bloomsbury Academic, 1998).
Löffler, Fritz, *Otto Dix. Life and Work*, trans. R. J. Hollingdale (New York and London: Holmes and Meier, 1982).
——, *Otto Dix und der Krieg* (Leipzig: Reclam, 1986).
——, "Otto Dix," *Zeitschrift fur Kunst* 3 (1949), 173–93.
——, Emilio Bertonati, and Johann Heuzinger von Waldegg, *Dresdner Sezession 1919–1923* (Munich: Galleria del Levante, 1977).
Lorenz, Ulrike, ed., *Otto Dix. Briefe* (Cologne: Wienand, 2013).
——, Beatrice von Bormann, and Roger Dierden, *Dix/Beckmann. Mythos der Welt* (Munich: Hirmer Verlag, 2014).
Lorenzer, Anna Barbara, "Studien zur Maltechnik von Otto Dix von 1910–1933," *Zeitschrift für Kunsttechnologie und Konservierung* 3 (1989), 113–148.
Lubin, David M., "Masks, Mutilation, and Modernity: Anna Coleman Ladd and the First World War," *Archives of American Art Journal* 47/3–4 (2008), 4–15.
Ludwig, W., "Beiträge zur Psychologie der Furcht im Kriege" in W. Stern and O. Lipmann, eds., *Behefte zur Zeitschrift für angewandte Psychologie* 21 (1920), 125–172.
Lyford, Amy, *Surrealist Masculinities. Gender Anxiety and the Aesthetics of Post-World War I Reconstruction in France* (Berkeley: University of California Press, 2007).
McGreevy, Linda F., *Bitter Witness: Otto Dix and the Great War* (Bern: Peter Lang, 2003).
Mackenzie, Michael, catalog entry for *Sailor and Prostitute* [*Matrose und Mädchen*] (1923), in Reinhold Heller, ed., *Stark Impressions: Graphic Production in Germany*, 1918–1933 (Evanston, IL: Northwestern University, 1993), 278.
März, Roland, "Das Gemälde 'Mondweib' von Otto Dix aus dem Jahr 1919. Eine Neuerwerbung der Nationalgalerie" *Forschungen und Berichte* 25 (1985), 71–81.
——, "Ja, das ist doch auch eine Lust am Grotesken," *Museumsjournal: Berichte aus Museen, Schlossern und Sammlungen in Berlin und Potsdam* 9/4 (October 1995) 52–55.

Maußer, Otto, *Deutsche Soldatensprache. Ihr Aufbau und ihre Probleme* (Strasbourg: Trübner, 1917).

Meier-Graefe, Julius, "Die Ausstellung in der Akademie," *Deutsche Allgemeine Zeitung* (2 July 1924, evening edition).

Merkatz, Friedrich v., ed., *Unterrichtsbuch für die Maschinengewehr-Kompagnien. Gerät 08* (Berlin: Eisenschmidt, 1917).

Merz, Jorg Martin, "Otto Dix' Kriegsbilder. Motivationen – Intentionen – Rezeptionen," *Marburger Jahrbuch für Kunstwissenschaft* 26 (1999), 189–226.

Mitchell, Claudine, "Facing horror: women's work, sculptural practice and the Great War," in Valerie Mainz and Griselda Pollack, eds., *Work and the Image, Volume II: Work in Modern Times: Visual Mediations and Social Processes* (Burlington: Ashgate, 2000), 33–55.

Möller, Klaus-Peter, *Der wahre E. Ein Wörterbuch der DDR-Soldatensprache* (Berlin: Lukas Verlag für Kunst- und Geistesgeschichte), 2000.

Morat, Daniel, "Kalte Männlichkeit? Weimarer Verhaltenslehren im Spannungsfeld von Emotionen- und Geschlechtergeschichte," in Manuel Borutta and Nina Verheyen, eds., *Die Präsenz der Gefühle. Männlichkeit und Emotion im 19. und 20. Jahrhundert* (Bielefeld: Transcript, 2010), 153–177.

Mosse, George, F*allen Soldiers. Reshaping the Memory of the World Wars* (Oxford: Oxford University Press, 1991).

Moxey, Keith, "Impossible Distance: Past and Present in the Study of Dürer and Grünewald," in Larry Silver and Jeffrey Chipps Smith, eds., *The Essential Dürer* (Philadelphia: University of Pennsylvania Press, 2010), 206–226.

Müller, Karsten, "The Charleston and the Prosthetic Leg: Otto Dix and the Art of the Balancing Act," in Olaf Peters, ed., *Otto Dix* (Munich: Prestel, 2010), 164–178.

Müller, Richard, "Spiegelbilder des Verfalls in der Kunst," *Dresdner Anzeiger* (23 September 1933).

Neue Züricher Zeitung (unsigned), 8 May 1938, e1.

Nevin, Thomas, *Ernst Jünger and Germany. Into the Abyss, 1914–1945* (Durham, NC: Duke University Press, 1996).

Niemeyer, Wilhelm, *Matthias Grünewald – der Maler des Isenheimer Altars* (Berlin: Furche, 1921).

Paret, Peter, "Machine-gun Section Advancing," in Peter Paret, *Imagined Battles. Reflections of War in European Art* (Chapel Hill: University of North Carolina Press, 1997), 99–115.

Pawly, Ronald, *Napoleon's Dragoons of the Imperial Guard* (Oxford: Osprey, 2012).

Pelnár, Josef, *Das Zittern. Seine Erscheinungsformen, seine Pathogenese und klinische Bedeutung*, trans. Gustav Mühlstein (Berlin: Springer, 1913).

Peters, Olaf, "Die Erfahrung des Krieges, 1914–1918," in Birgit Dalbajewa, Simone Fleischer, and Olaf Peters, eds., *Otto Dix. Der Krieg – Das Dresdner Triptychon* (Dresden: Sandstein, 2014), 47–53.
——, "Die ewige Wiederkehr des Gleichen. Zur Geschichtsauffasung des Gemäldes 'Der Krieg' von Otto Dix," in Uwe Fleckner, ed., *Bilder machen Geschichte: Historische Erignisse im Gedächtnis der Kunst* (Berlin: DeGruyter, 2014), 305–318.
——, "Eine Summe des Krieges. Otto Dix' Triptychon 'Der Krieg' (1929–1932)," in Birgit Dalbajewa, Simone Fleischer, and Olaf Peters, eds., *Otto Dix. Der Krieg – Das Dresdner Triptychon* (Dresden: Sandstein, 2014), 139–159.
——, "Intransigent Realism. Otto Dix between the World Wars," in Olaf Peters, ed., *Otto Dix* (Munich: Prestel, 2010), 13–31.
——, *Neue Sachlichkeit und Nationalsozialismus. Affirmation und Kritik 1931–1947* (Berlin: Reimer, 1998).
——, *Otto Dix. Der unerschrockene Blick* (Stuttgart: Reclam, 2013).
——, "Otto Dix – Otto Baumgärtel – Marga Kummer. Biographische Bemerkungen zum Frühwerk, zu Nietzsche, Mazdaznan und Ernst Heckel," in Ulrike Lorenz, ed., *Dix avant Dix. Das Jugend-und Frühwerk 1903–1914* (Jena: Glaux, 2000), 280–292.
——, "War 1924," in Olaf Peters, ed., *Otto Dix* (Munich: Prestel, 2010), 65.
——, ed., *Otto Dix* (Munich: Prestel, 2010).
Petropoulos, Jonathan, *Art as Politics in the Third Reich* (Chapel Hill: University of North Carolina Press, 1996).
——, *Artists Under Hitler. Collaboration and Survival in Nazi Germany* (New Haven, CT: Yale University Press), 2014.
——, *The Faustian Bargain: The Art World in Nazi Germany* (Oxford: Oxford University Press, 2000).
Pfäffle, Suse, *Otto Dix. Werkverzeichnis der Aquarelle und Gouachen* (Stuttgart: Hatje, 1991).
Pfeiler, Wilhelm, *War and the German Mind: The Testimony of Men of Fiction Who Fought at the Front* (New York: Columbia University Press, 1941).
Pietzsch, Henning, *Die Fronterfahrungen der deutschen Soldaten im Ersten Weltkrieg und ihre Ideologisierung zum ‚Fronterlebnis' in den zwanziger Jahren* (Stuttgart: Ibidem, 2005).
Pitzen, Jutta, *Jupp Rübsam, 1896–1976* (Krefeld: Kühlen, 1991).
Pol, Heinz, "Trommelfeur" *Die Weltbühne* 20/32 (7 August 1924), 236–237.
Potztal, Monkia, *Ludwig Dettmann: Zwischen Avantgarde und Anpassung* (Heide: Boyens, 2008).
Prior, Robin, and Trevor Wilson, *The Somme* (New Haven, CT: Yale University Press, 2005).

Probst, Volker G., *Bilder vom Tode. Eine Studie zum deutschen Kriegerdenkmal in der Weimarer Republik am Beispiel des Pièta-Motives und seiner profanierten Varianten* (Hamburg: Wayasbah, 1986).
——, *Das Pietà-Motiv bei Arno Breker* (Bonn: Marco, 1985).
Radkau, Joachim, *Das Zeitalter der Nervosität. Deutschland zwischen Bismarck und Hitler* (Munich: Propyläen Taschenbuch, 2000).
Ratzka, Thomas, "Dix, Grünewald, und die Neue Sachlichkeit," in Thomas Ratzka and Brigitte Schad, eds., *Grünewald in der Moderne. Die Rezeption Matthias Grünewalds im 20. Jahrhundert* (Cologne: Wienand, 2002), 51–62.
Remarque, Erich Maria, *All Quiet on the Western Front*, trans. A. W. Wheen (New York: Random House, 2013 edition). First published in German, *Im Westen Nichts Neues* (Berlin: Ullstein, 1928).
Renn, Ludwig, *Krieg* (Berlin: Aufbau, 2014, originally 1928).
Rewald, Sabine, Ian Baruma, and Matthias Eberle, *Glitter and Doom: German Portraits From the 1920s* (New Haven, CT: Yale University Press, 2006).
Ridderbos, Bernhard, "From Waagen to Friedländer," in Bernhard Ridderbos, Anne van Buren, and Henk van Veen, *Early Netherlandish Paintings. Rediscovery, Reception, and Research* (Los Angeles, CA: J. Paul Getty Museum, 2005), 218–251.
——, "Objects and Questions," in Bernhard Ridderbos, Anne van Buren, and Henk van Veen, *Early Netherlandish Paintings. Rediscovery, Reception, and Research* (Los Angeles, CA: J. Paul Getty Museum, 2005), 4–172.
Robinson, Philip, and Nigel Cave, *The Underground War: Vimy Ridge to Arras*, Vol. 1 (South Yorkshire: Pen and Sword Military Press, 2011).
Rosenfeld, Gavriel D., *Munich and Memory: Architecture, Monuments, and the Legacy of the Third Reich* (Oakland: University of California Press, 2000).
Rößler, Johannes, "Zwischen den Fronten. Der Genter Altar im Ersten Weltkrieg und im Friedensvertrag von Versailles," in Stephan Kemperdick and Johannes Rößler, eds., *Der Genter Altar der Brüder van Eyck, Geschichte und Würdigung* (Petersberg: Michael Imhof, 2014), 101–111.
Rossol, Nadine, "Commemoration of the Fallen (Germany)," *1914–1918-online. International Encyclopedia of the First World War*, <https://encyclopedia.1914-1918-online.net/article/commemoration_cult_of_the_fallen_germany> (updated 8 October 2014).
——, *Performing the Nation in Interwar Germany. Sport, Spectacle, and Political Symbolism, 1926–1936* (London: Palgrave Macmillan, 2010).
Rübsam, Jupp, "Unser Denkmal. Das Urteil eines Architekten," *Der 39er*, 3/11 (1928), 82.
Rüdiger, Ulrike, *Grüsse aus dem Krieg. Die Feldpostkarten der Otto-Dix-Sammlung in der Kunstgalerie Gera* (Gera: Kunstgalerie Gera, 1991).

Saalmann, Timo, *Kunstpolitik der Berliner Museen 1919–1959* (Berlin: de Gruyter, 2013).
Sacco, Joe, *The Great War: July 1, 1916, The First Day of the Battle of the Somme. An Illustrated Panorama* (New York: W. W. Norton, 2013).
Saehrendt, Christian, *Der Stellungskrieg der Denkmäler im Berlin der Zwischenkriegszeit 1919–1939* (Bonn: Dietz, 2004).
Salmony, Alfred, "Die neue Galerie des 17. Bis 20. Jahrhunderts im Museum Wallraf-Richartz in Köln," *Der Cicerone* 16/1, 6–11.
Schauwecker, Franz, *So war der Krieg. 200 Kampfaufnahmen aus der Front* (Berlin: Frundsberg, 1927).
Schmidt, Diether, *Otto Dix im Selbstbildnis* (East Berlin: Henschel, 1981).
Schmidt, Paul Ferdinand, "Der Schützengraben," *Die Weltbühne* 20/32 (7 August 1924), 235–236.
——, "Die deutschen Veristen," *Das Kunstblatt* 8 (1924), 373.
Schmidt, Rudolf, *Architekturplastik. Bildhauer Richard Kuöhl* (Berlin: Gebr. Mann, 1997).
Schmits, Walter, "Ein Bild des Krieges," *Kölnische Zeitung* (7 December 1923, early morning edition).
——, *Kölnische Zeitung* (14 December 1923, evening edition).
Schmitz, Britta, "Otto Dix' 'Flandern' 1934–1936," in Wulf Herzogenrath and Johann-Karl Schmidt, eds., Wulf Herzogenrath and Johann-Karl Schmidt, eds., *Otto Dix – zum 100. Geburtstag* (Stuttgart: Hatje-Cantz, 1991), 268–271.
Schneegans, Heinrich, *Geschichte der Grotesken Satire* (Strasbourg: Karl Trübner, 1894).
Schneider, Thomas F., "Die Meute hinter Remarque. Zur Diskussion um *Im Westen nichts Neues* 1928–1930," *Jahrbuch zur Literatur der Weimarer Republik*, 1 (1995), 143–170.
——, "'Sie werden auferstehen!' Otto Dix' Triptychon 'Der Krieg' im Kontext zeitgenössischer visueller und literarischer Repräsentationen des Ersten Weltkrieges," in Birgit Dalbajewa, Simone Fleischer, and Olaf Peters, eds., *Otto Dix. Der Krieg – Das Dresdner Triptychon* (Dresden: Sandstein, 2014), 125–135.
——, "The Weimar Republic and the Literature of the Great War," in Brian Murdoch, ed., *Critical Insights.* All Quiet on the Western Front *by Erich Maria Remarque* (Pasadena, CA: Salem Press, 2011), 23–37.
Scholz, Dieter, "Das Triptychon der Krieg," in Wulf Herzogenrath and Johann-Karl Schmidt, eds., *Otto Dix – zum 100. Geburtstag* (Stuttgart: Hatje-Cantz, 1991), 261–267.
Schröck-Schmidt, Wolfgang, "Der Schicksalsweg des 'Schützengraben'" in Wulf Herzogenrath and Johann-Karl Schmidt, eds., *Otto Dix – zum 100. Geburtstag* (Stuttgart: Hatje-Cantz, 1991), 159–164.
Schubert, "Rezeptions- und Stilpluralismus in die frühen Selbstbildnissen des Otto Dix," in Werner Hager and Norbert Knopp, eds., *Beiträge zum Problem des Stilpluralismus* (Munich: Prestel, 1977), 203–224.

Schubert, Dietrich, "Betrifft: O. Conzelmann, Der 'Andere' Dix," *Kritische Berichte* 12/1 (1984), 84–94.
——, "Death in the Trench: The Death of the Portrait? Otto Dix's Wartime Self-Portraits, 1915–1918," in Olaf Peters, ed., *Otto Dix* (Munich: Prestel, 2010), 33–55.
——, "Die Verfolgung des Gemäldes *Schützengraben* (1923) von Otto Dix," in Rolf Kloepfer and Burckhard Dücker, eds., *Kritik und Geschichte der Intoleranz* (Heidelberg: Syncron, 2000), 351–370.
——, "Krüppeldarstellungen im Werk von Otto Dix nach 1920: Zynismus oder Sarkasmus?," in Gertrude Cepl-Kaufmann and Gerd Krumeich, eds., *Krieg und Utopie. Kunst, Literatur und Politik im Rheinland nach dem Ersten Weltkrieg* (Essen: Klartext, 2006), 293–308.
——, *Künstler im Trommelfeuer des Krieges* (Heidelberg: Wunderhorn, 2013).
——, "Nietzsche-Konkretionsformen in der bildenden Kunst," Müller-Lauter and Volker Gerhardt, eds., *Nietzsche-Studien*, 10/11 (1981/82), 278–327.
——, *Otto Dix* (Reinbek: Rowohlt, 1980, revised edition, 2001).
——, "Otto Dix: Die Radierungen Der Krieg (Berlin 1924) oder: das "Yo lo vi," in Verein August Macke Haus, *Otto Dix. "Der Krieg" Radierwerk, 1924* (Bonn: August Macke Haus, 1999), 12–46.
——, "Otto Dix – das Triptychon 'Der Krieg' 1929–1932," in *Heidelberger Jahrbücher* 48 (2004), 311–331.
——, "Otto Dix, Die Radierungen 'Der Krieg' von 1924," *Kunsthistorische Arbeitsblätter*, 9 (September 2002), 39–46.
——, "Otto Dix und der Krieg," Dietrich Harth and Dietrich Schubert, eds., *Pazifismus zwischen den Weltkriegen: Deutscher Schriftsteller und Künstler gegen Krieg und Militarismus 1918–1933* (Heidelberg: HVA, 1985), 185–202.
——, "Otto Dix Zeichnet im Ersten Weltkrieg," in Wolfgang Mommsen, ed., *Kultur und Krieg, Die Rolle der Intellektuellen, Künstler und Schriftsteller im Ersten Weltkrieg* (Berlin: de Gruyter, 2015), 179–194.
Schwarz, Birgit, *Otto Dix. Großstadt* (Frankfurt: Insel, 1993).
Seiwert, Franz Wilhelm, Heinrich Hoerle, *et al.*, "Zu dem Artikel von Meier-Graefe: 'Die Ausstellung in der Akademie'," *Das Kunstblatt* 8 (October 1924), 317–318.
Sheldon, Jack, *The German Army on the Somme 1914–1916* (Barnsley, England: Pen & Sword Military, 2005).
Siebrecht, Claudia, *The Aesthetics of Loss. German Women's Art of the First World War* (Oxford: Oxford University Press, 2013).
——, "The *Mater Dolorosa* on the Battlefield – Mourning Mothers in German Women's Art of the First World War," *History of Warfare* 49 (2008), 259–291.

Simon, Olaf, "Wege zum Bild – die Kartons," in Birgit Dalbajewa, Simone Fleischer, and Olaf Peters, *Otto Dix. Der Krieg – Das Dresdner Triptychon* (Dresden: Sandstein, 2014), 169–172.

Simpson, Patricia Anne, *The Erotics of War in German Romanticism* (Lewisburg, PA: Bucknell University Press, 2006).

Smith, Helen Zenna, *Not So Quiet …* (New York: The Feminist Press, CUNY, 1993; first published 1930).

Söll, Änne, "'An die Schönheit' – Selbst, Männlichkeit und Moderne in Otto Dix Selbstbildnis von 1922" in Annette Geiger, ed., *Der Schöne Körper: Mode und Kosmetik in Kunst und Gesellschaft* (Cologne: Böhlau, 2008), 149–166.

——, *Der Neue Mann? Männerporträts von Otto Dix, Christian Schad und Anton Räderscheidt, 1914–1930* (Paderborn: Wilhelm Fink, 2016).

——, "Neue Männlichkeit. Die Matrosenbilder von Otto Dix," in Nils Büttner and Daniel Spanke, eds., *Das Auge der Welt. Otto Dix und die Neue Sachlichkeit* (Stuttgart: Hatje Cantz, 2012), 48–61.

Sommer, Robert, "Beseitigung funktioneller Taubheit besonders bei Soldaten durch eine experimental-psychologische Methode," *Schmidts Jarhbücher der in- und ausländischen gesamten Medizin* 84 (February 1917), 65–75.

Sozialistische Arbeiterjugend West-Sachsen, *Nie Wieder Krieg* (Leipzig: Roter Türmer, 1925).

Springer, Peter, *Hand and Head. Ernst Ludwig Kirchner's Self-Portrait as Soldier*, trans. Susan Ray (Berkeley: University of California Press, 2002).

Steinweis, Alan E., *Art, Ideology, and Economics in Nazi Germany. The Reich Chambers of Music, Theater, and the Visual Arts* (Chapel Hill: The University of North Carolina Press, 1993).

Stieglitz, Ann, "The Reproduction of Agony: Toward a Reception-History of Grünewald's Isenheim Altar after the First World War," *Oxford Art Journal* 12 (1989), 87–103.

Strachan, Hew, *First World War*, Vol. 1, *To Arms* (New York: Oxford, 2001).

Szejnmann, Claus-Christian W., *Nazism in Central Germany: The Brownshirts in 'Red' Saxony* (New York: Berghahn Books, 1999).

Tatar, Maria, *Lustmord: Sexual Murder in Weimar Germany* (Princeton, NJ: Princeton University Press, 1993).

Theweleit, Klaus, *Male Fantasies, Vol. 2: Male Bodies: Psychoanalyzing the White Terror*, trans. Erica Carter (Minneapolis: University of Minnesota Press, 1989).

Thomson, Richard, *The Troubled Republic* (New Haven, CT: Yale University Press, 2004).

Ulrich, Bernd, and Benjamin Ziemann, eds., "'Dann gehts wieder in die schöne Läuse-Schlampagne.' Otto Dix im ersten Weltkrieg," in Birgit Dalbajewa, Simone

Fleischer, and Olaf Peters, *Otto Dix. Der Krieg – Das Dresdner Triptychon* (Dresden: Sandstein, 2014), 35–45.

——, *Krieg im Frieden. Die umkämpfte Erinnerung an den Ersten Weltkrieg. Quellen und Dokumente* (Frankfurt: Fischer, 1997).

van Dyke, James, "Dix Petrified," in Deborah Ascher Barnstone and Barbara McCloskey, eds., *The Art of War* (Oxford: Peter Lang, 2017), 103–127.

——, "Erasure and Jewishness in Otto Dix's *Portrait of the Lawyer Hugo Simons*," in Warren Carter, Haran Barnaby, Frederic J. Schwartz, *et al.*, eds., *Renew Marxist Art History* (London: University College, 2013), 362–381.

——, *On the Grotesque Body in a Double-Sided Drawing by Otto Dix*, in Bettina Mathias, Eliza Garrison, and James A. van Dyke, eds, *Approaches to the Body in Early Twentieth-Century German and Austrian Art* (Hanover: University Press of New England, 2015), 61–77.

——, "Otto Dix's philosophical metropolis," in Olaf Peters, ed., *Otto Dix* (Munich: Prestel, 2010), 178–197.

——, "Otto Dix's *Streetbattle* and the Limits of Satire in Dusseldorf, 1928," *Oxford Art Journal* 32/1 (2009), 37–65.

van Lil, Kira, "Ein perfekter Skandal. Der 'Schützengraben' von Otto Dix zwischen Kritik und Verfemung," in Uwe Fleckner, ed., *Das verfemte Meisterwerk. Schicksalswege moderner Kunst im "Dritten Reich"* (Berlin: Akademie, 2009), 49–74.

——, *Otto Dix und der Erste Weltkrieg. Die Natur des Menschen in der Ausnahmesituation* (Ludwig Maximillian University Munich, dissertation, 2000).

Verein August Macke Haus, *Otto Dix. "Der Krieg" Radierwerk, 1924* (Bonn: August Macke Haus, 1999).

Verhey, Jeffrey, *The Spirit of 1914. Militarism, Myth and Mobilization in Germany* (Cambridge: Cambridge University Press, 2000).

Vinnen, Carl, *Ein Protest Deutscher Künstler* (Jena: Diedrichs, 1911).

von Killinger, Manfred, *Ernstes und Heiteres aus dem Putschleben* (Berlin: Vormarsch, 1928).

——, *Kampf um Oberschlesien 1921* (Leipzig: K. F. Koehler, 1934).

Wagner, Andreas, *Mutschmann gegen von Killinger. Konfliktlinien zwischen Gauleiter und SA-Führer während des Aufstiegs der NSDAP und der „Machtergreifung" im Freistaat Sachsen* (Beucha: Sax, 2001, dissertation).

Walter-Ris, Anja, *Die Geschichte der Galerie Nierendorf. Kunstleidenschaft im Dienst der Moderne. Berlin / New York 1920–1995* (Freie Universität Berlin, dissertation, 1999).

Watson, Alexander, *Enduring the Great War. Combat, Morale, and Collapse in the German and British Armies, 1914–1918* (Cambridge: Cambridge University Press, 2008).

Weikop, Christian, "Berlin Dada and the Carnivalesque. *Jedermann sein eigner Fussball* (1919) and *Der Dada* (1919–1920)," in Peter Brooker and Andrew Thacker, eds., *The Oxford Critical and Cultural History of Modernist Magazines: Europe 1880–1940* (Oxford: Oxford University Press, 2014), 816–854.

Weiß, Christian, "'Soldaten des Friedens'. Die pazifistischen Veteranen und Kriegsopfer des 'Reichsbundes' und ihre Kontakte zu den französischen *anciens combatants* 1919–1933" in Wolfgang Hardtwig, ed., *Politische Kulturgeschichte der Zwischenkriegszeit 1918–1939* (Göttingen: Vandenhoeck & Ruprecht, 2005), 183–204.

Weitz, Ulrich, "Kriegsgrüppel, Kapp-Putsch und Kunstlump-Debatte," in Galerie der Stadt Stuttgart, *Dix* (Stuttgart: Hatje, 1991), 95–100.

Werckmeister Otto Karl, "Radical Art History" *Art Journal* 42/4 (Winter 1982), 284–291.

Westecker, Wilhelm, *Krieg und Kunst. Das Erlebnis des Weltkrieges und des Großdeutschen Freiheitskrieges* (Vienna and Leipzig: Luser, 1940).

Westheim, Paul, "Dix," *Das Kunstblatt* 10 (1926), 142–146.

Wetzel, Maria, "Professor Otto Dix – Ein harter Mann, dieser Maler," *Diplotamischer Kurier* 14 (1965), 731–745. Reprinted in Schmidt, *Otto Dix im Selbstbildnis*, 269–270.

Whalen, Robert Weldon, *Bitter Wounds. German Victims of the Great War, 1914–1939* (Ithaca, NY: Cornell University Press, 1984), 164–165.

Winter, Jay, *Remembering War. The Great War Between Memory and History in the Twentieth Century* (New Haven, CT and London: Yale University Press, 2006).

——, *Sites of Memory, Sites of Mourning: The Great War in European Cultural History* (Cambridge: Cambridge University Press, 1995).

Wolfradt, Willi, "Otto Dix," *Der Cicerone* 16/20, 943–954.

——, *Otto Dix* (Leipzig: Klinkhardt & Biermann, 1924).

Worringer, Wilhelm, *Formprobleme der Gotik* (Munich: Piper, republished with 50 plates in 1919; a new edition was brought out in December 1926).

Wrobel, Ignaz (pseud. of Kurt Tucholsky), "Gesunder Pazifismus," *Das Andere Deutschland* (31 March 1928), 4.

Zacher, Inge, *Ewald Mataré: Der 'Tote Krieger' in Kleve* (Kleve: Boss, 1985).

Zeller, Ursula, "The Reception of Dix's Work," in Keith Hartley and Sarah O'Brien Twohig, eds., *Otto Dix, 1891–1969* (London: Tate Gallery, 1992), 49–60.

Ziemann, Benjamin, *Contested Commemorations, Republican War Veterans and Weimar Political Culture* (Cambridge: Cambridge University Press, 2012).

——, "Repbulikanische Kriegserinnerung in einer polarisierten Öffentlichkeit. Das Reichsbanner Schwarz-Rot-Gold als Veteranenverband der sozialistischen Arbeiterschaft," *Historische Zeitschrift* 267/2 (October 1998), 357–398.

zur Nieden, Susanne, "Homophobie und Staatsräson," in Susanne zur Nieden, ed., *Homosexualität und Staatsräson. Männlichkeit, Homophobie und Politik in Deutschland 1900–1945* (Frankfurt: Campus, 2005), 17–51.

Index

GERMAN VISUAL CULTURE

SERIES EDITOR

Dr Christian Weikop, Senior Lecturer,
Edinburgh College of Art, University of Edinburgh

German Visual Culture invites research on German art across different periods, geographical locations, and political contexts. Books in the series engage with aesthetic and ideological continuities as well as ruptures and divergences between individual artists, movements, systems of art education, art institutions, and cultures of display. Challenging scholarship that interrogates and updates existing orthodoxies in the field is desirable.

A guiding question of the series is the impact of German art on critical and public spheres, both inside and outside the German-speaking world. Reception is thus conceived in the broadest possible terms, including both the ways in which art has been perceived and defined as well as the ways in which modern and contemporary German artists have undertaken visual dialogues with their predecessors or contemporaries. Issues of cultural transfer, critical race theory and related postcolonial analysis, feminism, queer theory, and other interdisciplinary approaches are encouraged, as are studies on production and consumption, especially the art market, pioneering publishing houses, and the 'little magazines' of the avant-garde.

All proposals for monographs and edited collections in the history of German visual culture will be considered, although English will be the language of all contributions. Submissions are subject to rigorous peer review. The series will be promoted through the series editor's Research Forum for German Visual Culture (https://www.eca.ed.ac.uk/research/research-forum-german-visual-culture), which he founded at the University of Edinburgh in 2011, and which has involved various symposia and related publications, all connected to an international network of Germanist scholars.

Vol. 1 Deborah Ascher Barnstone and Thomas O. Haakenson (eds)
Representations of German Identity.
312 pages. 2013. isbn 978-3-0343-0841-0 (hb)
312 pages. 2018. isbn 978-1-78874-255-9 (pb)

Vol. 2 Jennifer L. Creech and Thomas O. Haakenson (eds)
Spectacle.
313 pages. 2015. ISBN 978-3-0343-1803-7

Vol. 3 Deborah Ascher Barnstone (ed.)
The Doppelgänger.
277 pages. 2016. ISBN 978-3-0343-1961-4

Vol. 4 Irene Noy
Emergency Noises: Sound Art and Gender.
336 pages. 2017. ISBN 978-3-0343-1987-4

Vol. 5 Deborah Ascher Barnstone and Barbara McCloskey (eds)
The Art of War.
318 pages. 2017. ISBN 978-1-78707-383-8

Vol. 6 Michael Mackenzie
Otto Dix and the First World War: Grotesque Humor, Camaraderie and Remembrance.
448 pages. 2019. ISBN 978-3-0343-1723-8

Vol. 7 Thomas O. Haakenson and Tirza True Latimer with Carol Hager and Deborah Barton (eds)
Becoming TransGerman: Cultural Identity Beyond Geography.
338 pages. 2019. ISBN 978-1-78874-426-3

Lightning Source UK Ltd.
Milton Keynes UK
UKHW021323061222
413484UK00001B/1

9 783034 317238